Cognitive Neuroscience

COGNITIVE
Neuroscience

A READER

EDITED BY

MICHAEL S. GAZZANIGA

First published 2000

2 4 6 8 10 9 7 5 3 1

Blackwell Publishers Inc.
350 Main Street
Malden, Massachusetts 02148
USA

Blackwell Publishers Ltd
108 Cowley Road
Oxford OX4 1JF
UK

British Library Cataloguing in Publication Data
A CIP catalogue record for this book is available from the British Library.

Library of Congress Cataloging-in-Publication Data

Cognitive neuroscience: a reader / edited by Michael S. Gazzaniga.
    p.   cm.
   Includes bibliographical references and index.
   ISBN 0–631–21659–6 (hbk : alk. paper) — ISBN 0–631–21660–X (pbk: alk. paper)
   1.   Cognitive neuroscience.   I. Gazzaniga, Michael S.
QP360.5.C639   1999
612.8'2—dc21   99–16563
                                              CIP

Typeset in 10.5 on 12.5pt Garamond
by Kolam Information Services Pvt. Ltd, Pondicherry.
Printed in Great Britain by MPG Books, Bodmin, Cornwall

This book is printed on acid-free paper

Contents

P A r t i i   **Perception**

Preface

Cognitive neuroscience is a booming new field that stands on the shoulders of giants. It is also a field of scientific enquiry that has more to do than has been done. At the core, the cognitive neuroscientist wants to understand how the brain enables mind. It is a very tricky business.

The successful student must know and study many things. First, there is the business about the brain, the basic facts of neuroscience. How does it get built, how easily can it rewire itself, what do the various structures manage or monitor at a functional level? Further, the student needs not only to read about these matters, but the student should dissect the brain, analyze the cytoarchitecture of the brain. It is only through such exercises that the enormous complexity of the brain is grasped. Warning: reading alone will not do the trick.

Just as importantly, one should listen to the brain. Electrophysiological recordings of neural activity reveal huge secrets about how the brain is organized to get its job done. This classic approach to brain science has recently been augmented with a variety of new brain imaging techniques such as positron emission tomography, functional magnetic brain imaging, etc. Each new technique adds to the power of analysis.

At the same time, even with all the magical and fantastically interesting new techniques, there is nothing as riveting and compelling as studying the neurologic patient. For years, the focal lesion patient who suffered a form of aphasia or apraxia or perceptual and attentional disorder was more or less seen only by behavioral neurologists and clinical neuropsychologists. It wasn't until the mid-1970s that the more cognitively oriented experimental psychologists saw how fascinating these patients were for understanding cognitive processes. Since then, there has been no turning back and the field of cognitive neuroscience found its center. One has not only to be trained in cognitive science, one also needs to understand brain science.

As these readings proceed through articles showing the origins of cognitive neuroscience and some of the basic facts of the nervous system, we tackle the functional issues of language, memory, attention, perception, and so on. Each section comprises both classic and seminal studies as well as current studies, using all the experimental approaches just mentioned. The new studies are providing the intellectual framework for the field of study.

When I first collected my favorite articles, there were three times as many as are now in this book. I whittled the list down to two times the current number and submitted that list to the publisher. Alas, the economics of book production forced me to make draconian cuts into that list, leaving us with the very high octane readings we now have.

Putting this set of readings together would not have been possible without the assistance of several people. First, Ian Wickersham's fine hand can be seen throughout. He prepared background reports on all topics and constantly made suggestions for changing order, groupings and even sometimes the content. Ian has developed his own style of thinking about cognitive neuroscience, and his wit and incisive thinking can be seen in each issue of the *Journal of Cognitive Neuroscience*.

Thanks also go to Alissa Surges and Meredith Cunningham. Both helped enormously in tracking down papers and other aspects of manuscript preparation. Finally, my deep thanks to Martin Davies for suggesting the project. Actually putting a collection of studies together focuses the mind and gives one the opportunity to appreciate both the beauty and the magnitude of the field of cognitive neuroscience. Good reading.

MICHAEL S. GAZZANIGA
Dartmouth College
Hanover, New Hampshire

Acknowledgments

The publishers and editor wish to thank the following for permission to reprint copyright material in this book:

Cambridge University Press: for Michael S. Gazzaniga, "Life with George: The Birth of the Cognitive Neuroscience Institute," in W. Hirst *et al* (eds), *The Making of Cognitive Science: Essays in Honor of George A. Miller* (Cambridge University Press, 1988), pp. 230–41; reprinted by permission of the publisher.

Science: for Patricia S. Churchland and Terrence J. Sejnowski, "Perspectives on Cognitive Neuroscience," in *Science*, 242: 4879 (1988), pp. 741–5; copyright © 1988 the American Association for the Advancement of Science. Reprinted by permission of the American Association for the Advancement of Science.

Current Biology: for Steven A. Hillyard, "Electrical and Magnetic Brain Recordings: Contributions to Cognitive Neuroscience," in *Current Opinion in Neurobiology*, 3:2 (1993), pp. 710–17; reprinted by permission of Elsevier Science Ltd.

National Academy of Sciences: for Marcus E. Raichle, "Behind the Scenes of Functional Brain Imaging: A Historical and Physiological Perspective," in *Proceedings of the National Academy of Sciences*, 95:3 (1988), pp. 765–72; copyright © 1998 National Academy of Sciences, USA. Reprinted by permission of the publisher via Copyright Clearance Center, Inc.

Nature: for David H. Hubel, "Exploration of the Primary Visual Cortex, 1955–78," in *Nature*, 299: 5883 (1982), pp. 515–24; copyright © 1982 Macmillan Magazines Ltd. Reprinted by permission of *Nature*.

Oxford University Press: for Vernon B. Mountcastle, "The Parietal System and Some

Higher Brain Functions," in *Cerebral Cortex*, 5 (1995), pp. 377–90; reprinted by permission of the author and publisher.

Academic Press: for Melvyn A. Goodale, Lorna S. Jakobson, and Philip Servos, "The Visual Pathways Mediating Perception and Prehension," in A. M. Wing *et al* (eds), *Hand and Brain: The Neurophysiology and Psychology of Hand Movements* (Academic Press, 1996), pp. 15–31; copyright © 1996 by Academic Press; reprinted by permission of the publisher.

Science: for C. Daniel Salzman and William T. Newsome, "Neural Mechanisms for Forming a Perceptual Decision," in *Science*, 264:5156 (1994), pp. 231–7; copyright © 1994 American Association for the Advancement of Science. Reprinted by permission.

American Psychological Association: for Ken Nakayama, "James J. Gibson – An Appreciation," *Psychological Review*, 10:2 (1994); reprinted by permission of the publisher.

Elsevier Science: for Michael I. Posner and Stanislas Dehaene, "Attentional Networks," in *Trends in Neurosciences*, 17:2 (1994), pp. 75–9; reprinted by permission of Elsevier Science.

Nature: for Sheng He, Patrick Cavanagh, and James Intriligator, "Attentional Resolution and the Locus of Visual Awareness," in *Nature*, 383: 6598 (1996), pp. 334–7; copyright © 1996 Macmillan Magazines Ltd. Reprinted by permission of *Nature*.

Nature: for Bruce T. Volpe, Joseph E. Ledoux, and Michael S. Gazzaniga, "Information Processing of Visual Stimuli in an 'Extinguished' Field," in *Nature*, 282: 5740 (1979), pp. 722–4; copyright © 1979 Macmillan Magazines Ltd. Reprinted by permission of *Nature*.

Memory & Cognition: for Steven P. Tipper and Jon Driver, "Negative Priming between Pictures and Words in a Selective Attention Task: Evidence for Semantic Processing of Ignored Stimuli," in *Memory & Cognition*, 16:1 (1988), pp. 64–70; reprinted by permission of the publisher.

Science: for Roger N. Shepard and Jacqueline Metzler, "Mental Rotation of Three-Dimensional Objects," in *Science*, 171:3972 (1971), pp. 701–3; copyright © 1971 American Association for the Advancement of Science. Reprinted by permission.

Nature: for Stephen M. Kosslyn *et al.*, "Topographical Representations of Mental Images in Primary Visual Cortex," from *Nature*, 378:6556 (1995), pp. 496–8; copyright © 1995 Macmillan Magazines Ltd. Reprinted by permission of *Nature*.

John Wiley & Sons: for Roger W. Sperry, "The Effect of Crossing Nerves to Antagonistic Muscles in the Hind Limb of the Rat," in *Journal of Comparative Neurology*, 75 (1941), pp. 1–19. Reprinted by permission of Wiley-Liss, Inc., a division of John Wiley & Sons, Inc.

National Academy of Sciences: for Charles D. Gilbert *et al.*, "Spatial Integration and Cortical Dynamics," in *Proceedings of the National Academy of Sciences*, 93 (1996), pp. 615–22; copyright © 1996 National Academy of Sciences, USA. Reprinted by permission of the publisher via Copyright Clearance Center, Inc.

Cambridge University Press: for Mark H. Johnson, "Cortical Mechanisms of Cognitive Development," in Jerry Hogan *et al.* (eds), *Causal Mechanisms of Behavioural Development* (Cambridge University Press, 1994), pp. 267–88; reprinted by permission of the author and publisher.

BMJ Publishing Group: for William Beecher Scoville and Brenda Milner, "Loss of Recent Memory after Bilateral Hippocampal Lesions," in *Journal of Neurology, Neurosurgery and Psychiatry*, 20 (1957), pp. 11–21; reprinted by permission of the publisher.

Larry R. Squire: for Larry R. Squire and Stuart M. Zola, "Episodic Memory, Semantic Memory, and Amnesia," in *Hippocampus*, 8:3 (1998), pp. 205–11; reprinted by permission of Larry R. Squire.

Alan Baddeley: for Alan Baddeley, "Working Memory: The Interface between Memory and Cognition," in *Journal of Cognitive Neuroscience*, 4:3 (1992), pp. 281–8; reprinted by permission of the author.

American Psychological Association: for Daniel L. Schacter, "Understanding Implicit Memory: A Cognitive Neuroscience Approach," in *American Psychologist*, 47:4 (1992), pp. 559–69; reprinted by permission of the publisher.

Science: for Apostolos P. Georgopoulos, Masato Taira, and Alexander Lukashin, "Cognitive Neurophysiology of the Motor Cortex," in *Science*, 260 (1993), pp. 47–52; copyright © 1993 the American Association for the Advancement of Science. Reprinted by permission.

Robert H. Wurtz: for Robert H. Wurtz, "Vision for the Control of Movement," in *Investigative Ophthalmology & Visual Science*, 37:11 (1996), pp. 2130–45; reprinted by permission of the author and the Association for Research in Vision and Ophthalmology.

Elsevier Science: for W. T. Thach *et al.*, "Combining versus Gating Motor Programs: Differential Roles for Cerebellum and Basal Ganglia?" in N. Mano *et al.* (eds), *Role of the Cerebellum and Basal Ganglia in Voluntary Movement* (Elsevier Science, 1993), pp. 235–45. Reprinted by permission of Elsevier Science.

Plenum Publishing: for Donald A. Norman and Tim Shallice, "Attention to Action: Willed and Automatic Control of Behavior," in R. J. Davidson *et al.* (eds), *Consciousness and Self-Regulation*, vol. 4 (Plenum Press, 1986), pp. 1–18; reprinted by permission of the publisher and authors.

New York Academy of Sciences: for Patricia S. Goldman-Rakic, "Architecture of the Prefrontal Cortex and the Central Executive," in J. Grafman, K. J. Holyoak and

F. Boller (eds), *Structure and Functions of the Human Prefrontal Cortex* (New York Academy of Sciences, 1995), pp. 71–83; reprinted by permission of the publisher.

Nature: for John Hart Jr, Rita Sloan Berndt, and Alfonso Caramazza, "Category-Specific Naming Deficit Following Cerebral Infarction," in *Nature*, 316: 6027 (1985), pp. 439–40; copyright © 1985 Macmillan Magazines Ltd. Reprinted by permission of *Nature*.

American Psychological Association: for Michael S. Gazzaniga, "Right Hemisphere Language Following Brain Bisection: A 20-Year Perspective," in *American Psychologist*, 38:5 (1983), pp. 525–37; reprinted by permission of the publisher.

Marta Kutas: for Marta Kutas, "Current Thinking on Language Structures," in *Cahiers de Psychologie Cognitive/Current Psychology of Cognition*, 17:4–5 (1998), pp. 951–69; reprinted by permission of the author.

The MIT Press: for Jon H. Kaas, "Why Does the Brain Have So Many Visual Areas?" in *Journal of Cognitive Neuroscience*, 1:2 (1989), pp. 121–35; © 1989 by the Massachusetts Institute of Technology; reprinted by permission of the publisher.

The Rockefeller University Press: for Niels Kaj Jerne, "Antibodies and Learning: Selection versus Instruction," in G. Quarton, T. Melnechuck and F. O. Schmitt (eds), *The Neurosciences: A Study Program*, vol. 1 (Rockefeller University Press, 1967), pp. 200–5; reprinted by permission of the publisher.

The MIT Press: for Todd M. Preuss, "The Argument from Animals to Humans in Cognitive Neuroscience," in Michael S. Gazzaniga *et al.* (eds), *The Cognitive Neurosciences* (MIT Press, 1995), pp. 1227–41; reprinted by permission of the publisher.

Every effort has been made to trace or contact all copyright holders. The publishers would be pleased to rectify any omissions brought to their notice at the earliest opportunity.

Part i

History and Methods of Cognitive Neuroscience

INTRODUCTION TO PART I

The push to understand the mind and brain is now one of the biggest and most dynamic struggles in science. There are many reasons for this: the lure of self-knowledge is ancient and obvious, but the introspective ape is now equipped with powerful technological tools and the increasingly intercommunicated insights of thousands of others in diverse and complementary fields. The result, largely a product of the last few decades, is an outrageous proliferation of discoveries.

In "Life with George: The Birth of the Cognitive Neuroscience Institute," I describe some groping towards meaningful cross-disciplinary collaboration at the outset of an endeavor we called "cognitive neuroscience." As should be apparent from reading the passage, what we meant by that was far from clear, but it was motivated by the instinct that scientists in the various camps needed to be talking to each other. This cross-pollination has turned out to be extremely fruitful.

By contrast, attempts to understand the mind while ignoring the brain have often died on the vine, despite the hype. Churchland and Sejnowski, speaking from the perspectives of a philosopher and a theoretical neuroscientist, respectively, argue that, though the software of the brain might in principle be abstractable from the hardware, this philosophical point will buy you nothing when it comes to figuring out how the system works. Theorizing is crucial, but it needs neurobiological reality for essential hints and pruning of ideas that are obviously wrong.

Conversely, cognitive thinking helps ensure that neuroscientists are studying something interesting. Marcus Raichle recounts a beautiful example of this kind of collaboration in his retrospective view of functional brain imaging. The new imaging techniques were seized upon by psychologists who had previously developed appropriate concepts and experimental approaches, and both functional imaging and psychologists were thus catapulted to stardom.

Steven Hillyard describes one of the oldest techniques for studying the working brain, the recording of electric (and now magnetic) fields from the scalp. Though not capable of producing the grippingly detailed images of activity that other techniques can provide, field recordings are far better at resolving events in time. Short of surgical intervention, they have no competitors for monitoring the time course of neural activity, and thus remain a mainstay of, for example, neurolinguistics. Hillyard presents results of investigations in a variety of areas, foreshadowing more detailed discussions in some of the following chapters.

Life with George: The Birth of the Cognitive Neuroscience Institute

Michael S. Gazzaniga

Introducing George Miller to clinical states of mind was my pleasure during the late 1970s. After arriving at Cornell Medical College and experiencing the whiteout of medical dress, I reached for the phone the first afternoon and called George. There was no one at Cornell who remotely resembled a psychologist, and I was in desperate need of someone who knew what a theory was all about. Propinquity governed once again, since George was also the closest psychologist.

I had never talked to or met the man before 1976, and I quite frankly did not know what to expect. As a general rule, I don't like meeting legends. Either they have removed themselves from the business of establishing new personal relationships or they are not what their metroself appears to suggest. (The concept of the "metroself" was introduced to me by Richmond Crinkley and serves well the problem of distinguishing the personal reality of a public person from his or her public reality, or "metroself.") When you are in a public business, and scholarship, alas, is that, the metroself can begin to drive the personal self and effectively run and ruin lives. When someone works only on the metroself and never on the real joys of a personal life, disaster ensues. But George put my worst fears to rest.

Shortly thereafter, we began to meet regularly after work at the bar in the Rockefeller Faculty Club. We talked about everything from neglect to neologisms. It was on one of those evenings that he coined the term "cognitive neuroscience"; shortly thereafter, we formed our small but lovable enterprise. What he meant by cognitive neuroscience was to emerge – slowly. What we already knew was that neuropsychology was not what we had in mind. Tying specific functions to lesioned brain areas was not going to be our enterprise. The bankruptcy and intellectual impoverishment of that idea seemed self-evident, especially with the advent of new brain-imaging techniques that revealed how much else was always damaged following what had previously been thought to be focal damage.

They used to say that Jack Benny, the world's funniest man, was the best audience in the world. Everyone loved to try his stuff out on Jack. If George is in an audience, he is usually asleep. If he *is* the audience, that is, if you are one on one, he is the best. It is like having an ongoing editor as one pours out one's story. He asks questions that elicit more, but then as you hear yourself, you begin to edit as silly formulations slide off his deadpan expression. There is not much new in this world, and certainly not much new about the psychological nature of human beings. What passes for discovery these days tends to be an individual scientist's rediscovery of some well-established phenomenon. Most of these have come and gone, and George knows all of them. Yet, on the hundredth trip to the well, one is overjoyed to see a glimmer in his eye. Perhaps there was something to that last idea!

We started exchanging stories, mine about episodes in the clinic and his about new experimental strategies. I would tell him about patients with high verbal IQs, as measured by the Wechsler Adult Intelligence Scale (WAIS), who lacked a grammar school child's ability to solve simple problems like the Raven's Progressive Matrices. He would tell me about people who talk a good game but really have nothing to say. He would also say that psychologists do not yet have anything resembling a theory of intelligence or mind. He urged the continued collection of dissociations in cognition, as seen in the clinic, in the hope that a theory would emerge from these bizarre facts.

I took him on my rounds one day and showed him a range of phenomena from perceptual disorders to language disorders. He had never seen anything like it and commented afterward that the neurologic patient was really what many psychologists were looking for. After all, he observed, psychologists try to break brains by making college sophomores work fast or by presenting stimuli rapidly so that errors are made. In the clinic, the errors pour out of largely highly responsive systems with little or no effort.

One patient we saw was a distinguished executive in New York who had fallen down a staircase after consuming too many martinis. He was reported to be globally aphasic, which means that he would not understand much, if anything, and would speak only a little. As we arrived in his room, the computer tomography technicians were fetching him for a scan, so we tagged along. The technician asked Mr. C to slide over to the gurney, to which he replied "Yes, sir." Once he was positioned and rolling down the hallway to the scanner, the technician inquired about his comfort. "Are you feeling Ok?" "Yes, sir," said Mr. C. After arriving at the scanner, the patient was again slid off the gurney onto the table and was again asked if he felt all right. "Yes, sir," said Mr. C. The scan took place and Mr. C was returned to his room by the technician. The technician, who was familiar with my interests, turned to me and asked why we were interested in this patient. He felt that there was nothing wrong with him. I turned to the patient and said, "Mr. C, are you the king of Siam?" "Yes, sir," he replied with great assuredness. George grinned and observed that getting anywhere with anything is simply a matter of asking the right question.

We started the formal aspect of our effort in cognitive neuroscience with a year-long lecture series. To pay for this, as well as for some of our subsequent ventures, George and I applied for and received funding from the Sloan Foundation for a training grant. They were in the midst of their "Particular Program in Cognitive Science," and the application seemed a reasonable way to incorporate the brain sciences into the topic of cognition. Mike Posner spent much of his time with us in an attempt to bring together the fields of brain science and cognitive science. There was plenty of talent on both sides of the fence that doggedly divides these two disciplines. Emilio Bizzi, Floyd

Bloom, Steven Hillyard, Russ Develois, John Marshall, and Rodolfo Llinas talked about the brain and Dave Premack, Leon Festinger, Roger Shepard, Edgar Zurif, and Donald MacKay talked about cognition. When Mike Posner summarized it all for us, it became clear that an integrated field of cognitive neuroscience was a goal, not a reality. The beauty of each separate contribution was best dealt with individually.

As it worked out, George and I were called upon to write something about cognitive neuroscience. We took to the mails. One evening in late May 1978, we were having drinks, and as the second martini was taking hold, I asked him, "Just what is it cognitive science wants to know?" He looked at me, alerted for action, and then said, "Let me think about that." The following week, the guiding ideas behind our Cognitive Neuroscience Institute took form:

To: Michael S. Gazzaniga
From: George A. Miller

Re: "COGNITIVE SCIENCE [*sic*]"

An intense undergraduate, in the sharp panic of an identity crisis, rushed to his professor: "I don't know who I am. Tell me, who am I?" The professor replied wearily, "Please, who's asking the question?"

The story flashed to mind recently when a friend, who watches science with the eyes of a biologist, asked: "What do cognitive scientists want to know?" Anyone capable of posing such a question must already know the answer. To know is to have direct cognition of. Obviously, scientists of cognition want to have direct cognition of having direct cognition. Any etymologist could tell you that. Indeed, the very phrase "cognitive science" invites a scholarly disquisition on the Latin verbs *scire* (whence "science"), *gnoscere* (whence "know"), and *cognoscere* (whence "cognition").

Habits of mind that lead one into biology, however, are not satisfied by verbal play. They demand serious answers. What do cognitive scientists want to know?

Who knows? Trying to speak for cognitive science, as if cognitive scientists had but one mind and one voice, is a bum's game.

Nevertheless, certain facts are beyond dispute. Somewhere out there is a group of people who, at appropriate tribal gatherings, regard themselves as cognitive scientists. Moreover, some of them edit journals like *Cognitive Science*. And recently a philanthropic foundation announced that it would contribute $15,000,000 to advance cognitive science. No wonder that even biologists are curious to know what cognitive scientists are up to. People, meetings, publications, money – given these trappings, can content be far behind? There must be something that cognitive scientists are trying to understand.

What would a biologist accept as an answer? Something deep is called for. My friend is not asking about computers, or simulations, or logical formalisms, or the latest methods of psychological experimentation – none of that ancillary horseshit that fills so much of the conversation of cognitive scientists. A deeper answer is that cognitive scientists want to know the cognitive rules that people follow and the knowledge representations that those rules operate on. But this language – cognitive rules, knowledge representations – is precisely the kind of smoke that started my friend looking for a fire.

Let us begin with a question that we can answer: What do biologists want to know? Biologists want to discover the molecular logic of the living state. What is the molecular logic of the living state? Simple. It is the set of principles that, in addition to the principles of physics and chemistry, operate to govern the behavior of inanimate matter in living systems. (That is an almost direct quotation from the introduction to a biochemistry textbook.)

Is this the kind of answer a biologist expects when he asks what cognitive scientists want to know? If so, perhaps we can construct an answer based on this model of what an answer should be. Because I am a little slow at these games, however, I shall take three steps to get where I am going.

First, I will substitute psychologists for biologists. No substitution seems required for molecular logic; I assume that "molecular" in this context means "susceptible to analysis," and is not limited to the analysis of matter into chemical molecules. And then I will substitute conscious for living, because I consider consciousness to be the constitutive problem for psychology, just as life is the constitutive problem for biology. Now I have achieved the following: Psychologists want to discover the molecular logic of the conscious state.

So far so good. But now what do we mean by molecular logic of the conscious state? Let's see if substitution leads anywhere: the set of principles that, in addition to the principles of physics, chemistry, and biology, operate to govern the behavior of inanimate matter in conscious systems. These substitutions say little more than that psychology is the next step in the positivistic hierarchy of sciences. The result sounds pretty good to me, but can I follow through? That is to say, the biochemist whose formulation I have borrowed as my model had a large and impressive textbook full of biological principles to illustrate what he was talking about. What do I have?

One thing I do not have is behaviorism, because most behaviorists are dedicated to the proposition that consciousness is irrelevant to the science of psychology. Another thing I do not have is artificial intelligence, because computer simulations have no need for the psychological distinction between living and nonliving systems, for that matter.

What I seem to have is a way of looking at psychology, a criterion to keep in mind while thumbing through psychological handbooks. It might be formulated like this: Any behavior that is unaffected by the state of consciousness of the behaving system is of no concern to psychology. Dreaming, for example, is a concern of psychology, because if you wake up – if your state of consciousness changes – dreaming is affected.

This reminds me of the opposite side of a challenge I have been giving my students for many years. I challenge them to give me any psychological principle that I cannot violate by a simple act of will. I have always seen this challenge as a devastating criticism of psychology as a science, and I have consumed many of my intellectual watts looking for inviolable principles – for limitations on short-term memory, for example, or sensory thresholds, or what have you. But always without success. Any lay subject who refuses to cooperate in my experiments can violate my conclusions. Now, however, I would simply change my value judgment. The ability to violate some principle by an act of will is now the critical test that the principle in question is one that is relevant to psychology.

A basic problem for this kind of psychology, however, is the characterization of different states of consciousness. If it is too difficult to differentiate a hungry consciousness from a thirsty one, we can postpone those refinements until we have some of the cruder differences under control: the difference between awake and asleep, say, or between asleep and hypnotized, or between hypnotized and anesthetized. These differences are important because, if we hope to follow the formulation we reached by substitution, we must have reliable ways of knowing whether states of consciousness have changed. Only then can we begin to study the effects of those changes on behavior.

I assume that most psychologists conform to this general proposition without stopping to think about it. When they publish the result of a rote memorization experiment, for example, the reader is generally safe in presupposing that the subjects were awake during the learning trials and that different results would have been obtained if they had been asleep. That presupposition is regarded as too obvious to bother mentioning. But perhaps we need to grab hold of a few obvious facts like that in order to provide a firm foundation for scientific psychology?

In most respects, our search for principles governing conscious systems would not change the research we do, although it might change the way we talk about it. The major place I would expect a change would be in those situations where what people do and what they say about what they do are different. Such situations have in the past been used primarily to illustrate the unreliability of introspective reports. Under the new regime, they would provide prime opportunities to explore how the state of consciousness is related to behavior, a question that could not even be raised if consciousness and behavior had always been correlated.

All of this could be elaborated in some detail, although psychologists are still a long way from any catalogue of principles comparable to those of biochemistry. The problem, however, is that my friend did not ask what psychologists want to know. He asked what cognitive scientists want to know.

A second set of substitutions can be tried, therefore. Suppose we substitute states of knowledge for the conscious state. Then we obtain: Cognitive psychologists want to discover the molecular logic of states of knowledge, where the molecular logic of states of knowledge refers to the set of principles that, in addition to the principles of physics and chemistry, govern the behavior of inanimate matter in knowledge systems. Reference to biological and psychological principles is here omitted, for the computers can instantiate knowledge systems; computers need obey no biological or psychological principles.

The criterion for looking at research would now become: Any behavior that is unaffected by the state of knowledge of the behaving system is of no concern to cognitive science. If you turn off the power in a computer, for example, the consequences will not depend on the state of knowledge of the computer, so they would be of no concern to cognitive scientists. I suspect that this criterion distinguishes rather sharply between those kinds of information that are imposed on the machine by its program and those imposed by its fixed architecture. This boundary can vary from one information processing device to the next, and the boundary of cognitive concern would vary correspondingly. I am not sure this is a happy result for cognitive scientists, since it seems to constrain the principles we can find to particular systems. For each system, a new science.

I have no desire to dissuade anyone who wants to develop cognitive science along these lines, but neither do I have any desire to join with them. I would prefer to take a different line, defining still another science more narrowly. So I will now take a third step, as follows: Cognitive neuroscientists want to discover the molecular logic of epistemic systems, where the molecular logic in question this time is the principle that, in addition to the principles of physics, chemistry, biology, and psychology, governs the behavior of inanimate matter in epistemic systems. (The term "epistemic system" is negotiable; I use it as a placeholder for something better.) A further substitution is possible: animate for inanimate in the final clause. I am unclear whether it would make any real difference.

By including the requirement that cognitive neuroscience is concerned only with living, conscious systems, we cut artificial intelligence free to develop in its own way, independent of the solutions that organic evolution happens to have produced. Now our concern is for a subset of conscious systems, and the criterion is whether or not the system's state of knowledge affects its behavior – what Pylyshyn has called its "cognitive penetrability." Perhaps cognitive penetrability should be paralleled by conative or affective penetrability, but since I don't really know what I am talking about, I will not try to pursue the contrasts.

One problem I feel with this formulation may be worth mentioning. Since the search is for principles that govern behavior, the definition presumably commits cognitive neuroscientists to the goal of predicting and controlling behavior. The inclusion of psychological principles, where "psychological" is defined in the way suggested earlier, allows for a considerable degree of mentalism in the methodology of cognitive science. A British psychologist named David Lieberman has recently argued that this is precisely the stance psychologists ought to take: behavioristic goals, but allowing introspective evidence. I agree with Lieberman that this describes the position of most cognitive psychologists at the present time, but it bothers me – it seems schizoid. If I could think of something other than behavior that cognitive principles would govern, I would opt for that, but everything I think of as an alternative is of questionable identifiability – that is, most mental contents are too hypothetical to let us observe what governs them. I know that this is the kind of trouble scientists don't get into unless they ask for it, but nevertheless I shall continue to ponder it in my own muddle-headed way.

It should be clear by now that I really don't have an answer to the question, what do cognitive scientists want to know? But I think that cognitive neuroscientists want to know something that is reasonably interesting, and that there really might be some promise in following up systematically the implications of the definitions that we arrived at by substitution into our biological model.

Unbelievable as it may seem, I attempted a response. It was spring.

To: George A. Miller
From: Michael S. Gazzaniga

Re: Exemplars of Cognitive Neuroscience

O.K., your claim is that our task is to understand those processes active in living systems that can exert control over the comings and goings of a variety of mental constituents that make up a cognitive agent. (Put differently, is it also fair to say that the defining qualities of a cognitive system are coincident with an information processing disorder?) Alternatively, it is our task to understand cerebral software, the programming stuff that orchestrates the spatial–temporal patterns of the neural network.

First, has your definition of cognitive neuroscience moved the ball down the field? I think it has. Consider what others have said about what cognition is, usually using other terminologies. Sperry, for example, used to argue that consciousness is an emergent property of the spatial–temporal interaction of the neuronal system subserving the phenomenon. He maintained that these emergent mental properties feed back, as it were, and control the activities of the system that produced it. To me this position is a neuroscientist's way of saying "cognitive act."

MacKay's hypothesis on what the cardinal feature of a cognitive system is goes like this: "the direct correlate of conscious experience is the self-evaluating, supervisory or metaorganizing activity of the cerebral system and it is this system that determines norms and priorities and organizes the internal state of readiness to reckon with the sources of sensory stimulation." That strikes me as a rather passive description of the conscious process and it takes on more of the character of a "jobber" or "dispatcher." He does not characterize the system as one that tries to penetrate the organism's natural tendency to reflexively respond to a command.

If I am right, your definition has advanced at least my understanding of some issues and has clearly stated that the task is to discover the rules that govern the epistemic system – the one living system that governs the biologic system. When thinking about that, I am maintaining that the epistemic system is supraordinate to the biologic system. Is that what you were driving at?

At any rate, you have set us to the task of actually trying to figure out the principles of not only how cognitive systems announce their products to consciousness, but also the criterion that a cognitive system is a process that can supersede the cerebral architecture. How else can we illuminate this dynamic other than by studying disruptive brain states? In some sense the cognitive neuroscientist is trying to trick out of the organism insight into that puzzling problem. But before raising some problems from studies on brain-damaged patients, let me make one other observation that I think needs up-front analysis.

The kind of analysis one would bring to understanding a New Yorker as opposed to understanding New York would be quite different. The kind of analysis one brings to understanding a serial system as opposed to a parallel system also seems to me to be quite different. Before we proceed with an intelligent analysis of cognitive function, do we have to face up to the issue of whether or not the system is in fact competing for the attention of the person? If we agree that this is a reasonable model, crudely put at this point, then it seems to me how one approaches problems in brain disease that merit consideration for a theory of cognition becomes quite different.

Let me now consider a brain disease situation that speaks to this notion of what constitutes a cognitive system. There can be in brain disease relatively discrete disruptions of one of the system properties of the cognitive agent. It is common, for example, to study patients with memory dysfunctions. On one level of analysis they are unable to (1) retain new information and (2) combine two new elements into a fresh concept. Looking into the pathophysiology underlying these disorders, one finds that both diffuse and focal disease states correlate in this psychologic disarray.

It is only on deeper probe that one begins to see differences at the psychologic level. Patients with focal disease possess a dense inability to transfer information from short-term to long-term memory, although lavishly assisted in their recall performance by cueing (e.g., categorical headings embedded in a long word list). On the other hand, patients with diffuse disease are not assisted by this cognitive strategy. Their recall performance stays down on the floor.

What are we to do with these observations? First of all, are we to dismiss the diffuse disease patients as still embodying a cognitive system? Has their agency been lost? If not, what is it about them that characterizes them as a member of this species? I don't have an answer.

It seems to me that brain-diseased patients tell us immediately that we must bring more specificity to the definition of "cognitive penetrability" as a criterion for a cognitive system. I have the strong feeling that there is a real insight here, but a nagging feeling that we can too easily dismiss a lot of cognitive agents.

To which George replied:

To: Michael S. Gazzaniga
From: George A. Miller

Re: There's a long, long trail awinding

Since you accept, at least tentatively, my definition of cognitive neuroscience, our next task is to try to put it to work. I want to restate the definition, but first I want to get rid of "epistemic system." Let me begin by pointing in the general direction I had in mind.

Organic Knowledge Systems.   A "knowledge base" is any tangible collection of signals that are arranged according to some accepted coding scheme in order to represent a given body of information. A knowledge base coupled with an information processing system for using it (for storing, retrieving, erasing, comparing, searching, etc.) is a "knowledge system." Obviously, a knowledge base is useless except as part of a knowledge system that (unlike libraries or computers) is governed by biological and psychological principles, i.e., a living, animate, agentive knowledge system.

Definition of Cognitive Neuroscience.   Cognitive neuroscientists attempt to discover the molecular logic of organic knowledge systems, i.e., the principles that, in addition to the principles of physics, chemistry, biology, and psychology, govern the behavior of inanimate matter in living knowledge systems.

The Cognitive Criterion.   It follows from this definition that any behavior unaffected by the state of knowledge of the behaving system is of no concern to cognitive neuroscience.

Implications of Definition.   This definition is compatible with various approaches to cognitive neuroscience: (1) Evolution of knowledge systems. For example, the evolutionary shift from genetically stored knowledge to knowledge acquired from experience. (2) Ontogenesis of knowledge systems. For example, the neural basis of personal memory. (3) Psychology of knowledge systems. For example, the effects of attention, as indicated by evoked potentials, perhaps, on knowledge-governed behavior. (4) Neurology of knowledge systems. For example, the correlation of different types of brain disease. And so on. None of these approaches is novel – which means that we could have something to say about each of them.

A philosophical objection to this approach is that, by introducing successive definitions of biology, psychology, and cognitive neuroscience in this manner, we have made it reductionistic. That is to say, the principles sought by the cognitive neuroscientist are also principles of psychology, and the principles sought by psychologists are also principles of biology. Since I have always thought of scientific psychology as a branch of biology, this objection carries little weight with me. It would carry greater weight, however, with such distinguished scientists as B. F. Skinner or H. A. Simon.

Implications of Criterion.   A central question in your memo of June 1 might be phrased as follows: What are the operational implications of the claim that "any behavior unaffected by the state of the behaving system is of no concern to cognitive neuroscience"?

Several things occur to me when you press this button. First, Zenon Pylyshyn should not have to assume responsibility for this phrasing of the criterion. As I understand his notion of "cognitive penetrability," it is intended to discriminate between the fixed "architecture" and the modifiable programs for a mental computer. We, on the other hand, are trying to distinguish what cognitive neuroscientists want to know from what they leave to others. It is not clear to me, in my ignorance of Pylyshyn's ideas, whether these two distinctions coincide, so the only line I can try to develop is our own.

Second, I see two obvious ways to apply the criterion: (1) Change an organism's state of knowledge and try to demonstrate a resultant change in its thinking or behaving. Or (2) leave the organism's knowledge alone, but vary the materials used in a task to see whether thought or behavior changes as a function of their familiarity.

If I have understood your example, the case of a patient with diffuse brain disease illustrates one of the difficulties of applying the criterion in manner (1) – since it is apparently impossible to change such a patient's state of knowledge, his memory-governed behavior was of no concern to cognitive neuroscience. For such a patient, therefore, it would be necessary to apply the criterion in manner (2) – essentially, to change the contents of the questions asked until we find something the patient does remember. Does this answer the disturbing question raised at the close of your memo?

Third, I would think of this criterion as something to guide us, as authors, in picking and choosing what studies to write about and how to organize them. I see nothing wrong with confessing that this is the criterion we used (if, indeed, we did), but it does not seem to me to be something that we must rub the reader's nose in.

Levels of Description.   One of the biggest problems I have in trying to get my thoughts straight about cognitive neuroscience is that different people work at different levels of description, and no one pays attention to how his level is related to descriptions at other levels. I assume this degree of incoherence is possible because the different levels are only loosely related, which, if true, is an interesting observation in its own right.

The closest discussions I have seen of the level problem have come from the MIT Artificial Intelligence Laboratory, where I assume that Minsky and Marr have been the guiding lights. It is forced on anyone who works with computers, I guess. For example, in P. H. Winston's *Artificial Intelligence* (Addison-Wesley, 1977) eight levels of description of the operation of a computer are distinguished: (1) transistors, (2) flip flops and gates, (3) registers and data paths, (4) machine instructions, (5) compiler or interpreter, (6) LISP, (7) embedded pattern matcher, and (8) intelligent programs. D. Marr and T. Poggio (A theory of human stereo vision, *Proc. Royal Soc. London*, 1977) bring this closer to neurology when they distinguish four levels of description that should apply both to computers and to brains: (1) transistors and diodes, or neurons and synapses, (2) assemblies made from elements at level (1), e.g., memories, adders, multipliers, (3) the algorithm, or scheme for computation, and (4) the theory of the computation.

Clearly, most neuroscientists today are gung ho for level (1); neurotransmitters are hot stuff. I have also encountered a little work at level (2) – e.g., Mountcastle's description of columnar assemblies – so I assume there is more that I don't know about. Level (3) is as abstract as any neuroscientist had dared to dream about – maybe it has been achieved in such cases as Vince Dethier's analysis of flies. Level (4) has been neglected, and Marr and Poggio propose that it is the responsibility of artificial intelligence to provide general theories by which the necessary structure of computation at level (3) can be defined.

I hold no brief for either of these analyses, but I do agree with them that anything as complicated as a nervous system can be understood at several levels. And the logic of levels is such that they must be only loosely connected to one another – otherwise they would not be distinct levels. Moreover, the processes described at level N could probably be achieved by many higher processes at level N + 1 – so a description at level N is never really an explanation of what is really going on at level N.

Problem. What do levels have to do with our definition of cognitive neuroscience? This is not a rhetorical question – I really need an answer.

For example, a particular drug known to affect synapses in a given way (manipulation at level 1) is observed to affect behavior governed by the patient's general knowledge of spatial relations (a consequence at level 4). It meets our criterion (applied in manner 2) for inclusion in cognitive neuroscience. But to include it is not to understand it! Help!

Years have intervened, and we wrote a different chapter. But the idea that neuroscience needed cognitive science has prevailed. I put it that way because that, after all, is what is at stake. The molecular approach in the absence of the cognitive context limited the fashionable neuroscientist to pursuing answers to biologic questions in a manner not unlike that of the kidney physiologist. Although such approaches represent an admirable enterprise, they do, when put in that light, make it impossible for the neuroscientist to attack the central integrative questions of mind–brain research.

The Cognitive Neuroscience Institute has taken all of this to heart. We plan yearly meetings. We were going to have more, but once a year is enough. We invite distinguished scientists from neuroscience and cognitive science to a far-off place and have them sit and think together for a week. None come to the meetings with the answers. We avoid inviting such people. Instead, we collect together people who want to know how to connect cognition with brain processes. The meetings are a pure delight, and tangible progress is being made. We have had two on the problem of memory, with the first effort representing the Institute's first monograph. Four more monographs are in the works. But our anxiousness and worry about the questions we badgered each other with went, ultimately, to make up the flavor of the Cognitive Neuroscience Institute. It continues to plug away, and we both love it. Yet, the concept and the means would not be without the modest but driving force of George Miller.

2

Perspectives on Cognitive Neuroscience

Patricia S. Churchland and Terrence J. Sejnowski

Neuroscience and cognitive science share the goal of trying to understand how the mind–brain works. In the past, discoveries at the neuronal level and explanations at the cognitive level were so distant that each often seemed of merely academic significance to the other. Symbol processing models based on the digital computer have been unpromising as a means to bridge the gap between neuroscience and cognitive science, because they did not relate to what was known about nervous systems at the level of signal processing. However, there is now a gathering conviction among scientists that the time is right for a fruitful convergence of research from hitherto isolated fields. The research strategy developing in cognitive neuroscience is neither exclusively from the top down, nor exclusively from the bottom up. Rather, it is a coevolutionary strategy, typified by interaction among research domains, where research at one level provides constraints, corrections, and inspiration for research at other levels (*1*).

Levels

There are in circulation at least three different notions of the term "levels," as it is used to describe scientific research, each notion carving the landscape in a different way – levels of analysis, levels of organization, and levels of processing.

Levels of analysis concern the conceptual division of a phenomenon in terms of different classes of questions that can be asked about it. A framework articulated by Marr and Poggio (*2*) drew upon the conception of levels in computer science and identified three levels: (i) the computational level of abstract problem analysis, decomposing the task into its main constituents (for example, determination of the three-dimensional structure of a moving object from successive views); (ii) the level of the algorithm, specifying a formal procedure to perform the task by providing the correct output for a given input; and (iii) the level of physical implementation. Marr (*3*) maintained that computational problems of the highest level could be analyzed independently of understanding the algorithm that performs the computation. Similarly, he thought the algorithmic problem of the second level was solvable independently of understanding its physical implementation.

Some investigators have used the doctrine of independence to conclude that neuroscience is irrelevant to understanding cognition. However, the independence that Marr emphasized pertained only to the formal properties of algorithms, not to how they might be discovered (*4*). Computational theory tells us that algorithms can be run on different machines and in that sense, and that sense alone, the algorithm is independent of the implementation. The formal point is straightforward: since an algorithm is formal, no specific physical parameters (for example, vacuum tubes or Ca^{2+}) are part of the algorithm. That said, it is important to see that the purely formal point cannot speak to the issue of how best to discover the algorithm used by a given machine, nor how best to arrive at the neurobiologically adequate task analysis. Certainly it cannot tell us that the discovery of the algorithms relevant to cognitive functions will be independent of a detailed understanding of the nervous system. Moreover, different implementations display enormous differences in speed, size, efficiency, and elegance. The formal independence of algorithm from architecture is something we can exploit to build other machines once we know how the brain works, but it is not a guide to discovery when we do not yet know how the brain works. Knowledge of brain architecture also can be the essential basis and invaluable catalyst for devising likely and powerful algorithms – algorithms that might explain how in fact the brain does its job.

Levels of organization. How do the three levels of analysis map onto the nervous system? There is organized structure at different scales: molecules, synapses, neurons, networks, layers, maps, and systems (*5*) (fig. 2.1). The range of structural organization implics, therefore, that there are many levels of implementation and that each has its companion task description. But if there are as many types of task description as there are levels of structural organization, this diversity will be reflected in a multiplicity of algorithms that characterize how the tasks are accomplished. This in turn means that the notion of *the* algorithmic level is as oversimplified as the notion of *the* implementation level. Structure at every scale in the nervous system – molecules, synapses, neurons, networks, layers, maps, and systems (fig. 2.1) – is separable conceptually but not detachable physically. Psychological phenomena may be associated with a variety of levels. Some perceptual states such as the "raw" pain of a toothache might be a low-level effect, whereas attention may depend on a variety of mechanisms, some of which can be found at the level of local neural networks and others at the level of larger neural systems that reside in many different locations in the brain.

Levels of processing. This concept could be described as follows: The greater the distance from cells responding to sensory input, the higher the degree of information processing. Thus the level assigned is a function of synaptic distance from the periphery. On this measure, cells in the primary visual area of the neocortex that respond to oriented bars of light are at a higher level than cells in the lateral geniculate nucleus (LGN), which in turn are at a higher level than retinal ganglion cells.

Once the sensory information reaches the cerebral cortex it fans out through cortico-cortical projections into a multitude of parallel streams of processing. In the primate visual system 24 visual areas have been identified (*6*). Many (perhaps all)

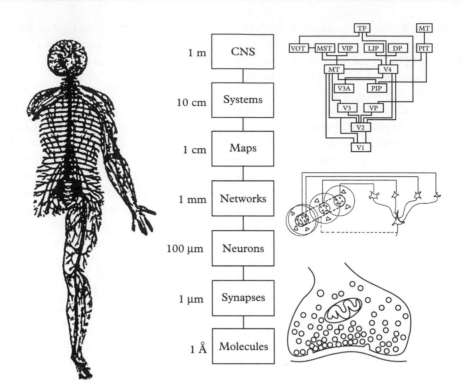

Figure 2.1   Structural levels of organization in the nervous system. The spatial scale at which anatomical organizations can be identified varies over many orders of magnitude. (*Left*) Drawing by Vesalius (*33*) of the human brain, the spinal column, and the peripheral nerves. (*Right*) Schematic diagrams illustrate (*top*) a processing hierarchy of visual areas in monkey visual vortex (*34*); (*center*) a small network model for the synthesis of oriented receptive fields of simple cells in visual cortex (*35*); and (*bottom*) the structure of a chemical synapse (*36*). Relatively little is known about the properties at the network level in comparison with the detailed knowledge we have of synapses and the general organization of pathways in sensory and motor system.

forward projections are accompanied by a back projection, and there are even massive feedback projections from primary visual cortex to the LGN. Given these reciprocal projections, it might seem that the processing levels do not really form a hierarchy, but there is a way to order the information flow by examining the layer of cortex into which fibers project. Forward projections generally terminate in the middle layers of cortex and feedback projections usually terminate in the upper and lower layers (*7*). However, we do not yet understand the function of these feedback pathways. If higher areas can affect the flow of information through lower areas, then the concept of sequential processing must be modified.

The hierarchical organization typical of earlier sensory areas is not adhered to everywhere. On the contrary, the anatomy of association areas and prefrontal cortex suggests a more "democratic" organization, and processing appears to take place in webs of strongly interacting networks (*8*). Decisions to act and the execution of plans and choices could be the outcome of a system with distributed control rather than a single control center. Coming to grips with systems having distributed control will require both new experimental techniques and new conceptual advances. Perhaps more appropriate metaphors for this type of processing will emerge from studying models of interacting networks of neurons.

Color Vision: A Case Study

As an illustration of fruitful interactions between psychology and physiology on a problem in perception, we have chosen several examples from color vision. Similar examples can also be found in the areas of learning and addiction (*9*) and sensory-motor integration (*10, 11*). Newton's ingenious prism experiment demonstrated that white light can be decomposed into a mixture of wavelengths and recombined to recover the white light. This physical description of color, however, did not satisfy artists, who were well aware that the perception of color involved complex spatial and temporal effects. As Goethe pointed out in *Zur Farbenlehre*, dark shadows often appear blue. The physical description of color and the psychological description of color perception are at two different levels: The link between them is at the heart of the problem of relating brain to cognition. Three examples will be given to illustrate how such links are being made in color vision.

The knowledge that mixtures of only three wavelengths of light are needed to match any color led Young to propose in 1802 (*12*) that there are only three types of photoreceptors. Quite a different theory of color vision was later proposed by Hering, who suggested that color perception was based on a system of color opponents, one for yellow versus blue, one for red versus green, and a separate system for black versus white (*13*). Convincing experiments and impressive arguments were marshaled by supporters of these two rival theories for nearly a century. The debate was finally settled by physiological studies proving that both theories were right – in different parts of the brain. In the retina three different types of color-sensitive photoreceptors were found, as predicted by Young, and the genes for the three cone photopigments have been sequenced (*14*). In the thalamus and visual cortex there are neurons that respond to Hering's color opponents (*15*). Evidently, even at this early stage of visual processing the complexity of the brain may lead to puzzles that can only be settled by knowing how the brain is constructed (*16*).

Recent progress in solving the problem of color constancy is a second example of converging physiological and psychological research. Red apples look red under a wide range of illumination even though the physical wavelengths impinging on the retina vary dramatically from daylight to interior lighting. Insights into color constancy have come from artists, who manipulate color contrasts in paintings, psychophysicists, who have quantified simultaneous contrast effects (*17*), and theorists, who have modeled them (*18*). Color constancy depends on being able to compute the intrinsic reflectance of a surface independently of the incident light. The reflectance of a patch of surface can be approximately computed by comparing the energy in wavelength bands coming from the patch of surface to the average energy in these bands from neighboring and distant regions of the visual field. The signature of a color-sensitive neuron that was performing this computation would be a long-range suppressive influence from regions of the visual field outside the conventional receptive field. Neurons with such color-selective surrounds have been reported in visual cortex area V4 (*19*); the first nonclassical surrounds were found for motion-selective cells in area MT (*20*). If these neurons are necessary for color constancy then their loss should result in impairments of color vision. Bilateral lesions of certain extrastriate visual areas in man do produce achromatopsia – a total loss of color perception (21) – although this condition is usually found with other deficits and the damaged areas may not be homologous with area V4 in monkeys.

The third example of a link between brain and cognition comes from research on how form, motion, and color information are processed in the visual system. If different parts of the system are specialized for different tasks, for example, for motion or color, then there should be conditions under which these specializations are revealed. Suppose the "color system" is good at distinguishing colors, but not much else, and, in particular, is poor at determining shape, depth, and motion, whereas the "shape system" is not sensitive to color differences but to brightness differences. When boundaries are marked only by color differences – all differences in brightness are experimentally removed – shape detection should be impaired. Psychophysical research has shown that this is indeed the case. The perceived motion of equiluminant contours is degraded (22); form cues such as shape-from-shading are difficult to interpret (23), and perceived depth in random-dot stereograms collapses (24). Physiological and anatomical research has begun to uncover a possible explanation for these phenomena (25). The separate processing streams in cerebral cortex mentioned earlier carry visual information about different properties of objects (6, 26). In particular the predominant pathway for color information diverges from those carrying information on motion and depth (fig. 2.2). The separation is not perfect, however, but equiluminant stimuli provide physiologists with a visual "scalpel" for tracking down the correlates of perceptual coherence in different visual areas.

The lessons learned from color perception may have significance for studying other cognitive domains. So far as we know, only a small fraction of the neurons in the visual system respond in a way that corresponds to our perceptual report of color. The locations in the brain where links between physiological states and perceptual states can be found vary from the retina to deep in the visual system for different aspects of color perception (27). New experimental techniques will be needed to study these links when the information is encoded in a large population of interacting neurons (10, 28).

Techniques and Research Strategies

Color vision is a problem that has been studied for hundreds of years; we know much less about the biological basis of other perceptual and cognitive states. Fortunately, new techniques, such as regional blood flow analysis with position emission tomography (PET) and magnetic resonance imaging (MRI) are becoming available for non-invasively measuring brain activity in humans. With these techniques the large-scale pattern of what is happening where and when in the brain can be determined; later, as techniques with higher resolution are developed they can be focused on the relevant areas to ask how the processing is accomplished.

A useful way to get an overview of the assorted techniques is to graph them with respect to temporal and spatial resolution. This permits us to identify areas where there do not yet exist techniques to get access to levels of organization at

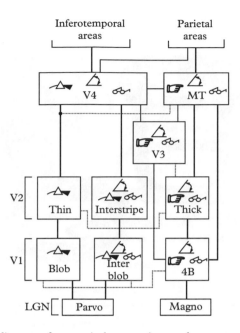

Figure 2.2 Schematic diagram of anatomical connections and response selectivities of neurons in early visual areas of the macaque monkey. Visual information from the retina is split into two parallel streams at the level of the lateral geniculate nucleus (LGN), the parvocellular and magnocellular divisions. The parvocellular stream projects to two divisions of primary visual cortex (V1): the cytochrome oxidase–rich regions (Blob) and cytochrome oxidase–poor regions surrounding the blobs (Interblob). The magnocellular stream projects to layer 4B of V1. These three divisions of V1 project into corresponding areas of V2: the "thin stripe," "interstripe," and "thick stripes" of cytochrome oxidase–rich and –poor regions in V2. These areas in turn project to visual areas V3, V4, and MT (middle temporal area, also called V5). Heavy lines indicate robust primary connections, and thin lines indicate weaker, more variable connections. Dotted lines indicate connections that require additional verification. Not all projections from these areas to other brain areas are represented. The neurons in each visual area respond preferentially to particular properties of visual stimuli as indicated by the icons: Prism, tuned or opponent wavelength selectivity; angle, orientation selectivity; spectacles, binocular disparity selectivity or strong binocular interactions; pointing hand, direction of motion selectivity. [Reprinted with permission from (6).]

those spatio-temporal resolutions and to compare their strengths and weaknesses (fig. 2.3). For example, it is apparent that we lack detailed information about processing in neural networks within cortical layers and columns over a wide range of time scales, from milliseconds to hours. There is also a pressing need for experimental techniques designed to address the dendritic and synaptic level of investigation in cerebral cortex. Without these data it will not be possible to develop realistic models of information processing in cortical circuits.

Although we need experimental data concerning the properties of neurons and behavioral data about psychological capacities, we also need to find models that explain how patterns of activity in neurons represent surfaces, optical flow, and objects; how networks develop and learn, store, and retrieve information; and how networks accomplish sensorimotor and other types of integration. Ideally, modeling and

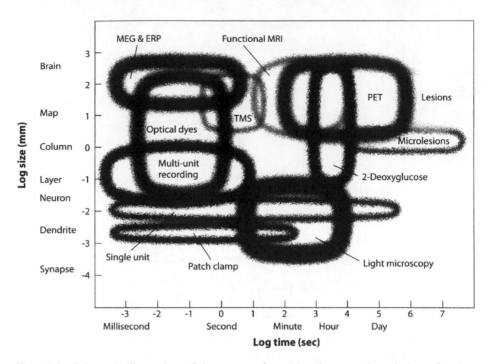

Figure 2.3   Schematic illustration of the ranges of spatial and temporal resolution of various experimental techniques for studying the function of the brain. The vertical axis represents the spatial extent of the technique, with the boundaries indicating the largest and smallest sizes of the region from which the technique can provide useful information. Thus, single-unit recording can only provide information from a small region of space, typically 10 to 50 μm on a side. The horizontal axis represents the minimum and maximum time intervals over which information can be collected with the technique. Thus, action potentials from a single neuron can be recorded with millisecond accuracy over many hours. Patch-clamp recording allows the ionic currents through single ionic channels to be measured. Optical and fluorescent dyes that can reveal membrane potential, ionic concentrations, and intracellular structure have been used with high resolution in tissue culture, where it is possible to obtain a clear view of single cells (*37, 38*). However, recordings from the central nervous system are limited in resolution by the optical properties of nervous tissue and only about 0.1-mm resolution has been achieved (*39*). Confocal microscopy is a recent development in light microscopy that could be used for improving the resolution of the technique for three-dimensional specimens (*40*). ERP (evoked response potential) and MEG (magnetoencephalography) record the average electrical and magnetic activity over large brain regions and are limited to events that take place over about 1 second (*41*). The temporal resolution of PET (positron emission tomography) depends on the lifetime of the isotope being used, which ranges from minutes to an hour. It may be possible to achieve a temporal resolution of seconds with ^{15}O to study fast changes in blood flow by using temporal binding of the gamma ray events (equivalent to the poststimulus time histogram for action potentials) (*42*). The 2-deoxyglucose (2-DG) technique has a time resolution of about 45 min and a spatial resolution of 0.1 mm with large pieces of tissue and 1 μm with small pieces of tissue (*43*). The 2-DG technique can also be applied to humans with PET (*44*). Lesions allow the interruption of function to be studied immediately after ablation of the tissue and for a long period of time after the ablation (*21, 45*). Microlesion techniques make selective modifications with substances such as ibotenic acid, which destroys neurons but not fibers of passage, and 4-amino-phosphonobutyric acid, which selectively and reversibly blocks a class of glutamate

experimental research will have a symbiotic relationship, such that each informs, corrects, and inspires the other.

Although many diverse kinds of things are presented as models for some part of the nervous system, it is useful to distinguish between realistic models, which are genuinely and strongly predictive of some aspect of nervous system dynamics or anatomy, and simplifying models, which though not so predictive, demonstrate that the nervous system could be governed by specific principles. Connectionist network models (*29*), which are simplifying models, are typically motivated by cognitive phenomena and are governed primarily by computational constraints, while honoring very general neuro-biological constraints such as number of processing units and time required to perform a task. Accordingly, they are more properly considered demonstrations of what could be possible and sometimes what is not possible. Realistic models of actual neural networks, by contrast, are primarily motivated by biological constraints, such as the physiological and anatomical properties of specific cell types (*30*). Despite their different origins and sources of dominant constraints, simplifying models and realistic neural models are both based on the mathematics of nonlinear dynamical systems in high-dimensional spaces (*31*). The common conceptual and technical tools used in these models should provide links between two rich sources of experimental data, and consequently, connectionist and neural models have the potential to coevolve toward an integrated, coherent account of information processing in the mind–brain.

The ultimate goal of a unified account does not require that it be a single model that spans all the levels of organization. Instead the integration will probably consist of a chain of models linking adjacent levels. When one level is explained in terms of a lower level, this does not mean that the higher level theory is useless or that the high-level phenomena no longer exist. On the contrary, explanations will coexist at all levels, as they do in chemistry and physics, genetics, and embryology.

Conclusions

It would be convenient if we could understand the nature of cognition without understanding the nature of the brain itself. Unfortunately, it is difficult if not impossible to theorize effectively on these matters in the absence of neurobiological constraints. The primary reason is that computational space is consummately vast, and there are many conceivable solutions to the problem of how a cognitive operation could be accomplished. Neurobiological data provide essential constraints on computational theories, and they consequently provide an efficient means for narrowing the search space. Equally important, the data are also richly suggestive in hints concerning what might really be going on and what computational strategies evolution might have chanced upon. Moreover, it is by no means settled what exactly are the functional categories at the cognitive levels, and theories of lower level function may well be crucial to the discovery of the nature of higher level organization. Accordingly, despite

---

receptors (*46*). Video-enhanced light microscopy has opened a window onto dynamical activity within neurons, such as the recent visualization of axonal transport of organelles on micro-tubules (*37, 47*). All of the boundaries drawn show rough regions of the spatio-temporal plane where these techniques have been used and are not meant to indicate fundamental limitations.

the fact that the brain is experimentally demanding, basic neurobiology is indispensable in the task of discovering the theories that explain how we perform such activities as seeing, thinking, and being aware.

On the other hand, the possibility that cognition will be an open book once we understand the details of each and every neuron and its development, connectivity, and response properties is likewise misconceived. Even if we could simulate, synapse for synapse, our entire nervous system, that accomplishment, by itself, would not be the same as understanding how it works. The simulation might be just as much of a mystery as the function of the brain currently is, for it may reveal nothing about the network and systems properties that hold the key to cognitive effects. Even simulations of small network models have capabilities that are difficult to understand (*32*). Genuine theorizing about the nature of neurocomputation is therefore essential.

Many major questions remain to be answered. Although some problems in vision, learning, attention, and sensorimotor control are yielding, this will be harder to achieve for more complex psychological phenomena such as reasoning and language. Nonetheless, once we understand some fundamental principles of brain function, we may see how to reformulate the outstanding problems and address them in ways that are impossible now to predict. Whatever the outcome, the results are likely to surprise us.

References and Notes

1   P. S. Churchland, *Neurophilosophy: Toward a Unified Science of the Mind–Brain* (MIT Press, Cambridge, MA, 1986); J. LeDoux and W. Hirst, *Mind and Brain: Dialogues in Cognitive Neuroscience* (Cambridge University Press, Cambridge, 1986); S. M. Kosslyn, *Science*, **240**, 1621 (1988).

2   The original conception of levels of analysis can be found in D. Marr and T. Poggio [*Neurosci. Res. Program Bull.* **15**, 470 (1977)]. Although Marr (*3*) emphasized the importance of the computational level, the notion of a hierarchy of levels grew out of earlier work by W. Reichardt and T. Poggio [*Q. Rev. Biophys.*, **9**, 311 (1976)] on the visual control of orientation in the fly. In a sense, the current view on the interaction between levels is not so much a departure from the earlier views as a return to the practice that was previously established by Reichardt, Poggio, and even by Marr himself, who published a series of papers on neural network models of the cerebellar cortex and cerebral cortex. See, for example, D. Marr, *J. Physiol. (London)*, **202**, 437 (1969); *Proc. R. Soc. London B*, **176**, 161 (1970). The emphasis on the computational level has nonetheless had an important influence on the problems and issues that concern the current generation of neural and connectionist models [T. J. Sejnowski, C. Koch, P. S. Churchland, *Science*, **241**, 1299 (1988)].

3   D. Marr, *Vision* (Freeman, San Francisco, 1982).

4   P. M. Churchland, *Dialogue*, **21**, 223 (1982).

5   F. H. C. Crick, *Sci. Am.*, **241**, 219 (September 1979); P. S. Churchland and T. J. Sejnowski, in *Neural Connections and Mental Computation*, L. Nadel, ed. (MIT Press, Cambridge, MA, 1988); G. M. Shepherd, *Yale J. Biol. Med.*, **45**, 584 (1972); P. Grobstein, *Brain Behav. Evol.*, **31**, 34 (1988).

6   E. A. DeYoe and D. C. Van Essen, *Trends Neurosci.*, **11**, 219 (1988).

7   J. H. R. Maunsell and D. C. Van Essen, *J. Neurosci.*, **3**, 2563 (1983).

8   P. S. Goldman-Rakie, *Annu. Rev. Neurosci.*, **11**, 137 (1988); V. B. Mountcastle, *Trends Neurosci.*, **9**, 505 (1986).

9 T. H. Brown, P. Chapman, E. W. Kairiss, C. L. Keenan, *Science*, **242**, 724 (1988); G. F. Koob and F. E. Bloom, ibid., p. 715; L. R. Squire, *Memory and Brain* (Oxford University Press, Oxford, 1987); E. R. Kandel et al.; in *Synaptic Function*, G. M. Edelman, W. E. Gall, W. M. Cowan, eds (Wiley, New York, 1987), pp. 471–518; M. Mishkin and T. Appenzeller, *Sci. Am.*, **256**, 80 (June 1987).

10 S. P. Wise and R. Desimone, *Science*, **242**, 736 (1988).

11 S. G. Lisberger, ibid., p. 728.

12 T. Young, *Philos. Trans. R. Soc. London*, **92**, 12 (1802).

13 E. Hering, *Zur Lehre vom Lichtsinn* (Berlin, 1878).

14 J. Nathans, T. P. Piantanida, R. L. Eddy, T. B. Shows, D. S. Hogness, *Science*, **232**, 203 (1986).

15 The possibility of a two-stage analysis for color vision was suggested as early as 1881, but no progress was made until physiological techniques became available for testing the hypothesis. There are still some issues that have not yet been fully resolved by this theory.

16 H. B. Barlow, *Q. J. Exp. Psychol.*, **37**, 121 (1985).

17 D. Jameson and L. M. Hurvich, *J. Opt. Soc. Am.*, **51**, 46 (1961).

18 E. H. Land, *Proc. Natl. Acad. Sci. USA*, **83**, 3078 (1986); A. Hurlbert and T. Poggio, *Science*, **239**, 482 (1988).

19 S. Zeki, *Neuroscience*, **9**, 741 (1983); R. Desimone, S. J. Schein, L. G. Ungerleider, *Vision Res.*, **25**, 441 (1985).

20 J. Allman, F. Miezin, E. McGuiness, *Annu. Rev. Neurosci.*, **8**, 407 (1985).

21 A. R. Damasio, in *Principles of Behavioral Neurology*, M. M. Mesulam, ed. (Davis, Philadelphia, 1985), pp. 259–88; O. Sacks, R. L. Wasserman, S. Zeki, R. M. Siegel, *Soc. Neurosci. Abstr.*, **14**, 1251 (1988).

22 V. S. Ramachandran and R. L. Gregory, *Nature*, **275**, 55 (1978).

23 P. Cavanagh and Y. Leclerc, *Invest. Ophthalmol. Suppl.*, **26**, 282 (1985).

24 C. Lu and D. H. Fender, ibid., **11**, 482 (1972).

25 M. S. Livingstone and D. H. Hubel, *Science*, **240**, 740 (1988).

26 S. Zeki, *Nature*, **335**, 311 (1988).

27 D. Y. Teller and E. N. Pugh, Jr, in *Color Vision: Physiology and Psychophysics*, J. D. Mollon and L. T. Sharpe, Eds (Academic Press, New York, 1983).

28 T. J. Sejnowski, *Nature*, **332**, 308 (1988).

29 T. Kohonen, *Self-Organization and Associative Memory* (Springer-Verlag, New York, 1984); J. J. Hopfield and D. W. Tank, *Science*, **233**, 625 (1986); S. Grossberg and M. Kuperstien, *Neural Dynamics of Adaptive Sensory-Motor Control* (North-Holland, Amsterdam, 1986); M. A. Arbib, *Brains, Machines and Mathematics* (McGraw-Hill, New York, edn 2, 1987); D. E. Rumelhart and J. L. McClelland, *Parallel Distributed Processing: Explorations in the Microstructure of Cognition* (MIT Press, Cambridge, MA, 1986).

30 T. J. Sejnowski, C. Koch, P. S. Churchland, *Science*, **241**, 1299 (1988); C. Koch and I. Segev, *Methods in Neuronal Modeling: From Synapse to Networks* (MIT Press, Cambridge, MA, in press).

31 R. F. Abraham and C. D. Shaw, *Dynamics, the Geometry of Behavior* (Aerial Press, Santa Cruz, CA, 1982).

32 G. Edelman, *Neural Darwinism* (Basic Books, New York, 1987); R. A. Andersen and D. Zipser, *Can. J. Physiol. Pharmacol.*, **66**, 488 (1988); S. R. Lehky and T. J. Sejnowski, *Nature*, **333**, 452 (1988).

33 A. Vesalius, *De Humani Corporis* (Brussels, 1543).

34 J. H. R. Maunsell and W. T. Newsome, *Annu. Rev. Neurosci.*, **10**, 363 (1987).

35 D. H. Hubel and T. N. Wiesel, *J. Physiol. (London)*, **160**, 106 (1962).

36 E. Kandel and J. Schwartz, *Principles of Neural Science* (Elsevier, New York, edn 2, 1984).

37 S. J. Smith, *Science*, **242**, 708 (1988).

38   J. Dodd and T. M. Jessell, ibid., **242**, 692 (1988); A. L. Harrelson and C. S. Goodman, ibid., p. 692.

39   G. G. Blasdel and G. Salama, *Nature*, **321**, 579 (1986); A. Grinvald, E. Lieke, R. D. Frostig, C. D. Gilbert, T. N. Wiesel, ibid., **324**, 361 (1986).

40   A. Fine, W. B. Amos, R. M. Durbin, P. A. McNaughton, *Trends Neurosci.*, **11**, 346 (1988).

41   S. J. Williamson, G. L. Romani, L. Kaufman, I. Modena, *Biomagnetism: An Interdisciplinary Approach* (Plenum, New York, 1983); 2-DG: S. A. Hillyard and T. W. Picton, in *Handbook of Physiology*, section 1, *Neurophysiology*, F. Plum, ed. (American Physiological Society, New York, 1987), pp. 519–84.

42   M. E. Raichle, *Trends Neurosci.*, **9**, 525 (1986); M. I. Posnet, S. E. Petersen, P. T. Fox, M. E. Raichle, *Science*, **240**, 1627 (1988).

43   L. Sokoloff, *Metabolic Probes of Central Nervous System Activity in Experimental Animals and Man* (Sinauer, Sunderland, MA, 1984).

44   M. E. Phelps and J. C. Mazziotta, *Science*, **228**, 799 (1985).

45   M. M. Mesulam, in *Principles of Behavioral Neurology*, M. M. Mesulam, ed. (Davis, Philadelphia, 1985), pp. 125–68; B. Milner, in *Amnesia*, C. W. M. Whitty and O. Zangwill, eds (Butterworth, London, 1966), pp. 109–33; R. W. Sperry and M. Gazzaniga, in *Brain Mechanisms Underlying Speech and Language*, C. Millikan and F. Darley, eds (Grune and Stratton, New York, 1967), pp. 108–15; E. H. Land, D. H. Hubel, M. S. Livingstone, S. H. Perry, M. M. Burns, *Nature*, **303**, 616 (1983); S. M. Kosslyn, J. D. Holtzman, M. S. Gazzaniga, M. J. Farrah, *J. Exp. Psychol. General*, **114**, 311 (1985).

46   P. Schiller, *Nature*, **297**, 580 (1982); J. C. Horton and H. Sherk, *J. Neurosci.*, **4**, 374 (1984).

47   B. J. Schnapp and T. S. Reese, *Trends Neurosci.*, **9**, 155 (1986).

48   We thank F. Crick whose insights as well as critical judgments were a major resource in writing this article. We also thank P. Churchland, R. Cone, C. Koch, and D. MacLeod for helpful suggestions. T. J. S. is supported by grants from the National Science Foundation, the Seaver Institute, the Air Force Office of Scientific Research, the Office of Naval Research, and the General Electric Corporation; P. S. C. is supported by grants from the National Science Foundation and the James S. McDonnell Foundation. Portions of this article are based on our chapter in *Foundations of Cognitive Science* [P. S. Churchland and T. J. Sejnowski, in *Foundations of Cognitive Science*, M. Posner, ed. (MIT Press, Cambridge, in press)].

3

Electrical and Magnetic Brain Recordings: Contributions to Cognitive Neuroscience

Steven A. Hillyard

Introduction

Several complementary approaches are currently available for recording and imaging the patterns of neural activity in the human brain that underlie perception and cognition. Methods for measuring regional cerebral blood flow or cellular metabolism (e.g. position emission tomography, functional magnetic resonance imaging) can provide a detailed anatomical mapping of active brain areas, but the time course of these events is too sluggish to reveal the rapid flux of neuronal communication. In contrast, surface recordings of the electric and magnetic fields emanating from active populations of neurons provide a high degree of temporal resolution (on the order of milliseconds), but yield a less complete picture of their anatomical sources. Recent methodological advances, however, have enabled the neural generators of surface recorded fields to be localized to specific brain sites with improved accuracy [1•, 2•, 3, 4•, 5]. This review will consider the emerging role of electrical and magnetic field recordings in delineating the neural systems and information processing operations that underlie human perception and cognition.

With appropriate instrumentation, it is possible to make non-invasive recordings of event-related electrical potentials (ERPs)* or event-related magnetic fields (ERFs)* that reflect patterns of neural activity time-locked to sensory, motor, or cognitive events. Both ERPs and ERFs originate from the flow of electrical (ionic) currents across the membranes of active nerve cells. The passage of these currents through elongated neuronal processes is responsible for generating ERFs, whereas the flow of transmembrane currents into or out of the extracellular fluid produces ERPs. When a sufficient number of similarly oriented neurons is active concurrently, the additive current flow may generate signals that can be recorded through the intact scalp. By

*Abbreviations: ERF – event-related magnetic field; ERP – event related electrical potential; LRP – lateralized readiness potential; M – magnetic; N – negative; P – positive.

mapping the surface distribution of the ERPs or ERFs and applying algorithms based on the physics of electrical volume conduction or magnetic field propagation, the three-dimensional coordinates of the underlying neural generator sources may be estimated with respect to anatomical structures in the brain [1•, 2•, 3, 4•, 5]. The validity of these estimated source locations, however, depends upon assumptions made about the number and geometry of the active cell populations and upon the anatomical constraints that may apply. At present, ERP studies of higher cognitive functions are more numerous than those using the more recently developed and technically demanding magnetic recording techniques, but both methods have had considerable success at localizing the brain regions involved in sensory, perceptual and attentive processing.

Sensory Processing

The transmission of sensory information from the receptors through the afferent relay nuclei to the primary and secondary cortical receiving areas engenders orderly sequences of surface-recorded ERPs/ERFs that are characteristic of each sensory

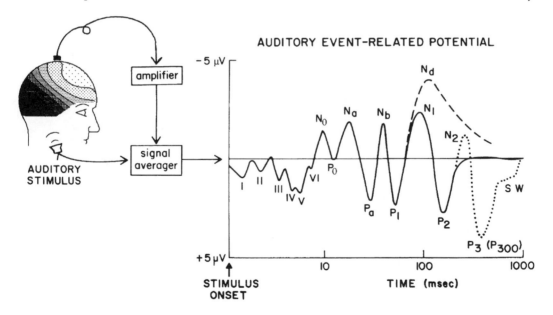

Figure 3.1 Characteristic waveform of the auditory ERP recorded from the scalp in response to a brief stimulus such as a click or tone. The brain's electrical responses to the sounds are first amplified and then signal-averaged over many stimulus presentations to produce an averaged waveform with an adequate signal/noise ratio. The logarithmic time axis allows visualization of the various components (voltage deflections) of the auditory ERP, which occur with typical latencies (time delays) after stimulus onset. These components include early waves 1–VI from the auditory brainstem pathways, early positive (P) and negative (N) cortical components N_a, P_a, N_b and P_1, and late cortical components N_1 and P_2. ERP components that vary dramatically according to the attentional and cognitive processing of the stimulus are shown in dotted and dashed lines (N_d, N_2, P_3 and SW). Shadings on the head represent the idealized voltage distribution over the scalp for the long-latency N_1 component at 100 ms, where lighter shades represent increasing electronegativity.

modality. Auditory stimuli elicit early (1–10 ms) components that originate in the brain-stem, followed by a sequence of rhythmic ERP/ERF components beginning at 15–20 ms that have been localized to the thalamo-cortical projections [6•] and supratemporal auditory cortex [7•]. The characteristic waveform of the scalp-recorded auditory ERP is shown in fig. 3.1. Longer latency components in the 50–200 ms range have similarly been localized to anatomically distinct subregions of the primary and secondary auditory cortext (Brodmann's areas 41 and 42) [1•, 3, 7•, 8–10]. Source localization studies have also revealed an orderly tonotopic organization in the human auditory cortex, reflecting the high anatomical resolution of these methods [11, 12•].

At least two of the longer latency components originating in the auditory cortex appear to reflect short-term sensory or "echoic" memory processes that last from one to several seconds and permit perceptual integration of successive sounds. Lu and colleagues [13•] observed an ERF component with a latency of 100 ms that showed a temporal decay function closely paralleling the time course of sensory memory. In addition, the "mismatch negativity" component that is triggered by any deviant stimulus in a repetitive auditory sequence signals a mismatch with the sensory memory trace of the immediately preceding stimulus features [5, 10, 14, 15••]. Several authors have concluded that the mismatch negativity component is unaffected by attention and thus provides evidence for the automatic feature analysis of all incoming stimuli [15••, 16•], but its automaticity has recently been questioned [17•, 18•].

Visual stimuli elicit complex patterns of ERPs/ERFs over the posterior scalp beginning at around 50 ms post-stimulus (depending on stimulus intensity). It has proven difficult to segregate and localize distinct neural generator sources in primary (striate) and secondary (extrastriate) cortical areas, mainly because multiple adjacent visual areas are activated with overlapping time courses. Studies using dipole source models and current density mappings have identified sources in or near striate cortex (Brodmann's area 17) that are active between 50–100 ms post-stimulus, with several extrastriate sources becoming active shortly thereafter [19–22, 23••]. Two extrastriate areas (occipito-temporal and mid-temporal) have been found to be specifically active during face perception [24]. Intracranial recordings of ERPs from the inferior occipital lobe have identified a cortical zone with a high specificity for color contrast, which the authors propose may be a homolog of area V4 in the macaque (T. Allison et al.: *Soc. Neurosci. Abstr.*, 1991, 18: 147).

Selective Auditory Attention

Because ERPs can track the flow of sensory information along the afferent pathways, they are well suited for studying the attentional mechanisms that determine which sensory inputs receive preferential processing at any given moment. Recent ERP/ERF studies have revealed both the anatomical levels of the sensory pathways at which attended stimuli are selected, and the time course of those selection processes [15••].

The neural substrates of auditory selective attention have been studied extensively using a dichotic listening task in which subjects attend to a sequence of rapidly presented tone pips in one ear and ignore a comparable sequence in the opposite ear. The earliest auditory ERP that is reliably affected by attention during dichotic listening is a positive (P) deflection between 20–50 ms (the P20–50 wave), which appears in magnetic (M) recordings as the M20–50 (M.G. Woldorff et al.: *Soc. Neurosci. Abstr.*, 1991, 17: 20) [25•]. The neural generators of the M20–50 attention effect have been localized to the auditory cortex in or near Heschl's gyrus (M.G. Woldorff et al.: *Soc. Neurosci. Abstr.*, 1991, 17: 20). The timing of the P20–50/M20–50 effect in humans corresponds closely to that observed in recordings of attention-sensitive single neurons from primary auditory cortex in monkeys [26, 27].

Selective listening also exerts a strong influence on the auditory ERP over the time interval 60–130 ms in the form of an enlarged negative (N) component that coincides in time with the evoked N100 wave [12•, 15••, 25•, 28]. Recordings of the magnetic counterpart of the N100 wave (the M100) during dichotic listening have identified the auditory cortex as its principal generator source (M. G. Woldorff et al.: *Soc. Neurosci. Abstr.*, 1991, 17: 20) [29•] (see fig. 3.2). Attention-related changes in M100 amplitude have also been localized to auditory cortex, supporting the hypothesis that selective listening acts to modulate the amplitude of sensory-evoked neural responses in modality-specific cortex, in the manner of a gain control mechanism. There is evidence, however, that a portion of the incremented N100/M100 response may arise from endogenous neural activity elicited only by attended sounds [12•, 15••, 28]. In any case, the finding that selective listening exerts control over sensory processing in the auditory cortex beginning as early as 20 ms post-stimulus, provides strong support for psychological theories that specify early selection of inputs before a full perceptual analysis.

Under appropriate conditions, the enlarged negative ERP elicited by attended stimuli includes an endogenous "processing negativity," which also originates from auditory cortex [30] and may persist for several hundred milliseconds as the relevant stimulus features are processed. The timing of the onset of the processing negativity provides a measure of how rapidly stimuli are selected or rejected on the basis of the sensory cues (e.g. pitch and location) that define an attended channel of tones [12•, 31, 32].

Selective Visual Attention

Human observers are adept at deploying their attention rapidly to relevant events in visual space, even when the eyes remain stationary. Behavioral studies of visual-spatial attention have shown that stimuli at attended locations are detected and discriminated more accurately than are stimuli distant from the focus of attention [33]. This improved perception is associated with a characteristic pattern of ERPs to stimuli at attended locations that includes enlarged "P1" and "N1" components over the occipital scalp (see fig. 3.3) [23••].

Mangun and colleagues [23••] have presented evidence that the earliest ERP component enhanced by visual-spatial attention (the P1 wave beginning at 70–80 ms) originates from neural generators in the lateral extrastriate visual cortex (Brodmann's areas 18–19), whereas subsequent attention-sensitive components (including the N1 at 130–190 ms) are generated in other extrastriate areas. An earlier component (beginning at around 50 ms) that displayed a surface topography consistent with a generator in primary visual (striate) cortex was unaffected by the direction of attention. These findings are consistent with neurophysiological studies in monkeys showing no attentional modulation at the level of the striate cortex [34], and with studies of cerebral blood flow in humans that have identified a lateral extrastriate area of increased

(a)

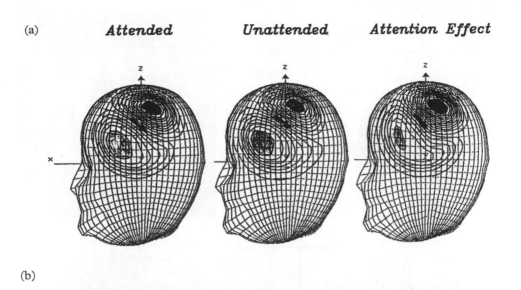

(b)

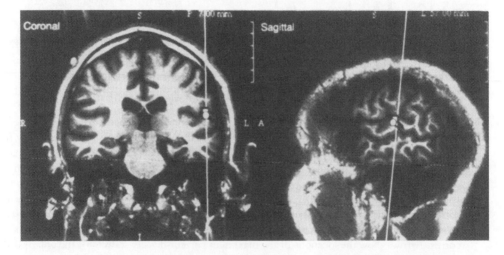

Figure 3.2 (**a**) Magnetic field distributions for the M100 component elicited by right ear tones in a dichotic listening experiment in subject M.W. Separate mappings are shown for the M100 elicited by (i) attended tones, (ii) unattended tones, and (iii) the "attention effect," which is the subtracted differential between the attended and unattended responses. These mappings show a dipolar field with magnetic field lines emerging from the head superiorly and entering inferiorly. The arrows indicate the direction and schematic positioning of the single equivalent dipole sources that were calculated to best fit these surface ERF distributions. (**b**) MRI scans showing the calculated location of the best-fit dipole sources for the subject shown in (**a**). The dipoles for the attended M100, the unattended M100, and the differential M100 attention effect were all situated within millimeters of one another in the auditory cortex of the supratemporal plane. Reproduced with permission from M. G. Woldorff et al. (*Soc. Neurosci. Abstr.*, 1991, 17: 20).

activation during tasks requiring attention to specific stimulus features [35, 36•]. Together, these studies suggest that a major mechanism of visual-spatial attention is the

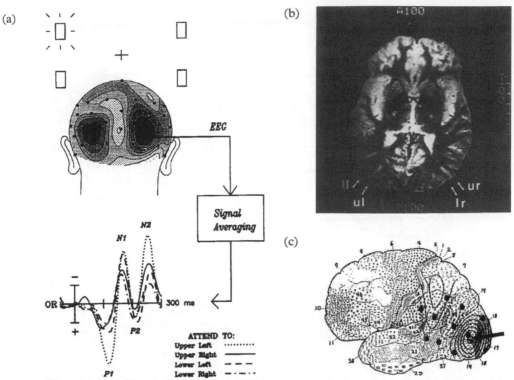

Figure 3.3   (**a**) Modulation of visual ERP components in the spatial attention task used by Mangun et al. [23••]. Stimuli (flashed rectangles) were presented to the four quadrants of the visual field in random order at intervals of 250–550 ms. Subjects were instructed to attend to only one of the quadrants during each 50ms run. ERPs were recorded and averaged separately for each type of stimulus and attention condition for each of 30 scalp sites (dots on the schematic head). The waveforms shown are grand average ERPs to the upper left quadrant flashes under each of the attention conditions. Note the enlargement of the P1, N1, and N2 waves when the flashes were attended. The head mapping shows the current density distribution of the P1 component, which has a maximal amplitude over the contralateral occipital scalp. (**b**) MRI scan showing a horizontal section of one subject's brain in a plane that includes the lateral extrastriate cortex. Arrows show the locations of the maximum current-density sources of the enlarged P1 attention effect at 100 ms for stimuli in the four visual quadrants: lower left (ll), upper left (ul), lower right (lr) and upper right (ur). Note that the MRI scan is left–right reversed. (**c**) Approximate superimposition of the average current density contours for the P1 component upon a classic map of Brodmann's cortical areas. The maximum source of the P1 attention effect overlies lateral prestriate visual cortex. Reproduced with permission from Mangun et al. [23••].

selective modulation of information flow from striate cortex to the multiple extrastriate areas, perhaps under the control of projections from the pulvinar nucleus of the thalamus [34, 37].

The same pattern of P1/N1 amplitude enhancement has been observed in other spatial attention tasks, including the cued orienting of attention to location [38, 39, 40•], and the identification of targets in visual search arrays [41, 42]. Together, these ERP findings have identified an early selection mechanism that is unique to visual-spatial attention and acts to facilitate the processing of all stimuli that fall within the "spotlight" of spatially focused attention [40•]. In contrast, paying attention to other visual features such as the color, orientation, brightness, and shape of a stimulus is manifested by longer-latency ERP/ERF components in the 150–300 ms range [43–45]. These later components demarcate the precise time course with which different visual features are selectively extracted and combined into whole percepts.

Mental Chronometry

Experimental psychologists have long sought to identify and isolate distinct stages of information processing that intervene between a sensory stimulus and a discriminative response. The study of the time course and sequencing of these processing stages, termed mental chronometry, has generally relied on reaction time as its main dependent measure [46]. The identification of ERP components that index a number of these processing stages provides a new source of data about their timing and organization. Whereas short-latency ERP components reflect the timing of early input and feature-selection processes, as described above, longer-latency components are closely coupled with processes of stimulus recognition and classification, and with response selection and execution [32, 44, 46, 47]. Among the most useful ERP components in mental chronometry are the N200 and P300 waves, which index perceptual discrimination processes, and the lateralized readiness potential (LRP), which is generated in the motor cortex contralateral to the responding hand and indexes covert response preparation.

Recent studies employing these ERP measures have helped resolve a basic question in mental chronometry, namely, whether each processing stage completes its own analysis before sending information to subsequent stages in a discrete all-or-none fashion, or whether partially analyzed information is passed along from one stage to the next in a more-or-less continuous "cascade." Clear evidence for the latter form of communication has been obtained from experiments in which an easily discriminable aspect of a stimulus (e.g. letter identity) signals to the subject which hand should respond, while a less discriminable feature (e.g. letter size) indicates whether or not the response should actually be carried out ("go") or withheld ("no-go") [48•–50•]. An early LRP signifying covert preparation of the appropriate hand arose with exactly the same onset latency for go and no-go stimuli, but this response activation was aborted on no-go trials as the less discriminable feature was discriminated. These studies demonstrate that covert response preparation can be initiated (in the absence of any peripheral muscle activity) on the basis of a preliminary analysis of one stimulus feature before the other features have been identified. In other words, partially analyzed sensory information is passed along to the response preparation stage before perceptual processing is complete. Miller and colleagues [51••] have found that preliminary perceptual information influences the discharge of single neurons in monkey motor cortex in exactly the same manner as with the human LRP. This provides strong converging evidence for the cortical localization and functional significance of the human LRP.

Memory Storage and Retrieval

The amplitude of a late positive ERP component elicited by stimuli being memorized has been found to be a reliable predictor of whether a given stimulus will be correctly recalled or recognized upon later testing (for examples, see [52–54, 55•]). This positivity has been interpreted as a neural sign of the initial encoding of the stimulus features in memory [54, 56], and the updating of the memory representation for the stimulus based on its distinctiveness [53]. Paller and colleagues [56, 57•] have found that the late positive amplitude predicted subsequent retrieval accuracy on explicit memory tests (e.g. recognition and recall) but not on implicit tests (e.g. stem completion priming and tachistoscopic identification). These ERP differences suggest that implicit and explicit forms of memory are associated with qualitatively different encoding processes.

Specific patterns of ERPs have also been observed when a previously presented stimulus is repeated and when it is correctly recognized as having been seen before (for example, see [52, 58, 59•]). These ERPs associated with memory retrieval include a late positive component (300–700 ms) associated with the conscious recollection of the stimulus, and a late negative component (N400) that reflects word repetition and contextual priming effects [55•, 57•, 60]. ERPs corresponding to these surface-recorded components have been recorded directly from the hippocampus and adjacent regions of the temporal lobe in patients implanted with depth electrodes [61, 62, 63•], thus revealing the timing of memory storage and retrieval operations mediated by temporal lobe structures.

Conclusion

Specific components of surface-recorded ERP/ERF activity have been reliably linked with sensory, perceptual, and cognitive processes in human subjects. Further refinement of techniques for localizing the neural circuitry giving rise to these activity patterns will lead to improved understanding of the anatomy and physiology of the underlying brain systems. The ERP/ERF methodologies allow the time course of human information processing to be delineated with high resolution, and complement the data available from other neuroimaging techniques. Recordings of ERPs/ERFs provide an important bridge between studies of the neural bases of human cognition and invasive studies in animal models that enable the corresponding neural mechanisms to be explored in more detail.

Acknowledgments

Supported by grants from NIMH (MH-25594), NINCDS (NS-17778) and the Human Frontier Science Program, and by ONR Contract N00014-89-J-1743. Thanks to S. Luck for helpful comments on the manuscript.

References and Recommended Reading

Papers of particular interest, published within the annual period of review, have been highlighted as:

● of special interest
●● of outstanding interest

1 Scherg, M. and Berg, P.: Use of Prior Knowledge in Brain Electromagnetic Source
● Analysis. *Brain Topog.*, 1991, **4**: 143–50.
Describes a quantitative approach for estimating the anatomical position and time course
of the neural generators (modelled as spatio-temporal dipoles) that contribute to surface-
recorded electrical and magnetic fields.

2 Williamson, S. J., Lu, Z-L., Karron, D. and Kaufman, L.: Advantages and Limitations of
● Magnetic Source Imaging. *Brain Topog.*, 1991, **4**: 169–80.
Considers methodological issues involved in deducing the distribution of neuronal activity
in the brain based on surface-recorded magnetic fields.

3 Papanicolaou, A. C., Baumann, S., Rogers, R. L., Saydjari, C., Amparo, E. G. and
Eisenberg, H. M.: Localization of Auditory Response Sources using Magnetoencephalography and Magnetic Resonance Imaging. *Arch. Neurol.*, 1990, **47**: 33–7.

4 Gevins, A., Le, J., Brickett, P., Reutter, B. and Desmond, J.: Seeing Through the Skull:
● Advanced EEGs use MRIs to Accurately Measure Cortical Activity from the Scalp. *Brain
Topog.*, 1991, **4**: 125–31.
Describes advanced techniques for estimating cortical sources of activity with high spatial
resolution.

5 Csepe, V., Pantev, C., Hoke, M., Hampson, S. and Ross, B.: Evoked Magnetic Responses
of the Human Auditory Cortex to Minor Pitch Changes: Localization of the Mismatch
Field. *Electroencephalog. Clin. Neurophysiol.*, 1992, **84**: 538–48.

6 Ribary, U., Ioannides, A. A., Singh, K. D., Hasson, R., Bolton, J. P. R., Lado, F., Mogilner,
● A. and Llinas, R.: Magnetic Field Tomography of Coherent Thalamocortical 40-Hz
Oscillations in Humans. *Proc. Natl. Acad. Sci. USA*, 1991, **88**: 11037–41.
Introduces a technique of magnetic field tomography to make a three dimensional
reconstruction of dynamic thalamo-cortical oscillations induced by repetitive sounds.

7 Pantev, C., Makeig, S., Hoke, M., Galambos, R., Hampson, S. and Gallen, C.: Human
● Auditory Evoked Gamma Band Magnetic Fields. *Proc. Natl Acad. Sci. USA*, 1991, **88**: 8996–
9000.
This study uses magnetic field recordings to localize oscillatory-evoked activity to the
auditory cortex as visualized on MRI scans of the subjects' brains.

8 Baumann, S. B., Rogers, R. L., Guinto, F. C., Saydjari, C. L., Papanicolaou, A. C. and
Eisenberg, H. M.: Gender Differences in Source Location for the N100 Auditory Evoked
Magnetic Field. *Electroencephalog. Clin. Neurophysiol.*, 1991, **80**: 53–9.

9 Lu, Z-L., Williamson, S. J. and Kaufman, L.: Human Auditory Primary and Association
Cortex have Differing Lifetimes for Activation Traces. *Brain Res.*, 1992, **572**: 236–41.

10 Sams, M., Kaukoranta, E., Hamalainen, M. and Naatanen, R.: Cortical Activity Elicited by
Changes in Auditory Stimuli: Different Sources for the Magnetic N100m and Mismatch
Responses. *Psychophysiology*, 1991, **28**: 21–9.

11 Pantev, C., Hoke, M., Lutkenhoner, B. and Lehnertz, K.: Tonotopic Organization of the
Auditory Cortex: Pitch versus Frequency Representation. *Science*, 1989, **246**: 486–8.

12 Woods, D. L., Alho, K. and Algazi, A.: Event-Related Potential Signs of Feature
● Conjunction during Human Auditory Selective Attention. *NeuroReport*, 1991, **2**: 189–92.
Demonstrates how the timing of auditory ERPs can be used to identify separate stages
of attentional selection. Changes in ERP scalp distribution as a function of tone
frequency were interpreted as reflecting a tonotopic organization of the human auditory
cortex.

13 Lu, Z.-L., Williamson, S. J. and Kaufman, L.: Behavioral Lifetime of Human Auditory
● Sensory Memory Predicted by Physiological Measures. *Science*, 1993, **258**: 1668–70.

Identifies a magnetically recorded component of auditory cortex activity that shows a time decay function corresponding to that of sensory (echoic) memory for the stimulus features.

14   Ritter, W., Paavilainen, P., Lavikainen, J., Reinikainen, K., Alho, K., Sams M. and Naatanen, R.: Event-Related Potentials to Repetition and Change of Auditory Stimuli. *Electroencephalog. Clin. Neurophysiol.*, 1992, **83**: 306–21.

15   Naatanen, R.: *Attention and Brain Function*. Hillsdale, New Jersey: Lawrence Erlbaum
••   Associates, 1992.
     A scholarly, comprehensive, and up-to-date analysis of the literature on neural mechanisms of selective attention in humans. The main emphasis is on the contributions of event-related potential and magnetic field recordings, but approaches based on measures of cerebral blood flow and metabolism are also covered.

16   Alho, K.: Selective Attention in Auditory Processing as Reflected by Event-Related Brain
•   Potentials. *Psychophysiology*, 1992, **29**: 247–63.
     A thorough and balanced review of recent studies of auditory ERPs related to selective attention.

17   Woldorff, M. G., Hackley, S. A. and Hillyard, S. A.: The Effects of Channel-Selective
•   Attention on the Mismatch Negativity Wave Elicited by Deviant Tones. *Psychophysiology*, 1991, **28**: 30–42.
     This study recorded the "mismatch negativity" (MMN) to deviant tones (of lower intensity) in the right and left ears in a dichotic listening task. Contrary to earlier reports that the MMN was unaffected by attention and thus reflected an automatic feature registration and comparator mechanism, it was found that the MMN was strongly suppressed to tones in the unattended ear.

18   Woods, D. L., Alho, K. and Algazi, A.: Intermodal Selective Attention. I: Effects on Event-
•   Related Potentials to Lateralized Auditory and Visual Stimuli. *Electroencephalog. Clin. Neurophysiol.*, 1992, **82**: 341–55.
     This study made a systematic comparison of ERP differences between intermodal (auditory–visual) and intramodal selective attention. It was concluded that intermodal attention depends primarily upon processing modulations in modality-specific cortex.

19   Aine, C. J., Bodis-Wollner, I. and George, J. S.: Generators of Visually Evoked Neuromagnetic Responses: Spatial-Frequency Segregation and Evidence for Multiple Sources. In *Advances in Neurology: Magnetoencephalography*, vol. 54, New York: Raven Press, 1990: 141–55.

20   Srebro, R. and Purdy, P. D.: Localization of Visually Evoked Cortical Activity using Magnetic Resonance Imaging and Computerized Tomography. *Vision Res.*, 1990, **30**: 351–58.

21   Simpson, G. V., Scherg, M., Ritter, W. and Vaughan, H. G. Jr: Localization and Temporal Activity Functions of Brain Sources Generating the Human Visual ERP. In *Psychophysiological Brain Research*, vol. 1, edited by Brunia, C. H. M., Gaillard, A. W. K., Kok, A., Tilburg University Press, 1990: 99–105.

22   Ossenblok, P., Reits, D. and Spekreijse, H.: Analysis of Striate Activity Underlying the Pattern Onset EP of Children. *Vision Res.*, 1992, **32**: 1829–35.

23   Mangun, G. R., Hillyard, S. A. and Luck, S. J.: Electrocortical Substrates of Visual Selective
••   Attention. In *Attention and Performance*, vol. XIV, Cambridge, Massachusetts: MIT Press, 1993, in press.
     This study employed ERP recordings with current source density mapping techniques to determine the level of the visual pathways at which spatial-selective attention modulates sensory inputs. Reviews recent ERP studies of spatial-selective attention.

24   Lu, S. T., Hari, R., Hamalainen, M., Ilmoniemi, R. J., Lounasmaa, O. V., Sams, M. and Vilkman, Vi: Seeing Faces Activates Three Separate Areas Outside the Occipital Visual Cortex in Man. *Neuroscience*, 1991, **43**: 287–90.

25 Woldorff, M. and Hillyard, S. A.: Modulation of Early Auditory Processing During
•   Selective Listening to Rapidly Presented Tones. *Electroencephalog. Clin. Neurophysiol.*, 1991,
    79: 170–91.
    Reports a dichotic listening experiment in which selective listening was found to affect
    short-latency auditory-evoked activity. The results are discussed in terms of "early
    selection" mechanisms of attention.

26 Goldstein, M. H., Jr, Benson, D. A. and Hienz, R. D.: Studies of Auditory Cortex in
    Behaviorally Trained Monkeys. In *Conditioning: Representation of Involved Neural Functions*,
    edited by Woody, C. D., New York: Plenum Press, 1982: 307–17.

27 Miller, J. M., Pfingst, B. E. and Ryan, A. F.: Behavioral Modification of Response
    Characteristics of Cells in the Auditory System. In *Conditioning: Representation of Involved
    Neural Functions*, edited by Woody, C. D., New York: Plenum Press, 1982, 345–61.

28 Naatanen, R., Teder, W., Alho, K. and Lavikainen, J.: Auditory Attention and Selective
    Input Modulation: A Topographical ERP Study. *NeuroReport*, 1992, **3**: 493–6.

29 Rif, J., Hari, R., Hamalainen, M. S. and Sams, M.: Auditory Attention Affects Two
•   Different Areas in the Human Supratemporal Cortex. *Electroencephalog. Clin. Neurophysiol.*,
    1991, **79**: 464–72.
    Magnetic field recordings were used to localize two different areas in auditory cortex in
    which evoked neural activity was modulated by selective attention.

30 Arthur, D. L., Lewis, P. S., Medvick, P. A. and Flynn, E. R.: A Neuromagnetic Study of
    Selective Auditory Attention. *Electroencephalog. Clin. Neurophysiol.*, 1991, **78**: 348–60.

31 Shelley, A. M., Ward, P. B., Michie, P. T., Andrews, S., Mitchell, P. F., Catts, S. V. and
    McConaghy, N.: The Effect of Repeated Testing on ERP Components during Auditory
    Selective Attention. *Psychophysiology*, 1991, **28**: 496–510.

32 Novak, G., Ritter, W. and Vaughan, H. G. Jr: The Chronometry of Attention-Modulated
    Processing and Automatic Mismatch Detection. *Psychophysiology*, 1992, **29**: 412–30.

33 Van Der Heijden, A. H. C.: *Selective Attention in Vision*. London, England: Routledge, 1992.

34 Desimone, R., Wessinger, M., Thomas, L. and Schneider, W.: Attentional Control of Visual
    Perception: Cortical and Subcortical Mechanisms. *Cold Spring Harbor Symp. Quant. Biol.*,
    1990, **55**: 963–71.

35 Corbetta, M., Miezin, F. M., Dobmeyer, S., Shulman, G. L. and Petersen, S. E.: Selective
    and Divided Attention during Visual Discriminations of Shape, Color, and Speed:
    Functional Anatomy by Positron Emission Tomography. *J. Neurosci.*, 1991, **11**: 2383–402.

36 Grady, C. L., Haxby, J. V., Horwitz, B., Schapiro, M. B. and Rapoport, S. I.: Dissociation of
•   Object and Spatial Vision in Human Extrastriate Cortex: Age-Related Changes in
    Activation of Regional Cerebral Blood Flow Measured with (150) Water and Positron
    Emission Tomography. *J. Cogn. Neurosci.*, 1992, **4**: 23–34.
    This study identifies an occipital-parietal focus of cortical activation during a visual-spatial
    task and an occipito-temporal focus during a face-matching task. These anatomical
    divisions relate to the concepts of dorsal and ventral "streams" of visual processing
    related to spatial and object vision, respectively.

37 LaBerge, D. and Buchsbaum, M. S.: Positron Emission Tomographic Measurements of
    Pulvinar Activity during an Attention Task. *J. Neurosci.*, 1990, **10**: 613–19.

38 Mangun, G. R. and Hillyard, S. A.: Modulation of Sensory-Evoked Brain Potentials
    Provide Evidence for Changes in Perceptual Processing during Visual-Spatial Priming. *J.
    Exp. Psychol. [Human Percept. Perform.]*, 1991, **17**: 1057–74.

39 Harter, M. R. and Anllo-Vento, L.: Visual-Spatial Attention: Preparation and Selection in
    Children and Adults. In *Event-Related Potentials of the Brain*, edited by Brunia, C. H. M.,
    Mulder, G., Verbaten, M. N., Amsterdam: Elsevier, 1991: 183–94.

40 Hillyard, S. A., Luck, S. J. and Mangun, G. R.: The Cuing of Attention to Visual Field
•   Locations: Analysis with ERP Recordings. In *Cognitive Electrophysiology: Event-Related Brain*

Potentials in Basic and Clinical Research, edited by Heinze, H. J., Munte, T. F., Mangun, G. R., Boston: Birkhausen, 1993, in press.

Reviews recent ERP evidence that the spatial cuing of attention affects early visual processing in extrastriate cortical areas. Increased ERP amplitudes to stimuli at cued locations are found to be associated with improved detectability of targets in relation to uncued locations.

41   Luck, S. J., Fan, S. and Hillyard, S. A.: Attention-Related Modulation of Sensory-Evoked Brain Activity in a Visual Search Task. *J. Cogn. Neurosci.*, 1993, in press.

42   Luck, S. J. and Hillyard, S. A.: The Role of Attention in Feature Detection and Conjunction Discrimination: An Electrophysiological Analysis. *Int. J. Neurosci.*, 1993, in press.

43   Harter, M. R. and Aine, C. J.: Brain Mechanisms of Visual Selective Attention. In *Varieties of Attention*, edited by Parasuraman, R., Davies, D. R., London: Academic Press, 1984: 293–321.

44   Wijers, A. A., Mulder, G., Okita, T. and Mulder, L. J. M.: Event-Related Potentials during Memory Search and Selective Attention to Letter Size and Conjunctions of Letter Size and Color. *Psychophysiology*, 1989, **26**: 529–47.

45   Kenemans, J. L., Kok, A. and Smulders, F. T. Y.: Event-Related Potentials to Conjunctions of Spatial Frequency and Orientation as a Function of Stimulus Parameters and Response Requirements. *Electroencephalog. Clin. Neurophysiol.*, 1993, **88**: 51–63.

46   Coles, M. G. H.: Modern Mind-Brain Reading: Psychophysiology, Physiology and Cognition. *Psychophysiology*, 1989, **26**: 251–69.

47   Gehring, W. J., Gratton, G., Coles, M. and Donchin, E.: Probability Effects on Stimulus Evaluation and Response Processes. *J. Exp. Psychol. [Human Percept. Perform.]*, 1992, **18**: 198–216.

48   Osman, A., Bashore, T. R., Coles, M., Donchin, E. and Meyer, D.: On the Transmission of
•   Partial Information: Inferences from Movement-Related Brain Potentials. *J. Exp. Psychol. [Human Percept. Perform]*, 1992, **18**: 217–32.

Recordings of the lateralized readiness potential were used to show that different features of an imperative cue are analyzed in parallel and passed along to the response-selection stage independently.

49   Smid, H., Mulder, G., Mulder, L. and Brands, G. J.: A Psychophysiological Study of the Use
•   of Partial Information in Stimulus-Response Translation. *J. Exp. Psychol. [Human Percept. Perform.]*, 1992, **18**: 1101–19.

This study used ERP markers to demonstrate a dissociation between the timing of stimulus identification and the communication of early feature analyses to the response-selection stages.

50   Miller, J. and Hackley, S. A.: Electrophysiological Evidence for Temporal Overlap Among
•   Contingent Mental Processes. *J. Exp. Psychol. [Gen.]*, 1992, **121**: 195–209.

This study used recordings of the lateralized readiness potential to show that response preparation can be initiated before perceptual processing is complete.

51   Miller, J., Riehle, A. and Requin, J.: Effects of Preliminary Perceptual Output on Neuronal
••   Activity of the Primary Motor Cortex. *J. Exp. Psychol. [Human Percept. Perform.]*, 1992, **18**: 1121–38.

Neurophysiological recordings from the monkey primary motor cortex show that preliminary perceptual information reaches the motor system before perceptual analysis is complete. Functionally separate classes of motor cortex cells are identified, which allow the authors to propose specific hypotheses about how sensory inputs are coupled to motor outputs within the motor cortex.

52   Neville, H., Kutas, M., Chesney, G. and Schmidt, A. L.: Event-Related Brain Potentials during Initial Encoding and Recognition Memory of Congruous and Incongruous Words. *J. Mem. Lang.*, 1986, **25**: 75–92.

53   Fabiani, M., Karis, D. and Donchin, E.: Effects of Mnemonic Strategy Manipulation in a
      Von Restorff Paradigm. *Electroencephalog. Clin. Neurophysiol.*, 1990, **75**: 22–35.
54   Sommer, W., Schweinberger, S. R. and Matt, J.: Human Brain Potential Correlates of Face
      Encoding into Memory. *Electroencephalog. Clin. Neurophysiol.*, 1991, **79**: 457–63.
55   Smith, M. E.: Neurophysiological Manifestations of Recollective Experience during
•   Recognition Memory Judgements. *J. Cogn. Neurosci.*, 1993, **5**: 1–13.
      ERPs recorded to words in a memory test show distinct waveforms according to whether
      the words are recollected or simply evoke a "sense of familiarity". The results are discussed
      in terms of both psychological theories of memory and underlying neural mechanisms.
56   Paller, K. A.: Recall and Stem-Completion Priming have Different Electrophysiological
      Correlates and are Modified Differentially by Directed Forgetting. *J. Exp. Psychol. [Learn.
      Memory Cogn.]*, 1990, **16**: 1021–32.
57   Paller, K. A. and Kutas, M.: Brain Potentials during Memory Retrieval Provide
•   Neurophysiological Support for the Distinction between Conscious Recollection and
      Priming. *J. Cogn. Neurosci.*, 1992, **4**: 373–92.
      Separate ERP components are shown to provide measures of different processes
      underlying memory performance. A late positive component appears to be a specific
      index of conscious recollection while earlier components index processes related to
      priming.
58   Friedman, D.: ERPs during Continuous Recognition Memory for Words. *Biol. Psychol.*,
      1990, **30**: 61–88.
59   Rugg, M. D. and Doyle, M. C.: Event-Related Potentials and Stimulus Repetition in Direct
•   and Indirect Tests of Memory. In *Cognitive Electrophysiology: Event-Related Brain Potentials in
      Basic and Clinical Research*, edited by Heinze, H. J., Munte, T. F., Mangun, G. R., Boston:
      Birkhausen, 1993, in press.
      An overview of recent studies from Rugg's laboratory, which have identified two separate
      ERP components that are modulated as a function of memory during word repetition. A
      late positive component is interpreted as signifying the "relative familiarity" of a repeated
      item, while a late negativity (N400) is considered to index processes of integrating the
      attributes of a repeated item with its context.
60   VanPetten, C., Kutas, M., Kleunder, R., Mitchiner, M. and McIssac, H.: Fractioning the
      Word Repetition Effect with Event-Related Potentials. *J. Cogn. Neurosci.*, 1991, **3**: 131–150.
61   Paller, K. A., Roessler, E. and McCarthy, G.: Potentials Recorded from the Scalp and from
      the Hippocampus in Humans Performing a Visual Recognition Memory Test. *J. Clin. Exp.
      Neuropsychol.*, 1990, **12**: 401.
62   Heit, G., Smith, M. E. and Halgren, E.: Neuronal Activity in the Human Medial Temporal
      Lobe during Recognition Memory. *Brain*, 1990, **113**: 1093–112.
63   Puce, A., Andrewes, D., Berkovic, S. and Bladin, P.: Visual Recognition Memory:
•   Electrophysiological Evidence for the Role of Temporal White Matter in Man. *Brain*,
      1991, **114**: 1647–66.
      Different classes of ERP components associated with memory were recorded from the
      temporal lobe of patients with implanted depth electrodes.

4

Behind the Scenes of Functional Brain Imaging: A Historical and Physiological Perspective

Marcus E. Raichle

Over the past 10 years the field of cognitive neuroscience has emerged as a very important growth area in neuroscience. Cognitive neuroscience combines the experimental strategies of cognitive psychology with various techniques to actually examine how brain function supports mental activities. Leading this research in normal humans are the new techniques of functional brain imaging: positron emission tomography (PET)* and magnetic resonance imaging (MRI)* along with event-related potentials obtained from electroencephalography or magnetoencephalography.

The signal used by PET is based on the fact that changes in the cellular activity of the brain of normal, awake humans and unanesthetized laboratory animals are invariably accompanied by changes in local blood flow (for a review, see ref. *1*). This robust, empirical relationship has fascinated scientists for well over a hundred years, but its cellular basis remains largely unexplained despite considerable research.

More recently it has been appreciated that these changes in blood flow are accompanied by much smaller changes in oxygen consumption (*2, 3*). This leads to changes in the actual amount of oxygen remaining in blood vessels at the site of brain activation (i.e., the supply of oxygen is not matched precisely with the demand). Because MRI signal intensity is sensitive to the amount of oxygen carried by hemoglobin (*4*), this change in blood oxygen content at the site of brain activation can be detected with MRI (*5–8*).

Studies with PET and MRI and magnetic resonance spectroscopy (MRS) have brought to light the fact that metabolic changes accompanying brain activation do not appear to follow exactly the time-honored notion of a close coupling between blood flow and the oxidative metabolism of glucose (*9, 10*). Changes in blood flow appear to be accompanied by changes in glucose utilization that exceed the increase in

*Abbreviations: PET, positron emission tomography; MRI, magnetic resonance imaging; MRS, magnetic resonance spectroscopy; fMRI, functional MRI; BOLD, blood-oxygen-level-dependent.

oxygen consumption (11, 12), suggesting that the oxidative metabolism of glucose may not supply all of the energy demands encountered transiently during brain activation. Rather, glycolysis alone may provide the energy needed for the transient changes in brain activity associated with cognition and emotion.

Because of the prominent role of PET and MRI in the study of human brain function in health and disease, it is important to understand what we currently know about the biological basis of the signals they monitor. Individuals using these tools or considering the results of studies employing them should have a working knowledge of their biological basis. This chapter reviews that information which is, at times, conflicting and incomplete.

Although it is easy to conclude that much of this work transpired over the past decade or so because of its recent prominence in the neuroscience literature, in truth work on these relationships and the tools to exploit them have been developing for more than a century. To place present work in its proper perspective, a brief historical review of work on the relationships between brain function, blood flow, and metabolism is included.

Historical Background

The quest for an understanding of the functional organization of the normal human brain, using techniques to assess changes in brain circulation, has occupied mankind for more than a century. One has only to consult William James' monumental two-volume text *Principles of Psychology* (*13*) on page 97 of the first volume to find reference to changes in brain blood flow during mental activities. He references primarily the work of the Italian physiologist Angelo Mosso (*14*) who recorded the pulsation of the human cortex in patients with skull defects following neurosurgical procedures. Mosso showed that these pulsations increased regionally during mental activity and concluded, correctly we now know, that brain circulation changes selectively with neuronal activity.

No less a figure than Paul Broca was also interested in the circulatory changes associated with mental activities as manifest by changes in brain temperature (*15*). Although best known for his seminal observations on the effect of lesions of the left frontal operculum on language function (*16*), Broca also studied the effect of various mental activities, especially language, on the localized temperature of the scalp of medical students (*15*). Although such measurements might seem unlikely to yield any useful information, the reported observations, unbiased by preconceived notions of the functional anatomy of the cortex, were remarkably perceptive. Also active in the study of brain temperature and brain function in normal humans were Mosso (*17*) and Hans Berger (*18*). Berger later abandoned his efforts in this area in favor of the development of the electroencephalogram.

Despite a promising beginning, including the seminal animal experimental observations of Roy and Sherrington (*9*), which suggested a link between brain circulation and metabolism, interest in this research virtually ceased during the first quarter of the twentieth century. Undoubtedly, this was due in part to a lack of tools sufficiently sophisticated to pursue this line of research. In addition, the work of Leonard Hill, Hunterian Professor of the Royal College of Surgeons in England, was very influential

(*19*). His eminence as a physiologist overshadowed the inadequacy of his own experiments that led him to conclude that no relationship existed between brain function and brain circulation.

There was no serious challenge to Leonard Hill's views until a remarkable clinical study was reported by John Fulton in the 1928 issue of the journal *Brain* (*86*). At the time of the report Fulton was a neurosurgery resident under Harvey Cushing at the Peter Bent Brigham Hospital in Boston. A patient presented to Cushing's service with gradually decreasing vision caused by an arteriovenous malformation of the occipital cortex. Surgical removal of the malformation was attempted but unsuccessful, leaving the patient with a bony defect over the primary visual cortex. Fulton elicited a history of a cranial bruit audible to the patient whenever he engaged in a visual task. Based on this history Fulton pursued a detailed investigation of the behavior of the bruit that he could auscultate and record over occipital cortex. Remarkably consistent changes in the character of the bruit could be appreciated depending upon the visual activities of the patient. Although opening the eyes produced only modest increases in the intensity of the bruit, reading produced striking increases. The changes in cortical blood flow related to the complexity of the visual task and the attention of the subject to that task anticipated findings and concepts that have only recently been addressed with modern functional imaging techniques (*20*).

At the close of World War II, Seymour Kety and his colleagues opened the next chapter in studies of brain circulation and metabolism. Working with Lou Sokoloff and others, Kety developed the first quantitative methods for measuring whole brain blood flow and metabolism in humans. The introduction of an *in vivo* tissue autoradiographic measurement of regional blood flow in laboratory animals by Kety's group (*21, 22*) provided the first glimpse of quantitative changes in blood flow in the brain related directly to brain function. Given the later importance of derivatives of this technique to functional brain imaging with both PET and functional MRI (fMRI) it is interesting to note the (dis)regard the developers had for this technique as a means of assessing brain functional organization. Quoting from the comments of William Landau to the members of the American Neurological Association meeting in Atlantic City (*21*): "Of course we recognize that this is a very secondhand way of determining physiological activity; it is rather like trying to measure what a factory does by measuring the intake of water and the output of sewage. This is only a problem of plumbing and only secondary inferences can be made about function. We would not suggest that this is a substitute for electrical recording in terms of easy evaluation of what is going on." With the introduction of the deoxyglucose technique for the regional measurement of glucose metabolism in laboratory animals (*23*) and its later adaptation for PET (*24*), enthusiasm was much greater for the potential of such measurements to enhance our knowledge of brain function (*1*).

Soon after Kety and his colleagues introduced their quantitative methods for measuring whole brain blood flow and metabolism in humans, David Ingvar, Neils Lassen and their Scandinavian colleagues introduced methods applicable to humans that permitted regional blood flow measurements to be made by using scintillation detectors arrayed like a helmet over the head (*25*). They demonstrated directly in normal human subjects that blood flow changed regionally during changes in brain functional activity. The first study of functionally induced regional changes in blood flow by using these techniques in normal humans was actually reported by Ingvar and

Risberg (*26*) at an early meeting on brain blood and metabolism and was greeted with cautious enthusiasm and a clear sense of its potential importance for studies of human brain function by Seymour Kety (*27*). However, despite many studies of functionally induced changes in regional cerebral blood that followed (*1, 28*), this approach was not embraced by most neuroscientists or cognitive scientists. It is interesting to note that this indifference was to disappear almost completely in the 1980s, a subject to which we will return shortly.

In 1973 Godfrey Hounsfield (*29*) introduced x-ray computed tomography, a technique based on principles presented in 1963 by Alan Cormack (*30, 31*). Overnight the way in which we looked at the human brain changed. Immediately, researchers envisioned another type of tomography, PET, which created *in vivo* autoradiograms of brain function (*32, 33*). A new era of functional brain mapping began. The autoradiographic techniques for the measurement of blood flow (*21, 22*) and glucose metabolism (*23*) in laboratory animals could now be performed safely in humans (*24, 34*). In addition, quantitative techniques were developed (*35, 36*) and, importantly, validated (*36, 37*) for the measurement of oxygen consumption.

Soon it was realized that highly accurate measurements of brain function in humans could be performed with PET (*38*). Although this could be accomplished with either measurements of blood flow or metabolism (*1*), blood flow became the favored technique because it could be measured quickly (<1 min) by using an easily produced radiopharmaceutical ($H_2^{15}O$) with a short half life (123 sec) that allowed many repeat measurements in the same subject.

The study of human cognition with PET was aided greatly by the involvement of cognitive psychologists in the 1980s whose experimental designs for dissecting human behaviors by using information-processing theory fit extremely well with the emerging functional brain imaging strategies (*38*). It may well have been the combination of cognitive science and systems neuroscience with brain imaging that lifted this work from a state of indifference and obscurity in the neuroscience community in the 1970s to its current role of prominence in cognitive neuroscience.

As a result of collaboration among neuroscientists, imaging scientists, and cognitive psychologists, a distinct behavioral strategy for the functional mapping of neuronal activity emerged. This strategy was based on a concept introduced by the Dutch physiologist Franciscus C. Donders in 1868 (reprinted in ref. *39*). Donders proposed a general method to measure thought processes based on a simple logic. He subtracted the time needed to respond to a light (say, by pressing a key) from the time needed to respond to a particular color of light. He found that discriminating color required about 50 msec. In this way, Donders isolated and measured a mental process for the first time by subtracting a control state (i.e., responding to a light) from a task state (i.e., discriminating the color of the light). An example of the manner in which this strategy has been adopted for functional imaging is illustrated in fig. 4.1.

One criticism of this approach has been that the time necessary to press a key after a decision to do so has been made is affected by the nature of the decision process itself. By implication, the nature of the processes underlying key press, in this example, may have been altered. Although this issue (known in cognitive science jargon as the assumption of pure insertion) has been the subject of continuing discussion in cognitive psychology, it finds its resolution in functional brain imaging, where changes in any process are directly signaled by changes in observable brain states. Events

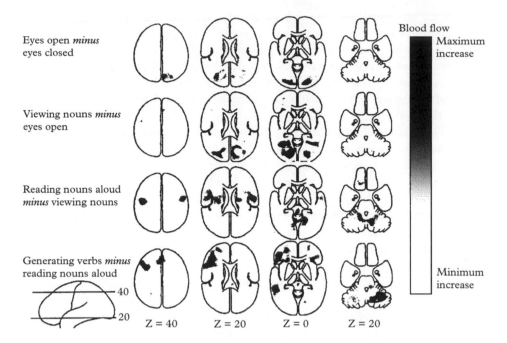

Eyes open *minus* eyes closed

Viewing nouns *minus* eyes open

Reading nouns aloud *minus* viewing nouns

Generating verbs *minus* reading nouns aloud

Blood flow
Maximum increase

Minimum increase

Z = 40   Z = 20   Z = 0   Z = 20

Figure 4.1 Four different hierarchically organized conditions are represented in these mean blood flow difference images obtained with PET. All of the changes shown in these images represent increases over the control state for each task. A group of normal subjects performed these tasks involving common English nouns (*40, 83, 84*) to demonstrate the spatially distributed nature of the processing by task elements going on in the normal human brain during a simple language task. Task complexity was increased from simply opening the eyes (row 1) through passive viewing of nouns on a television monitor (row 2); reading aloud the nouns as they appear on the screen (row 3); and saying aloud an appropriate verb for each noun as it appeared on the screen (row 4). These horizontal images are oriented with the front of the brain on top and the left side to the reader's left. The markings "Z = 40" indicate millimeters above and below a horizontal plane through the brain marked "Z = 0".

occurring in the brain are not hidden from the investigator as in the purely cognitive experiments. Careful analysis of the changes in the functional images reveals whether processes (e.g., specific cognitive decisions) can be added or removed without affecting ongoing processes (e.g., motor processes). Processing areas of the brain that become inactive during the course of a particular cognitive paradigm are illustrated in fig. 4.2. By examining the images in figs 4.1 and 4.2 together, a more complete picture emerges of the changes taking place in the cognitive paradigm illustrated together in these two figures. Clearly, some areas of the brain active at one stage in a hierarchically designed paradigm can become inactive as task complexity is increased. Although changes of this sort are hidden from the view of the cognitive scientist they become obvious when brain imaging is employed.

A final caveat with regard to certain cognitive paradigms is that the brain systems involved do not necessarily remain constant through many repetitions of the task. Although simple habituation might be suspected when a task is tedious, this is not the issue referred to here. Rather, when a task is novel and, more importantly, conflicts with a more habitual response to the presented stimulus, major changes can occur in

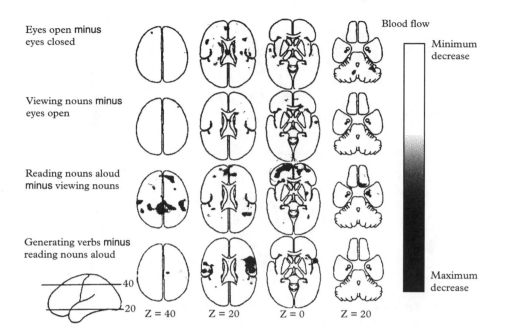

Eyes open minus eyes closed

Viewing nouns minus eyes open

Reading nouns aloud minus viewing nouns

Generating verbs minus reading nouns aloud

Blood flow
Minimum decrease
Maximum decrease

Z = 40   Z = 20   Z = 0   Z = 20

Figure 4.2 Hierarchically organized subtractions involving the same task conditions as shown in fig. 4.1 with the difference being that these images represent areas of decreased activity in the task condition as compared with the control condition. Note that the major decreases occurred when subjects read the visually presented nouns aloud as compared with viewing them passively as they appeared on the television monitor (row 3); and when they said aloud an appropriate verb for each noun as it appeared on the television monitor as compared with reading the noun aloud (row 4). Combining the information available in figs. 4.1 and 4.2 provides a fairly complete picture of the interactions between tasks and brain systems in hierarchically organized cognitive tasks when studied with functional brain imaging.

the systems allocated to the task. A good example relates to the task shown in figs 4.1 and 4.2 (row 4) where subjects are asked to generate an appropriate verb for visually presented nouns rather than simply read the noun aloud as they had been doing (*40*). In this task, regions uniquely active when the task is first performed (fig. 4.1, row 4 and fig. 4.3, row 1) are replaced by regions active when the task has become well practiced (fig. 4.3, row 2). Such changes have both practical and theoretical implications when it comes to the design and interpretation of cognitive activation experiments. Functional brain imaging obviously provides a unique perspective that is unavailable in the purely cognitive experiment.

Finally, another technology emerged contemporaneously with PET and computed tomography. This was MRI. MRI is based on yet another set of physical principles that have to do with the behavior of hydrogen atoms or protons in a magnetic field. These principles were discovered independently by Felix Block (*41*) and Edward Purcell and his colleagues in 1946 (*42*) and expanded to imaging by Paul Lauterbur in 1973 (*43*). Initially MRI provided superb anatomical information but inherent in the data also was important metabolic and physiological information. An opening for MRI in the area of functional brain imaging emerged when it was discovered that during changes in

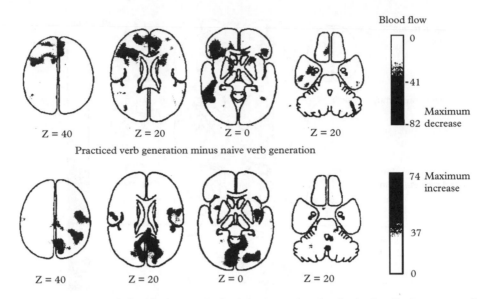

Figure 4.3 Practice-induced changes in brain systems involve both the disappearance of activity in systems initially supporting task performance (row 1) and the appearance of activity in other systems concerned with practiced performance (row 2). In this example, generating verbs aloud for visually presented nouns (see also row 4 of figs. 4.1 and 4.2 for changes during the naïve performance of the task), subjects acquired proficiency on the task after 10 min. of practice. This improved performance was associated with a disappearance of activity in areas of frontal and temporal cortex and the right cerebellum (row 1) and the appearance of activity in Sylvian-insular and occipital cortex (row 2). These images were created by subtracting the naïve performance of verb generation from the practiced performance of the task. More details on these changes can be obtained from Raichle et al. (*40*).

neuronal activity there are local changes in the amount of oxygen in the tissue (*2, 3*). By combining this observation with a much earlier observation by Pauling and Coryell (*44*) that changing the amount of oxygen carried by hemoglobin changes the degree to which hemoglobin disturbs a magnetic field, Ogawa et al. (*4*) were able to demonstrate that *in vivo* changes in blood oxygenation could be detected with MRI. The MRI signal (technically known as T2* or "tee-two-star") arising from this unique combination of brain physiology (*2*) and nuclear magnetic resonance physics (*44, 45*) became known as the blood-oxygen-level-dependent or BOLD signal (*4*). There quickly followed several demonstrations of BOLD signal changes in normal humans during functional brain activation (*5–8*), giving birth to the rapidly developing field of fMRI.

   In the discussion to follow it is important to keep in mind that when a BOLD signal is detected, blood flow to a region of brain has changed out of proportion to the change in oxygen consumption (*46*). When blood flow changes more than oxygen consumption, in either direction, there is a reciprocal change in the amount of deoxyhemoglobin present locally in the tissue, changing the local magnetic field properties. As you will see, both increases and decreases occur in the BOLD signal in the normal human brain.

Metabolic Requirements of Cognition

Although many had assumed that behaviorally induced increases in local blood flow would be reflected in local increases in the oxidative metabolism of glucose (*10*), evidence from brain imaging studies with PET (*2, 3*) and fMRI (*46*) have indicated otherwise. Fox and his colleagues (*2, 3*) demonstrated that in normal, awake adult humans, stimulation of the visual or somatosensory cortex results in dramatic increases in blood flow but minimal increases in oxygen consumption. Increases in glucose utilization occur in parallel with blood flow (*3, 12*), an observation fully anticipated by the work of others (*23, 47*). However, changes in blood flow and glucose utilization were much in excess of the changes in oxygen consumption, an observation contrary to most popularly held notions of brain energy metabolism (*10*). These results suggested that the additional metabolic requirements associated with increased neuronal activity might be supplied largely through glycolysis alone.

Another element of the relationship between brain circulation and brain function that was not appreciated before the advent of functional brain imaging was that regional blood flow and the fMRI BOLD signal not only increase in some areas of the brain appropriate to task performance but also decrease from a resting baseline in other areas (*48*) as shown in fig. 4.2. An appreciation of how these decreases arise in the context of an imaging experiment is diagrammatically represented in fig. 4.4. The possible physiological implications of these changes are discussed below.

Physiologists have long recognized that individual neurons in the cerebral cortex can both increase or decrease their activities from a resting, baseline firing pattern depending on task conditions. Examples abound in the neurophysiological literature (*49*). A parsimonious view of these decreases in neuronal activity is that they reflect the activity of inhibitory interneurons acting within local neuronal circuits of the cerebral cortex. Because inhibition is energy requiring (*50*), it is impossible to distinguish inhibitory from excitatory cellular activity on the basis of changes in either blood flow or metabolism. Thus, on this view a local increase in inhibitory activity would be as likely to increase blood flow and the fMRI BOLD signal as would a local increase in excitatory activity. How, then, might decreases in blood flow or the fMRI BOLD signal arise?

To understand the possible significance of the decreases in blood flow in functional imaging studies it is important to distinguish two separate conditions in which they might arise.[1] The less interesting and more usually referred to circumstance arises when two images are compared in which one contains a regional increase in blood flow caused by some type of task activity (e.g., let us consider hand movement that produces increases in contralateral motor cortex blood flow) and a control image that does not (i.e., in this example, no hand movement). In our example, subtracting the image associated with no hand movement from the image associated with hand movement reveals the expected increase in blood flow in motor cortex. Simply reversing the subtraction produces an image with a decrease in the same area. Although this example may seem trivial and obvious, such subtraction reversals are often presented in the analysis of very complex tasks and in such a manner as to be quite confusing even to those working the field. A diagrammatic representation of how this occurs is presented in fig. 4.4.

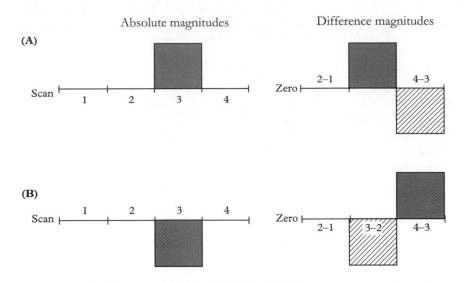

Figure 4.4   Functional images obtained with PET and fMRI represent comparisons between two conditions usually referred to as a control state and a task state. The task state is designed to contain specific mental operations of interest. Because the task state invariably contains additional mental operations not of interest, a control state is selected which contains those operations to be ignored yet does not contain the operations of interest in the task state. Depending on the actual changes in brain activity in each state and the comparison made between states, the resulting changes depicted in the functional image will have either a positive (fig. 4.1) or negative (fig. 4.2) sign. This figure is designed to illustrate how the sign (i.e., positive or negative change) arises from the primary image data. Absolute changes (Absolute Magnitudes) are represented on the left for a hypothetical area in the brain as monitored by either PET or fMRI. The horizontal axis on the left represents four states studied in the course of a hypothetical imaging experiment. An Absolute Magnitude above the horizontal axis (*A*) represents an increase over the other states studied whereas an Absolute Magnitude below this axis (*B*) represents a decrease. The comparisons (i.e. 2–1, 3–2, and 4–3) leading to the functional images themselves are shown on the right (Difference Magnitudes). It should be appreciated from this figure that the sign of the change in the functional image is dependent on both the change in activity within an area during a particular task (Absolute Magnitudes) and the particular comparison subsequently made between states (Difference Magnitudes). These general principles should be kept in mind when evaluating data of the type shown in figs. 4.1 to 4.3.

The second circumstance (fig. 4.4) in which decreases in blood flow and the fMRI BOLD signal appear is not caused by the above type of data manipulations (i.e., an active task image subtracted from a passive state image). Rather, blood flow and the fMRI BOLD signal actually decrease from the passive baseline state (i.e., the activity in a region of brain has not been first elevated by a task). The usual baseline conditions from which this occurs consist of lying quietly but fully awake in an MRI or PET scanner with eyes closed or passively viewing a television monitor and its contents, be it a fixation point or even a more complex stimulus (fig. 8.2, row 3). In the examples discussed by Shulman et al. (*48*), areas of the medial orbital frontal cortex, the posterior cingulate cortex, and the precuneus consistently showed decreased blood flow when subjects actively processed a wide variety of visual stimuli as compared with a passive baseline condition (compare with the example shown in fig. 4.2).

The hypothesis one is led to consider, regarding these rather large area reductions in blood flow, is that a large number of neurons reduce their activity together (for one of the few neurophysiological references to such a phenomenon, see ref. *52*). Such group reductions could not be mediated by a local increase in the activity of inhibitory interneurons as this would be seen as an increase in activity by PET and fMRI. Rather, such reductions are likely mediated through the action of diffuse projecting systems like dopamine, norepinephrine, and serotonin or a reduction in thalamic inputs to the cortex. The recognition of such changes probably represents an important contribution of functional brain imaging to our understanding of cortical function and should stimulate increased interest in the manner in which brain resources are allocated on a large systems level during task performance.

The metabolic accompaniments of these functionally induced decreases in blood flow from a passive baseline condition were not initially explored, and it was tacitly assumed that such reductions would probably be accompanied by coupled reductions in oxygen consumption. Therefore, it came as a surprise that the fMRI BOLD signal, based on tissue oxygen availability, detected both increases and decreases during functional activation (fig. 4.5). Decreases in the BOLD signal during a task state as compared with a passive, resting state have been widely appreciated by investigators using fMRI although, surprisingly, formal publications on the subject have yet to appear.

Complementing these observations from functional brain imaging on the relationship between oxygen consumption and blood flow during decreases are earlier quantitative metabolic studies of a phenomenon known as cerebellar diaschisis (*53, 54*). In this condition, there is a reduction in blood flow and metabolism in the hemisphere of the cerebellum contralateral to an injury to the cerebral cortex, usually a stroke. Of particular interest is the fact that blood flow is reduced significantly more than oxygen consumption (*53, 54*). The changes in the cerebellum are thought to reflect a reduction in neuronal activity within the cerebellum due to reduced input from the cerebral cortex. One can reasonably hypothesize that similar, large-scale reductions in systems-level activity are occurring during the course of normal functional brain activity (*48*).

Taken together the data we have at hand suggest that blood flow changes more than oxygen consumption in the face of increases as well as decreases in local neuronal activity (fig. 4.6). Glucose utilization also changes more than oxygen consumption during increases in brain activity (we presently have no data on decreases in glucose utilization) and may equal the changes in blood flow in both magnitude and spatial extent (*3, 12*). Although surprising to many, these results were not entirely unanticipated.

Experimental studies of epilepsy in well-oxygenated, passively ventilated experimental animals[2] (*56*) had indicated that blood flow increased in excess of the oxygen requirements of the tissue. During the increased neuronal activity of a seizure, discharge increase in the brain's venous oxygen content was routinely observed (*56*). Because of the increase in blood pressure associated with the seizure discharge, the fact that blood flow exceeded the oxygen requirements of the tissue was attributed to a loss of cerebral autoregulation (*56*). A similar concern was expressed about equally prescient experiments involving brain blood flow changes during sciatic nerve stimulation in rodents (*57, 58*). However, experiments by Ray Cooper and his colleagues largely circumvented that concern (*59, 60*). They demonstrated that oxygen availability

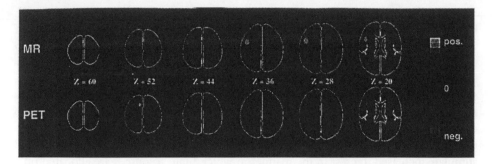

Figure 4.5 fMRI (*Upper*) of the BOLD signal (*4*) and PET (*Lower*) images of blood flow change. These images were obtained during the performance of a task in which subjects viewed three-letter word stems and were asked to speak aloud (PET) or think silently (fMRI) the first word to come to mind whose first three letters correspond to the stems [e.g., see cou, say or think couple (*85*)]. The color scale employed in these images shows activity increases in reds and yellows and activity decreases in greens and blues. Note that both PET and fMRI show similar increases as well as decreases. The fMRI images were blurred to the resolution of the PET images (18 mm full width at half maximum) to facilitate comparison.

measured locally in the cerebral cortex of awake patients undergoing surgery for the treatment of intractable epilepsy increased during changes in behavioral activity (e.g., looking at pictures, manual dexterity, reading). These changes in oxygen availability occurred in the absence of any change in blood pressure and were observed during normal brain function in humans. Surprisingly, these observations were largely ignored until the work of Fox and his colleagues called attention to the phenomenon in normal human subjects with PET (*2, 3*).

Interpretation of these blood flow–metabolism relationships during changes in functional brain activity are presently controversial. Several schools of thought have emerged. One hypothesis that addresses the role of glycolysis in brain functional activation is most eloquently articulated by Pierre Magistretti and colleagues based on their work with cultured astrocytes (*61, 62*). In this theory, increases in neuronal activity stimulated by the excitatory amino acid transmitter glutamate result in relatively large increases in glycolytic metabolism in astrocytes. The energy supplied through glycolysis in the astrocyte is used to metabolize glutamate to glutamine before being recycled to neurons. Coupled with estimates that increased firing rates of neurons require little additional energy over and above that required for the normal mainte-nance of ionic gradients (*63*) leads to the hypothesis that the primary metabolic change associated with changes (at least increases) in neuronal activity are glycolytic and occur in astrocytes.

In somewhat greater detail, neuronal activation results in sodium ion influx and potassium efflux. This is accompanied by an influx of protons into neurons, initially alkalinizing the extracellular space, which results in alkalinization of the astrocyte (*64*). Alkalinization of the astrocyte results in stimulation of glycolysis (*65*) with the break-down of glycogen (*66*) and the production of both pyruvate and lactate in excess of astrocyte metabolic needs and despite normal tissue oxygenation. The lactate can then leave the astrocyte and be taken up by neurons to be oxidatively metabolized by neurons (*67*). Because glucose metabolism exceeds oxygen consump-tion during increases in neuronal activity (*3*) another fate for lactate must also be

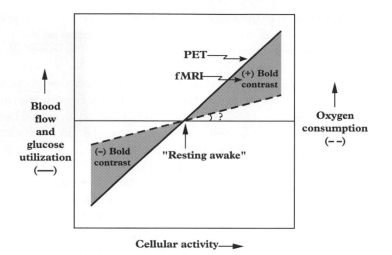

Figure 4.6 A summary of currently available data on the relationship of blood flow, glucose utilization, and oxygen consumption to the cellular activity of the brain during changes in functional activity is shown in this figure. The changes occurring in blood flow and glucose utilization exceed changes in oxygen consumption. The degree to which oxygen consumption actually changes, if at all, remains to be determined. PET measures the changes in blood flow; fMRI measures a BOLD (*4*) signal or contrast that arises when changes in blood flow exceed changes in tissue oxygen consumption.

sought. This might possibly occur through enhanced removal from the brain by flowing blood, an hypothesis for which we presently have only indirect evidence (*68*, *69*), or re-incorporation into astrocytic glycogen (*70*).

Additional support for this hypothesis comes from *in vivo* observations that increases in neuronal activity are associated with glycogenolysis in astrocytes (*71*), a convenient source of readily available energy for such a process, located in a cell uniquely equipped enzymatically for the process (*62, 71*). Finally, measurements of tissue lactate with MRS in humans (*72*) and with substrate-induced bioluminescence in laboratory animals (*73*) has shown localized increases in tissue lactate during physiologically induced increases in neuronal activity.

Not surprisingly, the above hypothesis has been challenged and alternatives offered to explain the observed discrepancy between changes in blood flow and glucose utilization, which appear to change in parallel, and oxygen consumption, which changes much less than either. One suggestion is that the observed discrepancy is transient (*74*). Measuring brain glucose and lactate concentrations and blood oxygenation with MRI and MRS in normal human volunteers, Frahm et al. (*74*) observed a rise in visual cortex lactate concentration that peaked after 3 min of visual stimulation and returned to baseline after 6 min of continuous stimulation. During this same period of time blood oxygen concentration was initially elevated but also returned to baseline by the end of the stimulation period. In a complementary study Hyder et al. (*75*) similarly suggest, on the basis of MRS studies of anesthetized rats during forepaw stimulation, that "oxidative CMRGlu supplies the majority of energy during sustained brain activation." However, in a very careful study of this question by Bandettini et al. (*76*) in awake humans, they conclude from their own data and a careful analysis of the literature that BOLD signal changes and blood flow remain elevated during prolonged periods of brain activation provided that there is no habituation to the presented stimulus. This conclusion is entirely consistent with the original observations of Fox and Raichle (2).

Another popular hypothesis is based on optical imaging work of physiologically stimulated visual cortex by Malonek and Grinvald (77). In their work they measure changes in reflected light from the surface of visual cortex in anesthetized cats. By using wavelengths of light sensitive to deoxyhemoglobin and oxyhemoglobin they note an almost immediate increase in deoxyhemoglobin concentration followed, after a brief interval, by an increase in oxyhemoglobin which, although centered at the same location as the change in deoxyhemoglobin, is greater in magnitude and extends over a much larger area of the cortex than do the changes in deoxyhemoglobin (77). They interpret these results to mean that increases in neuronal activity are associated with highly localized increases in oxygen consumption which stimulate a vascular response, delayed by several seconds, that is large in relation to both the magnitude of the increase in oxygen consumption and the area of cerebral cortex that is actually active. In other words, by their theory, increases in neuronal activity in the cerebral cortex are, actually, associated with increased oxidative metabolism of glucose. Because the blood flow response to the change in neuronal activity is relatively slow, oxygen reserves in the area of activation are temporarily depleted. When the blood flow response does occur, after a delay of 1–3 sec, it exceeds the needs of the tissue, delivering to the active area of cortex and its surroundings oxygen in excess of metabolic needs. This hypothesis has stimulated interest in the use of high field strength MRI systems to detect the initial oxygen depletion predicted by the small increases in deoxyhemoglobin (78). The hope would be that both spatial and temporal resolution of fMRI would be improved by focusing on this postulated early and spatially confined event.

Support for the hypothesis of Malonek and Grinvald (77) comes from theoretical work by Buxton and Frank (79). In their modeling work they show that in an idealized capillary tissue cylinder in the brain, an increase in blood flow in excess of the increased oxygen metabolic demands of the tissue is needed to maintain proper oxygenation of the tissue. This finding results from the poor diffusivity and solubility of oxygen in brain tissue. In this theory, blood flow remains coupled to oxidative metabolism but in a nonlinear fashion designed to overcome the diffusion and solubility limitations of oxygen in brain tissue to maintain adequate tissue oxygenation.

Although the hypothesis that reactive hyperemia is a normal and necessary consequence of increased neuronal activity merits careful consideration, several observations remain unexplained. First, it does not account for the increased glucose utilization that parallels the change in blood flow observed in normal humans (3, 12) and laboratory animals (73, 80, 81). Second, it does not agree with the observations of Woolsey et al. (80) as well as others (81) who have demonstrated a remarkably tight spatial relationship between changes in neuronal activity within a single, rat whisker barrel and the response of the vascular supply as well as glucose metabolism to that barrel. There is little evidence in these studies for spatially diffuse reactive hyperemia surrounding the stimulated area of cortex. Third, in the paper by Malonek and Grinvald (77), the initial rise in deoxyhemoglobin seen with activation is not accompanied by a fall in oxyhemoglobin as would be expected with a sudden rise in local oxygen consumption that precedes the onset of increased oxygen delivery to the tissue. In the presence of somewhat conflicting evidence on capillary recruitment in the brain (*80–82*), which could explain this observation, we should exercise caution in accepting uncritically the data of Malonek and Grinvald (*77*) until an explanation for this particular discrepancy is found and better concordance is achieved with other experiments. Clearly, more information is needed on the exact nature of the microvascular events surrounding functional brain activation. Finally, we are left without an explanation for the observation that when blood flow decreases below a resting baseline during changes in the functional activity of a region of the brain (fig. 4.2), a negative BOLD signal arises due to the fact that blood flow decreases more than the oxygen consumption (figs. 4.5 and 4.6).

One final caveat should be mentioned. From the perspective of this review it would be easy to assume that because blood flow and glucose utilization appear to increase together and more than oxygen utilization during increases in neuronal activity, the increase in blood flow serves to deliver needed glucose. Recent data from Powers et al. (*82*) suggest otherwise. They noted no change in the magnitude of the normalized regional blood flow response to physiological stimulation of the human brain during stepped hypoglycemia. They concluded that the increase in blood flow associated with physiological brain activation was not regulated by a mechanism that matched local cerebral glucose supply to local cerebral glucose demand (*82*).

So what are we to conclude at this point in time? Any theory designed to explain functional brain imaging signals must accommodate three observations (fig. 4.6). First, local increases and decreases in brain activity are reliably accompanied by changes in blood flow. Second, these blood flow changes exceed any accompanying change in the oxygen consumption. If this were not the case, fMRI based on the BOLD signal changes could not exist. Third, while paired data on glucose metabolism and blood flow are limited, they suggest that blood flow changes are accompanied by changes in glucose metabolism of approximately equal magnitude and spatial extent.

Several additional factors must be kept in mind in the evaluation of extant data and the design of future experiments. Anesthesia, a factor present in many of the animal experiments discussed in this review, may well have a significant effect on the relationships among blood flow, metabolism, and cellular activity during brain activation. Also, habituation of cellular activity to certain types of stimuli (*74, 76*) as well as rapid, practice-induced shifts in the neuronal circuitry used for the performance of a task (fig. 4.3) may well complicate the interpretation of resulting data if overlooked in experiments designed to investigate these relationships.

Presently we do not know why blood flow changes so dramatically and reliably during changes in brain activity or how these vascular responses are so beautifully orchestrated. These questions have confronted us for more than a century and remain incompletely answered. At no time have answers been more important or intriguing than presently because of the immense interest focused on them by the use of functional brain imaging with PET and fMRI. We have at hand tools with the potential to provide unparalleled insights into some of the most important scientific, medical, and social questions facing mankind. Understanding those tools is clearly a high priority.

Notes

I would like to acknowledge many years of generous support from the National Institute of Neurological Disorders and Stroke; the National Heart, Lung, and Blood Institute; the McDonnell Center for Studies of Higher Brain Function at Washington University; as well as the John D. and Katherine T. MacArthur Foundation and the Charles A. Dana Foundation.

1   Some have wondered whether these reductions in blood flow are merely the hemodynamic consequence of increases elsewhere (i.e., an intracerebral steal phenomenon). Such a hypothesis is very unlikely to be correct because of the tremendous hemodynamic reserve of the brain (51) and also because there is no one-to-one spatial or temporal correlation between increases and decreases (e.g., see figs. 4.1 and 4.2).

2   Wilder Penfield is frequently given credit for the observation that venous oxygenation increases during a seizure discharge (i.e., so-called "red veins on the cortex"). Careful reading of his many descriptions of the cortical surface of the human brain during a seizure fail to disclose such a description. Rather, he describes quite clearly the infrequent appearance of arterial blood locally in pial veins after a focal cortical seizure (55): "... the almost invariable objective alteration in the exposed hemisphere coincident with the onset of the fit is a cessation of pulsation in the brain" (p. 607).

References

1   Raichle, M. E. (1987) in *Handbook of Physiology: The Nervous System. V: Higher Functions of the Brain*, ed. Plum, F. (Am. Physiol. Soc., Bethesda, MD), pp. 643–74.

2   Fox, P. T. & Raichle, M. E. (1986) *Proc. Natl. Acad. Sci. USA*, **83**, 1140–44.

3   Fox, P. T., Raichle, M. E., Mintun, M. A. & Dence, C. (1988) *Science*, **241**.

4   Ogawa, S., Lee, T. M., Kay, A. R. & Tank, D. W. (1990) *Proc. Natl. Acad. Sci. USA*, **87**, 9868–72.

5   Ogawa, S., Tank, D. W., Menon, R., Ellermann, J. M., Kim, S.-G., Merkle, H. & Ugurbil, K. (1992) *Proc. Natl. Acad. Sci. USA*, **89**, 5951–5.

6   Kwong, K., Belliveau, J. W., Chesler, D. A., Goldberg, I. E., Weisskoff, R. M., Poncelet, B. P., Dennedy, D. N., Hoppel, B. E., Cohen, M. S., Turner, R., Cheng, H.-M., Brady, T. J. & Rosen, B. R. (1992) *Proc. Natl. Acad. Sci. USA*, **89**, 5675–9.

7   Bandettini, P. A., Wong, E. C., Hinks, R. S., Tikofsky, R. S. & Hyde, J. S. (1992) *Magn. Reson. Med.*, **25**, 390–7.

8   Frahm, J., Bruhn, H., Merboldt, K.-D. & Hanicke, W. (1992) *J. Magn. Reson. Imaging*, **2**, 501–5.

9   Roy, C. S. & Sherrington, C. S. (1890) *J. Physiol. (London)*, **11**, 85–108.

10   Siesjo, B. K. (1978) *Brain Energy Metabolism* (Wiley, New York).

11   Fox, P. T. & Raichle, M. E. (1988) *Proc. Natl. Acad. Sci. USA*, **83**, 1140–4.

12   Blomqvist, G., Seitz, R. J., Sjogren, I., Halldin, C., Stone-Elander, S., Widen, L., Solin, O. & Haaparanta, M. (1994) *Acta Physiol. Scand.*, **151**, 29–43.

13   James, W. (1890) *Principles of Psychology* (Henry Holt, New York), pp. 97–9.

14   Mosso, A. (1881) *Ueber den Kreislauf des Blutes im Menschlichen Gehirn* (von Veit, Leipzig).

15   Broca, P. (1879) *Bull. Acad. Med. (Paris)*, **2S**, 1331–47.

16   Broca, P. (1861) *Bull. Soc. Anatomique (Paris)*, **6**, 330–57, 398–407.

17   Mosso, A. (1894) *La Temperature del Cervello* (Milan).

18   Berger, H. (1901) *Zur Lehre von der Blutzirkulation in der Schandelhohle des Menschen* (von Gustav, Fischer, Jena, Germany).

19 Hill, L. (1896) *The Physiology and Pathology of the Cerebral Circulation: An Experimental Research* (Churchill, London).

20 Shulman, G. L., Corbetta, M., Buckner, R. L., Raichle, M. E., Fiez, J. A., Miezin, F. M. & Petersen, S. E. (1997a) *Cereb. Cortex*, **7**, 193–206.

21 Landau, W. M., Freygang, W. H. Jr, Roland, L. P., Sokoloff, L. & Kety, S. (1955) *Trans. Am. Neurol. Assoc.*, **80**, 125–9.

22 Kety, S. (1960) *Methods Med. Res.*, **8**, 228–36.

23 Sokoloff, L., Reivich, M., Kennedy, C., Des Rosiers, M. H., Patlak, C. S., Pettigrew, K. D., Sakurada, O. & Shinohara, M. (1977) *J. Neurochem.*, **28**, 897–916.

24 Reivich, M., Kuhl, D., Wolf, A., Greenberg, J., Phelps, M., Ido, T., Casella, V., Hoffman, E., Alavi, A. & Sokoloff, L. (1979) *Circ. Res.*, **44**, 127–37.

25 Lassen, N. A., Hoedt-Rasmussen, K., Sorensen, S. C., Skinhoj, E., Cronquist, B., Bodforss, E. & Ingvar, D. H. (1963) *Neurology*, **13**, 719–27.

26 Ingvar, G. H. & Risberg, J. (1965) *Acta Neurol. Scand. Suppl.*, **14**, 183–6.

27 Kety, S. (1965) *Acta Neurol. Scand. Suppl.*, **14**, 197 (abstr.).

28 Lassen, N. A., Ingvar, D. H. & Skinhoj, E. (1978) *Sci. Am.*, **239**, 62–71.

29 Hounsfield, G. N. (1973) *Br. J. Radiol.*, **46**, 1016–22.

30 Cormack, A. M. (1963) *J. Appl. Phys.*, **34**, 2722–7.

31 Cormack, A. M. (1973) *Phys. Med. Biol.*, **18**, 195–207.

32 Ter-Pogossian, M. M., Phelps, M. E., Hoffman, E. J. & Mulani, N. A. (1975) *Radiology*, **114**, 89–98.

33 Hoffman, E. J., Phelps, M. E., Mullani, N. A., Higgins, C. S. & Ter-Pogossian, M. M. (1976) *J. Nucl. Med.*, **17**, 493–502.

34 Raichle, M. E., Martin, W. R. W., Herscovitch, P., Mintun, M. A. & Markham, J. (1983) *J. Nucl. Med.*, **24**, 790–8.

35 Frackowiak, R. S. J., G. L., L., Jones, T. & Heather, J. D. (1980) *J. Comput. Tomogr.*, **4**, 727–36.

36 Mintun, M. A., Raichle, M. E., Martin, W. R. W. & Herscovitch, P. (1984) *J. Nucl. Med.*, **25**, 177–87.

37 Altman, D. I., Lich, L. L. & Powers, W. J. (1991) *J. Nucl. Med.*, **32**, 1738–41.

38 Posner, M. I. & Raichle, M. E. (1994) *Images of Mind* (Freeman, New York).

39 Donders, F. C. (1969) *Acta Psychol.*, **30**, 412–31.

40 Raichle, M. E., Fiez, J. A., Videen, T. O., MacLeod, A. M., Pardo, J. V. Fox, P. T. & Petersen, S. E. (1994) *Cereb. Cortex*, **4**, 8–26.

41 Block, F. (1946) *Physiol. Rev.*, **70**, 460–74.

42 Purcell, E. M., Torry, H. C. & Pound, R. V. (1946) *Physiol. Rev.*, **69**, 37.

43 Lauterbur, P. (1973) *Nature (London)*, **242**, 190–91.

44 Pauling, L. & Coryell, C. D. (1936) *Proc. Natl. Acad. Sci. USA*, **22**, 210–16.

45 Thulborn, K. R., Waterton, J. C., Matthews, P. M. & Radda, G. K. (1982) *Biochim. Biophys. Acta*, **714**, 265–70.

46 Kim, S. G. & Ugurbil, K. (1997) *Magn. Reson. Med.*, **38**, 59–65.

47 Yarowsky, P., Kadekaro, M. & Sokoloff, L. (1983) *Proc. Natl. Acad. Sci. USA*, **80**, 4179–83.

48 Shulman, G. L., Fiez, J. A., Corbetta, M., Buckner, R. L., Miezin, F. M., Raichle, M. E. & Petersen, S. E. (1997) *J. Cognit. Neurosci.*, **9**, 648–63.

49 Georgopoulos, A. P., Kalaska, J. F., Caminiti, R. & Massey, J. T. (1982) *J. Neurosci.*, **2**, 1527–37.

50 Ackerman, R. F., Finch, D. M., Babb, T. L. & Engel, J., Jr (1984) *J. Neurosci.*, **4**, 251–64.

51 Heistad, D. D. & Kontos, H. A. (1983) in *Handbook of Physiology: The Cardiovascular System*, eds Sheppard, J. T. & Abboud, F. M. (Am. Physio. Soc., Bethesda, MD), vol. 3, pp. 137–82.

52 Creutzfeldt, O., Ojemann, G. & Lettich, E. (1989) *Exp. Brain Res.*, **77**, 451–75.

53 Martin, W. R. & Raichle, M. E. (1983) *Ann. Neurol.*, **14**, 168–76.

54   Yamauchi, H., Fukuyama, H. & Kimura, J. (1992) *Stroke*, **23**, 855–60.

55   Penfield, W. (1937) *Res. Pub. Assoc. Res. Nervous Mental Disorder*, **18**, 605–37.

56   Plum, F., Posner, J. B. & Troy, B. (1968) *Arch. Neurol.*, **18**, 1–3.

57   Howse, D. C., Plum, F., Duffy, T. E. & Salford, L. G. (1973) *Trans. Am. Neurol. Assoc.*, **98**, 153–5.

58   Salford, L. G., Duffy, T. E. & Plum, F. (1975) in *Cerebral Circulation and Metabolism*, eds Langfitt, T. W., McHenry, L. C., Reivich, M. & Wollman, H. (Springer, New York), pp. 380–2.

59   Cooper, R., Crow, H. J., Walter, W. G. & Winter, A. L. (1966) *Brain Res.*, **3**, 174–91.

60   Cooper, R., Papakostopoulos, D. & Crow, H. J. (1975) in *Blood Flow and Metabolism in the Brain*, eds Harper, A. M., Jennett, W. B., Miller, J. D. & Rowan, J. O. (Churchill Livingstone, New York), pp. 14.8–14.9.

61   Tsacopoulos, M. & Magistretti, P. J. (1996) *J. Neurosci.*, **16**, 877–85.

62   Bittar, P. G., Charnay, Y., Pellerin, L., Bouras, C. & Magistretti, P. (1996) *J. Cereb. Blood Flow Metab.*, **16**, 1079–89.

63   Creutzfeldt, O. D. (1975) in *Brain Work: The Coupling of Function, Metabolism and Blood Flow in the Brain*, eds Ingvar, D. H. & Lassen, N. A. (Munksgaard, Copenhagen), pp. 21–46.

64   Chesler, M. & Kraig, R. P. (1987) *Am. J. Psychol.*, **253**, R666–R670.

65   Hochachka, P. W. & Mommsen, T. P. (1983) *Science*, **219**, 1391–7.

66   Swanson, R. A., Morton, M. M., Sagar, S. M. & Sharp, F. R. (1992) *Neuroscience*, **51**, 451–61.

67   Dringen, R., Wiesinger, H. & Hamprecht, B. (1993a) *Neurosci. Lett.*, **163**, 5–7.

68   Knudsen, G. M., Paulson, O. B. & Hertz, M. M. (1991) *J. Cereb. Blood Flow Metab.*, **11**, 581–6.

69   Lear, J. L. & Kasliwal, R. K. (1991) *J. Cereb. Blood Flow Metab.*, **11**, 576–89.

70   Dringen, R., Schmoll, D., Cesar, M. & Hamprecht, B. (1993) *Biol. Chem. Hoppe-Seyler*, **374**, 343–7.

71   Harley, C. A. & Bielajew, C. H. (1992) *J. Comp. Neurol.*, **322**, 377–89.

72   Prichard, J. W., Rothman, D. L., Novotny, E., Hanstock, C. C. & Shulman, R. G. (1991) *Proc. Natl. Acad. Sci. USA*, **88**, 5829–31.

73   Ueki, M., Linn, F. & Hossmann, K.-A. (1988) *J. Cereb. Blood Flow Metab.*, **8**, 486–94.

74   Frahm, J., Kruger, G., Merboldt, K.-D. & Kleinschmidt, A. (1996) *Magn. Reson. Med.*, **35**, 143–8.

75   Hyder, F., Chase, J. R., Behar, K. L., Mason, G. F., Rothman, D. L. & Shulman, R. G. (1996) *Proc. Natl. Acad. Sci. USA*, **93**, 7612–17.

76   Bandettini, P. A., Kwong, K. K., Davis, T. L., Tootell, R. B. H., Wong, E. C., Fox, P. T., Belliveau, J. W., Weisskoff, R. M. & Rosen, B. R. (1997) *Hum. Brain Mapping*, **5**, 93–109.

77   Malonek, D. & Grinvald, A. (1996) *Science*, **272**, 551–4.

78   Hu, X., Le, T. H. & Ugurbil, K. (1997) *Magn. Reson. Med.*, **37**, 877–84.

79   Buxton, R. B. & Frank, L. R. (1997) *J. Cereb. Blood Flow Metab.*, **17**, 64–72.

80   Woolsey, T. A., Rovainen, C. M., Cox, S. B., Henegar, M. H., Liang, G. E., Liu, D., Moskalenko, Y. E., Sui, J. & Wei, L. (1996) *Cereb. Cortex*, **6**, 647–60.

81   Greenberg, J. H., Sohn, N. W. & Hand, P. J. (1997) *J. Cereb. Blood Flow Metab.*, **17**, S561 (abstr.).

82   Powers, W. J., Hirsch, I. B. & Cryer, P. E. (1996) *Am. J. Physiol.*, **270**, H554–H559.

83   Petersen, S. E., Fox, P. T., Posner, M. I., Mintum, M. & Raichle, M. E. (1988) *Nature (London)*, **331**, 585–9.

84   Petersen, S. E., Fox, P. T., Posner, M. I., Mintun, M. & Raichle, M. E. (1989) *J. Cognit. Neurosci.*, **1**, 153–70.

85   Buckner, R. L., Petersen, S. E., Ojemann, J. G., Miezin, F. M., Squire, L. R. & Raichle, M. E. (1995) *J. Neurosci.*, **15**, 12–29.

86   Fulton, J. F. (1928) *Brain*, **51**, 310–20.

Perception

INTRODUCTION TO PART II

How the brain uses incoming information to experience the world is the subject of this part and part III. As dimly as we understand these processes now, it may be reassuring to note that a few decades ago we had not the slightest clue. David Hubel remarks in the opening article that "It is hard, now, to think back and realize just how free we were from any idea of what cortical cells might be doing in an animal's daily life." His work with Torsten Wiesel in revealing the behavior of neurons in primary visual cortex provided the first indications. Those have been followed by an avalanche of information about an embarrassment of different visual, auditory, and many other kinds of cortical areas, but the truth is that no convincing description of what the brain does with this babel of specialists has yet emerged.

A glimpse into this complexity is provided by Vernon Mountcastle, another pioneer in neuroscience. Recording from the posterior parietal cortex of awake monkeys engaged in trained hand movements, he observed a menagerie of neurons specialized for different components of the gestures. As discussed in the following section, the parietal lobe is critically involved in directing attention. The interaction of this clearly perceptual role with the motor specializations that Mountcastle and many other have described is not clear.

An idea, however, is suggested by Goodale, Jakobson, and Servos. Their basic notion is that a proposed fundamental division of the cortical visual system, into a "dorsal stream" responsible for representing the shifting spatial relationships of the visual scene and a "ventral stream" handling object recognition, is misguided. They maintain that the dorsal stream is far better described as being specialized for the visual guidance of movement, rather than for spatial perception. This debate remains lively.

Salzman and Newsome consider just what the effect of these cortical neurons' activity is on the organism's perceptual judgments. They electrically stimulated local patches of cortex in monkeys engaged in making decisions about a visual display. They were able to induce artificial percepts by activating cortical neurons directly. (A caveat: although this basic result still stands, further work from the same laboratory has brought some of the quantitative conclusions presented here into question, suggesting that "vector averaging" of signals may in fact be taking place.)

Finally, psychophysicist Ken Nakayama describes the brilliant and curmudgeonly late J. J. Gibson, who combined unique and prescient insights into vision with a willful and total lack of interest in neuroscience. Obviously attention to the hardware is not absolutely essential for psychological insight, and perhaps Gibson thought more clearly by restricting his scope. But, as Nakayama describes, Gibson's ideas have directly driven neurobiological investigations, and contribute to a deeper understanding of the brain.

5

Exploration of the Primary Visual Cortex, 1955–78

David H. Hubel

In the early spring of 1958 I drove over to Baltimore from Washington DC, and in a cafeteria at Johns Hopkins Hospital met Stephen Kuffler and Torsten Wiesel for a discussion that was more momentous for Torsten's and my future than either of us could have possibly imagined.

I had been at Walter Reed Army Institute of Research for 3 years, in the Neuropsychiatry Section headed by David Rioch, working under the supervision of M. G. F. Fuortes. I began at Walter Reed by developing a tungsten microelectrode and a technique for using it to record from cats with permanently implanted electrodes, and I had been comparing the firing of cells in the visual pathways of sleeping and waking animals.

It was time for a change in my research tactics. In sleeping cats, only diffuse light could reach the retina through the closed eyelids. Whether the cat was asleep or awake, diffuse light failed to stimulate the cells in the striate cortex. In waking animals I had succeeded in activating many cells with moving spots on a screen, and had found that some cells were very selective in that they responded to movement when a spot moved in one direction across the screen (for example, from left to right) but not when it moved in the opposite direction[1] (fig. 5.1). There were many cells that I could not influence at all. Obviously there was a gold mine in the visual cortex, but methods were needed that would permit recording of single cells for many hours, and with the eyes immobilized, if the mine were ever to begin producing.

I had planned to do a postdoctoral fellowship at Johns Hopkins Medical School with Vernon Mountcastle, but the timing was awkward for him because he was remodelling his laboratories. One day Kuffler called and asked if I would like to work in his laboratory at the Wilmer Institute of Ophthalmology at the Johns Hopkins Hospital with Torsten Wiesel, until the remodelling was completed. That was expected to take about a year. I did not have to be persuaded; some rigorous training in vision was just what I needed, and though Kuffler himself was no longer working in vision the tradition had been maintained in his laboratory. Torsten and I had visited each other's

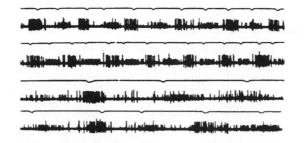

Figure 5.1 Continuous recording from the striate cortex of an unrestrained cat. In each dual trace, the lower member shows the microelectrode oscilloscope recording from two cells, one with large impulses, the other with smaller ones. The stimulus was small to-and-fro hand movements in front of the cat. Each movement interrupted a light beam falling on a photo-electric cell, producing the notches in the upper beam. The upper two pairs of records represent fast movements, the lower ones slower movements. Each line represents 4 s.[1]

laboratories and it was clear that we had common interests and similar outlooks. Kuffler suggested that I come over to discuss plans, and that was what led to the meeting in the cafeteria.

It was not hard to decide what to do. Kuffler had described two types of retinal ganglion cells which he called 'ON-centre' and 'OFF-centre'. The receptive field of each type was made up of two mutually antagonistic regions, a centre and a surround, one excitatory and the other inhibitory. In 1957, Barlow, FitzHugh and Kuffler had gone on to show that, as a consequence, retinal ganglion cells are less sensitive to diffuse light than to a spot just filling the receptive-field centre.[2] It took me some time to realize what this meant: that the way a cell responds to any visual scene will change very little when, for example, the sun goes behind a cloud and the light reflected from black and white objects decreases by a large factor. The cell virtually ignores this change, and our subjective assessment of the objects as black or white is likewise practically unaffected. Kuffler's centre–surround receptive fields thus began to explain why the appearance of objects depends so little on the intensity of the light source. Some years later Edwin Land showed that the appearance of a scene is similarly relatively independent of the exact wavelength composition of the light source. The physiological basis of this colour independence has yet to be worked out.

The strategy (to return to our cafeteria) seemed obvious. Torsten and I would simply extend Stephen Kuffler's work to the brain; we would record from geniculate cells and cortical cells, map receptive fields with small spots, and look for any further processing of the visual information.

My reception in Kuffler's office the first day was memorable. I was nervous and out of breath. Steve, at his desk, rotated around in his chair and said 'Hi David! Take off your coat, hang up your hat, do up your fly.' His manner was informal! But it took me a month, given my Canadian upbringing, to force myself to call him Steve. For the first three months no paycheque arrived, and finally I screwed up the courage to go in and tell him. He laughed and laughed, and then said, 'I forgot!'

Torsten and I did not waste much time. Within a week of my coming to Hopkins (to a dark and dingy inner windowless room at the Wilmer Institute basement, deemed ideal for visual studies) we did our first experiment. For the time being we finessed the geniculate (at Walter Reed I had convinced myself that the cells were centre–surround) and began right away with cortex. The going was rough. We had only the equipment for retinal stimulation and recording that had been designed a few years before by Talbot and Kuffler.[3] A piece of apparatus resembling a small cyclotron held the anaesthetized and paralysed cat with its head facing almost directly upward. A modified ophthalmoscope projected a background light and a spot stimulus onto the retina. The experimenter could look in, see the retina with its optic disk, area centralis, and blood vessels, and observe the background light and the stimulus spots. Small spots of light were produced by sliding 2×5 cm metal rectangles containing various sizes of holes into a slot in the apparatus, just as one puts a slide into a slide projector. To obtain a black spot on a light background one used a piece of glass like a microscope slide, onto which a black dot had been glued. All this was ideal for stimulating the retina and recording directly from retinal ganglion cells, since one could see the electrode tip and know where to stimulate, but for cortical recording it was horrible. Finding a receptive field on the retina was difficult, and we could never remember what part of the retina we had stimulated. After a month or so we decided to have the cat face a projection screen, as I had at Walter Reed and as Talbot and Marshall had in 1941.[4] Having no other head holder, we continued for a while to use the ophthalmoscope's head holder, which posed a problem since the cat was facing directly up. To solve this we brought in some bed sheets, which we slung between the pipes and cobwebs that graced the ceiling of the Wilmer basement, giving the setup the aura of a circus tent. On the sheets we projected our spots and slits. One day Mountcastle walked in on this scene, and was horror struck at the spectacle. The method was certainly inconvenient since we had to stare at the ceiling for the entire experiment. Then I remembered having seen in Mountcastle's laboratory a Horsley-Clarke head holder that was not only no longer being used but also had the name of the Wilmer Institute engraved on it. It was no other than the instrument that Talbot had designed for visual work when he and Marshall mapped out visual areas I and II in the cat in 1941.[4] For years Vernon had used it in his somatosensory work, but he had recently obtained a fancier one. Torsten and I decided to reclaim the Wilmer instrument, not without some trepidation. To give ourselves confidence we both put on lab coats, for the first and last times in our lives, and looking very professional walked over to Physiology. Though Mountcastle was his usual friendly and generous self, I suspect he was loath to part with this treasure, but the inscription on the stainless steel was not to be denied and we walked off with it triumphantly. It is still in use (now at Harvard; we literally stole it from the Wilmer), and has probably the longest history of uninterrupted service of any Horsley-Clarke in the world.

A short while before this adventure we had gone to a lecture by Vernon (this was a few years after the discovery of cortical columns)[5] in which he had amazed us by reporting on the results of recording from some 900 somatosensory cortical cells, for those days an astronomic number. We knew we could never catch up, so we catapulted ourselves to respectability by calling our first cell No. 3000 and numbering subsequent ones from there. When Vernon visited our circus tent we were in the middle of a three-unit recording, cells number 3007, 3008 and 3009. We made sure that we mentioned their identification numbers. All three cells had the same receptive-field orientation, but neither Vernon nor we realized, then, what that implied.

Our first real discovery came about as a surprise. We had been doing experiments for about a month. We were still using the Talbot–Kuffler ophthalmoscope and were not getting very far; the cells simply would not respond to our spots and annuli. One day we made an especially stable recording. [We had adapted my technique for recording, which used long-term implantations and the Davies closed chamber,[6] to the short-term experiments, and no vibrations short of an earthquake were likely to dislodge things.] The cell in question lasted 9 hours, and by the end we had a very different feeling about what the cortex might be doing. For 3 or 4 hours we got absolutely nowhere. Then gradually we began to elicit some vague and inconsistent responses by stimulating somewhere in the midperiphery of the retina. We were inserting the glass slide with its black spot into the slot of the ophthalmoscope when suddenly over the audiomonitor the cell went off like a machine gun. After some fussing and fiddling we found out what was happening. The response had nothing to do with the black dot. As the glass slide was inserted its edge was casting onto the retina a faint but sharp shadow, a straight dark line on a light background. That was what the cell wanted, and it wanted it, moreover, in just one narrow range of orientations.

This was unheard of. It is hard, now, to think back and realize just how free we were from any idea of what cortical cells might be doing in an animal's daily life. That the retinas mapped onto the visual cortex in a systematic way was, of course, well known, but it was far from clear what this apparently unimaginative remapping was good for. It seemed inconceivable that the information would enter the cortex and leave it unmodified, especially when Kuffler's work in the retina had made it so clear that interesting transformations took place there between input and output. One heard the word 'analysis' used to describe what the cortex might be doing, but what one was to understand by that vague term was never spelled out. In the somatosensory cortex, the only other cortical area being closely scrutinized, Mountcastle had found that the cells had properties not dramatically different from those of neurons at earlier stages.

Many of the ideas about cortical function then in circulation seem in retrospect almost outrageous. One has only to remember the talk of 'suppressor strips', reverberating circuits, or electrical field effects. This last notion was taken so seriously that no less a figure than our laureate-colleague Roger Sperry had had to put it to rest, in 1955, by dicing up the cortex with mica plates to insulate the subdivisions, and by skewering it with tantalum wire to short out the fields, neither of which procedures seriously impaired cortical function.[7,8] Nevertheless, the idea of ephaptic interactions was slow to die out. There were even doubts as to the existence of topographic representation, which was viewed by some as a kind of artefact. One study, in which a spot of light projected anywhere in the retina evoked potentials all over the visual cortex, was interpreted as a refutation of topographic representation, but the result almost certainly came from working with a dark-adapted cat and a spot so bright that it scattered light all over the retina. It is surprising, in retrospect, that ideas of nonlocalization could survive in the face of the masterly mapping of visual fields onto the cortex in rabbit, cat and monkey done by Talbot and Marshall far back in 1941.[4]

It took us months to convince ourselves that we were not at the mercy of some optical artefact, such as anyone can produce by squinting their eyes and making vertical rays emanate from street lights. We did not want to make fools of ourselves quite so early in our careers. But recording in sequence in the same penetration several cells, with several different optimal orientations would, I think, have convinced anyone. By January we were ready to take the cells we thought we could understand (we later called them 'simple cells') and write them up. Then, as always, what guided and sustained us was the attitude of Kuffler, who never lectured or preached but simply reacted with buoyant enthusiasm whenever he thought we had found something interesting, and acted vague and noncommittal when he found something dull.

Hierarchy of Visual Cells

During the years 1959–62, first at the Wilmer Institute and then at Harvard Medical School, we were mainly concerned with comparing responses of cells in the lateral geniculate body and primary visual cortex of the cat. In the lateral geniculate we quickly confirmed my Walter Reed finding that the receptive fields are like those of retinal ganglion cells in having an antagonistic concentric centre–surround organization. But now we could directly compare the responses of a geniculate cell with those of a fibre from an afferent retinal ganglion cell, and we found that in geniculate cells the power of the receptive-field surround to cancel the input from the centre was increased. This finding was subsequently confirmed and extended in a beautiful set of experiments by Cleland et al.,[9] and for many years it remained the only known function of the lateral geniculate body.

In the cat striate cortex it soon became evident that the cells were more complex than geniculate cells, and came in several degrees of complexity.[10] One set of cells could be described by techniques similar to those used in the retina by Kuffler; we called these 'simple'.[11,12] Their receptive fields, like the fields of retinal ganglion cells and of lateral geniculate cells, were subdivided into antagonistic regions, illumination of any one of which tended to increase or decrease the rate of firing. But simple cells differed from retinal ganglion cells and lateral geniculate cells in the striking departure of their receptive fields from circular symmetry; instead of a single circular boundary between centre and surround, the antagonistic subdivisions were separated by parallel straight lines whose orientation (vertical, horizontal or oblique) soon emerged as a fundamental property (fig. 5.2). The optimal stimulus – a slit, dark bar or edge – was easily predictable from the geometry of the receptive field, so that a stationary line stimulus worked optimally when its boundaries coincided with the boundaries of the subdivisions (fig. 5.3), and displacing the line to a new position parallel to the old one generally resulted in a sharp decline in the response. Perhaps most remarkable was the precision of the spatial distribution of excitatory and inhibitory effects: not only did diffuse light produce no response (as though the excitatory and inhibitory effects were mutually cancelling with the precision of an acid–base titration), but any line oriented $90°$ to the optimal was also without effect, regardless of its position along the field, suggesting that the subpopulations of receptors so stimulated also had precisely mutually cancelling effects.

In the cat, simple cells are mostly found in layer 4, which is the site of termination of the bulk of the afferents from the lateral geniculate body. The exact connections that lead to orientation specificity are still unknown, but it is easy to think of plausible circuits. For example, the behaviour of one of the commonest kinds of simple cells may be explained by supposing that the cell receives convergent excitatory input from a set of geniculate cells whose ON-centres are distributed in overlapping fashion over a straight line (fig. 5.4). In the monkey, the cells of layer 4C (where most geniculate fibres terminate) all seem to be concentric centre–surround, and the simple layers

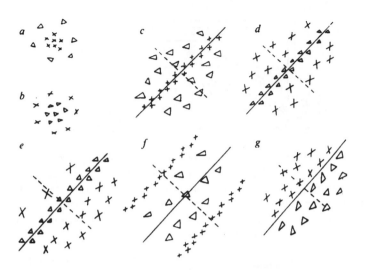

Figure 5.2   Common arrangements of lateral geniculate (*a, b*) and simple cortical (*c–g*) receptive fields. Symbols: X, areas giving excitatory (ON) responses; △, areas giving inhibitory (OFF) responses. Receptive-field orientations are shown by continuous lines through field centres; in this figure these are all oblique, but each arrangement occurs in all orientations (Fig. 2 in ref. 10).

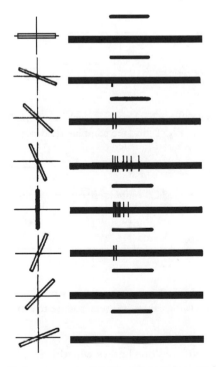

Figure 5.3   Responses to shining a rectangular slit of light 1 deg ×8 deg, so that centre of slit is superimposed on centre of receptive field in various orientations. Receptive field is of type C (see fig. 5.2), with the axis vertically oriented (Fig. 3 in ref. 12).

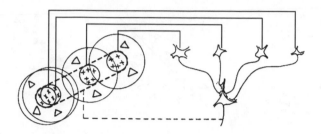

Figure 5.4   Possible scheme for explaining the organization of simple receptive fields. A large number of lateral geniculate cells, of which four are illustrated on the right, have receptive fields with ON-centres arranged along a straight line on the retina. All of these project onto a single cortical cell, and the synapses are supposed to be excitatory. The receptive field of the cortical cell will then have an elongated ON-centre, indicated by the interrupted lines in the receptive-field diagram (left) (Fig. 19 in ref. 10).

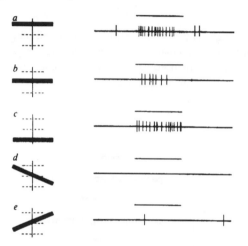

Figure 5.5   *a–c*, Complex cell responding best to a black, horizontally oriented rectangle placed anywhere in the receptive field. *d, e*, Tilting the stimulus rendered it ineffective.

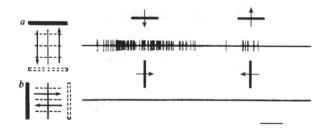

Figure 5.6   Same cell as for fig. 5.5, showing response to a moving horizontal bar. *a*, Downward movement was superior to upward; *b*, there was no response to a moving vertical bar (Figs 7 and 8 in ref. 10).

immediately superficial to 4C. No one knows why this extra stage of centre–surround cells is intercalated in the monkey's visual pathway.

The next set of cells we called 'complex' because their properties cannot be derived in a single logical step from those of lateral geniculate cells (or, in the monkey, from the

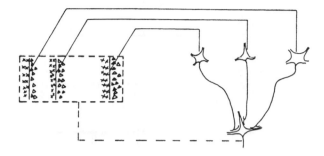

Figure 5.7   Possible scheme for explaining the organization of complex receptive fields. A number of cells with simple fields, of which three are shown schematically, are imagined to project to a single cortical cell of higher order. Each projecting neuron has a receptive field arranged as shown to the left: an excitatory region to the left and an inhibitory region to the right of a vertical straight-line boundary. The boundaries of the fields are staggered within an area outlined by the interrupted lines. Any vertical-edged stimulus falling across this rectangle, regardless of its position, will excite some simple-field cells, leading to excitation of the higher-order cell (Fig. 20 in ref. 10).

concentric cells of layer 4C). For the complex cell (compared with the simple cell), the position of an optimally oriented line need not be so carefully specified: the line works anywhere in the receptive field, evoking about the same response wherever it is placed (fig. 5.5). This can most easily be explained by supposing that the complex cell receives inputs from many simple cells, all of whose receptive fields have the same orientation but differ slightly in position (fig. 5.7). Sharpness of tuning for orientation varies from cell to cell, but the optimal orientation of a typical complex cell in layer 2 or 3 in the monkey can be easily determined to the nearest 5–10°, with no more stimulating equipment than a slide projector and a screen.

For a complex cell, a properly oriented line produces especially powerful responses when it is swept across the receptive field (fig. 5.6). The discharge is generally well sustained as long as the line keeps moving, but falls off quickly if the stimulus is stationary. About half of the complex cells fire much better to one direction of movement than to the opposite direction, a quality called 'directional selectivity', which probably cannot be explained by any simple projection of simple cells onto complex cells, but seems to require inhibitory connections with time delays of the sort proposed for rabbit retinal ganglion cells by Barlow and Levick.[13]

Many cat or monkey cells, perhaps 10 to 20 per cent in area 17, respond best to a line (a slit, an edge, or a dark bar) of limited length; when the line is prolonged in one direction or both, the response falls off. This is called 'end stopping'. In some cells the response to a very long line fails completely (fig. 5.8).[14] We originally called these cells 'hypercomplex' because we looked on them as next in an ordered hierarchical series, after the simple and the complex. We saw hypercomplex cells first in areas 18 and 19 of the cat, and only later in area 17. Dreher subsequently found cells, in all other ways resembling simple cells, that showed a similar fall-off in response as the length of the stimulus exceeded some optimum.[15] It seems awkward to call these cells hypercomplex: they are probably better termed 'simple end-stopped', in contrast to 'complex end-stopped'.

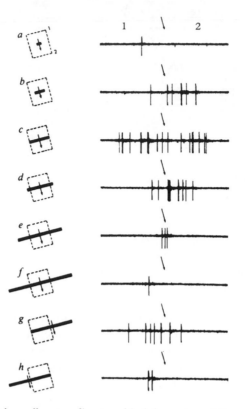

Figure 5.8 Hypercomplex cell responding to a black bar oriented from 2:30 to 8:30, moving downward. The optimum response occurred when a stimulus swept over area outlined (*c*); stimulating more than this region (*d–h*), or less (*a* or *b*), resulted in a weaker response. Sweep duration, 2.5 s (Fig. 19 in ref. 14).

Complex cells come in a wide variety of subtypes. Typical cells of layers 2 and 3 have relatively small receptive fields and low spontaneous activity, and in the monkey may be not only highly orientation-selective but also fussy about wavelength, perhaps responding to red lines but not white. They may or may not be end-stopped. Cells in layers 5 and 6 have larger fields. Those in layer 5 have high spontaneous activity, and many respond just as well to a very short moving line as to a long one. Many cells in layer 6 respond best to very long lines.[16] These differences are doubtless related to the important fact, first shown with physiological techniques by Toyama et al.[17] and confirmed and extended by anatomical techniques, that different layers project to different destinations – the upper layers mainly to other cortical regions; layer 5 to the superior colliculus, pons and pulvinar; and layer 6 back to the lateral geniculate body and to the claustrum.

Since the 1960s the subject of cortical receptive-field types has become rather a jungle, partly because the terms simple and complex are used differently by different people and partly because the categories themselves are not cleanly separated. Our original idea was to emphasize the tendency towards increased complexity as one moves centrally along the visual path and the possibility of accounting for a cell's behaviour in terms of its inputs. The circuit diagrams we proposed were just a few examples from a number of plausible possibilities. Even today the actual circuit by which orientation specificity is derived from centre–surround cells is unknown, and indeed the techniques necessary for solving this may still not be available. One can nevertheless say that cells of different complexities whose receptive fields are in the same part of the visual field and which have the same optimal orientation are likely to be interconnected, whereas cells with different optimal orientations are far less likely to be interconnected. In the monkey, a major difficulty with the hierarchical scheme outlined here is the relative scarcity of simple cells, compared with the huge numbers of cells with concentric fields in layer 4C or with the large number of complex cells above and below layer 4. The fact that the simple cells have been found mainly in layer 4B also agrees badly with Jennifer Lund's finding that layer $4C\beta$ projects not to layer 4B but to layer 3. One has to consider the possibility that in the monkey the simple-cell step may be skipped, perhaps by summing the inputs from cells in layer 4 on dendrites of complex cells. In such a scheme each main dendritic branch of a complex cell would perform the function of a simple cell. All such speculation only emphasizes our ignorance of the exact way in which the properties of complex cells are built up.

Knowing how cortical cells respond to some visual stimuli and ignore others allows us to predict how a cell will react to any given visual scene. Most cortical cells respond poorly to diffuse light, so that when I gaze at a white object, say an egg, on a dark background I know that those cells in my area 17 whose receptive fields fall entirely within the boundaries of the object will be unaffected. Only the fields that are cut by the borders of the egg will be influenced, and then only if the local orientation of a border is about the same as the orientation of the receptive field. Slightly changing the position of the egg without changing its orientation will produce a dramatic change in the population of activated simple cells, but a much smaller change in the activated complex cells.

Orientation-specific simple or complex cells are specific for the direction of a short line segment. The cells are thus best not thought of as line detectors: they are no more line detectors than they are curve detectors. If our perception of a certain line or curve depends on simple or complex cells it presumably depends on a whole set of them, and how the information from such sets of cells is assembled at subsequent stages in the path to build up what we call percepts of lines or curves (if indeed anything like that happens at all) is still a complete mystery.

Architecture

By the early 1960s, our research had extended into four different but overlapping areas. Closest to conventional neurophysiology was the working out of response properties (receptive fields) of single cells. We became increasingly involved with architecture – the grouping of cells according to function into layers and columns, studied by electrode track reconstructions. This led in turn to experiments in which single-cell recording was combined with experimental anatomy. It began when one day James Sprague called to tell us that his chief histological technician, Jane Chen, was moving to Boston and needed a job: could we take her? Luckily we did (despite our not possessing anatomical union cards), and so acquired an expert in the Nauta method of making lesions in nervous tissue and selectively staining the degenerating axons. It seemed a terrible waste not to use this method and we soon got the idea of working out detailed pathways by making microelectrode lesions that were far smaller than conventional lesions and could be precisely placed by recording with the same electrodes. It became possible to make lesions in single layers of the lateral geniculate body, with results to be discussed shortly. Finally, another phase of our work involved studies of newborn animals' postnatal development and the effects of distorting normal sensory experience in young animals. This began in 1962 and grew steadily.

Orientation Columns

What our three simultaneously recorded cells, numbers 3009, 3010 and 3011, mapped out on the overhead sheet in September 1958 with their parallel orientation axes and separate but overlapping field positions, were telling us was that neighbouring cells have similar orientations but slightly different receptive-field positions. We of course knew about Mountcastle's somatosensory columns, and we began to suspect that cells might be grouped in the striate cortex according to orientation; but to prove it was not easy (fig. 5.9).

Our first indication of the beauty of the arrangements of cell groupings came in 1961 in one of our first recordings from the striate cortex of monkey, a spider monkey named George. In one penetration, which went into the cortex at an angle of about 45° and was 2.5 mm long, we were struck right away by something we had only seen hints of before. As the electrode advanced, the orientations of successively recorded cells progressed in small steps of about 10° for every advance of 50 μm. We began the penetration about 8:00 p.m.; 5 hours later we had recorded 53 successive orientations without a single large jump in orientation (fig. 5.10). During the entire time, in which

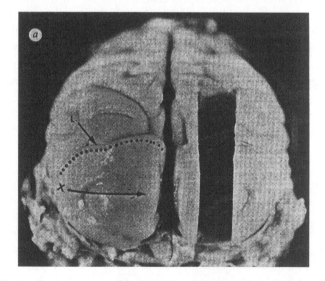

Figure 5.9   *a*, Brain of a macaque, perfused with formalin, viewed from above and behind. The occipital lobe is demarcated in front by the lunate sulcus (L) and consists mainly of the striate cortex, area 17, which occupies most of the smooth surface, extending forward to the dotted line (the 17–18 border). If followed medially, area 17 curves around the medial surface of the

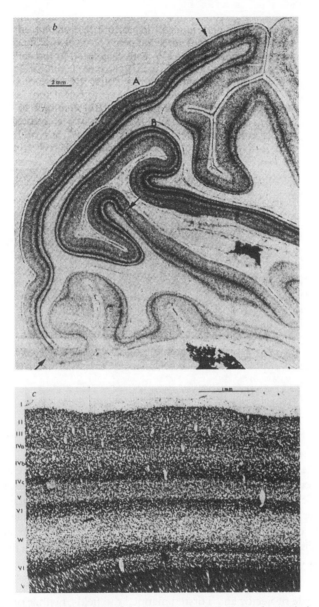

brain and continues in a complex buried fold, a part of which lies underneath the convexity and parallel to it. X marks the projection of the fovea; movement in the direction of the arrow corresponds to movement along the horizon; movement along the dotted line, to movement down along the vertical midline of the visual field. The groove in the right hemisphere was made by removing a parasagittal block of tissue to produce the cross-section of *b* (fig. 6a in ref. 29). *b*, Low power Nissl-stained section from a parasagittal block. It is what would be seen if one could stand in the groove of *a* and look to the left. A, outer convexity; B, the buried fold; arrows indicate the 17–18 borders, the upper right one of which is indicated by the dotted line in *a* (fig. 6b in ref. 29). *c*, Cross-section through the monkey striate cortex stained with cresyl violet and showing conventional layering designations. W, white matter. Deeper layers (5 and 6) of the buried fold of the cortex are shown in the lower part of the figure (compare *b*) (figure 10 in ref. 29).

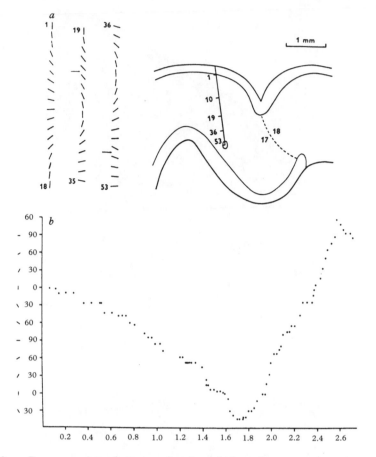

Figure 5.10   a, Reconstruction of a penetration through the striate cortex about 1 mm from the 17–18 border, near the occipital pole of a spider monkey called George. To the left of the figure, the lines indicate receptive-field orientations of cells in the columns traversed; each line represents one or several units recorded against a rich unresolved background activity. Arrows indicate reversal of directions of shifts in orientation.[32] *b*, Graph of stimulus orientation in degrees versus distance along the electrode track in millimetres, in the experiment shown in *a*. Vertical is taken as 0°, clockwise is positive and anticlockwise negative.

I wielded the slide projector and Torsten mapped the fields, neither of us moved from our seats. Fortunately, our fluid intake that day had been modest. Though I have shown this illustration many times, so far only Francis Crick has asked why there was no interruption in layer 4C, where according to dogma the cells are not orientation-specific. The answer is that I do not know.

In the cat we had had occasional suggestions of similar orderliness, and so we decided to address directly the problem of the shape and arrangement of the groupings.[18] By making several closely spaced oblique parallel penetrations, we convinced ourselves that the groupings were really columns in that they extended from the surface to white matter and had walls that were perpendicular to the layers. We next made multiple close-spaced penetrations, advancing the electrode just far enough in each penetration to record one cell or a group of cells. To map a few square millimetres of cortex this way required 50 to 100 penetrations, each of which took 10 to 15 minutes. We decided it might be better to change careers, perhaps to chicken farming. But although the experiments were by our standards exhausting they did succeed in showing that orientation columns in the cat are not generally pillars but parallel slabs that intersect the surface as either straight parallel stripes or swirls.

Reversals in direction of orientation shift (fig. 5.10*a*) are found in most penetrations. They occur irregularly, on the average about once every millimetre, and not at any particular orientation such as vertical or horizontal. We still do not know how to interpret them. Between reversals the plots of orientation against electrode position are remarkably linear.[19] Once, to exercise a new programmable calculator, I actually determined the coefficient of linear correlation of such a graph. It was 0.998, which I took to mean that the line must be very straight indeed.

For some years we had the impression that regular sequences like the one shown in fig. 5.10 are rare – that most sequences are either more or less random or else the orientation hovers around one angle for some distance and then goes to a new angle and hovers there. Chaos and hovering do occur but they are exceptional, as are major jumps of 45° to 90°. It took us a long time to realize that regularity is the rule, not the exception, probably because we did not begin making very oblique or tangential penetrations until the mid-1970s. For these experiments to be successful requires electrodes coarse enough to record activity throughout a penetration, and not simply every 100 μm or so. Such electrodes look less aesthetically pleasing, a fact that I think has happily tended to keep down the competition.

Our attempts to learn more about the geometry of orientation columns in the monkey by using the 2-deoxy-D-glucose technique[20] suggest that iso-orientation lines form a periodic pattern but are far from straight, being full of swirls and interruptions. Experiments done since then[21] suggest that the deoxyglucose is probably also labelling the cytochrome blobs (see below). Similar work in the tree shrew by Humphrey et al.[22] has shown a much more regular pattern, and Stryker, Wiesel and I have seen more regularity in the cat (unpublished data). Both tree shrew and cat lack the cytochrome blobs.

Ocular Dominance Columns

A major finding in our 1959 and 1962 papers,[10,12] besides the orientation selectivity, was the presence in the striate cortex of a high proportion of binocular cells. Since recordings from the lateral geniculate body had made it clear that cells at that stage are for all practical purposes monocular, this answered the question of where, in the retinogeniculocortical pathway, cells first received convergent input from the two eyes. More interesting to us than the mere binocularity was the similarity of a given cell's receptive fields in the two eyes in size, complexity, orientation and position. Presumably this forms the basis of the fusion of the images in the two eyes. It still seems remarkable that a cell should not only be wired with the precision necessary to produce complex or hypercomplex properties, but should have a duplicate set of such connections, one from each eye.

Although the optimum stimulus is the same for the two eyes, the responses evoked are not necessarily equal; for a given cell one eye is often consistently better than the other. It is as if the two sets of connections were qualitatively similar, but, for many cells, different in density. We termed this relative effectiveness of the two eyes 'eye preference' or 'relative ocular dominance'.

In the macaque it was evident from the earliest experiments that neighbouring cells have similar eye preferences. In vertical penetrations the preference remains the same all the way through the cortex. In layer 4C the cells are monocular, and here any cell is monopolized by the eye that merely dominates the cells in the layers above and below. In penetrations that run parallel to the layers eye preference alternates, with shifts roughly every 0.5 mm. The conclusion is that the terminals from cells of the lateral geniculate distribute themselves in layer 4C according to eye of origin, in alternating patches about 0.5 mm wide. In the layers above and below layer 4, horizontal and diagonal connections lead to a mixing that is incomplete, so that a cell above a given patch is dominated by the eye supplying that patch but receives subsidiary input from neighbouring patches (fig. 5.11).

The geometry of these layer-4 patches was finally determined by several independent anatomical methods, the first of which[23] was the Nauta method and its modifications for staining terminals worked out first by Fink and Heimer and then by a most able and energetic research assistant, Janet Wiitanen. By making small lesions in single geniculate layers, we were able to see the patchy distribution of degenerating terminals in layer 4, which, in a face-on view, takes the form not of circumscribed patches but of parallel stripes. We also showed that the ventral (magnocellular) pair of layers projects to the upper half of layer 4C (subsequently called 4Cα by Jennifer Lund), whereas the dorsal four layers project to the lower half (4Cβ), and that the line of Gennari (4B), once thought to receive the strongest projection, is actually almost bereft of geniculate terminals.

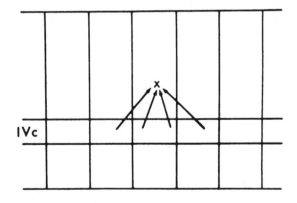

Figure 5.11   Wiring of a binocular cell in a layer above (or below) layer 4C. In the macaque, the bulk of the afferents to the striate cortex from the lateral geniculate body, themselves monocular, are strictly segregated by eye affiliation in layer 4C, and thus the cells in this layer are strictly monocular. A cell outside layer 4C (X) receives its input connections, directly or indirectly by one or more synapses, from cells in layer 4C (to some extent also, perhaps, from layers 4A and 6). Cells in layer 4C will be more likely to feed into X the closer they are to it; consequently X is likely to be binocular, dominated by the eye corresponding to the nearest patch in 4C. The degree of dominance by that eye is greater, the closer X is to being centred in its ocular dominance column, and cells near a boundary may be roughly equally influenced by the two eyes (Fig. 12 in ref. 29).

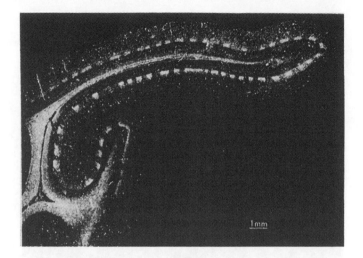

Figure 5.12 Dark-field autoradiograph of the striate cortex in an adult macaque in which the ipsilateral eye had been injected with tritiated proline-fucose 2 weeks previously. Labelled areas show white. The section passes in a plane roughly perpendicular to the exposed surface of the occipital lobe and to the buried part immediately beneath (roughly, through the arrow of fig. 5.9*a*). In all, about 56 labelled patches can be seen (Fig. 22 in ref. 29).

While the Nauta studies were still in progress, we read Bernice Grafstein's report that radioactive label injected into the eye of a rat could be detected in the contralateral visual cortex, as though transneuronal transport had taken place in the geniculate.[24] (The rat retinogeniculocortical pathway is mainly crossed.) It occurred to us that if we injected the eye of a monkey we might be able to see autoradiographic label in area 17. We tried it, but could see nothing. Soon after, while visiting Ray Guillery in Wisconsin, I saw some amino acid transport autoradiographs which showed nothing in light field, but in which label was obvious in dark field. I rushed back, we got out our slides, borrowed a dark-field condenser and found beautiful alternating patches throughout all the binocular part of area 17[25] (fig. 5.12). This method allowed us to reconstruct ocular dominance columns over much wider expanses than could be mapped with the Nauta method (fig. 5.13). It led to a study of the pre- and postnatal visual development of ocular dominance columns and the effects of visual deprivation on the columns, which Torsten Wiesel will describe.

Relationship between Columns, Magnification and Field Size

To me the main pleasures of doing science are in getting ideas for experiments, doing surgery, designing and making equipment, and above all the rare moments in which some apparently isolated facts click into place like a Chinese puzzle. When a collaboration works, as ours has, the ideas and the clicking into place often occur simultaneously or collaboratively; usually neither of us has known (or cared about) which of us originally produced an idea, and sometimes one idea has occurred to one of us, only to be forgotten and later resurrected by the other. One of the most exciting moments was the realization that our orientation columns, extending through the full thickness

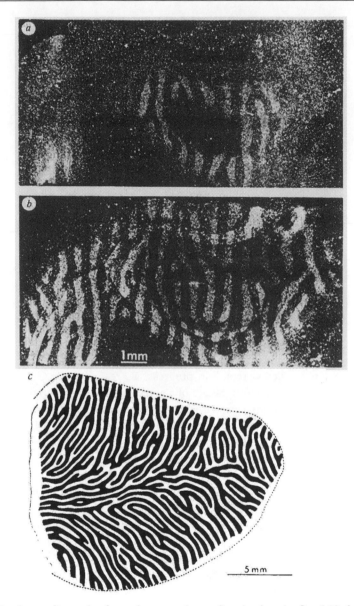

Figure 5.13 Autoradiographs from the same (normal) animal as in fig. 5.12, but from the hemisphere contralateral to the injected eye (dark field). *a*, A section tangential to the exposed dome-like surface of the occipital lobe, just grazing layer 5, which appears as an oval, surrounded by layer 4C, which appears as a ring containing the labelled parallel bands, which appear light against the dark background. *b*, A composite made by cutting out layer 4C from a number of parallel sections such as the one shown in *a* and pasting them together to show the bands over an area some millimetres in extent. *c*, Reconstruction of layer 4C ocular dominance columns over the entire exposed part of area 17 in the right occipital lobe, made from a series of reduced-silver sections.[33] The region represented is the same as the part of the right occipital lobe shown in fig. 5.9*a*. The line on the left represents the midsagittal plane, where the cortex bends around. The dashed reversed c-shaped curve is the 17–18 border, whose apex, to the extreme right, represents the fovea. Every other column has been blacked in to exhibit the twofold nature of the set of subdivisions. Note the relative constancy of column widths.

of the cat cortex, contain just those simple and complex cells (later we could add the hypercomplex) that our hierarchical schemes had proposed were interconnected.[10] This gave the column a meaning: a little machine that takes care of contours in a certain orientation in a certain part of the visual field. If the cells of one set are to be interconnected, and to some extent isolated from neighbouring sets, it makes obvious sense to gather them together. As Lorente de Nó showed,[26] most of the connections in the cortex run up and down; lateral or oblique connections tend to be short (mostly limited to 1–2 mm) and less rich. These ideas were not entirely new since Mountcastle had clearly enunciated the principle of the column as an independent unit of function. What was new in the visual cortex was a clear function for the columns, the transformation of information from circularly symmetric form to orientation-specific form, and the stepwise increase in complexity.

A similar argument applies to the ocular dominance columns, a pair of which constitutes a machine for combining inputs from the two eyes – combining, but not completely combining, in a peculiar grudging way for reasons still not at all clear, but probably related in some way to stereopsis. (Whatever the explanation of the systematically incomplete blending, it will have to take into account the virtual but not complete absence of dominance columns in squirrel monkeys.) If the eyes are to be kept to some extent functionally separate, it is economical of connections to pack together cells of a given eye preference.

To my mind our most aesthetically attractive and exciting formulation has been the hypercolumn and its relation to magnification. The idea grew up gradually, but took an initial spurt as a result of a question asked by Werner Reichardt during a seminar that I gave in Tübingen. I had been describing the ordered orientation sequences found in monkeys like George, when Werner asked how one avoided the difficulty arising from the fact that as you move across the cortex, visual field position is changing in addition to orientation. Could this mean that if you looked closely you would find, in one small part of the visual field, only a small select group of orientations represented? The question seemed silly (at first), and I explained that in any one part of the visual field all orientations are represented, in fact probably several times over. Afterwards the question nagged me. There must be more to it than that. We began to put some seemingly isolated facts together. The visual fields map systematically onto the cortex but the map is distorted: the fovea is disproportionately represented, with 1 mm about equivalent to 1/6° of visual field. As one goes out in the visual field the representation falls off logarithmically, as Daniel and Whitteridge had shown,[27] so that in the far periphery the relationship is more like 1 mm = 6°. Meanwhile the average size of receptive fields grows from centre of gaze to periphery. This is not unexpected when one considers that in the fovea our acuity is much higher than in the periphery. To do the job in more detail takes more cells, each looking after a smaller region; to accommodate the cells takes more cortical surface area. I had always been surprised that the part of the cortex representing the fovea is not obviously thicker than that representing the periphery: surprised, I suppose, because in the retina near the fovea, the ganglion is, in fact, many times thicker than in the periphery. The cortex must be going out of its way to keep its uniformity by devoting to the detailed tasks more area rather than more thickness.

We decided to look more carefully at the relationship between receptive field size and area of cortex per unit area of visual field.[28] When an electrode pushed vertically

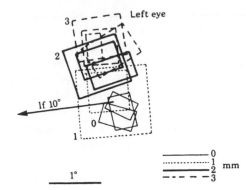

Figure 5.14   Receptive-field drift. Receptive fields mapped during an oblique, almost tangential, penetration through the striate cortex. A few fields were mapped along each of four 100-μm segments, spaced at 1-mm intervals. These four groups of fields are labelled 0, 1, 2, and 3. Along any one of these 100-μm segments no systematic progression of receptive fields could be seen; any such movement was obscured by the random scatter. But from one segment to the next there was a clear movement: each new set of fields was slightly above the other in the visual field, as predicted from the direction of movement of the electrode and from the topographic map of visual fields onto the cortex. Roughly a 2-mm movement through cortex was required to displace the fields from one region to an entirely new region (fig. 2 in ref. 28).

through the cortex encounters a hundred or so cells in traversing the full thickness, the receptive fields vary to some extent in size, and in a rather random way in position, so that the hundred maps when superimposed cover an area several times that of an average receptive field. We call this the 'aggregate receptive field' for a particular point on the cortex. On making a penetration parallel to the surface, a gradual drift in field positions is superimposed on the random staggering, in a direction dictated by the topographic map (fig. 5.14). We began to wonder whether any law connected the rate of this drift in aggregate position and the size of the fields. It turned out that for layers 2 and 3 a movement of about 2 mm across the cortex is just sufficient to produce a displacement, in the visual field, out of the region where one started and into an entirely new region. This held across the entire striate cortex (and consequently over the whole visual field). In the fovea the displacement was tiny and so were the fields. As one went out, both increased in size, in parallel fashion (fig. 5.15). Now things seemed to mesh. George and other monkeys had taught us that a 1–2-mm movement across the cortex is accompanied by an angular shift in receptive field orientation of 180° to 360°, more than one full complement of orientations. We have termed such a set of orientation columns (180°) a hypercolumn. Meanwhile, the ocular dominance shifts back and forth to take care of both eyes every millimetre – a hypercolumn for ocular dominance. Thus in 1 or 2 mm^2 there seems to exist all the machinery necessary to look after everything the visual cortex is responsible for, in a certain small part of the visual world. The machines are the same everywhere; in some parts the information on which they do their job is less detailed, but covers more visual field (fig. 5.16).

Uniformity is surely a huge advantage in development, for genetic specifications need only be laid down for a 1–2-mm block of neural tissue, together with the instruction to make a thousand or so.

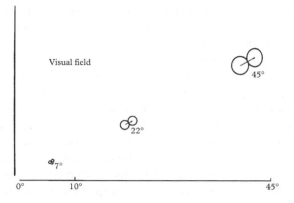

Figure 5.15 Variation of receptive-field drift with eccentricity. The diagram represents one quadrant of the field of vision, and the circles represent aggregate receptive fields – the territory collectively occupied by receptive fields of cells encountered in a micro-electrode penetration perpendicular to the cortical surface. Each pair of circles illustrates the movement in aggregate receptive fields accompanying a tangential movement along the cortex of 1–2 mm. Both the displacement and the aggregate field size vary with distance from the fovea (eccentricity), but they do so in parallel fashion. Close to the fovea the fields are tiny, but so is the displacement accompanying a 1–2 mm movement along the cortex. (At 0° eccentricity, displacement and aggregate field size are both too small to be reproduced in this figure.) The greater the distance from the fovea, the greater the two become, but they continue to remain roughly equal.[28]

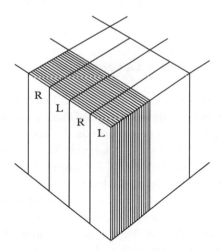

Figure 5.16 Model of the striate cortex, to show roughly the dimensions of the ocular dominance slabs (L and R) in relation to the orientation slabs and the cortical thickness. Thinner lines separate individual columns: thicker lines demarcate the two pairs of ocular dominance columns and two sets of orientation columns. The placing of these hypercolumn boundaries is arbitrary: one could as well begin the orientation hypercolumn at horizontal or at any of the obliques. The decision to show the two sets of columns as intersecting at right-angles is also arbitrary, since there is at present no evidence of the relationship between the two sets. For convenience, the slabs are shown as plane surfaces, but whereas the dominance columns are indeed more or less flat, the orientation columns are not known to be so, and when viewed from above, they may have the form of swirls (Fig. 27 in ref. 29).

We could have called the entire machine a hypercolumn, but we did not. The term as we define it refers to a complete set of a given column. I mention this because in terminology, too, uniformity has some obvious advantages. Perhaps one could use 'module' to refer to the complete machine.

There are three qualifications to all of this. (1) I do not mean to imply that there need really be 2,000 separate definable entities. It need not matter whether one begins a set of orientation columns at vertical, horizontal or any one of the obliques; the decision is arbitrary. One requires two dominance columns, a left and a right, and it makes no difference which one begins with. (In fact, as will become apparent when I discuss cytochrome blobs, it now looks as though the blocks of tissue may really be discrete, to a degree that we could not have imagined 2 years ago.) (2) Because receptive fields are larger and connections longer in layers 5 and 6, compared with those of layers 2 and 3, a module defined for the deeper layers would be somewhat larger than 2 × 2 mm. In this sense, to think of modules as small chunks of cortex was an oversimplification. (3) There may well be some differences in cortical machinery between the centre and periphery of the visual field. Colour vision and stereopsis, for example, probably decline in importance far out in the visual fields. I say this not to be obsessively complete but because in the next few years someone will probably find some difference and pronounce the general concept wrong. It may of course be wrong, but I hope it will be for interesting reasons.

The retina must be nonuniform if it is to do a more detailed job in the centre. To have more area devoted to the centre than to the periphery is not an option open to it, because it is a globe. Were it anything else the optics would be awkward and the eye could not rotate in its socket.

New Developments

A few years ago, in a Ferrier Lecture,[29] Torsten and I ended by saying that the striate cortex was probably, in broad outline, understood. This was done deliberately: one did not want the well to dry up. When one wants rain the best strategy is to leave raincoat and umbrella at home. So the best way to guarantee future employment was to declare the job finished. It certainly worked. In 1978, Margaret Wong-Riley observed regular intermittent puff-like densities in the upper layers of monkey striate cortex stained for the enzyme cytochrome oxidase, and 2 years ago Anita Hendrickson and her group and our laboratory independently discovered that if cytochrome-stained cortex was cut parallel to the surface through layer 3 these densities took the form of a polka-dot pattern of dark blobs quasi-regularly spaced about 0.5 mm apart (fig. 5.17).[21,30] It is as if the animal's brain had the measles. The pattern has been seen with several other enzymatic stains, suggesting that either the activity or the machinery is different in the blob regions. The pattern has been found in all primates examined, including humans, but not, so far as I know, in any non-primates. In the macaque the blobs are clearly lined up along ocular dominance columns.[21] Over the past year Margaret Livingstone and I have shown that the cells in the blobs lack orientation selectivity, resembling, at least superficially, cells of layer 4C.[31] They are selectively labelled after large injections of radioactive proline into the lateral geniculate body, so it is clear that their inputs are not identical to the inputs to the rest of layers 2 and 3. Thus an entire system has

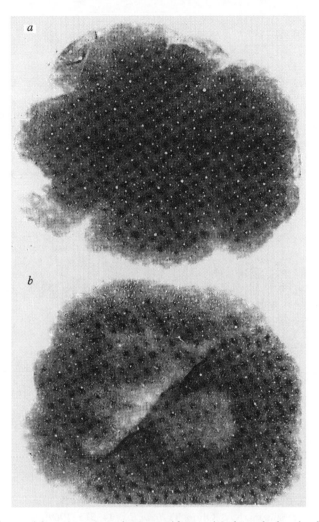

Figure 5.17 Tangential sections (cytochrome oxidase stain) through the visual cortex of the squirrel monkey. The sections pass through the 17–18 border, which runs obliquely in the figure, with area 17 below and to the right and 18 above and to the left. (D.H.H. and M.S.L., unpublished data). *a,* The section passes through layer 3, and the blobs can be seen easily in area 17. *b,* The section is tangential to layer 5, where the blobs can again be seen, though faintly; these lie in register with the upper-layer blobs.

opened up, whose existence we were previously unaware of and whose anatomy and functions we do not yet understand. We are especially anxious to learn what, if any, relationship exists between the cytochrome blobs and the orientation columns.

Things are at an exciting stage. There is no point leaving the umbrella home; it is raining, and raining hard.

Acknowledgements

I thank the Eye Institute of the National Institutes of Health, the US Air Force, the Klingenstein Fund, and the Rowland Foundation for their generous support of our research; also, the Faculty of Harvard University for tolerating such a truculent colleague. I thank many research assistants who have helped Torsten Wiesel and me over the past 22 years, especially Jane Chen, Janet Wiitanen, Bea Storai, Jaye Robinson, Martha Egan, Joan Weisenbeck, Karen Larson, Sharon Mates, Debra Hamburger, Yu-Wen Wu, Sue Fenstemaker, Stella Chow, Sarah Kennedy, Maureen Packard and Mary Nastuk. For photographic assistance I thank Sandra Spinks, Carolyn Yoshikami and Marc Peloquin; in electronics and computers David Freeman; and Sheila Barton, Pat Schubert and Olivia Brum for secretarial help.

References

1 Hubel, D. H. *Am. J. Ophthal.*, **46**, 110 (1958).
2 Barlow, H. B., FitzHugh, R. & Kuffler, S. W. *J. Physiol., Lond.*, **137**, 327 (1957).
3 Talbot, S. A. & Kuffler S. W. *J. Opt. Soc. Am.*, **42**, 931 (1952).
4 Talbot, S. A. & Marshall, W. H. *Am. J. Ophthal.*, **24**, 1255 (1941).
5 Mountcastle, V. B. *J. Neurophysiol.*, **20**, 408 (1957).
6 Davies, P. W. *Science*, **124**, 179 (1956).
7 Sperry, R. W., Miner, N. & Myers, R. E. *J. Comp. Physiol. Psychol.*, **48**, 50 (1955).
8 Sperry, R. W. & Miner, N. *J. Comp. Physiol. Psychol.*, **48**, 463 (1955).
9 Cleland, B. G., Dubin, M. W. & Levick, W. R. *Nature New Biol.*, **231**, 191 (1971).
10 Hubel, D. H. & Wiesel, T. N. *J. Physiol. Lond.*, **160**, 106 (1962).
11 Hubel, D. H. & Wiesel, T. N. *21st Int. Congr. Physiol.*, Buenos Aires (1959).
12 Hubel, D. H. & Wiesel, T. N. *J. Physiol. Lond.*, **148**, 574 (1959).
13 Barlow, H. B. & Levick, W. R. *J. Physiol. Lond.*, **178**, 477 (1965).
14 Hubel, D. H. & Wiesel, T. N. *J. Neurophysiol.*, **28**, 229 (1965).
15 Dreher, B. *Invest. Ophthal.*, **11**, 355 (1972).
16 Gilbert, C. D. *J. Physiol, Lond.*, **268**, 391 (1977).
17 Toyama, T., Matsunami, K. & Ohno, T. *Brain Res.*, **14**, 513 (1969).
18 Hubel, D. H. & Wiesel, T. N. *J. Physiol., Lond.*, **165**, 559 (1963).
19 Hubel, D. H. & Wiesel, T. N. *J. Comp. Neurol.*, **158**, 267 (1974).
20 Sokoloff, L. et al. *J. Neurochem.*, **28**, 897 (1977).
21 Horton, J. C. & Hubel, D. H. *Nature*, **292**, 762 (1981).
22 Humphrey, A. L., Skeen, L. C. & Norton, T. T. *J. Comp. Neurol.*, **192**, 549 (1980).
23 Hubel, D. H. & Wiesel, T. N. *J. Comp. Neurol.*, **146**, 421 (1972).
24 Grafstein, B. *Science*, **172**, 177 (1971).
25 Wiesel, T. N., Hubel, D. H. & Lam, D. M.-K. *Brain Res.*, **79**, 273 (1974).
26 Lorente de Nó, R. in *Physiology of the Nervous System*, 3rd edn, ed. Fulton, J. F. (Oxford University Press, 1949).
27 Daniel, P. M. & Whitteridge, D. *J. Physiol., Lond.*, **159**, 203 (1961).
28 Hubel, D. H. & Wiesel, T. N. *J. Comp. Neurol.*, **158**, 295 (1974).
29 Hubel, D. H. & Wiesel, T. N. *Proc. R. Soc.*, **B198** (1977).
30 Hendrickson, A. E., Hunt, S. P. & Wu, J.-Y. *Nature*, **292**, 605 (1981).
31 Hubel, D. H. & Livingstone, M. S. *Soc. Neurosci. Abstr.*, **7**, 357 (1981).
32 Hubel, D. H. & Wiesel, T. N. *J. Physiol., Lond.*, **195**, 215 (1968).
33 LeVay, S., Hubel, D. H. & Wiesel, T. N. *J. Comp. Neurol.*, **159**, 559 (1975).

6

The Parietal System and Some Higher Brain Functions

Vernon B. Mountcastle

A quarter century has passed since electrophysiological studies of the homotypical cortex in waking monkeys began. These are made as monkey subjects emit behavioral acts sufficiently complex to qualify as those generated and controlled by the "higher" functions of the neocortex. The general experimental plan is an extension to the study of higher functions of an approach proven successful in earlier studies of the neocortical mechanisms in sensation and perception, and the control of movement. The early phase of exploratory experiments on the homotypical cortex has now given way to more precise experiments, quantitative analysis, and model testing, and it is clear that we can look forward to a rapid acquisition of knowledge of these complex neocortical operations. If progress during the early phase was less rapid than had been hoped for, the reasons are easy to find. At the experimental level the linkage between behavioral events and neural activity in homotypical cortical areas is always less precise than in primary areas; in many cases it is conditional in nature and influenced by central state functions of the brain, and interpretations are plagued by the ever difficult transition from causation to causality. Interpretations are always beset by varying concept; command or re-afference, attention or neglect, active intention or passive reception, and so on. Indeed, the neurophysiologist who ventured into the homotypical cortex in the 1970s entered a foreign country in which new and unlabeled neural events were encountered at every turn, or rather, in nearly every microelectrode penetration!

This issue of *Cerebral Cortex* [Sept./Oct. 1995] brings together a number of descriptions of these new studies of the homotypical cortex, restricted to a sample of the many now underway on the posterior parietal cortex. I preface them with an account of my own adventures into the parietal lobe, now long ago.

My Adventures in the Parietal Lobe

Edward Evarts and the transition to the waking monkey experiment

Given a highball or two even the most reserved of scientists may be persuaded to reveal a tale of serendipity in research, often with some embellishments that add measurably to its telling. I have observed this quite often among the high priests of molecular biology, and even on rare occasions among my colleagues in neuroscience. I assert, however, that the following is a true account of my first adventures into the posterior parietal cortex of the waking monkey. Many living witnesses impose constraint.

It began on a bright Monday morning in April of 1968. I had spent the previous Friday visiting my friend the late Edward Evarts, watching as he recorded the activity of neurons in the motor cortex of a waking monkey as the latter executed motor tasks. I had left Bethesda somewhat despondent, for I saw difficulty in delivering mechanical stimuli in a precise way to the glabrous skin of the hand of a waking monkey.

That Monday morning changed it all. I glanced down the hall from my laboratory in Baltimore to see none other than that same Edward Evarts striding toward me, his face wreathed in that wonderful smile, with a large wooden box on his shoulder. He had brought me all the gadgets required for recording from the waking monkey. With that encouragement I could not do otherwise; I used his gifts for a year, and began a long series of adventures.

Technical preparations, and our first study of the somatic sensory cortex in the waking monkey

The next two years were filled with technical and behavioral development, particularly with William H. Talbot, that genius of the computer-controlled laboratory experiment (with an original Linc, memory = 1000 bytes; and only later a PDP); with Robert H. LaMotte, whom I am convinced can read monkeys' brains and train even the most cantankerous one to execute difficult tasks; and with an extraordinary engineer, John Chubbuck. Thus, with improved methods we began to record the electrical signs of the activity of single neurons in the postcentral somatic sensory cortex of monkeys as they executed sensory tasks, in this case the detection of a sine wave mechanical oscillation at the flutter frequency (10–40 Hz) superimposed upon a 0.5 mm step indentation of the glabrous skin of the hand. All went well, and by the summer of 1970 we had established a correlation between the increasing probability of correct detection with increasing stimulus amplitude, and an increase in the cyclic entailment of the cortical neuronal activity at the stimulus frequency (see figs. 6.1, 6.2; Carli et al., 1971a, b). Alas! When we examined neuronal responses to stimuli detected only 50% of the time, we found no differences between those evoked by stimuli detected and those missed! Where was the critical neural event upon which detection depended?

Transition to study of the posterior parietal areas

Thus, it was more in frustration than in a planned experimental foray that on 8 September 1970 in monkey BM 19 we (Robert LaMotte, now at Yale University;

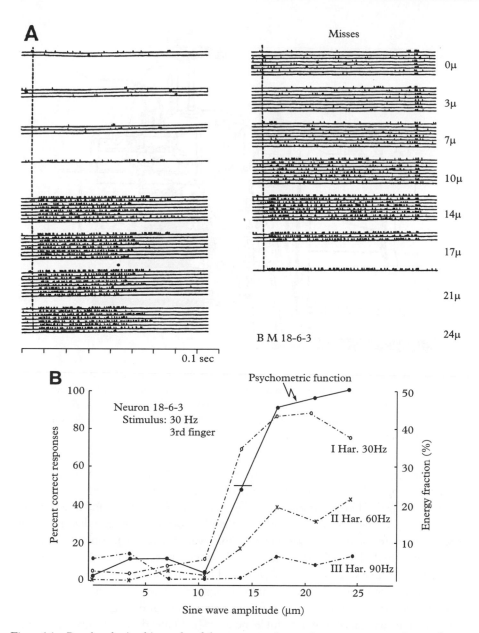

Figure 6.1 Results obtained in study of the postcentral somatic sensory cortex of a monkey as he worked in a flutter detection task. Stimuli were delivered to the glabrous skin of the hand in the arrangement shown in figure 6.2. **A**, Impulse replicas of a cortical neuron. Each *line* was obtained during a single trial; each *short upstroke* indicates the instant at which the neuron discharged an impulse. Peak-to-peak amplitudes of the mechanical sinusoid imposed on a 500 μm step indentation of the glabrous skin are shown to the *right*. Trials at different amplitudes were sequenced randomly. Trials are separated into those detected (HITS) and those not detected (MISSES). **B**, Analysis of power in the neuronal signals by Fourier shows growth of the first harmonic *pari passu* with the increasing certainty of correct detection. However, analysis of hits and misses at the 50% point of detection revealed no difference. Data from Carli et al. (1971a).

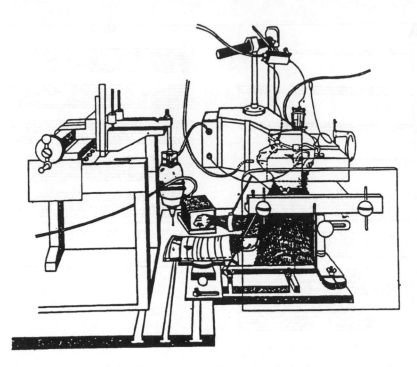

Figure 6.2 Apparatus used for the experiment the results of which are shown in figure 6.1. Tactile stimulator shown to the *left* poised over the glabrous skin of the restrained hand of the waking monkey subject. Microdrive and cathode follower are shown *upper right*. *Box surrounding the head*, shown cutaway, contained signal lights indicating trial onset, and so on. Reprinted with permission, from Mountcastle et al. (1972).

Carlos Acuna, now at the University of Santiago de Compestella in Spain; and I) suddenly changed the locus of recording from the postcentral somatic sensory area to the posterior parietal homotypical cortex, first on that day to area 5, and a few months later to area 7. What we observed in those exploratory experiments determined my experimental life for fifteen years: neurons that were active if and only if the animal "had a mind" to deal with the stimulus in a behaviorally meaningful way! In *area 5*, there were neurons active when the animal projected his arm toward a target of interest, but not during random arm movements; and neurons active when the animal worked with his fingers to extract a morsel of food from a recess, but not during other hand actions like pinching (we called them "winkle neurons"). Quite different sets of neurons appeared to drive the transport and grasping phases of reaching movements. Other sets of neurons were activated by joint rotation, more intensely during his active joint rotations than when the joints were rotated passively by us; still others by cutaneous stimulation, frequently from large, bilateral receptive fields, often with directional selectivity. In *area 7*, there were neurons active during visual fixation of objects of interest, but not during casual fixations, and insensitive to visual stimuli; neurons active during visually evoked but not during spontaneous saccadic eye movements; neurons active during smooth pursuit visual tracking; and neurons that responded to visual stimuli, per se, with unusual receptive fields and response properties. We called them "light-sensitive" or "visual space" neurons, leaving open for the time being the question of whether they played an active role in visual perceptions.

The major source of information about the putative functions of the parietal systems was in the descriptions of patients with lesions of the parietal lobe (Critchley, 1953). I began to attend the neurological ward rounds in the hospital, and soon my colleagues Guy McKhann and Richard Johnson showed me a patient who had sustained a vascular lesion of his right posterior parietal cortex, and who displayed all the classical signs of optic ataxia and contralateral neglect. He loudly complained of a foreign arm in his bed – it was his own! I followed this patient's history, and observed his remarkable degree of recovery, such that one year later it was not easy to demonstrate either his neglect or his optic ataxia. This was of great interest to me in relation to the function of distributed systems. I obtained and reviewed all the case histories in the Johns Hopkins Hospital filed under the label "parietal lobe syndrome," and I reviewed the relatively sparse literature on studies of the effects of parietal lobe lesions in nonhuman primates, as well as that describing the connectivity of these regions. These reviews provided a base for a series of studies of the parietal lobe system I then carried out with a succession of extraordinarily able collaborators, in temporal sequence: W. H. Talbot, R. H. LaMotte, C. Acuna, J. C. Lynch, H. Sakata, A. P. Georgopoulos, T. T. C. Yin, B. C. Motter, C. J. Duffy, R. A. Andersen, M. A. Steinmetz, and A. K. Sestokas.

These exploratory experiments indicated how useless it was to study the posterior parietal cortex in a qualitative way, or with the standard sensory stimuli available to us. John Chubbuck designed the test apparatus shown in figure 6.3. This provided a target light carried on a car moved at different speeds for selected arcs of the circle, all under program control. We then studied the reach neurons of areas 5 and 7, as the monkey made arm projections at different angles for the same distances, and tracked the moving target with eye and hand. For the reach neurons we also combined the tactile stimulator of figure 6.2 in the apparatus of figure 6.3, and discovered that the activity of a typical reach neuron is independent of the sensory channel – somesthetic or visual – evoking the movement, in both a lighted and a darkened environment. This was at least for us compelling evidence that in areas 5 and 7 we dealt with a higher order of cortical function than we had hitherto encountered, and that our deeply embedded concepts derived from studies of primary sensory areas were too simple for the new tasks. We managed some preliminary reports in 1973 (Lynch et al., 1973a, b), but our first full-length report was delayed until 1975 (Mountcastle et al., 1975).

Several things became clear early in our studies: first, that it is possible to study the higher functions of the brain in nonhuman primates, but only if the complex properties of the homotypical cortex are matched by equally complex behavioral tasks, and that quantitative studies under controlled conditions are essential; second, that although the properties of posterior parietal neurons do provide a limited positive image of the defects of the parietal lobe syndrome, the functions inferred are embedded in dynamic neuronal processes in widely distributed systems of the forebrain, in which the parietal lobe is but one of several essential nodes; third, what is important for experimental design, that in any given experimental arrangement one cannot study quantitatively all of the many classes of parietal neurons, perhaps at best only two. This makes especially acute the ubiquitous sampling problem that dogs all electrophysiological studies of the cerebral cortex, and emphasizes that conclusions drawn from any small sample of neurons are especially hazardous. This is, I believe, the explanation of why in so many cases different investigators describe populations of parietal neurons with quite different properties, even though recording from what are putatively the same areas of cortex. These differences provide no grounds for polemic controversy.

Cerebral Cortical Mechanisms in the Transport Phase of Directed Reaching

Psychophysical studies of reaching and grasping in humans and in nonhuman primates have documented the decomposition of reaching to a target into a transport phase of projection of the arm and hand, and a grasping phase in which the hand adapts to the spatial contours of the target. Studies of this sort have been made in many laboratories, and with particular elegance and insight by our colleagues in France, particularly by Paillard (1982; 1991). Jeannerod et al. (1988), and Perenin and Vighetto (1988). These two phases have been selectively damaged by lesions located in different parts of the parietal lobe in human subjects.

It was the perceptive insight of Georgopoulos that visually guided reaching movements of the arm could be studied in the waking monkey experiment, both for the

Figure 6.3   Drawing of a *Macaca arctoides* working in the test apparatus used in our first studies of the reach, hand manipulation, fixation, and tracking neurons of the posterior parietal cortex. The head-fixation apparatus, implanted microdrive, cathode follower, and reward tube are shown *upper left*. The signal key is seen through the cutaway of the circular race. The animal has just released the key with his left hand and projected his arm and hand forward to contact the light switch mounted on the moving carriage, *upper right*. The carriage could be moved from any preset position in either direction at speeds of 12 or 21 degrees/sec for preset distances. All parameters were under PDP 11 control. Drawing by Mrs E. Bodian, from Mountcastle et al. (1975), reprinted with permission.

immediate problem of the motor and premotor cortical activity controlling directed reaches (Georgopoulos et al., 1982; 1986; Georgopoulos, 1991; 1994), and for the more general problem of the sensory-motor interface, in this case the population codings between the parietal and frontal lobe mechanisms involved. He used a directional vector to define the population signal in the motor cortex driving reaching movements, a method devised by K. O. Johnson, and it was Georgopoulos who observed neuronal activity directly correlated with a silent and unexpressed "mental" activity, mental rotation (Georgopoulos et al., 1989). Since then research on the posterior parietal and motor cortical mechanisms in reaching has reached a level of sophistication rarely matched by any other body of neurophysiological studies of the neocortex in waking monkeys.

The problem of the neural mechanisms in reaching to visual targets opened for study several major themes in the physiology of the neocortex. How are precise signals for action generated in a population of imprecise neural elements? How are the neural signals for different parts of a complex action – like the transport and grasping phases of reaching – processed in parallel in different parts of a widely distributed system, yet finally converge (but never to a single point) to drive a smoothly phased temporal evolution of the action? How are different neural operations composed in different frames of reference, yet coordinate transforms between them achieved? Understanding of these matters is still incomplete, but the major problems are all in play in the experimental arena, and discoveries flow in rapid succession from many laboratories. This area of research has been characterized by an unusual convergence of psychophysical, anatomical, neurophysiological, and modeling methods and concepts that accounts in large part, I believe, for the rapid progress that has been made (for reviews, see Jeannerod, 1988; Paillard, 1991). Some aspects of the role of the posterior parietal cortical areas in reaching to visual targets are described in three articles, two in this issue of *Cerebral Cortex*.

In an article in a forthcoming issue of *Cerebral Cortex*, Caminiti et al. (1996) provide a review of a host of new studies of the neural connections between several recently defined areas of the posterior parietal cortex. The results described resolve a long-standing problem in understanding the cortical mechanisms in visually guided reaching. That is, that while projections are known to link area 5 to the dorsal premotor area of the frontal lobe, and also directly to the motor cortex itself, no connections had hitherto been shown to link the visual mechanisms of the inferior to the motor mechanisms of the superior parietal lobule. The new studies made with tracing methods have now revealed strong projections from the prestriate and posterior parietal visual areas to a more medial parietal area, PO, which projects forward upon the region of area 5 lining the anterior bank in the medial portion of the intraparietal sulcus. This provides the link from the visual to the somesthetic and motor mechanisms involved in visually guided reaching. It is of special importance, for a major class of visual neurons of area 7a is optimally suited by virtue of its motion and directional sensitivities to guide the movement of the arm through the periphery of the visual field during the transport phase of visually guided reaching (Motter and Mountcastle, 1981).

The cortex of area 7a lining the posterior bank of the intraparietal sulcus in its more medial extent contains a significantly large population of reach neurons. These resemble those of area 5, described above, but differ in that they are more likely to be active with reaches of either arm (Mountcastle et al., 1975). MacKay (1992) has studied these cells and observed that when "bilateral" reach neurons have a directional preference, that direction is similar for the two.

Lacquaniti et al. (pp. 391–409 in this issue) present a new and penetrating analysis of a population of reach neurons in area 5 studied in Caminiti's laboratory, in the three-work-space arrangement shown in their Figure 1. They show that the directional vector tuning is much less precise for the parietal population than it is for neurons of the motor and premotor areas of the frontal lobe. For example, only 22% of parietal reach neurons fit the directional vector model for all three of the cubed work spaces, versus the 75% of motor cortical neurons that do so. Moreover, when a parietal neuron is directionally tuned in at least two of the work spaces, the preferred directions for individual neurons change in an idiosyncratic way from one space to the next, with average but disorganized rotations of 50°. This contrasts with the motor cortex population, where the preferred directions change in a uniform and systematic way from one work space to the adjacent one, to a degree determined by the angular rotation of the shoulder required by the change.

Lacquaniti et al. base their analysis upon the results of psychophysical studies indicating that the transformation from sensory signals to motor commands for reaching movements is specified in a body-centered coordinate system. They then demonstrate that the activity of area 5 reach neurons is monotonically tuned in a way encoding the start position of the hand, its movement through successive way points in space; and its final location at the target, all in a body-centered frame of reference probably centered on the shoulder. Several models were tested, and the spherical angular one centered at the shoulder achieved the best prediction of the experimental observations. A finding of considerable interest is a strong tendency for the individual spatial coordinates (whether angular or Cartesian) to be encoded in separate subpopulations of parietal reach neurons. This is a particularly concise example of parallel processing, for the total movement is signaled in quasi-separate populations, and I conjecture that these three never converge to any summing or nodal points, but engage directly the premotor/motor cortical mechanisms of the frontal lobe. This emphasizes the need for further study of the population-to-population interface in the sensory-motor transformation.

All current and past studies of area 5 leave unresolved the question of its relative position and role in the distributed network controlling projection movements of the arm and hand to visual targets. Although the responses of area 5 reach neurons to passive stimulation of the contralateral arm are very weak, nevertheless 80% of those analyzed by Lacquaniti et al. were responsive at some level to such stimuli. Are we to conclude that the area 5 activity is largely produced by sensory re-afference from peripheral receptors during movement, and used in some matching operation for correction of the actual to the intended movement? Unhappily, no separate analyses have ever been made of the 20% (or more) of area 5 reach neurons insensitive to sensory stimulation, nor of those (are they the same?) shown by earlier studies of several investigators to remain active during visually evoked reaching movements after section of the dorsal roots.

On the assumption that an area 5 reach neuron population exists that is not driven directly from the moving arm, the question remains unsettled whether that population is driven by a central reentry – and used for the matching operations described above – or whether that population is an essential node in the command operations linking visual signals of the target and motor cortical compositions of the reach movement. Measurements of relative timing of onset of activity in relation to movement onset may not settle the matter, for they have usually been made in highly overtrained monkeys working in reaction time tasks. Indeed, Kalaska (1991) has now shown in studies using an instructed delay task that the activity of reach neurons of area 5 consistently leads that of neurons of area 4, and Burbaud et al. (1991) found that the "early" area 5 reach neurons lead all other cortical neuronal populations active in reaching. It appears that these time relations depend critically upon the task in which the animal is engaged.

It was Kalaska and his colleagues who first discovered that area 5 reach neurons are virtually unaffected by loads that oppose the movements of the contralateral arm in visually guided reaching (Kalaska et al., 1990). The area 5 population appears to encode movement kinematics, good evidence that they are not driven, or not driven only, by sensory re-afference during movement, for certainly that afferent barrage will be changed markedly during load-opposed movements. Neurons of the motor cortical areas, by contrast, include many whose discharge is markedly changed by opposing loads, particularly under dynamic conditions (Evarts et al., 1983; Georgopoulos et al., 1992). This dissociation suggests that area 5 reach neurons are not driven by a centrally contained reentrant discharge derived from the motor cortex, although it does not rule out the unlikely possibility that such a reentrant discharge might originate elsewhere. Kalaska and Crammond (pp. 410–28 in this issue) now describe another remarkable difference between parietal and frontal populations of reach neurons. They studied these neuronal sets as monkeys worked in instructed delay tasks in which, cued by earlier appropriate signals for each trial, they either emitted or withheld movement at the end of the delay: the go/no-go paradigm. Both sets of neurons develop significant directionalities during the delay in go trials, but only the parietal neurons do so during no-go trials. The signal not to go appears to be inserted "central" to the parietal lobe, perhaps in the premotor and motor cortical areas. This provides further evidence against the central reentrant hypothesis of parietal lobe function in visually guided reaching.

In summary, a number of important discoveries have been made in recent years concerning the role of parietal lobe mechanisms in visually guided reaching movements of the arm. Neuroanatomical tracing studies have revealed a robust, multistaged projection linking the prestriate visual areas to the putative motor mechanisms of area 5 of the superior parietal lobule. The population vector describes the parietal activity during movement less precisely than it does for neurons of the dorsal premotor and motor areas of the frontal lobe. A model based on positional coding in a body-centered reference frame anchored on the shoulder fits the activities of parietal neurons adequately. The three dimensions of movement in this space appear to be encoded by separate but overlapping sets of area 5 reach neurons. The demonstration of kinematic coding by the area 5 population and dynamic coding by the premotor and motor populations argues against the peripheral re-afferent explanation of parietal activity. A new experiment made in both frontal and parietal areas as monkeys worked in instructed-delay, go/no-go reaching tasks exposed a second dissociation. The signal not to move appears to be inserted between parietal and motor populations, or perhaps in the motor cortical areas themselves. Further progress will now depend, I suggest, upon development of accurate methods for identifying the types and laminar localizations of neurons from which recordings are made (Taira and Georgopoulos, 1993; Wilson et al., 1994).

Cerebral Cortical Mechanisms of the Grasping Phase of Directed Reaching

Our first experiments on the posterior parietal cortex of the waking monkey yielded a number of unusual observations; among them was the discovery of the hand manipulation neurons (HM) of areas 5 and 7 (Lynch et al., 1973a; Mountcastle et al., 1975). HM neurons are virtually silent during the transport phase of visually guided reaches. They discharge intensely during the grasping phase, as the hand is molded to the target, or during other exploratory manipulations. Our first observations of HM neurons were made as a monkey shaped his hand to obtain a raisin from a receptacle slightly smaller than the resting palm diameter (it was a 100-ml beaker). This activity was particularly intense when the receptacle was presented 15–20 cm in front of the face, associated with visual fixation of as well as manipulation for the food object. We soon discovered that the activity of the majority of HM neurons was undiminished when the animal's view of the target was occluded before arm release, and this became one of the defining characteristics of HM neurons. Other neurons of area 7, but not of area 5, are active only during visual fixation, and another set appears to sum the effects of visual fixation and hand manipulations.

Sakata and his colleagues have pursued study of the area 7 HM neurons, with results described in a series of reports (Taira et al., 1990; Sakata et al., 1992; Jeannerod et al., 1995), and in Sakata et al., pp. 429–38 in this issue). These investigators discovered that area 7 HM neurons are selectively tuned to several broad categories of the shapes of targets. Moreover, they found that certain of the special HM/visual fixation neurons referred to above are sensitive to the same shapes, whether viewed or manipulated. The spatial patterns selected appear to be very broad, with considerable overlap in selectivity for individual neurons. It is still unknown whether or not the selectivities observed are samples of a wide range existing a priori, though this appears unlikely. It remains to be determined whether the selectivity for objects in these experiments resulted from prolonged preexperimental training, and whether training with different objects might produce posterior parietal neurons with spatial selectivities fitting the form of the training objects.

The HM neurons studied by Sakata et al. were located in the anterolateral limb of the posterior bank of the intraparietal sulcus, in a region he calls the anterior intraparietal area, AIP. However, his illustrations show that more than 50% of the HM neurons studied were located in the lateral intraparietal area, LIP, a region studied by Andersen (pp. 457–69 in this issue) and by Colby et al. (pp. 470–81 in this issue) for quite different purposes and with what must certainly be quite different and differentially selected populations of cells.

The zone of area 7 HM neurons is heavily and reciprocally connected with the inferior premotor area of the frontal lobe, where Rizzolatti and Gentilucci (1988) studied neurons with properties similar to those of area AIP. The inferior premotor area projects heavily upon the hand area of the motor cortex itself. How area AIP of the parietal lobe and the inferior premotor area of the frontal lobe are fitted into the distributed system controlling grasping is still uncertain. What is clear is that the two parietofrontal systems concerned respectively with the transport and the grasping phases of visually directed reaching are to a considerable degree independent until

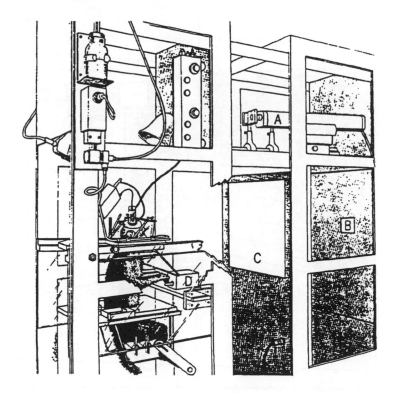

Figure 6.4   Drawing of the apparatus used by Yin and Mountcastle (1977a) in our first study of the visual neurons of the inferior parietal lobule. A laser beam is projected from above via stationary and galvanometer-driven mirrors upon the tangent screen placed 57 cm from the monkey's eyes. The beam spot (1 mm diameter) could be moved at speeds up to 360 degrees/ sec, dimmed, and turned on or off, all under computer control. For study of saccade neurons, the tangent screen was replaced by another containing 16 LEDs in a static spatial array. The LEDs could be turned on or off in a large number of spatial and temporal sequences. Drawing by Mrs E. Bodian, from Yin and Mountcastle (unpublished observations).

their final convergence upon the motor cortex. Yet the result is a smooth and neatly ordered sequence of skilled movements. How that conjunction is effected is a major subject for continuing study.

Nevertheless, the general conclusion appears certain, that the transformation of the intrinsic spatial properties of objects – their three-dimensional form – into efferent signals driving a matching shaping of the hand takes place in a distributed system that includes parietal areas AIP and LIP, and the inferior premotor area of the frontal lobe.

The HM neurons of area 5, in the anterior bank of the intraparietal sulcus, have apparently not been studied further since their original description.

The Parietal Lobe System and Visuospatial Perception

It is an ancient problem in philosophy and psychology whether we perceive space as such, or, indeed, for some philosophers whether space itself exists outside our brains!

Figure 6.5   Behavioral test apparatus used in our special studies of the visual, tracking, and saccade neurons of the inferior parietal lobule. The headholder allowed positioning in the neutral position shown, or turned 60° left or right, or freed in the horizontal plane for periods of rest during recording sessions. Microdrive and chamber are not shown. Two back projectors were used. The first positioned the target laser spot wherever desired or moved in any direction at velocities up to 800 degrees/sec. The second projected luminous stimuli of variable sizes, intensities, and directions of movement over the same velocity range. A panel of 600 LEDs could be inserted in front of the screen along guide rails, for studies of saccade neurons. Drawing by Mrs E. Bodian, from Motter and Mountcastle (1981), reprinted with permission.

These matters need not detain us here, except to say what is obvious, that we do not sense/perceive space as such. No sets of afferent fibers we possess are activated by "space." When a human subject is placed in a structureless visual surround, a *ganzfeld*, he is visually aware of only a gray, fog-like surround. We perceive space in terms of the spatial locations and relations between objects and events within that space, and the relations of these to our own bodies, and the relations between our body parts, and our relation to the direction of gravity. Thus, spatial perception requires the integration of signals in many different afferent systems, visual, vestibular, somesthetic, proprioceptive, auditory. And we interpret these in relation to our stored and continually updated central image of the body form, what Head and Holmes called the "body schema," a happy metaphor disguising ignorance.

The parietal lobe syndrome

The syndrome produced by lesions of the parietal lobe system in humans is so well known it needs no detailed description. The feature attracting the attention of experimentalists is that it comprises a variety of disorders in the perceptual, attentional, intentional, and motor spheres, frequently without defects in what are loosely termed primary sensory and motor functions; that is, they are disorders of "higher functions." Given the variations in the locations and severity of naturally occurring lesions in human brains, quite different samples of the full panorama of defects appear in different patients. Briefly, there are disorders of attention with neglect of the contralateral body and immediately surrounding space, often with denial of neglect or indeed of any disease at all. Disorders of volition are common, with reluctance to move a contralateral body part but with retention of primary motor capacity. Errors are seen in both the transport and grasping phases of visually guided reaching movements of the arms into contralateral space, called optic ataxia. The disorders of visuospatial perception are striking; for many such patients cannot identify the spatial relations between objects seen, are defective in the topographical sense, and are unable to recognize or reach to even familiar objects in the periphery of the visual fields. There is a slowness in visual fixation of objects in the contralateral visual field, but equal difficulty in disengaging fixation once achieved, and in shifting gaze and attention to new objects. Many of these disorders have been produced in more pallid forms by parietal lobe lesions in nonhuman primates; that of optic ataxia has been easiest to produce and measure. It is important to emphasize that these disorders are produced by lesions in a widely and heavily interconnected distributed system (see Caminiti et al., 1996) in which the posterior parietal cortex is one of several nodes. Equally important is the fact we have known since the landmark report of Bisiach and Luzzati (1978) that information concerning the spatial surround is not irretrievably lost after parietal lobe lesions. The deficit is one of access. Bisiach et al. now describe, in their article on pp. 439–47 of this issue, a dissociation between two forms of neglect: an ophthalmokinetic one associated with parietal lobe damage and a myelokinetic one associated with frontal or subcortical brain damage.

Problems posed in the transition to the study of higher functions

The first is the transition required in thinking from that appropriate for study of sensory and motor systems to a completely new arena. Here conditionality is prevalent, relations of neuronal activity to behavioral states and actions obscure, and powerful general state control functions affect both behavior and its relevant neuronal mechanisms. The latter are thought to result from the "integration" of a variety of afferent inputs with stored records of experience, and lead through states of intentionality to motor output. We found this transition difficult at first, and it is clear that some investigators are still in transition, while others retain the attitude that all neurons of the neocortex are either *directly* sensory or *directly* motor.

A second problem is how we define in neural terms what is meant by phrases like "the body schema," or "construct a viridical image of surrounding space" – a phrase

(A)

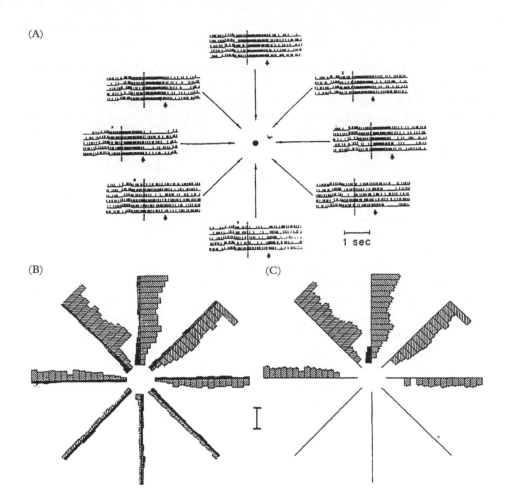

1 sec

(B)   (C)

I

Figure 6.6   Impulse replicas (*A*) and radially oriented discharge histograms (*B, C*) for a parietal visual neuron, evoked by a $10° \times 10°$ luminous stimulus, 0.6 log units more intense than the $2cd/m^2$ background, moved inwardly and then outwardly with respect to the fixation point, in each of eight radial directions for $100°$ through the visual field (*long arrows*), as the monkey fixated a small central light. Trials along different axes were sequenced randomly. *Vertical dashed lines* in A indicate stimulus onset; *small vertical arrows*, the instants when the moving stimuli crossed the fixation point. Each *line* shows the result for a single trial; each *small upstroke*, the instant at which the neuron discharged an impulse. The radially oriented impulse histograms of B and their statistically reduced form in C (rates significantly above background control levels) show discharge frequencies as stimuli moved inwardly toward the fixation point (*hatched*) and outwardly (*solid*) away from it in each of the eight radial directions. Bin size, 50 msec; *vertical bar*, 100 impulses/sec; stimulus velocity, 60 degrees/sec. Reprinted with permission, from Mountcastle et al. (1984).

I myself have used. One simple meaning is that all the particular elements required for such "neural constructs" must converge upon or reside in the memory-induced repertoires of different but overlapping distributed systems. Well and good, but what next? How is such a "neural construct" brought to and maintained in action, and how does it flow through stages of intentionality to output motor commands? I know of no

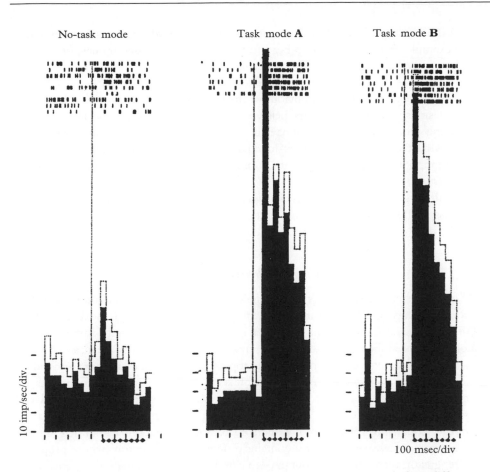

No-task mode   Task mode **A**   Task mode **B**

10 imp/sec/div.

100 msec/div

Figure 6.7 Comparison of the responses of a parietal visual neuron evoked in different attentional states, to illustrate the strong facilitation by attention of responses evoked from the nonfoveal receptive field. In the *no-task mode*, the animal is not working, and makes spontaneous saccades to and oculomotor pauses at randomly distributed locations on the tangent screen. In *task mode A*, the animal is steadily fixating a target light whose dimming he cannot predict in time, but which he must detect for reward. In *task mode B*, the target light blinks off before and during stimuli, and the animal maintains steady fixation of the location at which he knows it will reappear, before dimming. The neuron subtended a receptive field in the upper half of the visual field; all stimuli were delivered close to the point of fixation, in identical retinotopic coordinates on all trials. The facilitation ratio between responses evoked in the task modes and the no-task mode was 8.3. The responses in the no-task mode and in task mode A were also studied in total darkness, with similar results. *Above*, impulse replicas: each *line* represents recording in a single trial; each *short upstroke*, the instant of neuronal discharge. *Dashed lines*, 1 SEM for each bin; bin size, 50 msec. *Diamonds* indicate bins of the left histogram significantly different from similarly marked bins in the histograms at center and right. Reprinted with permission, from Mountcastle et al. (1981).

way in which this central problem can be studied directly with presently available neurophysiological methods. Thus, for the time being, the most productive approach may be to close in on the problem by studying one by one things that can be identified as constituent elements.

A third is the problem of spatial constancy: how are coordinate transforms executed, for example, from retinotopic to head to body to external space frames, or, as some believe, whether such transforms are needed at all.

A fourth is the problem of the direction and redirection of attention. Defects in attention are among the most obvious of the behavioral defects produced by parietal lobe lesions, and some scholars believe that all the defects can be interpreted as primarily those of attention. What have been observed until now in neurophysiological studies of the parietal lobe cortex in waking monkeys are the pervasive effects of attention, not its mechanism. Efforts to infer the latter from the former have so far been fruitless.

A fifth is the problem of visually guided reaching and grasping, which I have discussed above and which is undoubtedly at the present time the best understood of the many functions of the parietal lobe system.

Survey studies of the inferior parietal lobe neurons

Our first systematic recordings in the inferior parietal lobule began in monkey BM 25, from February 8, 1972 onward, first with James Lynch, now at the University of Mississippi, and Carlos Acuna, and later in a long series of experiments with other colleagues listed above. We encountered a new and for us unusual problem: a vast area of neocortex in which we could make out no topographic pattern of any sort, and indeed, none has been discovered there to this day. It is remarkable that there is no topographic mapping of space in those cortical areas and systems preeminently concerned with spatial perception, as defined above, and for the generation of intentions and, conditionally, commands for visuomotor and somatomotor operations within that immediately surrounding space. The area contains different sets of neurons whose properties differ greatly; these sets are encountered in closely adjacent (1 mm or less) penetrations of the exposed cortical surface, and appear in *en bloc* sequences during penetrations made down sulcal walls, parallel to the cortical surface. We therefore undertook two survey studies, I and II of table 6.1, made in sets of apparatus shown in figures 6.3 and 6.4, for we quickly learned that what is called "clinical" examination is virtually useless in defining the functional properties of parietal neurons. We attempted to make those definitions for every neuron whose action potential we could bring under study.

The major classes we identified are listed in table 6.1: the fixation, oculomotor, reach/hand-manipulation, visual, and special neurons. However, no certainty attaches to the proportions of neurons in each of the classes of table 6.1, save that each class is present in substantial numbers. There remained a very large number whose properties we could not define at all. The special class consists more often of neurons that combined the properties of two of the other classes, for example, oculomotor or reach neurons with visual receptive fields. These appear to have attracted considerable attention from later investigators, so much so that some have been led to believe that they are the only class that exists in the inferior parietal lobule, where every neuron is said to possess a visual receptive field! While the special neurons may be more plentiful than our experience indicated, the suggestion that only they exist in the inferior parietal lobule is simply absurd.

Visual fixation neurons increase their discharge rates with the visual grasping of desired objects, or of the surrogate target light in a trained paradigm. The increment is

Table 6.1 Summary of studies of the posterior parietal cortex

	Survey studies		Special studies				
	I[a]	II[b]	III[c]	IV[d]	V[e]	VI[f]	Sums
Hemispheres	7	10	6	20	10	3	56
Penetrations	43	107	NA	204	141	22	517
Neuron types							
Fixation	155	521		266			942
Oculomotor	88	218		163			469
Visual	75	NA	98	462	613	105	1353
Reach/HM	128	136		206			470
Special	21	32		67			120
Unidentified	94	369		519			981
Sums	*561*	*1276*	*98*	*1683*	*610*	*105*	*4335*

[a]   Lynch et al., 1973a, b; Mountcastle et al., 1975.
[b]   Lynch et al., 1977.
[c]   Yin and Mountcastle, 1977a, b.
[d]   Motter and Mountcastle, 1981; Mountcastle et al., 1981; Andersen and Mountcastle, 1983.
[e]   Mountcastle et al., 1984; Motter et al., 1987; Steinmetz et al., 1987.
[f]   Mountcastle et al., 1987; Mountcastle and Steinmetz, 1990.

sustained until reward, then subsides even without change in the line of gaze. These neurons are inactive during fixations of bland objects in the surround. The gaze fields of fixation neurons are most often confined to a quarter or half of the visual field, the result of a powerful angle of gaze effect. Control experiments showed that fixation neurons are insensitive to visual stimuli per se. Nearly half of the fixation neurons are suppressed when fixation is interrupted by a saccade, and those suppressed are preferentially located in the infragranular layers. Thus, a superimposed saccade loosens the output fixation signal descending from the parietal cortex to brainstem structures (Mountcastle et al., 1975; Lynch et al., 1977).

Two classes of oculomotor neurons were identified. *Tracking neurons* are active during eye pursuits of slowly moving objects, and are inactive during steady fixations. They are directionally oriented, are suppressed by a saccade superimposed upon the tracking movement, but are relatively insensitive to tracking speed. The *saccade neurons* are active before and during visually evoked but not spontaneous saccades; the discharge leads and peaks during the eye movement. Many saccade neurons are preferentially active with saccades directed contralateral to the hemisphere in which they are located. The discharge rate is relatively insensitive to saccade amplitude. A powerful angle of gaze effect influences the activity of both classes of oculomotor neurons. Tracking neurons differ in discharge rate during tracks of similar length and speed located in different parts of the gazefield, as do saccade neurons for differently located saccades of equal amplitude and direction.

Special studies of the visual neurons of the inferior parietal lobule

My colleagues and I then initiated a series of special studies of the visual neurons of the parietal lobe (table 6.1). We first mapped their receptive fields with small stationary stimuli, in the apparatus shown in figure 6.4 (Yin and Mountcastle, 1977a, b). We

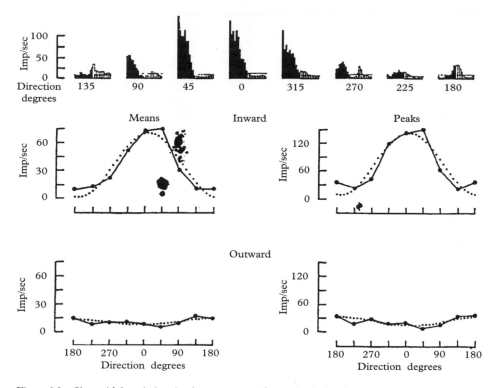

Figure 6.8 Sinusoidal variation in the response of a parietal visual neuron to stimuli moving along radial axes through the visual field and across the fixation point, during a task requiring attentive fixation. The *histograms* show the time course of the change in discharge frequency during the inward (*solid*) and outward (*open*) halves of the 100° stimulus movement in each of the eight directions indicated. The mean and peak frequencies of discharge are plotted as functions of the directions of stimulus movements for both inward and outward halves of stimulus movement. *Solid lines* connect data points; *dashed lines* show sine waves fitted to the data by periodic regression. Reprinted with permission, from Steinmetz et al. (1987).

identified two classes of visual neurons. The first subtends large and frequently bilateral receptive fields, in which the loci of greatest sensitivity are at the far periphery, exempting the foveal-parafoveal regions. Class I neurons respond with mean latencies of about 80 msec, and adapt slowly to steadily maintained stimuli. Class II visual neurons respond at longer latencies (115 msec), subtend smaller usually contralateral receptive fields in which the most sensitive loci are near the center of the field, and are enhanced when the stimulus becomes the target for a saccade. Of the first 98 receptive fields mapped, not a one included the foveal region.

Our attention was riveted by the large class I parietal visual neurons (PVNs), for their properties indicated that the representation of the visual world in the inferior parietal lobule differs strikingly from that in the temporal lobe component of the transcortical visual systems. We studied them in the apparatus shown in figure 6.5. PVN receptive fields are frequently large, bilateral, exempt the fovea, and cover from a quarter to – in the limit – the entire visual field, from one monocular rim to the other (Motter and Mountcastle, 1981). Bilateral receptive fields of this extent are not known

A

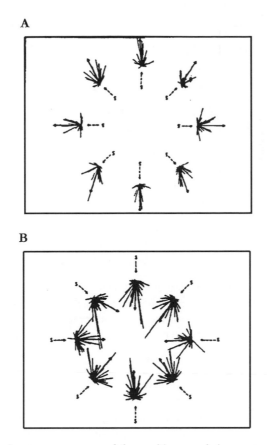

B

Figure 6.9 Individual response vectors and the resulting population vectors (*solid arrows*) for the sets of parietal visual neurons sensitive to outwardly (A; $n = 42$) and inwardly (B: $n = 78$) moving visual stimuli. Direction of stimulus movement shown by *dashed arrows*. Each neuron is assumed to provide a signal of movement in its best direction, at various frequencies depending upon stimulus direction, and thus contribute more or less to the population vector for each stimulus direction. Reprinted with permission, from Steinmetz et al. (1987).

to occur in any of the way-stations between the striate cortex and the inferior parietal lobule, so that the interhemispheric convergence required to construct them must occur within the inferior parietal lobule itself. Such a field is illustrated by the impulse replicas and radial histograms of figure 6.6, which illustrates also another unusual property of PVNs: they are exquisitely sensitive to stimuli moving inwardly or, for a different set, outwardly across the rim of the visual field. And, they respond rather indiscriminately over a wide range of stimulus speeds (Motter et al., 1987).

We then discovered the powerful effect of attentive fixations upon the excitability of PVNs: the absence of a response in the foveal-perifoveal region is produced by an active and powerful suppression, associated with an equally strong facilitation of the responses to moving stimuli in the field periphery (figs 6.6, 6.7; Mountcastle et al., 1981). Thus, the effect of attention upon the parietal system is reciprocal to that it exerts upon the striate-temporal lobe component, for in the parietal system there is a

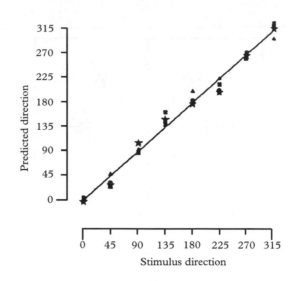

Figure 6.10   Population vectors (the directions predicted by the neuronal populations) plotted as functions of actual stimulus directions. The near-identify relation indicates the accuracy of the population signal, on this analysis, in contrast to the imprecise signal of stimulus direction provided by any single parietal visual neuron. Reprinted with permission, from Steinmetz et al. (1987).

suppression of response to the object fixated, and a strong facilitation of response to novel stimuli appearing in the periphery. Thus, the head of the attending primate is surrounded by a halo of high sensitivity to moving objects entering or leaving the visual field, a mechanism of great survival value to primates who spend long periods of time in intensely attentive close-in hand and eye work, for example, the monkey during feeding. This effect also provides a suitable neuronal base for the flow field guidance of locomotion, and perhaps also for the illusions of vection. Indeed, we observed in unpublished experiments that when balanced symmetrical stimuli are delivered along the same axis, for example, inwardly pairs of stimuli moving along the horizontal meridian, they may together evoke no PVN response at all, when either alone evokes a vigorous one: a null detector mechanism for signaling symmetrical flow on either side of the head during linear advance.

Steinmetz and Constantinidas describe, in their article on pp. 448–56 of this issue, the results of an ingenious experiment in which they have been able to dissociate under well-controlled conditions the line of gaze and the line of attention. Their result is that the central suppression and facilitatory surround are anchored to the line of attention, not that of gaze.

It is obvious from their huge receptive fields that any single PVN can provide only a very inexact signal of a stimulus moving across the visual field periphery. This is shown by the analysis of figure 6.8, which reveals the neat fit to the sine function of the intensity of responses to stimuli moving along different radial axes. This allows one to define a best direction for such a neuron along a preferred radial axis, but shows also what an imprecise signal it is, for stimuli moving along axes at $90°$ on either side of the best direction evoked responses at 50% of that evoked by the stimulus at best direction. We therefore applied to the population of PVNs the vector summation

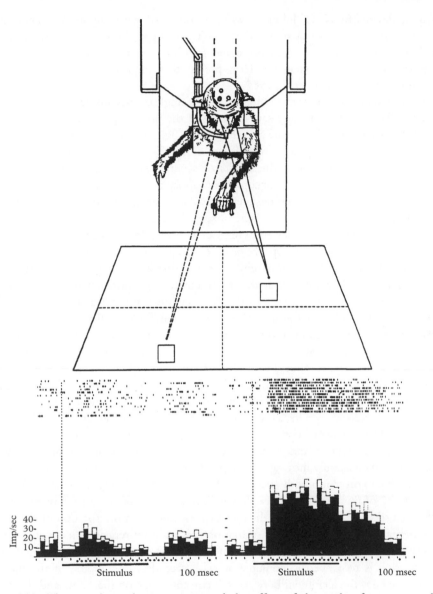

Figure 6.11 The experimental arrangement and the effect of the angle of gaze upon the responses of a parietal visual neuron to light stimuli. The monkey fixated a small target light placed at a series of positions on the tangent screen, with head fixed. The results obtained at two fixation positions are shown. At each, a 6° × 6° test stimulus of 1 sec duration was flashed 10° above the fixation point, as the monkey attentively fixated the target light to detect its dimming. Tests at different spatial positions were interleaved randomly in a single run. Impulse replicas are shown *below* the screen. Each *line* represents a single trial; each *small upstroke*, the instant of impulse discharge. Impulse replicas and histogram to the *right* show the intense response evoked during fixations 20° down and 20° to the left; those to the *left*, the responses with fixation 20° right, 20° up. *Dotted lines above histogram bins*, SE of the means. *Diamonds below* corresponding bins of the two histograms indicate that a significant difference exists between the means of those bins ($p < 0.05$). *Time marks*, 100 msec; *divisions on ordinates*, 10 impulses/sec. Reprinted with permission, from Andersen and Mountcastle (1983)

analysis devised by K. O. Johnson, with the result shown in figure 6.9. There is no evidence at all that such a summation is carried out in the cerebral cortex, but the analysis shows that a very precise signal for direction could be extracted from a population of imprecise elements. How precise that might be is shown by the graph of figure 6.10 (Steinmetz et al., 1987).

We found in our earliest experiments that the angle of gaze influenced in a powerful way the fixation, tracking, and saccade cells of the inferior parietal lobule. Andersen and I discovered that this is true also for PVNs (fig. 6.11; Andersen and Mountcastle, 1983). Andersen has exploited further the angle of gaze effect, and described in a number of important reports the results of several experiments made in the lateral intraparietal area (LIP), which occupies the upper part of the posterior bank of the intraparietal sulcus. This area is designated by Andersen as one specialized for saccadic eye movement, for 63% of the cells he observed there are saccade related. The results of these experiments are reviewed in his article on pp. 457–69 of this issue of *Cerebral Cortex*. Andersen's general hypothesis is consonant with classical ideas about the function of the parietal lobe system, that it forms a neural image of surrounding space. The central theme is that this representation is constructed from visual and eye position signals and, it is conjectured, from auditory, vestibular, and proprioceptive signals as well. Andersen and his colleagues present evidence that the visual and eye position signals are combined to form "planar gain fields" that compose a population code for localizing visual targets in orbital coordinates. This initial coordinate transform is thought to be combined with others for converting it to a body-centered frame. Andersen has enlarged this general hypothesis to include the concept that the parietal system is part of an essential sensory-motor interface dealing with intentions, an idea that fits with Sakata's results, as well as with those of Lacquaniti and Caminiti.

The problem of spatial constancy is a vexed one of long standing in visual science. Many investigators, like Andersen, follow the idea that the stability of the visual world seen through constantly moving eyes depends upon a series of coordinate transforms from retinal to orbital to body space, and so on. Colby et al. present, in their article on pp. 470–81 of this issue, evidence they believe supports quite a different hypothesis, that each saccadic movement of the eyes evokes concurrently a rotation of the central representation of the visual field, so that objects within it remain in a constant spatial position relative to head and body. That is, in their own words, that "stored visual information is remapped in conjunction with saccades. Remapping of the memory trace maintains the alignment between the current image on the retina and the stored representation in cortex." This is a novel and interesting idea that deserves continued study. It is reminiscent of the old observation that a voluntary effort to move the eyes in the direction of a paralyzed extraocular muscle evokes a transient rotation of the visual field. How this general area of study will play out is still uncertain, but it will certainly provide fruitful opportunities for future research.

This problem of spatial constancy and the associated one of coordinate transformation both here and in the motor sphere are among the most difficult of the many difficult problems in the study of the neocortical mechanisms in the higher functions. Progress has been slow, particularly, I believe, because of the complexity and diversity of the neuronal operations that have been observed in the posterior parietal cortex. How to sort them out and how to put them together in a coherent and generalized scheme have, up to now, been impossible. Some investigators take the position that the inferior parietal lobule is divided into a large number of relatively small and independent cortical areas, each specialized for a particular mode of neuronal processing, and each exerting its influence upon behavior via its own particular set of extrinsic connections. Indeed, some evidence supports this view, but other evidence does not.

A major conceptual problem is what is to be called visual, if as is customary we define as visual something directly involved in the perception of seen objects. How, then, should we designate the large number of other cortically controlled operations in which light ("visual") stimuli play an important but perhaps not a singular role. For example, the largely unconscious "visual" guidance of the arm during the transport phase of reaching. I first encountered this problem when I observed reach neurons indiscriminately brought to action by either somesthetic or visual stimuli. And Andersen (pp. 457–69 in this issue) has now made a similar observation, that parietal saccade neurons may be activated by either visual or auditory stimuli. This led him to the concept of the role of the parietal cortex in intentional operations, an idea with which I heartily agree. Intentionality leads, conditionally, to what I originally called the command function of the parietal system, command regarded here as something more general than impulses, in motoneurons, or motor cortical cells of origin of the pyramidal tract! This brings to mind the old observation that in a distributed system command may reside from time to time in different nodes of the system, and at any one time in the node with the most and the most urgent information.

References

Andersen, R. A., Mountcastle, V. B. (1983) The influence of the angle of gaze upon the excitability of the light-sensitive neurons of the posterior parietal cortex. *J. Neurosci.*, **3**: 532–48.

Bisiach, E., Luzzati, C. (1978) Unilateral neglect of representational space. *Cortex*, **14**: 129–33.

Burbaud, P., Doegle, C., Gross, C., Bioulac, B. (1991) A quantitative study of neuronal discharge in areas 5, 2, and 4 of the monkey during fast arm movements. *J. Neurophysiol.*, **66**: 429–43.

Caminiti, R., Ferraina, S., Johnson, P. B. (1996) The sources of visual information to the primate frontal lobe: A novel role for the superior parietal lobule. *Cereb. Cortex*, **6** (2), in press.

Carli, G., LaMotte, R. H., Mountcastle, V. B. (1971a) A comparison of sensory behavior and the activity of postcentral neurons, observed simultaneously, elicited by oscillating mechanical stimuli delivered to the contralateral hand. *Proc. Int. Congr. Physiol.*, **25**.

Carli, G., LaMotte, R. H., Mountcastle, V. B. (1971b) A simultaneous study of somatic sensory behavior and the activity of sensory cortical neurons. *Fed. Proc.*, **30**: 664.

Critcheley, M. (1953) *The parietal lobes.* London: Arnold; reprint, New York: Hafner, 1969.

Evarts, E. V., Fromm, C., Kroller, J., Jennings, V. A., (1983) Motor cortex control of finely graded forces. *J. Neurophysiol.*, **49**: 1199–215.

Georgopoulos, A. P. (1991) Higher order motor control. *Annu. Rev. Neurosci.*, **14**: 361–77.

Georgopoulos, A. P. (1994) New concepts in the generation of movement. *Neuron*, **13**: 257–68.

Georgopoulos, A. P., Kalaska, J. F., Caminiti, R., Massey, J. T. (1982) On the relations between the direction of two-dimensional arm movements and cell discharge in primate motor cortex. *J. Neurosci.*, **2**: 1527–37.

Georgopoulos, A. P., Schwartz, A. B., Kettner, R. E. (1986) Neuronal population coding of movement direction. *Science*, **233**: 1416–19.

Georgopoulos, A. P., Lurito, J., Petrides, M., Schwartz, A. B., Massey, J. T. (1989) Mental rotation of the neuronal population vector. *Science*, **243**: 234–6.

Georgopoulos, A. P., Ashe, J., Smyris, N., Taira, M. (1992) Motor cortex and the coding of force. *Science*, **256**: 1692–5.

Jeannerod, M. (1988) *The neural and behavioral organization of goal directed movements*. New York: Oxford University Press.

Jeannerod, M., Arbib, M. A., Rizzolatti, G., Sakata, H. (1995) The neural mechanisms of grasping. *Trends Neurosci.*, in press.

Kalaska, J. F. (1991) Parietal area 5: A neuronal representation of movement kinetics for kinesthetic perception and movement control. In: *Brain in space* (Paillard, J., ed.), pp. 133–46, London: Oxford University Press.

Kalaska, J. F., Cohen, D. A. D., Prud'homme, M., Hyde, M. L. (1990) Parietal area 5 neuronal activity encodes movement kinematics, not movement dynamics. *Exp. Brain Res.*, **80**: 351–64.

Lynch, J. C., Acuna, C., Sakata, H., Georgopoulos, A. P., Mountcastle, V. B. (1973a) The parietal association cortex and immediate extrapersonal space. *Proc. Annu. Meet. Soc. Neurosci.*, **3**.

Lynch, J. C., Sakata, H., Georgopoulos, A., Mountcastle, V. B. (1973b) Parietal association cortex neuron activity during hand and eye tracking of objects in the immediate extrapersonal space. *Physiologist*, **16**: 384.

Lynch, J. C., Mountcastle, V. B., Talbot, W. H., Yin, T. C. T. (1977) Parietal lobe mechanisms for directed attention. *J. Neurophysiol.*, **40**: 362–89.

MacKay, W. A. (1992) Properties of reach-related neuronal activity in cortical area 7A. *J. Neurophysiol.*, **67**: 1335–45.

Motter, B. C., Mountcastle, V. B. (1981) The functional properties of the light-sensitive neurons of the posterior parietal cortex studied in waking monkeys: foveal sparing and opponent vector organization. *J. Neurosci.*, **1**: 3–36.

Motter, B. C., Steinmetz, M. A., Duffy, C. J., Mountcastle, V. B. (1987) Functional properties of parietal visual neurons: Mechanisms of directionality along a single axis. *J. Neurosci.*, **7**: 154–76.

Mountcastle, V. B., Steinmetz, M. A. (1990) The parietal visual system and some aspects of visuospatial perception. In: *From neuron to action* (Deeke, R., Eccles, J. C., Mountcastle, V. B., eds), pp. 193–209, Berlin: Springer.

Mountcastle, V. B., LaMotte, R. H., Carli, G. (1972) Detection thresholds for vibratory stimuli in humans and monkey: Comparison with threshold events in mechanoreceptor afferents innervating the monkey hand. *J. Neurophysiol.*, **35**: 122–36.

Mountcastle, V. B., Lynch, J. C., Georgopoulos, A., Sakata, H., Acuna, C. (1975) Posterior parietal association cortex of the monkey: Command functions for operation within extra-personal space. *J. Neurophysiol.*, **38**: 871–908.

Mountcastle, V. B., Andersen, R. A., Motter, B. C. (1981) The influence of attentive fixation upon the excitability of the light-sensitive neurons of the posterior parietal cortex. *J. Neurosci.*, **1**: 1218–35.

Mountcastle, V. B., Motter, B. C., Steinmetz, M. A., Duffy, C. J. (1984) Looking and seeing: The visual functions of the parietal lobe. In: *Dynamic aspects of neocortical function* (Edelman, G. M., Gall, E., Cowan, W. M., eds), pp. 159–93, New York: Wiley.

Mountcastle, V. B., Motter, B. C., Steinmetz, M. A., Sestokas, A. K. (1987) Common and differential effects of attentive fixation on the excitability of parietal and prestriate (V4) cortical visual neurons in the macaque monkey. *J. Neurosci.*, **7**: 2239–55.

Paillard, J. (1982) The contribution of central and peripheral vision to visually guided reaching. In: *Analysis of visual behavior* (Ingle, D. J., Goodale, M. A., Mansfield, R. J., eds), pp. 3767–385, Cambridge, MA: MIT Press.

Paillard, J., ed. (1991) *Brain and space*. London: Oxford University Press.

Perenin, M. T., Vighetto, A. (1988) Optic ataxia: A specific disruption in visuomotor mechanisms. I: Different aspects of the deficit in reaching for objects. *Brain*, **111**: 643–74.

Rizzolatti, G., Gentilucci, M. (1988) Motor and visual-motor functions of the pre-motor cortex. In: *Neurobiology of neocortex* (Rakic, P., Singer, W., eds), pp. 268–84, New York: Wiley.

Sakata, H., Taira, M., Mine, S., Murata, A. (1992) Hand-movement-related neurons in the posterior parietal cortex of the monkey: Their role in the visual guidance of hand movements. In: *Control of arm movement in space: Neurophysiological and computational approaches* (Caminiti, R., Johnson, P. B., Burnod, Y., eds), pp. 185–98, Berlin: Springer.

Steinmetz, M. A., Motter, B. C., Duffy, C. J., Mountcastle, V. B., (1987) Functional properties of parietal visual neurons: Radial organization of directionalities within the visual field. *J. Neurosci.*, **7**: 177–91.

Taira, M., Georgopoulos, A. P. (1993) Cortical cell types from spike trains. *Neurosci. Res.*, **17**: 39–45.

Taira, M., Mine, S., Georgopoulos, A. P., Murata, A., Sakata, H. (1990) Parietal cortex neurons of the monkey related to the visual guidance of hand movements. *Exp. Brain Res.*, **83**: 29–36.

Wilson, A. W., O'Scalaidhe, S. P., Goldman-Rakic, P. S. (1994) Functional synergism between putative gamma-aminobutyrate-containing neurons and pyramidal neurons in prefrontal cortex. *Proc. Natl Acad. Sci. USA*, **91**: 4009–13.

Yin, T. C. T., Mountcastle, V. B. (1977a) Visual inputs to the visuomotor mechanisms of the monkey's parietal lobe. *Science*, **197**: 1381–3.

Yin, T. C. T., Mountcastle, V. B. (1977b) Mechanisms of neural integration in the parietal lobe for visual attention. *Fed. Proc.*, **37**: 2251–57.

7

The Visual Pathways Mediating Perception and Prehension

Melvyn A. Goodale, Lorna S. Jakobson, and Philip Servos

1 Introduction

The higher primates, especially humans, are capable of reaching out and grasping objects with considerable accuracy. Vision plays a critical role in the control of this important skill. Only recently, however, has there been much investigation of the organization of the visual pathways mediating the control of the different components of manual prehension. Accumulating evidence from both neuropsychological studies of patients and electrophysiological and behavioral work in the monkey suggests that these pathways, particularly at the level of the cerebral cortex, may be quite distinct from those underlying what we traditionally think of as visual "perception." In this chapter, we review some of this evidence. The chapter is based on material previously covered in detail in Goodale (1993a, 1993b) and Jakobson and Goodale (1994).

2 Two Visual Systems in Primate Visual Cortex?

Beyond primary visual cortex (V1) in the primate brain the ascending visual pathways within the cerebral cortex project to a complex mosaic of interconnected areas, each of which contains visually sensitive neurons with rather different response properties (for review, see Felleman and Van Essen, 1991; Zeki, 1993). Despite the high degree of interconnectivity between the different cortical visual areas, work on the monkey has revealed that there are two main streams of projections emanating from primary visual cortex and projecting to different cortical regions (Ungerleider and Mishkin, 1982): a *ventral* stream, which leaves V1 and projects via a series of cortico-cortical projections to the inferotemporal cortex; and a *dorsal* stream, which projects from V1 to the posterior parietal cortex. A simplified diagram of these two streams of projections is presented in figure 7.1.

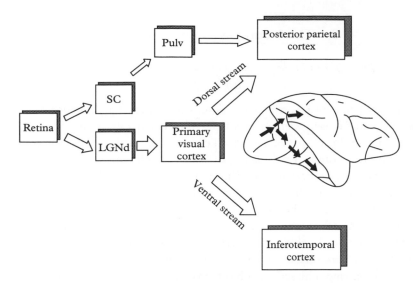

Figure 7.1 Major routes whereby retinal input reaches the dorsal and ventral streams. The diagram of the macaque brain (right hemisphere) on the right of the figure shows the approximate routes of the cortico-cortical projections from the primary visual cortex to the posterior parietal and the inferotemporal cortex, respectively. LGNd: lateral geniculate nucleus, pars dorsalis; Pulv: pulvinar: SC: superior colliculus.

Ungerleider and Mishkin (1982) proposed that anatomical separation of the cortical visual projections into two distinct streams reflects a fundamental division of labor in visual processing. According to their original account, the ventral stream plays a special role in the visual identification of objects, while the dorsal stream is responsible for localizing objects in visual space. This "Two Visual Systems" model of cortical visual processing was one of the most influential accounts of visual function throughout the 1980s, and is still regarded as an important organizing principle for a wide variety of visual phenomena in visual neuroscience and cognitive psychology. In this chapter, however, we argue that Ungerleider and Mishkin's original distinction between object vision and spatial vision (or *what* vs. *where*) fails to capture the essential difference between the functions of the ventral and dorsal streams of processing. We introduce a recent proposal by Goodale and Milner (1992; Milner and Goodale, 1993), which invokes instead the distinction between visual perception and the visual control of skilled action and, in so doing, puts greater emphasis on differences in the output requirements of the dorsal and ventral streams. As we shall see, according to this account, both streams process information about object characteristics, such as size, orientation, and shape, and both process information about spatial location. Each stream, however, uses this visual information in different ways. Transformations carried out in the ventral stream permit the formation of perceptual and cognitive representations that embody the enduring characteristics of objects and their spatial relations with each other; those carried out in the dorsal stream, which utilize instantaneous object features that are organized within egocentric frames of reference, mediate the control of goal-directed actions.

3   The Neuropsychological Evidence

3.1   *Dissociations in the processing of object size, orientation, and location for perception and prehension*

The initial evidence for this reinterpretation of the functional distinction between the dorsal and ventral streams came from a series of recent investigations of visually guided behavior in neurological patients in which damage appeared to be largely confined to one stream or the other. Traditionally, of course, work with such patients has been offered as part of the evidence for Ungerleider and Mishkin's (1982) original Two Visual Systems model. Thus, patients with damage to the superior portions of the posterior parietal cortex (which is thought to be a region within the human homolog of the dorsal stream in the monkey) often show *optic ataxia*. That is, they are unable to use visual information to reach out and grasp objects in the hemifield contralateral to the lesion, and make large directional errors. At the same time, such patients often have no difficulty recognizing or describing objects that are presented in that part of the visual field. Conversely, patients with *visual form agnosia*, following damage to the occipito-temporal region (which is thought to correspond to the monkey's ventral stream), are unable to recognize or describe common objects, faces, drawings, or abstract designs, even though they often have no difficulty using vision to avoid obstacles as they move through the world. On the face of it, these clinical observations certainly appear to support the what-versus-where dichotomy originally proposed by Ungerleider and Mishkin (1982): a ventral stream supporting object vision but not spatial vision, and a dorsal stream supporting spatial vision but not object vision. When the behavior of these patients is examined more closely, however, a different picture emerges.

3.1.1   *Optic ataxia*

Consider the patients with optic ataxia following parietal damage. As was just indicated, the fact that they have difficulty reaching toward objects has often been interpreted as a deficit in spatial vision – a kind of disorientation that makes it impossible for them to localize an object in visual space. The problem with this interpretation, however, is that in many patients the disorientation shows effector specificity. Thus, in some patients, the deficit shows up when one hand is used but not the other (Bàlint, 1909; Perenin and Vighetto, 1988). Even when reaching is impaired, whichever *hand* is used, several patients with optic ataxia can direct their *eyes* accurately toward targets that they cannot accurately reach for (Ratcliff and Davies-Jones, 1972; Riddoch, 1935). Such results show clearly that in no sense can the misreaching in optic ataxia be attributed to a loss of *the* sensory representation of space in such patients. Indeed, as we shall see later, these observations suggest that there are *multiple* spatial codings, each controlling a different effector system.

Observations in several laboratories have also shown that some patients with optic ataxia not only have difficulty reaching in the right direction, but they also show deficits in their ability to position their fingers or adjust the orientation of their hand when reaching toward an object, even though they have no difficulty in verbally describing the orientation of the object (Perenin and Vighetto, 1988). Other clinical reports suggest that patients with damage to the posterior parietal region can also have trouble adjusting their grasp to reflect the size of an object they are asked to pick up. Such deficits were observed, for example, in a patient (VK) who was recovering from Bàlint's syndrome, in which bilateral parietal lesions had resulted in a profound disorder of spatial attention, gaze, and visually guided reaching (Jakobson, Archibald, Carey, and Goodale, 1991). While VK was able to identify line drawings of common objects with little difficulty, her ability to pick up objects remained grossly impaired. Unlike neurologically intact subjects, for example, the size of her grasp was only weakly related to the size of the objects she was asked to pick up and she often opened her hand as wide for small objects as she did for large ones. Moreover, compared with normal control subjects, VK took much longer to initiate and execute her movements and also made a large number of adjustments in grip aperture as she closed in on the target. Similar deficits have also been observed in another patient (RV) with bilateral lesions in the occipitoparietal region (Goodale, Murphy, Meenan, Racicot, and Nicolle, 1993). (It is important to note that the grasping deficits in patients like RV and VK cannot be explained by motor weakness or by a problem in the selection of appropriate hand postures. Both patients showed normal finger tapping and hand-strength scores in the hand used for grasping and neither patient was apraxic [i.e., they could follow instructions such as "Show me how you eat soup with a spoon"]. In short, the deficit was visuomotor, not motor, in nature.)

Such studies suggest that it is not only the spatial location of the object that is apparently inaccessible for controlling manual prehension in such patients, but the intrinsic characteristics of the object as well. These data, like the effector-specific deficits in localization, make it clear that one cannot explain the behavior of these patients by appealing to disorientation or spatial vision deficits. In fact, in at least one way, the spatial vision of some of these patients is demonstrably intact, since they can often describe the relative location of objects that they cannot pick up (Jeannerod, 1988). These dissociations between visual perception and the visual control of skilled movements, which cut across both object vision and spatial vision, are not easily accommodated within the original Ungerleider and Mishkin (1982) framework. Such dissociations are consistent, however, with the proposal put forward by Goodale and Milner (1992).

As Goodale and Milner (1992) point out, the visual control of prehension requires more than spatial location information; it also requires information about the size and orientation of the goal object. After all, we do not reach to locations in space but to objects! Thus, if the dorsal stream is important in the mediation of such actions (as Goodale and Milner propose), then the deficits in the visual control of grasping shown by VK and other patients with posterior parietal lesions are exactly what one would expect to see. It should be emphasized, however, that not all patients with damage in this region have difficulty shaping their hand to correspond to the size and orientation of the target object. Some have difficulty with hand postures, some with controlling the direction of their grasp, and some with foveating the target. Indeed, depending on the size and locus of the lesion, a patient can demonstrate any combination of these visuomotor deficits (for review, see Milner and Goodale, 1995). Different subregions of the posterior parietal cortex, it appears, support different visuomotor components of a skilled act.

3.1.2   *Visual form agnosia*

If patients with optic ataxia can identify objects that they cannot pick up, can patients with visual form agnosia pick up objects that they cannot identify? Goodale, Milner, Jakobson, and Carey (1991) studied the behavior of one such patient (DF) who developed a profound visual form agnosia following carbon monoxide poisoning. Although MRI brain scanning revealed a pattern of widespread damage consistent with anoxia, most of the damage was evident in areas 18 and 19, with area 17 apparently remaining largely intact (Milner et al., 1991). Despite her profound inability to recognize the shape, size, and orientation of objects, DF showed strikingly accurate guidance of hand and finger movements directed at these very same objects. Thus, when she was presented with a pair of rectangular blocks of the same or different dimensions, she was unable to distinguish between them. (Pairs of blocks were selected from two sets of five blocks, each with a surface area of 25 cm² but with dimensions ranging from 5 × 5 cm to 2.5 × 10 cm.) When she was asked to indicate the width of a single block by means of her index finger and thumb, her matches bore no relationship to the dimensions of the object and showed considerable trial-to-trial variability (see figure 7.2A). In contrast, when she was asked simply to reach out and pick up the block, the aperture between her index finger and thumb changed systematically with the width of the object as the movement unfolded, just as in normal subjects (see figure 7.2B). In other words, DF scaled her grip to the dimensions of the object she was about to pick up, even though she appeared to be unable to perceive those object dimensions.

A similar dissociation was seen in DF's responses to the orientation of stimuli. Thus, when presented with a large slot that could be placed in one of a number of different orientations, she showed great difficulty in indicating the orientation of the slot either verbally or even manually by rotating a hand-held card (see figure 7.3A). Nevertheless, when she was asked simply to reach out and insert the card, she performed as well as normal subjects, rotating her hand in the appropriate direction as soon as she began the movement (see figure 7.3B).

Findings such as these are difficult to reconcile with Ungerleider and Mishkin's (1982) idea that object vision is the preserve of the ventral stream of projections, for here we have a patient in whom a profound loss of object perception exists alongside the ability to use object features such as size and orientation to guide skilled actions. Such a dissociation, of course, is consistent with Goodale and Milner's (1992) proposal that there are separate neural pathways for transforming incoming visual information into representations for action and representations for perception.

3.2   *Dissociations in the processing of object shape for perception and prehension*

So far, we have presented evidence to suggest that the visual perception of an object's size, orientation, and location may depend on neural mechanisms that are independent from those involved in using these same object features for the control of manual prehension. But the size, orientation, and location of an object are not the only features that control the parameters of a grasping movement. To pick up an object successfully, it is not enough to orient the hand and scale the grip appropriately and direct the grasp in the correct direction; the fingers and thumb must also be placed at appropriate

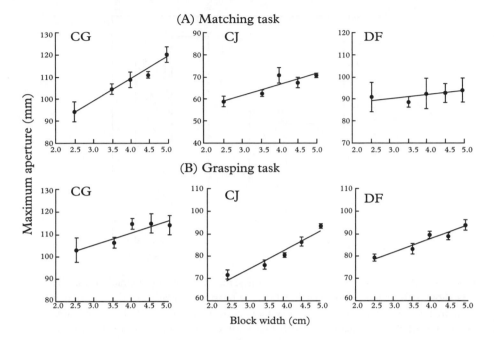

Figure 7.2 The relationship between object width and thumb–index finger aperture on a matching task and a grasping task for the patient DF and two age-matched control subjects (CG and CJ). When DF was required to indicate how wide the block was by opening her finger and thumb, her matches were unrelated to the object width and showed considerable trial-to-trial variability. When she picked up the block, however, the size of her grasp was well correlated with the width of the block.

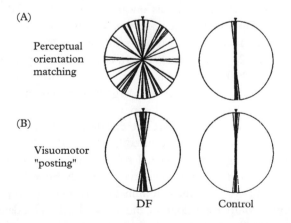

Figure 7.3 Polar plots of the orientation of the hand-held card when DF and a control subject were each asked to rotate the card to match the orientation of the slot (A) or to post the card into the slot (B). The orientation of the card on the visuomotor task was measured at the instant before the card was placed in the slot. In both plots, the actual orientations of the slot have been normalized to vertical.

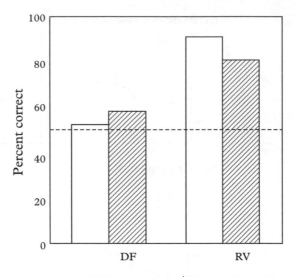

Figure 7.4   Performance of DF and RV on the same/different discrimination tests. The open bars show performance on the task in which the relative orientation of the two shapes on the same trial was identical; the hatched bars show performance on the task in which the relative orientation of the twin shapes varied between same trials. The control subject (not shown) scored perfectly on both tests although she took longer when the two shapes on the same trials were presented at different orientations. The dotted line indicates chance performance. (From Goodale, M. A., Meenan, J. P., et al., 1994.)

opposition points on the object's surface. Computation of these grasp points must take into account the surface boundaries or shape of the object. In fact, even casual observations of grasping movements suggest that the posture of the fingers and hand are remarkably sensitive to object shape. But does the visual analysis of object shape for grasping, like the related analyses of object size and orientation, depend on neural mechanisms that are relatively independent of those underlying the perceptual identification of objects? To answer this question, the ability of the patient DF to discriminate objects of different shape was compared with her ability to position her fingers correctly on the boundaries of those same objects when she was required to pick them up (Goodale, Meenan et al., 1994). In addition, DF's performance on these tasks was compared with that of patient RV, mentioned earlier, who had developed optic ataxia after strokes, which left her with large bilateral lesions of the occipitoparietal cortex, with no involvement of the temporal cortex.

The shapes that were used to compare the discrimination and grasping abilities of DF and RV were based on the templates used by Blake (1992) to develop algorithms for the control of grasping in two-fingered robots working in novel environments. These shapes were chosen because they have smoothly bounded contours and an absence of clear symmetry. Thus, the determination of stable grasp points requires an analysis of the entire contour envelope of the shape. In the Goodale, Meenan, et al. (1994) experiment, the shapes were made from wood, were painted white, and were designed so that they could be picked up using the index finger and thumb in a precision grip. DF and RV were first presented with a series of pairs of these shapes (on a black background) and they were simply asked to indicate whether the two shapes were the same or different. As figure 7.4 illustrates, their performances on this discrimination task were strikingly different. DF hovered just above chance and she seemed quite unable to distinguish one shape from another; in contrast, RV achieved scores well above 80% correct. In other words, whereas DF apparently failed to perceive whether two objects had the same or different outline shapes, RV had little difficulty in making such a discrimination.

Quite the opposite pattern of results was observed when DF and RV were asked to pick up the shapes. Even though DF had failed to discriminate between these different objects, she had no difficulty in placing her finger and thumb on stable grasp points on the circumference of these objects when any one of them was placed in different orientations in front of her. In fact, the grasp points she selected were remarkably similar to those chosen by a neurologically intact control subject (see figure 7.5). In addition, DF showed the same systematic shift in the selection of grasp points as the control subject when the orientation of the object was changed. Moreover, there were other similarities between DF's grasps and those of the control subject: the line joining the two grasp points tended to pass through the center of mass of the object; these grasp lines often corresponded to the axes of minimum or maximum diameter of the object; and finally, the grasp points were often located on regions of the object boundary that would be expected to yield the most stable grip – regions of maximum convexity or concavity (Blake, 1992; Iberall, Bingham, and Arbib, 1986).

RV's grasping was different from DF's (see figure 7.5); RV often chose unstable grasp points and she stabilized her grasp only after her finger and thumb made contact with the object. Thus, despite her apparent ability to perceive the shape of an object, RV was unable to use visual information about object shape to control the placement of her finger and thumb as she attempted to pick up that object. Once she had made contact with the object, however, her manipulation of it appeared essentially normal. This suggests that, despite her problems in visuomotor control, she was able to use tactile and haptic information to control the placement of her fingers. It was only her visuomotor performance that was disturbed. In order to quantify differences between

SH: Control   DF: Visual   RV: Optic
subject   agnosic   ataxic

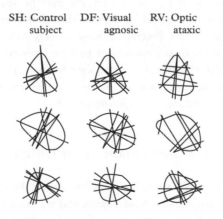

Figure 7.5 The grasp lines (joining points where the index finger and the thumb first made contact with the shape) selected by the optic ataxic patient (RV), the visual form agnosic patient (DF), and the control subject (SH) when picking up three of the twelve shapes. The four different orientations in which each shape was presented have been rotated so that they are aligned. No distinction is made between the points of contact for the thumb and finger in these plots. (From Goodale, M. A., Meenan, J. P., et al., 1994.)

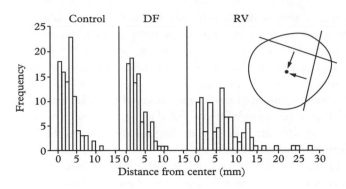

Figure 7.6   The frequency distributions of the distances between the grasp lines and the center of mass of the shape for DF, RV, and the control subject for all twelve shapes. The inset shows how those distances were calculated for two different grasp lines. (From Goodale, M. A., Meenan, J. P., et al., 1994.)

the performance of RV and DF (and the control subject), the shortest distance between the grasp line (connecting opposing grasp points) on each trial and the object's center of mass was measured. As figure 7.6 illustrates, whereas DF and the control subject did not differ on this measure, both differed significantly from RV, who often chose grasp lines that were some distance from the object's center of mass.

These findings provide clear evidence that the visual control of prehension is sensitive to the shape (as well as the size, orientation, and spatial location) of the goal object and that this analysis appears to depend on neural systems that are independent of those underlying the visual perception of object shape. The pattern of deficits and spared visual abilities in DF and RV in this study (together with the results of the earlier work reviewed in the previous section) is consistent with the idea that the human homolog of the ventral stream may be specialized for the visual perception of objects in the world, while the dorsal stream is specialized for the visual control of skilled actions directed at those objects (Goodale and Milner, 1992). But at least two important questions remain to be addressed. Why should the brain have developed two different visual systems, one for perception and one for action? What are the important differences in the kinds of transformations that each of these systems carries out on incoming visual information?

4   Different Transformations for Different Purposes

Consider first the task of the perceptual system. Its fundamental task is to identify objects and their relations, classify those objects and relations, and attach meaning and significance to them. Such operations are essential for engaging in social interactions, exchanging information with others, accumulating a knowledge base about the world, and choosing among different courses of action. In short, perception provides the foundation for the cognitive life of the animal. As a consequence, perception tends to be more concerned with the enduring characteristics of objects (and their relations) so that they can be recognized when they are encountered again in different visual contexts or from different vantage points. To generate these long-term representations, perceptual mechanisms must be object based; that is, constancies of size, shape, color, lightness, and relative location need to be maintained across different viewing conditions. Some of these mechanisms might use a network of viewer-centered representations of the same object (e.g., Bülthoff and Edelman, 1992); others might use an array of canonical representations (e.g., S. Palmer, Rosch, and Chase, 1981); still others might be truly "object centered" (Marr, 1982).

Whatever the particular coding might be, it is the identity of the object, not its disposition with respect to the observer, that is of primary concern to the perceptual system. This is not the case for the visuomotor mechanisms that support actions directed at that object. In this case, the underlying visuomotor transformations have to be viewer centered; in other words, both the location of the object and its disposition and motion must be encoded relative to the observer in egocentric coordinates (e.g., retinocentric, head-centered, or shoulder-centered coordinates; see Soechting et al., chapter 8). (One constancy that must operate, however, is object size; in order to scale the grasp during prehension, the underlying visuomotor mechanisms must be able to compute the real size of the object independent of its distance from the observer.) Finally, because the position and disposition of a goal object in the action space of an observer are rarely constant, such computations must take place de novo every time an action occurs (for a discussion of this issue, see Goodale, Jakobson, et al., 1994). In other words, action systems do most of their work on-line; perceptual systems do most of their work off-line. To summarize then, while similar (but not identical) visual information about object shape, size, local orientation, and location is available to both systems, the transformational algorithms that are applied to these inputs are uniquely tailored to the function of each system. According to Goodale and Milner (1992), it is the nature of the functional requirements of perception and action that lies at the root of the division of labor in the ventral and dorsal visual projection systems of the primate cerebral cortex.

5 Evidence from Monkey Studies

5.1 The dorsal stream

Electrophysiological studies of the dorsal and ventral streams in the monkey lend considerable support to the distinction outlined above (for a more detailed account of the electrophysiology, see Goodale 1993a; Milner and Goodale, 1993). For example, in sharp contrast to the activity of cells in the ventral stream, the responses of cells in the dorsal stream are greatly dependent on the concurrent behavior of the animal with respect to the visual stimulus. In fact, while it is difficult to record any visually driven activity in the dorsal stream of anesthetized monkeys, recordings from alert monkeys have revealed a rich array of cells whose activity is affected by both visual stimulation and motor activity. Separate subsets of visual cells in the posterior parietal cortex, the major terminal zone for the dorsal stream, have been shown to be implicated in visual fixation, pursuit and saccadic eye movements, visually guided reaching, and the manipulation of objects (Hyvärinen and Poranen, 1974; Mountcastle, Lynch, Georgopoulos, Sakata, and Acuña, 1975). In reviewing these studies, R. A. Andersen (1987) has pointed out that most neurons in these areas "exhibit both sensory-related and movement-related activity." For example, many cells in the posterior parietal cortex have gaze-dependent responses; in other words, where the animal is looking determines the amplitude of the cell's response to a visual stimulus (e.g., R. A. Andersen, Asanuma, Essick, and Siegel, 1990; R. A. Andersen, Essick, and Siegel, 1985). Modulation by gaze direction is important because it permits the computation of the spatial (head-related) coordinates of the stimulus independent of retinal location.

Recent work by Duhamel, Colby, and Goldberg (1992) has also shown that some cells in the posterior parietal cortex (in area LIP, the lateral intraparietal sulcus) appear to shift their receptive field transiently just before the animal makes a saccadic eye movement, so that stimuli that will fall on that receptive field after the eye movement is completed will begin to modulate the cell's activity before the eye movement occurs. In addition, many cells will respond when an eye movement brings the site of a previously flashed stimulus into the cell's receptive field. Taken together, these results suggest that networks of cells in the posterior parietal cortex anticipate the retinal consequences of saccadic eye movements and update the cortical representation of visual space to provide a continuously accurate representation of the location of objects in the world. The egocentric spatial coding generated by these cells and the gaze-dependent cells described earlier would be of value only over short time spans, since every time the animal moved its head, eyes, or body, the representation would be updated. This kind of short-term coding could provide critical information about the location of a goal object for calibrating the amplitude and direction of a reaching movement, but not for the long-term storage of information about the allocentric (or relative) location of that object with respect to other objects in the world.

Many of the well-known motion-sensitive cells in the dorsal pathway seem remarkably well suited to providing inputs for continually updating information about the disposition and structural features of objects in egocentric space (e.g., Newsome, Wurtz, and Komatsu, 1988; Saito et al., 1986). Also, a subset of these cells seem quite capable of monitoring limb position during manual prehension (Mountcastle, Motter, Steinmetz, and Duffy, 1984), while motion-sensitive cells in the temporal lobe have been reported not to respond to such self-produced visual motion, although they do respond to moving objects (Hietanen and Perrett, 1993).

In a particularly interesting recent development (Sakata, Taira, Mine, and Murata, 1992; Taira, Mine, Georgopoulos, Murata, and Sakata, 1990), some cells in the posterior parietal region that fire when the monkey manipulates an object have also been shown to be sensitive to the intrinsic object features, such as size and orientation, that determine the posture of the hand and fingers during a grasping movement. These cells are not tied to a particular spatial or retinal location; indeed, many do not have a definable receptive field. Nevertheless, they are visually driven, responding selectively to the size and/or orientation of the object. Thus, these manipulation neurons are tied both to object properties and to the movements of the hands and fingers that are appropriate for those properties. The route by which the visual information required for the coding of the object shape reaches the posterior parietal cortex is at present unknown. It is unlikely, however, that the shape coding in manipulation cells is dependent on input from the higher-level modules within the ventral stream that support the perception of object qualities. Evidence against this possibility is that monkeys with profound deficits in object recognition following inferotemporal lesions are nevertheless as capable as normal animals at picking up small food objects (Klüver and Bucy, 1939), at catching flying insects (Pribram, 1967), and at orienting their fingers in a precision grip to grasp morsels of food embedded in small oriented slots (Buchbinder, Dixon, Hyang, May, and Glickstein, 1980). In short, these animals behave much the same way as the patient DF described earlier: they are unable to discriminate between objects on the basis of visual features that they can clearly use to control their grasping movements.

Many of the neurons in the dorsal stream receive visual inputs both from the geniculostriate pathway and from the superior colliculus, via the pulvinar and/or the lateral geniculate nucleus (Gross, 1991). These inputs would be classified as largely broad-band or magnocellular in origin (with high temporal and low spatial resolution) (Livingstone and Hubel, 1988). The dorsal stream also sends extensive projections to the superior colliculus. Area LIP, for example, projects strongly to the intermediate and deep layers of the superior colliculus, which are intimately involved in oculomotor control (C. Asanuma, Andersen, and Cowan, 1985; Lynch, Graybiel, and Lobeck, 1985). Many regions in the posterior parietal cortex, including area LIP, also send extensive projections to nuclei lower in the brain stem, especially those in the dorso-lateral region of the pons (e.g., Glickstein, May, and Mercier, 1985). These pontine nuclei, which are closely linked with the cerebellum, have been implicated in the subcortical organization of skilled visuomotor behavior (Glickstein and May, 1982). The pattern of downstream projections from the dorsal stream suggests that one way this processing stream may mediate the control of skilled actions is by modulating more phylogenetically ancient brain stem networks.

The posterior parietal region is also strongly linked, in a reciprocal fashion, with those premotor regions of the frontal cortex directly implicated in oculomotor control, reaching movements of the limb, and grasping actions of the hand and fingers (e.g., C. J. Bruce, 1990; C. J.Bruce and Goldberg, 1984; Cavada and Goldman-Rakic, 1989; Gentilucci and Rizzolatti, 1990; Petrides and Pandya, 1984). In addition, there are projections from the posterior parietal cortex to various regions in the striatum (Cavada and Goldman-Rakic, 1991). Recent work by Graziano and Gross (1993) has shown that neurons in those regions of the striatum receiving dorsal-stream inputs not only show visuomotor properties but also code space in body-centered coordinates. Thus, in addition to its connections with subcortical motor regions, the dorsal stream appears to be intimately connected with a number of telencephalic structures involved in motor control.

5.2   The ventral stream

In contrast to the dorsal stream, the primary source of visual input to the ventral stream comes from the geniculostriate pathway; input from the superior colliculus (via the pulvinar) appears to be of little importance in determining the receptive field characteristics of cells in this stream (Gross, 1991). The geniculostriate input to the ventral stream is about equally divided between magnocellular (high temporal and low spatial resolution) and parvocellular (low temporal and high spatial resolution) channels (Ferrera, Nealey, and Maunsell, 1992). Unlike the cells in the posterior parietal cortex, visually sensitive cells in the inferotemporal cortex, the major terminus of the ventral stream, are unaffected by anesthesia and the ongoing behavior of the animal. Many of the cells in this region and in neighboring areas of the superior temporal sulcus also show remarkable categorical specificity (Gross, 1973), and some of them maintain their selectivity irrespective of viewpoint, retinal image size, and even color (Hasselmo, Rolls, Baylis, and Nalwa, 1989; Hietanen, Perrett, Oram, Benson, and Dittrich, 1992; Perrett et al., 1991). Cells in the anterior region of the inferotemporal cortex also show a columnar arrangement (much like the columns in the primary visual cortex) in which cells responsive to similar visual features of objects are clustered together (Fujita, Tanaka, Ito, and Cheng, 1992). In addition, cells in the inferotemporal cortex and the adjacent regions of the superior temporal sulcus typically have exceptionally large receptive fields that most often include the fovea and usually extend across the vertical meridian well into both half-fields, a feature that is consistent with the idea that these cells generalize their response across the visual field and code the intrinsic features of an object independent of its location (Gross, 1973).

Cells in the ventral stream, far from providing the "real-time" information needed for guiding action, specifically ignore changing details. Such observations are entirely consistent with the suggestion that networks of cells in the inferotemporal cortex, in sharp contrast to the action systems in the dorsal stream, are more concerned with the enduring characteristics of objects than they are in the moment-to-moment changes in the visual array. The object-based descriptions that the ventral stream delivers would appear to form the basic raw material for recognition memory and other long-term representations of the visual world. In line with this idea is the observation that the responsivity of cells in the ventral stream can be modulated by the reinforcement history of the stimuli employed to study them (Richmond and Sato, 1987; Sakai and Miyashita, 1992). Indeed, it has recently been suggested that cells in this region might play a role in comparing current visual inputs with internal representations of recalled images (Eskandar, Optican, and Richmond, 1992; Eskandar, Richmond, and Optican, 1992), which are themselves presumably stored in other regions, such as neighboring regions of the medial temporal lobe and related limbic areas (Fahy, Riches, and Brown, 1993; Nishijo, Ono, Tamura, and Nakamura, 1993).

Unlike the dorsal stream, the ventral stream has no significant projections to either the superior colliculus or the pontine nuclei (Baizer, Desimone, and Ungerleider, 1993; Glickstein et al., 1985; Schmahmann and Pandya, 1993). There are, however, strong reciprocal connections between the inferotemporal cortex and the amygdala, a structure that has few if any connections with the posterior parietal cortex (Baizer et al., 1993). The amygdala, a limbic structure lying deep in the temporal lobe, has been implicated in the mediation of social and emotional reponses to visual signals in both monkeys and humans (Adolphs, Tranel, Damasio, and Damasio, 1994; Brothers and Ring, 1993; Kling and Brothers, 1992). The inferotemporal cortex also projects heavily to the perirhinal and parahippocampal cortices and other regions of the medial temporal lobe that appear to be important for storing information about objects in memory, while the projections from the posterior parietal cortex to these regions are not nearly so prominent (Suzuki and Amaral, 1994). Thus, the ventral stream shows none of the evidence for direct modulation of subcortical visuomotor systems evident in the dorsal stream; instead, the ventral stream appears to be connected quite directly with neural mechanisms that are critically involved in associative learning, long-term memory, and social behavior.

6   Separate Streams for Perception and Action

In summary, then, the monkey work converges rather well on the neuropsychological studies described earlier. Both sets of evidence suggest that different transformations are carried out on the information that reaches the ventral and dorsal streams of visual projections in primate cerebral cortex – differences that reflect the requirements of the different output systems served by the two streams (Goodale and Milner, 1992). To reiterate this distinction once more: the ventral stream delivers the perceptual and cognitive representations underlying (visual) knowledge of objects and events in the world, and the dorsal stream, which utilizes the moment-to-moment information about the location and disposition of objects in egocentric frames of reference, mediates the on-line (visual) control of goal-directed actions. Of course, the dorsal and ventral streams work in a highly integrated fashion in the behaving organism and there is considerable anatomical evidence for a complex interconnectivity between the two streams (for review, see Milner and Goodale, 1995). What needs to be done now is to investigate in detail the differences in the processing characteristics of these two functional systems and the way in which they work together to control behavior.

References

Adolphs, R., Tranel, D., Damasio, H., and Damasio, A. (1994). Impaired recognition of emotional facial expressions following bilateral damage to the human amygdala. *Nature* (London), **372**, 669–672.

Andersen, R. A. (1987). Inferior parietal lobule function in spatial perception and visuomotor integration. In V. B. Mountcastle, F. Plum, and S. R. Geiger (eds), *Handbook of Physiology: Sect. 1. The Nervous System*, vol. 5, part 2, pp. 483–518. Bethesda, MD: American Physiological Association. [2]

Andersen, R. A., Asanuma, C., Essick, G., and Siegel, R. M. (1990). Corticocortical connections of anatomically and physiologically defined subdivisions within the inferior parietal lobule. *Journal of Comparative Neurology*, **296**, 65–113.

Andersen, R. A., Essick, G. K., and Siegel, R. M. (1985). The encoding of spatial location by posterior parietal neurons. *Science*, **230**, 456–8.

Asanuma, C., Andersen, R. A., and Cowan, W. M. (1985). The thalamic relations of the caudal inferior parietal lobule and the lateral prefrontal cortex in monkeys: divergent cortical projections from cell clusters in the medial pulvinar nucleus. *Journal of Comparative Neurology*, **241**, 357–81.

Baizer, J. S., Desimone, R., and Ungerleider, L. G. (1993). Comparison of subcortical connections of inferior temporal and posterior parietal cortex in monkeys. *Visual Neuroscience*, **10**, 59–72.

Bàlint, R. (1909). Seelenlähmung des "Schauens," optische Ataxie, räumliche Störung der Aufmerksamkeit. *Monatsschrift fuer Psychiatrie und Neurologie*, **25**, 51–81.

Blake, A. (1992). Computational modelling of hand-eye coordination. *Philosophical Transactions of the Royal Society of London*, **337**, 351–60.

Brothers, L., and Ring, B. (1993). Mesial temporal neurons in the macaque monkey with responses selective for aspects of social stimuli. *Behavioural Brain Research*, **57**, 53–61.

Bruce, C. J. (1990). Integration of sensory and motor signals in primate frontal eye fields. In G. M. Edelman, W. E. Gall, and W. M. Cowan (eds), *Signal and Sense: Local and Global Order in Perceptual Maps* (pp. 261–314). New York: Wiley-Liss.

Bruce, C. J., and Goldberg, M. E. (1984). Physiology of the frontal eye fields. *Trends in Neurosciences*, **7**, 436–41.

Buchbinder, S., Dixon, B., Hyang, Y.-W., May, J. G., and Glickstein, M. (1980). The effects of cortical lesions on visual guidance of the hand. *Society for Neuroscience Abstracts*, **6**, 675.

Bülthoff, H. H., and Edelman, S. (1992). Psychophysical support for a two-dimensional view interpolation theory of object recognition. *Proceedings of the National Academy of Sciences of the USA*, **89**, 60–4.

Cavada, C., and Goldman-Rakic, P. S. (1989). Posterior parietal cortex in rhesus monkey: II. Evidence for segregated corticocortical networks linking sensory and limbic areas with the frontal lobe. *Journal of Comparative Neurology*, **287**, 422–45.

Cavada, C., and Goldman-Rakic, P. S. (1991). Topographic segregation of corticostriatal projections from posterior parietal subdivisions in the macaque monkey. *Neuroscience*, **42**, 683–96.

Duhamel, J.-R., Colby, C. L., and Goldberg, M. E. (1992). The updating of the representation of visual space in parietal cortex by intended eye movements. *Science*, **255**, 90–2.

Eskandar, E. M., Optican, L. M., and Richmond, B. J. (1992). Role of inferior temporal neurons in visual memory. II. Multiplying temporal waveform related to vision and memory: *Journal of Neurophysiology*, **68**, 1296–306.

Eskandar, E. M., Richmond, B. J., and Optican, L. M. (1992). Role of inferior temporal neurons in visual memory. I. Temporal encoding of information about visual images, recalled images, and behavioral context. *Journal of Neurophysiology*, **68**, 1277–95.

Fahy, F. L., Riches, I. P., and Brown, M. W. (1993). Neuronal signals of importance to the performance of visual recognition memory tasks: evidence from recordings of single neurones in the medial thalamus of primates. *Progress in Brain Research*, **95**, 401–16.

Felleman, D. J., and Van Essen, D. C. (1991). Distributed hierarchical processing in the primate cerebral cortex. *Cerebral Cortex*, **1**, 1–47.

Ferrera, V. P., Nealey, T. A., and Maunsell, J. H. R. (1992). Mixed parvocellular and magnocellular geniculate signals in visual area V4. *Nature (London)*, **358**, 756–8.

Fujita, I., Tanaka, K., Ito, M., and Cheng, K. (1992). Columns for visual features of objects in monkey inferotemporal cortex. *Nature (London)*, **343**, 343–6.

Gentilucci, M., and Rizzolatti, G. (1990). Cortical motor control of arm and hand movements. In M. A. Goodale (ed.), *Vision and Action: The Control of Grasping* (pp. 147–62). Norwood, NJ: Ablex.

Glickstein, M., and May, J. G. (1982). Visual control of movement: the circuits which link visual to motor areas of the brain with special reference to the visual input to the pons and cerebellum. In W. D. Neff (ed.), *Contributions to Sensory Physiology* (vol. 7, pp. 103–45). New York: Academic Press.

Glickstein, M., May, J. G., and Mercier, B. E. (1985). Corticopontine projection in the macaque: the distribution of labelled cortical cells after large injections of horseradish peroxidase in the pontine nuclei. *Journal of Comparative Neurology*, **235**, 343–59.

Goodale, M. A. (1993a). Visual pathways supporting perception and action in the primate cerebral cortex. *Current Opinion in Neurobiology*, **3**, 578–85.

Goodale, M. A. (1993b). Visual routes to knowledge and action. *Biomedical Research*, **14** (Suppl. 4), 113–24.

Goodale, M. A., Jakobson, L. S., and Keillor, J. M. (1994). Differences in the visual control of pantomimed and natural grasping movements. *Neuropsychologia*, **32**, 1159–78.

Goodale, M. A., Jakobson, L. S., Milner, A. D., Perrett, D. I., Benson, P. J., and Hietanen, J. K. (1994). The nature and limits of orientation and pattern processing supporting visuomotor control in a visual form agnosic. *Journal of Cognitive Neuroscience*, **6**, 45–55.

Goodale, M. A., Meenan, J. P., Bülthoff, H. H., Nicolle, D. A., Murphy, K. S., and Racicot, C. I. (1994). Separate neural pathways for the visual analysis of object shape in perception and prehension. *Current Biology*, **4**, 604–10.

Goodale, M. A., and Milner, A. D. (1992). Separate visual pathways for perception and action. *Trends in Neurosciences*, **15**, 20–5.

Goodale, M. A., Milner, A. D., Jakobson, L. S., and Carey, D. P. (1991). A neurological dissociation between perceiving objects and grasping them. *Nature (London)*, **349**, 154–6.

Goodale, M. A., Murphy, K., Meenan, J.-P., Racicot, C., and Nicolle, D. A. (1993). Spared object perception but poor object-calibrated grasping in a patient with optic ataxia. *Society for Neuroscience Abstracts*, **19**, 775.

Graziano, M. S. A., and Gross, C. G. (1993). A bimodal map of space: somatosensory receptive fields in the macaque putamen with corresponding receptive fields. *Experimental Brain Research*, **97**, 96–109.

Gross, C. G. (1973). Visual functions of inferotemporal cortex. In R. Jung (ed.), *Handbook of Sensory Physiology* (vol. 7, part 3B, pp. 451–82). Berlin: Springer-Verlag.

Gross, C. G. (1991). Contribution of striate cortex and the superior colliculus to visual function in area MT, the superior temporal polysensory area and inferior temporal cortex. *Neuropsychologia*, **29**, 497–515.

Hasselmo, M. E., Rolls, E. T., Baylis, G. C., and Nalwa, V. (1989). Object-centered encoding by face-selective neurons in the cortex in the superior temporal sulcus of the monkey. *Experimental Brain Research*, **75**, 417–29.

Hietanen, J. K., and Perrett, D. I. (1993). Motion sensitive cells in the macaque superior temporal polysensory area. I. Lack of response to the sight of the monkey's own limb movement. *Experimental Brain Research*, **93**, 117–28.

Hietanen, J. K., Perrett, D. I., Oram, M. W., Benson, P. J., and Dittrich, W. H. (1992). The effects of lighting conditions on responses of cells selective for face views in the macaque temporal cortex. *Experimental Brain Research*, **89**, 157–71.

Hyvärinen, J., and Poranen, A. (1974). Function of the parietal associative area 7 as revealed from cellular discharges in alert monkeys. *Brain*, **97**, 673–92.

Iberall, T., Bingham, G., and Arbib, M. A. (1986). Opposition space as a structuring concept for the analysis of skilled hand movements. *Experimental Brain Research*, **15**, 158–73.

Jakobson, L. S., Archibald, Y. M., Carey, D. P., and Goodale, M. A. (1991). A kinematic analysis of reaching and grasping movements in a patient recovering from optic ataxia. *Neuropsychologia*, **29**, 803–9.

Jakobson, L. S., and Goodale, M. A. (1994). The neural substrates of visually guided prehension: The effects of focal brain damage. In K. M. B. Bennett and U. Castiello (eds), *Insights into the Reach to Grasp Movement* (pp. 199–214). Amsterdam: Elsevier.

Jeannerod, M. (1988). *The Neural and Behavioral Organization of Goal-directed Movements*. Oxford: Clarendon Press.

Kling, A., and Brothers, P. C. (1992). The amygdala and social behavior. In J. Aggleton (ed.), *The Amygdala: Neurobiological Aspects of Emotion, Memory, and Mental Dysfunction* (pp. 353–77). New York: Wiley-Liss.

Klüver, H., and Bucy, P. C. (1939). Preliminary analysis of functions of the temporal lobes of monkeys. *Archives of Neurological Psychiatry*, **42**, 979–1000.

Livingstone, M. S., and Hubel, D. H. (1988). Segregation of form, color, movement, and depth: anatomy, physiology, and perception. *Science*, **240**, 740–9.

Lynch, J. C., Graybiel, A. M., and Lobeck, L. J. (1985). The differential projection of two cytoarchitectural subregions of the inferior parietal lobule of macaque upon the deep layers of the superior colliculus. *Journal of Comparative Neurology*, **235**, 241–5.

Marr, D. (1982). *Vision*. San Francisco: Freeman.

Milner, A. D., and Goodale, M. A. (1993). Visual pathways to perception and action. *Progress in Brain Research*, **95**, 317–38. [2]

Milner, A. D., and Goodale, M. A. (1995). *The Visual Brain in Action*. Oxford: Oxford University Press.

Milner, A. D., Perrett, D. I., Johnston, R. S., Benson, P. J., Jordan, T. R., Heeley, D. W., Bettucci, D., Mortara, F., Mutani, R., Terazzi, E., and Davison, D. L. W. (1991). Perception and action in visual form agnosia. *Brain*, **114**, 405–28.

Mountcastle, V. B., Lynch, J. C., Georgopoulos, A., Sakata, H., and Acuña, C. (1975). Posterior parietal association cortex of the monkey: command functions for operations within extra-personal space. *Journal of Neurophysiology*, **38**, 871–08.

Mountcastle, V. B., Motter, B. C., Steinmetz, M. A., and Duffy, C. J. (1984). Looking and seeing: the visual functions of the parietal lobe. In G. Edelman, W. E. Gall, and W. M. Cowan (eds), *Dynamic Aspects of Neocortical Function* (pp. 159–93). New York: Wiley.

Newsome, W. T., Wurtz, R. H., and Komatsu, H. (1988). Relation of cortical areas MT and MST to pursuit eye movements: II. Differentiation of retinal from extraretinal inputs. *Journal of Neurophysiology*, **60**, 604–20.

Nishijo, H., Ono, I., Tamura, R., and Nakamura, K. (1993). Amygdalar and hippocampal neuron response related to recognition and memory in monkey. *Progress in Brain Research*, **95**, 339–58.

Palmer, S., Rosch, E., and Chase, P. (1981). Canonical perspective and the perception of objects. In J. Long and A. Baddeley (eds), *Attention and Performance IX* (pp. 135–51). Hillsdale, NJ: Earlbaum.

Perenin, M.-T., and Vighetto, A. (1988). Optic ataxia: A specific disruption in visuomotor mechanisms: I. Different aspects of the deficit in reaching for objects. *Brain*, **111**, 643–74.

Perrett, D. I., Oram, M. W., Harries, M. H., Bevan, R., Hietanen, J. K., Benson, P. J., and Thomas, S. (1991). Viewer-centred and object-centred coding of heads in the macaque temporal cortex. *Experimental Brain Research*, **86**, 159–73.

Petrides, M., and Pandya, D. N. (1984). Projections to the frontal cortex from the posterior parietal region in the rhesus monkey. *Journal of Comparative Neurology*, **228**, 105–16.

Pribram, K. H. (1967). Memory and the organization of attention. *UCLA Forum in Medical Sciences*, **6**, 79–122.

Ratcliff, G., and Davies-Jones, G. A. B. (1972). Defective visual localization in focal brain wounds. *Brain*, **95**, 49–60.

Richmond, B. J., and Sato, T. (1987). Enhancement of inferior temporal neurons during visual discrimination. *Journal of Neurophysiology*, **58**, 1292–1306.

Riddoch, G. (1935). Visual disorientation in homonymous half-fields. *Brain*, **58**, 376–82.

Saito, H., Yukie, M., Tanaka, K., Hikosaka, D., Fukada, Y., and Iwai, E. (1986). Integration of direction signals of image motion in the superior temporal sulcus of the macaque monkey. *Journal of Neuroscience*, **6**, 145–57.

Sakai, K., and Miyashita, Y. (1992). Neural organization for the long-term memory of paired associates. *Nature (London)*, **354**, 152–5.

Sakata, H., Taira, M., Mine, S., and Murata, A. (1992). Hand-movement-related neurons of the posterior parietal cortex of the monkey: their role in visual guidance of hand movements. In R. Caminiti, P. B. Johnson, and Y. Burnod (eds), *Control of Arm Movement in Space: Neuro-physiological and Computational Approaches* (pp. 185–98). Berlin: Springer-Verlag.

Schmahmann, J. D., and Pandya, D. N. (1993). Prelunate, occipitotemporal, and parahippo-campal projections to the basis pontis in rhesus monkey. *Journal of Comparative Neurology*, **337**, 94–112.

Soechting, J. F., and Terzuolo, C. A. (1986). An algorithm for the generation of curvilinear wrist motion in an arbitrary plane in three-dimensional space. *Neuroscience*, **19**, 1395–405.

Suzuki, W., and Amaral, D. G. (1994). Perirhinal and parahippocampal cortices of the macaque monkey: Cortical afferents. *Journal of Comparative Neurology*, **350**, 497–533.

Taira, M., Mine, S., Georgopoulos, A. P., Murata, A., and Sakata, H. (1990). Parietal cortex neurons of the monkey related to the visual guidance of hand movement. *Experimental Brain Research*, **83**, 29–36.

Ungerleider, L. G., and Mishkin, M. (1982). Two cortical visual systems. In D. J. Ingle, M. A. Goodale, and R. J. W. Mansfield (eds), *Analysis of Visual Behavior* (pp. 549–86). Cambridge, MA: MIT Press.

Zeki, S. (1993). *A Vision of the Brain*. Oxford: Blackwell.

8

Neural Mechanisms for Forming a Perceptual Decision

C. Daniel Salzman and William T. Newsome

Within the cerebral cortex, the visual environment is encoded by the electrical activity of neurons in topographically organized maps of visual space. Little is known, however, about how the neuronal signals within a sensory representation are interpreted to form perceptual decisions that guide behavior. Such decision processes have been extensively modeled in cognitive psychology and psychophysics to provide quantitative accounts of human performance in a variety of discrimination tasks (1). Physiological approaches that test and refine such models are essential for understanding the neural basis of cognitive behavior. Here we describe a physiological experiment that explores how sensory signals are evaluated to judge the direction of moving visual stimuli in a specific psychophysical task.

In monkeys, neural signals related to the perception of motion are carried within a specialized pathway in the visual cortex (2). Neurons in this motion pathway are predominantly direction-selective; they respond maximally to visual stimuli moving in a preferred direction but little or not at all to motion in the opposite direction. Within the motion pathway, the middle temporal area of dorsal extrastriate cortex (MT, or V5) contains a systematic representation of motion direction (3). Almost all MT neurons are direction-selective, and these neurons are organized in a columnar fashion so that neighboring neurons tend to have a similar preferred direction and receptive field location. Each cortical column therefore encodes a particular direction of motion in a restricted region of the visual field. Cortical columns may differ in receptive field location and preferred direction, thus forming a topographic representation of all directions of motion (4).

In a direction discrimination task, at least two competing hypotheses – vector averaging and winner-take-all – could explain how activity within this system of columns is evaluated in order to form a perceptual decision. In a vector averaging model, the responses of neurons encoding all directions of motion are weighted and pooled to obtain an accurate estimate of motion direction. In this model, each neuron "votes" for its preferred direction with a weight proportional to its response intensity.

The average of all individual neuronal vectors yields a population vector, indicating the direction of stimulus motion that elicited the observed pattern of activity in MT (*5*, *6*). This proposal is similar to motor mechanisms that control the metrics of saccadic eye movements (*7*) and also, perhaps, of reaching arm movements (*8*).

Although a vector averaging model may be correct for some moving stimuli, it cannot account for perceptual phenomena like motion transparency in which two directions of motion are perceived simultaneously when two moving dot patterns are spatially superimposed (*9*). Motion transparency indicates that directional signals need not be averaged together, but can be kept segregated in the neural representation of motion.

The segregation of signals is a central feature of a winner-take-all model, in which the direction of stimulus motion is identified by monitoring several direction-specific channels. Decisions are cast in favor of the channel generating the largest signal. In the present context, a channel may be considered to be one or a few columns in MT that encode a particular motion direction (*10*). Winner-take-all models account nicely for perceptual data acquired in several common psychophysical procedures (*1*), and they can also be applied to physiological data to predict accurately psychophysical performance (*11*, *12*).

To distinguish between vector averaging and winner-take-all mechanisms in a specific perceptual task, we applied electrical microstimulation to directional columns in MT, while rhesus monkeys performed an eight-alternative direction discrimination (*13–15*). Evidence for vector averaging could emerge when the direction of visual stimulus motion differed by 90 or 135 degrees from the preferred direction of the stimulated neurons. Under these conditions, a vector averaging model predicts that the monkeys' choices will be biased toward directions of motion intermediate between the two directional signals. In contrast, a winner-take-all model predicts that the two directional signals will compete with each other, with choices being made in favor of the channel of neurons responding most strongly. In this case, microstimulation and the visual stimulus exert independent effects on the monkeys' choices. Decisions will tend to be cast in favor of one of the two directional signals if these directions are separated sufficiently. Our data support the winner-take-all mechanism; the monkeys' performance could be accounted for by independent contributions from microstimulation and the visual stimulus. We observed no interactions between microstimulation and the visual stimulus that could support a vector averaging mechanism.

Stimulation Sites and the Behavioral Task

For each experiment, we positioned a microelectrode within a cortical column encoding a particular direction of motion (*16–18*). The multiunit receptive field was mapped with a bar of light, and we then presented visual stimuli consisting of dynamic random dot patterns within an aperture placed directly over the neurons' receptive field (*11*). The strength of a motion signal within the random dot display was determined by the percentage of dots carrying a unidirectional motion signal. We refer to this percentage as the correlation of the motion signal, and the correlation could vary from 0 to 100 percent. The remaining uncorrelated dots were displaced randomly in the display, creating a masking motion noise. Thus the difficulty of the eight-alternative discrimination could be adjusted simply by presenting a different correlation of the motion signal.

Before starting a microstimulation experiment, we used a dot pattern with 100 percent correlation to measure the directional turning properties of neurons at the stimulation site. Multiunit responses were measured for each of eight directions of motion separated by 45 degrees while monkeys performed a fixation task (*19*).

During a discrimination experiment, a monkey fixated a point of light (fig. 8.1A, FP) while viewing the dynamic random dot stimulus presented within the visual stimulus aperture placed over the neurons' receptive field. For an individual trial, the direction of motion in the visual stimulus was one of the eight possible directions (fig. 8.1A, arrows). The direction was selected randomly on each trial, and the speed of the correlated motion signal was the optimal speed of the neurons under study. At the end of a 1-s viewing interval, the visual stimulus and fixation point were extinguished, and eight light-emitting diodes (LEDs) were turned on, one corresponding to each possible direction of motion. The monkey indicated its judgment of motion direction by making a saccadic eye movement to one of the LEDs. Correct choices were rewarded with drops of water or juice. We trained two monkeys on this task until their performance under a wide range of stimulus conditions no longer improved. The monkeys usually performed almost perfectly (> 90 percent correct) when the correlation was high (> 50 percent correlated dots). At low correlation values (below 10 percent correlated dots, for example), performance approached chance values.

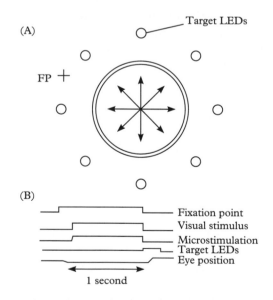

Figure 8.1 (**A**) The experimental set-up for the eight-alternative direction discrimination. The monkey fixated a light-emitting diode (LED) labeled FP and viewed the visual stimulus presented within an aperture (outer circle) placed directly over the receptive field of neurons at the stimulation site (inner circle). Motion in the stimulus could occur in any of eight directions (arrows) over a range of correlation levels. (**B**). The timing of events within a trial containing microstimulation. Microstimulation was applied simultaneously with the presentation of the visual stimulus.

While a monkey performed the eight-alternative discrimination, we attempted to introduce a directionally specific signal into the cortex by activating neurons at the stimulation site with trains of small-amplitude stimulating pulses (10 μA, biphasic pulses) (*20*). Microstimulation was applied for 1 s, beginning and ending simultaneously with the onset and offset of the visual stimulus (fig. 8.1B). In a typical experiment, the monkey discriminated the direction of motion at six or seven correlation values spanning 0 to 100 percent correlation. Microstimulation usually occurred on half of the trials at all but the two highest correlation values; the values excluded from the microstimulation regime helped ensure that the monkey's reward rate was sufficiently high to maintain motivated performance. For both the stimulated and nonstimulated conditions, an equal number of trials (usually five) was presented in each direction for each correlation value. At 0 percent correlation, where the stimulus cannot cue a correct choice, we rewarded the monkey randomly. Reward contingencies were identical for stimulated and nonstimulated trials, and all trial types were randomly interleaved.

Performance on the Eight-Alternative Discrimination

Microstimulation frequently had a striking effect on the monkeys' decisions (for example, fig. 8.2). Data from this experiment have been collapsed across the eight visual stimulus directions to indicate the overall proportion of decisions made in each direction. The monkey's choices were influenced by at least three factors: (i) an inherent "choice bias," (ii) microstimulation, and (iii) the visual stimulus. The monkey's inherent choice bias can be observed in the nonstimulated condition at very low correlation values, where the visual stimulus supplies little or no directional information. Under these conditions, the monkey chose the rightward direction more frequently than would be expected by chance (> 12.5 percent of the decisions) (fig. 8.2, A and B), revealing an inherent choice bias toward the right. The choice bias could be overcome either by microstimulation or by the presence of a strong motion stimulus. The effect of microstimulation on the choices is demonstrated by the large increase in decisions made down and to the left on stimulated trials (fig. 8.2, A through D). The effect of the visual stimulus, while large, is not directly obvious in these polar plots because the data have been collapsed across visual stimulus direction. However, the monkey made approximately equal numbers of choices in each direction at high correlation values (51.2 percent and 100 percent) (fig. 8.2, E and F), reflecting nearly perfect performance when the visual stimulus contained a strong motion signal. (Equal numbers of trials were presented in each direction for each correlation value.)

Analysis of these data had to accommodate the large number of test conditions within an experiment (usually 528 combinations of stimulus and response options). We developed a statistical model, based on polychotomous logistic regression, that predicted performance from three types of parameters, corresponding to the three influences evident in fig. 8.2 – choice bias, microstimulation, and the visual stimulus (*21*).

In its simplest form, the statistical model assumed independent contributions from each free parameter. Eight parameters described choice bias, one for each choice direction. If the data from an experiment revealed no choice bias, the eight bias

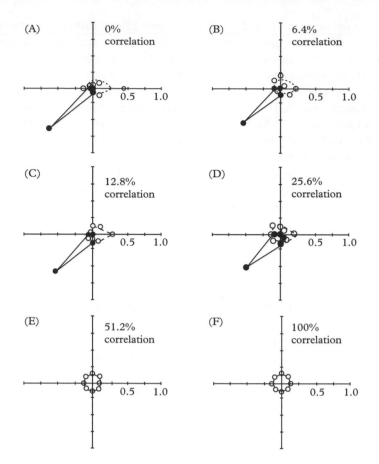

Figure 8.2   Polar plots showing monkey performance (circles) and model predictions (lines) for an eight-alternative microstimulation experiment. The preferred direction of neurons at this stimulation site was down and to the left. The data have been collapsed across visual stimulus direction so that one polar plot describes all choices made at a particular correlation. Open circles, performance on nonstimulated trials; closed symbols, the data from stimulated trials. Dashed lines, model predictions for nonstimulated data; solid lines, predictions for stimulated data. Data predicted by the model are at the vertices of each of the line plots; the vertices are connected with lines only for the purpose of presentation. Microstimulation was not applied at 51.2 percent and 100 percent correlation, and therefore only data and predictions for the nonstimulated condition appear. Eighty trials were performed at each correlation value.

coefficients were equal. An additional eight parameters described the effect of micro-stimulation, one corresponding to each of the eight possible directions. Finally, five parameters described the relation between the direction and strength of motion in the visual stimulus and a monkey's decisions. The first of these five parameters modeled the influence of the visual stimulus on decisions made to the same direction as the visual stimulus. The remaining four parameters modeled the effect of the visual stimulus on decisions made to directions ±45, ±90, ±135, and ±180 degrees away from the direction of stimulus motion. Because the monkeys accurately reported the direction of motion in the stimulus at high correlation values, the fitting of the model to the data always estimated the first stimulus parameter to have the largest value, with the values of the other parameters tending to decrease as the angle between stimulus and choice directions increased. The use of these five parameters to model the contribution of the visual stimulus to performance required two assumptions: (i) the monkey's sensitivity to the visual stimulus on average does not vary with the direction of the motion signal, and (ii) given motion in a particular direction, the monkey's decisions are symmetrically distributed about that direction in the absence of bias.

We used a maximum likelihood fitting method to provide quantitative estimates and measures of statistical significance for each parameter (*22*). Our criterion for statistical significance of a parameter in the model was $P < 0.01$. The model provided an excellent description of the data for every experiment (*23*), with model predictions closely matching observed data (for example, fig. 8.2, dashed and solid lines).

Interaction between Microstimulation and the Visual Stimulus

To distinguish between vector averaging and winner-take-all mechanisms for forming decisions about motion direction, we examined conditions where the visual stimulus and microstimulation both influenced decisions. We could not detect vector averaging if either the visual stimulus or the microstimulation effect was sufficiently strong to overwhelm the other signal. We therefore analyzed a subset of data chosen to maximize our chances of detecting interaction effects; in this subset both microstimulation and the visual stimulus had a statistically significant impact on performance (*24*).

The selected subset of data comprised 27 stimulus correlation values from 23 experiments. For each selected condition, we extracted the data when the direction of visual stimulus motion was 90 or 135 degrees away from the preferred direction of the microstimulation effect and analyzed the pattern of decisions made under these conditions (*25*) (fig. 8.3, A and B). Each of the 27 selected conditions actually contributed two sets of data in this analysis, as stimulus motion was presented both clockwise and counterclockwise from the microstimulation effect direction.

When the direction of stimulus motion and microstimulation effect differed by 135 degrees, the monkeys made the most decisions in favor of the visual stimulus direction, with somewhat fewer decisions made to the microstimulation effect direction (fig. 8.3A, open symbols). As expected from a winner-take-all mechanism, fewer decisions were made in favor of directions intermediate between the two directional signals. The model predictions closely matched the observed data (fig. 8.3A, solid symbols). Recall that the model estimates the effects on decisions of microstimulation, the visual stimulus, and choice bias under the assumption that these factors contribute independently to decisions. The model cannot incorporate specific interactions such as vector averaging between different directional signals (*26*). Since independent contributions of microstimulation and the visual stimulus account for psychophysical performance, our data support a winner-take-all decision mechanism.

When the visual stimulus and microstimulation effect directions differed by 90 degrees, the monkeys made slightly more decisions to the direction intermediate between the two-directional signals than one might intuitively expect (fig. 8.3B, open symbols). A winner-take-all mechanism, however, would predict an increase in choices to intermediate directions when the two directional signals are broadly tuned and not substantially separated (*27*). In fact, the statistical model, which does not incorporate

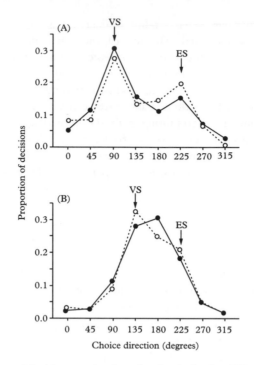

Figure 8.3   The pattern of decisions made when the visual stimulus (VS) differed by (**A**) 135 or (**B**) 90 degrees from the preferred direction of the microstimulation effect (ES). Open symbols, the average proportion of the decisions made in each of eight response directions; closed symbols, model predictions for the same data points. Before averaging the selected data, each data set was rotated so that the preferred direction of the microstimulation effect corresponded to 225 degrees. The data were also symmetrically folded over so that visual stimulus motion clockwise to the microstimulation effect direction could be represented on the same plots as motion counterclockwise.

vector averaging, predicts a higher proportion of decisions in favor of the intermediate direction than was observed in the data (fig. 8.3B, solid symbols). Thus the monkeys made even fewer choices to the intermediate direction than would be expected if microstimulation and the visual stimulus contributed independently to decisions. This might occur if the subpopulation of neurons encoding the intermediate direction was inhibited by the visual stimulus and microstimulation (*28*).

To confirm that the averaged data in fig. 8.3 did not disguise vector averaging effects in individual experiments, we explicitly tested the interaction hypothesis on an experiment-by-experiment basis. For each of the 27 selected conditions, we fit the experiment containing the selected condition with an expanded version of the model containing two interaction terms (*29*). One of the new terms estimated interaction effects when the direction of visual stimulus motion was orthogonal to the preferred direction of the microstimulation effect. The second new term assessed interaction when the visual stimulus moved in a direction 135 degrees from the preferred direction of the microstimulation effect. The interaction terms only modeled choices made when the visual stimulus was at the correlation value specified by the screening tests described above. The new terms allowed the model to capture nonlinear interactions between the visual stimulus and the microstimulation signal that would not be fit under the assumption of independence of the two signals. Positive interaction terms would reflect increased choices relative to the original model toward directions intermediate between the visual and microstimulation signals. This result would be consistent with the vector averaging model.

In 52 of the 54 conditions tested (96 percent), the interaction term was not significantly different from zero. Of the two significant interaction terms, one was positive and the other was negative. In addition, the mean of the interaction terms was not significantly different from zero for the 27 conditions where the direction of stimulus motion differed from the direction of the microstimulation effect by 135 degrees. The mean of the interaction terms was significantly less than zero when visual stimulus motion was orthogonal to the direction of the microstimulation effect. Negative interaction terms imply that fewer decisions were made to the intermediate direction than expected on the assumption of independence. This result is consistent with the averaged data in fig. 8.3B, which show that fewer decisions were made in favor of the intermediate direction (180 degrees) than predicted by the original model.

Our data therefore provide no evidence for vector averaging between the visual and microstimulation signals. Considering the data set as a whole, the pattern of choices made by the monkeys is well described by modeling the visual stimulus and micro-stimulation signal as independent influences on performance.

Characterization of the Microstimulation Effects

MT is thus far unusual in that psychophysical performance can be manipulated predictably by activating functionally defined cortical circuits with microstimulation. Because microstimulation exerts an independent influence on performance, the model enabled us to compute the directional properties of each microstimulation effect without the confounding influences of choice bias and the visual stimulus. To accomplish this, we calculated for each experiment the probability of decisions occurring in each of the eight possible directions assuming microstimulation was the only factor affecting the monkey's choices. The bias and visual stimulus coefficients in the model were set equal to zero. For the experiment in fig. 8.2, the computed microstimulation effect was specific for the preferred direction of neurons at the stimulation site, and the directional tuning of the behavioral effect was substantially narrower than that of the neurons (*30*) (fig. 8.4).

To compare quantitatively the microstimulation tuning curve to the visual tuning curve of neurons at the stimulation site, we fit separate Gaussian functions to the two sets of data (*31*). The fit Gaussian functions produced a mean and standard deviation (σ) for both the neuronal and microstimulation data, allowing us to compare directly the preferred directions and bandwidths of the microstimulation and visual response data. For the experiment in fig. 8.4, the preferred directions differed by only 6 degrees, but the bandwidth of the visual tuning curve was 43 degrees wider than that of the microstimulation tuning curve ($\sigma = 70.8$ degrees for visual responses; $\sigma = 27.5$ degrees for microstimulation).

We performed this analysis for each of the 44 experiments (out of 66 total) in which microstimulation had a significant effect on the monkey's choices. Since the visual responses of MT neurons are broadly tuned, the preferred direction of the

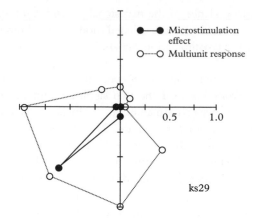

Figure 8.4 The behavioral effect of microstimulation compared to the directional tuning of neurons at the stimulation site (experiment from fig. 8.2). To describe the microstimulation effect (filled circles and solid lines), for each response direction the predicted probabilities were plotted under the assumption that the only factor affecting the monkey's choices was microstimulation. In the plot of neuronal response as a function of visual stimulus direction, the maximum response was normalized to equal 1.0 (open circles and dashed lines). Monkey ks29.

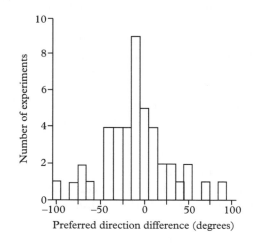

Figure 8.5 The difference between the preferred direction of microstimulation effect and that of the neurons recorded at the stimulation site in each experiment in which microstimulation had a significant effect. This difference is defined as the preferred direction of the neurons minus the preferred direction of the behavioral effect, as characterized by the Gaussian fits to neuronal and behavioral data.

microstimulation effect generally fell within the excitatory bandwidth of the visual tuning curve (fig. 8.5). In fact, 80 percent of the behavioral effects (35 out of 44) had a preferred direction within 45 degrees of the preferred direction of neurons at the stimulation site. The absolute value of the difference in preferred direction was inversely correlated with the size of effects ($r = -0.46$; $P < 0.01$) (*32*), indicating

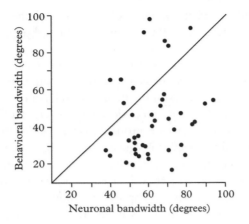

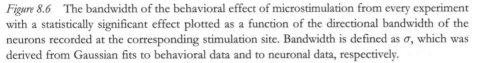

Figure 8.6 The bandwidth of the behavioral effect of microstimulation from every experiment with a statistically significant effect plotted as a function of the directional bandwidth of the neurons recorded at the corresponding stimulation site. Bandwidth is defined as σ, which was derived from Gaussian fits to behavioral data and to neuronal data, respectively.

that the alignment of the preferred directions was more precise when a large effect occurred.

As in the experiment in fig. 8.4, the microstimulation tuning curves tended to be narrower than the visual tuning curves of neurons at the stimulation site. When the microstimulation tuning bandwidth was plotted as a function of visual tuning bandwidth (fig. 8.6), the bandwidth of the behavioral effect was usually narrower than that of the visual responses (data points below the diagonal). The mean difference in bandwidth was 18 degrees, indicating a 29 percent decrease in behavioral bandwidth relative to visual tuning bandwidth (paired t test; $P \leq 0.0001$) (*33*). The narrow tuning of microstimulation effects was even more striking for experiments showing large effects, as the size of the effect was inversely correlated with behavioral bandwidth ($r = -0.49$; $P < 0.001$). For the 22 experiments with the largest effects, the difference in bandwidth was 27 degrees, corresponding to a 44 percent decrease in behavioral relative to neuronal bandwidth. Experiments with large effects therefore tended to produce narrow tuning curves well aligned with the preferred direction of neurons at a stimulation site. These conditions probably arise when the stimulating electrode is particularly well positioned, perhaps in the middle of a cortical column.

Neural Mechanisms for Forming a Perceptual Decision

Our results provide physiological evidence that distinguishes between two mechanisms for forming a perceptual decision on an eight-alternative direction discrimination. We found that the directional signals elicited by microstimulation and the visual stimulus exerted independent effects on performance. These effects may be explained if monkeys used a winner-take-all mechanism to form decisions on the task. In this mechanism, a comparison of activity in distinct subpopulations of neurons, each encoding a particular direction of motion, results in a decision favoring the largest signal. The independent effects of microstimulation and the visual stimulus arise directly from their differential influence on specific subpopulations of direction selective neurons.

Our data do not rule out the possibility that vector averaging of neuronal signals occurs within each subpopulation of neurons. In fact, the narrow tuning of microstimulation effects, as compared with the tuning of MT neurons, could result from a local vector computation. We found no evidence, however, that decisions on this task rely on a vector computation across neurons encoding all directions of motion. Our results therefore show that directional signals can be segregated and evaluated independently to support performance on tasks like our eight-alternative direction discrimination. The segregation of directional signals, however, does not imply that microstimulation caused a subjective impression similar to motion transparency in our experiments. The perception of a second transparent dot field would almost certainly require intricate patterns of activity in V1 and other extrastriate areas that microstimulation in MT cannot replicate.

Although our data clearly demonstrate the existence of a winner-take-all decision process for the eight-alternative direction discrimination, both vector averaging and winner-take-all mechanisms probably operate in the visual system, depending upon the nature of the visual stimuli and the demands of the task being performed. For example, a stimulus in which dots move randomly within a restricted range of directions results in a unidirectional motion percept, suggesting that a vector averaging mechanism underlies perception of this stimulus (*34*). More complicated mechanisms than either vector averaging or winner-take-all must also exist. For example, the psychophysical phenomenon of motion coherence, in which a single direction of motion is perceived when two sine wave gratings moving in different directions are spatially superimposed, suggests a sophisticated "intersection of constraints" mechanism (*35*). It is interesting that some neurons in MT respond to the superimposed gratings as predicted by this mechanism (*36*). Thus neural signals for visual motion are probably combined in multiple ways to form decisions in different perceptual tasks with greatly varying demands.

Sensory systems represent diverse stimuli present simultaneously in the environment. Motor control, by contrast, is inherently more serial because movements of any body part are executed one at a time. Thus motor systems may rely more on broadly based averaging mechanisms (*7, 8, 37, 38*), having no need to code different movements simultaneously. From this point of view, a critical problem in sensorimotor integration is the selection of single targets for movement from a large array of environmental stimuli. The decision mechanisms that accomplish this selection are becoming an increasingly important subject of investigation for cognitive neuroscience.

References and Notes

1   For a detailed discussion of decision mechanisms in the context of visual discriminations see N. V. S. Graham, *Visual Pattern Analyzers* (Oxford Univ. Press, Oxford, 1989).

2   J. H. R. Maunsell and W. T. Newsome, *Annu. Rev. Neurosci.*, **10**, 363 (1987); T. D. Albright, in *Visual Motion and Its Role in the Stabilization of Gaze*, F. A. Miles and J. Wallman, eds (Elsevier, New York, 1993), pp. 177–201.

3   S. M. Zeki, *J. Physiol.* (London), **236**, 549 (1974); J. F. Baker, S. E. Petersen, W. I. Newsome, J. M. Allman, *J. Neurophysiol.*, **45**, 397 (1981); D. C. Van Essen, J. H. R. Maunsell, J. L. Bixby. *J. Comp. Neurol.*, **199**, 293 (1981); J. H. R. Maunsell and D. C. Van Essen, *J. Neurophysiol.*, **49**, 1127 (1983); T. D. Albright ibid., **52**, 1106 (1984).

4   T. D. Albright and R. Desimone, *Exp. Brain Res.*, **65**, 582 (1987); J. H. R. Maunsell and D. C. Van Essen, *J. Comp. Neurol.*, **266**, 535 (1987); T. D. Albright, R. Desimone, C. G. Gross, *J. Neurophysiol.*, **51**, 16 (1984); R. T. Born and R. B. H. Tootell, *Nature*, **357**, 497 (1992).

5   For the purposes of this article, we do not distinguish between vector averaging models and vector summation models. It is not clear that the two models would produce distinct predictions concerning the perception of motion of a visual stimulus.

6   For example, see M. A. Steinmetz, B. C. Motter, C. J. Duffy, and V. B. Mountcastle., *J. Neurosci.*, **7**, 177 (1987).

7   J. T. McIlwain, *Int. Rev. Physiol.*, **10**, 223 (1976); *J. Neurophysiol.*, **47**, 167 (1982); *Vis. Neurosci.*, **6**, 3 (1991); D. L. Sparks, R. Holland, B. L. Guthrie, *Brain Res.*, **113**, 21 (1976); D. A. Robinson, *Vision Res.*, **12**, 1795 (1972). D. A. Robinson and A. F. Fuchs, *J. Neurophysiol.*, **32**, 637 (1969); D. L. Sparks and L. E. Mays, ibid., **49**, 45 (1983); P. H. Schiller and J. H. Sandell, *Exp. Brain Res.*, **49**, 381 (1983); C. Lee, W. H. Rohrer, D. L. Sparks, *Nature*, **332**, 357 (1988); V. Henn and B. Cohen, *Brain Res.*, **108**, 307 (1976).

8   A. P. Georgopoulos, A. B. Schwartz, R. E. Kettner, *Science*, **233**, 1416 (1986); A. P. Georgopoulos, R. E. Kettner, A. B. Schwartz, *J. Neurosci.*, **8**, 2928 (1988).

9   W. Marshak and R. Sekuler, *Science*, **205**, 1399 (1979).

10   The precision with which a winner-take-all model may estimate motion direction is limited by the number of monitored channels and the "distance" between channels.

11   K. H. Britten, M. N. Shadlen, W. T. Newsome, J. A. Movshon, *J. Neurosci.*, **12**, 4745 (1992).

12   M. N. Shadlen, W. T. Newsome, K. H. Britten, E. Zohary, J. A. Movshon, *Abstr. Soc. Neurosci.*, **18**, 1101 (1992); W. T. Newsome, M. N. Shadlen, E. Zohary, K. H. Britten, J. A. Movshon, in *The Cognitive Neurosciences*, M. S. Gazzaniga, ed. (MIT Press, Cambridge, MA, in press).

13   Enhancing the activity of neurons encoding a particular direction of motion biases monkeys' choices on a two-alternative task in which monkeys discriminate between two opposite directions of motion (*14*, *15*). These results may be explained by either vector averaging or winner-take-all models. In a winner-take-all model, choices would be made by monitoring two channels, with the decision being cast in favor of the channel offering the strongest signal. On the other hand, a decision mechanism based on vector averaging would first compute the vector average of all directional signals available. This would produce a population vector pointing to a particular direction of motion. A decision rule would then be applied to the population vector to generate an actual choice on the two-alternative discrimination. Assuming a decision rule that chooses the direction closest to the population vector, the two models can produce similar predictions.

14   C. D. Salzman, C. M. Murasugi, K. H. Britten, W. T. Newsome, *J. Neurosci.*, **12**, 2331 (1992).

15   C. D. Salzman, K. H. Britten, W. T. Newsome, *Nature*, **346**, 174 (1990); C. M. Murasugi, C. D. Salzman, W. T. Newsome, *J. Neurosci.*, **13**, 1719 (1993).

16   Our techniques for physiological recording and behavioral control have been described (*14*). Eye movements were monitored with the scleral search coil technique (*17*). During recording sessions a monkey sat in a primate chair facing a cathode ray tube (CRT) monitor 57 cm away, upon which we presented visual stimuli. For each experiment, the monkey's

head was held stationary by connecting a surgically installed head implant to the primate chair. A recording cylinder located over the occipital lobe permitted electrode access to visual cortex. Electrodes were inserted into MT through a transdural guide tube (*18*). Monkeys were required to fixate a point of light while we searched for a stimulation site. Our formal criterion for positioning the electrode was that neurons had to have similar physiological properties for at least 150 μm of electrode travel. We then positioned our electrode in the middle of such a cluster.

17 D. A. Robinson, *IEEE Trans. Biomed. Eng.*, **10**, 137 (1963); S. J. Judge, B. J. Richmond, F. C. Chu, *Vision Res.*, **20**, 535 (1980).

18 C. F. Crist, D. S. G. Yamasaki, H. Komatsu, R. H. Wurtz, *J. Neurosci. Methods*, **26**, 117 (1988).

19 Multiunit responses were measured with a window discriminator. The lower boundary of the window was set at approximately half the amplitude of the maximum signal observed.

20 We used the same microstimulation parameters as in previous experiments involving two-choice direction discriminations (*14*, *15*): 10-μA biphasic pulses, each with a duration of 200 μs, with a 100-μs interval between the cathodal leading pulse and the anodal pulse. See (*14*) for a discussion of issues concerning neuronal activation with microstimulation. For all experiments, we used tungsten microelectrodes (Microprobe, Inc.) with 20 to 30 μm of exposed tip (resistance usually < 1.0 Mohm at 1 kHz). We typically plated the tip of an electrode with gold before an experiment, substantially reducing the electrode's resistance.

21 For a brief discussion of polychotomous logistic regression see D. R. Cox and E. J. Snell, *Analysis of Binary Data* (Methuen, London, 1989). In the specific model that we used, the probability of a decision in the ith direction, P_i, is a function of the visual stimulus presented and microstimulation

$$P_i = \frac{\exp(y_i)}{\sum\limits_{j=1}^{8} \exp(y_j)} \{i = 1 \ldots 8\} \tag{1}$$

where

$$y_j = \alpha_j + \beta_j Z_1 + \gamma_d X \tag{2}$$

In these equations, α_j represents the contribution of choice bias for the jth response direction, and β_j models the effects of microstimulation for the same direction. β_j is multiplied by Z_1, which equals 1 when microstimulation is applied, but when there is no microstimulation the visual stimulus parameters are represented notationally by γ_{1-5}. These terms are specified in Eq. 2 by γ_0 where d indicates a particular visual stimulus parameter according to the difference in angle between a response direction, j, and the direction of the visual stimulus. γ_1 is used when stimulus direction and response direction are identical (that is, when stimulus motion is in the jth direction). Similarly, when motion is 45 degrees from the jth direction, γ_2 is included. For motion 90, 135, and 180 degrees away from the jth direction, γ_3, γ_4, and γ_5, respectively, are used. In each instance, the designated γ parameter is multiplied by x, the correlation of the visual stimulus. This system of equations estimates the proportion of choices in eight directions for each combination of visual and electrical stimulation. We used maximum likelihood methods to find the best fitting parameters α_{1-8}, β_{1-8}, and γ_{1-5}.

22 To permit quantitative estimation of the parameters in the model, we arbitrarily set three parameters (α_8, β_8, and γ_5) equal to 0. The other parameters are therefore estimated relative to the three preset parameters. Presetting these parameters in this manner did not affect the predictions of the model nor the identification of experiments containing significant microstimulation effects.

23 To assess the fit of the model to data from each experiment, we performed a goodness-of-fit test based on log-likelihood ratios. This test failed to reject the fit from any experiment ($P > 0.5$ in all cases).

24 For each experiment in which microstimulation had a significant effect (at least one significant β term), we screened correlation values by performing two chi-square tests of association. The first analysis tested the null hypothesis that the direction of the monkeys' choices on stimulated trials was unrelated to the direction of the visual stimulus. The second analysis tested the null hypothesis that the direction of choices was unrelated to the presence or absence of microstimulation. A correlation value was included in the interaction analysis only if both tests revealed a significant association ($P < 0.05$).

25 The preferred direction of the microstimulation effect was determined by the fit of the model described by Eqs. 1 and 2. We defined this direction according to which stimulation coefficient β_j was greatest.

26 To confirm that the model could not account for interactions such as vector averaging, we performed an analysis of residual errors. One might think that vector averaging could be incorporated into the model by increasing the estimate of microstimulation parameters corresponding to directions 45 or 90 degrees from the microstimulation effect direction. Choices to these directions would be affected by a vector averaging mechanism when visual stimulus motion is 90 or 135 degrees away from the microstimulation effect direction. The change in parameter estimates would thereby permit accurate description of the effects of vector averaging. But predicted choices in this case would be affected independent of visual stimulus direction, because the increased estimates of microstimulation parameters would influence predictions regardless of visual stimulus direction. This would lead to systematic errors in the predicted choices for those conditions in which vector averaging is irrelevant (for example, when the visual stimulus was in the same direction as the microstimulation effect or in a direction 45 degrees away). Examination of data and predictions for the 27 selected correlation values revealed no evidence of systematic error under such conditions (the mean value of each set of residual errors was not significantly different from 0; t test, $P > 0.1$). This analysis confirmed that an interaction such as vector averaging between signals generated by microstimulation and the visual stimulus cannot be described with this version of the model. To account for a vector averaging effect, the model must include terms allowing a specific interaction between the visual stimulus and microstimulation.

27 A winner-take-all mechanism is based on a comparison of the sum of activity in distinct subpopulations of neurons encoding different motion directions. If two broadly tuned directional responses, differing in preferred direction by 90 degrees, are introduced into cortex, then the peak of activity across the entire population of neurons may correspond to the direction intermediate between the two preferred directions. In this case, a winner-take-all mechanism will decide in favor of this intermediate direction.

28 Consistent with this finding, psychophysical experiments have shown that the perceived angle between two patterns of spatially superimposed random dots is overestimated for angle differences of up to 90 degrees, also suggesting a mechanism that relies on inhibition (*12*). In addition, a model of the perception of motion in plaid grating patterns incorporates inhibition between adjacent direction channels [H. R. Wilson, V. P. Ferrera, C. Yo, *Visual Neurosci.*, **9**, 79 (1992)].

29 To implement the interaction analysis, the model described by Eqs. 1 and 2 was first fit to determine the preferred direction of the microstimulation effect; we defined this direction according to which stimulation coefficient β_j was greatest. The interaction terms were then added to the model in an appropriate manner given the direction of the microstimulation effect. The model including interaction terms is still described by Eq. 1, but the equation for y_j (Eq. 2) was modified to

$$y_j = \alpha_j + \beta_j Z_1 \gamma_d X + \delta_1 Z_2 + \delta_2 Z_3 \qquad (3)$$

Here δ_1 is the interaction coefficient when the two directional signals differ by 90 degrees, and δ_2 is the term for a difference of 135 degrees. Z_2 and Z_3 are dummy variables that allow δ_1 and δ_2 to affect model predictions only when conditions are appropriate for vector averaging. Specifically, Z_2 assumes a value of unity when the response direction (j) is intermediate between two orthogonal directional signals. Otherwise, Z_2 is zero. Similarly, Z_3 is unity only when j is intermediate between directional signals separated by 135 degrees. For the four experiments that contained two correlation values appropriate for analysis, we performed separate fits of the model to test interaction at each correlation value independently. Note that the interaction terms assumed symmetry; the value of the coefficient was the same regardless of whether the visual stimulus was clockwise or counterclockwise to the preferred direction of the microstimulation effect.

30   In the experiment in fig. 8.4, the effect of microstimulation was sufficiently strong that the modeled microstimulation effect was very similar to the plot of actual performance on stimulated trials at 0 percent correlation (compare with fig. 8.2A). For experiments with smaller effects, however, microstimulation did not completely overcome the effects of choice bias, as the monkey made choices on stimulated trials both toward the bias direction and toward the direction of the microstimulation effect. In those cases, the model provides an accurate description of the microstimulation effect independent of choice bias.

31   We fit the data with a Gaussian function that had four free parameters: a baseline parameter allowing the tails of the function to asymptote at non-zero values, a parameter characterizing the center of the distribution, a parameter that quantified the bandwidth of the distribution (σ), and a parameter that allowed the amplitude of the function to vary. To fit the functions, we first "clipped open" the circular tuning curves for the microstimulation effect and for the visual responses and plotted each on linear axes. We used a fitting algorithm based on chi-square minimization. Errors on the microstimulation data points were calculated from the model parameter estimates (β_{1-8}) by using the delta method for calculating asymptotic distributions [Y. M. M. Bishop, S. E. Feinberg, P. W. Holland, *Discrete Multivariate Analysis* (MIT Press, Cambridge, MA, 1975)]. For the visual response data, errors were calculated on the basis of the standard deviation of the mean firing rate in a particular direction across eight trials.

32   For this analysis, we estimated the size of each effect by calculating the proportion of decisions changed by microstimulation.

33   The mean multiunit neuronal bandwidth in the significant experiments was 61.7 degrees. This is similar to a mean single-unit bandwidth of 66.0 degrees measured in MT with the same stimuli ($n = 163$ cells) (K. H. Britten and W. T. Newsome, unpublished data).

34   D. W. Williams and R. Sekuler, *Vision Res.*, **24**, 55 (1984).

35   E. H. Adelson and J. A. Movshon, *Nature*, **300**, 523 (1982).

36   J. A. Movshon, E. H. Adelson, M. S. Gizzi, W. T. Newsome, in *Pattern Recognition Mechanisms*, C. Chagas, R. Gattass, C. Gross, eds. (Springer-Verlag, New York, 1985); H. R. Rodman and T. D. Albright, *Exp. Brain Res.*, **75**, 53 (1989); G. R. Stoner and T. D. Albright, *Nature*, **358**, 412 (1992).

37   W. Becker and R. Jurgens, *Vision Res.*, **19**, 967 (1979); F. P. Ottes, J. A. M. Van Gisbergen, J. J. Eggermont, ibid., **24**, 1169 (1984); J. M. Findlay, ibid., **22**, 1033 (1982).

38   R. H. Schor, A. D. Miller, D. L. Tomko, *J. Neurophysiol.*, **51**, 136 (1984); V. J. Wilson, K. Ezure, S. J. B. Timerick, ibid., p. 567; I. Suzuki, S. J. B. Timerick, V. J. Wilson, ibid., **54**, 123 (1985).

39 We thank K. H. Britten, L. Maloney, J. A. Movshon, and M. N. Shadlen for comments and suggestions during this work; B. Efron and J. Halpern for statistical advice; S. G. Lisberger, E. Seidemann, and E. Zohary for criticism of the manuscript; and J. Stein for technical assistance. Supported by the National Eye Institute (EY 5603). C.D.S. was supported by the Howard Hughes Medical Institute and subsequently by an NIH training grant (NS 07158–14).

9

James J. Gibson – An Appreciation

Ken Nakayama

I saw Gibson just once and immediately formed a negative impression. That was back in 1963. I was a beginning graduate student in physiological psychology at the University of California at Los Angeles (UCLA), eager to understand the mind and behavior in terms of brain function. I attended Gibson's lecture, aware only that he was a well-known psychologist. Other than some mention of slant perception, I recall little of the content. I had, however, an impression of a man impervious to new information, old fashioned, perhaps reactionary. But of course I was young and opinionated, I knew very little about perception, and I had just learned of the spectacular discoveries of Lettvin (Lettvin, Maturana, McCulloch, and Pitts, 1959), Hubel and Wiesel (1959), and others. Someone raised the issue of Lettvin's work during the question period, and I was struck by Gibson's uninterested, dismissive tone. Either he did not seem to understand the findings or, if he did, he thought them irrelevant. "Hmm," I thought to myself, "another traditional psychologist, old fashioned, maybe on the defensive, not able to keep up with things."

I walked out of the room somewhat puzzled. How could such a renowned person have turned his back on such amazing results? No matter. In the next several years, I was to follow my dream and set up a single-unit neurophysiology laboratory to map receptive fields and to try to link the behavior of single cells to visual psychophysics.

Just before leaving graduate school, I happened to come across Gibson's (1966) newly published book, *The Senses Considered as Perceptual Systems*. Since Gibson's lecture in 1963, I had not thought much about Gibson. I did have the uneasy feeling, however, that maybe I was missing something. Perhaps my original opinion needed reassessment.

I bought the book, and I remember I could not stop reading it. It was hard to place. It did not seem scientific, but it read more like a philosophical essay. Yet it really was not like contemporary philosophy; it was more broadly synthetic. The language was very plain, free from the usual buzzwords or scientific jargon. Initially, the ideas had a distinct sense of the everyday about them, a description of the earth below, sky above, certainly not revealing any obvious hidden "secrets" about vision, at least not then. Nevertheless, Gibson's views did not seem unreasonable, despite his claim to have a very radical position. It was his main point, the primacy of "perception" over "sensation," that was generally the most memorable, but I also recalled, in passing, the emphasis of the mobile observer and the accompanying change in the optic array. I remember conveying a very tentative enthusiasm to a perception graduate student at UCLA. By then I realized that I really did not know much about perception and wanted his opinion. He scoffed, "Oh Gibson, that mystical stuff, where are the experiments? No testable hypothesis, no quantitative predictions."

It was not until I became a postdoctoral student at the University of California–Berkeley that at least one of Gibson's ideas began to sink in. Intending to record from the lateral geniculate nucleus, I often noticed that above the nucleus (in a then uncharacterized extrastriate cortical area), it was very easy to isolate single cells and that virtually all the neurons there were insensitive to form yet were clearly sensitive to motion. I thought, "Perhaps Gibson is right, maybe the function of motion is much more than the mere registration of moving objects in the world, but is also used for the perception of space and self motion. There seem to be too many neurons just for the registration of moving objects." Not too long afterward, I had the pleasure of collaborating with Jack Loomis. We read Gibson again and made an effort to bridge the gap between his ideas and those of Barlow (1961), who suggested that visual neurons should code meaningful regularities in the environment, thus reducing redundancy. We postulated the existence of a class of velocity-sensitive neurons that could obtain information about the boundaries of surfaces during observer locomotion (Nakayama and Loomis, 1974). Such was the beginning of a growing appreciation of Gibson's contributions and a recognition that, far from being old fashioned, his ideas about visual motion could provide the foundation for entirely new research directions. I suspected that I would do well to reread Gibson from time to time because it was apparent that buried in this deceptively simple prose were some of the most interesting thoughts on vision that I had ever encountered. I would just have to reread these books at intervals to grasp their full meaning.

Over the intervening decades, I have not been disappointed. This occasion to comment on Gibson's 1954 article, "The Visual Perception of Objective Motion and Subjective Movement," certainly gives me another opportunity to both hear him out and to urge the reader to do so. The strength of Gibson's short article is that it anticipates and brings together issues and questions that had been previously neglected and that have now become recognized as critical questions. However, it also appears that Gibson was severely constrained, having to write a piece to be both short and understood entirely on its own. So by itself it lacks the depth of some of Gibson's longer writings, acquiring more significance in the broader context of Gibson's more sustained thinking. Thus, to be fair to Gibson, I comment on his article in the larger context of his more systematic writings on perception, primarily his books.

In his *The Perception of the Visual World*, Gibson (1950) proposed a psychophysics of vision, a research program that differed markedly from the prevailing practice of visual psychophysics. Traditional psychophysics began with Fechner, who invented an approach to link elementary physical quantities to what he thought were the simplest mental events. The absolute and differential threshold provided an operational, objective method to establish a relationship between physical intensity and sensation. Later, the structuralists would attempt to understand perception and higher processes in terms of elementary sensations, as if to build mental molecules out of atomic sensations. Logical and reasonable as it may have sounded at the time, the search for a "mental chemistry" failed. A description of "elementary sensations" did not lead to an understanding of perception.

Although the specific enterprise of the structuralists did not succeed, a much more broadly based program, motivated by a similar desire to understand perception in terms of elementary constituents, has emerged in the past 30 years. Calling itself by various names, such as vision, visual science, and visual neuroscience, this program forms a large, vigorous, and growing interdisciplinary field embracing neurophysiology, anatomy, psychophysics, and perceptual psychology. It also reaches out to computer vision and cognitive psychology. It was boosted by Hubel and Wiesel's (1959) description of visual receptive fields at various anatomical loci. Their catalogue of receptive field types held out the promise of a hierarchical progression, where cells with simple properties would then go on to bestow succeeding cells with complex, then hyper-complex, properties simply on the basis of excitatory and inhibitory connections. Lettvin et al. (1959) implied that the successive logical operations of differentiation and generalization had the hallmarks of logical thought. Extending this attractive idea to link it to the everyday facts of perception, however, began to run aground fairly early. Hubel and Wiesel, wisely, sidestepped the issue as to the specific functional role of these cells and directed their energies toward anatomical investigations, using novel techniques to reveal the intricacies of cortical architecture with convincing detail. This was accompanied and followed with the important discovery that the posterior portion of the brain consisted of many maps of the visual field (Allman and Kaas, 1974; Van Essen, 1985; Zeki, 1978). However, this tremendous increase in knowledge has told researchers mainly about the "nuts and bolts" of the visual system, not about how visual perception itself might work or what its specific functions might be.

During this time, psychophysics became informed by these neurophysiological developments, and a parallel concept of an orientation-selective spatial frequency channel emerged, one that provided a link to the receptive fields of cortical neurons (DeValois and DeValois, 1990). Such channels could explain simple detection and discrimination experiments, and some combination of channels provided some explanation of simple pattern discriminations as well as providing some foundation to understanding motion encoding and stereopsis. However, it was a far cry from everyday perception. Marr (1980), keenly sensing the crises in the playing out of the separate fields of physiology and psychophysics, articulated a synthetic view of how these findings might fit into a larger conception of visual function.

Meanwhile, Gibson appeared to all but ignore these developments. Early on he wrote, "The writer has elected to study psychophysics rather than psychophysiology because he believes that it offers the more promising approach in the present state of knowledge" (Gibson, 1950). Although using the term psychophysics, the psychophysics of Gibson was altogether different from the traditional variety just described. To review Gibson's psychophysics, I consider what he meant by each component – the physical first, then the psychological.

Gibson's Physics

All through his long scientific life, Gibson the psychologist would show a deep interest in physics, endeavoring to find a broad and more principled framework within which to place psychology. However, for Gibson it is a physics not recognizable to physicists, at least not then. Gibson's physics is the physics of the everyday on the scale of the everyday. It spans the distances traversed by animals, not those traversed by atoms or galaxies. It spans durations of the present, not infinitesimal instants or epochs. It deals with forces of the everyday and with its materials.

It is a physics more tied to the macroscopic phenomenon, largely ignored by physicists. For example, against Eddington's (1928) *The Nature of the Physical World*, Gibson argued,

> Some thinkers, impressed by the success of atomic physics, have concluded that the terrestrial world of surfaces, objects, places and events is a fiction. They say that only the particles and their fields are "real." The very ground under one's feet is said to be "merely" the bombardment of molecules.   (Gibson, 1966, p. 22)

Ground, the earth on which we stand, is physical and very real to Gibson and would become a cornerstone of his environmental physics.

Thus, Gibson's physics differed in at least two significant ways from conventional physics. It was a physics restricted to a scale comparable to the animal. In addition, it possessed a particularity not usually associated with physics, consisting of those physical features of our earthbound environment relevant to animate life. Thus, it consisted of a firm ground below, but with numerous and often dramatic deformations and outcroppings (terrain), air and illumination above, and large bodies of water (oceans, rivers, puddles, etc.). Even more specific and most emphasized in later work (Gibson, 1979) is the description of the physical world exclusively considered in terms of its potential functional relation to an animal's existence. The focus remained rooted in the physical world, but it now became fused with psychology because Gibson felt a need for an environmental physics defined specifically in relation to animate life. For this purpose, he developed his well-known theory of affordances:

> The affordances of the environment are what it offers the animal, what it provides or furnishes, either for good or ill. The verb to afford is found in the dictionary, but the noun affordance is not. I have made it up.   (Gibson, 1979, p. 127)

Gibson linked his ideas explicitly to evolutionary biology and behavioral ecology, indicating that a particular set of affordances comprised an "ecological niche" for that animal. Affordances and niches to Gibson had an objective meaning freed from mentalism and subjectivity: "The niche for some species should not be confused with what some animal psychologists have called the 'phenomenal environment of the species in which the species is supposed to live'" (Gibson, 1979, p. 128).

Surfaces for Gibson are one of the most important generic physical features of the physical environment:

The surface is where most of the action is. The surface is where light is reflected or absorbed, not the interior of the substance. The surface is what touches the animal not the interior.... If a terrestrial surface is nearly horizontal (instead of slanted), nearly flat (instead of convex or concave) and its substance is rigid (relative to the weight of the animal), then the surface affords support.... If its surface of support with the few properties is also knee-high above the ground, it affords sitting. We call it a seat in general, or a stool, bench, chair.   (Gibson, 1979, p. 23)

Thus, Gibson's physics is not about the physical world by itself, but only in its relation to potential physical actions of animals. Locomotion, a major focus of Gibson's 1954 *Psychological Review* article, constituted one class of actions common to all animals and was of major concern to Gibson. His interest can be separated into two components. First is the issue of how locomotion with respect to the physical environment is controlled, the issue of proprioception. Second are the consequences of locomotion for perception, the effect of a changing optic array. When considered jointly, they would provide a major source of new ideas about vision.

Gibson's Psychology of Information Pickup

Hand in hand with Gibson's very different approach to physics, his conception of perceptual psychology and the nature of the visual stimulus differed greatly from traditional psychophysics. Gibson's conception was to make a tight linkage between *his* physics and *his* psychology. As such, he rejected the traditional route on which most of researchers' current understanding of vision now rests. Referring to that tradition, he wrote,

The visual exposition of the sense of sight begins with the anatomy of the eye. There follows an account of the visual sensations, with emphasis on color, brightness and form as they are related to the photosensitive cells of the retina.... The whole treatment is in terms of human vision. We shall begin, however, with the question of what eyes are good for.   (Gibson, 1966, p. 155)

In short, for Gibson this meant getting information from the layout of surfaces and controlling behavior in this environment, particularly locomotion. So rather than light intensity, spatial extent, spectral content (all of the physical variables of interest to vision researchers in the past), Gibson would be concerned with surfaces, in particular reference to the actions of animals.

Ignoring the conventional approach taken in perceptual psychology and psycho-physics, with its preoccupation with visual angle in the two-dimensional retinal image and the needed reconstruction of the third dimension by means of binocular parallax, Gibson's space perception repudiates any scheme based on Cartesian coordinate axes:

Visual space, unlike abstract geometrical space, is perceived by virtue of what fills it.... The surfaces, slopes, and edges of the world have correlates in the retinal image specifically related to their objective counterparts by a lawful transformation. If this is correct, the problem of the restoration of the lost 3rd dimension in perception is a false problem.... There is literally no such thing as the perception of space without the perception of continuous background surface. This hypothesis might be called a "ground" theory to distinguish it from the "air" theory. (Gibson, 1950, pp. 5–11)

Gibson thus saw light "itself," not as a stimulus but as a carrier of information about the surrounding environment of surfaces. Perhaps one of the most controversial ideas was that the pickup of information from surfaces was "direct," not mediated by some kind of synthesis or set of inferences. What led Gibson to this view was his notion of the higher order variable of the optic array, a variable of optical stimulation that if directly measured, would give an immediate and informative reading. Consider his well-known example of size. An object of a given size cuts x units of texture elements with respect to the surface that it sits on, no matter how far it is placed. No measurement of distance is necessary for an appreciation of equivalent size to be registered. To obtain the slant of a surface, Gibson saw the gradient of texture as particularly important, providing a direct measure of surface slant.

Thus, Gibson was concerned with obtaining information about surfaces in the world; he was not concerned with providing an exact copy between the information about surfaces and one's visual experience. Not requiring a replica, he went on to ask whether a psychophysical bottom-up approach to perception is possible:

If, contrary to past teaching, there are exact concomitant variations in the image for the important features in the visual world a psychophysical theory will be possible.... The question is not how much it resembles the visual world but whether it contains enough variations to account for all the features of the visual world. (Gibson, 1950, pp. 61–2)

These views anticipate by over 25 years one of the most important tenets of computational vision, articulating the nature of the stimulus information required for vision (Marr, 1980).

As revolutionary and more immediately influential was Gibson's suggestion that spatial gradients of motion were sensed directly because in fact, these gradients of motion, like gradients of texture, could provide direct information regarding surface layout and extent. To appreciate the boldness of these assertions about motion, one has to understand the prevailing view of vision at the time. Then and even now, vision is seen in terms of the static retinal image, a set of light intensities across the photoreceptor mosaic, stimulating local retinal points, or "signs," from which perception must be built.

So sure was Gibson of his own views that as early as 1950, he could turn his back to this established thinking and calmly yet prophetically assert,

Every photographer is aware that even a slight movement of his camera during exposure will shift the image on the film, for it ruins the picture. The same kind of shifting of the image on the retina occurs all the time during vision with the difference that vision is enriched rather than spoiled. (Gibson, 1950, p. 117)

The weight of the scientific tradition that Gibson had to repudiate is described by Lombardo (1987):

Because the analogy between the retinal image and a static picture became popularized, the perceiver was not thought to be sensitive to optical change, a property of optical change or an invariant of optical change as such. Only those instantaneous properties of one given retinal image were thought of as stimuli. Perceived change, such as movement, always required memory images, integration, inference, or some process of metatemporal organization. (p. 216)

For Gibson, the memory image of the immediately preceding retinal image was deemed unnecessary: The observer could directly sense change and the gradient of change.

Although the idea of a motion gradient did not receive an adequately precise definition by Gibson (it is more complicated than the usual gradient of scalar fields described by vector analysis), his basic intuitions have proved to be largely correct, at least mathematically. Evidently aware of contemporary ideas of mathematical invariance and group structure, and citing Courant and Robbins (1941) and Ernst Cassirer (1944) in his 1950 book, Gibson argued that a higher order variable of the motion field would be more explicitly informative about surface layout than motion itself. He also made the same claim for binocular disparity, suggesting that the gradient of disparity rather than disparity itself was more informative. In a highly influential set of mathematical articles in the mid-1970s, Koenderink and van Doorn (1976a; 1976b) examined the nature of motion parallax and binocular parallax fields and were able to show that a certain higher order component of the gradient of these fields was indeed more explicitly informative about surface orientation. Since then, Koenderink in similar spirit has gone far beyond Gibson, essentially creating a mathematics of vision, describing how images from surfaces either vary or remain invariant with viewer position.

Gibson's Impact: Relative Motion and the Control of Locomotion

For those younger scientists coming of age after the discovery of motion sensitive neurons, Gibson's ideas might not seem particularly startling until they realize that his detailed thinking about motion antedated the physiology. Only now has the physiology begun to catch up with and to address the class of questions asked by Gibson, and only now has the physiology begun to discover otherwise unforeseen properties of visual neurons that appear to vindicate his emphasis on motion and relative motion.

In my own case, I was very interested in whether neurons in the visual system of animals might analyze the moving image to pick out surfaces for the moving observer. As mentioned earlier, Jack Loomis and I, directly influenced by Gibson, postulated the existence of higher order visual neurons that would take differences in velocity between the center and surround of a receptive field, independent of direction. Such cells could highlight the boundaries of surfaces for a wide range of observer and eye motions (Nakayama and Loomis, 1974). Our analysis rested on the fact that the velocity fields created by observer translation could be mathematically distinguished from those created by observer or eye rotation. Later, Barrie Frost and I (Frost and

Nakayama, 1983), looked for cells that might generalize velocity differences between center and surround and indeed found neurons with spectacularly complex properties that were almost but not identical to those anticipated. Essentially, all cells of the pigeon optic tectum fired only when the motion of the center was in the opposite direction to that of the surround, generalizing this property over a wide range of motion directions. In detail, it became quite clear that such cells would not outline the edges of surfaces during motion, say flight, because they would be unresponsive if center and surround were both stimulated by motion in the same direction. Yet the eyes of the walking pigeon are mostly stationary with respect to the environment because of the head-bobbing reflex. As such, these neurons could well serve to address one of the key questions asked in Gibson's 1954 article. He asked how we can determine self motion from the motion of objects when both lead to image motion on the retina. These cells will distinguish the motions of small objects from large background motions at least during walking. Despite the highly specific and complex requirements for cell firing, the exact function of these cells remains unexplained. Nevertheless, without the Gibsonian framework it is clear that we would never have looked for or found cells with such remarkable properties.

More closely relating to our original idea of outlining surface boundaries, John Allman and associates found cells in monkey visual areas that preferentially responded when the velocities of center and surround were different (Allman, Miezin, and McGuinness, 1985). More recently, and echoing Koenderink and van Doorn (1976b), cells with higher order properties of the velocity field (divergence or curl) have been identified in monkey extrastriate cortex (Tanaka and Saito, 1989).

It is in the control of locomotion, however, that the most complete vindication of the Gibsonian outlook is evident, at least so far. In his 1954 article, Gibson asked about the visual perception of locomotion in a stable environment. Shortly thereafter, Gibson (1958) proposed that the focus of expansion, the point in the velocity field where all motion vectors originate, constituted an optical invariant that would identify for an observer his own heading, his direction of motion with respect to a visual environment. Although this is not true if the animal rotates his eyes during locomotion or moves in a curvilinear path (see Nakayama, 1982), one can conceive of isolating the focus of expansion from the added rotational component purely from operations of the velocity field itself or by taking account of eye rotations. Psychophysical studies have in broad outline confirmed Gibson's imaginative hypotheses, showing that observers can sense their own direction of motion in a computer-simulated display (Warren and Hannon, 1988). For complex conditions where the eye does not undergo pure translational motion, the sense of eye position is also required (Royden, Banks, and Crowell, 1992). As yet, however, researchers have not gone beyond these psycho-physical observations to show that humans or animals actually use this information to perform real locomotor tasks.

A more spectacular vindication of Gibson's approach concerns the timing of impending collision as one approaches surfaces or when projectiles are moving toward observers. Symmetrically growing images simulate a direct hit, a very primitive visual spatiotemporal pattern to which human infants are differentially responsive (Yonas, 1981). Building on Gibson's theory of invariances, Lee (1976) described the optical parameter *tau*, the angular extent of an approaching object divided by its first time derivative. This variable provides exact information as to the time when the target will collide with the observer (see also Hoyle, 1957). It is remarkable that this variable provides reliable information independent of distance or speed, thus providing not mediated but direct information of obvious behavioral relevance. Lee later found that this variable could account for the behavior of diving birds, who must streamline their wings just before plunging into the water at high velocities (Lee and Reddish, 1981). Most recently, in a very exciting set of physiological experiments, Wang and Frost (1992) found neurons in the pigeon visual system that fire at a fixed interval of time before an impending collision, independent of distance or speed. This sequence of remarkable studies is perhaps one of the most dramatic of the recent success stories emerging from the Gibsonian framework.

The Perceptual Primacy of Surfaces

For Gibson, surfaces were all-important, both in the realm of the physics relevant to animate life and in the psychology of information pickup. Not surprisingly, the traditional approach of psychophysics and neurophysiology, with its preoccupation with visual angle, luminance, and spectral content, ignored surfaces. They were not forgotten, however, by perceptual phenomenologists, who created many demonstrations showing the importance of surface phenomena (Kanizsa, 1979; Metelli, 1974). Yet, so buried was this awareness of surfaces that Marr's (1980) theoretical formulation of the 2.5-dimensional (2.5 D) sketch (essentially a revival of surfaces) became a high point in his ambitious enterprise to "explain" vision. It is of interest to quote Marr directly: "For all these reasons, the emergence during the autumn of 1976 of the idea of the 2.5 D sketch, which first appeared in Marr and Nishihara...was for me the most exhilarating moment of the whole investigation" (Marr, 1980, p. 269).

Over the past 7 years and with the close collaboration of several colleagues, I have developed a very strong interest in surfaces. Our work, however, did not start from Gibsonian principles or outlook but began as a set of phenomenological explorations. Yet, a set of conclusions emerged from our work that I think show clear parallels to ideas promulgated by Gibson years earlier. First, we argued that the pickup of information about surfaces is more or less an autonomous process, accomplished before object recognition (Nakayama, Shimojo, and Silverman, 1989), which may begin as early as cortical area V1 (Nakayama and Shimojo, 1990a, 1990b). Second, and strongly echoing Gibson's philosophical views on the primacy of perception over sensation (Gibson, 1966), we showed that observers are more immediately responsive to surface properties in an image, not features. Thus, surface shape, not features, determines performance in visual search (He and Nakayama, 1992), visual texture segregation (He and Nakayama, 1994), and apparent motion experiments (He and Nakayama, in press; Shimojo and Nakayama, 1990). Finally, and more directly influenced by Gibson through Koenderink and van Doorn's (1976c) formal description of the sampling of images from different vantage points, we developed a theoretical framework to understand the perceptual learning of surfaces (Nakayama and Shimojo, 1992).

Locomotion in a World of Surfaces?

In reviewing Gibson and his successors, I note that two of his most persistent interests, locomotion and the pickup of information about surfaces, have been, in at least one respect, curiously isolated from each other. To my knowledge, the control of locomotion and the perception of a world of surfaces have not been considered together. Perhaps this is because the parameters relevant to control the direction of locomotion (the focus of expansion) and the estimation of the time of collision (*tau*) have been considered as image properties with only an indirect relation to the composition of surfaces. Furthermore, more recent analyses within the Gibsonian framework have identified other potential optical parameters that could control locomotion. For example *tau*-dot (the first derivative of *tau*) provides information to control braking (Lee, 1976; see Yilmaz and Warren, 1992); changing image orientation has been identified as an optical parameter for a pilot landing an aircraft on a straight runway (Loomis and Beall, 1992). In all of these cases, one might be drawn to the conclusion that locomotion could be controlled independently of a surface representation. To my knowledge, this supposition has never been explicitly raised or tested. Researchers need to ask whether locomotion in general must be considered within a world of perceived surfaces or whether there might be primitive processes of motor control, perhaps the ones cited here, that might be driven by image information alone.

Summing Up

It should be evident from what I have written that I hold Gibson in the highest esteem. I should. At critical moments in my scientific career, I have benefited immensely from his theoretical perspective. However, his influence of course is far broader.

In fact, for sheer breadth, incisiveness, originality, and influence, I cannot imagine anyone more qualified to be recognized as the most important perceptual psychologist of the last 100 years. Spanning many levels – philosophy, physics, behavior, specifics of the stimulus – the sweep is without parallel. Then there is the obvious originality: surfaces, texture, invariance, motion, the moving observer, and ecological optics, to mention a few. Moreover, I would argue that Gibson's influence in perception, psychophysics, neurophysiology, and computer vision runs very deep, although not always fully acknowledged.

That said, and aside from noting my own first impressions of Gibson, I have avoided one aspect of Gibson's views that has received the greatest criticism. Gibson and especially his followers have scrupulously avoided reference to any form of internal representation. Whether this reflects a defensible ideological position as articulated by his followers (Turvey, Shaw, Reed, and Mace, 1981), a pragmatic ordering of research priorities as indicated by Gibson himself (1950), or a fundamental naïveté as suggested by Marr (1980, p. 30), this almost blatant disinterest in the face of steady and often brilliant progress in the fields of neuroscience and psychophysics strikes me as a major limitation, particularly now. Nonetheless, I have turned a blind eye to this uncompromising stance because, early on, I decided that Gibson's ideas were just too good to pass up. For whatever valid reasons Gibson may have had against internal representation, the discovery of new and unexpected forms of internal representation have been the happy result.

So, Gibson's influence has had some paradoxical features. Throughout his career, he has more or less ignored internal representation, the very thing that most of us non-Gibsonians have been looking for. Yet, he has had quite a few admirers from within "our" ranks. Why should this be so?

The answer is apparent as soon as researchers realize that the search for internal representation cannot proceed in isolation, divorced from behavior or from an analysis of that which has to be represented. Recall that Marr (1980) outlined different levels of explanation required for complex processes like vision. They were (a) the computational level, (b) the algorithmic level, and (c) the level of implementation. In grudging acknowledgment, Marr noted that Gibson's main contribution was restricted to the computational level but faulted Gibson for underestimating the difficulties posed beyond. My own view is that even Marr, his followers, and most of contemporary visual science might be comparably faulted for underestimating difficulties at the computational – I prefer the word functional – level.

Whatever the faults or limitations of studies conducted at these various levels, those of us who have chosen to study vision are very fortunate in having such rich traditions from which to draw. As a field, we need to think hard about internal representation and to continue to look to physiological findings. We also need the approach advocated by Gibson: clear and original thinking about the nature and purpose of visual function linked to a rigorous analysis of the optical information required.

Acknowledgments

Thanks to Zijiang J. He, Jack Loomis, and Shinsuke Shimojo for stimulating conversation, to Shimsuke Shimojo for reading a draft of this article, and to the Air Force Office of Scientific Research for financial support.

References

Allman, J., & Kaas, J. (1974). The organization of the second visual area (V2) in the owl monkey: A second order transformation of the visual hemifield. *Brain Research*, **76**, 247–65.

Allman, J., Miezin, F., & McGuinness, E. (1985). Stimulus specific responses from beyond the classical receptive field: Neurophysiological mechanisms for local–global comparisons in visual neurons. *Annual Review of Neuroscience*, **8**, 407–30.

Barlow, H. B. (1961). Possible principles underlying the transformations of sensory messages. In W. A. Rosenblith (ed.), *Sensory communication* (pp. 217–34), New York: Wiley.

Cassirer, E. (1944). The concept of group and the theory of perception. *Philosophical and Phenomenological Research*, **5**, 1–35.

Courant, R., & Robbins, H. (1941). *What is mathematics?* New York: Oxford University Press.

DeValois, R. L., & DeValois, K. K. (1990). *Spatial vision*. New York: Oxford University Press.

Eddington, A. S. (1928). *The nature of the physical world*. New York: Macmillan.

Frost, B. J., & Nakayama, K. (1983). Single neurons code opposing motion independent of direction. *Science*, **220**, 744–5.

Gibson, J. J. (1950). *The perception of the visual world*. Boston: Houghton Mifflin.

Gibson, J. J. (1954). The visual perception of objective motion and subjective movement. *Psychological Review*, **61**, 304–14.

Gibson, J. J. (1958). Visually controlled motion and visual orientation in animals. *British Journal of Psychology*, **49**, 182–94.

Gibson, J. J. (1966). *The senses considered as perceptual systems*. Boston: Houghton Mifflin.

Gibson, J. J. (1979). *The ecological approach to visual perception*. Boston: Houghton Mifflin.

He, Z. J., & Nakayama, K. (1992). Surfaces vs. features in visual search. *Nature*, **359**, 231–3.

He, Z. J., & Nakayama, K. (1994). Perceiving textures: Beyond filtering *Vision Research*, **34**, 151–62.

He, Z. J., & Nakayama, K. (in press). Perceived shape not features determines apparent motion correspondence. *Vision Research*.

Hoyle, F. (1957). *The black cloud*. New York: Harper & Row.

Hubel, D. H., & Wiesel, T. N. (1959). Receptive fields, binocular interaction and functional architecture in cat's visual center. *Journal of Physiology*, **160**, 106–54.

Kanizsa, G. (1979). *Organization in vision*. New York: Praeger.

Koenderink, J. J., & van Doorn, A. J. (1976a). Geometry of binocular vision and a model for stereopsis. *Biological Cybernetics*, **21**, 29–35.

Koenderink, J. J., & van Doorn, A. J. (1976b). Local structure of movement parallax in the plane. *Journal of the Optical Society of America*, **66**, 717–23.

Koenderink, J. J., & van Doorn, A. J. (1976c). The singularities of the visual mapping. *Biological Cybernetics*, **24**, 51–9.

Lee, D. N. (1976). A theory of the visual control of braking based on information about time-to-collision. *Perception*, **5**, 437–59.

Lee, D. N., & Reddish, P. E. (1981). Plummeting gannets: A paradigm of ecological optics. *Nature*, **293**, 293–4.

Lettvin, J. Y., Maturana, H. R., McCulloch, W. S., & Pitts. W. H. (1959). What the frog's eye tells the frog's brain. *Proceedings of the Institute of Radio Engineers*, **47**, 1940–51.

Lombardo, T. J. (1987). *The reciprocity of perceiver and environment: The evolution of James J. Gibson's ecological psychology*. Hillsdale, NJ: Erlbaum.

Loomis, J. M., & Beall, A. C. (1992). Optic flow rule for controlling a curvilinear approach to a straight path. *Investigative Ophthalmology and Visual Science Annual Meeting Abstract Issue*, **33–4**, 1370.

Marr, D. (1980). *Vision*. New York: Freeman.

Metelli, F. (1974). The perception of transparency. *Scientific American*, **230**, 90–8.

Nakayama, K. (1982). Motion parallax sensitivity and space perception. In A. Hein & M. Jeannerod (eds), *Spatially coordinated behavior* (pp. 223–42), San Diego, CA: Academic Press.

Nakayama, K., & Loomis, J. M. (1974). Optical velocity patterns, velocity-sensitive neurons, and space perception: A hypothesis. *Perception*, **3**, 63–80.

Nakayama, K., & Shimojo, S. (1990a). DaVinci stereopsis: Depth and subjective contours from unpaired monocular points. *Vision Research*, **30**, 1811–25.

Nakayama, K., & Shimojo, S. (1990b). Towards a neural understanding of visual surface representation. In T. Sejnowski, E. R. Kandel, C. F. Stevens, & J. D. Watson (eds), *The brain: Cold Spring Harbor Symposium on Quantitative Biology* (pp. 911–24), Cold Spring Harbor, NY: Cold Spring Harbor Laboratory Press.

Nakayama, K., & Shimojo, S. (1992). Experiencing and perceiving visual surfaces. *Science*, **257**, 1357–63.

Nakayama, K., Shimojo, S., & Silverman, G. H. (1989). Stereoscopic depth: Its relation to image segmentation, grouping and the recognition of occluded objects. *Perception*, **18**, 55–68.

Royden, C., Banks, M. S., & Crowell, J. A. (1992). The perception of heading during eye movements. *Nature*, **360**, 583–4.

Shimojo, S., & Nakayama, K. (1990). Amodal presence of partially occluded surfaces determines apparent motion. *Perception*, **19**, 285–99.

Tanaka, K., & Saito, H. (1989). Analysis of motion of the visual field by direction, expansion/contraction, and rotation cells clustered in the dorsal part of the medial superior temporal area of the macaque monkey. *Journal of Neurophysiology*, **62**, 626–41.

Turvey, M. T., Shaw, R. E., Reed, E. S., & Mace, W. M. (1981). Ecological laws of perceiving and acting: In reply to Fodor and Pylyshyn (1981). *Cognition*, **9**, 237–304.

Van Essen, D. C. (1985). Functional organization of primate visual cortex. In A. Peters & E. G. Jones (eds), *Cerebral Cortex* (vol. 3, pp. 259–329), New York: Plenum.

Wang, Y., & Frost, B. J. (1992). Time-to-collision is signalled by neurons in the nucleus rotundus of pigeons. *Nature*, **356**, 236–8.

Warren, W. H., & Hannon, D. J. (1988). Direction of self-motion is perceived from optical flow. *Nature*, **336**, 162–3.

Yilmaz, E. H., & Warren, W. H. (1992). Second-order optical expansion (tau-dot) is used to control braking. *Investigative Ophthalmology and Visual Science* (Suppl. 33), 1145.

Yonas, A. (1981). Infants' responses to optical information for collision. In R. N. Aslin, J. Alberts, & M. Petersen (eds), *Development of perception: Psychobiological perspectives: The visual system* (vol. 2, pp. 313–34), San Diego, CA: Academic Press.

Zeki, S. (1978). Functional specialization in the visual cortex of the rhesus monkey. *Nature*, **274**, 423–8.

INTRODUCTION TO PART III

We deal with the constant barrage of incoming sensory information by ignoring most of it. The nineteenth-century psychologist William James wrote: "Everyone knows what attention is. It is the taking possession by the mind, in a clear and vivid form, of one out of what seem several simultaneously possible objects or trains of thought." Multiple brain mechanisms now seem responsible for this kind of thing. The "trains of thought" James refers to are not so well studied as the selective processing of objects; first things first, perhaps. What happens when we attend to something, and what happens to the things that we ignore, are addressed in these papers.

Michael Posner and Stanislas Dehaene describe in macroscopic terms the brain regions that seem to be most involved in these effects. The most obvious human brain region that is involved in selective attention is the parietal lobe of the cerebral cortex; damage here can produce a curious "neglect" of the side of the world opposite the lesion. (This is almost always due to right hemisphere damage, with a resulting neglect of the left side of space; apparently the right hemisphere has a sufficient "map" of both sides of space to cover for a damaged left hemisphere. That the left hemisphere evidently can't do the same for the right hemisphere probably stems from a crowding out of the left's spatial abilities by the expanding language areas during human evolution.)

Using PET (and more recently fMRI), Posner and his collaborators have also demonstrated the involvement of a frontal region known as the anterior cingulate gyrus, which increases its activity, apparently, when subjects struggle with self-control, suppressing one form of processing in favor of another.

The involvement of the primary visual cortex (V1) in attention is a matter of debate. Until recently, as mentioned earlier in the paper by Hillyard, there was no evidence of any modulation of neuronal responses by attention or, as in the paper here by He, Cavanagh, and Intriligator, evidence of awareness of the V1 neuron's activity. Recent work suggests that attention is probably as relevant to V1 as to anywhere else in the cortex. He et al.'s compelling demonstration that activation of V1 can occur without conscious perception might therefore be not so much a demonstration of V1's immunity to attention as another demonstration that unconscious processing can occur without attention.

Both the other papers in this section present evidence along these latter lines. Volpe, Ledoux, and Gazzaniga examined patients with "extinction," a milder form of unilateral neglect that permits focusing on the left side of space if nothing interesting on the right hand side competes for attention. We found that despite some patients' strenuous denials that they had seen anything on the left side, they were nevertheless very good at comparing it with what they had seen on the right side. Working with healthy subjects, Tipper and Driver demonstrate an impressively deep level of processing of ignored stimuli. These and other findings indicate that attention, while extremely important to perception and thought, is not the whole story.

1

Attentional Networks

Michael I. Posner and Stanislas Dehaene

The study of selective attention has been an important area of research since the inception of psychology in the late 1800s. However, it has remained controversial whether there are any separate brain mechanisms that subserve attention. Attention does not give rise to a unique qualitative experience like vision or touch, nor does it automatically produce motor responses. While we appear to be able to select sensory stimuli, information in memory, or motor responses, this might not indicate a separate attention system, since all brain systems play a role in selection.

There has been evidence of more general mechanisms related to visual selection. One way to select information is to orient to it. Eye movements to foveate a visual stimulus is a clear case, since without foveation there is little ability to examine details of the visual scene. There are also brain mechanisms for visual orienting that do not involve any overt changes in head or eye. In the 1970s, it was found that cells in the parietal lobe increased their firing rate in response to stimulation of their receptive field when monkeys attended to peripheral stimuli even when no eye movements were allowed.[1] It was also shown that humans could covertly shift attention to peripheral stimuli and when they did so they responded more rapidly, at lower threshold and with enhanced electrical activity to stimuli at the attended location. Lesions of the parietal lobe specifically damaged this covert orienting ability on the side of space opposite the lesion. These findings supported the idea that portions of the parietal lobe were involved in covert orienting to visual stimuli.[2]

Since 1987, when we last reviewed this topic,[2] it has become possible to use neuroimaging methods to observe the networks of brain areas that become active when people perform complex tasks.[3,4] Certain brain areas appear active when subjects have to orient, select or transform information in ways that would be said, by most psychological models, to involve attention. These brain areas appear to fit quite well with the idea of selection and control as properties of attention outlined in our previous work. In this article, we use the neuroimaging data to outline what is known about networks of brain areas involved in selection during visual search and then extend the discussion to mechanisms of selection and control more generally.

Visual Search

Throughout this article, we use the example of a simple visual-search task in order to illustrate the role of attention in finding objects.[5] Data indicate that the time for a subject to locate a target (for example, the vertical rectangle in fig. 10.1) increases almost linearly with the number of distractors, as though the subject attended to each item in turn. The reaction time when there is no target has twice the slope found for "yes" responses, indicating that one stops as soon as the target is found.[5]

A simplified view of the problem faced by the brain in this task is presented in Fig. 10.2. The visual array is processed through a diverging tree of cortical areas.[6] Cortical cells early in the stream have narrow receptive fields and respond mechanically whenever their preferred stimuli are present, whether they correspond to a target or not. As one moves up in the hierarchy, however, receptive fields widen and the cells become more sensitive to attentional and intentional influences, and react less effectively to the passive presentation of a stimulus.

The simple illustration in Fig. 10.2 makes it clear that selective attention serves at least two distinctive functions. First, the brain must enhance the processing of the selected stimulus relative to other stimuli present, otherwise all stimuli would be processed to a similar degree (Fig. 10.2, top). Second, processing of the selected stimulus must be actively oriented or guided towards the cortical areas appropriate for a given task. The diverging tree of cortical areas, each of which specializes for a distinct aspect of the stimuli, must be selectively "pruned" to focus only on those stimulus characteristics that are relevant to the task. This "pruning" is depicted on the bottom of Fig. 10.2 in a static manner, but in complex tasks such as serial search, the appropriate processing stream might change as a function of time (for example, the subject might attend to each stimulus in turn or to all vertical items first and then to all horizontal items).

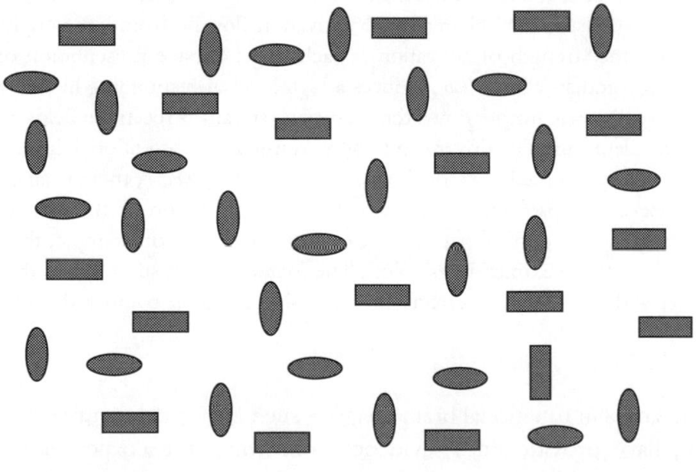

Figure 10.1   Visual search for a vertical rectangle among a large number of distractors (horizontal and vertical ellipses and rectangles). The target is defined by a conjunction of form and orientation. In most cases, selective attention is used to sequentially search the display until the target is found.[5]

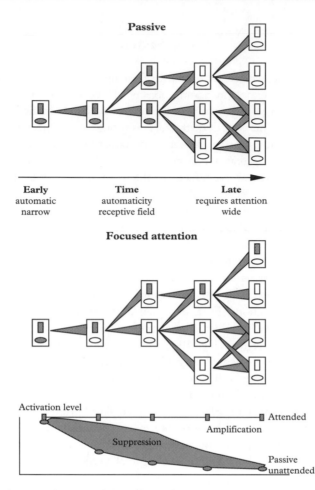

Figure 10.2   Schematic diagram of the effects of attention on visual processing. Boxes depict the diverging tree of visual cortical areas, with activation flowing from left to right. Shading is used to represent the strength of activation at each stage. Passive presentation of two visual objects, a rectangle and an ellipse (*top*), induces a high level of responding in early visual areas, with a progressive decrease further down the processing stream as receptive fields widen and the neurons become less stimulus-driven and more sensitive to attentional influences. When attention is selectively oriented towards the vertical rectangle (*middle*), there is an early suppression of the irrelevant ellipse. This is followed by an amplification of the activity evoked by the target rectangle in the cortical pathways relevant to the task (for example, those extracting its location, but not those extracting its color). The *bottom* diagram summarizes the time course of suppression and amplification effects in successive areas as compared with the passive situation.

Recent advances in functional brain imagery, such as positron emission tomography (PET) scan, have provided new evidence concerning the cortical and subcortical networks responsible for these two functions of selective attention. As it turns out, the two functions seem to be carried out by two distinct systems:[7] the posterior attention system (superior parietal cortex, pulvinar and superior colliculus) is largely responsible for selecting one stimulus location among many and for shifting from one stimulus to the next, whereas the anterior attention system (anterior cingulate and basal ganglia) serves a more executive function (attention for action) and is involved in the attentional recruitment and control of brain areas to perform complex cognitive tasks. This network is also involved in selecting visual objects when the instructions emphasize properties of the object. Ultimately, however, the effect of both systems is relative amplification of activity within the cortical areas relevant to a given task.

Attentional Amplification

In the visual display of fig. 10.1, if you are attending to the correct location it is easy to see the target. Otherwise, the target is not seen. How does the brain implement such target detection? It appears that brain activity, in many cortical areas, can be selectively amplified or suppressed as a function of attentional set. When subjects are instructed to pay attention to one particular dimension of the stimuli, the brain areas that specialize in the processing of this stimulus dimension are selectively enhanced. These findings are striking in the prestriate areas of the visual system. In one experiment, subjects viewed passively either stationary or moving objects, presented every second for a minute.[8] When blood flow during the stationary control condition was subtracted from that found in the moving condition, a prestriate area of the midtemporal lobe was found to have a significant increase in blood flow. This might be the human equivalent of area V5 or MT which, in the monkey, contains cells with a strong selectivity for moving stimuli. In a different experiment,[9] subjects always viewed moving objects of varying color and form, but in one set of trials they were instructed to detect differences in velocity, whereas in a control set they had to detect changes in other stimulus parameters. Even though the physical stimuli were the same in the two conditions, the instruction to attend to velocity activated a brain area that was similar to that found in the comparison of moving and stationary targets. In other words, attention to velocity activates a brain area that is similar in location to what is found when motion is physically added to the stimulus.

The same general correspondence also occurs between brain areas activated by presenting color and form stimuli and those activated when the person is instructed to selectively process color or form information.[9] Increases in blood flow have also been reported in motor areas[10] when subjects are instructed to attend to motor actions. In general, there appears to be a relative increase in blood flow in nearly any area of the brain when subjects are instructed to attend to a sensory or motor computation thought to be related to that brain area. A possible exception is the primary visual cortex, which does not seem to be affected by attentional manipulations.[1,9]

So far we have looked at the effects of attention when people are instructed to attend to sensory dimensions such as color, form or motion. But in the search task above, neither the orientation nor the form of the target is sufficient to find it. Only a combination of the two dimensions at the same location will work.[5] Under these conditions, subjects often search serially by shifting their attention from location to location. If there are no eye movements allowed, these shifts must be mediated covertly, and they should produce a sequence of amplification at each successive location. Indeed, electrical recordings of the scalp have been used to measure such location-specific amplification.[11,12] First, the time for subjects to find a target con-junction was found. At this time, a white square was presented as a probe stimulus, either at this attended target location or at another unrelated location that did not contain a target, and the brain event-related potential generated by this probe was recorded. The results showed that by 80 ms after the probe, the potential elicited over the posterior regions of the scalp was greater when the probe occurred at the target location. The covert shift of attention to the target location had amplified the scalp electrical activity for probes presented at this location. The scalp amplification was strongest over posterior sites contralateral to the hemifield where the probe appeared. In other studies, where attention was deliberately cued to a location, a similar ampli-fication of target ERPs at the cued location was also found.[13] In these cueing studies,[13] current source density analysis has shown that the amplification originates from prestriate areas similar in location to those shown to be activated in the above cited PET studies.[9]

Cellular recordings in awake monkeys have shown that the relative amplification of the attended stimulus might actually involve suppression of activity evoked by unattended events. When monkeys were required to attend to a particular location in order to respond to a change in color at that location, cells in area V4 stopped responding to a stimulus at an unattended location that would otherwise be optimal in initiating cell firing.[14] Similar suppression effects have been observed in the inferior temporal cortex during a visual search task: cells that initially fired strongly to a given visual object stopped responding when the monkey attended to a different object at another location, even though the preferred object was still present in the receptive field.[15]

Based on the model in fig. 10.2, we speculate that attentional effects should generally appear as a suppression of unattended information early on in the processing stream, and as an enhancement of relevant information later on. The reason is that neurons in earlier visual areas are already activated to a near optimal level by visual stimuli even in a passive situation (or in the anesthetized animal), and that therefore there is little room for firing enhancement of the target, but more room for firing suppression of the non-targets. Neurons in the retina, lateral geniculate and area V1 fire strongly to their preferred stimuli whether they are attended or not. Extra-striate areas such as V4 seem to be the first visual areas to show the influence of attention.[14] Because the neurons in early visual areas already respond at a high-firing rate even in a passive condition, attention has the effect of selectively suppressing some or all of this automatic activation. Later on, as the cell responses become less automatic, attention can have the effect of boosting the activation of cells coding for the attended stimulus, as well as suppressing those coding for unattended stimuli. Finally, even further downstream, in cortical areas that activate only during specific tasks and not in a passive situation, attention appears necessary for any activation to occur.

Indeed this predicted sequence of suppression followed by enhancement has been observed recently in studies of event-related potentials during cued attention tasks.[12] The task involved three conditions. In the correctly cued condition, attention was brought to the correct location prior to presentation of the target. In the neutral condition, the cue provided no information on target location. In the miscued condi-tion, attention was brought to a location other than that at which the target was presented. The P1 component of the evoked potential, an early positive electrical event which appears about 80 ms following stimulus presentation, was the same for correctly cued and neutral conditions and both were larger than when the target occurred following a miscue. For this component, activity is suppressed when attention is located at the wrong location. However, for the subsequent N1, a negative component that arises about 150–200 ms after the stimulus, there was increased electrical activity for correctly cued stimuli with respect to the neutral or miscued conditions. In the N1 component of the evoked potential, the relative amplification appears due to boosting the attended location.

According to our interpretation, this suppression-enhancement sequence should be observed most readily with stimuli that are sufficiently intense to passively activate the early visual system and therefore leave little room for an early enhancement by attention. On the contrary, with low-intensity stimuli that cause little passive activation, enhancement should be seen earlier in time and suppression should hardly be perceptible at all.

Control of Orienting

In visual search, attention moves from location to location until the target is detected. How is the internal focus of attention moved? In order to isolate the attentional network responsible for searching locations, a cue can be used to direct attention to that location. Such cueing experiments have shown that stimuli that are presented at the cued location are responded to more rapidly, have a lower perception threshold and generate brain potentials of a larger amplitude.[7,16] When brain-lesioned patients are tested in this form of cued attention, different forms of deficit are found depending on the site of the lesion. For example, patients with lesions of the right parietal lobe are severely impaired when cues are in the good right visual field and targets in the bad left visual field, but not much impaired in other situations, suggesting a deficit of disengaging attention from a cued location.[16]

Recent PET data[17] from normal subjects show that when attention is shifted from location to location either voluntarily or as a result of being summoned by external events, the major focus of increased blood flow is in the left and right superior parietal lobes. This is the only activation to be specifically related to the attention shift. As mentioned earlier, cellular recordings in the parietal lobe of awake monkeys have also supported the involvement of parietal neurons in visual attention. Parietal areas appear to be implementing aspects of the act of shifting attention rather than being sites at which attention is affecting target detection.[1,7]

The PET data also support the clinical observation that the attentional functions of the two hemispheres are not symmetric. The right superior parietal lobe increases in blood flow for attention shifts in both fields, while the left increases only for right field shifts.[17] This finding might explain the clinical observation that right-hemisphere lesions produce greater attention deficits than do left-hemisphere lesions. In the normal subject however, the left and right parietal areas are integrated into a single mechanism, so that covert attention has a single focus. The corpus callosum appears crucial in unifying the attentional focus. In visual search tasks, normal subjects are not faster when the same number of distractors is distributed across the two visual fields than when all are concentrated in one field. However, patients whose corpus callosum is cut can search at twice the rate when distractors are split evenly between the two visual fields in comparison to when they are concentrated within a single field.[18] This suggests that attentional mechanisms in the left and right hemispheres can become decoupled after callosotomy.

Positron emission tomography studies suggest that the anatomical circuitry which enables the parietal areas to selectively modulate brain activity in other prestriate areas passes through the pulvinar nucleus of the thalamus. When one visual field contains an array with only one large target, while the other contains a target surrounded by distractors, there is evidence of increased metabolism specific to the thalamus of the side opposite the complex array. The act of filtering out the distractors or amplifying the target seems to produce a larger effect in the pulvinar of the opposite side than in other structures.[19]

Guiding and Controlling Search

Suppose you are asked to locate the vertical rectangle. Must you search all the target locations or can you confine your search to the vertical objects only? There is considerable evidence that search can be guided by information about the color or orientation or other non-locational features of the target.[20] How is this implemented in the brain? It seems that the recruitment and control of posterior brain areas, in this case, is supervised by an anatomically distinct system which has been called the anterior attention system.[7] In the study of attentional amplification of color, form or motion, mentioned above, there was evidence for activation of a frontal attentional system, but no parietal activation was found.[9] It thus appears that two different attentional systems serve as sources of activation for color or form (frontal areas) and for location (parietal), although both might enter and amplify activity within the visual system at the same site (for example, V4).

In guided search, selection by location and selection by color or form occur simultaneously with relatively little interference,[20] unlike the situation for location when the corpus callosum is intact in which attention cannot be shared between the two fields.[18] One speculative possibility would be that time sharing is possible when two anatomically distinct attentional sources are involved.

The frontal areas that serve to guide search appear to involve a network that includes at least portions of the basal ganglia and of the anterior cingulate gyrus.[7,21] The anterior portion of the cingulate gyrus appears to be involved in a wide range of activities that have been termed collectively "executive function".[21] In PET language studies, when subjects were required to name the use of familiar nouns (for example, pound to hammer), activation of the anterior cingulate along with left lateral areas were most prominent.[4,22] When subjects were required to respond to the ink color in which a conflicting color name was presented (Stroop effect) there was strong activation of the anterior cingulate along with prestriate color areas.[23,24] The detection of multiple color form or motion targets in comparison to passive viewing of the same stimuli also activated the anterior cingulate.[9] All of these situations involve selection of targets from competing inputs, which is considered a traditional role of attention. In the case of this area of the brain, the nature of the target does not seem to matter very much.

The term "executive" suggests two important overall functions. First, an executive is informed about the processes taking place within the organization. A system that would be related to our subjective experience of focal attention would clearly play this function for a subset of current (sensory) and stored (memory) information. There are reasons for relating anterior cingulate function to focal awareness of the target.[25] The strongest reason is that the intensity of cingulate activity tends to increase with the number of targets in a set of stimuli[3] and decreases with practice on any single stimulus set.[4] These findings correspond to cognitive theories linking focal attention to number and difficulty of target detection.[25]

A second function of an executive is to exercise some control over the system. The anatomy of the anterior cingulate provides pathways for connecting it to both the posterior parietal area and to anterior areas active during language tasks.[26] Working memory is generally thought to involve both a representation of past events and an executive system involved in sustaining and transforming this representation.[27] Recent PET (refs 28 and 29) and neurophysiological[30,31] studies show that lateral areas of the prefrontal cortex play a key role in holding online a representation of past events. Cellular recordings in the awake monkey indicate that cells within the dorsolateral prefrontal cortex maintain a representation of the spatial environment when monkeys have to hold in mind a location to which to move their eyes after the stimulus disappears.[24] Lateral areas of the frontal and posterior cortex are also active in studies when people must obtain a quick association to word stimuli.[3,4,22] While specialized areas of the prefrontal cortex appear to hold the relevant information on-line, the anterior cingulate is playing a role in the executive functions of awareness and control discussed in cognitive studies and often found impaired in subjects with frontal damage.

Concluding Remarks

Recent brain-imaging and neurophysiological data indicate that attention is neither a property of a single brain area, nor that of the entire brain. While attentional effects seem mediated by a common principle of attentional amplification at all levels of the cortical circuitry, the origins of these amplification effects are to be found in specialized cortical areas of the frontal and parietal lobes. These results represent substantial progress in the effort to determine how brain activity is regulated through attention. While many philosophical and practical issues remain in developing such an understanding, the new tools now available should provide the basis for the efforts still ahead.

Selected References

1   Wurtz, R. H., Goldberg, M. E. and Robinson, D. L. (1980) *Prog. Psychobiol. Physiol. Psychol.*, **9**, 43–83.
2   Posner, M. I. and Presti, D. (1987) *Trends Neurosci.*, **10**, 12–17.
3   Posner, M. I., Petersen, S. E., Fox, P. T. and Raichle, M. E. (1988) *Science*, **240**, 1627–31.
4   Raichle, M. E. et al., *Cerebral Cortex* (in press).

5   Treisman, A. and Sato, S. (1990) *J. Exp. Psychol.*, **17**, 652–76.
6   Felleman, D. J. and Van Essen, D. C. (1991) *Cerebral Cortex*, **1**, 1–47.
7   Posner, M. I. and Petersen, S. E. (1990) *Annu. Rev. Neurosci.*, **13**, 25–42.
8   Zeki, S. et al. (1991) *J. Neurosci.*, **11**, 641–9.
9   Corbetta, M., Miezin, F. M., Dobmeyer, S., Schulman, G. L. and Petersen, S. E. (1991) *J. Neurosci.*, **11**, 2338–2402.
10   Roland, P. E. (1984) *Human Neurobiol.*, **3**, 1–12.
11   Luck, S. J., Fan, S. and Hillyard, S. A. (1993) *J. Cog. Neurosci.*, **5**, 188–98.
12   Luck, S. J. et al. *J. Exp. Psychol.*, (in press).
13   Mangun, G. R., Hillyard, S. A. and Luck, S. J. (1983) in *Attention and Performance*, xiv, pp. 219–44, MIT Press.
14   Moran, J. and Desimone, R. (1985) *Science*, **229**, 782–4.
15   Chelazzi, L., Miller, E. K., Duncan, J. and Desimone, R. (1993) *Nature*, **363**, 345–7.
16   Posner, M. I. (1988) *Master Lectures in Clinical Neuropsychology and Brain Function: Research, Measurement and Practice*, pp. 171–202, American Psychology Association.
17   Corbetta, M., Miezin, F. M., Shulman, G. L. and Petersen, S. E. (1993) *J. Neurosci.*, **13**, 1202–26.
18   Luck, S. J., Hillyard, S. A., Mangun, G. R. and Gazzaniga, M. S. (1989) *Nature*, **342**, 543–5.
19   LaBerge, D. and Buchsbaum, M. S. (1990) *J. Neurosci.*, **10**, 613–19.
20   Wolfe, J. K. M., Cave, K. R. and Franzel, S. L. (1989) *J. Exper. Psychol.*, **15**, 419–33.
21   Vogt, B. A., Finch, D. M. and Olson, C. R. (1992) *Cerebral Cortex*, **2**, 435–43.
22   Fiez, J. A. and Petersen, S. E. (1993) *Psychol. Sci.*, **5**, 287–93.
23   Pardo, J. V., Pardo, P., Janer, K. and Raichle, M. E. (1990) *Proc. Natl Acad. Sci. USA*, **87**, 256–9.
24   Bench, C. J. et al. (1993) *Neuropsychologia*, **31**, 907–31.
25   Posner, M. I. and Rothbart, M. K. (1992) in *The Neuropsychol. of Conscious.*, pp. 91–112, Academic Press.
26   Goldman-Rakic, P. S. (1988) *Annu. Rev. Neurosci.*, **11**, 137–56.
27   Baddeley, A. D. (1990) *Working Memory*, Oxford University Press.
28   Jonides, J. et al. (1993) *Nature*, 623–35.
29   Paulesu, E., Frith, C. D. and Frackowiak, R. S. (1993) *Nature*, **363**, 342–5.
30   Funahashi, S., Chafee, M. V. and Goldman-Rakic, P. (1993) *Nature*, **365**, 753–6.
31   Wilson, F. A. W., Scalaidhe, S. P. O. and Goldman-Rakic, P. (1993) *Science*, **260**, 1955–8.

Attentional Resolution and the Locus of Visual Awareness

Sheng He, Patrick Cavanagh, and James Intriligator

Visual spatial resolution is limited by factors ranging from optics to neuronal filters in the visual cortex,[1, 2] but it is not known to what extent it is also limited by the resolving power of attention. To investigate this, we studied adaptation to lines of specific orientation, a process that occurs in primary visual cortex.[3] When a single grating is presented in the periphery of the visual-field, human observers are aware of its orientation, but when it is flanked by other similar gratings ('crowding'), its orientation becomes impossible to discern.[4,5] Nevertheless, we show that orientation-specific adaptation is not affected by crowding, implying that spatial resolution is limited by an attentional filter acting beyond the primary visual cortex. Consistent with this, we find that attentional resolution is greater in the lower than in the upper visual field, whereas there is no corresponding asymmetry in the primary visual cortex. We suggest that the attentional filter acts in one or more higher visual cortical areas to restrict the availability of visual information to conscious awareness.[6]

A high-contrast adapting grating patch of one cycle per degree was presented 25° above the point of visual fixation. When presented alone, the orientation of the grating was clearly visible even at contrasts of less than 10%. When the same adapting grating was presented fourth in a linear array of five similar grating patches (maximizing the crowding effect[5,7]), subjects identified the orientation at chance levels, even with unlimited viewing time at full contrast (fig. 11.1a). We tested whether there was any orientation-specific analysis of the grating when the subjects were unaware of the orientation. Observers were adapted to a target grating presented alone or with flanking gratings (one above and three below the target), and then were tested on their ability to identify the orientation of a grating either at the same or orthogonal orientation presented at the target position (fig. 11.1a). When observers were adapted to a crowded grating (and were unaware of its orientation), the contrast thresholds in tests in which the grating was of the same orientation as the adapting grating were roughly 2 to 3 times higher than for tests using the orthogonal orientation (see fig.

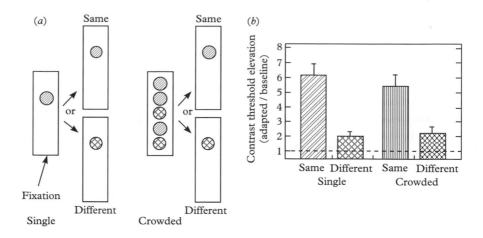

Figure 11.1   Orientation-selective adaptation when subjects could and could not perceive the orientation of the adapting grating (fourth grating from the fixation point). In all experiments, stimuli were circular patches of sinusoidal gratings. *a*, Contrast thresholds were measured for three conditions: adapted to a single grating; adapted to the fourth stimulus in a linear array of five; no adaptation (baseline). The adapting grating and test grating were centred 25° above the point of visual fixation. The radius for each grating was 2.67°, and the centre-to-centre distance between neighbouring gratings was 6.67°. Except in the baseline condition, subjects were exposed to a continuous 5-s adaptation, 300-ms interstimulus interval, 180-ms test cycle, during which threshold contrast for the test grating was set by the subjects. Settings were not recorded during the first 10 cycles to ensure that subjects could achieve a stable adapted state. For each adapting–testing cycle, the orientation of the first grating was randomly chosen to be either 45° or 135°, and the orientations of the other distractors were successively rotated by 90°. Orientation of the fourth target grating was predetermined and remained the same for each session. *b*, Threshold contrast elevation after adaptation, compared with baseline contrast threshold before adaptation. Mean of four subjects; error bars show s.e.m. The difference between same adapt–test orientation and different adapt–test orientation represents the strength of orientation selective adaptation. The data show that a flanked grating (orientation not perceivable) and a single grating (orientation readily perceivable) were almost equally effective in orientation-specific adaptation.

11.1*b*). We found this same orientation-specific threshold elevation when observers were adapted to a single grating, and were aware of its orientation. There is a clear dissociation between perceptual awareness of orientation and orientation-specific adaptation (located at or beyond the primary visual cortex (area V1), the first site of orientation processing). The results indicate that visual awareness, and the 'crowding' that blocks it, occur after orientation analysis in the visual information processing stream. Others have reported that unresolvable high-frequency gratings can produce orientation-specific adaptation,[2] and orientation information can be used for segmentation without the explicit knowledge of the subject.[8] Our results indicate further that activation of neurons in V1 is insufficient for conscious perception.[6]

Conventionally, the reduced sensitivity to targets embedded in a field of similar items is termed 'lateral masking' and is often attributed to lateral inhibition between neighbouring neurons at early stages of processing.[9] We show that the information that is inaccessible to perceptual awareness because of crowding, is in fact processed by the primary visual cortex without disruption, ruling out the simplest sensory lateral masking explanation. We believe that this crowding effect reflects the limited resolution of the spatial attention mechanism.

The crowding effect seemed stronger in the upper visual field than in the lower field. Lesion[10] and functional magnetic resonance imaging (fMRI)[11,12] studies show that human primary visual cortex devotes roughly the same area to the representations of the upper and lower visual fields. Consequently, we would not expect any asymmetry in crowding effects if performance were determined principally in the primary visual cortex. To test this prediction, we compared performance in the upper and lower visual fields directly in an orientation discrimination task. Rather than maximizing the crowding effect with a radial stimulus organization[5,7] as in the first experiment, we arranged the stimuli horizontally to reduce crowding and to expose any modulation by visual field. The stimulus consisted of either a single grating patch or the same grating patch flanked by four similar patches, two on each side (fig. 11.2a). The target grating was tilted either to the right (45°) or to the left (135°). Subjects were asked to fixate a point above the stimulus pattern in half of the trials, and a point the same distance below it on the other half. The stimulus was presented briefly (180 ms), and subjects were asked to press one of two keys to indicate which way the central grating was tilted, guessing if necessary. The results (fig. 11.2b) reveal a strong asymmetry in performance: crowding reduced the accuracy of report significantly more when the target was in the upper visual field than when it was in the lower field.

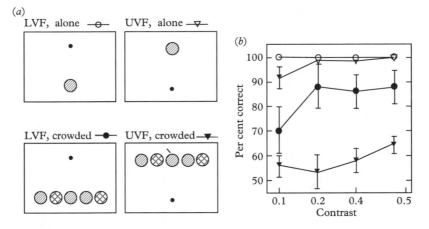

Figure 11.2 Discrimination of grating orientation. *a*, Examples of four stimulus conditions. All gratings were 1 cycle per degree. Grating patches had a 2° radius, and the centre of the target grating was 20° from the point of fixation. In the crowding condition, the centre-to-centre distance between neighbouring gratings was 5°. Stimuli were presented for 180ms. Subjects were instructed to always report (and hence attend to) only the orientation of the grating patch in the middle, ignoring the flanking gratings when they appeared. Visual field positions were fixed during each session, and varied between sessions. Stimuli were presented at 4 different contrast levels (target and flanking stimuli always had the same contrast). *b*, Mean ± s.e.m. accuracy from three subjects. Symbols correspond to the conditions depicted in *a*. Whereas subjects could see the grating orientation almost equally well in both the upper and lower visual field (open symbols), their ability to identify the orientation of the target grating was much more affected by flanking stimuli when presented in the upper visual field (filled triangles) than in the lower visual field (filled circles).

If crowding is a result of insufficient spatial resolution of attention, then performance in tasks that require more focused attention should be better when the stimulus is presented in the lower visual field than in the upper visual field, whereas tasks that demand little focused attention should show little or no asymmetry. Visual search tasks provide examples of both attentional categories. Many studies have shown that searches for feature-defined targets (where the target has the odd feature in an otherwise homogeneous array) require little focused attention, whereas searches for conjunction targets (where targets and distractors share features but differ in how they are combined) often require focused attention.[13] We used two simplified versions of these tasks. Five items were presented along a vertical line above or below the point of visual fixation. In half of the trials, the item in the centre was the prespecified target, and in the other trials, the central item was a distractor. In the feature detection condition, the target was a line angled at 45° among 135° distractors, and in the conjunction detection condition, the target was a vertical and a horizontal line arranged in a 'T' shape rotated by 90° to the right, with distractors of the same shape in the three other orientations (upright, upside down, 90° rotation to the left). The target and distractors all contain the same features and are distinguished only by the conjunction of their positions (fig. 11.3*a*). In the feature detection task, subjects performed equally well when targets were presented in the upper and lower visual field, whereas in the conjunction detection task, subjects showed the predicted, improved detection ability in the lower visual field (fig. 11.3*b*).

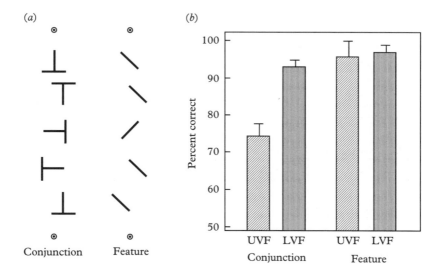

Figure 11.3   *a*, Schematic examples of stimuli used in the feature detection and the conjunction detection condition. Subjects attended to the central stimulus, and responded to the presence or absence of the prespecified target (in this example, the 45° bar is the target in the feature case and the T tilted 90° clockwise is the conjunction target). Line segments in both cases subtended 2° and vertical centre-to-centre distance between elements was 3°. To reduce the contribution of global shape recognition on detection ability, the horizontal position of each element was randomly centred 1° to the left or right of the vertical midline. Stimuli were presented for 150 ms and feedback about whether the response was correct was given in each trial. *b*, Accuracy data collected in four conditions. Each bar is the mean ± s.e.m. of 4 subjects. Conjunction detection suffers a large asymmetry between upper (UVF) and lower visual field (LVF), whereas feature detection is equally good in both the upper and lower visual field.

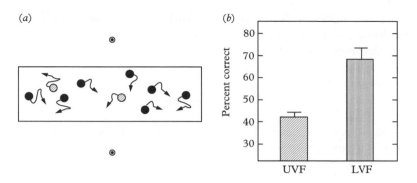

Figure 11.4 Attentional tracking task and accuracy data. *a*, Subjects fixated 10° above or below the centre of a 6.6° × 30° area in which nine green moving discs were presented. At the start of each trial, two of the discs were changed to red for 1s, and then turned back to green. Subjects were required to track these two discs with their attention while keeping their gaze steady on the fixation dot. After 5 s, all nine discs stopped moving, and subjects were asked to identify the target discs. Chance performance was 22.2%. *b*, Subjects performed much better when the discs were presented in the lower visual field. Mean ± s.e.m. of 4 subjects.

Finally we used an attentional tracking task that places strong and constant demands on the attentional system.[14,15] Subjects were presented with 9 green discs moving randomly in a rectangular area in the upper or lower visual field. At the start of each trial, two discs were identified as targets by briefly turning red. They then turned back to green and subjects were asked to track the two targets with their attention while fixating a central dot. At the end of 5 seconds, all discs stopped moving and subjects were required to report which were the original targets. Tracking performance was significantly better in the lower visual field than in the upper visual field (fig. 11.4).

Without distractors, perception of spatial details is limited by conventional visual resolution. However, when several items are presented, perception of the spatial details of a particular item seems to depend on the ability of attentional processes to isolate the item. This suggests that attentional resolution limits the access of spatial details to perceptual awareness. We believe that the frequently reported degradation of spatial information when several items are present in the visual field may be a result of this limitation.[16,17] The asymmetry in attentional resolution between the upper and lower visual field may also contribute to the reported lower visual field advantage for the perception of global shape in tasks involving hierarchical structures where several elements are used.[18–20]

We attempted to locate the cortical area that mediates visual attention and limits the final access to our conscious vision. We show that stimuli not available to conscious perception could produce undiminished orientation-specific adaptation, a process that first occurs in primary visual cortex. Clearly, neuronal activity in the primary visual cortex is not sufficient for conscious perception. This is further supported by the fact that although there is little anatomical asymmetry between the upper and lower visual fields in human primary visual cortex,[10–12] crowding and other manipulations of attentional load produced a large asymmetry favouring the lower visual field. The same holds for V2 as well. The dorsal parietal system has classically been associated with attentional processes[21, 22] and the projections from early visual areas to the parietal regions are more numerous for the lower visual field than the upper field.[23] We suggest that the dorsal parietal area may control attentional resolution and the information entering our conscious vision.

Acknowledgments

We thank K. Nakayama, N. Rubin, M. Chun, C. Moore, F. Verstraten and C. Koch for useful discussions. This work was supported by NIH grants to S.H. and P.C.

References

1   Campbell, F. W. & Gubisch, R. W. *J. Physiol.*, **186**, 558–78 (1966).
2   He, S., Smallman, H. S. & MacLeod, D. I. A. *Invest. Ophthalmol. Vis. Sci. Suppl.*, **36**, 2010 (1995).
3   Blakemore, C. B. & Campbell, F. W. *J. Physiol.*, **203**, 237–60 (1969).
4   Bouma, H. *Nature*, **226**, 177–8 (1970).
5   Toet, A. & Levi, D. M. *Vision Res.*, **32**, 1349–57 (1992).
6   Crick, F. & Koch, C. *Nature*, **375**, 121–3 (1995).
7   Chambers, L. & Wolford, G. *Bull. Psychonom. Soc.*, **21**, 459–61 (1983).
8   Kolb, F. C. & Braun, J. *Nature*, **377**, 336–8 (1995).
9   Chastain, G. *Psychol. Res.*, **45**, 147–56 (1983).
10 Horton, J. C. & Hoyt, W. F. *Archives Ophthalmol.*, **109**, 816–24 (1991).
11 Sereno, M. I. et al. *Science*, **268**, 889–93 (1995).
12 DeYoe, E. A. et al. *Proc. Natl Acad. Sci. USA*, **93**, 2382–6 (1988).
13 Treisman, A. Q. *J. Exp. Psychol. Human Exp. Psychol.*, **40**, 201–37 (1988).
14 Pylyshyn, Z. W. & Storm, R. W. *Spatial Vis.*, **3**, 179–97 (1988).
15 Intriligator, J., Nakayama, K. & Cavanagh, P. *Invest. Ophthalmol. Vis. Sci. Suppl.*, **32**, 1040 (1991).
16 Butler, B. E. & Currie, A. *Psychol. Res.*, **48**, 201–9 (1986).
17 Taylor, S. G. & Brown, D. R. *Percept. Psychophys.*, **12**, 97–9 (1972).
18 Previc, F. H. *Behav. Brain Sci.*, **13**, 519–75 (1990).
19 Christman, S. D. *Bull. Psychonom. Soc.*, **31**, 275–8 (1993).
20 Rubin, N., Nakayama, K. & Shapley, R. *Science*, **271**, 651–3 (1996).
21 Gazzaniga, M. S. & Ladavas, E. in *Neurophysiological and Neuropsychological Aspects of Spatial Neglect* (ed. Jeannerod, M.) 203–13 (Elsevier, Amsterdam, 1987).
22 Posner, M. I. *Neuropsychol. Rehab.*, **4**, 183–7 (1994).
23 Maunsell, J. H. & Newsome, W. T. *Annu. Rev. Neurosci.*, **10**, 363–401 (1987).

Information Processing of Visual Stimuli in an 'Extinguished' Field

Bruce T. Volpe, Joseph E. Ledoux, and
Michael S. Gazzaniga

Lesions of the right parieto-occipital cortex in man produce a variety of behavioural disturbances which interfere with the detection of, and orientation to, external stimuli.[1] One striking example is extinction to double simultaneous stimulation (DSS), in which presentation of a single stimulus in any area of the visual field results in its accurate description, but lateralized simultaneous presentation of two stimuli, one in each field, results in the verbal description of only the stimulus in the right visual field (RVF).[2] While extinction to DSS can also be demonstrated in other (non-visual) sensory modalities,[3] and is occasionally seen following left-hemisphere lesions[4] our concern here is with visual extinction to DSS following right parieto-occipital lesions, whose precise nature is poorly understood although a variety of theories have been proposed to account for it.[5-7] One of the critical, yet unexplored questions about extinction concerns the fate of the extinguished stimulus. The following observations demonstrate that although the extinguished stimulus often goes completely unnoticed by the patient, the patients are able to utilize the extinguished stimulus in an interfield comparison task. Accurate same/different judgements between the visual fields could be made in situations in which the patients did not know the identity of, and at times even denied the presence of, the left field stimulus.

The subjects were four right-handed female patients ranging in age from 56 to 70 years who were selected for study by routine neurologic examination. Although all patients had full visual field capacity when tested by a standard perimetry mapping with a single 1-cm, white object, each patient extinguished LVF* stimuli on DSS,* and left-sided touch stimuli under double simultaneous tactile stimulation. Each patient was alert and oriented and without language disturbance. Patients were tested on the third hospital

---

*Abbreviations: LVF, left visual field; DSS, double simultaneous stimulation.

day, before therapeutic manoeuvres (two cases). Patient no. 3 received steroids over the 36 hours before testing. Patient no. 4 had a persistent defect that remained unchanged during the weeks following surgery. Angiographic analysis and/or computerized tomography[8] revealed that all four patients had tumours in the right parietal lobe. (Cerebral angiography is a standard neuroradiologic procedure in which contrast material is injected into each discrete arterial system of the brain. This procedure aids the neurologist in diagnosis and the neurosurgeon in treatment. Computerized tomography is a brain imaging technique.) Neuropathologic analysis of tissue biopsies confirmed the clinical diagnosis of tumour in all patients.

In the test conditions, all tasks involved the lateralized presentation of visual stimuli in a manner previously reported.[9] All experiments were carried out in a room in which it was not possible to control the level of background lighting completely. The room was generally as dim as possible, but allowed the experimenter to record the results. The subject was seated 1 m from an opaque screen and instructed to fixate on a dot in the centre of the screen. By means of a standard slide projector fitted with an electronic shutter, stimuli were presented 3° to the right and/or left of fixation for 150 ms. The stimuli were positive photographic slides of three- or four-letter words or simple line-drawn pictures that were rear-projected onto a screen, which the subject faced. A representative series of word stimuli subtended 2° of horizontal visual angle and 5° of vertical visual angle. Because of the line-drawn nature of the picture and word stimuli, measurements of luminosity varied less than 0.5% on all bilateral simultaneously projected trials irrespective of similarity or difference. Due to restraints regarding the medical care of these patients, testing sessions were 30 minutes in duration, and the variability in the number of trials among the patients reflects this primary factor.

Each patient was seated in front of the screen and after fixation on the centre point, the words or pictures were presented randomly to either the left or right visual field. All patients named the stimuli with high accuracy when singly presented to either visual field (see table 12.1).

The next series of tachistoscopic test trials was preceded by a group of illustrative trials where words or pictures were, simultaneously, bilaterally projected to the right and left of the exation point. The patients were shown several such examples under prolonged exposure conditions (5–10 s) so they could identify both stimuli. They were

Table 12.1   Single visual field naming

| | Visual field | |
| | | |
Patient no.	Left	Right
1	1.00 (15)	1.00 (12)
2	0.94 (16)	0.89 (9)
3	0.86 (14)	1.00 (15)
4	0.91 (33)	0.88 (33)

The proportion of trials that were correctly named by each patient in each visual field is shown. Numbers in parentheses represent total number of trials presented to each visual field. Performance differences between the visual fields were not significant ($t(3) = 1.12, P < 0.4$). Variation in total number of trials presented to each patient is described in the text.

Table 12.2   Same/different judgement with double simultaneous visual field presentation

Patient no.	Same/different judgements	'Different' trials correct	'Same' trials correct
1	1.00 (17)	1.00 (7)	1.00 (10)
2	0.88 (26)	0.88 (16)	0.90 (10)
3	0.95 (39)	0.96 (25)	0.93 (14)
4	0.90 (68)	0.89 (35)	0.91 (33)

Proportion of same/different judgements that were correct is shown. Correct proportions for trials judged as 'same' and 'different' are separately indicated. Numbers in parentheses represent total number of trials. Each patient compared the bilaterally projected stimuli with high accuracy, and errors occurred with equal frequency on the 'same' and 'different' trials.

then told that on each subsequent trial there would be two stimuli, one on each side on exation, and that their task was simply to judge whether the two stimuli were the 'same' or 'different'. In addition to representing quite different items on the 'different' trials, the simultaneously flashed picture stimuli bore no semantic relationships to one another (for example, bicycle and comb). The words flashed on the 'different' trials were three or four letters in length, semantically unrelated, and spelled differently, with, at most, only a single similar letter (HOT and WON for example). On these bilateral DSS trials all patients performed both the 'same' and 'different' comparison with high accuracy (see table 12.2). Proportion of same/different judgements that were correct is shown. Correct proportions for trials judged as 'same' and 'different' are separately indicated. Numbers in parentheses represent total number of trials. Each patient compared the bilaterally projected stimuli with high accuracy, and errors occurred with equal frequency on the 'same' and 'different' trials.

After verbally reporting in the 'same/different' test situation, the patients were then asked to respond again and name the stimuli. On the trials in which the stimuli were identical, naming of the item in the LVF was an easily accomplished deduction from naming the RVF stimulus. On the 'same' response trials that were correct, there were no LVF naming errors. On the trials in which the stimuli were different, the LVF stimulus could not be deduced from the RVF stimulus. Patients nos 1 and 2 could not name the left visual field stimuli, although they had performed accurately on the 'same/different' judgements. In fact, during bilateral simultaneous projection, these two patients could not name any of the left visual field stimuli (table 12.3), and asserted

Table 12.3   LVF naming after same/different judgements on double simultaneous visual field presentation trials

Patient no.	Same/different judgements	LVF naming in 'different' trials
1	1.00 (17)	0.00 (7)
2	0.88 (26)	0.00 (16)
3	0.95 (39)	0.48 (25)
4	0.90 (68)	0.23 (35)

The proportion of correct 'same/different' judgements and proportion of 'different' trials in which LVF stimulus was correctly named are shown. Numbers in parentheses represent total number of trials. The accuracy of the 'same/different' judgements was significantly greater than the accuracy of LVF naming ($t(3) = 3.53, P < 0.05$).

further that the task was 'silly', since there was no stimulus in the LVF with which to compare the RVF stimulus. Patients nos 3 and 4 performed as accurately as the previous two on the 'same/different' judgements, but were able to name some of the left visual field stimuli on the critical 'different' trials (table 12.3). Although these latter two patients were more often aware of the presence and nature of the LVF stimuli than the first two patients, all patients' accuracy on 'same/different' judgements was statistically greater than their accuracy at naming the LVF stimulus ($t(3) = 3.53, P < 0.05$).

These experimental observations focused on the residual cognitive abilities of four patients with right parietal lesions. Manipulation of exposure duration below 250 ms, the use of single digits, and the use of nonsense pictures and nonsense syllables did not alter the pattern of results. The patients uniformly made accurate judgements when comparing information simultaneously presented to both visual fields, in spite of their inability to verbally characterize with a similar level of accuracy the left visual field information. These data bear relation to the results of studies showing that under certain test conditions normal subjects can be influenced by information they frequently are unable to identify.[10–13]

Our patients responded to information presented to the extinction field in two ways. In some instances, especially with patients 3 and 4, they felt that something had appeared in the LVF, but they were unable to characterize it. In other instances, as with patients 1 and 2, they were completely unaware that anything had been presented in the LVF. Yet, it is clear that some features of the extinguished stimuli were attended to and perceived, for the 'same/different' judgements were accurately made on the basis of these stimuli. It thus becomes difficult to assert that the so-called extinguished stimulus is extinguished at all. Rather, this disturbance seems to involve a selective

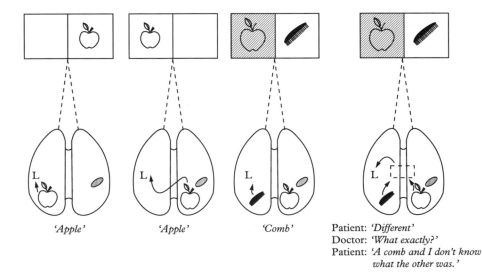

'Apple'   *'Apple'*   *'Comb'*   Patient: *'Different'*
                                                                Doctor: *'What exactly?'*
                                                                Patient: *'A comb and I don't know
                                                                what the other was.'*

Figure 12.1   This composite picture represents each of four experimental parameters. The two pictures on the left describe the identical left and right single visual field naming trials. The two pictures on the right describe a verbal response during two simultaneous bilateral visual field trials, in the 'same/different' paradigm.

breakdown in a mechanism through which information which is attended to and perceived reaches some level of neuronal processing which allows for verbal description, if not conscious awareness (see fig. 12.1).

Parietal lobe extinction thus offers the possibility of observing, under appropriate test conditions, a breakdown in the flow of information between conscious and non-conscious mental systems. The stimulus comparison task in our study appears to have been carried out at a post-perceptual, pre-verbal level, with only the resultant comparison entering consciousness. Extension of this paradigm may provide a mechanism for studying non-conscious information processing in man.

References

1   Friedland, R. P. & Weinstein, E. A. in *Hemi-Inattention and Hemisphere Specialization* (eds Weinstein, E. A. & Friedland, R. P.) 1–31 (Raven, New York, 1977).

2   Bender, M. B. in *Hemi-Inattention and Hemisphere Specialization* (eds Weinstein, E. A. & Friedland, R. P.) 107–10 (Raven, New York, 1977).

3   Critchley, M. *Brain*, **72**, 538–61 (1949).

4   Denny-Brown, D. & Banker, B. *Archs neurol. Psychiat.*, **71**, 302–13 (1954).

5   Eidelberg, E. & Schwartz, A. S. *Brain*, **94**, 91–108 (1971).

6   Heilman, K. M. & Valenstein, E. *Neurology*, **22**, 660–4 (1972).

7   Battersby, W. S., Bender, M. B. & Pollack, M. *Brain*, **79**, 68–93 (1956).

8   New, P. F. J. & Scott, W. R. *Computerized Tomography of the Brain* (Williams and Wilkins, Baltimore, 1975).

9   Gazzaniga, M. S. *The Bisected Brain* (Appleton-Century-Croft, New York, 1970).

10   Treisman, A. M. *J. Verb. Learning Verb. Behav.*, **3**, 449–59 (1964).

11   Lewis, J. L. *J. Exp. Psych.*, **85**, 225–8 (1970).

12   MacKay, D. G. *Q. J. Exp. Psych.*, **25**, 22–8 (1973).

13   Lackner, J. R. & Garrett, M. F. *Cognition*, **1**, 359–74 (1973).

Negative Priming between Pictures and Words in a Selective Attention Task: Evidence for Semantic Processing of Ignored Stimuli

Steven P. Tipper and Jon Driver

The study of visual selective attention is concerned with how organisms select particular objects for action and successfully ignore other objects potentially capable of controlling action. This problem can be subdivided into two issues. The first issue is the role that attention plays in the perceptual processes that produce internal representations of the visual environment with which the organism interacts. Two opposing theories try to explain this role. The precategorical view (Broadbent, 1982; Johnston and Dark, 1986) holds that attention is critical for the perceptual processes involved in object recognition. Thus, if an object is ignored, only low-level features such as color are encoded, and the object's identity is not internally represented. The alternative, postcategorical selection theory (Allport, 1980; Deutsch and Deutsch, 1963; Van der Heijden, 1981) holds that attention plays a limited role in object recognition. If an object is familiar, with well-established internal representations, the perceptual system will encode the identity of the object whether or not it is attended.

The second issue concerns the mechanism of selection. Precategorical selection theories were predicated upon filter models (Broadbent, 1958; 1971; 1982) in which objects were selected on a physical basis and only then received further "semantic" processing. Kahneman and Treisman (1984) argued that postcategorical selection theories underspecify the mechanisms that allow an organism to direct its actions to one object from a set, because equivalent information is available for both relevant and irrelevant objects. Two models of postcategorical selection have been proposed. In the passive decay model, the activation level of the representation of the relevant object is maintained until irrelevant activation has passively decayed. In this model, selection is selective remembering (Van der Heijden, 1981). Alternatively, Neill (1977) proposed that representations of ignored objects may be actively inhibited.

Tipper (1985) broached these two issues. To examine whether passive decay or active inhibition occurs, it was necessary to observe the fate of the representations of the ignored object subsequent to the initial encounter with that object. A priming paradigm was therefore employed. Subjects were presented with two pictures (the prime display) and told by means of a physical cue (color) which to select and name and which to ignore. Both pictures were above threshold, and thus both were capable of controlling action. Shortly afterward a probe display, similarly containing two pictures, was presented. In the crucial condition, the selected picture in the probe display was identical to the ignored picture in the previous prime display. Tipper predicted that if the representations of ignored pictures are inhibited during selection, then processing of a subsequent picture requiring these same representations would be impaired. This prediction was supported; there was a reaction-time cost in naming the probe picture for the condition described, relative to the control condition. This effect was termed negative priming.

Negative priming was also observed when the ignored picture was not physically identical to the probe picture, but was in the same category (e.g., cat–dog). This was tentatively attributed to a process of spreading inhibition in semantic memory (Roediger and Neely, 1982). In terms of the postcategorical selection theories, the categorical negative priming was interpreted as evidence that ignored objects are processed beyond the level of physical properties to that of categorical representations, and that inhibition takes place at or beyond this level. (See Schneider and Fisk, 1984, for similar views of automatic categorical processing and inhibition of ignored information.)

The claim that categorical internal representations are achieved independent of attention may, however, be premature. Rosch, Mervis, Gray, Johnson, and Boyes-Braem (1976) and Sperber, McCauley, Ragain, and Weil (1979) pointed out that pictures within the same semantic category have many features in common (see also Snodgrass and McCollough, 1985). Examination of figure 13.1, which contains examples of the figures employed by Tipper (1985), would tend to support these suggestions. Clearly the pictures depicting objects within the semantic category of *tool* have features and overall shape in common, relative to objects in other categories, such as *furniture*. It is feasible, therefore, that the influence between pictures within a category is

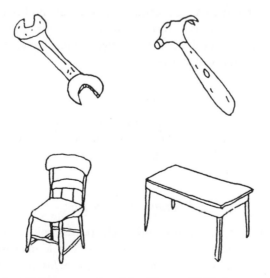

Figure 13.1 Examples of figures employed by Tipper (1985) demonstrating the structural similarity between pictures within the same semantic category.

at the physical-feature level of representation rather than at an abstract categorical level.

The present experiment attempts to identify the level of internal representation achieved by ignored objects, while controlling the confounding variable of physical properties. To this end, priming effects are observed between objects represented in different symbolic domains (pictures and words) that have *no* features in common. As Anderson (1980) pointed out, pictures are an analog representation that reflects the physical properties of the objects they represent. Words, on the other hand, are arbitrary symbolic representations. Therefore, any priming effects observed between words and pictures must be beyond the physical level of internal representation; the effect must be at some abstract semantic level. Such priming effects would support postcategorical theories of attention, and suggest that inhibition is late in the sequence of processes from perception to action (Tipper and Cranston, 1985).

Method

The method for the experiment described here is based on that of Tipper (1985, Experiment 3). The essential difference is that in this study priming effects were observed across symbolic domain (from pictures to words, and from words to pictures), preventing any possible contribution from physical similarity. For comparison, we included within-domain priming conditions (from pictures to pictures, and from words to words) in which physical similarity between prime and probe clearly exists. As in previous research (Allport, Tipper, and Chmiel, 1985; Tipper, 1985), priming effects were observed both for ignored stimuli and for stimuli selected for response. In the latter case, any priming effects are typically facilitatory (e.g., Sperber et al., 1979). The subjects' task was to give the superordinate category of the selected stimulus (e.g., *animal* in response to *dog*). This categorization response was chosen in an attempt to maximize the chance of observing negative priming across symbolic domains. In the facilitatory priming literature (D. I. Irwin and Lupker, 1983), priming between words and pictures is more robust with this categorization response than with naming. Moreover, we have evidence that negative priming between words is obtained with categorization but not with naming.

Subjects

Fifty-six subjects (36 females) from the long-term University of Oxford subject pool were each paid £1.50 to participate. They ranged in age from 18 to 32, and had normal color vision (as determined by the Ishihari color test) and normal or corrected-to-normal visual acuity in both eyes.

Apparatus and materials

A six-field tachistoscope having two three-field power units (Electronic Developments Ltd) was used for stimulus presentation. A hand-held microswitch was used by subjects for starting each trial. A voice key and a millisecond timer (Behavioral Research and Development Electronics Ltd) were used to measure oral categorization latencies.

The 10 pictures used to create the experimental stimuli were adjusted with a reducing photocopier to be approximately equal in size. Visual angles ranged between 4.7° and 7.9°. They were drawn with Bic biro pens. The related pairs were cat–dog, chair–table, trumpet–guitar, hammer–spanner (wrench), and hand–foot. The selected picture was drawn in red and superimposed over the ignored green picture. The superimposed pictures of a given display were always in different categories. (For examples of superimposed objects in selective attention tasks, see Goldstein and Fink, 1981; J. Irwin, 1979; Rock and Gutman, 1981; Tipper, 1985.) Each picture was superimposed over every other picture employed in the experiment, except for the other picture in its own category, yielding 80 displays. Twenty of these displays were selected to be the probe displays; thus each picture appeared twice as the selected picture. This limited set of probes was employed so that each priming condition was observed within the same stimulus display. The remaining displays constituted the prime displays, 10 of which were used for practice trials and 50 for experimental trials.

The 10-word stimuli were simply the names of the pictures, and prime and probe displays were prepared in a similar way. The selected red word partially overlapped the ignored green word such that it was equally likely to be above and to the right, above and to the left, below and to the right, or below and to the left. The visual angles of the words were 1.3° vertical and 3.3° to 7.5° horizontal.

Design

The experiment manipulated three independent variables. The first was between subjects: half of the subjects received between-domain priming, that is, picture displays as primes and word displays as probes (picture–word) or word primes and picture probes (word–picture), and half received within-domain priming (word–word or picture–picture). The second between-subjects variable was whether the probe was a word or a picture. In all four groups the subject was to select and categorize a red stimulus, while ignoring an overlapping green stimulus. The difference between the groups was whether the subjects selected pictures, words, a picture and then a word, or

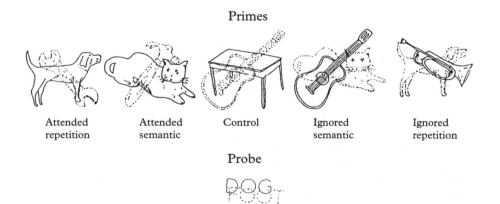

Primes

Attended   Attended   Control   Ignored   Ignored
repetition   semantic   semantic   repetition

Probe

Figure 13.2   Examples of the priming and probe displays in the picture–word group. The lines depicted as solid were red (selected) and those depicted as broken were green (ignored).

a word and then a picture. Assignment of the subjects to these four groups was random. There were 14 subjects in each group.

The third independent variable, priming condition, was within subjects. The following description is of the picture–word group. The conditions were as follows (except as mentioned, other components of the displays were unrelated): *Attended repetition* (AR) – The selected prime picture had the same name as the selected probe word. *Attended semantic* (AS) – The selected prime picture was in the same category as the selected probe word. *Control* (C) – The selected and ignored prime pictures were both unrelated to the selected probe word. *Ignored semantic* (IS) – The ignored prime picture was in the same category as the selected probe word. *Ignored repetition* (IR) – The ignored prime picture had the same name as the selected probe word.

There were 20 trials in each condition. Each probe display appeared once in each condition. Stimulus presentation was randomized for each subject. Each experimental prime display appeared twice. Figure 13.2 provides examples of the stimuli and conditions in the picture–word group.

Procedure

The subjects were initially shown a series of five cards, each containing two pictures or two words in the within-domain groups or both sets of materials in the between-domain groups. The pictures and words were in their associate pairs on each card (e.g., cat–dog). Subjects were required simply to name each stimulus.

Tachistoscopic presentation was used to establish the appropriate masking stimulus onset asynchrony (SOA) for each subject. These durations were approximate minimum viewing times required to identify the selected picture and/or selected word in the absence of any other interfering or intervening task. Brief exposure durations and pattern masking were employed to reduce the possibility of switching attention to the ignored stimulus after selection of the attended stimulus, and also for compatibility with previous research (Allport et al., 1985; Tipper, 1985).

When the subject pressed the microswitch, a fixation cross appeared for 600 msec, followed by the superimposed selected and ignored pictures (or words); both were presented monoptically to the left eye. This was followed by a pattern mask to the left eye for 100 msec. All presentation fields in the tachistoscope were adjusted to be of equal luminance.

SOA was titrated for picture and word displays in separate blocks of trials for the subjects in the between-domain groups. Within each group, half the subjects underwent picture SOA setting followed by word SOA setting, and vice versa for the other half. Subjects in the within-domain groups received SOA setting only for the stimulus domain they would experience. Stimulus-mask SOA began at 10 msec and was increased using the method of ascending limits by 10-msec steps. The same picture (or word) display was repeatedly presented until subjects correctly named the red stimulus. The longest SOA for the five displays presented was recorded, and 5 msec was added to this figure. The resulting SOAs were then used throughout the experimental trials. Mean SOA was 118 msec (range 80–200) for the pictures and 125 msec (range 80–230) for the words.

The next stage consisted of the experimental trials. When the subject pressed the microswitch, he/she saw a series of events as follows: (1) A fixation cross was presented to the subject's left eye for 600 msec. (2) The prime display containing either a red line drawing superimposed on a green drawing or red word over a green word was displayed. This also was presented to the subject's left eye. (3) A pattern mask was presented for 100 msec to the left eye. (4) A fixation cross was presented to the right eye for 1,100 msec. (5) The probe display containing either pictures or words was presented to the right eye. (4) Finally, a pattern mask was presented for 100 msec to the right eye.

The subjects were informed that the stimuli would alternate between eyes. This alternation of presentation was included for compatibility with previous research (Tipper, 1985).

The subjects in the picture–word group were then given instructions concerning the stimulus sequence. They were told that they should correctly identify the first red picture, as they would have to recall its category shortly afterward. (For example, if the picture was of a dog, the subjects were to report the superordinate category of *animal*. The category labels to be used were explicitly stated: *animal, furniture, music, tool,* and *body*.) However, it was stressed that they should not overtly categorize the picture when it was presented. When the word probe appeared, the subjects were requested to categorize the red word as fast as possible. They were then asked to recall the category of the selected prime picture. The recall of the category of the selected prime was requested to ensure that the subjects attended to the red picture. The subjects were informed that trials counted only if they could correctly report the category of the red (selected) prime. Furthermore, the subjects were informed that green stimuli would also be present in the displays; they were instructed that these were irrelevant to the task and should be ignored. The same instructions were given to the subjects in the other three groups, accounting for the changes in stimuli.

The intertrial interval was approximately 15–20 seconds, during which time the subjects noted their own reaction times (RTs), thus receiving feedback on categorization latency performance; these were verified by the experimenter. The subjects were also informed of any errors. The initial 10 trials in this procedure were practice, although subjects were not informed of this.

The final stage, adapted from the procedures used by Rock and Gutman (1981) and Tipper (1985), was a test for the subjects' awareness of the ignored priming picture or word. On the last trial only, there was no probe picture or word to be categorized. It was replaced by a white card. As this blank white card was presented, subjects were asked the surprise question of what the previous green picture (or word) had been. Thus they were asked to recall any information that may have been available for conscious scrutiny at about the time when the probe would have been presented (see Tipper, 1985, for further details).

Results and Discussion

One subject who appeared to be unable to carry out the selection task (34% errors) was dropped from data analysis. In the catch trial recall task, 21% (3 subjects) were able to recall the ignored picture and 14% (2 subjects) recalled the ignored word in the between-domain groups. Similarly, 14% recalled the ignored picture and 21% recalled the word in the within-domain groups. As discussed by Tipper (1985), with this small set of stimuli repeatedly presented, there is an 11% chance of guessing the ignored stimulus. The observed recall in these groups is not above this chance level based on Fisher's exact test. Such failure to recall the ignored stimulus supports previous findings (Allport et al., 1985; Tipper, 1985) using the same catch trial methodology, and is consistent with previous research demonstrating that subjects cannot recognize ignored stimuli from such displays (Goldstein and Fink, 1981; Rock and Gutman, 1981; Tipper, 1985).

Errors for both recall of the selected prime and response to the selected probe are shown in table 13.1. Analysis of the prime recall errors produced no significant effects for any of the factors: between–within domain [$F(1, 52) = 2.6$], word–picture probe [$F(1, 52) = 0.831$], and priming conditions [$F(4, 208) = 0.758$]. Analysis of probe errors produced a similar pattern: between–within domain [$F(1, 52) = 0.257$], word–picture probe [$F(1, 52) = 0.047$], and priming condition [$F(4, 208) = 1.803$]. Further analysis compared the control condition with each of the priming conditions using the Wilcoxon test. No significant contrasts were revealed, which discounts a speed–accuracy interpretation of the RT data to be discussed.

Trimmed mean RT (minus the 5.2% extreme scores above two standard deviations) are also represented in table 13.1. RT was analyzed in a three-way mixed ANOVA. It should be noted that the analysis of RT with outliers included produced the same pattern of results as those to be reported.

The between-subjects factor of within–between domain was significant [$F(1, 52) = 4.18, p < 0.04$]. Overall mean RT was longer when subjects had to switch domain from prime to probe than when they remained within a symbolic domain (917 msec and 841 msec for between and within domains, respectively). The second between-subjects factor of word–picture probe was nonsignificant [$F(1, 52) = 0.90$]. The within-subjects priming factor was highly significant [$F(4, 208) = 196.183, p < 0.001$]. The only

Table 13.1   Mean reaction time to categorize probes and percent errors in recalling primes and categorizing probes

	Attended repetition	Attended semantic	Control	Ignored semantic	Ignored repetition
	Picture prime–word probe				
Reaction time (msec)	754	767	998	1023	1038
% Errors–prime	0.7	1.07	1.4	1.8	0.70
% Errors–probe	0.7	2.86	2.5	1.4	1.79
	Word prime–picture probe				
Reaction time (msec)	837	809	956	985	1005
% Errors–prime	1.8	2.5	2.5	2.5	0.4
% Errors–probe	2.1	1.1	3.2	3.57	1.4
	Word prime–word probe				
Reaction time (msec)	714	752	953	972	996
% Errors–prime	1.8	3.9	2.9	1.8	2.5
% Errors–probe	1.0	1.8	1.8	2.1	2.5
	Picture prime–picture probe				
Reaction time (msec)	701	745	828	875	873
% Errors–prime	2.1	1.8	0.7	3.2	4.3
% Errors–probe	0.7	2.5	1.4	.5	3.9

interaction that was significant was between word–picture probes and priming [F(4, 208) = 13.16, $p < 0.001$].

To examine the priming effects for each group, comparison of each of the priming conditions with the relevant control condition was undertaken by Wilcoxon test (the number of subjects demonstrating the effect from the total of 14 in each cell is also reported). All of the selected primes produced substantial facilitatory priming. In the picture–word group AR and AS were significant ($p < 0.01$: AR = 14 and AS = 14 subjects, showing facilitation), as they were for the word–picture group ($p < 0.01$: AR = 14 and AS = 12 subjects), the word–word group ($p < 0.01$: AR = 14 and AS = 13 subjects), and the picture–picture group ($p < 0.01$: AR = 14 and AS = 13 subjects).

The ignored primes produced clear evidence for negative priming. In the picture–word group both IS and IR were significant ($p < 0.02$: 11 and 12 subjects, respectively, showing negative priming). In the word–picture group IR produced significant negative priming ($p < 0.01$: 13 subjects), whereas IS was marginally significant ($p < 0.1$: 10 subjects). In the picture–picture group both IR and IS produced significant negative priming ($p < 0.01$: 12 and 11 subjects, respectively). Finally in the word–word group IR was significant ($p < 0.01$: 11 subjects), but IS was nonsignificant. No other comparisons were significant. Figure 13.3 summarizes all the above priming effects.

The observation of facilitatory priming between symbolic domain for attended pictures and words in the present experiment is consistent with previous research (D. I. Irwin and Lupker, 1983; Sperber et al., 1979), which reported such priming to be a robust phenomenon at short interstimulus intervals with a categorization response. Similarly, the within-domain facilitatory priming observed here has previously been well established (Meyer and Schvaneveldt, 1971; Warren and Morton, 1982). The consistency of the attended (facilitatory) and ignored (inhibitory) priming effects reported are equivalent, but the overall size of the attended priming effect is much larger than that of the ignored primes. This can plausibly be attributed to response repetition, for the categorization response is identical for prime and probe displays in the attended priming conditions only.

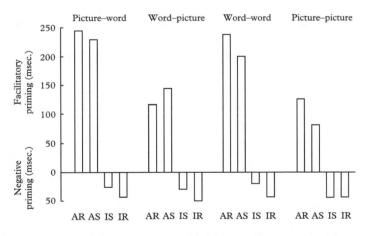

Figure 13.3 A summary of the facilitatory and inhibitory effects produced by attended and ignored primes. AR = attended repetition; AS = attended semantic; IS = ignored semantic; IR = ignored repetition.

The overall attended priming effect for the word probes, however, was substantially larger than that for the picture probes (228 msec vs. 122 msec; see figure 13.3). This accounts for much of the unpredicted interaction in the ANOVA, as the contrast between word and picture probes is primarily observed in the effects of attended primes. One post hoc explanation for this unpredicted result is in terms of the speed to categorize words and pictures. It has been consistently demonstrated that pictures can be categorized faster than can words (Potter and Faulconer, 1975; Smith and Magee, 1980; Glaser and Dungelhoff, 1984). Therefore, the more difficult process of categorizing word probes is differentially advantaged relative to picture probes when subjects identify and maintain the categorically related prime. Only in the attended priming conditions is there response repetition between prime and probe. This suggests that the contrast producing the interaction is due to these response factors.

Such attended priming effects have been well established and discussed elsewhere. In the present context, their significance is that they demonstrate the qualitative change in the priming effects of a stimulus depending on whether the stimulus receives attentional processing or is ignored. The important result of this study is the demonstration of negative priming between pictures and words, that is, across symbolic domain. As previously discussed, there is no physical resemblance between pictures and words representing the same object or related objects. The negative priming observed from the ignored primes in this case is clearly abstract in nature, which entails that the ignored prime must have achieved an abstract level of representation.

Thus, the between-domain groups conclusively demonstrate that physical resemblance is not a necessary condition for negative priming to be observed. One can ask further whether physical resemblance makes *any* contribution to negative priming. The size of the negative priming effect was similar in both between- and within-domain groups; analysis of only the control, ignored semantic, and ignored repetition conditions reveals no evidence for any interaction [$F(2, 104) = 0.143$]. More specifically, in the ignored repetition condition, overall negative priming was 44 msec in both the between- and within-domain conditions. Thus, the presence of physical similarity in within-domain conditions does not affect the ignored repetition negative priming observed. This suggests that there is little or no contribution of physical/structural information to negative priming over and above that of semantic information. If negative priming is interpreted as reflecting a selective mechanism of active inhibition (Tipper, 1985), then the inhibition clearly is late in the sequence of processes from perception to action (Tipper and Cranston, 1985).

The abstract nature of the negative priming observed provides support for post-categorical selection theories of attention (Allport, 1980; Deutsch and Deutsch, 1963; Van der Heijden, 1981), which predict that an ignored prime will achieve abstract levels of representation. The results for the picture–word group entail that pictures that subjects ignore while attending to another picture nevertheless achieve abstract levels of internal representation. In the case of ignored words, we must be more cautious. Although we observe negative priming between ignored words and a picture with the same identity, there is only partial evidence for negative priming when the word is categorically related to the subsequent picture. Thus, the weight of our evidence favors the postcategorical view, but is less compelling than in the case of ignored pictures.

The data provide a good fit to the model of Tipper and Cranston (1985). In this model, the initial analysis of two objects takes place in parallel at least to the level of categorical representation if they are familiar and have well-established internal representations. Subsequent to this analysis, the selected object receives further processing, enabling overt action to be directed to it. Such processes result in activated perceptual and response representations that facilitate the processing of subsequent objects requiring the same, or semantically related, representations. The internal representations of the ignored objects also receive further processing, rather than passively decaying back to resting levels. In this case, however, the internal representations are inhibited. Such inhibition prevents action from being inappropriately directed to ignored objects.

Several questions remain about the nature of the inhibited internal representations of the ignored object. The observation of negative priming between categorically related objects in the ignored semantic condition could suggest a process of spreading inhibition in semantic memory networks, analogous to that of spreading activation (Collins and Loftus, 1975). The possibility that inhibition spreads between related concepts in semantic memory has been proposed by other theorists, notably Roediger and Neely (1982). Our current observations do not establish whether the spread of inhibition in such a model is best characterized as associative or categorical in nature (Lupker, 1979), because the ignored prime and attended probe in the ignored semantic condition (e.g., cat and dog) are related associatively and categorically.

An alternative to the above spreading inhibition explanation of the negative priming effect would locate the inhibition at response rather than in semantic memory. With the categorizing response used in the present experiment, the response that would be given to the ignored prime is the same as that required to the attended probe, for the ignored semantic condition as well as the ignored repetition condition. In both cases, therefore, the negative priming could be accounted for if the subject inhibited the response subsequently required to the probe upon presentation of the prime. Such a response inhibition process has been suggested by Eriksen and his associates (Eriksen and Eriksen, 1974; Eriksen and Schultz, 1979). It is not clear how peripherally such a mechanism would be located; for example, Eriksen, Coles, Morris, and O'Hara (1985) reported that response competition may not be resolved until the point of flexor muscles in the case of a manual keypress response. It remains for future research to examine whether negative priming can still be observed when, say, a different modality of response is required to the prime and the probe.

Thus, the present results do not establish whether the inhibition of ignored objects is located at semantic memory or response. However, it should be noted that either locus corresponds to a postcategorical theory of attention. The between-domain negative priming we observed must be operating at, or beyond, an abstract semantic level of representation of the ignored object.

Acknowldgments

We gratefully acknowledge the assistance of Maxine Cresswell and Wendy Perkins with data collection, and Glenda MacQueen and an anonymous reviewer for comments on a draft of this paper. The research was supported by M.R.C. Grant G8313910N.

References

Allport, D. A. (1980). Attention and performance. In G. Claxton (ed.), *Cognitive psychology: New directions* (pp. 112–53), London: Routledge & Keegan Paul.

Allport, D. A., Tipper, S. P., & Chmiel, N. (1985). Perceptual integration and post-categorical filtering. In M. I. Posner & O. S. M. Marin (eds), *Attention and performance, XI* (pp. 107–132), Hillsdale, NJ: Erlbaum.

Anderson, J. R. (1980). *Cognitive psychology and its implications*. San Francisco: W. H. Freeman.

Broadbent, D. E. (1958). *Perception and communication*. London: Pergamon Press.

Broadbent, D. E. (1971). *Decision and stress*. London: Academic Press.

Broadbent, D. E. (1982). Task combination and selective intake of information. *Acta Psychologica*, **50**, 253–90.

Collins, A. M., & Loftus, E. (1975). A spreading activation theory of semantic memory. *Psychological Review*, **82**, 407–28.

Deutsch, J. A., & Deutsch, D. (1963). Attention: Some theoretical considerations. *Psychological Review*, **70**, 80–90.

Eriksen, C. W., Coles, M. G. H., Morris, L. R., & O'Hara, L. P. (1985). An electromyographic examination of response competition. *Bulletin of the Psychonomic Society*, **23**, 165–8.

Eriksen, B. A., & Eriksen, C. W. (1974). Effects of noise letters on identification of a target letter in a nonsearch task. *Perception & Psychophysics*, **16**, 143–9.

Eriksen, C. W., & Schultz, D. W. (1979). Information processing in visual search: A continuous flow model and experimental results. *Perception & Psychophysics*, **25**, 249–63.

Glaser, W. R., & Dungelhoff, F. J. (1984). The time course of picture–word interference. *Journal of Experimental Psychology: Human Perception & Performance*, **10**, 640–54.

Goldstein, E. B., & Fink, S. I. (1981). Selective attention in vision: Recognition memory for superimposed line pictures. *Journal of Experimental Psychology: Human Perception & Performance*, **7**, 954–67.

Irwin, D. I., & Lupker, S. J. (1983). Semantic priming of pictures and words: A level of processing approach. *Journal of Verbal Learning & Verbal Behavior*, **22**, 45–60.

Irwin, J. (1979). A method for testing selective attention in vision. *Perception & Motor Skills*, **48**, 899–902.

Johnston, W. A., & Dark, V. J. (1986). Selective attention. *Annual Review Psychology*, **37**, 43–75.

Kahneman, D., & Treisman, A. M. (1984). Changing views of attention and automaticity. In R. Parasuraman, R. Davies, & J. Beaty (eds.), *Varieties of attention* (pp. 29–61), New York: Academic Press.

Lupker, S. J. (1979). The semantic nature of response competition in the picture–word interference task. *Memory & Cognition*, **7**, 485–95.

Meyer, D. E., & Schvaneveldt, R. W. (1971). Facilitation in recognizing pairs of words: Evidence of a dependence between retrieval operations. *Journal of Experimental Psychology: General*, **90**, 227–34.

Neill, W. T. (1977). Inhibitory and facilitatory processes in selective attention. *Journal of Experimental Psychology: Human Perception & Performance*, **3**, 444–50.

Potter, M. C., & Faulconer, B. A. (1975). Time to understand pictures and words. *Nature*, **253**, 437–8.

Rock, I., & Gutman, D. (1981). Effect of inattention on form perception. *Journal of Experimental Psychology: Human Perception & Performance*, **7**, 275–85.

Roediger, H. L., & Neely, J. H. (1982). Retrieval blocks in episodic and semantic memory. *Canadian Journal of Psychology*, **36**, 213–42.

Rosch, E., Mervis, C. B., Gray, W. D., Johnson, D. M., & Boyes-Bream, P. (1976). Basic objects in natural categories. *Cognitive Psychology*, **8**, 382–439.

Schneider, W., & Fisk, A. D. (1984). Automatic category search and its transfer. *Journal of Experimental Psychology: Learning, Memory, & Cognition*, **10**, 1–15.

Smith, M. C., & Magee, L. E. (1980). Tracing the time course of picture word processing. *Journal of Experimental Psychology: General*, **4**, 373–92.

Snodgrass, J. G., & McCullough, B. (1985). The role of visual similarity in picture categorization. *Journal of Experimental Psychology: Learning, Memory, & Cognition*, **12**, 147–54.

Sperber, R. D., McCauley, C., Ragain, R. D., & Weil, C. M. (1979). Semantic priming effects on picture and word processing, *Memory & Cognition*, **7**, 339–45.

Tipper, S. P. (1985). The negative priming effect: Inhibitory priming by ignored objects. *Quarterly Journal of Experimental Psychology*, **37A**, 571–90.

Tipper, S. P., & Cranston, M. (1985). Selective attention and priming: Inhibitory and facilitatory effects of ignored primes. *Quarterly Journal of Experimental Psychology*, **37A**, 591–611.

Van der Heijden, A. H. C. (1981). *Short-term visual information forgetting*. London: Routledge & Keegan Paul.

Warren, C., & Morton, J. (1982). The effect of priming on picture recognition. *British Journal of Psychology*, **73**, 117–29.

Imagery

INTRODUCTION TO PART IV

The virtual world of considered possibilities, remembered scenes, and imagined hypotheticals is one of the fundamental aspects of the mind. The ability to step out of the moment at hand and dwell on a previous event or probable outcome enough to influence current decisions or behavior is a hallmark of intelligence. How do we do this? The answer is still a deep mystery, but some issues, at least, have been illuminated. One fundamental question is whether the processes, and the same cortical areas, that are responsible for perceiving a scene in the first place are also involved in its subsequent recall in the mind's eye.

This question has been fairly convincingly answered in the affirmative. The first paper to clearly address the topic was by Shepard and Metzler, reprinted here. These investigators had subjects view paired pictures of geometric objects which might or might not be rotated versions of one another; the time required to decide that two rotated but otherwise identical objects were the same increased linearly with the angle by which they were offset. This is generally taken as evidence that the process of mentally rotating shows some strong similarities with the process of observing a rotation.

More direct evidence for the involvement of perceptual cortical areas in imagery was provided by Kosslyn, Thompson, Kim, and Alpert: by PET-scanning subjects engaged in visualizing objects, they observed changes in primary visual cortex activity that correlated with the size of the visualized image. That even V1 is recruited in virtual vision implies a wholesale flexibility of the cerebral cortex, with possibly every area of it serving both to perceive immediate reality and to enable the consideration of alternatives.

The unilateral neglect touched on in the previous section is revisited in a startling light by Bisiach and Luzzatti. They took the simple but ingenious step of asking neglect patients to imagine themselves in a familiar environment and to describe their surroundings. The patients exhibited precisely the same unilateral neglect of their imagined surroundings as of anything that was actually in front of them. Whatever was broken in their perception was awry in their imagination as well; they could not even conceive of the left side of space.

Mental Rotation of Three-Dimensional Objects

Roger N. Shepard and Jacqueline Metzler

Human subjects are often able to determine that two two-dimensional pictures portray objects of the same three-dimensional shape even though the objects are depicted in very different orientations. The experiment reported here was designed to measure the time that subjects require to determine such identity of shape as a function of the angular difference in the portrayed orientations of the two three-dimensional objects.

This angular difference was produced either by a rigid rotation of one of two identical pictures in its own picture plane or by a much more complex, nonrigid transformation, of one of the pictures, that corresponds to a (rigid) rotation of the three-dimensional object in depth.

This reaction time is found (i) to increase linearly with the angular difference in portrayed orientation and (ii) to be no longer for a rotation in depth than for a rotation merely in the picture plane. These findings appear to place rather severe constraints on possible explanations of how subjects go about determining identity of shape of differently oriented objects. They are, however, consistent with an explanation suggested by the subjects themselves. Although introspective reports must be interpreted with caution, all subjects claimed (i) that to make the required comparison they first had to imagine one object as rotated into the same orientation as the other and that they could carry out this "mental rotation" at no greater than a certain limiting rate; and (ii) that, since they perceived the two-dimensional pictures as objects in three-dimensional space, they could imagine the rotation around whichever axis was required with equal ease.

In the experiment each of eight adult subjects was presented with 1600 pairs of perspective line drawings. For each pair the subject was asked to pull a right-hand lever as soon as he determined that the two drawings portrayed objects that were congruent with respect to three-dimensional shape and to pull a left-hand lever as soon as he determined that the two drawings depicted objects of different three-dimensional shapes. According to a random sequence, in half of the pairs (the "same" pairs) the two objects could be rotated into congruence with each other (as in fig. 14.1, A and B),

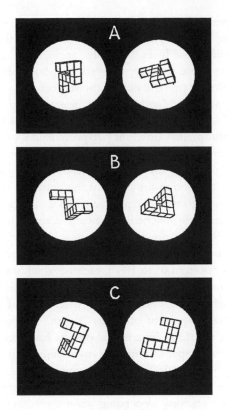

Figure 14.1 Examples of pairs of perspective line drawings presented to the subjects. (**A**) A "same" pair, which differs by an 80° rotation in the picture plane; (**B**) a "same" pair, which differs by an 80° rotation in depth; and (**C**) a "different" pair, which cannot be brought into congruence by *any* rotation.

and in the other half (the "different" pairs) the two objects differed by a reflection as well as a rotation and could not be rotated into congruence (as in fig. 14.1C).

The choice of objects that were mirror images or "isomers" of each other for the "different" pairs was intended to prevent subjects from discovering some distinctive feature possessed by only one of the two objects and thereby reaching a decision of noncongruence without actually having to carry out any mental rotation. As a further precaution, the ten different three-dimensional objects depicted in the various perspective drawings were chosen to be relatively unfamiliar and meaningless in overall three-dimensional shape.

Each object consisted of ten solid cubes attached face-to-face to form a rigid armlike structure with exactly three right-angled "elbows" (see fig. 14.1). The set of all ten shapes included two subsets of five: within either subset, no shape could be transformed into itself or any other by any reflection or rotation (short of 360°). However, each shape in either subset was the mirror image of one shape in the other subset, as required for the construction of the "different" pairs.

For each of the ten objects, 18 different perspective projections – corresponding to one complete turn around the vertical axis by 20° steps – were generated by digital computer and associated graphical output. Seven of the 18 perspective views of each object were then selected so as (i) to avoid any views in which some part of the object was wholly occluded by another part, and yet (ii) to permit the construction of two pairs that differed in orientation by each possible angle, in 20° steps, from 0° to 180°. These 70 line drawings were then reproduced by photo-offset process and were attached to cards in pairs for presentation to the subjects.

Half of the "same" pairs (the "depth" pairs) represented two objects that differed by some multiple of a 20° rotation about a vertical axis (fig. 14.1B). For each of these pairs, copies of two appropriately different perspective views were simply attached to the cards in the orientation in which they were originally generated. The other half of the "same" pairs (the "picture-plane" pairs) represented two objects that differed by some multiple of a 20° rotation in the plane of the drawings themselves (fig. 14.1A). For each of these, one of the seven perspective views was selected for each object and two copies of this picture were attached to the card in appropriately different orientations. Altogether, the 1600 pairs presented to each subject included 800 "same" pairs, which consisted of 400 unique pairs (20 "depth" and 20 "picture-plane" pairs at each of the ten angular differences from 0° to 180°), each of which was presented twice. The remaining 800 pairs, randomly intermixed with these, consisted of 400 unique "different" pairs, each of which (again) was presented twice. Each of these "different" pairs corresponded to one "same" pair (of either the "depth" or "picture-plane" variety) in which, however, one of the three-dimensional objects had been reflected about some plane in three-dimensional space. Thus the two objects in each "different" pair differed, in general, by both a reflection and a rotation.

The 1600 pairs were grouped into blocks of not more than 200 and presented over eight to ten 1-hour sessions (depending upon the subject). Also, although it is only of incidental interest here, each such block of presentations was either "pure," in that all pairs involved rotations of the same type ("depth" or "picture-plane"), or "mixed," in that the two types of rotation were randomly intermixed within the same block.

Each trial began with a warning tone, which was followed half a second later by the presentation of a stimulus pair and the simultaneous onset of a timer. The lever-pulling response stopped the timer, recorded the subject's reaction time and terminated the visual display. The line drawings, which averaged between 4 and 5 cm in maximum linear extent, appeared at a viewing distance of about 60 cm. They were positioned, with a center-to-center spacing that subtended a visual angle of 9°, in two circular apertures in a vertical black surface (see fig. 14.1, A to C).

The subjects were instructed to respond as quickly as possible while keeping errors to a minimum. On the average only 3.2 percent of the responses were incorrect (ranging from 0.6 to 5.7 percent for individual subjects). The reaction-time data presented below include only the 96.8 percent correct responses. However, the data for the incorrect responses exhibit a similar pattern.

In fig. 14.2, the overall means of the reaction times as a function of angular difference in orientation for all correct (right-hand) responses to "same" pairs are plotted separately for the pairs differing by a rotation in the picture plane (fig. 14.2A) and for the pairs differing by a rotation in depth (fig. 14.2B). In both cases, reaction time is a strikingly linear function of the angular difference between the two three-dimensional objects portrayed. The mean reaction times for individual subjects increased from a value of about 1 second at 0° of rotation for all subjects to values

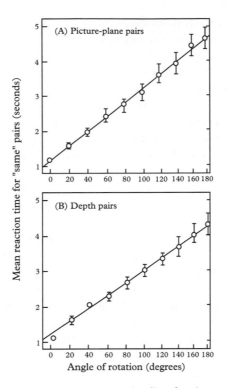

Figure 14.2   Mean reaction times to two perspective line drawings portraying objects of the same three-dimensional shape. Times are plotted as a function of angular difference in portrayed orientation: (**A**) for pairs differing by a rotation in the picture plane only; and (**B**) for pairs differing by a rotation in depth. (The centers of the circles indicate the means and, when they extend far enough to show outside these circles, the vertical bars around each circle indicate a conservative estimate of the standard error of that mean based on the distribution of the eight component means contributed by the individual subjects.)

ranging from 4 to 6 seconds at 180° of rotation, depending upon the particular individual. Moreover, despite such variations in slope, the *linearity* of the function is clearly evident when the data are plotted separately for individual three-dimensional objects or for individual subjects. Polynomial regression lines were computed separately for each subject under each type of rotation. In all 16 cases the functions were found to have a highly significant linear component ($P > 0.001$) when tested against deviations from linearity. No significant quadratic or higher-order effects were found ($P > 0.05$, in all cases).

The angle through which different three-dimensional shapes must be rotated to achieve congruence is not, of course, defined. Therefore, a function like those plotted in fig. 14.2 cannot be constructed in any straightforward manner for the "different" pairs. The *overall* mean reaction time for these pairs was found, however, to be 3.8 seconds – nearly a second longer than the corresponding overall means for the "same" pairs. (In the postexperimental interview, the subjects typically reported that they attempted to rotate one end of one object into congruence with the corresponding end of the other object; they discovered that the two objects were *different* when, after this "rotation," the two free ends still remained noncongruent.)

Not only are the two functions shown in fig. 14.2 both linear but they are very similar to each other with respect to intercept and slope. Indeed, for the larger angular differences the reaction times were, if anything, somewhat shorter for rotation in depth than for rotation in the picture plane. However, since this small difference is either absent or reversed in four of the eight subjects, it is of doubtful significance. The determination of identity of shape may therefore be based, in both cases, upon a process of the same general kind. If we can describe this process as some sort of "mental rotation in three-dimensional space," then the slope of the obtained functions indicates that the average rate at which these particular objects can be thus "rotated" is roughly 60° per second.

Of course the plotted reaction times necessarily include any times taken by the subjects to decide how to process the pictures in each presented pair as well as the time taken actually to carry out the process, once it was chosen. However, even for these highly practiced subjects, the reaction times were still linear and were no more than 20 percent lower in the "pure" blocks of presentations (in which the subjects knew both the axis and the direction of the required rotation in advance of each presentation) than in the "mixed" blocks (in which the axis of rotation was unpredictable). Tentatively, this suggests that 80 percent of a typical one of these reaction times may represent some such process as "mental rotation" itself, rather than a preliminary process of preparation or search. Nevertheless, in further research now underway, we are seeking clarification of this point and others.

Unilateral Neglect of Representational Space

Edoardo Bisiach and Claudio Luzzatti

Discussions of unilateral neglect following brain injuries have generally disregarded the question of whether the phenomenon is only manifest in the egocentrical perspective of the physical environment (including one's own body) or evident in representational space as well. An answer to this question would somehow contribute to the understanding of the nature of unilateral neglect. A simple procedure, recently applied to two patients who exhibited left unilateral neglect, provided some insight into the question. The patients were asked to describe a familiar place, the Piazza del Duomo in Milan (figure 15.1), according to definite perspectives. First (*a*), they were requested to imagine themselves looking at the front of the cathedral from the opposite side of the square; then the reverse perspective (*b*) had to be described, i.e. the perspective seen from the front doors of the cathedral. In one patient, the same procedure was followed in relation to the studio where he had spent most of his life (figure 15.2).

Case Reports

Case 1

I.G., a retired manager of 86, had a stroke without loss of consciousness on July 24th, 1977. Neurological examination revealed a left hemiplegia with left hemianopia and severe global left hemihypesthesia. Tested a few days later, she was found to be minimally anosognosic concerning her motor disorder, while she denied any defect of visual field. She was requested to touch all 13 dots composing a symmetrical pattern, 23 cm in width, starting from the center. After having scanned the whole right side, she said: "I think I have touched all of them." After a few seconds' hesitation, however, she went on spontaneously, correctly completing the task.

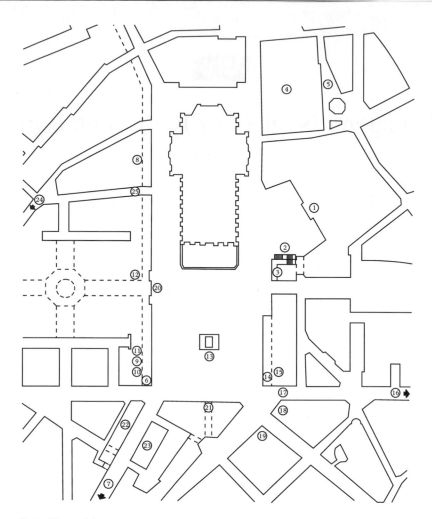

Figure 15.1 Plan of the town.

Description of the square (see figure 15.1 for references)

Perspective *a*. "The cathedral with its steps in front of me; the Royal Palace (1); the stairs (2); ... the Arengario (3); the Royal Palace; further on, the Archiepiscopal Palace (4); then Via delle Ore (5)." Perspective *b*. "The arcades with the shops" (she is probably referring to the northern arcades (6) rather than to the southern, as it is customary for Milanese people to allude to the former when no further specifications are added, due to their much greater significance and extension); "Via Dante (7); Rinascente (8); the jewellers' shops (9) (10); a shirt shop (11) Motta (12)."

Computerized tomography

Two areas of abnormal attenuation with mixed changes and ill defined margins are seen in the right hemisphere. In the frontal lobe the lesion is mainly decreased in density, involving the white matter lateral to the frontal horn, with some increased density dots at the level of the head of the caudate nucleus. In the temporoparietal region, lateral to the trigone there is a small cortical increased density area with decreased density in the underlying white matter. These findings are compatible with hemorragic infarction in the vascular supply area of the lenticulostriate arteries and of the angular branch of the sylvian artery.

Case 2

N.V., a lawyer of 72, had a stroke on December 2nd, 1977. Neurological examination revealed a very slight left hemiparesis with left hemianopia and severe left hemihypesthesia. He was completely anosognosic for the above-mentioned deficits. The tests were begun on the same evening. The scanning task elicited complete neglect of the left half of the pattern, which could not be overcome in spite of the examiner's remarks.

Description of the square

Perspective *a*. "The cathedral; the corner of the Royal Palace (1); the Arengario (3); the Vittorio Emanuele II monument (13); the northern (6) and southern (14) arcades; the lamps; Galtrucco (15); Piazza Missori (16) at the end of Via Mazzini (17); Al Duomo stores (18),...but they are no longer there; Alemagna (19)." After the examiner's invitation to continue his description, he added: "The front of the Galleria (20) with the terraces and Motta (12)." Perspective *b*. "The palace with the arcade to Via Orefici (21); the Palazzo dei Giureconsulti (22); the Loggia dei Mercanti (23); Motta (12); Rinascente (8); Piazza San Fedele (24); Via San Raffaele (25)." The last 4 items were provided after the examiner's incitement to go on.

Description of the studio *(see figure 15.2 for references)*

Perspective *a* (Sitting at the desk). "Behind me there is a book-case (1); I am sitting in a Savonarola chair (2), behind a carved Renaissance table (3); in front of me there is an unknown master's painting representing Jesus Christ's flagellation (4); I have many books, some armchairs, a chandelier with false candles (5); on the right, the window on *** street (6); on the left, the door to the passageway (7)." Prompted to go on, he added: "An enclosed book-case (8)," and, after several seconds, "an upright piano (9)." It must be pointed out that the patient was very fond of music and used to spend a couple of hours at his piano every afternoon after working. Perspective *b* (Facing the desk; this part of the test was carried out on the following day). "In front of me, the book-case (1) and the carved table (3); on the right, the upright piano (9), some chairs, paintings on the walls, the door to the passageway (7); beyond the piano, a large room (10) hung with old tapestries, with old chests of drawers and some paintings...a Madonna and Child;...in the studio there are no paintings besides the Flagellation...there are some water-colours (11) hung over the piano; then a copy from Titian...no, from Giorgione, a beautiful Lady, maybe it is by Palma il Vecchio, her name is Violante (12)." After being asked for further details, he added: "A French pendulum-clock (13); the flowered velvet armchair (14); Dante's bust on the book-case (15)."

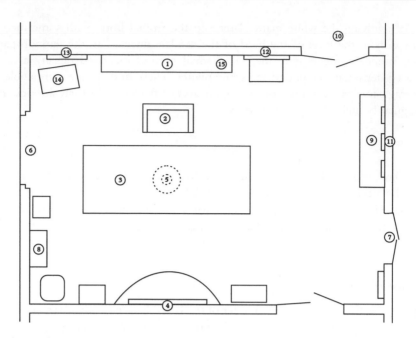

Figure 15.2   Plan of the room.

Computerized tomography

Right intracerebral hematoma, approximately 4 cm in diameter, involving the grey and white matter of the postero temporal and inferior parietal areas (carrefour).

Discussion

Though the more or less complete neglect of left-sided details in the descriptions of the imagined surroundings by our two patients is per se sufficiently eloquent, something may be added about patient N.V.'s exposition of the parts of remembered scenes: while central and right-sided items were enumerated in a rather lively manner and sometimes dwelt upon, the few left-sided items were mentioned in a kind of absent-minded, almost annoyed tone.

A full discussion of the findings would exceed the scope of this note. For the present purpose it is enough to consider briefly some of their theoretical implications. There is reason to suggest that unilateral neglect cannot be reduced to a disorder confined to the input–output machinery of the organism interacting with its physical environment, once it seems to affect mental events whose occurrence is not contingent upon actual stimulation from the outside or actions of the organism on his environment; at least, not upon their spatial attributes. Moreover, our findings support the view that the mechanisms underlying the mental representation of the environment are topologically structured in the sense that the processes by which a visual image is conjured up by the mind may split between the two cerebral hemispheres, like the projection of a real scene onto the visual areas of the two sides of the brain. It might therefore be argued that even stimulus-unbounded properties of the mind such as those at issue here do have *extension* and are built in a substrate which scarcely conforms to the holographic model suggested by Pribram (1971, p. 140).

Summary

Two patients showing left unilateral neglect were asked to describe imagined perspectives of familiar surroundings. Left-sided details were largely omitted in the descriptions. Some theoretical implications of the occurrence of unilateral neglect in representational space are briefly considered.

Reference

Pribram, K. H. (1971) *Languages of the Brain.* Englewood Cliffs, New Jersey: Prentice-Hall.

Topographical Representations of Mental Images in Primary Visual Cortex

Stephen M. Kosslyn, William L. Thompson, Irene J. Kim, and Nathaniel M. Alpert

INTRODUCTION

We report here the use of positron emission tomography (PET) to reveal that the primary visual cortex is activated when subjects close their eyes and visualize objects. The size of the image is systematically related to the location of maximal activity, which is as expected because the earliest visual areas are spatially organized.[1–5] These results were only evident, however, when imagery conditions were compared to a non-imagery baseline in which the same auditory cues were presented (and hence the stimuli were controlled); when a resting baseline was used (and hence brain activation was uncontrolled), imagery activation was obscured because of activation in visual cortex during the baseline condition. These findings resolve a debate in the literature about whether imagery activates early visual cortex[6–11] and indicate that visual mental imagery involves 'depictive' representations, not solely language-like descriptions.[12–14] Moreover, the fact that stored visual information can affect processing in even the earliest visual areas suggests that knowledge can fundamentally bias what one sees.

We tested 12 right-handed male volunteers in five conditions while local cerebral blood flow was monitored using PET. The resting baseline task followed the procedure and instructions of ref. 10. Subjects were blindfolded with a dark cloth, and told to close their eyes, relax and to 'have it black in front of their mind's eye'. Such an uncontrolled rest state probably corresponds to many states that do not preclude some form of imagery. The other four conditions used the same type of auditory stimuli, which either were listened to passively or used as prompts to form images of previously memorized pictures (figure 16.1). Subjects received three imagery conditions, each of which consisted of four practice trials and 24 experimental trials. The imagery conditions differed only in the size at which images were formed, at 0.25, 4.0 or 16.0 degrees of

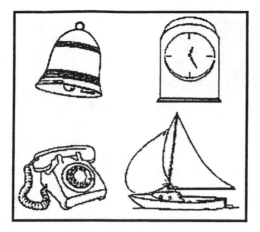

Figure 16.1 Stimuli used in four of the five conditions. In the listening baseline condition, subjects received trials of the following sort. First they heard the name of a common object (such as 'anchor'), and 4 seconds later heard a spatial comparison term (such as 'right higher'), and then responded. One second later, another trial was presented. Subjects were told to close their eyes and respond as quickly as possible on hearing the comparison terms, alternating feet from trial to trial; they were told not to visualize anything during these 28 trials. The order of this baseline and the resting baseline was counterbalanced. Half of the subjects received the resting-baseline at the beginning of the experiment, and half received it at the end of the experiment; in both cases, the listening baseline always preceded the first imagery condition (this was necessary because once subjects knew the meanings of the cues, they would be unlikely to listen passively). Immediately before the imagery conditions, subjects studied 28 pictures, adapted from (*19*), as illustrated here. Each picture appeared on the screen when its name was read aloud by the computer. After memorizing the pictures, four spatial judgements were defined; for example, 'right higher' required them to decide whether the rightmost point was higher than the leftmost point. Pictures of objects (not used in the actual experiment) illustrated 'yes' and 'no' judgements. At the beginning of each set of imagery trials, subjects memorized the size of a square piece of cardboard taped to the screen. Subjects heard the same type of stimuli used in the listening baseline condition, but now closed their eyes and visualized each named picture at the size of the square. Subjects were urged to visualize each object at the correct size and to maintain the image at this size. When they heard the spatial comparison term, they evaluated the imaged picture as quickly and accurately as possible. Four different sets of 28 pictures were used, and counterbalancing ensured that the names and associated spatial comparison terms occurred equally often in the listening baseline and in each imagery condition in each order, and that the spatial comparison terms and yes/no responses appeared equally often in each condition.

visual angle. We compared activation in the three imagery conditions with each of the two baselines.

Here we focus entirely on activation in the medial occipital region. First, when activation in the resting baseline was subtracted from the imagery conditions, the only occipital activation was in area 19 (only for medium-sized images), including the parieto-occipital sulcus and precuneus. This is very similar to the region reported previously with this baseline condition;[15] the $X\ Y\ Z$ Talairach coordinates were 20–68–28. Second, figures 16.2 and 16.1 present the results of subtracting activation in the listening baseline from the three imagery conditions; we focus here on activation within 15 mm of the midline (the smoothness parameter used in analysis was 14 mm)

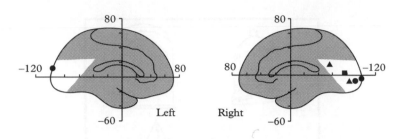

Figure 16.2 Left and right PET results in medial occipital cortex; points indicate the most activated pixel using statistical parametric mapping (*20*) with Z > 3.0. Small imagery (closed circle), medium imagery (closed square), and large imagery (closed triangle), all minus listening baseline. Activation for the smallest images was very posterior, –102 mm from the anterior commissure for left- and right-hemisphere area 18, which included area 17 in the right hemisphere, as well as –88 mm in a more medial portion of area 18. Activation for medium images was –79 mm in area 17 in the right hemisphere. Finally, activation for the largest images was –60 mm in a region that includes area 17 and the precuneus, and –83 mm in another part of area 17 and 18, which may have been activated by internal details of the images. The PET machine was a GE Scanditronix PC4096 15-slice whole-body tomograph in its stationary mode (see (*21*)). Contiguous slices were 6.5 mm apart (centre-to-centre; the axial field was 97.5 mm); the axial resolution was 6.0 mm full width at half maximum. Each subject was fitted with a custom moulded face mask (TRUE SCAN, Annapolis, MD), and his head was aligned relative to the CM (cantho-meatal) line. Nasal cannulae were connected to a radiolabelled gas inflow, and a face mask, attached to a vacuum, was placed over the subject's nose. On each PET run, 20 measurements were taken: the first 3 were 10 seconds and the remaining 17 were 5 seconds long. The PET protocol was as follows: (1) the camera acquisition program was started (which measured residual background from past studies); (2) stimulus presentation began 15 seconds later, and the subject began the task; (3) sup 15 O-CO sub 2 gas was administered 15 seconds after this; and (4) 60 seconds later, scanning ended and the gas was stopped (for additional details, see experiment 2 of (*7*)).

in the occipital lobe, and consider only activations that had Z scores greater than 3.0. Locations are specified using the stereotactic coordinate system.[16] As is evident, we find very posterior activation only for the small images, and very anterior activation only for the largest images, with medium images activating intermediate regions. Inspection of the scans from each individual indicated that activation was in fact in the primary visual cortex.

We next compared the two baselines by subtracting blood flow during the listening baseline from that during the resting baseline. We found more blood flow during the resting baseline in area 17 (primary visual cortex), $t(11) = 3.94$, $P = 0.002$ (two-tailed) (figure 16.3). To examine the possible effects of practice in both baselines, we compared only the first condition for each subject, and found greater activation in area 17 during the resting baseline, $F(1, 10) = 5.65$, $P = 0.039$; we also compared only the second baseline condition for each subject, and again found more activation in area 17 during the resting baseline, $F(1, 10) = 7.06$, $P = 0.024$. Moreover, when baseline and order were considered in a single analysis of variance, there was no interaction between the two factors, $F < 1$.

We also considered the variability associated with each baseline, and found comparable variances (5.91 and 7.65 for the listening and resting baselines, respectively).

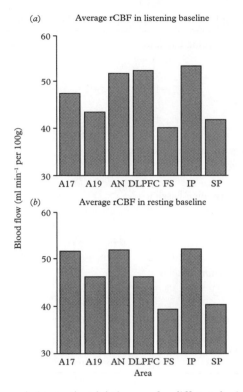

Figure 16.3   Blood flow relative to the global mean for different brain areas during the two baseline conditions. Each brain was normalized to the same value, 50 ml min sup −1 per 100 g, and the relative flows in area 17 and other cortical areas were analysed relative to the mean. Activation in area 17 (A17) was average in the listening baseline (*a*), but above average in the resting baseline (*b*). The activation in area 17 was compared to the mean blood flow in the previously activated regions (7) of area (A19), the angular gyrus (AN), dorsolateral prefrontal cortex (DLPFC), the fusiform gyrus (FS), the inferior parietal lobe (IP), and the superior parietal lobe (SP), not the normalized value of 50 ml min sup −1 per 100 g; thus, the mean blood flow in A17 (47.4) is not different (F < 1) from the mean blood flow in those other brain areas (46.8) during the listening baseline, whereas the mean blood flow in A17 (51.3) is higher than that in the other brain areas (45.6) during the resting baseline (F = 59.8; P = 0.0001). Most of the same extrastriate regions were activated during each of the three sizes, but not all such areas were activated in common.

Moreover, we found more blood flow in area 17, relative to the global mean, than in the average of the other cortical areas we examined in the resting baseline condition (consistent with ref. 17), but not in the listening baseline condition (see figure 16.3).

The present findings do not imply that visual images are stored in primary visual cortex. About 32 cortical areas have now been shown to process visual information in the macaque monkey brain, and the spatially organized early areas not only send information to areas later in the processing stream, but also receive information from those later areas;[18] indeed, the feedback connections are of comparable size to the feedforward connections.[4] Thus, it is possible that higher-level areas that actually store visual information can evoke activity in earlier areas.

Table 16.1 Data showing blood flow under experimental conditions

	X	Y	Z	Z-score
(a) Small-sized images – listening baseline				
Left hemisphere regions				
Area 18	−13	−102	8	3.20
Right hemisphere regions				
Area 18/17	15	−102	−4	3.40
Area 18	6	−88	−8	3.42
(b) Medium-sized images – listening baseline				
Right hemisphere regions				
Area 17	8	−79	4	3.00
(c) Large-sized images – listening baseline				
Midline				
Area 17*	2	−83	0	3.25
Area 18*	−4	−83	−8	3.30
Precuneus/17	−2	−60	16	3.09
(d) Resting baseline – listening baseline				
Left hemisphere regions				
Area 18/Cuneus	−7	−102	8	3.79
Area 17*	−11	−69	8	3.21
Area 18*	−6	−67	4	3.39
Right hemisphere regions				
Area 19/18	12	−92	24	3.65
Area 18	6	−81	0	3.60

Notes: Blood flow in the listening baseline condition was subtracted from blood flow in the small (a) medium (b) and large (c) visual mental imagery conditions and from blood flow in the resting baseline condition (d; $Z > 3.0$).
*Part of the same continuous area of activation.

The fact that the size of the image systematically affected the locus of activation rules out the possibility that hypometabolism in visual cortex artefactually produced the appearance of imagery activation when the listening baseline was used. Moreover, the use of three sizes eliminates the possibility that different sizes activated different brain areas (as could have occurred in ref. 7, in which two sizes were examined, and which also did not include any baseline conditions but rather examined activation only relative to the other size, and thereby did not allow precise localization of activity). Finally, the relatively high occipital activation during the resting baseline explains why previous researchers using this baseline failed to find evidence that imagery activates area 17. By using three sizes of pictures of common objects, comparing them to a baseline that had the same physical stimuli (but different, non-imagery, mental processing), and showing that the three sizes induce activation along a continuum (but only when we compare them to the listening baseline), we circumvent the problems inherent in the earlier designs, thereby convincingly demonstrating that visual imagery activates primary visual cortex.

Acknowledgments

We thank A. Loring, S. Weise and the MGH Cyclotron Unit for technical assistance.

References

1 Daniel, P. M., and Whittridge, D. J., *Physiol.*, **159**, 203–21 (1961).
2 Fox, P. T. et al., *Nature*, **323**, 806–9 (1986).
3 Tootell, R. B. H., Silverman, M. S., Switkes, E., and De Valois, R. L., *Science*, **218**, 902–4 (1982).
4 Felleman, D. J., and Van Essen, D. C., *Cereb. Cortex*, **1**, 1–47 (1991).
5 Fox, P. T. et al., *Nature*, **323**, 806–9 (1986).
6 Damasio, H. et al., *Soc. Neurosci. Abstr.*, **19**, 1603 (1993).
7 Kosslyn, S. M. et al., *J. Cogn. Neurosci.*, **5**, 263–87 (1993).
8 Menon, R. et al., In *Functional MRI of the Brain: A Workshop Presented by the Society of Magnetic Resonance in Medicine and the Society for Magnetic Resonance Imaging*, 2nd edn (eds Le Bihan, D., Turner, R., Mosley, M., and Hyde, J.) (Arlington, VA: Society of Magnetic Resonance in Medicine Inc, 1993).
9 Charlot, V., Tzourio, M., Zilbovicius, M., Mazoyer, B., and Denis, M. *Neuropsychologia*, **30**, 565–80 (1992).
10 Roland, P. E., and Gulyas, B. *Cereb. Cortex*, **5**, 79–93 (1995).
11 Le Bihan, D. et al., *Proc. Natn. Acad. Sci. USA*, **5**, 11802–5 (1993).
12 Pylyshyn, Z. W., *Psychol. Bull.*, **80**, 1–24 (1973).
13 Kosslyn, S. M., and Pomerantz, J. R., *Cogn. Psychol.*, **9**, 52–76 (1977).
14 Kosslyn, S. M., *Image and Brain: The Resolution of the Imagery Debate* (Cambridge, MA: MIT Press, 1994).
15 Roland, P. E., and Friberg, L. J., *Neurophys.*, **53**, 1219–43 (1985).
16 Talairach, J., and Tournoux, P., *Co-planar Stereotaxic Atlas of the Human Brain* (trans. M. Rayport) (New York: Thieme, 1988).
17 Roland, P. E., *Brain Activation* (New York: Wiley-Liss, 1993).
18 Douglas, K. L., and Rockland, K. S., *Soc. Neurosci. Abstr.*, **18**, 390 (1992).
19 Snodgrass, J. G., and Vanderwart, M. A., *J. Exp. Psychol. Hum. Learn. Mem.*, **6**, 174–215 (1980).
20 Friston, K. J., Frith, C. D., Liddle, P. F., and Frackowiak, R. S. J., *J. Cereb. Blood Flow Metab.*, **11**, 690–9 (1991).
21 Kops, E. R., Herzog, H. H., Schmid, A., Holte, S., and Feinendegen, L. E., *J. Comput. Assist. Tomogr.*, **14**, 437–45 (1990).

Development and
Plasticity

INTRODUCTION TO PART V

Change is a major part of the brain; a mind that learns nothing is not a mind. The learning that makes us intelligent and interesting must be embodied in physical changes in the brain, and many of the processes involved in such changes may well also be used to wire the brain during development. Study of the rules of development may therefore reveal some rules of the dynamic mind.

These studies have been going on a long time. Roger Sperry, another neuroscientific patriarch, demonstrated, as part of his doctoral thesis, that rats can be remarkably inflexible: he surgically switched the nerve connections of opposing flexor and extensor muscles in their legs and reported that they never learned to compensate for the switch, ever. This contrasts with the greater plasticity seen, for example, in juvenile amphibians, in which nerves that are rerouted to unnatural contacts are transformed by their targets to produce wiring that is appropriate to them.

Mark Johnson discusses the basics of cortical development, drawing on anatomical and physiological studies as well as infant psychophysics. He describes an apparently remarkable sophistication of infant cognition at birth, almost inexplicable if the cortex is as underdeveloped at that point as is generally believed. He suggests that the relatively mature subcortical structures handle most cognition at this stage, tutoring the cortex as it grows.

Back in the perception section, David Hubel's description of the first observations of neurons in the primary visual cortex may have left an impression of them as fairly mechanical, boring things. Charles Gilbert and colleagues redress this misconception with a picture of a constantly changing cortex, with neurons communicating by long-range connections that both enable perceptual integration and allow neurons to shift their response profiles with changing circumstances.

The Effect of Crossing Nerves to Antagonistic Muscles in the Hind Limb of the Rat

Roger W. Sperry

When nerves to limb muscles are forced by operative measures to activate opposing muscles in amphibians, no corresponding disturbance results in the response pattern of the limb muscles (Weiss, 1936). Contrary to the view that specific connections between nerve centers and end organs are important in determining the pattern of response, the muscles or limbs so operated contract normally in timing and in intensity regardless of the experimental distortion of their nerve connections. It has been demonstrated further that this return to normal function after crossing of limb nerves in amphibians is not the result of reeducation or of any kind of automatic reflex adjustment (Weiss, 1937).

The only tenable explanation of the phenomenon yet suggested is that offered by Weiss himself in terms of modulation of nerve by muscle. When nerve fibers growing out in ontogenetic development make contact with peripheral organs, they are presumably induced by those end organs to undergo a further cell differentiation according to the specific biochemical properties of the end organ. Nerves to different muscles thus become differentiated qualitatively from each other. When a nerve is severed from its muscle and forced to regenerate into a foreign muscle, the nerve cells, under the influence of the new muscle, undergo a process of cell modulation losing the specific properties induced by the original muscle and acquiring those specific to the new muscle. These specific properties of motor nerves result in selective sensitivity of the nerves of the various muscles to different central excitatory agents. According to the Resonance Principle this selective sensitivity, rather than the anatomical connections in the ventral horn, links the individual muscles with their respective central activators. Normal function thus reappears after experimental disarrangement of the peripheral nerve connections as soon as the nerves are modulated by the muscles into which they regenerate. Evidence has been presented that nerves undergo these muscle-specific changes also in embryonic stages of human development (Weiss, 1935).

Apparent recovery of normal function after nerve crossing in birds and mammals has in the past been attributed to reeducation or to automatic reflex regulation without testing for other possible factors such as modulation of nerve by muscle. Flourens (1842) crossed the medial and ulnar nerves in the fowl. Rawa (1885) crossed the peroneal and tibial nerves in rabbits, cats, dogs, and pigs. Osborne and Kilvington (1910) crossed the peroneal and tibial nerves in dogs. These investigators all report a restoration of normal function and attribute it to reeducation. Barron (1934) in summarizing the literature concludes that the crosses between spinal nerves have been more successful than those between cranial nerves in being followed by a complete independence of the movements of the muscle groups involved. He made anastomoses between fore and hind limb nerves in the rat and reported that a gradual dissociation of movement occurred as the result of a learning process. Kennedy (1914) after crossing flexor and extensor nerves in the front leg of the dog, states that recovery occurred without any evidence of a training period and that it was probably due to an immediate reflex adjustment to the altered periphery rather than to learning. Although the numerous clinical reports are somewhat controversial, the predominating opinion in neuro-surgery seems to be that the crossing of limb nerves in human patients results in a corresponding distortion of sensation or response which can be corrected in time by reeducation provided there are not numerous axon bifurcations to non-synergic muscles or to receptors of different modality.

These reports imply a plasticity of the nerve centers that is directly at variance with the results of muscle transposition in rats (Sperry, 1940). When flexor and extensor muscles of the hind foot of 50-day-old rats are transposed, a reversal of foot movement follows which persists permanently without the slightest corrective modification. Even after amputation of the front legs and 8 months of special training, the foot action remains unalterably reversed. In view of the fact that foot coordination in these cases proved completely refractory to reeducation, it seems questionable that the ready restoration of apparently normal foot function following nerve crosses in rabbits, cats, dogs, and pigs could actually have been due to learning or reflex regulation. Persistence of the correction in foot movement after cord transection in Osborne and Kilvington's dogs suggests, in itself, that the adjustment was due to some factor other than reeducation, because spinal conditioning has never been conclusively demonstrated elsewhere. Modulation of nerve by muscle is another such factor that would result in recovery of normal function. In amphibians an age difference has been demonstrated; modulation occurs quickly in larval stages but may require as long as several months in older animals (Weiss, 1936). A corresponding slow modulation of crossed nerves in post-embryonic mammals would be practically indistinguishable in effect from reeducation.

To date no study has been undertaken to determine for certain whether or not such a modulation process occurs. In the present experiments nerves were crossed in the hind limb of the rat to the same set of muscles which was used previously in muscle transposition for the purpose of (1) comparing the functional effects of nerve crossing and muscle transposition under similar conditions, and (2) discovering whether the limb nerves of postnatal mammals have become irreversibly determined or are still capable of undergoing muscle-specific changes on regeneration into foreign muscles.

Method

A reversal of hind foot movement was produced by crossing nerves to flexor and extensor muscles of the shank. In the previous investigations of other authors on the crossing of limb nerves, large compound nerve trunks have been employed containing fibers to several different groups of muscles as well as a large number of cutaneous and other sensory components. Reeducation was favored and general confusion avoided in the present work by isolating and crossing the pure individual branches to single muscles. All remaining shank muscles, whose nerves were not crossed, were excised. This clarifies, for study, the action of the test muscles and also eliminates reflex inhibition of reeducation by the continued action of shank muscles with normal innervation.

Because both modulation and reeducation result in restoring normal limb function after nerve crossing, critical conditions were established to separate the two factors so that one could clearly tell of any adjustment in function that occurred whether it was due to modulation or to reeducation: Correction of reversed foot movement following the crossing of nerves, when it had been shown not to follow the transposition of the muscles supplied by those nerves, would, in itself, suggest that some factor other than reeducation was responsible. Spinal cord transection should abolish the adjustment if due to learning, but not if due to modulation. Furthermore, by first crossing the nerves and then transposing those muscles supplied by the crossed nerves, a crucial test situation was established under the conditions of which modulation could not possibly be mistaken for reeducation. Foot movement in normal phase is the immediate result on recovery from such a double operation (see Sperry, 1940). Subsequent modulation of nerve by muscle would have to show up as a shift from normal to reversed action, which could hardly be interpreted as reeducation.

Operation

The nerve branch to the soleus muscle, a plantar flexor, was dissected out carefully back to its emergence from the tibial trunk. The nerve was then cut distally next to the muscle, pulled anteriorly, and inserted into the anterior tibial muscle, a dorsi-flexor, after the original nerve to that muscle had been severed. Similarly, the distal cut end of the nerve to the extensor digitorum longus muscle, a dorsi-flexor, was pulled posteriorly and inserted into the medial gastroenemius muscle, a plantar flexor, after its original nerve had been severed.

All other shank muscles, whose nerves had not been crossed, were excised. The loose ends of the original nerves to the intact muscles and those of the excised muscles were ligated with fine silk thread and tied to tissues away from the intact muscles to prevent undesired regeneration. The nerves were inserted in the muscles directly at the motor point in an attempt to bring the cut end of the foreign nerve into contact with the distal stump of the original nerve whose degenerating ramifications through the muscle provide pathways for regeneration. More complete reinnervation of the muscle is thus insured than when the insertion is made elsewhere.

Another technique was also used in crossing the nerves, in which the cut end of the foreign nerve instead of being inserted directly into the muscle, was sutured to the distal stump of the original nerve. The sutures were tubulated in a small piece of artery obtained from another rat according to the method of Weiss (1941). The artery itself was sufficient to hold the two cut ends of nerve together provided a little slack was allowed in the length of nerve. Extra length when needed was obtained by separating the muscular branch from the main trunk farther proximally after removing the common connective tissue sheath. In anticipation of the operation for muscle trans-position to be made on some of the cases after regeneration of the crossed nerves, the nerves were cross-sutured to the lateral head of the gastroenemius muscle which is more easily transposed than the medial head.

In a number of the first trials ankylosis of the joint set in before muscular activity was restored by nerve regeneration. It was found preferable to leave the deep plantar-flexor muscles intact in the first operation and excise them in a second operation after regeneration of the crossed nerves had taken place. Contraction of the deep plantar-flexor muscles maintains the mobility of the joint and helps prevent ankylosis.

The operations were performed under sodium amytal anesthesia with a single lateral incision from above the knee to the ankle. A short incision along the medial side of the tibia bone under ether anesthesia was made for removal of the deep plantar-flexor muscles in the second operation.

Recovery

After the operation the foot hung limply in those cases in which all the extra muscles had been excised. After a period, varying in different cases from $3\frac{1}{2}$ to 6 weeks, active foot movement began to reappear in the operated limbs. This movement from the start was in reverse. Plantar flexion instead of the normal dorsi-flexion occurred in the withdrawal reflex. When the rats tried to rise upright on their toes, the foot was dorsi-flexed instead of plantar-flexed so that the toes swung up in the air and the body weight fell on the back point of the heel. The reversed action gradually became stronger and occurred regularly in all reflex and spontaneous leg movements.

In the remaining cases the deep plantar-flexor muscles were excised at the end of 8 weeks. These rats began to move the foot in reverse a few days after the second operation, as soon as the leg had healed.

Ten successful cases were obtained with complete reversal of hind foot movement unrestricted by ankylosis. In eight of these cases, six unilateral, two bilateral, the nerves had been inserted directly into the muscles. In the remaining two, both unilateral, the nerves had been cross-sutured in arterial tubes. Two more successful cases were obtained in which the muscles had been transposed 8 weeks after the nerves were cross-sutured. The muscles were transposed and the tendons re-inserted in such position that contraction of the gastrocnemius muscle produced dorsi-flexion of the foot instead of the normal plantar flexion, and contraction of the anterior tibial muscle produced plantar flexion instead of dorsi-flexion. In these animals the reversal of muscle action cancelled the reversal produced by nerve crossing, so that dorsi-flexion and plantar flexion occurred in normal phase in all active leg movement. The twelve cases at the time the nerves were crossed varied in age from 40 to 250 days. No age difference appeared in the results except that there was some indication of more rapid and complete nerve regeneration in the younger animals.

The animals were kept under close observation in large cages with a deep flooring of sawdust to protect the operated feet. Once a week for the first 2 weeks and monthly thereafter, the animals were put through a series of twelve specific test reactions involving plantar flexion and dorsi-flexion of the foot. These reactions included the suspended and supporting phases of locomotion and climbing, the withdrawal reflex, placing reaction, scratch reflex, rising upright on the hind legs, escape movements when the rat is held down on its back by pressing across the abdomen, and braking movements of the hind feet when the rat is pulled forward across the floor by its forequarters. These test reactions furnish a reliable index of the contraction of the shank muscles in both voluntary and reflex activity. They have been described in detail with the corresponding foot movements in normal and in reverse phase (Sperry, 1940). Moving pictures of some of the test reactions taken 3 weeks after the appearance of reversed foot movement were compared with pictures of the same reactions taken 1 year later.

Results

Cases tested for modulation of nerve by muscle

Six of the unilateral nerve cross cases were left till their deaths without further treatment. They were kept 6, 10, 13, 15 and 18 months after the operation, respectively. No adjustment in foot movement appeared. The reversal was fully as vigorous and consistent just before death as at the beginning. Likewise no change occurred in those two special cases in which the muscles supplied by the crossed nerves had also been transposed. Flexion and extension of the foot continued in the normal phases of leg coordination. The foot movements, though slightly weakened by incomplete reinner-vation, were very similar to those in controls in which all muscles of the shank had been removed except the lateral gastrocnemius and the anterior tibial. There had been no sign of a shift back toward reversal of foot movement when they were sacrificed 15 months after the operation.

The results in regard to nerve modulation in these cases are clear and may be dispensed with briefly. Modulation of nerve by muscle obviously does not occur in rats of 40 days or older. The motor nerves, already specifically determined by their original muscles, are no longer in a sufficiently labile condition to be respecified by foreign muscles. Consequently, in connection with the problem of possible restoration of function after nerve crossing, modulation of nerve by muscle may be discounted as a factor operating in rats at this age.

Cases in which reeducation was attempted

The reversal of foot movement which follows nerve crossing is quite similar in all respects to the reversal which follows muscle transposition. The factors involved in reeducation after crossing nerves should be very much the same as after transposing the muscles activated by those nerves. It was thought, however, that because the position of the muscles is not changed by nerve crossing the array of proprioceptive and kinesthetic stimuli might possibly be more favorable for reeducation after nerve crossing than after muscle transposition. The two-joint gastrocnemius muscle with its origin on the femur bone is mechanically stretched in normal phase by movement of the knee joint. This normal stretching of the muscle is, in most responses, simply exaggerated after nerve crossing by the reversal of foot movement, whereas such mechanical effects of knee action were completely abolished in the muscle transposition experiments by attaching the origin of the gastrocnemius muscle to the tibia bone.

With the purpose of forcing out reeducational correction if possible, special treatment was administered to four cases, two unilateral and two bilateral, in which as indicated by palpation, full reinnervation of the muscles had taken place. In the two unilateral cases the contralateral hind foot was immobilized in a neutral position of slight dorsi-flexion by operations causing adhesions and ankylosis of the joint. Four weeks after the appearance of reversed movement, the front legs of one unilateral and one bilateral case were amputated at the shoulder. Because this operation made the animals entirely dependent on the hind legs for support and for locomotion and provided a continuous condition of training where the alteration demanded for the animals' well-being involved the simple sustained contraction of one muscle and inhibition of its antagonist, this test was considered crucial of the rats' ability to correct by a learning process the reversed foot movement. When these rats tried to support themselves on their hind feet, contraction of the anterior tibial muscle activated by the soleus nerve produced dorsi-flexion of the foot so that the toes and sole of the foot were lifted up in the air. The rats continued to balance and hobble about awkwardly on the back points of their heels with the toes pointing upward. They never learned to bring the toes and ball of the foot down to the floor and use them for support. Forty-nine and 63 days of age at the time of the first operation when the nerves were crossed, these two cases died 17 and 16 months, respectively, after amputation of the front legs without any sign of reeducation.

The other two cases, 40 and 83 days old at the time of the first operation, were compelled to rise upright on their hind legs to obtain food. Hard food which could be gnawed only a small bit at a time from a self-feeder was gradually raised so high that it was almost out of reach. When the rats stretched upright to reach the food, their feet were dorsi-flexed so that they could not get up off their heels. By straining upward to their utmost they were able only to barely nibble at the food. The animals were watched to see if they would learn to contract the gastrocnemius on rising upright, as rats do normally, and thus raise themselves to a position from which the food would be more accessible. They continued to struggle and strain to reach the food from the back points of their heels without ever learning to contract the gastrocnemius muscle at the correct time or even to inhibit contraction of the anterior tibial muscle which kept the toes and ball of the foot in the air and prevented use of the flat of the foot as an aid in balancing. At the end of 6 months the animals had become quite thin and training was discontinued. Up to the time of their deaths $10\frac{1}{2}$ and 9 months later, the reversal of foot movement persisted without modification. In being unable to correct or even to inhibit the reversal of foot movement, which was more of a hindrance to them than no foot movement at all, these rats in which the muscles had been left in normal position and only the nerves crossed, were entirely similar to those previous cases in which the muscles had been transposed.

Checks and controls

Post-mortem dissection showed that nerve regeneration had been as intended. There were no stray fibers to the muscles from the original nerve stumps or from other foreign nerves. In two cases which were showing signs of senility and were ready to be sacrificed, the peroneal and tibial nerves were cut and the distal ends stimulated electrically above the point at which the nerves had been sutured. Stimulation of the peroneal nerve caused strong contraction of the gastrocnemius muscle and none of the anterior tibial muscle, while stimulation of the tibial nerve caused strong contraction of the anterior tibial muscle and none of the gastrocnemius muscle. Since the gastrocnemius muscle is normally supplied by the tibial nerve and the anterior tibial muscle by the peroneal nerve, these physiological tests also showed that nerve regeneration had taken place as intended.

The incision was then closed in one of these cases and the anesthesia removed. After healing, 1 week later, it was obvious that the reversal of foot movement had been completely abolished by cutting the nerves. In an extra case in which the operation had not been successful because the reversed movement occurred only in the plantar direction, dorsi-flexion being absent, dissection revealed that the nerve crossed to the anterior tibial muscle had pulled loose, the nerve to the gastrocnemius muscle remaining intact. From this evidence there was no doubt that the reversed foot movement was caused by active contraction of the muscles to which the nerves had been crossed and not by any extraneous mechanical factors.

In control animals in which all the shank muscles had been removed except the anterior tibial and medial gastrocnemius muscles, these two muscles were strong enough to allow the foot to be used to good advantage in coordination very close to that of the normal rat. Two controls similar to the above except that the nerves were cut and connected again to their original muscles in one case and to muscles of the same action in the other, in the former by suture and in the latter by direct insertion, also showed good coordination in normal phase.

In the experimental group reinnervation of the anterior tibial muscle was sufficient in all cases to cause good strong dorsi-flexion of the foot against gravity. That reinnervation of the gastrocnemius muscle was sufficient to lift the body weight of the rat off its heels was questionable in three cases since at death the muscles were only about one-quarter normal size. In the remainder of the cases reinnervation was more complete and in the cases in which reeducation was attempted, palpation previous to training and post-mortem dissection and weighing indicated no appreciable loss of muscle mass. Strong plantar flexion of the foot in the reverse phase was present in all cases.

That sensory as well as motor nerves had regenerated into the foreign muscles was shown by the fact that pinching the exposed muscles under light anesthesia with a blunt forceps, produced reflex responses. Reflex responses elicited by pricking the skin and pulling the hair over all regions of the shank, ankle, and foot, and to flexing the toes and ankle about a month after return of function showed that the operation had not impaired the sensitivity of the limb.

Crosses between Peroneal and Tibial Nerves

Since regeneration of nerves is unselective (Weiss, 1936), the crossing of large nerve trunks such as the peroneal and tibial must result in a random redistribution of the motor fibers of any one muscle of the shank or foot to a large number of foreign muscles. Likewise any one foreign muscle must be reinnervated by a heterogeneous lot of fibers that originally were spread among many different muscles. A similar random dispersal must occur among the sensory fibers. For reeducation or reflex regulation to occur in the face of such confused reinnervation would imply an extreme plasticity, homogeneity, and adaptability on the part of the nerve centers that is directly negated by the results of muscle transposition and nerve crosses between individual muscular nerve branches. The latter results show that contraction of the shank muscles as a group cannot be dissociated in the nerve centers from that of the rest of the leg musculature. It seems improbable that this same dissociation plus the much finer dissociations between different groups of shank and intrinsic foot muscles and even between individual neurons, as would be required after unselective regeneration of the peroneal and tibial nerve trunks, could be made after crossing these nerves. Learning would be simpler presumably after reconnecting the fibers of one muscle directly to another single muscle. However, since reeducational adjustment has been reported to follow the crossing of the compound peroneal and tibial nerve trunks in dogs by Osborne and Kilvington and in dogs, cats, rabbits, and pigs by Rawa, this operation also was performed on a number of rats.

Anatomically the dorsi-flexor muscles of the foot are supplied by the peroneal nerve and the plantar flexors by the tibial nerve. In the normal rat electrical stimulation under light anesthesia of the distal cut end of the peroneal nerve causes sharp strong dorsi-flexion of the foot. Likewise, stimulation of the tibial nerve causes vigorous clear-cut plantar flexion of the foot.

Twenty cases were prepared. They were operated at ages ranging from 15 to 80 days. After cutting the nerves the proximal end of the peroneal was sutured to the distal end of the tibial and the proximal end of the tibial to the distal end of the peroneal. The sutures were enclosed in artery tubes and, because the nerve trunks lie side by side, a long sheet of beef allantoic membrane (Bauer and Black's "insultoic membrane") was placed between the sutured nerves to prevent cross regeneration of fibers to their original branches.

Regeneration occurred as intended. When the legs were reopened after $2\frac{1}{2}$ months, the two nerve trunks were distinctly separable with no sign of stray fibers crossing from one suture to the other. The shank muscles had regained their full size. After cutting the nerve trunks proximal to the point of suture in three cases, electrical stimulation of the cut ends produced dorsi-flexion when the crossed tibial nerve was stimulated, and plantar flexion when the crossed peroneal nerve was stimulated. Clearly the mass of structures normally supplied by the tibial fibers had been reinnervated by the peroneal fibers, and vice-versa.

Flaccid paralysis with muscular atrophy immediately followed the operation. On regeneration of the nerves with resultant recovery of muscular strength and tonus, the foot was moved abnormally but not in reverse as after crosses between individual muscles. There were no loose free reciprocal movements of the foot. Active dorsi-flexion was never seen. Only when the rats were at rest with the leg muscles relaxed did the foot attain a normal position of dorsi-flexion, passively flexed underneath the animals by the body weight. Whenever leg movement occurred, the foot was held rather stiffly and moved only through varying degrees of plantar flexion. As time went on, the plantar flexion became more predominant. During activity the foot was kept stiffly extended. In the supporting phase of locomotion the body weight was supported on the digits instead of on the sole of the foot. The result of this rigid plantar flexion in locomotion was to make the leg coordination of the rats similar to that of digitigrade mammals such as the cat, dog and pig. In the rat, however, the toes are long and become permanently curled after the operation so that the rats walked on the dorsal rather than on the plantar surface of the toes.

The reason for the predominance of plantar flexion with curling of the toes and rigidity of the ankle joint is not entirely clear, though the following factors are probably in part responsible. The peroneal and tibial trunks contain, besides fibers to the directly opposed flexor and extensor muscles, fibers to the peroneal group of muscles and to the group of deep flexor muscles and also to all the small muscles intrinsic to the foot which groups probably do not all function in perfect synchrony with the primary plantar and dorsi-flexors. If, for example, the posterior tibial and the short and long peroneal muscles contract during plantar flexion as they apparently do in man (Wright, 1928), then, after crossing their fibers along with those of the dorsi-flexors into the plantar-flexor muscles, one would expect to get a continuous plantar-flexor contraction persisting through both phases of locomotion. Also, because the plantar flexors are much more powerful than the dorsi-flexors, any generalized pull on all muscles produced by prolonged contraction, contracture, or even by muscle tonus, after disruption of the myotatic reflex mechanisms for controlling that tonus, would tend to result in predomination of plantar flexion. Whether cause or result, there was an anatomical shortening of the plantar-flexor muscles. This shortening was not so severe in the majority of cases as to prevent reeducational adjustment since good dorsi-flexion of the foot could be obtained by electrical stimulation of the nerve. In most of those cases operated at about 15 days of age, however, when growth is still very rapid, the condition became so severe that complete dorsi-flexion was impossible even by forcible manipulation.

The leg coordination following the crossing of peroneal and tibial nerves was quite similar in all twenty rats save for the age difference mentioned above. Fifteen of the animals were kept longer than a year, nine of them as long as 18 months after the operation. Foot movement remained abnormal to the end with no evidence of correction.

One must conclude either that the nervous system of cats, dogs, rabbits, and pigs is considerably more efficient in regard to reeducation than that of rats, which seems very unlikely particularly in the case of pigs, whose central nervous system is decidedly more primitive (Kappers, Huber and Crosby, 1936), or that the adjustment observed in these other animals was actually due to anatomical and mechanical peripheral effects rather than to central adjustment. In this regard it should be noted that passive extension of a dog's, cat's, rabbit's, or pig's knee mechanically forces an extension of the foot because of the pronounced two-joint action of the plantar-flexor muscles. Dorsi-flexion is mechanically impossible with the knee extended and can occur only, as it does normally, when the knee is flexed. After crossing peroneal and tibial nerves, knee movement which is unaffected by the operation would thus tend on regeneration of the nerves to control foot movement mechanically as the two-joint muscles gradually recovered their strength and tonus. The effects observed after crossing the peroneal and tibial nerves in the rat, obviously not normal in this animal, would be functionally very adaptive in a short-toed digitigrade animal, and might easily be mistaken for a restoration of normal coordination.

There was no indication of nerve modulation in these cases. Unfortunately the effect of modulation of the few fibers that had not yet reached their end-organs at the time of operation in the youngest animals would have been so weak that it would have been overshadowed by the action of the fibers already established.

Conclusion

No adaptive functional adjustment of the nervous system took place in these rats after the connections from the spinal centers to antagonistic limb muscles had been exchanged. The crossing of the peroneal and tibial nerves and the crossing of the pure muscular branches of these nerves resulted in an awkward and thoroughly abnormal foot movement in the former case and in a complete reversal of foot movement in the latter, neither of which was ever corrected by automatic reflex regulation or by a gradual learning or conditioning process. These results are in agreement with those of Cunningham (1898) who crossed the median and ulnar nerves in dogs and stood alone in maintaining that recovery of normal muscular coordination does not follow the crossing of limb nerves. They indicate that the more numerous reports implying a surprising plasticity and regulatory adaptability of the central nervous system to disarrangements of the normal peripheral relations are not to be accepted without question, and show in contrast an extremely unplastic fixation of the basic motor patterns for hind limb coordination.

Persistence of the original patterns of discharge to the limb musculature after peripheral alterations that thoroughly disrupted the normal array of afferent stimuli from the limb supports the contention that the control of limb coordination is in large part central. As pointed out by Gray (1939), peripheral stimuli are extremely important in the timing of limb responses, in controlling the intensity of limb responses, and in determining in many cases which of various possible limb responses as wholes will be set off. But since the elementary patterns of limb coordination persist in the rat after extreme distortion of peripheral conditions produced by nerve crossing, muscle transposition, and even complete deafferentation of the limb; the organization of the intrinsic motor patterns themselves must depend primarily on central rather than peripheral factors.

Permanent retention of the original incidence of discharge of the motor nerve fibers after their regeneration into foreign antagonistic muscles also demonstrates that nerve cells in juvenile and adult stages of the rat are no longer in a sufficiently labile condition to be respecified by foreign muscles. In amphibians where modulation of nerve by muscle has been most thoroughly studied it has been shown that in larval stages respecification takes place quite readily, while in newly metamorphosed toads it occurs only very slowly (Weiss, 1936, p. 516), and in fully grown toads the capacity of nerve cells to undergo modulation is completely lost (Weiss, unpublished). Mammalian tissues in general are less labile than those of amphibians and their nerves probably become irreversibly determined in an earlier stage of development soon after reaching the muscles.

The results in the rat are not necessarily contradictory to the results in larval amphibians in their implications regarding the role of inter-neuron connections in reflex activity and central nervous function. Nerve modulation may be considered an embryological inductive influence which affects development of the central connections of motor cells in the cord rather than a factor which selectively modifies the nerves' sensitivity to central excitatory agents. According to this interpretation, the formation of synaptic terminations on motor cells by the telodendria of internuncial neurons is conditioned by the specific biochemical properties induced in the different motor cells by their muscles. End-organ connection formed by outgrowing nerve fibers in ontogeny becomes, on this basis, an important factor in the laying down and differentiation of central reflex relations. The influence of peripheral organs on the quantitative development of the central nervous system has already been well demonstrated (see Detwiler, 1936).

After crossing peripheral nerves, one would expect a restoration of normal function due to modulation of nerve by muscle, according to this interpretation, only in cases where the peripheral nerves had not already become irreversibly determined by their original end-organs and where the central nervous system was still in a sufficiently labile condition to permit compensatory growth readjustments in the central connections and also where the central terminations of the nerves crossed were located in the same region of the central nervous system. At present there is no crucial evidence to indicate whether modulation affects the selective sensitivity of the motor neurons or the central connections of these neurons. But because this alternative explanation of the phenomenon of homologous response is consistent with both the amphibian and mammalian experiments and also with the classical conceptions of central nervous physiology it is mentioned here as a working hypothesis.

Summary

1. In ten rats (eight unilateral and two bilateral cases, operated at ages ranging from 40 to 250 days) exchanging the nerve connections of flexor and extensor muscles in the shank produced a reversal of foot movement.

2. In all ten cases the foot movement remained fixedly reversed to the end with no corrective modification whatever. Seven cases were kept longer than 15 months after the operation. Immobilization of the contralateral hind foot, training the rats to rise upright on their hind legs for food, and amputation of both front legs at the shoulder all failed to induce reeducation.

3. Post-mortem examination and physiological tests showed that nerve regeneration had been as intended, that sensitivity of the shank and foot had not been impaired by the operation, and that sensory as well as motor fibers had reinnervated the muscles. Severance of the crossed nerves abolished the reversed movement. Control animals, similarly operated except that the nerves were reconnected to the original muscles, showed foot movement in normal phase in all activity.

4. In two additional rats, both unilateral, transposition of flexor and extensor muscles after the nerves to these muscles had previously been crossed resulted in foot movement in normal phase. No change toward reversal occurred after 15 months.
5. In twenty rats, ranging in age from 15 to 80 days, the peroneal and tibial nerves were crossed instead of the single nerve branches to individual muscles. This operation produced an abnormal limb coordination characterized by indiscriminate contraction of the shank muscles and a predomination of plantar flexion of the foot. This abnormal coordination persisted for 18 months without any sign of a central nervous adjustment.
6. The results furnish new evidence of the rigid organization in the rat of the basic motor patterns for hind limb coordiantion. They also show that, in a mammal, motor nerve cells in post-embryonic condition do not have the capacity to undergo muscle-specific modulation after regeneration into foreign muscles.

References

Barron, D. H. (1934). The results of peripheral anastomoses between the fore and hind limb nerves of albino rats. *J. Comp. Neur.*, vol. 59, pp. 301–23.

Cunningham, R. H. (1898). The restoration of coordinated, volitional movement after nerve "crossing." *Am. J. Physiol.*, vol. 1, pp. 239–54.

Detwiler, S. R. (1936). *Neuroembryology*. New York: Macmillan.

Flourens, J. P. (1842). *Recherches expérimentales sur les propriétés et les fonctions du système nerveux dans les animaux vertébrés*. Ed. 2. Paris: J. B. Baillière.

Gray, J. (1939). Aspects of animal locomotion. *Proc. Roy. Soc. Lond., ser. B*, vol. 128, pp. 28–62.

Kappers, C. U. Ariëns, G. Carl Huber and E. C. Crosby (1936). *The comparative anatomy of the nervous system of vertebrates, including man*. New York: Macmillan.

Kennedy, R. (1914). Experiments on the restoration of paralysed muscles by means of nerve anastomosis. *Proc. Roy. Soc. Lond., ser. B*, vol. 87, pp. 331–5.

Osborne, W. A., and Basil Kilvington (1910). Central nervous response to peripheral nervous distortion. *Brain*, vol. 33, pp. 288–92.

Rawa, A. L. (1885). Über das Zusammenwachsen der Nerven verschiedener Bestimmungen und verschiedener Functionen. *Arch. für Anat. u. Physiol., Physiol. Abt.*, Bd. 9, S. 296–328.

Sperry, R. W. (1940). The functional results of muscle transposition in the hind limb of the rat. *J. Comp. Neur.*, vol. 73, pp. 379–404.

Weiss, Paul (1935). Homologous (resonance-like) function in supernumerary fingers in a human case. *Proc. Soc. Exp. Biol. and Med.*, vol. 33, pp. 426–30.

—— (1936). Selectivity controlling the central–peripheral relations in the nervous system. *Biol. Rev.*, vol. 11, pp. 494–531.

—— (1937). Further experimental investigations on the phenomenon of homologous response in transplanted amphibian limbs. *J. Comp. Neur.*, vol. 67, pp. 269–315.

—— (1941). Reunion of stumps of small nerves by tubulation instead of suture, *Sci.*, vol. 93, pp. 67–8.

Wright, W. G. (1928). *Muscle function*. New York: Paul B. Hoeber, Inc.

Spatial Integration and Cortical Dynamics

Charles D. Gilbert, Aniruddha Das, Minami Ito, Mitesh Kapadia, and Gerald Westheimer

The visual cortex analyzes information coming from the retina, transforms it in a way that makes it possible to identify objects within the visual image, and stores a representation of these objects for later recall. The visual cortex as a whole consists of multiple areas. It has been suggested that each area is specialized for analyzing a particular aspect of the visual image, though the relative contribution of each of these areas for image analysis is only beginning to be understood. Even so, the conceptual framework by which we view the cortical mechanisms of vision is undergoing a radical change. It had been thought that information about object identity was analyzed progressively, through a series of areas, culminating in the areas situated in the temporal lobe. The nature of functional deficits following lesions of the temporal lobe, including prosopagnosia, the inability to recognize faces, suggests that these areas are responsible for the categorization and identification of objects. This led to the supposition that the plasticity of circuits required to store this information would be a property of these higher-order areas and that at the earliest stages of visual processing, especially the primary visual cortex (V1), the properties of cells would be considerably simpler and fixed in adulthood. In support of this idea, work on the development of the functional properties of cells in V1 and of its cortical circuits showed cortical plasticity to be limited to a critical period in the first few months or years of life. During this period, abnormal visual experience can produce a change in the balance of input from the two eyes, which is mediated by a change in the pattern of input to the cortex from the thalamus (1). After the end of that period, these properties and connections become fixed. This led to the assumption that in adulthood, all of the properties and connections in V1 would be fixed and that this area performs a fixed, stereotyped operation on the retinal input regardless of the characteristics of the visual stimulus. The emerging view, however, is that even in V1, and even in adulthood, many functional properties of cells, the strength and density of connections, and the functional architecture are highly dynamic. The dynamic nature of the functional properties of cortical cells is seen at several levels: the response specificity of a cell is dependent on

Abbreviations: PS, point spread; RF, receptive field.

the context within which local features are presented, and is dependent on the previous history of stimulation over time scales ranging from seconds to months.

Another change in the view of cortical processing, which is likely to be related to the dynamic properties of visual cortex, concerns the ability to link the components of a visual image into a unified percept. One of the fundamental requirements of the visual system is to integrate the line segments of which object boundaries are composed, and the surfaces of which three-dimensional structures are made, into identifiable objects. It had long been believed that the sizes of receptive fields (RFs) for cells at early stages in the visual pathway were very tiny and discrete, providing a minute window on an object's contour. This rather atomistic view of visual processing left a major issue unresolved: how the line segments of which an object is composed are integrated in a way that enables us to deal with the object as a whole. The traditional viewpoint would have held that the process of spatial integration is left to high-order stages in the visual pathway, such as those found in the temporal lobe. Several lines of evidence indicate that, quite to the contrary, spatial integration begins at the earliest stages, even in primary visual cortex (V1), and builds progressively at consecutive stages as the signal is processed from one area to the next. For several reasons one can view the process of object recognition as being distributed across all visual cortical areas, rather than taking place at one final stage, so that a strictly hierarchical view of processing is an over-simplification. The integrative, dynamic nature of even the first visual cortical area points toward a considerable degree of complexity in the properties of V1 cells. Visual information is present at the finest spatial grain within V1, so the perceptual attributes involving the most detailed spatial information are likely to be based in V1. The presence of feedback loops to V1 from numerous areas along the visual cortical pathway allows the analysis of complex properties of the visual image, such as surface segmentation, to be referred back to earlier stages.

Anatomical evidence shows that at the early cortical levels the substrate exists for providing cells with input from relatively large parts of the visual field. From physiological studies, it now appears that the response properties of cells are modulated by stimuli lying outside of the "classical" RF. The structure and specificity of RFs and of cortical functional architecture are increasingly seen as context dependent. This may represent the cellular mechanism of perceptual studies showing that the visual system is capable of linking contours and surfaces in a process of perceptual fill-in (*2–6*), that our perception of the attributes of local features is influenced by context (*7–14*), and that simple contours can be picked out of a noisy background (*15–18*). The perceptual phenomena obey rules that are consonant with the patterns of connectivity in primary visual cortex, supporting the idea that a major component of the process of spatial integration occurs there. One can characterize a host of processes, referred to as intermediate-level vision, that occur between the discrimination of simple visual attributes, such as orientation, and the identification of complex objects. The neural mechanisms may be found at earlier stages than previously believed.

Long-Range Cortical Connections

Our initial evidence of a cellular substrate for spatial integration was a pattern of long-range horizontal connections formed by the axons of pyramidal cells in V1 (*19–23*).

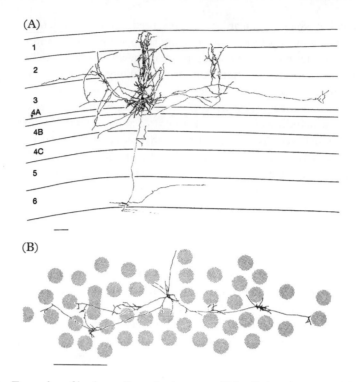

Figure 18.1   Examples of horizontally projecting pyramidal cells in primate area V1, labeled by intracellular injection of horseradish peroxidase. The cell in *A* is seen in a transverse view of cortex, with the cell and dendritic field located in the superficial layers. Its axon spread for > 4 mm parallel to the cortical surface, and within this area the axon's collaterals were distributed in discrete clusters. The cell in *B* is seen in tangential view, with only the axon shown. The axonal field is shown in relation to the cytochrome oxidase blobs, a feature of histochemical staining in V1 that correlates with the ocular dominance columns, giving a sense of the scale of the horizontal connections. This axon traversed 6 mm of cortex, mediating communication between cells with widely separated RFs. (Bars = 1 mm.) [Reprinted with permission from ref. *24* (copyright 1992, Cell Press).]

The extensive plexus of horizontal connections was revealed in experiments which mapped the intrinsic cortical circuit and related cortical connections to RF properties by labeling the full axonal arbor of functionally characterized cells (fig. 18.1). The findings were quite surprising, since they seemed to violate the principles of RF structure and cortical topography. Because of the extensive spread of the horizontal connections, their cellular targets are capable of integrating input over an area of cortex that represents an extent of visual field roughly an order of magnitude larger in area than the cells' own RFs. This finding contrasted with the belief that all the connections in the cortex are vertical, between cells with overlapping RFs and similar orientation preference, with relatively little lateral transfer of information. In effect it posed a contradiction in the definition of the RF, in that it suggested that cells should be sensitive to stimuli lying outside of the RF. The resolution to this conflict lies in the way the RF is defined, which is highly dependent on the stimulus used. When one uses a simple stimulus, such as a single short line segment of the appropriate orientation, one can activate a cell to suprathreshold levels over a very limited area, the classical RF. If,

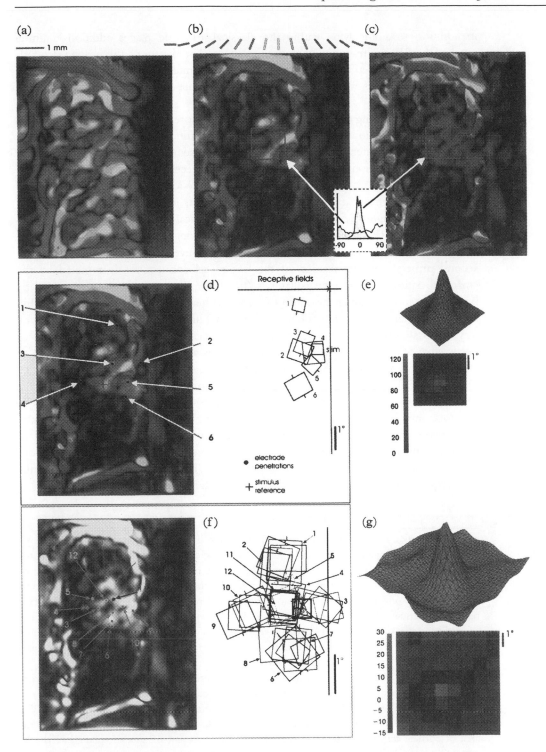

Figure 18.2 Functional interactions mediated by horizontal connections visualized in cat visual cortex with optical recording of cortical PS. (*a*) Optical image of orientation columns, based on stimulation with a global stimuli of gratings of different orientations. Optical PS, the area of

in addition to a line lying within the classical RF, one places additional stimuli outside the RF, the response of the cell changes. The nature of the change depends on the precise geometric relationship between the stimuli lying within and outside the RF, and it correlates well with the influence of context on the perception of local features.

The rules governing contextual influences are mirrored by the registration between the long-range horizontal connections and cortical functional architecture. The first relationship is the extent of visual space that is represented by the area of cortex over which these connections spread. The horizontal connections spread laterally up to 6–8 mm (*19, 20, 25*). As was shown by Hubel and Wiesel (*26*), a distance of two hypercolumn diameters (a hypercolumn is defined as a complete set of orientation columns), or roughly 1.5 mm, is the minimal cortical distance between cells with nonoverlapping RFs. The distance covered by the longest-range horizontal connections, therefore, separates cells with RFs that are several RF diameters apart. The second principle of organization of the horizontal connections is revealed by the clustered nature of their axon collaterals (fig. 18.1). These clusters are separated by 0.5–1 mm, approximating the width of an individual hypercolumn. The relationship between the clusters and the columnar functional architecture was shown in several ways. Cross-correlation analysis, which is a statistical technique relating the time of occurrence of action potentials in pairs of neurons and which provides a measure of effective connection strength between the neurons, showed that cells with correlated firing had similar orientation preference (*27, 28*). Correlated firing was found even for cell pairs with nonoverlapping RFs, as would be expected for the distances spanned by the horizontal connections. The registration between the clustering of the horizontal connections and orientation columns was revealed anatomically by labeling the orientation columns by 2-deoxyglucose autoradiography and marking the horizontal connections with extracellularly applied tracers (*25*). This showed that the horizontal connections ran between columns of similar orientation specificity.

---

cortical activation in response to a small, 0.5° light bar, is 3.2 mm in diameter. (*c*) Optical PS subtracted from image of orientation columns, showing close correspondence over the entire area of the PS, consistent with a pattern of lateral interactions between columns of similar orientation specificity. This image is also multiplied by the strength of the signal, so that only sites of strong orientation preference and good visual responses are seen in the subtracted pattern. (*d*) Visual field representation of optical PS, obtained by electrophysiological recordings around its perimeter. The area of activation represents an area of visual field that is much larger than the stimulus used to generate the optical PS. (*e*) RF profile, showing close correspondence to the hand-mapped RFs, and reinforcing the discrepancy between RF size and the visual representation of the area of cortical activation. (*f*) Interaction profile of RF, using a conditioning stimulus to elevate the level of firing of the cell, and a test stimulus placed in and around the RF. This procedure brings out the subthreshold inhibitory influences surrounding the RF. The overall profile, including both excitation and inhibition, is equivalent in size to the area of cortical activation measured optically. (*g*) Measurement of area of spiking activity by closely spaced electrode penetrations. The area of cortex activated to spiking levels by the test stimulus (bold square) is 0.5 mm × 1.0 mm, much smaller than the area measured with optical recording, which includes regions of subthreshold and suprathreshold activation. (Adapted from ref. 34.)

Visualization of lateral cortical interactions with optical recording

More recently we have used optical recording to obtain a functional measure of the extent and specificity of the horizontal connections. Optical recording reveals *in vivo* the pattern of activity, projected onto the cortical surface, elicited by a given stimulus. It relies on changes in surface reflectance, referred to as the "intrinsic signals," that are linked to metabolic changes resulting from local neural activity. Optical recordings of this signal have been used to visualize the cortical functional architecture, in particular the arrangement of orientation columns (*29–32*). We used optical recording to visualize the area of cortex activated by a minimal visual stimulus, known as the cortical point spread (PS; ref. *33*). The PS was a useful tool to analyze the lateral interactions in cortex. In addition to the optically measured PS, we determined the area of cellular spiking activity, the spiking PS, by recording with extracellular electrodes.

The striking result in these studies was that the optical PS was much larger than the spiking PS (fig. 18.2; refs. *34* and *35*). The diameter of the optical PS averaged 4 mm, while that of the spiking PS averaged 750 μm. This finding was consistent with the idea that the optical PS revealed areas of cortex where cells were activated to subthreshold levels, and that the area of subthreshold activation represented > 95% of the total area covered by the optical PS. The visual field representation of the optical PS was determined electrophysiologically by measuring RF size and positions of cells at its boundary. For the example shown in fig. 18.2, this corresponded to an area of visual field 4° in diameter, as compared to the 0.5° size of the stimulus used and the similar size of RFs in the region. This supported the idea that the lateral interactions within V1 provide an order-of-magnitude-larger area of visual integration than that covered by the classical RF.

The discrepancy between the area of visual field over which cells receive input and the area of the classical RF emphasizes the stimulus dependency of the RF definition. Ordinarily, the RF boundaries are determined by using a short line segment of a particular orientation as the visual stimulus. When using multiple stimuli, however, one can see evidence for modulatory regions surrounding the RF. This is shown again in fig. 18.2, where a conditioning stimulus was placed within the classical RF, and a second test bar was placed in various positions outside the RF. This revealed the existence of a large inhibitory "moat" surrounding the RF, which includes regions mediating end- or side-band inhibition (*36, 37*). The diameter of the central excitatory core and the surrounding inhibitory region for this cell was ≈4°, equivalent to the visual field representation of the optical PS. If we assumed that connections between the spiking region and the surrounding area of subthreshold activation are reciprocal, the correspondence between the area of the RF surround and the representation of the area of cortical activation suggested that lateral cortical interactions play a part in the extended RF measured with complex visual stimuli.

Further evidence for the relationship between the horizontal connections and the cortical columnar architecture is also revealed by the comparison between the optical PS and the optical image of orientation columns (fig. 18.2). The close match between the two, as seen in the uniform blue color in the difference image, showed that the distant patches of subthreshold activation had the same orientation specificity as the central zone of spiking activity. That is, when a stimulus of a particular orientation activates a small patch of spiking cells, these cells have axons projecting outside the area of spiking activity, which leads to subthreshold activation of satellite patches of the same orientation preference. The subthreshold signal could arise from inhibitory as well as excitatory activity, either of which could lead to the metabolic signal which induces the change in surface reflectance.

Synaptic physiology of horizontal connections

The suggestion from the RF map obtained by using paired stimuli is that much of the extended RF surround is inhibitory. Is it plausible that some of this inhibition could be mediated by the horizontal connections? Though the longest-range connections in the cortex are formed by pyramidal cells, which produce direct excitation, the effect of the horizontal plexus can involve both excitation and inhibition. The reason for this is seen in both anatomical studies and physiological studies of the horizontally evoked synaptic potentials in cortical slices. Roughly 80% of the targets of the horizontal connections are other spiny, pyramidal cells and 20% are inhibitory interneurons (*38*). Though the inhibitory limb of this circuit represents the minority of connections, it can have a disproportionate effect in terms of the resultant synaptic potentials. When the horizontal connections are weakly activated, the synaptic potential is exclusively excitatory, but as additional horizontal inputs are recruited by increasing the strength of stimulation, the excitatory postsynaptic potential (epsp) initially is truncated and reversed by a disynaptic inhibitory postsynaptic potential (ipsp) and, at the highest stimulus strengths, becomes strongly inhibitory (*39*). Another important feature of the horizontally evoked epsp is that it increases substantially as the cell is depolarized. This increases the strength of the horizontal inputs when the cell is simultaneously depolarized by other inputs, and suggests that the effect of horizontal inputs is state dependent (*39*). These nonlinear properties at the synaptic level may account in part for the nonlinear RF properties described below.

Contextual Influences in Psychophysics and Physiology

The interactions revealed by the anatomy of the horizontal connections and their relationship with orientation columns suggest a possible role in visual spatial integration. The process of integration was evaluated in terms of the threshold level of contrast required to detect a target line. In psychophysical experiments, the contrast level required to detect a target line is influenced by the presence of a second line adjacent to the target. When the flanking line is located near the target line, is colinear with it, and has the same orientation, the required contrast level for detection of the target is reduced by $\approx 40\%$. Shifting the flanking line away from the target along the colinear axis reduces its influence. Similarly, shifting it laterally, along an axis orthogonal to its orientation, also abolishes the effect. In addition to the influence of changing position, there is also a dependency on orientation, such that changing the relative orientation of the two lines from parallel to $> 30°$ abolishes the threshold reduction (*11, 13, 14*).

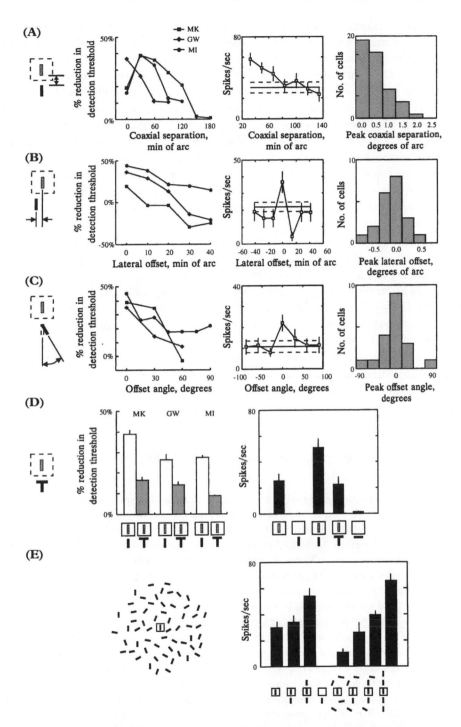

Figure 18.3 Contextual effects on perception of local features and on RF properties of cells in superficial layers of primary visual cortex. The effects illustrated here show the effect of context on the perception of the visual attributes of local features and the underlying facilitatory effect of contours lying outside the classical RF. The psychophysical studies were done in human

Analogous effects are seen at the level of single cells in V1. The long-range horizontal connections in the cortex raise the possibility for extensive facilitatory influences from outside the classical RF, and these have been seen in a number of studies *(40–47)*. Also, contextual alteration of a cell's response specificity, such as orientation preference, has been suggested to play a role in the tilt illusion *(45, 48)*. To determine whether facilitation from outside the RF, in area V1, might account for contextual influences on perception, we explored whether they showed similar dependency on position and orientation. These experiments were done in alert, fixating monkeys, with the idea that making a comparison between human and monkey experiments requires using animals that are at levels of alertness comparable to those of the human subjects. In these studies, > 40% of the complex cells in the superficial layers of cortex showed facilitation when, in addition to the stimulus within the RF, a second nearby, colinear, iso-oriented line was placed outside the excitatory core of the RF (fig. 18.3; ref. *14*). The median level of facilitation was 2.3-fold. For most of the cells showing facilitation, the greatest effect occurred when the flanking line was near the boundary of the RF, and the effect decreased as the line was separated from the target line in directions along the orientation axis or orthogonal to it (fig. 18.3*A* and *B*). In addition, the effect was maximal when the lines were parallel, and it decreased as the flanking line was tilted relative to the target line (fig. 18.3*C*). The physiological results not only showed a similar dependency on position and angle as the psychophysical studies, but the effects operated over comparable spatial scales. Thus the substrate for the psychophysical effects of context may be present as early as V1.

How might the facilitatory effect of a single line outside the classical RF relate to the process of binding the components of a contour along its length, and to the segmentation of a contour from its background? One way to interrupt a contour is to place an orthogonal line across one of the component line segments. When, instead of a flanking line, one placed a T-shaped figure outside the RF, with the crossbar of the

---

observers, and the physiological studies were done on superficial layer complex cells in primary visual cortex of alert, fixating monkeys. (*A*) When two lines were placed in close proximity and were colinear and similarly oriented, there was a reduction in the contrast level needed to detect a target line, and this effect diminished as the lines were separated along the colinear axis (*left*). Individual cells could show a 2-fold or greater increase in their responses to lines outside the classical RF (*center*), and over the population the facilitatory effect dropped off as the lines were separated (*right*). (*B*) There was a loss of the threshold-lowering effect as the lines were shifted laterally (*left*), and a corresponding loss of facilitation at the level of single cells (*center*), which was seen for the overall population (*right*). (*C*) The effect was also dependent on orientation, as seen in both the psychophysical (*left*) and physiological (*center* and *right*) experiments, with the strongest effect seen when the lines were parallel. (*D*) Breaking the continuity between the lines by introducing a cross bar between them caused a loss of the perceptual effect (*left*) and an elimination of the facilitation seen with individual cells (*right*). (*E*) The effects described above with pairs of lines might be related to the ability for salient contours to emerge from a noisy background. The effect of a background of randomly placed and oriented lines was to inhibit the response of the cell, but when elements of the background were shifted to positions that were near, colinear and parallel with the line that lay within the RF, the cell's response was lifted from inhibition. Thus with the appropriate configuration of contours lying within and outside the RF, cells could respond in a visual context that would otherwise be strongly inhibitory. (Adapted from ref. *14*.)

T lying between the two lines, the psychophysical effect was greatly reduced. Similarly, placing the T outside the classical RF often abolished the facilitation seen with a simple line (fig. 18.3*D*). In more complex visual environments, the presence of stimuli outside the RF often inhibited cells' responses, due to the flanking inhibitory regions surrounding the core excitatory region of the RF. When the classical RF was surrounded by a background of randomly positioned and oriented lines, the effect of one or more lines of the appropriate position and orientation outside the RF counteracted the inhibition caused by the random background. These results suggest that with the appropriate configuration of contours surrounding the RF, the cell is lifted from a rather profound level of inhibition and its excitatory inputs are unmasked, allowing it to respond to the stimulus. The push–pull nature of the surround effects, operating over the cortical sheet, would promote the activation of cells whose RFs are superimposed on a salient contour, and would suppress the activity of cells whose RFs cover a random background.

These findings emphasize the nonlinear nature of complex cells in primary visual cortex: the response of these cells in a complex visual environment cannot be predicted from their responses to a single line, presented at different positions and orientations. In this sense the response specificity of cells is dynamic, changing with alterations in context, but not necessarily requiring changes in synaptic weights. The mechanism underlying the contextual sensitivity is likely to involve nonlinearities in the integration ascending interlaminar inputs, which carry information about the more local stimuli, and the horizontal inputs, which carry information about contextual stimuli lying over a larger area.

Long-Term Cortical Plasticity

An expanding body of evidence indicates that even in adulthood some fundamental properties of cortical cells, and cortical functional architecture itself, are mutable and subject to alteration by experience. The initial evidence came from studies in the somatosensory system, which, like the visual system, has a map of the sensory surface on the cortical surface. Amputation of a finger leads to an alteration of this map, such that the area of cortex originally receiving input from the amputated finger changes its representation to the adjacent fingers (*49–51*). We performed similar studies in the visual system, driven by our knowledge of the existence of the long-range horizontal connections, which seemed a likely substrate for the map alterations.

To study experience-dependent plasticity in the visual system, we made focal retinal lesions at homologous positions in the two eyes, thereby removing visual input from a focal area of visual cortex. Over a period of several months, the silenced area of cortex, or cortical scotoma, recovered functioning visual input. The RFs of cells that recovered visual responses shifted from the lesioned part of the retina to positions immediately surrounding it. Effectively, the cortical topography had reorganized, expanding the representation of the perilesion retina and shrinking the representation of the lesioned part of the retina (fig. 18.4; refs. *52–9*).

The substrate for the reorganization was explored by recording at various stages along the visual pathway. At a time when the cortex had been remapped, the lateral geniculate nucleus (LGN, the major source of input to primary visual cortex) still

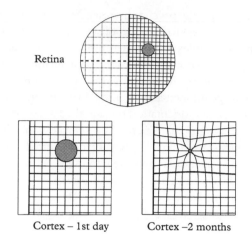

Figure 18.4   Schematic representation of pattern of recovery following binocular retinal lesions. Initially a region was silenced, but over a period of a few months it recovered visually driven activity. This recovery involved a shrinkage in the representation of the lesioned part of the retina and an expansion in the representation of the part of the retina surrounding the lesion. The recovery was due to mechanisms that were intrinsic to the cortex, involving intracortical connections, and over the time course of the full effect involved sprouting of axonal collaterals and synaptogenesis. Much shorter-term changes, over a smaller cortical scale, were seen within minutes. [Reprinted with permission from ref. *66* (copyright 1992, Cell Press).]

sustained a large silent area. Hence one could conclude that the reorganization was due to processes intrinsic to the cortex and not to changes at antecedent levels of visual processing (*53, 55*). The extent of reorganization, roughly 6–8 mm in diameter, could not be explained by the lateral spread of thalamic afferents, which are up to about 1.5–2 mm wide, unless they had increased their projection pattern into the center of the reorganized region. On the other hand, the extent of the long-range horizontal connections did approximate that of the area of reorganization, so these were likely candidates for the cellular substrate of topographic plasticity. We were able to rule out a significant role of thalamocortical projections, leaving the long-range horizontal connections as the most likely substrate (*53, 55*).

The idea that the horizontal connections were responsible for the reorganization was supported by the finding that after recovery, the pattern of orientation columns was similar to that seen before the lesion was made, despite the fact that the RFs of the cells in this region had shifted considerably in visual space (*34*). Given that the horizontal connections run between columns of similar specificity, the involvement of a preexisting framework of horizontal connections would cause the reorganized cortex to recover its original pattern of orientation columns. In addition, the recovery was associated with an increase in the size of the spiking PS, with a larger area of cortex representing a particular part of the visual field. The spiking PS expanded to a size similar to the size of the optical PS in normal cortex, indicating that the reorganization occurred by strengthening existing lateral interactions from subthreshold to suprathreshold levels.

We next attempted to determine the mechanism accounting for the strengthening of the connection from cells lying outside the cortical scotoma to those within the scotoma. The length of time required to see the full extent of reorganization, 2 months or more, raised the possibility of a morphological change. To explore this, we placed injections of biocytin, an anterograde label, at several sites immediately outside the boundary of the original scotoma and compared the pattern of projection into the scotoma with projections into normal (unreorganized) cortex. After about a year, the density of the horizontal projection into the reorganized region had doubled, indicating that the strengthening was mediated by a process of sprouting of axon collaterals and synaptogenesis (*54*). The change observed here did not entail an increase in the extent of the horizontal arbor, but an increase in the density of collateral arborization within the existing clusters of axon collaterals. To see sprouting in the adult brain as a result of alteration in visual experience was quite a contrast with the limitations on alterations in connectivity to the critical period (*60*). Clearly, even in adulthood, brain plasticity results from a continuing process of experience-dependent synaptogenesis.

Rapid Cortical Dynamics

The kind of plasticity discussed to this point involves changes occurring over a period of months. These same experiments revealed a much faster plasticity, occurring within minutes after the retinal lesions were made. Although we saw the expected silencing of activity within the center of the cortical representation of the lesioned part of the retina, there was still visually driven activity for cells whose RFs were originally located within what was later to become the boundary of the retinal lesion. Within minutes of making the lesion, the RFs of these cells had expanded an order of magnitude in area and had shifted to positions outside the lesion (*53, 55, 59*). Thus, substantial changes in RF size and position can be induced, as a result of alteration in visual experience, over a time course of minutes. That one could see these changes so quickly – and that they could be generated without a cutting of the connections to the cortex, but merely by destroying the retinal photoreceptor layer – suggested that one did not need to make lesions in order to induce changes in RF properties.

To test this idea, we generated an "artificial scotoma," a masked part of the visual field including and surrounding the RFs of cells isolated in electrophysiological recordings. The stimulus consisted of a pattern of moving lines or dynamic (twinkling) random dots, within which a blank area or occluder was located. The occluder was sized and positioned to lie over the RF of a cell isolated with a recording electrode, and was roughly three times the diameter of the classical RF. The RF boundary was measured before stimulation with this pattern, during stimulation with the occluder present, and after stimulation of the RF center. The effect after stimulation with this pattern for a few minutes was to expand the size of the RF severalfold, and stimulation within the RF caused it to collapse back down to its original size (fig. 18.5; refs. *61* and *62*). Fig. 18.5 shows that the RF expanded into parts of the visual field where no response had been elicited previously, and demonstrates that the effect is a true RF expansion and not simply gain control. This effect reveals that the structure of the RF is dependent on the history of previous visual stimulation of the cell, and reinforces the fact that stimuli in one part of the visual field influence the response properties of cells with RFs located some distance away. It points out the existence of a problem in neurobiology analogous to the uncertainty principle in physics, that whatever one does

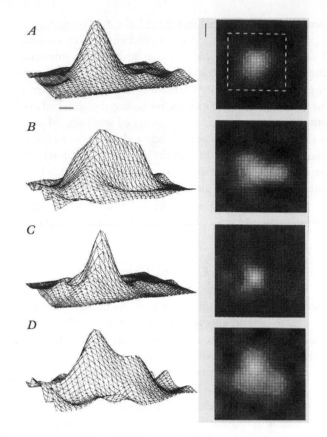

Figure 18.5   Short-term plasticity of RF size induced by an artificial scotoma, an occluded area of visual field surrounded by a pattern of lines or random dots. When placed within the scotoma, the RF expands severalfold in area, and when stimulated in its center, it collapses toward its original size. The RF profile was mapped by placing a small bar at different positions in an 8 × 8 grid. The responses are shown as three-dimensional contour plots on the left, with response rate represented on the vertical axis, and as two-dimensional plots on the right, with response rate represented by the brightness of each pixel. The scale markers represent 1° of visual angle. (*A*) The original size of the RF. The dashed white square on the two-dimensional plot indicates the size and position of the boundary of the artificial scotoma during subsequent conditioning with a dynamic random dot display that surrounded the scotoma. Peak response rate was 40 spikes/sec. (*B*) After a few minutes of conditioning, the RF expanded, as indicated in both the three-dimensional and two-dimensional plots. Peak response rate was 24 spikes/sec. (*C*) After visual stimulation within the RF center, the RF collapsed down to its preconditioned size. Peak response rate was 20 spikes/sec. (*D*) Placing the RF again within the artificial scotoma resulted in its re-expansion. Peak response rate was 60 spikes/sec.

to measure the response properties of a cell may change them. The perceptual consequences of the short-term RF plasticity were explored using psychophysical techniques. It is plausible to think, given the nature of these changes, that the expansion of RFs could explain the phenomenon of perceptual fill-in, in which an occluder appears to fill-in with the color or texture pattern surrounding it (*6*). Cells represent "line labels" indicating, when the cell is active, the presence of a stimulus somewhere within their RFs. When the RFs inside an artificial scotoma expand, the cells become activated by the stimuli lying outside the scotoma, erroneously signaling the presence of the stimuli within the boundary of the scotoma. In addition to perceptual fill-in, the phenomenon of RF expansion might be expected to produce a distortion in the spatial position sense in the vicinity of the scotoma. Due to the imbalance in RF size, a line located near the boundary of the scotoma would activate more cells with RFs within the scotoma than outside, and it would, therefore, be perceived as being shifted inward toward the center of the scotoma. This was shown in human observers, where viewing an artificial scotoma causes the perceived position of objects located near its boundary to be pulled in towards its center (*63*). Thus, in human visual perception one can observe the effects of RF plasticity within a short period of time. These experiments provided insight into the time course of the plasticity, in that viewing the artificial scotoma for a period as short as 1 second caused a significant shift in perceived position. In addition, the task showed a learning effect, with subjects showing an increased accuracy in the determination of position. Both the short-term plasticity evidenced by the perceptual shift and the longer-term learning effects may be associated with the RF expansion and the associated increase in the cortical representation of the trained portion of visual field.

Given the extent of the long-range horizontal connections, the mechanism of the shortest-term plasticity is likely to involve a change in the effectiveness of existing connections, rather than a formation of new synapses. Rather, one can think of the long-range connections in a context similar to that seen in development, where the connections are exuberant, having a broader functional potential than that expressed at any one time. By varying the effective strength of a subset of connections formed by a cell, the functional properties of the target cells can be shifted around within a larger domain. The changing strength of the connections was measured by using the technique of cross-correlation analysis referred to above. When two cells are isolated and their RFs are placed within an artificial scotoma and caused to expand after a period of stimulation, the peak in correlated firing increases in size (*62*). The increase in the peak in the correlogram indicates that there was an associated increase in the effective connection strength between the neurons. The observed plasticity is likely to involve intrinsic cortical connections, since the effect shows interocular transfer (*64*). Here again it is tempting to attribute the change to the horizontal connections.

This increase in effectiveness may be achieved in various ways at the synaptic level, including a strengthening of excitatory connections and an adaptation of inhibitory connections (*65*). Since the horizontal connections, as described above, involve push–pull interactions between excitation and inhibition, a reduction in the inhibition would unmask the connections, boosting their strength from a subthreshold influence to a suprathreshold, driving influence. Moreover, since the ability to strengthen these connections is itself under inhibitory control, where with less inhibition there is an increased probability of producing a use-dependent change in the excitatory connection (*66*), one might produce an increase in the strength of the horizontal connections by a cascade of mechanisms. The precise synaptic mechanisms governing plasticity in this system, however, remain to be worked out.

Summary

The response properties of cells in primary visual cortex are considerably more complex than was previously believed. The complexity is manifest as both a context dependency and a dependency on the prior history of stimulation. As a result of these findings it is clear that the primary visual cortex carries information about higher-order characteristics of the visual stimulus rather than a mere representation of the line segments of which it is composed. Instead, it provides information about the character of the conjunctions between contours and surfaces in the visual image. The perceptual consequences of the dynamic changes in RF structure and cortical functional architecture depend on the time scale of the plasticity. Changes occurring over the longest time periods may play a role in recovery of function after lesions of the central nervous system, but under normal circumstances may be involved in perceptual learning. Over shorter time scales, the effect may represent a continuing process of normalization and calibration of the visual system, as well as the linkage of contours and fill-in of surfaces common to a single object. Several characteristics of the phenomena described above bear emphasizing: cells in area V1 are increasingly being seen as being involved in complex perceptual tasks, mediating the process of linkage of contours and integrating visual information over visual space. These processes are likely to involve a differential strengthening and weakening of subsets of connections within extensive axonal fields, the long-range horizontal connections representing a likely substrate for many of the observed effects. Because of these connections any cortical cell has a wider range of potential properties it can potentially express than is manifest at any given time. An important question to be addressed is to differentiate those contextual effects and dynamic changes in RFs that are due to the intrinsic horizontal connections, hence reflecting bottom-up processes, from those that arise from feedback connections, reflecting top-down influences. Though the precise synaptic mechanisms remain to be worked out, the fact that the effects have been observed in primary visual cortex, where much of the detailed functional architecture, connectivity, and RF properties have been worked out in considerable detail, makes accessible an understanding of the mechanisms of higher-order perceptual phenomena.

References

1   Hubel, D. H. & Wiesel, T. N. (1970) *J. Physiol. (London)*, **206**, 419–36.

2   Kanizsa, G. (1979) *Organization in Vision: Essays on Gestalt Perception* (Praeger, New York).

3   Yarbus, A. L. (1957) *Biophysics*, **2**, 683–90.

4   Krauskopf, J. (1961) *Am. J. Psychol.*, **80**, 632–7.

5   Crane, H. D. & Piantanida, T. P. (1983) *Science*, **221**, 1078–9.

6   Ramachandran, V. S. & Gregory, T. L. (1991) *Nature (London)*, **350**, 699–702.

7   Gibson, J. J. & Radner, M. (1937) *J. Exp. Psychol.*, **20**, 453–67.

8   Badcock, D. R. & Westheimer, G. (1985) *Vision Res.*, **25**, 1259–69.

9   Westheimer, G., Shimamura, K., & McKee, S. P. (1976) *J. Opt. Soc. Am.*, **66**, 332–8.

10   Westheimer, G. (1986) *J. Physiol. (London)*, **370**, 619–29.

11   Polat, U. & Sagi, D. (1993) *Vision Res.*, **33**, 993–9.

12 Polat, U. & Sagi, D. (1994) *Vision Res.*, **28**, 115–32.

13 Dresp, B. (1993) *Spatial Vision*, **7**, 213–25.

14 Kapadia, M. K., Ito, M., Gilbert, C. D., & Westheimer, G. (1995) *Neuron*, **15**, 843–56.

15 Wertheimer, M. (1938) *Laws of Organization in Perceptual Forms* (Harcourt, Brace & Jovanovich, London).

16 Grossberg, S. & Mingolla, E. (1985) *Percept. Psychophys*, **38**, 141–71.

17 Ullman, S. (1990) *Cold Spring Harbor Symp. Quant. Biol.*, **55**, 889–98.

18 Field, D. J., Hayes, A., & Hess, R. F. (1993) *Vision Res.*, **33**, 173–93.

19 Gilbert, C. D. & Wiesel, T. N. (1979) *Nature (London)*, **280**, 120–5.

20 Gilbert, C. D. & Wiesel, T. N. (1983) *J. Neurosci.*, **3**, 1116–33.

21 Rockland, K. S. & Lund, J. S. (1982) *Brain Res.*, **169**, 19–40.

22 Rockland, K. S. & Lund, J. S. (1983) *J. Comp. Neurol.*, **216**, 303–18.

23 Martin, K. A. C. & Whitteridge, D. (1984) *J. Physiol. (London)*, **353**, 463–504.

24 Gilbert, C. D. (1992) *Neuron*, **9**, 1–20.

25 Gilbert, C. D. & Wiesel, T. N. (1989) *J. Neurosci.*, **9**, 2432–42.

26 Hubel, D. H. & Wiesel, T. N. (1974) *J. Comp. Neurol.*, **158**, 295–306.

27 Ts'o, D. Y., Gilbert, C. D., & Wiesel, T. N. (1986) *J. Neurosci.*, **6**, 1160–70.

28 Ts'o, D. Y. & Gilbert, C. D. (1988) *J. Neurosci.*, **8**, 1712–27.

29 Grinvald, A., Lieke, E., Frostig, R. D., Gilbert, C. D., & Wiesel, T. N. (1986) *Nature (London)*, **324**, 361–4.

30 Frostig, R. D., Lieke, E. E., Ts'o, D. Y., & Grinvald, A. (1990) *Proc. Natl Acad. Sci. USA*, **87**, 6082–6.

31 Ts'o, D. Y., Frostig, R. D., Lieke, E. E., & Grinvald, A. (1990) *Science*, **249**, 417–20.

32 Bonhoeffer, T. & Grinvald, A. (1991) *Nature (London)*, **353**, 429–31.

33 McIlwain, J. T. (1975) *J. Neurophysiol.*, **38**, 219–30.

34 Das, A. & Gilbert, C. D. (1995) *Nature (London)*, **375**, 780–84.

35 Grinvald, A., Lieke, E., Frostig, R. D., & Hildesheim, R. (1994) *J. Neurosci.*, **14**, 2545–68.

36 Hubel, D. H. & Wiesel, T. N. (1962) *J. Physiol. (London)*, **160**, 106–54.

37 Bishop, P. O., Coombs, J. S., & Henry, G. H. (1971) *J. Physiol. (London)*, **219**, 659–87.

38 McGuire, B. A., Gilbert, C. D., Rivlin, P., & Wiesel, T. N. (1991) *J. Comp. Neurol.*, **305**, 370–92.

39 Hirsch, J. A. & Gilbert, C. D. (1991) *J. Neurosci.*, **11**, 1800–9.

40 Maffei, L. & Fiorentini, A. (1976) *Vision Res.*, **16**, 1131–9.

41 Nelson, J. I. & Frost, B. (1985) *Exp. Brain Res.*, **61**, 54–61.

42 Allman, J. M., Miezin, F., & McGuinnes, E. (1985) *Perception*, **14**, 105–26.

43 Tanaka, K., Hikosaka, K., Saito, H., Yukiem, M., Fukada, Y., & Iwai, E. (1986) *J. Neurosci.*, **6**, 134–44.

44 Gulyas, B., Orban, G. A., Duysens, J., & Maes, H. (1987) *J. Physiol. (London)*, **57**, 1767–91.

45 Gilbert, C. D. & Wiesel, T. N. (1990) *Vision Res.*, **30**, 1689–1701.

46 Knierim, J. J. & Van Essen, D. C. (1992) *J. Neurophysiol.*, **67**, 961–80.

47 Lamme, V. A. F. (1995) *J. Neurosci.*, **15**, 1605–15.

48 Westheimer, G. (1990) *Vision Res.*, **30**, 1913–21.

49 Merzenich, M. M., Kaas, J. H., Wall, J. T., Nelson, R. J., Sur, M., & Felleman, D. (1983) *J. Neurosci.*, **8**, 33–55.

50 Merzenich, M. M., Kaas, J. H., Wall, J. T., Sur, M., Nelson, R. J., & Fellemen, D. (1983) *J. Neurosci.*, **10**, 639–65.

51 Merzenich, M. M., Nelson, R. J., Stryker, M. P., Cynader, M. S., Schoppmann, A., & Zook, J. M. (1984) *J. Comp. Neurol.*, **224**, 591–605.

52 Gilbert, C. D., Hirsch, J. A., & Wiesel, T. N. (1990) *Cold Spring Harbor Symp. Quant. Biol.*, **55**, 663–77.

53 Gilbert, C. D. & Wiesel, T. N. (1992) *Nature (London)*, **356**, 150–2.

54   Darian-Smith, C. & Gilbert, C. D. (1994) *Nature (London)*, **368**, 737–40.

55   Darian-Smith, C. & Gilbert, C. D. (1995) *J. Neurosci*, **15**, 1631–47.

56   Heinen, S. J. & Skavenski, A. A. (1991) *Exp. Brain Res.*, **83**, 670–4.

57   Kaas, J. H., Krubitzer, L. A., Chino, Y. M., Langston, A. L., Polley, E. H., & Blair, N. (1990) *Science*, **248**, 229–31.

58   Chino, Y. M., Smith, E. L., III, Wada, H., Ridder, W. L., III, Langston, A. L., & Lesher, G. A. (1991) *J. Neurophysiol.*, **65**, 841–59.

59   Chino, Y. M., Kaas, J. H., Smith, E. L., III, Langston, A. L., & Cheng, H. (1992) *Vision Res.*, **32**, 789–96.

60   Hubel, D. H., Wiesel, T. N., & LeVay, S. (1977) *Philos. Trans. R. Soc. London B*, **278**, 377–409.

61   Pettet, M. W. & Gilbert, C. D. (1992) *Proc. Natl. Acad. Sci. USA*, **89**, 8366–70.

62   Das, A. & Gilbert, C. D. (1995) *J. Neurophysiol.*, **74**, 779–92.

63   Kapadia, M. K., Gilbert, C. D., & Westheimer, G. (1994) *J. Neurosci.* **14**, 451–7.

64   Volchan, E. & Gilbert, C. D. (1995) *Vision Res.*, **35**, 1–6.

65   Xing, J. & Gerstein, G. L. (1994) *Vision Res.*, **34**, 1901–11.

66   Hirsch, J. A. & Gilbert, C. D. (1993) *J. Physiol. (London)*, **461**, 247–62.

Cortical Mechanisms of Cognitive Development

Mark H. Johnson

Introduction

The region of the primate brain which shows the greatest extent of postnatal development is the cerebral cortex, with detectable changes occurring within the region in humans until the teenage years. Not unrelatedly, the cerebral cortex is also the region of the mammalian brain most suspectible to the effects of postnatal experience. While the exact role of cerebral cortex in psychological processes is still unclear, several authors have argued that extent of the cerebral cortex may be correlated with 'intelligence' across species (e.g. MacPhail, 1982). Thus, the main evolutionary development within the brain across mammals is the relative expansion of the area of cerebral cortex. For example, the area of the cortex in the cat is about 100 cm^2, whereas that of the human is about 2400 cm^2 (24 times the size). This suggests that the extra cortex possessed by primates, and especially humans, is related to the higher cognitive functions they possess. The aim of this chapter is to describe some of the progressive and regressive events which occur during the postnatal development of the primate cortex, and to discuss how these neural developments may relate to advances in perceptual, attentional, and memory abilities in human infants.

Until recently, the study of the development of cognitive abilities such as attention, language, and object recognition had proceeded largely independently of any considerations of their neural concomitants. This lack of interest in the brain by cognitive developmentalists may be due to an implicit assumption that identifiable neural developments which correspond in time or age to a cognitive change may allow the inference that the cognitive change was caused by the maturation of a neural structure (see discussion in Johnson and Morton, 1991). As will become clear later in this chapter, this assumption is not always correct, since many aspects of cortical development appear to be extremely sensitive to the effects of experience. Furthermore, the particular experiences that the animal has early in life are partly determined by its existing cognitive abilities.

Both progressive and regressive events are characteristic of the postnatal development of the cortex, and both classes of event may have their effects on psychological abilities. In this chapter, I shall suggest that while most of the progressive events in postnatal cortical development are relatively impervious to experiential factors, the majority of regressive events are shaped by sensory input. Further, I shall argue that the relation between neural and cognitive development is two-way. Not only do neural developments bring about cognitive changes, but aspects of neural development may be shaped by the interaction between neurocognitive systems within the organism and its external environment.

The Postnatal Development of the Cerebral Cortex

The cortex is basically a thin flat sheet (about 3–4 mm thick) which becomes increasingly convoluted with both phylogenetic and ontogenetic development. It has a fairly consistent internal structure throughout its extent. This does not mean, however, that this structure is simple. It is not. In fact, we still have no widely accepted computational theories of how the cortex works. Figure 19.1 shows a schematic section through an area of primate cortex, the primary visual cortex of the adult macaque monkey. This section is cut at right-angles to the surface of the cortex, and reveals its laminar structure. Each of the laminae has particular cell types within it, and has particular patterns of inputs and outputs. For example, with regard to inputs and outputs, layer 4 is where inputs to the cortex from thalamic regions terminate. This is the layer where most of the inputs from regions other than the cortex arrive. The deeper layers, 5 and 6, often project back to subcortical regions that project to the corresponding layer 4, as well as other subcortical areas. More superficial layers, 2 and 3, commonly project forward to neighbouring regions of cortex. Layer 1 is very diffuse and may be involved in long-range cortico–cortico and cortico–limbic connections. We shall see later that the differential structure of layers in the cortex may be used to analyse developmental changes at the cognitive level.

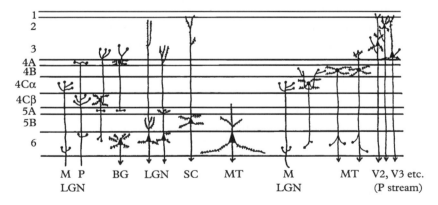

Figure 19.1   A schematic representation of primary visual cortex. Not all cell types or connections are shown. Abbreviations: LGN = lateral geniculate nucleus; SC = superior colliculus; BG = basal ganglia; MT = middle temporal area; M = broad band (magnocellular) stream; P = colour opponent (parvocellular) stream. (Reprinted from *Journal of Cognitive Neuroscience* (Johnson, 1990) by permission of the MIT Press.)

Progressive events in cortical development

Rakic (1988) has proposed a 'radial unit model' of neocortical development which gives an account of how the structure of the mammalian cerebral cortex arises during ontogeny. According to this model, the vertical columnar organization of the cerebral cortex is determined by the fact that each proliferative unit (a cell that gives birth to many others in the subventricular zone, just below the region that subsequently becomes the cortex) gives rise to approximately 100 neurones that all migrate up the same radial glial fibre, with the latest to be born travelling past their older relatives. This results in an inside-out pattern of growth. Thus, radial glial fibres act like a climbing rope to ensure that cells produced by one proliferative unit all contribute to one ontogenetic column. Rakic has speculated that regulatory genes, known as homeobox genes, may be involved in parcellating the proliferative zone into a basic protomap of cortical cytoarchitectonic areas. The scaffolding provided by the radial glial fibres simply enables the translation of this two-dimensional map from one location (the thalamus) to another (the cortex).

Although most cortical neurones are in their appropriate locations by the time of birth in the primate, the 'inside-out' pattern of growth extends into postnatal development. Extensive descriptive neuroanatomical studies of cortical development in the human infant by Conel over a 30-year period led him to the conclusion that the postnatal growth of cortex proceeds in an 'inside-out' pattern with regard to the extent of dendrites, dendritic trees and myelinization (Conel, 1939–1967). In more recent years, the general conclusions which Conel reached have been largely substantiated by more modern neuroanatomical methods (e.g. Rabinowicz, 1979; Purpura, 1975; Becker et al., 1984). In particular, the maturation of layer 5 in advance of layers 2 and 3 seems to be a very reliably observed sequence for several cortical regions in the human infant (Rabinowicz, 1979; Becker et al., 1984). For example, the dendritic trees of cells in layer 5 of primary visual cortex are already at about 60% of their maximum extent at birth. In contrast, the mean total length for dendrites in layer 3 is only at about 30% of maximum at birth. Furthermore, higher orders of branching in dendritic trees are observed in layer 5 than in layer 3 at birth (Becker et al., 1984; Huttenlocher, 1990). Interestingly, this inside-out pattern of growth is not evident in the later-occurring rise and fall in synaptic density. For this measure, there are no clear differences between cerebral cortical layers. We will return to this issue later.

The differential development of cortical areas

In many of the neuroanatomical variables mentioned so far, there appears to be differential development not only between different brain structures, but also between regions within the same structure. For example, Huttenlocher (1990) reports clear evidence of a difference in the timing of postnatal neuroanatomical events between the primary visual cortex and the frontal cortex in human infants, with the latter reaching the same developmental landmarks considerably later in postnatal life than the former. It is worth noting that this differential development within the cerebral cortex has not always been reported in other primate species (Rakic et al., 1986).

Consistent with the reports from postmortem tissue, a study in which the functional development of the human brain was investigated by positron emission tomography (PET) has also found differential development between regions of cortex (Chugani and Phelps, 1986; Chugani, Phelps and Mazziotta, 1987). In infants under 5 weeks of age, glucose uptake was highest in sensorimotor cortex, thalamus, brainstem and the cerebellar vermis. By 3 months of age there were considerable rises in the parietal, temporal and occipital cortices, basal ganglia, and cerebellar cortex. Maturational rises were not found in the frontal and dorsolateral occipital cortex until approximately 6 to 8 months.

Regressive events in cortical development

Regressive events are commonly observed by those studying the development of nerve cells and their connections in the brain. Within the cortex, these events commonly occur some time after the layer-wise dendritic development discussed earlier. For example, in primary visual cortex the mean density of synapses per neurone only starts to decrease at the end of the first year of life (e.g. Huttenlocher, 1990). In humans, most cortical regions and pathways undergo this postnatal loss, which can sometimes exceed 50% (for reviews see: Clarke, 1985; Cowan et al., 1984; Hopkins and Brown, 1984; Janowsky and Findlay, 1986; Purves and Lichtman, 1985).

That selective loss is a significant influence on postnatal primate brain development is evident in a number of different quantitative measures. For example, in the PET study alluded to above, the authors found a somewhat surprising result. This was that the absolute rates of glucose metabolism rise postnatally until they *exceed* adult levels, before returning to adult levels after about 9 years of age. For most cerebral cortical regions the levels reached are about double those found in the adult. One possibility is that this developmental pattern of glucose uptake reflects the over-production of synapses known to occur in many primate brain regions (Chugani et al., 1987).

Consistent with the PET findings of Chugani and colleagues, Huttenlocher (1990) reports quantitative neuroanatomical evidence from two comparatively well-studied regions of the human brain – the primary visual cortex and a part of the prefrontal cortex. In both regions the density of synapses shows a characteristic increase to levels about twice that found in the adult. This is then followed by a period of synaptic loss. Huttenlocher suggests that this initial overproduction of synapses may have an important role in the apparent plasticity of the young brain, a matter which will be discussed in more detail later. There is no strong evidence for this pattern of rise and fall either for density of dendrites or for the number of neurones themselves in humans or other primates. However, in rodents and other vertebrates, postnatal cell loss may be more significant.

Support for the proposal that the peak in density of synapses coincides with the peak in glucose uptake as identified by PET has been obtained in a recent developmental study conducted with cats (Chugani et al., 1991). In this study, the peak of glucose uptake in cat visual cortex was found to coincide with the peak in overproduction of synapses in this region. However, when similar data from human visual cortex are plotted together (figure 19.2), it is apparent that the peak of glucose uptake lags behind synaptic density. Clearly, further work on the relation between these two measures of cortical development is required.

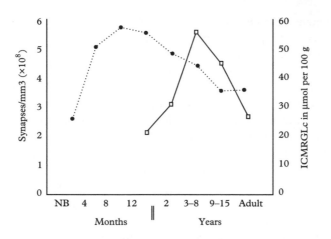

Figure 19.2   Graph showing the development of density of synapses in human primary visual cortex (dotted line – data taken from Huttenlocher, 1990), and resting glucose uptake in the occipital cortex as measured by positron emission tomography (solid line – data taken from Chugani et al., 1987). (ICMRGlc refers to the local cerebral metabolic rates for glucose.)

Cortical Growth and the Development of Perceptual and Cognitive Abilities

Progressive events and perceptual development

The subcortical to cortical shift

Since the classic studies on motor development by McGraw (1943) and others, it has been argued that development in early infancy can be characterized as a shift from subcortical to cortical control over behaviour. Bronson (1974; 1982) proposed that the primary visual pathway does not gain control over visuomotor behaviour in the human infant until between 2 and 4 months after birth. Prior to this age, the infant was thought to respond to visual stimuli primarily by means of the subcortical visual pathway. The detailed evidence in support of this contention has been discussed and extensively reviewed elsewhere (Atkinson, 1984; Bronson, 1974; 1982; Johnson, 1990). Briefly, a variety of neuroanatomical, electrophysiological and lesion evidence indicates that structures on the subcortical visual pathway are developmentally in advance of those on the cortical visual pathway in early infancy. Bronson used this evidence to account for the differences between visually guided behaviour in the newborn infant, as compared to the infant of 3 or 4 months old. The general claim of a shift from subcortical to cortical processing has been reinforced by evidence from the PET studies discussed earlier (Chugani et al., 1987). Assuming that there is some validity to the general claim that there is a shift from subcortical to cortical processing in early infancy, then this should have implications not only for simple aspects of visually guided behaviour, but also for more 'cognitive' aspects of perception, such as the ability to recognize faces. With this in mind, my colleagues and I investigated changes in face-recognition abilities that coincide with the period of rapid cortical visual pathway maturation around 2 months of age. When we began our work on this topic, the existing literature appeared somewhat contradictory. The prevailing view, and most of the evidence, supported the contention that it takes the infant about 2 or 3 months to learn about the arrangement of features that compose a face. Clearly, this is consistent with the idea that this ability is subserved by cortical mechanisms. However, one study provided evidence that newborn infants about 10 minutes old would track (by means of head and eye movements) a face-like pattern further than various 'scrambled' face patterns (Goren, Sarty and Wu, 1975). My colleagues and I attempted to replicate the claims made by Goren et al. As in the original study, newborn infants (around 30 minutes old) were required to track different visual stimuli. This testing procedure differs markedly from that employed by the majority of other investigators. Rather than the infant viewing one or more stimuli in static locations and measuring the length of time spent looking at the stimuli, in the Goren et al. tracking procedure the dependent measure is how far the infant will turn its head and eyes in order to keep a moving stimulus in view. The stimulus is moved slowly away from the midline and the angle at which the infant disengages its eyes from the stimulus is recorded. We used similar stimuli to those used in the original study, and replicated the effect reported (Johnson, Dziurawiec, Ellis and Morton, 1991: Experiment 1).

The replication of the Goren et al. effect raised two questions. First, how specifically face-like does the test stimulus require to be in order to elicit the preferential tracking? Second, what is the developmental time course of this preferential tracking response? In an attempt to begin to address the first of these two questions, we performed a series of experiments using similar procedures to the one just mentioned except that we expanded the set of stimuli to include various forms of 'degraded' face stimuli and optimal spatial frequency patterns (Johnson et al., 1991: Experiment 2; see chapter 5 of Johnson and Morton, 1991). Although there is much work still to be done in defining the exact characteristics of the face-like patterns that are important, at present it appears that high-contrast 'blobs' in the correct relative spatial locations for eyes and a mouth are sufficient. Spatial frequency components of the stimuli alone cannot account for the preference (see Morton, Johnson and Maurer, 1990).

The second question raised by the newborn findings related to the time course of the preferential tracking response. Although it is not feasible to test older infants with exactly the same procedure we used with newborns, we devised an equivalent situation in which the infant was still required to track similar stimuli by means of head and eye turning (Johnson et al., 1991: Experiment 3). Using this procedure, the results indicated that the preferential tracking of faces declines sharply between 4 and 6 weeks after birth.

Why should this decline occur at this age? We have proposed that the preferential tracking response in newborns is primarily mediated by the subcortical visual pathway (Johnson, 1988; Johnson and Morton, 1991; Morton and Johnson, 1991). Apart from considerations of developmental neuroanatomy and neurophysiology alluded to earlier, the time course of the preferential tracking is similar to that of other responses of newborns thought to be mediated by subcortical circuits, e.g. the imitation of facial gestures (Vinter, 1986) or prereaching (Von Hofsten, 1984). The disappearance of these early reflex-like behaviours in the second month of life has been proposed to be due to inhibition of subcortical circuits by developing cortical circuits (see also Muir, Clifton and Clarkson, 1989).

Other sources of evidence support the conclusion that the newborns' face tracking is primarily mediated by subcortical circuits. The temporal visual field feeds more directly into the subcortical pathway, whereas the nasal feeds mainly into the cortical pathway. In a tracking task such as that described, the stimulus is continually moving out of the central visual field and toward the periphery. It may be that this movement into the temporal field initiates a saccade to re-foveate the stimulus in newborns (for details see Bronson, 1974; Johnson, 1990). This consistent movement toward the periphery would not necessarily arise with static presentations, and therefore preferences will rarely be elicited. Thus, the tracking task may effectively tap into the capacities of subcortical structures such as the superior colliculus.

It appears, then, that the development of face recognition in human infants may be accounted for in terms of two mechanisms with independent time courses of neural development. First, there is a system accessed via the subcortical visual pathway that underlies the preferential tracking in newborns, but whose influence wanes by 6 weeks. Second, there is a system dependent upon cortical maturity and requiring exposure to faces that appears around 8 weeks of age. The notion of a shift from subcortical to cortical processing over the first few months of life, therefore, may be useful when considering even apparently complex perceptual abilities.

In recent years, the notion of a shift from subcortical to cortical visual processing in early infancy has come under criticism for several reasons. First, the increasing evidence for apparently sophisticated perceptual abilities in early infancy (e.g. Slater, Morison and Somers, 1988; Bushnell, Sai and Mullin, 1989). Second, recent knowledge about cortical visual processing has brought into question the notion of one cortical visual pathway: recent evidence suggests that multiple distinct cortical pathways should be considered (e.g. Van Essen, 1985; de Yoe and Van Essen, 1988). These considerations have led several authors to propose some form of partial cortical functioning in the newborn (e.g. Maurer and Lewis, 1979; Posner and Rothbart, 1980; Atkinson et al., 1988). As yet, however, this partial cortical functioning remains poorly specified. This consideration motivated some recent attempts to relate differential maturation intrinsic to the cortex to aspects of perceptual and cognitive development. One of my own attempts in this direction is discussed in the following section.

The 'inside-out' pattern of growth and the development of visual attention

The inside-out pattern of postnatal growth of the cortex is crucial for the proposals reviewed in this section. This is because, as mentioned earlier, particular afferents and efferents to any cortical area terminate and depart from particular layers. Thus, if only some layers are functionally mature, then there is a restriction on the afferent and efferent connectivity of the area concerned. Figure 19.1 is a highly schematized diagram of the inputs and outputs of primary visual cortex of the macaque. Several things are worth noting about this section through the visual cortex. As development proceeds upwards through the layers, more output pathways will come 'on line'. In fact, in primary visual cortex this effect may be exacerbated since the afferents from the lateral geniculate nucleus (LGN) slowly grow through the deeper layers (possibly forming temporary synapses on the way) until they reach their adult termination sites in layer 4 at about 2 months of age in the human infant (Conel, 1939–1967). Therefore, as the innervation passes up through the layers, different output pathways may start to feed-forward information to other cortical areas. Since the primary visual cortex is the 'gateway' to nearly all cortical visual processing (Schiller, 1985; but see Johnson, in press a, for caveats to this), this differential maturation has some profound consequences for the control of visually guided behaviour.

Schiller (1985) proposed, on the basis of electrophysiological and lesion data, that there are four pathways underlying oculomotor control in adult primates. These four pathways are: (i) A pathway from the retina to the superior colliculus, the *SC pathway*, thought to be involved in the generation of eye movements toward simple, easily discriminable stimuli, and fed mainly by the peripheral visual field. (ii) A cortical pathway that goes both directly to the superior colliculus from the primary visual cortex and also via the middle temporal area (MT), the *MT pathway*. (iii) A cortical pathway where both magnocellular and parvocellular streams of processing converge in the frontal eye fields, the *FEF pathway*, and which is involved in the detailed and complex analysis of visual stimuli such as the temporal sequencing of eye movements within complex arrays. (Neurophysiological and psychophysical evidence suggests that there are two relatively independent pathways for visual signals from the retina, through the LGN, and within some cortical structures. One of these pathways, the magnocellular pathway, is thought to be concerned with motion processing, while the other, the parvocellular pathway, may be more concerned with colour and form processing.) (iv) The fourth pathway for the control of eye movements is an inhibitory input to the colliculus from several cortical areas via the substantia nigra, the *inhibitory pathway*. Schiller proposes that this final pathway ensures that the activity of the colliculus can be regulated.

The specific proposal made by Johnson (1990) is that, first, the characteristics of visually guided behaviour in the human infant at particular ages is determined by which of these pathways is functional, and second, which of these pathways is functional is determined in turn by the maturational state of the visual cortex. In this chapter only one of the transitions will be illustrated, that which is attributed to the onset of the FEF pathway between 2 and 4 months of age.

There are two types of transitions observed between 2 and 4 months of age which are indicative of FEF pathway functioning. The first of these is that the control over eye movements becomes less input-driven, and more anticipatory in nature, while the second concerns the onset of the ability to perform so-called anti-saccades.

(i)   *The onset of anticipatory eye movements.* This onset of anticipatory eye movements can be demonstrated both in tasks which require the tracking of a moving object, and also in tasks where the infant shows savings to react to predictable sequences of stimuli. By around 2 months, infants begin to be able to track moving objects smoothly and respond readily to stimuli placed in the nasal visual field (Aslin, 1981). Only after 2 months, however, do infants start to show anticipatory tracking in that their eye movements 'predict' the trajectory and speed of a stimulus which moves in a regular repeating fashion (see Johnson, 1990). Other studies, which involve presenting stimuli on one of two different screens in regular or irregular sequences, have shown that only after about 2 months of age do infants show faster reaction times to orient toward stimuli when they are part of regular repeating sequences of presentation (Haith, Hazan and Goodman, 1988). Using a different procedure, Johnson, Posner and Rothbart

(1991) demonstrated that only by 4 months of age do infants show clear evidence of the ability to make predictive eye movements.

(ii)   *The onset of anti-saccades.* The frontal eye fields contain neurones which often discharge in relation to saccadic eye movements, and increase their response to targets within their visual field when that stimulus serves as a target for a subsequent saccade (Goldberg and Bushnell, 1981; Bruce, 1988). A proportion of cells respond prior to a saccade being made. These observations have led to the proposal that the region is involved in the planning of saccadic eye movements. Consistent with this suggestion is the finding that frontal cortex damage in humans results in an inability to suppress involuntary saccades toward targets, and an apparent inability to control volitional saccades (Guitton, Buchtel and Douglas, 1985; Fischer and Breitmeyer, 1987). Guitton et al. (1985) studied patients with frontal lobe lesions, temporal lobe lesions, and normal subjects in an 'anti-saccade' task. In such a task, subjects are instructed not to look at a briefly flashed cue, but rather to look in the opposite direction. Guitton et al. (1985) reported that while normal subjects, and patients with temporal lobe damage, could do this easily, patients with frontal damage, and especially those with damage around the FEF, were severely impaired. The frontal patients had difficulty in suppressing the unwanted saccades toward the cue stimulus.

Clearly, one cannot give verbal instruction to a young infant to look to the side opposite from where the cue stimulus appears. Fortunately, however, as discussed in the previous section, infants of around 4 months or older will rapidly acquire expectations for sequences of stimuli. In order to test for anti-saccades in young infants, I trained them on a series of trials with a predictable sequence of presentation. Figure 19.3 illustrates the sequence of stimuli used by Johnson (in preparation). The infant faces three video monitors. At the beginning of each trial, infants are presented with an attractive fixation stimulus on the centre of the three screens. Once the infant is gazing at this stimulus, a second stimulus is briefly flashed on one of the two side screens. If this stimulus is presented for long enough, infants will make a saccade toward it. After a

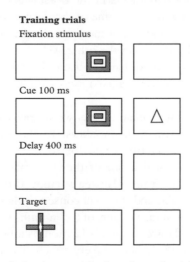

Figure 19.3   The sequence of stimulus presentations for each trial in the 'anti-saccade' experiment. (See text for details.)

brief gap in which no stimuli are presented, an attractive, dynamic, target stimulus is presented on the opposite screen to that on which the brief stimulus had appeared. While infants will commonly make a saccade toward the briefly presented stimulus over the first few trials to which they are exposed, they rapidly learn to ignore this less interesting stimulus and make saccades directly from the central fixation stimulus to the interesting target stimulus. That is, despite the presence of a stimulus that we know normally elicits a saccade, 4-month-old infants are able to suppress an eye movement toward it in order to look toward a more attractive target stimulus.

The differential development of cortical areas

As discussed earlier in the chapter, the frontal area is, in general, the latest region of the cortex to develop postnatally, with detectable changes occurring until the teenage years in the human. This suggests that many aspects of cognitive development may have their neural concomitants in this region. One aspect of cognitive development which has been related to the development of the prefrontal cortex is the ability to retrieve an object in certain situations.

Piaget (1954) discovered a phenomenon which has become known as the 'A not B error'. In this object-retrieval task, infants watch a toy being hidden in one of two wells, or under one of two cups. After a delay of several seconds the infant is allowed to reach toward where he or she thinks that the toy is. From an early age infants will successfully reach to the appropriate location and retrieve the toy. If, however, after a number of such trials, the experimenter switches the side on which the toy is hidden in full view of the infant, infants will continue to reach to the location in which they originally saw the toy being hidden. That is, they make a perseverative error. Once infants are about 8 to 10 months old, they begin to be able to perform this task quite successfully.

Diamond and Goldman-Rakic (1983; 1985; Diamond, 1988) have gathered evidence from a variety of sources in support of the contention that this advance in infant behaviour is mediated by developments in the dorsolateral prefrontal cortex. These authors noticed the similarity between some of the delayed response tests sensitive to prefrontal damage in human adults and monkeys on the one hand, and the object permanence test devised by Piaget on the other. When they administered a monkey version of Piaget's task, they found that infant monkeys appeared to show the same developmental progression between 1 and 4 months as human infants show between 7 and 12 months.

The next question was how human infants would behave in a task known to be sensitive to frontal cortex damage in monkeys. In this simple task the subject is required to reach for an object (food item or toy). The object is in a box with transparent plastic walls, except that one of the side walls is open. An earlier study had shown that monkeys with frontal damage attempt to reach straight for the food through the solid perspex walls, and thus will consequently fail to retrieve the object. Diamond (1988) reports that human infants of 6–7 months were also unable to retrieve the reward in this situation. However, by 11–12 months infants were successful at the task. The younger infants, then, behave very much like the brain-damaged adult monkeys, leading to the conclusion that the developmental changes seen in the infants can be attributed to the maturation of the frontal cortex.

Regressive events in cortical development and perceptual development

The mammalian cerebral cortex is composed of a variety of vertical units referred to variously as blobs, columns, stripes, and modules. It has recently become clear that some of these structures, such as the ocular dominance columns found in the primary visual cortex, emerge during postnatal development. Furthermore, the increasing separation of one cortical column from another may be achieved by the selective loss of dendritic processes and synapses discussed earlier. This functional segregation, which has been referred to as parcellation (Ebbesson, 1984), often results in the separation of previously combined projections. What effects does this process in cortical development have on infant perception?

Ocular dominance columns and binocular vision

Held (1985) has reviewed converging evidence that binocular vision comes in toward the end of the fourth month of life in human infants (although it is worth noting that this can vary from 2 months to 5 months in different infants). One of the abilities associated with binocular vision, stereoacuity, increases very rapidly from the onset of stereopsis, such that it reaches adult levels within a few weeks. This is in contrast to other measures of acuity, such as grating acuity, which increase much more gradually. Held suggests that this very rapid, sudden spurt in stereoacuity requires some radical change in the neural substrate supporting it. On the basis of evidence from animal studies, he proposes that this substrate is the development of ocular dominance columns found in layer 4 of the primary visual cortex.

Neurophysiological studies in monkeys and cats have demonstrated that the geniculocortical afferents from the two eyes are initially mixed so that they synapse on common cortical neurones in layer 4. These layer 4 cells project to disparity selective cells (possibly in cortical layers 2 and 3). During ontogeny, geniculate axons originating from one eye withdraw from the region leaving behind axons from the other eye. Thus, clusters of layer 4 cells become 'captured' by one of the two eyes. Held posits that it is these events at the neural level that give rise to the sudden increase in stereoacuity observed by behavioural measures at around 4 months of age in the human infant.

More recently, Held (1993) explores implications of the fact that prior to segregation of neuronal input, both eyes project to the same cells in layer 4 of the primary visual cortex. Thus, there will be a certain degree of integration between the eyes that will decline once each neurone only receives innervation from one eye. This is elegantly shown in an experiment in which Held and colleagues demonstrate that younger infants (under 4 months) can perform certain types of integration between the two eyes that older infants cannot (Shimojo, Bauer, O'Connell and Held, 1986).

Held and colleagues first of all demonstrated that infants during the first few months of life prefer to look at grid patterns over grating patterns of comparable spatial frequencies. The logic of the experiment depended on the fact that when two orthogonal grating patterns are combined together they form a grid pattern. If inputs from the two eyes are combined, then a grating in one eye orthogonal to that in the other will form a gridlike representation. In the experiment, interocularly orthogonal gratings were paired with parallel ones in a two-alternative preferential looking test.

Infants might be expected to prefer the orthogonal gratings before segregation of ocular dominance columns since they summate to some approximation of the preferred grid pattern. However, upon the formation of ocular dominance columns, the infants should prefer binocularly fusible stimuli over competing ones. The results of the experiment bore out the prediction. The infants shifted suddenly, at about the same age as they acquired stereopsis, from a preference for the orthogonal gratings to one for the parallel gratings. In fact, this shift in preference often occurred from one testing session to another only 1 or 2 weeks apart.

Regression of sensory afferents and visuo-spatial processing

In an attempt to account for the loss of processes and synapses that occurs during cortical development, Changeux has proposed a mechanism hypothesized to underlie the ontogeny of neural circuits (Changeux, Courrege and Danchin, 1973; Changeux and Dehaene, 1989). In brief, he argues that connections between classes of cells are specified genetically, but are initially labile. Synapses in their labile state may either become stabilized or regress, depending on the total activity of the postsynaptic cell. The activity of the postsynaptic cell is, in turn, dependent upon its input. Initially, this input may be the result of spontaneous activity in the network, but rapidly it is evoked by environmental input. The critical concept here is that of *selective stabilization*. In other words, Changeux proposes that: 'to learn is to eliminate', as opposed to learning taking place by instruction. What might the consequence of such a neural process be?

Neville (1991) has attempted to provide evidence concerning the mechanisms proposed by Changeux, the elimination of exuberance by sensory input, by using event-related potentials (ERPs) to study intersensory competition. In her experiments, she provides evidence from visual and spatial tasks with deaf subjects that cortically mediated visual processing is different among subjects reared in the absence of auditory input. Specifically, the congenitally deaf seem more sensitive to events in the peripheral visual field than are hearing subjects. ERPs recorded over classical auditory regions, such as the temporal lobe, are two or three times larger for deaf than for hearing subjects following peripheral visual field stimulation.

Neville suggests that her data support the idea that, in the absence of auditory input to auditory and polysensory areas of cortex, visual afferents that are normally lost, stabilize or increase. This is clearly consistent with the general position put forward by Changeux and colleagues. In particular, Changeux and Dehaene (1989) proposed that the stabilization of afferents requires neural activity. Consistent with this, Neville argues that the acquisition of competence in grammar is essential for the left hemisphere specialization in language. This specialization may not otherwise emerge. The evidence for this comes from ERP studies of language and hemispheric specialization. ERP studies reveal greater activation of areas of the left hemisphere in normal hearing subjects during a word-reading task. In contrast to this, deaf subjects did not show this lateralization. A group of subjects that had learned sign language as their first language, but who were not themselves deaf, showed the lateralization found in the normal hearing subjects, suggesting that it is not the acquisition of sign language *per se* that gives rise to this difference. Rather, the difference may index the activity of processes involved in either phonological or grammatical decoding. However, the lateralization effect was found in deaf signers when they were presented with sign language, indicating that the left hemisphere becomes specialized for language regardless of the modality involved, and may develop in association with the acquisition of competence in the grammar.

Constructive Processes in Neurocognitive Development

While much of the discussion so far has centred on cases in which a development in cortical structure may be said to give rise to, or at least provide the necessary substrate for, a cognitive or perceptual advance, I have also alluded to the fact that many aspects of postnatal cortical development are extremely sensitive to the effects of experience. In this concluding section I will review evidence in support of two contentions about the relation between cortical growth and cognitive development:

(i)   regressive events in neural development, such as synaptic loss, are those most sensitive to postnatal experience;

(ii) while in some cases neural developments in the cortex may be said to cause or allow cognitive changes, in other cases neurocognitive systems may shape the pattern of neural developments within the cortex. That is, there is a two-way interaction between neural and cognitive development.

Regressive events in the cortex and plasticity

As mentioned earlier, Changeux and others (Changeux et al., 1973; Changeux and Dehaene, 1989; Held, 1985; 1993; Johnson and Karmiloff-Smith, 1992) have argued that regressive events in neural development, such as the 'pruning' of synapses, are a crucial substrate for the plasticity of the cortex. For example, several authors have proposed that a distinction should be made between effects of experience that are common to all members of a species, which the genes of the species have evolved to expect, and changes which are caused by experience likely to be unique to an individual, 'learning' (Greenough, Black and Wallace, 1987; Johnson and Morton, 1991). Greenough and colleagues have referred to effects of experience common to most or all members of a species as 'experience-expectant', and have provided evidence from rats reared in impoverished and enriched environments that this is associated with the blooming and pruning of synapses. (Johnson and Morton's (1991) term 'species-typical environment' corresponds to Greenough's 'experience-expectant', with the difference that the former refers to an aspect of environmental input, while the latter also refers to the neural consequence of that experience.)

While Greenough and colleagues (Greenough et al., 1987; Greenough, 1993) have argued that progressive events in cortical development such as dendritic growth may be influenced by individual learning, or 'experience-dependent' information storage, most of the examples of progressive developments discussed in this chapter have been associated with cognitive and perceptual changes which may be comparatively impervious to the effects of postnatal experience. For example, the development of components of visual attention which were accounted for by the inside-out growth of the primary visual cortex over the first few months of life (Johnson, 1990) may be only accelerated or decelerated to a small extent by environmental factors (Johnson, 1992).

Diamond (1991) similarly allows for some limited role for experience in the beha-vioural transitions which she attributes to progressive developments in the prefrontal cortex. She reports that repeated testing on any of the tasks can accelerate the performance of human infants by 2 or 3 weeks. However, she argues that these accelerations are limited by the maturational state of the brain, since transitions attributed to frontal development occur at around the same age in three tasks which appear to require very different forms of experience. Diamond suggests that the underlying maturation of neural circuitry allows certain types of experience to have effects at certain points only. One piece of evidence for this is that in an object-retrieval task, the infants always go through the same sequence of stages before finally succeed-ing. Experience cannot push them straight to the final behaviour.

While distinctions between forms of plasticity in the cortex are unlikely to be absolute (Johnson and Morton, 1991), the examples discussed in this chapter lead to the view that while progressive growth of the cortex can only be accelerated or retarded by effects of experience, regressive events such as the 'pruning' of synapses may be more sensitive to postnatal experience (see also Johnson and Karmiloff-Smith, 1992).

The role of neurocognitive systems in cortical development

While the traditional approach to understanding the relation between brain develop-ment and behaviour has been to assume that the former causes, or allows, the latter, it has recently become evident that behaviour can affect brain development also (John-son and Morton, 1991; Johnson, 1992). Let us take the example of the development of face recognition which was discussed earlier.

Evidence was presented consistent with the notion that there are two independent systems involved in face recognition in early infancy; first, a predisposition for new-borns to orient toward face-like stimuli (probably subserved by subcortical structures in the brain), and second, a cortically mediated attention toward faces that emerges around the second month of life. Thus, the first system may be said to 'tutor', or select the appropriate input for, the second. Johnson and Morton (1991) suggest that this 'bootstrapping' phenomenon may also apply to other domains of perceptual and cognitive development. By this view it is clear that orienting and attention systems have a vital role in development (Johnson, 1992). By orienting the sensory organs toward particular classes of stimuli while the cortical circuits are still developing, these neurocognitive systems ensure that the cortex develops specializations for processing information about biologically relevant classes of stimuli.

While the view that newborn predispositions 'tutor' the developing cortex has also been put forward by others (e.g. Horn, 1985; Gibson, 1991), one challenge for the future lies in understanding the influence of cortically mediated components of visual and auditory attention on other aspects of cortical development.

Acknowledgments

Sections of this chapter were begun while I was a Research Fellow at the Center for Cognitive Neuroscience, University of Oregon. I wish to thank Johan Bolhuis, Annette Karmiloff-Smith,

Mike Posner, and Mary Rothbart for their comments on earlier versions of this chapter, and Leslie Tucker and Kathy Sutton for their assistance in its preparation. Financial assistance from the Human Frontiers Scientific Foundation, Carnegie Mellon University, and NSF (grant DBS-9120433) is gratefully acknowledged.

References

Aslin, R. N. (1981). Development of smooth pursuit in human infants. In *Eye Movements: Cognition and Visual Perception*, ed. D. F. Fisher, R. A. Monty, & J. W. Senders, pp. 31–51, Hillsdale, NJ: Lawrence Erlbaum.

Atkinson, J. (1984). Human visual development over the first six months of life: A review and a hypothesis. *Human Neurobiology*, **3**, 61–74.

Atkinson, J., Hood, B., Wattam-Bell, J., Anker, S. & Tricklebank, J. (1988). Development of orientation discrimination in infants. *Perception*, **17**, 587–95.

Becker, L. E., Armstrong, D. L., Chan, F. & Wood, M. M. (1984). Dendritic development on human occipital cortex neurones. *Brain Research*, **315**, 117–24.

Bronson, G. W. (1974). The postnatal growth of visual capacity. *Child Development*, **45**, 873–90.

Bronson, G. W. (1982). Structure, status and characteristics of the nervous system at birth. In *Psychobiology of the Human Newborn*, ed. P. Stratton, pp. 99–104, Chichester: John Wiley & Sons.

Bruce, C. J. (1988). Single neuron activity in the monkey's prefrontal cortex. In *Neurobiology of Neocortex*, ed. P. Rakic & W. Singer, pp. 297–331. Chichester: John Wiley & Sons.

Bushnell, I. W. R., Sai, F. & Mullin, J. T. (1989). Neonatal recognition of the mother's face. *British Journal of Developmental Psychology*, **7**, 3–15.

Changeux, J.-P., Courrege, P. & Danchin, A. (1973). A theory of the epigenesis of neuronal networks by selective stabilization of synapses. *Proceedings of the National Academy of Sciences of the USA*, **70**, 2974–8.

Changeux, J.-P. & Dehaene, S. (1989). Neuronal models of cognitive functions. *Cognition*, **33**, 63–109.

Chugani, H. T., Hovda, D. A., Villablanca, J. R., Phelps, M. E. & Xu, W-F. (1991). Metabolic maturation of the brain: A study of local cerebral glucose utilization in the developing cat. *Journal of Cerebral Blood Flow and Metabolism*, **11**, 35–47.

Chugani, H. T. & Phelps, M. E. (1986). Maturational changes in cerebral function infants determined by (18)FDG positron emission tomography. *Science*, **231**, 840–3.

Chugani, H. T., Phelps, M. E. & Mazziotta, J. C. (1987). Positron emission tomography study of human brain functional development. *Annals of Neurology*, **22**, 487–97.

Clarke, P. G. H. (1985). Neuronal death in the development of the vertebrate nervous system. *Trends in Neurosciences*, **8**, 345–9.

Conel, J. L. (1939–1967). *The Postnatal Development of the Human Cerebral Cortex*, vols I–VIII. Cambridge, MA: Harvard University Press.

Cowan, M. W., Fawcett, J. W., O'Leary, D. M., & Stanfield, B. B. (1984). Regressive events in neurogenesis, *Science*, **225**, 1258–65.

de Yoe, E. A. & Van Essen, D. C. (1988). Concurrent processing streams in monkey visual cortex. *Trends in Neurosciences*, **11**, 219–26.

Diamond, A. (1988). Differences between adult and infant cognition: Is the crucial variable presence or absence of language? In *Thought without Language*, ed. L. Weiskrantz, pp. 335–66, Oxford: Clarendon Press.

Diamond, A. (1991). Neuropsychological insights into the meaning of object concept development. In *The Epigenesis of Mind: Essays on Biology and Cognition*, ed. S. Carey & R. Gelman, pp. 67–107, Hillsdale, NJ: Lawrence Erlbaum.

Diamond, A. & Goldman-Rakic, P. S. (1983). Comparison of performance on a Piagetian object permanence task in human infants and rhesus monkeys: Evidence for involvement of prefrontal cortex. *Society for Neuroscience Abstracts*, **9**, 641.

Diamond, A. & Goldman-Rakic, P. S. (1985). Evidence for the involvement of the prefrontal cortex in cognitive changes during the first year of life. *Society for Neuroscience Abstracts*, **11**, 832.

Ebbesson, S. O. (1984). The evolution and ontogeny of neural circuits. *Behavioral and Brain Sciences*, **7**, 321–6.

Fischer, B. & Breitmeyer, B. (1987). Mechanisms of visual attention revealed by saccadic eye movements. *Neuropsychologia*, **25**, 73–83.

Gibson, K. R. (1991). New perspectives on instincts and intelligence: Brain size and the emergence of hierarchical mental constructional skills. In *'Language' and Intelligence in Monkeys and Apes*, ed. S. T. Parker & K. R. Gibson, pp. 97–128, Cambridge: Cambridge University Press.

Goldberg, M. E. & Bushnell, M. C. (1981). Behavioral enhancement of visual responses in monkey cerebral cortex. II: Modulation in frontal eye fields specifically related to saccades. *Journal of Neurophysiology*, **46**, 773–87.

Goren, C. C., Sarty, M. & Wu, P. Y. K. (1975). Visual following and pattern discrimination of face-like stimuli by newborn infants. *Pediatrics*, **56**, 544–9.

Greenough, W. T. (1993). Brain adaptation to experience: An update. In *Brain Development and Cognition: A Reader*, ed. M. H. Johnson, pp. 319–22, Oxford: Blackwell.

Greenough, W. T., Black, J. E. & Wallace, C. S. (1987). Experience and brain development. *Child Development*, **58**, 539–59.

Guitton, H. A., Buchtel, H. A. & Douglas, R. M. (1985). Frontal lobe lesions in man cause difficulties in suppressing reflexive glances and in generating goal-directed saccades. *Experimental Brain Research*, **58**, 455–72.

Haith, M. M., Hazan, C. & Goodman, G. S. (1988). Expectation and anticipation of dynamic visual events by 3.5-month old babies. *Child Development*, **59**, 467–79.

Held, R. (1985). Binocular vision – Behavioral and neural development. In *Neonate Cognition: Beyond the Blooming, Buzzing Confusion*, ed. J. Mehler & R. Fox, pp. 37–44, Hillsdale, NJ: Lawrence Erlbaum.

Held, R. (1993). Development of binocular vision revisited. In *Brain Development and Cognition: A Reader*, ed. M. H. Johnson, pp. 159–65, Oxford: Blackwell.

Hopkins, W. G. & Brown, M. C. (1984). *Development of Nerve Cells and their Connections*. Cambridge: Cambridge University Press.

Horn, G. (1985). *Memory, Imprinting and the Brain*. Oxford: Clarendon Press.

Huttenlocher, P. R. (1990). Morphometric study of human cerebral cortex development. *Neuropsychologia*, **28**, 517–27.

Janowsky, J. S. & Findlay, B. L. (1986). The outcome of perinatal brain damage: The role of normal neuron loss and axon retraction. *Developmental Medicine and Child Neurology*, **28**, 375–89.

Johnson, M. H. (1988). Memories of mother. *New Scientist*, **1600**, 60–2.

Johnson, M. H. (1990). Cortical maturation and the development of visual attention in early infancy. *Journal of Cognitive Neuroscience*, **2**, 81–95.

Johnson, M. H. (1992). Cognition and development: Four contentions about the role of visual attention. In *Cognitive Science and Clinical Disorders*, ed. D. J. Stein & J. E. Young, pp. 45–62, New York: Academic Press.

Johnson, M. H. (in press a). Dissociating components of visual attention: A neurodevelopmental approach. In *The Neural Basis of High-level Vision*, ed. M. Farah & G. Radcliffe, Hillsdale, NJ: Lawrence Erlbaum.

Johnson, M. H. (in press b). The development of attention. In *The Cognitive Neurosciences*, ed. M. S. Gazzaniga, Cambridge, MA: MIT Press.

Johnson, M. H., Dziurawiec, S., Ellis, H. D. & Morton, J. (1991). Newborns' preferential tracking of face-like stimuli and its subsequent decline. *Cognition*, **40**, 1–19.

Johnson, M. H. & Karmiloff-Smith, A. (1992). Can neural selectionism be applied to cognitive development and its disorders? *New Ideas in Psychology*, **10**, 35–47.

Johnson, M. H. & Morton, J. (1991). *Biology and Cognitive Development: The Case of Face Recognition*. Oxford: Blackwell.

Johnson, M. H., Posner, M. I. & Rothbart, M. (1991). The development of visual attention in infancy: Contingency learning, anticipations and disengaging. *Journal of Cognitive Neuroscience*, **3**, 335–44.

MacPhail, E. (1982). *Brain and Intelligence in Vertebrates*. Oxford: Oxford University Press.

Maurer, D. & Lewis, T. L. (1979). A physiological explanation of infants' early visual development. *Canadian Journal of Psychology*, **33**, 232–52.

McGraw, M. B. (1943). *The Neuromuscular Maturation of the Human Infant*. New York: Columbia University Press.

Morton, J. & Johnson, M. H. (1991). Conspec and Conlern: A two-process theory of infant face recognition. *Psychological Review*, **98**, 164–81.

Morton, J. & Johnson, M. H. & Maurer, D. (1990). On the reasons for newborns, responses to faces. *Infant Behavior & Development*, **13**, 99–103.

Muir, D. W., Clifton, R. K. & Clarkson, M. G. (1989). The development of a human auditory localization response: A U-shaped function. *Canadian Journal of Psychology*, **43**, 199–216.

Neville, H. (1991). Neurobiology of cognitive and language processing: Effects of early experience. In *Brain Maturation and Cognitive Development*, ed. K. R. Gibson & A. C. Peterson, pp. 335–80, Hawthorne, NY: Aldine de Gruyter.

Piaget, J. (1954). *The Construction of Reality in the Child*. New York: Basic Books.

Posner, M. I. & Rothbart, M. K. (1980). The development of attentional mechanisms. In *Nebraska Symposium on Motivation*, ed. J. H. Flower, pp. 1–52, Lincoln, Nebraska: University of Nebraska Press.

Purpura, D. P. (1975). Normal and aberrant neuronal development in the cerebral cortex of human fetus and young infant. In *Brain Mechanisms of Mental Retardation*, ed. N. A. Buchwald & M. A. B. Brazier, pp. 141–69, New York: Academic Press.

Purves, D. & Lichtman, J. W. (1985). *Principles of Neural Development*. Sunderland, MA: Sinauer.

Rabinowicz, T. (1979). The differential maturation of the human cerebral cortex. In *Human Growth*, vol. 3: *Neurobiology and Nutrition*, ed. F. Falkner & J. M. Tanner, pp. 141–69, New York: Plenum Press.

Rakic, P. (1988). Intrinsic and extrinsic determinants of neocortical parcellation: A radial unit model. In *Neurobiology of Neocortex*, ed. P. Rakic & W. Singer, pp. 5–27, New York: John Wiley & Sons.

Rakic, P., Bourgeois, J.-P., Eckenhoff, M. F., Zecevic, N. & Goldman-Rakic, P. S. (1986). Concurrent overproduction of synapses in diverse regions of the primate cerebral cortex. *Science*, **232**, 232–4.

Schiller, P. H. (1985). A model for the generation of visually guided saccadic eye movements. In *Models of the Visual Cortex*, ed. D. Rose & V. G. Dobson, pp. 62–71, Chichester: John Wiley & Sons.

Shimojo, S., Bauer, J. A., O'Connell, K. M. & Held, R. (1986). Pre-stereoptic binocular vision in infants. *Vision Research*, **26**, 501–10.

Slater, A., Morison, V. & Somers, M. (1988). Orientation discrimination and cortical function in the human newborn. *Perception*, **17**, 597–602.

Van Essen, D. C. (1985). Functional organisation of primate visual cortex. In *Cerebral Cortex*, vol. 3, ed. A. Peters & E. G. Jones, pp. 259–329, New York: Plenum Press.

Vinter, A. (1986). The role of movement in eliciting early imitations. *Child Development*, **57**, 66–71.

Von Hofsten, C. (1984). Developmental changes in the organisation of prereaching movements. *Developmental Psychology*, **20**, 378–88.

Memory

INTRODUCTION TO PART VI

One of the main reasons for having a brain is the ability to adapt behavior on the basis of experience. There are many ways of doing this: it turns out that a diverse array of neural structures are modifiable, and that there are correspondingly many different kinds of memory. The main reason that we know this is the strange and remarkable fact that the anatomical structures responsible for some of these memory types can be selectively damaged, leaving patients with a glaring lack of something that we usually take for granted.

The most famous such case is the patient H. M., whose experimental surgical treatment for epilepsy left him unable to recall any event that happened to him from the time of his operation onward. As described by Scoville and Milner, he retained some memories for events prior to his surgery, so that the problem seems to be one of creating new memories rather than of accessing ones that are already there. The existence of "vivid and intact" memories from his early years has generated the notion of the medial temporal lobes as a temporary storage site of memory for facts and events, with such knowledge slowly being transferred to the cortex.

It was subsequently revealed that, despite this profound lack of recognition and recall, H.M. and other amnesics apparently retained normal abilities to learn new motor tasks and skills. What other forms of memory may remain intact in such patients remains a matter of debate. Squire and Zola's article gives a taste of one of these issues, namely the question of whether memory for events can be clearly dissociated from memory for facts.

Quite a different form of memory is considered by Daniel Schacter. In contrast to the more obvious types of memory that result in conscious awareness of some fact or event, other types of experience-driven neural change do not. This would include the motor and skill learning just mentioned, as well as the family of phenomena referred to as "priming": the influence of neural activity on subsequent processing whether or not one remembers the original activity. We have already encountered priming effects in two papers in the attention section, where they were used as clues to processing in the absence of conscious awareness. One very interesting bottom line from these studies seems to be that factors that strongly affect conscious recall, such as considering an object or word more deeply, have no effect on priming. Another main point is that, despite this, priming can occur at a variety of levels, such as those of the superficial perceptual attributes of a stimulus and of deeper meaning – as described before by Tipper and Driver. A big question would seem to be whether every patch of cortex is intrinsically capable of being primed.

In addition, Alan Baddeley describes a different beast altogether: working memory. This denotes the moment-to-moment contents of consciousness that are maintained over the time scale of thought processes despite changing sensory input. Here, presumably, is the train of thought. It is preserved in amnesics such as H.M., who can keep a thought in mind for several minutes, "if care [is] taken not to distract them in the interval." As it seems to co-opt the perceptual apparatus to attend to an internal stimulus, as well as to direct behavior, this topic could as comfortably be discussed in the context of attention or executive control, and in fact we will hear much more about it in Part VII.

Loss of Recent Memory after Bilateral Hippocampal Lesions

William Beecher Scoville and Brenda Milner

In 1954 Scoville described a grave loss of recent memory which he had observed as a sequel to bilateral medial temporal-lobe resection in one psychotic patient and one patient with intractable seizures. In both cases the operations had been radical ones, undertaken only when more conservative forms of treatment had failed. The removals extended posteriorly along the mesial surface of the temporal lobes for a distance of approximately 8 cm from the temporal tips and probably destroyed the anterior two-thirds of the hippocampus and hippocampal gyrus bilaterally, as well as the uncus and amygdala. The unexpected and persistent memory deficit which resulted seemed to us to merit further investigation. We have therefore carried out formal memory and intelligence testing of these two patients and also of eight other patients who had undergone similar, but less radical, bilateral medial temporal-lobe resections.[1] The present paper gives the results of these studies which point to the importance of the hippocampal complex for normal memory function. Whenever the hippocampus and hippocampal gyrus were damaged bilaterally in these operations some memory deficit was found, but not otherwise. We have chosen to report these findings in full, partly for their theoretical significance, and partly as a warning to others of the risk to memory involved in bilateral surgical lesions of the hippocampal region.

Operations

During the past seven years in an effort to preserve the overall personality in psycho-surgery some 300 fractional lobotomies have been performed, largely on seriously ill schizophrenic patients who had failed to respond to other forms of treatment. The aim in these fractional procedures was to secure as far as possible any beneficial effects a complete frontal lobotomy might have, while at the same time avoiding its undesirable side-effects. And it was in fact found that undercutting limited to the orbital surfaces of both frontal lobes has an appreciable therapeutic effect in psychosis and yet does not

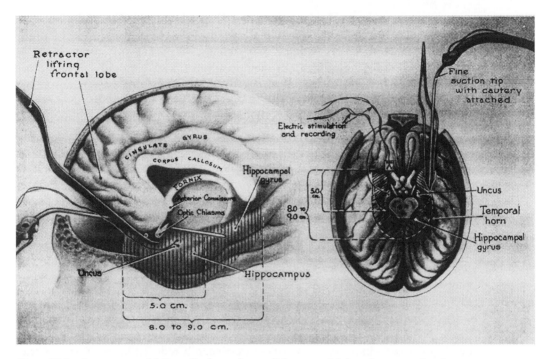

Figure 20.1   Area removed bilaterally from the medial temporal lobes demonstrating 5 cm as well as 8 cm removals through supra-orbital trephines.

cause any new personality deficit to appear (Scoville, Wilk, and Pepe, 1951). In view of the known close relationship between the posterior orbital and mesial temporal cortices (MacLean, 1952; Pribram and Kruger, 1954), it was hoped that still greater psychiatric benefit might be obtained by extending the orbital undercutting so as to destroy parts of the mesial temporal cortex bilaterally. Accordingly, in 30 severely deteriorated cases, such partial temporal-lobe resections were carried out, either with or without orbital undercutting. The surgical procedure has been described elsewhere (Scoville, Dunsmore, Liberson, Henry, and Pepe, 1953) and is illustrated anatomically in figs. 20.1 to 4. All the removals have been bilateral, extending for varying distances along the mesial surface of the temporal lobes. Five were limited to the uncus and underlying amygdaloid nucleus; all others encroached also upon the anterior hippo-campus, the excisions being carried back 5 cm or more after bisecting the tips of the temporal lobes, with the temporal horn constituting the lateral edge of resection. In one case only in this psychotic group all tissue mesial to the temporal horns for a distance of at least 8 cm posterior to the temporal tips was destroyed, a removal which presumably included the anterior two-thirds of the hippocampal complex bilaterally.

An equally radical bilateral medial temporal-lobe resection was carried out in one young man (H.M.) with a long history of major and minor seizures uncontrollable by maximum medication of various forms, and showing diffuse electro-encephalographic abnormality. This frankly experimental operation was considered justifiable because the patient was totally incapacitated by his seizures and these had proven refractory to a medical approach. It was suggested because of the known epileptogenic qualities of the uncus and hippocampal complex and because of the relative absence of post-operative seizures in our temporal-lobe resections as compared with fractional lobotomies in other areas. The operation was carried out with the understanding and approval of the patient and his family, in the hope of lessening his seizures to some extent. At operation the medial surfaces of both temporal lobes were exposed and recordings were taken from both surface and depth electrodes before any tissue was removed; but again no discrete epileptogenic focus was found. Bilateral resection was then carried out, extending posteriorly for a distance of 8 cm from the temporal tips.

Results

The psychiatric findings bearing upon the treatment of schizophrenia have already been reported (Scoville and others; 1953). Briefly, it was found that bilateral resections limited to the medial portions of the temporal lobes were without significant therapeutic effect in psychosis, although individual patients (including the one with the most radical removal) did in fact show some improvement. There have been no gross changes in personality. This is particularly clear in the case of the epileptic, non-psychotic patient whose present cheerful placidity does not differ appreciably from his pre-operative status and who, in the opinion of his family, has shown no personality change. Neurological changes in the group have also been minimal. The incidence and severity of seizures in the epileptic patient were sharply reduced for the first year after operation, and although he is once again having both major and minor attacks, these attacks no longer leave him stuporous, as they formerly did. It has therefore been possible to reduce his medication considerably. As far as general intelligence is concerned, the epileptic patient has actually improved slightly since operation, possibly because he is less drowsy than before. The psychotic patients were for the most part too disturbed before operation for finer testing of higher mental functions to be carried out, but certainly there is no indication of any general intellectual impairment resulting from the operation in those patients for whom the appropriate test data are available.

There has been one striking and totally unexpected behavioural result: a grave loss of recent memory in those cases in which the medial temporal-lobe resection was so extensive as to involve the major portion of the hippocampal complex bilaterally. The psychotic patient having the most radical excision (extending 8 cm from the tips of the temporal lobes bilaterally) has shown a profound post-operative memory disturbance, but unfortunately this was not recognized at the time because of her disturbed emotional state. In the non-psychotic patient the loss was immediately apparent. After operation this young man could no longer recognize the hospital staff nor find his way to the bathroom, and he seemed to recall nothing of the day-to-day events of his hospital life. There was also a partial retrograde amnesia, inasmuch as he did not remember the death of a favourite uncle three years previously, nor anything of the period in hospital, yet could recall some trivial events that had occurred just before his admission to the hospital. His early memories were apparently vivid and intact.

This patient's memory defect has persisted without improvement to the present time, and numerous illustrations of its severity could be given. Ten months ago the family moved from their old house to a new one a few blocks away on the same street;

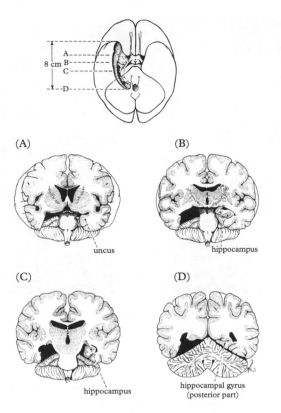

Figure 20.2 Diagrammatic cross-sections of human brain illustrating extent of attempted bilateral medial temporal lobe resection in the radical operation. (For diagrammatic purposes the resection has been shown on one side only.)

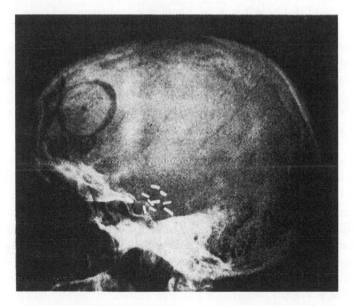

Figure 20.3 Post-operative skull radiograph with silver clip markers outlining extent of bilateral resections limited to the uncus and amygdala.

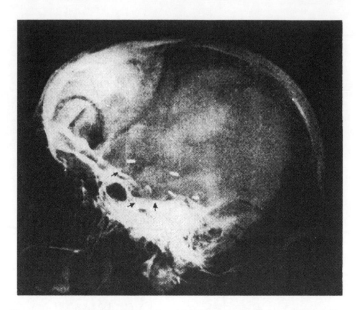

Figure 20.4   Post-operative skull radiograph with silver clip markers outlining the extent of the bilateral resections including the anterior hippocampal complex (approximately 6 cm posterior to the tip of the anterior temporal fossa).

he still has not learned the new address, though remembering the old one perfectly, nor can he be trusted to find his way home alone. Moreover, he does not know where objects in continual use are kept; for example, his mother still has to tell him where to find the lawn mower, even though he may have been using it only the day before. She also states that he will do the same jigsaw puzzles day after day without showing any practice effect and that he will read the same magazines over and over again without finding their contents familiar. This patient has even eaten luncheon in front of one of us (B.M.) without being able to name, a mere half-hour later, a single item of food he had eaten; in fact, he could not remember having eaten luncheon at all. Yet to a casual observer this man seems like a relatively normal individual, since his understanding and reasoning are undiminished.

The discovery of severe memory defect in these two patients led us to study further all patients in the temporal-lobe series who were sufficiently cooperative to permit formal psychological testing. The operation sample included, in addition to the two radical resections, one bilateral removal of the uncus, extending 4 cm posterior to the temporal tips, and six bilateral medial temporal-lobe resections in which the removal was carried back 5 or 6 cm to include also a portion of the anterior hippocampus; in three of these six cases the temporal-lobe resection was combined with orbital under-cutting. One unilateral case was also studied in which right inferior temporal lobectomy and hippocampectomy had been carried out for the relief of incisural herniation due to malignant oedema (fig. 20.5). We found some memory impairment in all the bilateral cases in which the removal was carried far enough posteriorly to damage the hippo-campus and hippocampal gyrus, but in only one of these six additional cases (D.C.) did the memory loss equal in severity that seen in the two most radical excisions. The case with bilateral excision of the uncus (in which the removal can have involved only the

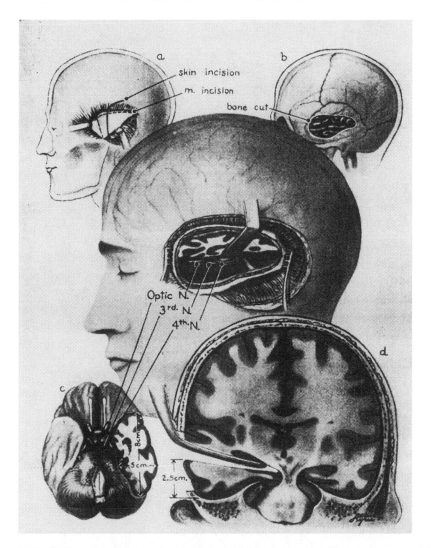

Figure 20.5   Unilateral inferior horizontal temporal lobectomy extending a distance of 8cm posterior to the tip of the anterior temporal fossa. This operation is performed for incisural herniation of the temporal lobes (Case 10)

amygdaloid and peri-amygdaloid areas) showed excellent memory function. The unilateral operation, extensive as it was, has caused no lasting memory impairment, though some disturbance of recent memory was noted in the early post-operative period (Scoville, 1954); we now attribute this deficit to temporary interference with the functioning of the hippocampal zone of the opposite hemisphere by contralateral pressure.

The histories and individual test results for these 10 cases are reported below, and table 20.1 summarizes the principal findings. For purposes of comparison the cases have been divided into three groups representing different degrees of memory impairment.

Table 20.1   Classification of cases

Cases	Age at time of follow-up (yrs)	Sex	Diagnosis	Operation	Bi- or unilateral	Approximate extent of removal along medial temporal lobes (cm)	Time between operation and testing (mth)	Wechsler Scale Intelligence quotient	Memory quotient
Group 1: Severe Memory Defect									
Case 1, H.M.	29	M	Epilepsy	Medial temporal	B	8	20	112	67
Case 2, D.C.	47	M	Paranoid schizophrenia	Medial temporal and orbital undercutting	B	5.5	21	122	70
Case 3, M.B.	55	F	Manic-depressive psychosis	Medial temporal	B	8	28	78	60
Group II: Moderate Memory Defect									
Case 4, A.Z.	35	F	Paranoid schizophrenia	Medial temporal	B	5	40	96	84
Case 5, M.R.	40	F	Paranoid schizophrenia	Medial temporal and orbital undercutting	B	5	39	123	81
Case 6, A.R.	38	F	Hebephrenic schizophrenia	Medial temporal and orbital undercutting	B	4.5	47	Incomplete	
Case 7, C.G.	44	F	Schizophrenia	Medial temporal	B	5.5	41	Incomplete	Incomplete
Case 8, A.L.	31	M	Schizophrenia	Medial temporal	B	6	38	Incomplete	Incomplete
Group III: No Memory Defect									
Case 9, I.S.	54	F	Paranoid schizophrenia	Uncectomy	B	4	53	122	125
Case 10, E.G.	55	F	Incisural herniation	Inferior temporal lobectomy	U-Rt.	9	16	93	90

Group I: Severe Memory Defect

In this category are those patients who since operation appear to forget the incidents of their daily life as fast as they occur. It is interesting that all these patients were able to retain a three-figure number or a pair of unrelated words for several minutes, if care was taken not to distract them in the interval. However, they forgot the instant attention was diverted to a new topic. Since in normal life the focus of attention is constantly changing, such individuals show an apparently complete anterograde amnesia. This severe defect was observed in the two patients having the most radical bilateral medial temporal-lobe excisions (with the posterior limit of removal approximately 8 cm from the temporal tips) and in one other case, a bilateral 5.5 cm medial temporal excision. These three cases will now be described.

Case 1: H.M.

This 29-year-old motor winder, a high school graduate, had had minor seizures since the age of 10 and major seizures since the age of 16. The small attacks lasted about 40 seconds, during which he would be unresponsive, opening his mouth, closing his eyes, and crossing both arms and legs; but he believed that he could 'half hear what was going on.' The major seizures occurred without warning and with no lateralizing sign. They were generalized convulsions, with tongue-biting, urinary incontinence, and loss of consciousness followed by prolonged somnolence. Despite heavy and varied anti-convulsant medication the major attacks had increased in frequency and severity through the years until the patient was quite unable to work.

The aetiology of this patient's attacks is not clear. He was knocked down by a bicycle at the age of 9 and was unconscious for five minutes afterwards, sustaining a laceration of the left supra-orbital region. Later radiological studies, however, including two pneumo-encephalograms, have been completely normal, and the physical examination has always been negative.

Electro-encephalographic studies have consistently failed to show any localized epileptogenic area. In the examination of 17 August 1953, Dr T. W. Liberson described diffuse slow activity with a dominant frequency of 6 to 8 per second. A short clinical attack was said to be accompanied by generalized 2 to 3 per second spike-and-wave discharge with a slight asymmetry in the central leads (flattening on the left).

Despite the absence of any localizing sign, operation was considered justifiable for the reasons given above. On 1 September 1953, bilateral medial temporal-lobe resection was carried out, extending posteriorly for a distance of 8 cm from the midpoints of the tips of the temporal lobes, with the temporal horns constituting the lateral edges of resection.

After operation the patient was drowsy for a few days, but his subsequent recovery was uneventful apart from the grave memory loss already described. There has been no neurological deficit. An electro-encephalogram taken one year after operation showed increased spike-and-wave activity which was maximal over the frontal areas and bilaterally synchronous. He continues to have seizures, but these are less incapacitating than before.

Psychological examination

This was performed on 26 April 1955. The memory defect was immediately apparent. The patient gave the date as March 1953, and his age as 27. Just before coming into the examining room he had been talking to Dr Karl Pribram, yet he had no recollection of this at all and denied that anyone had spoken to him. In conversation, he reverted constantly to boyhood events and seemed scarcely to realize that he had had an operation.

On formal testing the contrast between his good general intelligence and his defective memory was most striking. On the Wechsler–Bellevue Intelligence Scale he achieved a full-scale IQ rating of 112, which compares favourably with the pre-operative rating of 104 reported by Dr Liselotte Fischer in August 1953, the improvement in arithmetic being particularly striking. An extensive test battery failed to reveal any deficits in perception, abstract thinking, or reasoning ability, and his motivation remained excellent throughout.

On the Wechsler Memory Scale (Wechsler, 1945) his immediate recall of stories and drawings fell far below the average level and on the 'associate learning' subtest of this scale he obtained zero scores for the hard word associations, low scores for the easy associations, and failed to improve with repeated practice. These findings are reflected in the low memory quotient of 67. Moreover, on all tests we found that once he had turned to a new task the nature of the preceding one could no longer be recalled, nor the test recognized if repeated.

In summary, this patient appears to have a complete loss of memory for events subsequent to bilateral medial temporal-lobe resection 19 months before, together with a partial retrograde amnesia for the three years leading up to his operation; but early memories are seemingly normal and there is no impairment of personality or general intelligence.

Case 2: D.C.

This 47-year-old doctor was a paranoid schizophrenic with a four-year history of violent, combative behaviour. Before his illness he had been practising medicine in Chicago, but he had always shown paranoid trends and for this reason had had difficulty completing his medical training. His breakdown followed the loss of a lawsuit in 1950, at which time he made a homicidal attack on his wife which led to his admission to hospital. Since then both insulin and electro-shock therapy had been tried without benefit and the prognosis was considered extremely poor. On 13 May 1954, at the request of Dr Frederick Gibbs and Dr John Kendrick, a bilateral medial temporal-lobe resection combined with orbital undercutting was carried out at Manteno State Hospital (W.B.S., with the assistance of Dr John Kendrick). The posterior limit of the removal was 5 cm from the sphenoid ridge, or roughly 5.5 cm from the tips of the temporal lobes, with the inferior horns of the ventricles forming the lateral edges of resection. Recording from depth electrodes at the time of operation showed spiking from the medial temporal regions bilaterally with some spread to the orbital surfaces of both frontal lobes, but after the removal had been completed a normal electro-encephalographic record was obtained from the borders of the excision.

Post-operative recovery was uneventful and there has been no neurological deficit. Since operation the patient has been outwardly friendly and tractable with no return of his former aggressive behaviour, although the paranoid thought content persists; he is considered markedly improved. But he too shows a profound memory disturbance. At Manteno State Hospital he was described as 'confused', because since the operation he had been unable to find his way to bed and seemed no longer to recognize the hospital staff. However, no psychological examination was made there, and on 29 November 1955, he was transferred to Galesburg State Research Institute where he was interviewed by one of us (B.M.) on 12 January 1956.

Psychological findings

This patient presented exactly the same pattern of memory loss as H.M. He was courteous and cooperative throughout the examination, and the full-scale Wechsler IQ rating of 122 showed him to be still of superior intellect. Yet he had no idea where he was, explaining that naturally the surroundings were quite unfamiliar because he had only arrived there for the first time the night before. (In fact, he had been there six weeks.) He was unable to learn either the name of the hospital or the name of the examiner, despite being told them repeatedly. Each time he received the information as something new, and a moment later would deny having heard it. At the examiner's request he drew a dog and an elephant, yet half an hour later did not even recognize them as his own drawings. On the formal tests of the Wechsler Memory Scale his immediate recall of stories and drawings was poor, and the memory quotient of 70 is in sharp contrast to the high IQ level. As with H.M., once a new task was introduced there was total amnesia for the preceding one; in his own words, the change of topic confused him. This man did not know that he had had a brain operation and did not recall being at Manteno State Hospital, although he had spent six months there before the operation as well as six months post-operatively. Yet he could give minute details of his early life and medical training (accurately, as far as we could tell).

Case 3: M.B.

This 55-year-old manic depressive woman, a former clerical worker, was admitted to Connecticut State Hospital on 27 December 1951, at which time she was described as anxious, irritable, argumentative, and restless, but well-orientated in all spheres. Her recent memory was normal, in that she knew how long she had been living in Connecticut and could give the date of her hospital admission and the exact times of various clinic appointments. On 18 December 1952, a radical bilateral medial temporal-lobe resection was carried out, with the posterior limit of removal 8 cm from the temporal tips. Post-operatively she was stuporous and confused for one week, but then recovered rapidly and without neurological deficit. She has become neater and more even-tempered and is held to be greatly improved. However, psychological testing by Mr I. Borganz in November 1953, revealed a grave impairment of recent memory; she gave the year as 1950 and appeared to recall nothing of the events of the last three years. Yet her verbal intelligence proved to be normal.

She was examined briefly by B.M. in April 1955, at which time she showed a global loss of recent memory similar to that of H.M. and D.C. She had been brought to the examining room from another building, but had already forgotten this; nor could she describe any other part of the hospital although she had been living there continuously for nearly three and a half years. On the Wechsler Memory Scale her immediate recall of stories and drawings was inaccurate and fragmentary, and delayed recall was impossible for her even with prompting; when the material was presented again she failed to recognize it. Her conversation centred around her early life and she was unable to give any information about the years of her hospital stay. Vocabulary, attention span, and comprehension were normal, thus confirming Mr Borganz's findings.

Group II: Moderately Severe Memory Defect

In this second category are those patients who can be shown to retain some impression of new places and events, although they are unable to learn such arbitrary new associations as people's names and cannot be depended upon to carry out commissions. Subjectively, these patients complain of memory difficulty, and objectively, on formal tests, they do very poorly irrespective of the type of material to be memorized. The five remaining patients with bilateral medial temporal-lobe removals extending 5 or 6 cm posteriorly from the temporal tips make up this group. Only two of these patients were well enough to permit thorough testing, but in all five cases enough data were obtained to establish that the patient did have a memory defect and that it was not of the gross type seen in Group I. The individual cases are reported below.

Case 4: A.Z.

This 35-year-old woman, a paranoid schizophrenic, had been in Connecticut State Hospital for three years and extensive electro-shock therapy had been tried without lasting benefit. She was described as tense, assaultative, and sexually preoccupied. On 29 November 1951, bilateral medial temporal-lobe resection was carried out under local anaesthesia, the posterior limit of the removal being approximately 5 cm from the tips of the temporal lobes. During subpial resection of the right hippocampal cortex the surgeon inadvertently went through the arachnoid and injured by suction a portion of the right peduncle, geniculate, or hypothalamic region with immediate development of deep coma. The injury was visualized by extra-arachnoid inspection. Post-operatively the patient remained in stupor for 72 hours and exhibited a left spastic hemiplegia, contracted fixed pupils, strabismus and lateral nystagmus of the right eye; vital signs remained constant and within normal limits. She slowly recovered the use of the left arm and leg and her lethargy gradually disappeared. By the seventh post-operative day she could walk without support and pupillary responses had returned to normal. The only residual neurological deficit has been a left homonymous hemianopia. Of particular interest was the dramatic post-operative improvement in her psychotic state with an early complete remission of her delusions, anxiety, and paranoid behaviour. At the same time she showed a retrograde amnesia for the entire period of her illness.

This patient was discharged from the hospital nine months after operation and is now able to earn her living as a domestic worker. However, she complains that her memory is poor, and psychological examination (27 April 1955) three and a half years post-operatively confirms this. But the deficit is less striking than in the three cases reported above. This patient, for example, was able to give the address of the house where she worked although she had been there only two days, and she could even describe the furnishings in some detail although she had not yet learned the name of her employer. She was also able to give an accurate, though sketchy, description of a doctor who had spoken to her briefly that morning and whom she had never seen before. However, she could recall very little of the conversation.

Formal testing at this time showed her intelligence to lie within the average range with no impairment of attention or concentration. The Wechsler–Bellevue IQ rating was 96. On the Wechsler Memory Scale her immediate recall of stories was normal, but passing from one story to the next was enough to make her unable to recall the first one, though a few fragments could be recovered with judicious prompting. She showed the same rapid forgetting on the 'visual retention' subtest, indicating that the memory impairment was not specific to verbal material. Finally, she was conspicuously unsuccessful on the 'associate learning' subtest, failing to master a single unfamiliar word association. This examination as a whole provides clear evidence of an impairment of recent memory.

Case 5: M.R.

This 40-year-old woman, a paranoid schizophrenic with superimposed alcoholism, had been a patient at Norwich State Hospital for 11 years, receiving extensive electro-shock therapy. Bilateral medial temporal-lobe resection combined with orbital undercutting was carried out on 17 January 1952, the posterior extent of removal being roughly 5 cm from the temporal tips. The patient has shown complete remission of psychotic symptoms and was discharged from the hospital on 16 September 1954, to the care of her family.

Psychological examination

This was performed on 29 April 1955. Tests showed this woman to be of superior intelligence, with a full-scale IQ rating of 123 on the Wechsler Scale. However, she complained of poor memory, adding that she could remember faces and 'the things that are important', but that, to her great embarrassment, she forgot many ordinary daily happenings. Upon questioning she gave the year correctly but did not know the month or the day. She knew that she had had an operation in 1952 but did not recognize the surgeon (W.B.S.) nor recall his name. Formal testing revealed the same pattern of memory disturbance as A.Z. had shown, and the memory quotient of 81 compares most unfavourably with the high IQ rating. In conversation, she reverted constantly to discussion of her work during the years of depression and showed little knowledge of recent events.

Case 6: A.R.

This 38-year-old woman had been in hospital for five years with a diagnosis of hebephrenic schizophrenia. Before operation she was said to be noisy, combative, and suspicious, and electro-shock therapy had caused only transient improvement in this condition. On 31 May 1951, bilateral medial temporal-lobe resection combined with orbital undercutting was carried out, the posterior limit of removal being slightly less than 5 cm from the bisected tips of the temporal lobes. After operation the patient gradually became quieter and more cooperative and on 29 September, 1952, she was discharged to her home. There have been no neurological sequelae.

Psychological examination

This was performed in April 1955. Examination revealed a hyperactive woman, too excited and talkative for prolonged testing. She showed a restricted span of attention but scores on verbal intelligence tests were within the dull normal range. Moreover, she appeared to recall some recent happenings quite well. Thus, she knew that her daughter had caught a 7 o'clock train to New York City that morning to buy a dress for a wedding the following Saturday. She could also describe the clothes worn by the secretary who had shown her into the office. However, on formal testing some impairment of recent memory was seen, although unlike the other patients in this group she did succeed on some of the difficult items of the 'associate learning' test. As with A.Z. and M.R., the deficit appeared most clearly on tests of delayed recall after a brief interval filled with some other activity. Thus, on the 'logical memory' test she gave an adequate version of each story immediately after hearing it, but passing from one story to the next caused her to forget the first almost completely; similar results were obtained for the recall of drawings. We conclude that this patient has a memory impairment identical in type to that of the other patients in this group, but somewhat milder. It is interesting that she had a relatively small excision.

Case 7: C.G.

This 44-year-old schizophrenic woman had been in the hospital for 20 years without showing any improvement in her psychosis. On 19 November, 1951, bilateral medial temporal-lobe resection was carried out under local anaesthesia, the posterior limit of removal being 5.5 cm from the tips of the temporal lobes. There was temporary loss of consciousness during the resection but the patient was fully conscious at the end of the procedure and post-operative recovery was uneventful. There has been no neurological deficit. She is considered to be in better contact than before but more forgetful.

This patient was examined at Norwich State Hospital in April 1955, and although she was too distractable for prolonged testing, it was possible to show that she remembered some recent events. For example, she knew that she had been working in the hospital beauty parlour for the past week and that she had been washing towels that morning. Yet formal memory testing revealed the same deficit as that shown by A.Z. and M.R., though less extensive data were obtained in this case.

Case 8: A.L.

This 31-year-old schizophrenic man had been a patient at Norwich State Hospital since October 1950. He had first become ill in August 1950, demonstrating a catatonic type of schizophrenia with auditory and visual hallucinations. On 31 January, 1952, bilateral medial temporal-lobe resection combined with orbital undercutting was carried out, the removal extending posteriorly for a distance of 6 cm along the mesial surface of the temporal lobes. Recovery was uneventful and no neurological deficit ensued. The patient has been more tractable since the operation but he is still subject to delusions and hallucinations. He is said to have a memory defect. When interviewed by B.M. in April 1955, he was found to be too out of contact for extensive formal testing. However, he was able to recall the examiner's name and place of origin 10 minutes after hearing them for the first time, and this despite the fact that the interval had been occupied with other tasks. He could also recognize objects which had been shown to him earlier in the interview, selecting them correctly from others which he had not seen before. But his immediate recall of drawings and stories was faulty and these were forgotten completely once his attention was directed to a new topic.

In this patient we stress the negative findings: despite his evident psychosis he did not show the severe memory loss typical of the patients in Group I. Yet the brief psychological examination and the hospital record both indicate some impairment of recent memory, though no reliable quantitative studies could be made.

Group III: No Persistent Memory Defect

Case 9: I.S.

This 54-year-old woman had a 20-year history of paranoid schizophrenia, with auditory hallucinations and marked emotional lability. She had attempted suicide on several occasions. On 16 November, 1950, six months after admission to a state hospital, a bilateral medial temporal lobectomy was carried out under local anaesthesia with sectioning of the tips of the temporal lobes and subpial suction removal of the medial portion, extending back 4 cm to include the uncus and amygdala. Thus this was a conservative bilateral removal, sparing the hippocampal region. The operation was complicated by accidental damage to the midbrain from the electrocautery, causing the patient to give a convulsive twitch which was followed by coma and extensive rigidity. After operation she was somnolent for a time with continuing rigidity, more marked on the left side than on the right. Vital signs were normal. She required traction to prevent flexure spasm contractures. There was slow improvement over the ensuing two months, with some residual clumsiness and spasticity of gait. For a time the patient's mental state was worse than before operation, but within three months she had improved markedly, with increased gentleness, diminished auditory hallucinations, and no depression. She ultimately showed the best result of all the cases in this series and was discharged from the hospital five months after operation.

This patient was re-examined on 11 May, 1956. She shows a complete remission of her former psychotic behaviour and is living at home with her husband and leading a normal social life. Her hallucinations have ceased. Upon neurological examination she shows some 25% residual deficit, manifested chiefly by spastic incoordination of gait and similar but less marked incoordination of the arms. The deep leg reflexes are increased to near clonus, but there is no Babinski sign. Arm reflexes are moderately increased and abdominal reflexes absent. Smell is completely lost but all other sense modalities are intact and other cranial nerves normal.

Psychological Findings

The patient was examined psychologically in April 1955. From the standpoint of memory, this patient presents a complete contrast to the cases reported above, obtaining excellent scores for both immediate and delayed recall of stories, drawings, and word associations, and describing accurately episodes from the relatively early post-operative period. The memory quotient of 125 is consistent with the IQ level of 122, and both would be classed as superior. This is so despite prolonged psychosis, intensive electro-shock therapy, and brain-stem damage of undetermined extent.

Case 10: E.G.

This 55-year-old woman developed malignant oedema after removal of a huge, saddle-type meningioma from the right sphenoid ridge; the pupils were dilated, she lost consciousness, and vital signs began to fail. A diagnosis of incisural hippocampal herniation was made, and, as a life-saving measure, unilateral non-dominant inferior temporal lobectomy was carried out, with deliberate resection of the hippocampus and hippocampal gyrus to a distance of 9 cm from the tip of the temporal lobe. (The operative procedure is illustrated in fig. 20.5.) Vital signs improved immediately and consciousness gradually returned, but for a few weeks the patient showed a disturbance of recent memory resembling that seen in our bilateral cases. However, follow-up studies in April 1955, 16 months after operation, showed no residual memory loss. Both immediate and delayed recall were normal and the memory quotient of 90 was completely consistent with the IQ level of 93. Neurological examination at this time showed a left homonymous visual field defect with macular sparing but no other deficit.

Discussion

The findings in these 10 cases point to the importance of the hippocampal region for normal memory function. All patients in this series having bilateral medial temporal-lobe resections extensive enough to damage portions of the hippocampus and hippo-campal gyrus bilaterally have shown a clear and persistent disturbance of recent memory, and in the two most radical excisions (in which the posterior limit of removal was at least 8 cm from the temporal tips) the deficit has been particularly severe, with no improvement in the two or more years which have elapsed since operation. These observations suggest a positive relationship between the extent of destruction to the hippocampal complex specifically and the degree of memory impairment. The correlation is not perfect, since D.C., who had only a 5.5 cm removal, showed as much deficit as did the two cases of most radical excision. Moreover, in the absence of necropsy material we cannot be sure of the exact area removed.

In all these hippocampal resections the uncus and amygdala have also of course been destroyed. Nevertheless the importance of the amygdaloid and periamygdaloid region for memory mechanisms is open to question, considering the total lack of memory impairment in the bilateral uncectomy case (I.S.), in which a 4 cm medial-temporal lobe removal was made. But not enough is known of the effects of lesions restricted to the hippocampal area itself to permit assessment of the relative contributions of these two regions. This is a question on which selective ablation studies in animals could well shed important light, but unfortunately the crucial experiments have yet to be done (Jasper, Gloor, and Milner, 1956).

The role of the hippocampus specifically has been discussed in some clinical studies. Glees and Griffith (1952) put forward the view that bilateral destruction of the hippocampus in man causes recent-memory loss and mental confusion, citing in support of this a somewhat unconvincing case of Grünthal (1947) and also a case of their own in which the hippocampus, the hippocampal and fusiform gyri, and 75% of the fornix fibres had been destroyed bilaterally by vascular lesion, but in which the rest of the brain appeared normal at necropsy. Interestingly enough, the amygdaloid nuclei were found to be intact as were the mamillary bodies. This patient showed marked anterograde and retrograde amnesia.

More recently Milner and Penfield (1955) have described a memory loss similar in all respects to that shown by our patients, in two cases of unilateral partial temporal lobectomy in the dominant hemisphere. In one case the removal was carried out in two stages separated by a five-year interval, and the memory loss followed the second operation only, at which time the uncus, hippocampus, and hippocampal gyrus alone were excised. Although these authors had carried out careful psychological testing in over 90 other cases of similar unilateral operation, only in these two cases was a general memory loss found. To account for the unusual deficit, they have assumed that there was in each case a pre-operatively unsuspected, but more or less completely destructive lesion of the hippocampal area of the opposite hemisphere. The unilateral operation would then deprive the patient of hippocampal function bilaterally, thus causing memory loss. The present study provides strong support for this interpretation.

Memory loss after partial bilateral temporal lobectomy has been reported by Petit-Dutaillis, Christophe, Pertuiset, Dreyfus-Brisac, and Blanc (1954) but in their patient the deficit was a transient one, a finding which led these authors to question the primary importance of the temporal lobes for memory function. However, their temporal lobe removals were complementary to ours in that they destroyed the lateral neocortex bilaterally but spared the hippocampal gyrus on the right and the uncus and hippocampus on the left. It therefore seems likely that the memory loss was due to temporary interference with the functioning of the hippocampal system, which later recovered.

We have stated that the loss seen in patients with bilateral hippocampal lesions is curiously specific to the domain of recent memory; neither in our cases nor in those of Milner and Penfield was there any deterioration in intellect or personality as a result of hippocampal resection. It appears important to emphasize this, since Terzian and Dalle Ore (1955) have described gross behavioural changes (affecting memory, perception, and sexual behaviour) after bilateral temporal lobectomy in man; they consider these changes comparable to Klüver and Bucy's (1939) findings after radical bilateral temporal lobectomy in the monkey. But Terzian and Ore included not only the uncal and hippocampal areas, but also the lateral temporal cortex in their bilateral removal. In contrast to the grossly deteriorated picture they describe, we find that bilateral resections limited to the mesial temporal region cause no perceptual disturbance, even on visual tests known to be sensitive to unilateral lesions of the temporal neocortex (Milner, 1954).

The findings reported herein have led us to attribute a special importance to the anterior hippocampus and hippocampal gyrus in the retention of new experience. But the hippocampus has a strong and orderly projection to the mamillary bodies (Simpson, 1952), and as early as 1928 Gamper claimed that lesions of the mamillary bodies were commonly found in amnesic states of the Korsakoff type. Moreover, Williams and Pennybacker (1954) have carried out careful psychological studies of 180 patients with verified intracranial lesions and find that a specific deficit in recent memory is most likely to occur when the lesion involves the mamillary region. It is possible, then, that when we have two interrelated structures (hippocampus and mamillary bodies) damage to either can cause memory loss, a point which has been emphasized by Jasper and others (1956). In view of these findings it is interesting that sectioning the fornix bilaterally, and thereby interrupting the descending fibres from the hippocampus, appears to have little effect on behaviour (Dott, 1938; Garcia Bengochea, De la Torre, Esquivel, Vieta, and Fernandez, 1954), though a transient memory deficit is sometimes seen (Garcia Bengochea, 1955).

To conclude, the observations reported herein demonstrate the deleterious effect of bilateral surgical lesions of the hippocampus and hippocampal gyrus on recent memory. The relationship between this region and the overlying neocortex in the temporal lobe needs further elucidation, as does its relationship to deeper-lying structures.

Summary

Bilateral medial temporal-lobe resection in man results in a persistent impairment of recent memory whenever the removal is carried far enough posteriorly to damage portions of the anterior hippocampus and hippocampal gyrus. This conclusion is based on formal psychological testing of nine cases (eight psychotic and one epileptic) carried out from one and one-half to four years after operation.

The degree of memory loss appears to depend on the extent of hippocampal removal. In two cases in which bilateral resection was carried to a distance of 8 cm posterior to the temporal tips the loss was particularly severe.

Removal of only the uncus and amygdala bilaterally does not appear to cause memory impairment.

A case of unilateral inferior temporal lobectomy with radical posterior extension to include the major portion of the hippocampus and hippocampal gyrus showed no lasting memory loss. This is consistent with Milner and Penfield's negative findings in a long series of unilateral removals for temporal-lobe epilepsy.

The memory loss in these cases of medial temporal-lobe excision involved both anterograde and some retrograde amnesia, but left early memories and technical skills intact. There was no deterioration in personality or general intelligence, and no complex perceptual disturbance such as is seen after a more complete bilateral temporal lobectomy.

It is concluded that the anterior hippocampus and hippocampal gyrus, either separately or together, are critically concerned in the retention of current experience. It is not known whether the amygdala plays any part in this mechanism, since the hippocampal complex has not been removed alone, but always together with uncus and amygdala.

Note

1   These further psychological examinations by one of the authors, B.M., were made possible through the interest of Dr Wilder Penfield.

References

Dott, N. M. (1938). In Clark, W. E., Le Gros, Beattie, J., Riddoch, G., and Dott, N. M. *The Hypothalamus: Morphological, Functional, Clinical and Surgical Aspects*, Oliver and Boyd, Edinburgh.

Gamper, E. (1928). *Disch. Z. Nervenheilk.*, **102**, 122.

Garcia Bengochea, F. (1955). Personal communication.

——, De La Torre, O., Esquivel, O., Vieta, R., and Fernandez, C. (1954). *Trans. Amer. neurol. Ass.*, **79**, 176.

Glees, P., and Griffith, H. B. (1952). *Mschr. Psychiat. Neurol.*, **123**, 193.

Grünthal, E. (1947). Ibid., **113**, 1.

Jasper, H., Gloor, P., and Milner, B. (1956). *Ann. Rev. Physiol.*, **18**, 359.

Klüver, H., and Bucy, P. C. (1939). *Arch. Neurol. Psychiat. (Chicago)*, **42**, 979.

MacLean, P. D. (1952). *Electroenceph. Clin. Neurophysiol.*, **4**, 407.

Milner, B. (1954). *Psychol. Bull.*, **51**, 42.

——, and Penfield, W. (1955). *Trans. Amer. Neurol. Ass.*, **80**, 42.

Petit-Dutaillis, D., Christophe, J., Pertuiset, B., Dreyfus- Brisac, C., and Blanc, C. (1954). *Rev. Neurol. (Paris)*, **91**, 129.

Pribram, K. H., and Kruger, L. (1954). *Ann. N. Y. Acad. Sci.*, **58**, 109.

Scoville, W. B. (1954). *J. Neurosurg.*, **11**, 64.

——, Dunsmore, R. H., Liberson, W. T., Henry, C. E., and Pepe, A. (1953). *Res. Publ. Ass. Nerv. Ment. Dis.*, **31**, 347.

——, Wilk, E. K., and Pepe, A. J. (1951). *Amer. J. Psychiat.*, **107**, 730.

Simpson, D. A. (1952). *Journal of Neurology, Neurosurgery and Psychiatry*, **15**, 79.

Terzian, H., and Dalle Ore, G. (1955). *Neurology*, **5**, 373.

Wechsler, D. (1945). *J. Psychol.*, **19**, 87.

Williams, M., and Pennybacker, J. (1954). *Journal of Neurology, Neurosurgery and Psychiatry*, **17**, 115.

Episodic Memory, Semantic Memory, and Amnesia

Larry R. Squire and Stuart M. Zola

Introduction

Recently there has been renewed interest in the distinction between episodic memory and semantic memory (Tulving, 1972; 1992). Episodic memory refers to the capacity for recollecting happenings from the past, for remembering events that occurred in particular spatial and temporal contexts. Semantic memory refers to the capacity for recollecting facts and general knowledge about the world. A critical question has been how this distinction might be reflected in the organization of memory functions in the brain.

Episodic memory and semantic memory are two types of declarative memory (Tulving, 1983; 1991; Squire, 1987). One view is that episodic memory and semantic memory are both dependent on the integrity of medial temporal lobe and midline diencephalic structures,[1] and that episodic memory depends additionally on the frontal lobes (Shimamura and Squire, 1987; Squire, 1987; Tulving, 1989; Knowlton and Squire, 1995). According to this view, amnesic patients with medial temporal lobe/diencephalic damage should be deficient in remembering both events and facts (episodic and semantic memory). Amnesic patients who in addition have frontal lobe damage should be especially deficient in episodic memory, because the frontal lobes are involved in an important aspect of episodic remembering, that is, associating the content of an event with its source (when and where the event occurred) in order to construct an autobiographical recollection (Janowsky et al., 1989; Schacter, 1987). Under this view, episodic memory is the gateway to semantic memory. New information is always presented initially as part of some event, but through repetition or rehearsal the new information can be abstracted from its original context and be represented as semantic memory. Thus, when episodic memory is impaired as the result of medial temporal lobe/diencephalic amnesia, semantic memory should be correspondingly impaired. However, when episodic memory is impaired because of frontal lobe dysfunction, then new semantic learning should be possible.

An alternative view is that episodic memory is not critical for the formation of semantic memory (Cermak, 1984; Kinsbourne and Wood, 1975; Parkin, 1982). This view is based in part on the observation that amnesic patients can acquire some semantic knowledge successfully after much repetition (Kovner et al., 1983; Glisky et al., 1986a, b; Shimamura and Squire, 1987; Tulving et al., 1991; Hayman et al., 1993). Drawing on such observations, Tulving (1991) proposed that new information can enter semantic memory through the perceptual systems and independently of the medial temporal lobe/diencephalic brain structures that are damaged in amnesia. This account holds semantic memory to be partially or wholly preserved in amnesia. "The hypothesis that semantic learning ability is preserved in some amnesics implies that these amnesics would perform normally in all semantic learning tasks in which normal subjects could not rely on their intact episodic memory" (Tulving, 1991: 24). A more specific version of this idea is that semantic memory is relatively preserved in amnesic patients who have damage limited to the hippocampus (Vargha-Khadem et al., 1997).

The views outlined above are based on two kinds of data. The first are cases where amnesia has occurred early in childhood, before much of an individual's semantic knowledge has been acquired. The question of interest is whether such individuals can acquire semantic knowledge, for example as a result of formal schooling, more successfully than would be expected from their impairment in moment-to-moment episodic memory. The second kind of data come from experimental studies of amnesic patients where the ability to accomplish fact learning and event learning have been directly compared, studies where retrieval from episodic and semantic memory have been directly compared, and studies of remote memory. This article reviews the available data and considers their implications for the neurologic foundations of episodic and semantic memory.

Reports of Amnesia Occurring Early in Childhood

There have been three reports of early childhood amnesia. One report concerned an amnesic patient (T.C.) who developed amnesia at the age of 9 years, after an episode of herpes simplex encephalitis (Wood et al., 1989). The patient continued to attend school and graduated from high school with her class. Yet her academic progress occurred against a severe memory impairment for moment-to-moment memory which gave the impression of preserved, or partially preserved, semantic memory capacity in the absence of episodic memory. However, a closer analysis of this case reveals that T.C. was capable of some episodic learning and her progress in school was abnormally slow. With respect to episodic memory, on the Rey Auditory Verbal Learning task, she managed to recall eight of fifteen words on the fifth trial, and after a delay with a distractor list she was still able to recall three of the words. Thus, her episodic memory was impaired, but it was not altogether absent. With respect to progress in school (semantic memory), two assessments (one at age 14 and another at age 20) indicated that during these 6 years she progressed only two grade levels in reading and spelling ability (from grade six to grade eight). In addition, during the same period, she did not progress at all in mathematics, as measured by the Wide Range Achievement Test.

An early commentary on this case report suggested that T.C.'s ability to learn in school (semantic memory) was not obviously better than would have been expected from her performance on standard tests of anterograde memory ability, i.e., her ability to remember moment-to-moment information (episodic memory) (Ostergaard and Squire, 1990). The real difficulty, of course, is that no formula exists for determining what level of school achievement should in fact be expected, given an impairment in moment-to-moment memory. Accordingly, case reports like this one cannot establish whether semantic memory is spared relative to episodic memory or whether they are affected similarly.

A second report of childhood amnesia concerned a patient (C.C.) who developed amnesia at the age of 10 years as the result of an anoxic episode (Ostergaard, 1987). Formal testing during a 4-year period indicated that C.C. had persistent and severely impaired declarative memory, both episodic and semantic. With respect to episodic memory, for free recall of 10 different 10-word lists, each tested after a 20-s distraction-filled interval, C.C. averaged only 1.1 words correct. Also, after a 45-min delay he could recall nothing of short prose passages and virtually nothing of the Rey-Osterrieth figure. With respect to semantic memory, C.C. did improve in school, but his progress was not normal and as time passed he fell further and further behind his peers. For example, he required 52 months to progress 25 months in reading age. In the laboratory, he was impaired relative to age-matched control subjects on several tests of semantic memory, including tests of verbal fluency, reading, spelling, vocabulary, and semantic classification. On the latter test, which involved classifying the names of living and nonliving things, his performance was poorer for names that are ordinarily learned after the age of 8 than for names that are ordinarily learned earlier. As with T.C., there is no basis for deciding whether the semantic knowledge that C.C. accrued over the years is unusual or simply what would have been expected from estimates of his moment-to-moment (episodic) memory ability.

For these two patients, there was minimal documentation concerning the locus and extent of brain damage. Patient T.C. was assumed to have medial temporal lobe damage, though a computerized tomography (CT) scan taken 2 years after the onset of her amnesia was interpreted as normal (Wood et al., 1989). For patient C.C., a CT scan suggested bilateral medial temporal lobe damage and additional damage in the left occipital lobe, right orbitofrontal cortex, and right neostriatum (Ostergaard, 1987).

The third report described three patients who early in life sustained bilateral injury to the hippocampus (as determined by magnetic resonance imaging) (Vargha-Khadem et al., 1997). The damage was judged to have spared the perirhinal, entorhinal, and parahippocampal cortices. In one of the three cases the damage occurred at birth (Beth), in another at age 4 years (Jon), and in the third at age 9 years (Kate), "before they had acquired the knowledge base that characterizes semantic memory" (Vargha-Khadem et al., 1997: 376). All three patients were reported to have considerable capacity for semantic memory (speech and language competence, literacy, and factual knowledge) despite pronounced amnesia for episodes of everyday life. Accordingly, the authors interpreted their findings as evidence that "early bilateral pathology that is limited largely to the hippocampus produces severe loss of episodic memory but leaves general cognitive development, based mainly on semantic memory functions, relatively intact" (Vargha-Khadem et al., 1997: 373). They further suggested that episodic memory ordinarily depends primarily on the integrity of the hippocampal component of the medial temporal lobe memory system, whereas semantic memory ordinarily depends primarily on the adjacent cortical areas of the medial temporal lobe memory system, e.g., the entorbinal and perirhinal cortex. If true, this finding would be important because of the implication that the hippocampal region is critical for only one aspect of declarative memory.

Evidence for impaired episodic memory in the three patients was documented by their low scores on delayed recall of the stories from the logical memory subtest of the Wechsler Memory Scale (WMS), and on delayed reproduction of the WMS designs. All three patients also obtained close to the lowest possible scores on other standardized tests, including delayed recall of the word list from the Children's Auditory Verbal Learning Test, despite performing within normal limits on immediate memory for the word list. Additionally, questionnaires completed by the patients' parents revealed everyday memory difficulties, including difficulty finding their way in familiar surroundings, difficulty remembering where objects and belongings were placed, impaired orientation for date and time, and difficulty recounting recent telephone conversations, television programs, or the day's activities.

Against this background of impaired episodic memory, all three individuals were reported to have fared well in mainstream education and to have acquired considerable semantic knowledge. For example, their verbal IQ scores (which depend on acquired knowledge) were 82 (Beth), 109 (Jon), and 86 (Kate). On the Wechsler Objective Reading Dimensions (WORD) Test (normal mean scores for the subtests are 100, with a standard deviation of 15; Rust et al., 1993), the three patients obtained competent scores in reading (Beth = 85; Jon = 102; Kate = 102), spelling (Beth = 77; Jon = 84; Kate = 99), and reading comprehension (Beth = 84; Jon = 97; Kate = 88). All of their scores (with the exception of Jon's spelling) were reported as commensurate with their verbal IQ scores. In addition, all three patients scored within the normal range for the population on the Vocabulary, Information, and Comprehension subtests of the Wechsler Intelligence Scale for Children (WISC-III) and the Wechsler Adult Intelligence Scale – Revised (WAIS-R).

Given the fund of knowledge that the children had acquired, Vargha-Khadem et al. (1997) asked how sensory information can enter a semantic memory store in the face of early-onset amnesia and a disabling loss of episodic memory. They suggested that semantic memories were stored partly independently of episodic memory by way of the intact perirhinal and entorhinal cortices. However, it is also possible to propose that each patient had some residual episodic memory and that even a little episodic memory is able, in the fullness of time and after sufficient repetition, to support the acquisition of a good deal of semantic knowledge. If so, then episodic and semantic memory may actually have been affected in these three patients to the same degree.

The neuropsychological data presented by Vargha-Khadem et al. (1997) are not inconsistent with this possibility. Like most amnesic patients, their patients did exhibit some residual moment-to-moment (episodic) memory ability. They scored above zero on most of the recall tests (story recall, WMS design recall, and the Rivermead Behavioural Memory Test). Moreover, they reportedly scored quite well on all but two of the 12 recognition memory tests that were given. Regardless whether recognition memory function is considered to be relatively spared in these patients or impaired in proportion to their recall scores, it is notable that these patients exhibited good recognition performance on memory tests for words, faces, and other material that had been presented only once. Thus, before one interprets the ability of these patients to accrue factual knowledge during their years in school, it is important to keep in mind that the patients have considerable capacity for moment-to-moment memory, which could provide a foundation for the acquisition of factual knowledge.

With respect to acquiring information in school, the level of semantic memory that the patients were able to achieve may not be as high as first appears. First, because one does not know what IQ scores would have been obtained by these patients if they had not sustained early brain damage, it is unclear what it means when the performance of these patients on knowledge tests is sometimes found to be commensurate with their IQ scores. Second, their scores on knowledge tests are not always commensurate with their IQ scores. On the WORD Test, Jon's scores for basic reading, spelling, and reading comprehension are all below what would be predicted from his verbal IQ score, and Beth's spelling score is below what would be predicted by her IQ score. Third, for two of the patients (Beth and Kate), the verbal and performance IQ scores themselves range from one to three standard deviations below the mean scores obtained by the control subjects included in this report.

Thus, just as for T.C. and C.C., it is unclear that Beth, Jon, or Kate have achieved more in school (i.e., acquired more semantic memory) than might be expected from their ability to remember moment-to-moment information (episodic memory). The difficulty is that one simply does not know what can be achieved in school over the years, on the basis of residual episodic memory ability. Accordingly, documentation of progress in school, in the face of impaired episodic memory, cannot on its own provide a critical test of the relationship between episodic and semantic memory.

Experimental Studies of Amnesic Patients

Another kind of data relevant to the organization of episodic and semantic memory comes from experiments comparing the performance of amnesic patients and control subjects. One approach has been to assess the ability of amnesic patients to acquire new factual information as well as new information about specific episodes. The question of interest is whether the semantic memory that amnesic patients can acquire is disproportionately better than the event memory that they can acquire. A second approach has been to compare two kinds of retrieval in amnesic patients, remembering and knowing, which are thought to reflect the operation of episodic and semantic memory, respectively. The question of interest is whether amnesia affects remembering more than it affects knowing. A third approach has been to assess remote memory in amnesic patients. The question of interest is whether patients have difficulty remembering factual information from the past. Each of these approaches will now be considered in turn.

Acquiring factual knowledge vs. learning about specific events

In a study that compared fact and event learning (Hamann and Squire, 1995), amnesic patients with diencephalic lesions or lesions of the hippocampal formation were taught new factual knowledge (40 three-word sentences such as "MEDICINE cured HIC-CUP"). Training occurred during four weekly sessions (two training trials/session). For testing, sentence fragments were presented with the instruction to complete each fragment with a word that had been studied (e.g., MEDICINE cured ———). The patients learned at an abnormally slow rate, progressing from 0% correct to 19% correct, as measured 1 week after their fourth training session. Control subjects achieved better than 75% correct performance 1 week after their second session. Event memory was tested in the second session by asking about specific events that had occurred during the first session. The finding was that amnesic patients were impaired on both fact memory and event memory to a similar degree. Indeed, their performance on both the fact and event tests one week after the first training session closely matched the performance of control subjects who had the same training on facts and events but who were tested after a delay of four weeks. Thus, unlike the situation where one observes children in school, in formal experiments one can establish whether the level of fact memory ability attained by amnesic patients is or is not what it should have been given their ability to remember specific events. In this study, there was no indication that the capacity for fact learning reflects some spared or partially spared ability, relative to the capacity for event memory.

A different conclusion about fact and event memory in amnesia was reached by Tulving (1991) on the basis of his work with a severely amnesic patient (K.C.). This work introduced a novel learning method for amnesic patients, which was designed to facilitate the acquisition of new semantic knowledge by reducing interference. This method (the study-only procedure) prevents incorrect, potentially interfering responses during learning by testing retention for the first time after several distributed study sessions. The important finding was that across several weeks K.C. was able to acquire considerable semantic knowledge (e.g., the three-word sentences described earlier) using the study-only procedure, despite what was described as a completely dysfunctional episodic memory for specific past events (Tulving et al., 1991). The rate at which K.C. acquired semantic knowledge was far from normal, but what he did learn was striking, given his severe deficit in episodic memory.

Extensive study of K.C.'s fact learning ability led to the proposal that semantic learning is spared, or partially spared, in amnesia (Tulving, 1991). To explain earlier failures to demonstrate good semantic learning in amnesia, Tulving (1991) raised two important points. First, the poor performance of amnesic patients in earlier studies (e.g., patient H.M.; Gabrieli et al., 1988) might be attributable to the conventional learning methods that were used. Second, the performance of amnesic patients on tests of semantic learning may compare poorly to the performance of normal subjects, because normal subjects (but not amnesic patients) are able on such tests to draw on their intact episodic memory.

There are three reasons why the results for patient K.C. cannot be taken as clear evidence for sparing, or partial sparing, of semantic memory in amnesia. First, Hamann and Squire (1995) also used the study-only method to teach amnesic patients three-word sentences. Although the study-only method resulted in better learning than conventional learning methods (32% correct vs. 19% correct after the fourth weekly session), the amount of acquired knowledge was commensurate with the ability of the patients to recollect events that had occurred on the previous day. Second, Hamann and Squire (1995) also tested E.P., a severely amnesic patient with no detectable episodic memory (Squire and Knowlton, 1995). E.P. was given four separate training sessions during a 2-week period using the study-only procedure. He exhibited no learning at all, obtaining a score of zero. Thus, in a patient with no detectable capacity for episodic memory, there was also no detectable capacity for acquiring semantic knowledge.

Third, some questions can be raised about the claim that K.C.'s episodic memory is "completely dysfunctional" (Hayman et al., 1993). On yes/no recognition tests involving 107–116 target items, K.C. failed to endorse a single item as familiar (Tulving et al., 1991). This observation could reflect actual at-chance memory performance or a strong "no" bias. Additional memory tests based on forced-choice recognition could settle the issue by showing whether K.C. can discriminate at all between familiar and novel test items. However, little documentation was provided concerning K.C.'s performance on forced-choice recognition tests. In addition, it was stated: "Most of his [K.C.'s] scores on the WMS-R [Wechsler Memory Scale – Revised] are comparable to the mean scores of amnesic subjects used in experiments in other laboratories" (Tulving et al., 1991: 598). Yet, most amnesic study patients do not have completely dysfunctional episodic memory.

An additional difficulty is that the neuropathology in this (closed head injury) patient is complicated. Magnetic resonance imaging studies of K.C. revealed "a predominance of observable abnormal signal in the left hemisphere.... Abnormal signal in the right hemisphere is less severe, observable only in a small portion of the medial temporal region and in superior aspects of the medial parietal region" (Tulving et al., 1991: 597). Thus, K.C.'s medial temporal lobe damage, while bilateral, is asymmetric and present in only a small portion of the right medial temporal lobe. Moreover, his brain damage involves other cortical areas in the left hemisphere, including frontal, parietal, retrosplenial, and occipital cortices, and it involves the right parietal cortex.

One way to understand K.C.'s capacity for gradual semantic learning, in the face of his severely impaired episodic memory, is that his episodic memory problems, and especially his apparent inability to have autobiographical recollections, are due especially to his left frontal damage. This scenario is consistent with our finding that patient E.P., who is profoundly amnesic (and has extensive bilateral damage in the medial temporal lobe, but does not have K.C.'s frontal lobe damage), could not accomplish semantic learning at all. It would be interesting to use forced-choice recognition testing to ask whether K.C. could learn about single events (episodic memory), so long as the test did not require that he place himself autobiographically within any past episode. If so, perhaps K.C.'s main difficulty is his inability to personally experience his past through autobiographical remembering. Perhaps he has some capacity to learn about single events, just as he has some capacity to acquire semantic knowledge through repetition. In summary, the findings for patient K.C. are interesting, but it is not clear that his findings illuminate the status of episodic and semantic memory in other amnesic patients or the relative dependence of episodic and semantic memory on the medial temporal lobe or diencephalon.

Remembering and knowing in amnesia

Remembering and knowing are thought to reflect the operation of episodic memory and semantic memory, respectively (Tulving, 1989). When a recently presented item evokes a recollection of having specifically encountered that item, an individual is said to "remember." By contrast, when one has simply a sense of familiarity about a previously presented item, without actually recollecting a specific prior encounter with the item, one is said to experience "knowing." In other words, "remember" (R) responses measure the recollection of information about an item that is embedded within or associated with the learning episode, whereas "know" (K) responses measure context-free item familiarity.

With this framework in mind, the pattern of R and K responses provides a method for determining the status of episodic and semantic memory in amnesia. If semantic memory is relatively preserved following damage to medial temporal lobe/diencephalic structures, then the accuracy of K responses in recognition memory tests should be less affected than the accuracy of R responses. In a study that directly tested this idea, 13 amnesic patients were given a yes/no recognition test 10 minutes after studying 36 words. For each word that was endorsed as a study item, subjects indicated whether they remembered it (R) or whether they simply knew that the word had been presented but had no specific recollection about it (K). Amnesic patients were impaired in the accuracy of both R and K responses, and they performed like control subjects who were tested after a 1-week delay interval. That is, amnesic patients tested 10 minutes after learning and control subjects tested 1 week after learning exhibited similar reductions in R and K responses (Knowlton and Squire, 1995). Of the thirteen patients in this study, four had bilateral damage to the hippocampal formation as determined by quantitative MRI. These four patients also had similar reductions in R and K accuracy (controls: d' for R = 1.96 ± 0.11; d' for K = 0.93 ± 0.13; four amnesic patients: d' for R = 0.33 ± 0.25; d' for K = 0.30 ± 0.22; controls tested after a 1-week delay: d' for R = 0.64 ± 0.21; d' for K = 0.31 ± 0.25).

A recent reanalysis of the available R and K data from three studies of amnesic patients reached a similar conclusion that both R and K accuracy are impaired in amnesia (Kroll and Yonelinas, 1997). These findings provide strong evidence that the components of memory that support R and K responses (episodic and semantic memory) both depend on the integrity of the medial temporal lobe/diencephalic brain structures damaged in amnesia. Most important, the data for the four patients studied by Knowlton and Squire (1995) suggest that R and K accuracy depends similarly on the hippocampal formation. There is no indication in the data that hippocampal formation lesions spare, or partially spare, K responses (semantic memory) relative to R responses (episodic memory).

Studies of remote memory

Performance on remote memory tests provides another test of the idea that episodic and semantic memory can be differentially affected in amnesia. As mentioned earlier, it has been suggested that the reported advantage of normal subjects over amnesic patients in tests of semantic memory is due to the fact that normal subjects can perform these tests by drawing upon episodic memory (Tulving, 1991). Arguing against this point of view, however, is the finding that amnesic patients, including patients with histologically confirmed lesions limited to the hippocampal formation (patients L.M. and W.H., Rempel-Clower et al., 1996), can be impaired on factual questions about news events that occurred more than a decade before the onset of their amnesia (Squire et al., 1989; Beatty et al., 1987; Salmon et al., 1988). It is unclear how normal subjects could gain advantage over amnesic subjects by using episodic memory in this kind of test. The point is that amnesic patients have difficulty retrieving factual information even when the contribution of episodic retrieval is quite unlikely (for additional evidence, see Verfaellie et al., 1995; Schmidtke and Vollmer, 1997).

Remote memory performance is also relevant to episodic and semantic memory in the case of patients who have been amnesic for many years. Vargha-Khadem et al. (1997) suggest that semantic learning can proceed rather well despite damage to the hippocampus. Reed and Squire (1998) studied two patients, A.B. and L.J., who have been amnesic for 22 and 9 years, respectively. MRI findings for L.J. suggest that damage is limited to the hippocampal region (see next section for limitations of MRI). A.B.'s lesion is presumed to be hippocampal on the basis of etiology (anoxia and cardiac arrest). Compared with control subjects who were asked about the same past time periods as the patients, these two patients were found to have acquired an abnormally small amount of new factual knowledge about vocabulary, famous people, and news events during the years since they became amnesic (Reed and Squire, 1998). The finding that A.B. and L.J. possess deficient fact knowledge about the years since the onset of their amnesia shows that factual knowledge does not inevitably accrue to normal levels in the face of hippocampal pathology.

Conclusion

The proposal that episodic and semantic memory are affected differently in amnesia (Tulving, 1991) or, more specifically, that they are affected differently by hippocampal damage (Vargha-Khadem et al., 1997), is an interesting idea and in the spirit of current efforts to find specificity within the medial temporal lobe memory system. There appear to be two reasons why it has been difficult to arrange a decisive test of this proposal. First, rather stringent neuropsychological evidence is required to support such a claim. Either double dissociations between episodic and semantic memory are needed, or compelling evidence is required that episodic memory is disproportionately affected relative to semantic memory.

Second, with human material one seldom has available the requisite neuropathological detail. MRI data are essential, but even high-resolution MRI cannot detect cell loss that is easily detected in histological examination. For example, MRI indicated clearly that amnesic patients L.M. and W.H. had damage to the hippocampal region (Squire et al., 1990). Subsequent neurohistological analysis confirmed this finding but also provided additional information: W.H., but not L.M., had damage to the subicular complex, and both patients had cell loss in the entorhinal cortex (Rempel-Clower et al., 1996). Accordingly, it is doubtful that the neuroimaging techniques currently available can reliably identify patients who have damage limited to the hippocampal and no damage to adjacent structures such as entorhinal cortex. Yet this level of resolution is required to evaluate the hypothesis advanced by Vargha-Khadem et al. (1997).

With respect to the two specific proposals under consideration – that semantic and episodic memory are differentially affected following either medial temporal lobe lesions (Tulving, 1991) or more restricted hippocampal lesions (Vargha-Khadem et al., 1997) – there is at this time no compelling support for these proposals and some evidence against them. (1) Reported cases of childhood amnesia have not yet provided the kind of rigorous comparison between episodic and semantic memory that is needed to test the hypothesis. The cases described to date are inconclusive because there is no basis for judging whether the amount of semantic knowledge eventually acquired by amnesic patients is unusual or simply what would be expected after repeated effort over many years. (2) Experiments comparing the ability of amnesic patients to acquire episodic and semantic memory suggest that both kinds of memory are impaired to the same degree. (3) Experiments comparing the ability to retrieve from episodic and semantic memory suggest that episodic and semantic retrieval are impaired similarly. (4) Amnesic patients can have difficulty remembering factual knowledge that occurred more than a decade prior to the onset of their amnesia, direct evidence that semantic memory is impaired. Also, amnesic patients do not inevitably acquire factual knowledge to the degree that normal individuals do, during the years after they become amnesic.

Thus, the data suggest that episodic and semantic memory depend similarly on the medial temporal lobe/diencephalic structures damaged in amnesia. Although episodic and semantic memory do not appear to be dissociable in medial temporal lobe/ diencephalic amnesia, the distinction remains useful for understanding the contribution of the frontal lobes to episodic memory. Indeed, the findings from patient K.C. might be viewed in this light – as support for the idea that episodic and semantic memory are dissociable in amnesic patients with severe frontal lobe damage.

Note

1 Within the diencephalon, the most important structures for declarative memory are in the medial thalamus: the anterior thalamic nucleus, the mediodorsal nucleus, and the connections to and from the medial thalamus that lie within the internal medullary lamina (Zola-Morgan and Squire, 1993). Within the medial temporal lobe, the important structures are the hippocampal formation (the hippocampus proper, the denlate gyrus, the subicular complex, and entorhinal cortex) and adjacent, anatomically related cortex, i.e., perirhinal and para-hippocampal cortices (Squire and Zola-Morgan, 1991).

References

Beatty, W. W., Salmon, D. P., Bernstein, N., Butters, N. Remote memories in a patient with amnesia due to hypoxia. *Psychol. Med.* (1987) 17: 657–65.

Cermak, I. S. The episodic–semantic distinction in amnesia. In: Squire, I. R., Butters, N. (eds), *Neuropsychology of memory* (New York: Guilford Press, 1984): 55–62.

Gabrieli, J. D. E., Cohen, N. J., Corkin, S. The impaired learning of semantic knowledge following medial temporal-lobe resection. *Brain Cogn.* (1988) 7: 157–77.

Glisky, F. I., Schacter, D. L., Tulving, E. Computer learning by memory-impaired patients: Acquisition and retention of complex knowledge. *Neuropsychologia* (1986a) 27: 173–8.

Glisky, F. I., Schacter, D. L., Tulving, E. Learning and retention of computer-related vocabulary in memory-impaired patients: Method of vanishing cues. *J. Clin. Exp. Neuropsychol.* (1986b) 8: 292–312.

Hayman, C. A., MacDonald, C. A., Tulving, E. The role of repetition and associative interference in new semantic learning in amnesia: A case experiment. *J. Cogn. Neurosci.* (1993) 5: 375–89.

Hamann, S. B., Squire, I. R. On the acquisition of new declarative knowledge in amnesia. *Behav. Neurosci.* (1995) 109: 1027–44.

Janowsky, J. S., Shimamura, A. P., Squire, L. R. Source memory impairment in patients with frontal lobe lesions. *Neuropsychologia* (1989) 27: 1043–56.

Kinsbourne, M., Wood, E. Short-term memory processes and the amnesic syndrome. In: Deutsch, D., Deutsch, J. A., (eds), *Short-term memory* (San Diego: Academic Press, 1975): 258–91.

Knowlton, B. J., Squire, L. R. Remembering and knowing: Two different expressions of declarative memory. *J. Exp. Psychol.* [Learn. Mem. Cogn.] (1995) 21: 699–710.

Kovner, R., Mattis, S., Goldmeier, E. A technique for promoting robust free recall in chronic organic amnesia. *J. Clin. Neuropsychol.* (1983) 5: 65–71.

Kroll, N. F. A., Yonelinas, A. P. The contribution of recollection and familiarity to recognition memory in normals and amnesiacs. *Soc. Neurosci. Abs.* (1997), 23: 1580.

Ostergaard, A. L. Episodic, semantic, and procedural memory in a case of amnesia at an early age. *Neuropsychologia* (1987) 25: 341–57.

Ostergaard, A. L., Squire, I. R. Childhood amnesia and distinctions between forms of memory. *Brain Cogn.* (1990) 14: 127–33.

Parkin, A. J. Residual learning capability in organic amnesia. *Cortex* (1982) 18: 417–40.

Reed, J. M., Squire, L. R. Retrograde amnesia for facts and events: Findings from four new cases. *J. Neurosci.* (1998) 18: 3943–54.

Rempel-Clower, N., Zola, S. M., Squire, L. R., Amaral, D. G. Three cases of enduring memory impairment following bilateral damage limited to the hippocampal formation. *J. Neurosci.* (1996) 16: 5233–55.

Rust, J., Golombok, S., Trickey, G. *Wechsler Objective Reading Dimensions Test* (Psychological Corporation) (Sidcup, UK, 1993).

Salmon, D. P., Lasker, B. R., Butters, N., Beatty, W. W. Remote memory in a patient with circumscribed amnesia. *Brain Cogn.* (1988) 7: 201–11.

Schacter, D. L. Memory, amnesia, and frontal lobe dysfunction. *Psychobiology* (1987) 15: 21–36.

Schmidtke, K., Vollmer, H. Retrograde amnesia: A study of its relation to anterograde amnesia and semantic memory deficits. *Neuropsychologia* (1997) 35: 505–18.

Shimamura, A. P., Squire, I. R. A neuropsychological study of fact memory and source amnesia. *J. Exp. Psychol.* [Learn. Mem. Cogn.] (1987) 13: 464–73.

Squire, I. R. *Memory and brain* (New York: Oxford University Press, 1987).

Squire, I. R., Haist, P., Shimamura, A. P. The neurology of memory: Quantitative assessment of retrograde amnesia in two groups of amnesic patients. *J. Neurosci.* (1989) 9: 828–39.

Squire, L. R., Knowlton, B. Learning about categories in the absence of memory. *Proc. Natl. Acad. Sci. USA* (1995) 92: 12470–4.

Squire, I. R., Zola-Morgan, S. The medial temporal lobe memory system, *Science* (1991) 253: 1380–6.

Squire, I. R., Amatal, D. G., Press, G. A. Magnetic resonance measurements of hippocampal formation and mammillary nuclei distinguish medial temporal lobe and diencephalic amnesia. *J. Neurosci.* (1990) 10: 3106–17.

Tulving, E. Episodic memory. In: Squire, I. (ed.), *Encyclopedia of learning and memory* (New York: Macmillan, 1992): 161–3.

Tulving, E. Episodic and semantic memory. In: Tulving, F. Donaldson, W. (eds), *Organization of memory* (New York: Academic Press, 1972): 381–403.

Tulving, E. *Elements of episodic memory* (Oxford: Oxford University Press, 1983).

Tulving, E. Remembering and knowing the past. *Am. Scientist* (1991) 77: 361–7.

Tulving, E. Concepts in human memory. In: Squire, I. R., Weinberger, N. M., Lynch, G., McGaugh, J. (eds), *Memory: Organization and locus of change* (New York: Oxford University Press, 1991): 3–32.

Tulving, E., Hayman, C. A. G., MacDonald, C. A. Long-lasting perceptual priming and semantic learning in amnesia: A case experiment. *J. Exp. Psychol.* [Learn. Mem. Cogn.] (1991) 17: 595–617.

Vargha-Khadem, E. Gadian, D. G., Watkins, K. E., Connely, A., Van Paesschen, W., Mishkin, M. Differential effects of early hippocampal pathology on episodic and semantic memory. *Science* (1997) 277: 376–80.

Verfaellie, M., Reiss, L., Roth, H. L. Knowledge of new English vocabulary in amnesia: An examination of premorbidly acquired semantic memory. *J. Int. Neuropsychol. Soc.* (1995) 1: 443–53.

Wood, F. B., Brown, I. S., Felton, R. H. Long-term follow-up of a childhood amnesic syndrome. *Brain Cogn.* (1989) 10: 76–86.

Zola-Morgan, S., Squire, J. R. Neuroanatomy of memory. *Ann. Rev. Neurosci.* (1993) 16: 547–63.

Working Memory: The Interface between Memory and Cognition

Alan Baddeley

Human Memory: A Speculative Overview

I assume that memory, along with other cognitive capacities, has evolved to allow the organism to cope with a complex but structured world. The world is never entirely predictable, but has sufficient regularity to make it advantageous for the organism to use the past in order to predict the future, that is, to make use of learning and memory.

Working memory and perception

Before learning can take place, an organism must be able to perceive the world, and preferably take advantage of the fact that the information from the range of sensory channels is likely to be correlated. Objects have not only visual and spatial characteristics, but are likely also to have associated tactile features, and quite possibly to have a characteristic smell and taste. It seems likely that perceiving and integrating these various sources of information would benefit from at least a temporary form of storage, both to allow for extended processing, and also for the fact that the evidence from the various channels may not always be available simultaneously. Indeed in some cases, such as the subsequent taste of an orange, or the sound emitted by a cat, information on one channel such as vision, may arrive substantially before that of others. It could be argued that this capacity to integrate sensory information requires some form of working memory, particularly if the system is one that actively attempts to build up information about a perceived object. Furthermore, it can be argued that conscious awareness provides a convenient way of simultaneously representing such diverse streams of information about a common object, although it is almost certainly not the only way (see Baddeley, 1992a; b, for a discussion).

Aspects of learning

Whereas a working memory system that coordinates information from a number of sources is likely to aid perceptual organization of the world, it would not necessarily benefit from experience. Hence, it would not form concepts such as would be necessary to recognize a cat as such, nor would it allow one to learn that cats tend to hiss rather than bark. More importantly perhaps, it would not allow one to know whether cats were dangerous, or indeed to recognize one's own cat, or of course to remember whether it had already been fed or not. It is now widely accepted that long-term memory is not a simple unitary system, although there is considerably less agreement as to how it should be conceptualized (Richardson-Klavehn and Bjork, 1988).

There are two major dimensions along which it has in the past been proposed to dichotomize long-term memory: one is the proposed distinction between *semantic* and *episodic* memory, and the other uses a rather broader range of terminology of which the *implicit* and *explicit* memory distinction is one of the most widely adopted. Semantic memory is the term applied by Tulving to the storage of information about the world, the name of the capital of France, or the chemical formula for salt, for example. Episodic memory, on the other hand, refers to the recollection of a personally experienced event. In its earlier formulations, the theoretical emphasis tended to be on the basic separability of the underlying systems (Tulving, 1972). Later developments have tended rather to emphasize the more phenomenological aspects of episodic memory, which is assumed to be associated with the *conscious recollection* of the earlier episode (Tulving, 1983).

The implicit–explicit memory distinction, which is also sometimes described as a procedural–declarative or direct–indirect memory distinction, has developed more recently to reflect the observation that certain types or aspects of memory (implicit) appear to differ markedly from the pattern of function typically observed in laboratory learning and memory studies (explicit). Such traditional studies are typically concerned with the subject's explicit capacity to recall or recognize material; they show that performance is a function of variables such as the depth of processing of the material, its meaningfulness, and its degree of active organization.

In contrast, implicit or indirect memory measures are able to reveal other aspects of learning, which appear to be insensitive to depth of processing, and much less influenced by strategies and organizational variables. This latter type of learning also tends to be relatively intact in a wide range of neuropsychological patient groups who typically have impairment in explicit declarative or directly tested memory. Although there is considerable agreement as to the existence and importance of such distinctions, there is considerably less agreement as to the best way of theoretically interpreting this rich and rapidly growing research area. Broadly speaking, proponents fall into two categories; the first attempt to explain the data as reflecting different aspects of a unitary memory system (e.g., Jacoby, Baker, and Brooks, 1989; Roediger, 1990), and typically concentrate on data from normal subjects. On the other hand, those who argue for two, or possibly more separate memory systems (e.g., Squire and Zola-Morgan, 1988; Tulving and Schacter, 1990) are typically concerned to account for both normal and neuropsychological evidence. As will become clear, my own views tend to be of this kind.

Given that the world is to some extent a predictable place, then it makes sense for the organism to be able to capitalize on such predictability, to learn, for example, that food of one kind is typically found in one location, water in another, while a third may be associated with danger. The organism will also find it advantageous to be able to acquire novel skills, allowing hunting to be carried out more effectively, or in the case of humans, for language to develop. At a rather more basic level, there may be advantages to priming, whereby the operation of a particular cognitive process may facilitate the subsequent operation of that process (positive priming), or may cause it to be inhibited (negative priming). Although these various forms of learning may employ different underlying neural systems, they tend to have in common the fact that they can in principle be acquired by a process of gradual accumulation of experience. Such learning of the varied probabilities of events can readily be simulated using connectionist networks, employing one of a range of possible learning algorithms (Rumelhart, 1991).

Episodic memory

The limitation of such basic accumulative learning processes, however, is that they do not allow the organism to select one specific episode from the agglomeration of prior experience. For this a different form of associative learning is required (Rumelhart, 1991), which I would like to suggest corresponds to episodic memory. If the organism is to retrieve a specific episode, then it must have a means of specifying that episode. The most likely mechanism would seem to be via the use of context. It is assumed that the episodic learning mechanism is capable of very rapidly forming links between stimuli that are experienced at the same time. Such a link will allow one such experience to evoke the other, hence if I met Charlie and Gladys together at the Green Dragon pub, then meeting Charlie is likely to remind me of both Gladys and the pub.

Clearly the extent of such retrieval needs to be limited, otherwise the regulars at the Green Dragon, on entering the pub, would be overcome by a bombardment of memories of everyone they had ever met there, potentially causing serious interference with the main purpose of their visit. The study of the utilization and operation of such retrieval cues has, of course, formed one of the most active and successful areas of recent memory research (Tulving, 1983).

I assume that this process of retrieval from episodic memory makes a representation of an earlier episode accessible to working memory, allowing the central executive component of working memory to reflect on its implications and choose an appropriate action. Suppose that I had chatted to Gladys and been told that Charlie always went to that particular pub on Tuesday evenings, then recollection of that experience would be rather useful if I wanted to make sure that I met him. In contrast, a learning mechanism that simply strengthened the association between Charlie and the pub would be much less helpful.

Predicting the future

So far we have discussed the role of memory as providing information about the past; however, the principal value of such information is for the light it throws on the future, and here again working memory becomes crucial in two ways. First, it provides a system for representing the past in a way that allows the organism to reflect on it, and actively choose a further action, rather than simply responding to the highest probability. Second, it offers the capacity to set up and utilize models to predict the future. Johnson-Laird (1983) has argued that mental models play an important role in comprehension, thinking, and problem solving. In cases such as the problem of trying to meet Charlie, the model of his visiting the pub every week is so simple as to hardly constitute thinking, but it does of course involve most of the elements of problem solving, identifying the problem, retrieving the relevant information, setting up a simple model, and extrapolating to the solution of going to the pub on Tuesday.

I assume, therefore, that episodic memory relies on a rather special kind of learning that is capable of associating arbitrary events, that happen to be present at the same time in conscious awareness. This allows the capacity for the recollection of individual episodes, and the use of such episodes to plan future behavior, again through the operation of working memory.

Semantic memory in this framework is assumed to result from the accumulation of many episodes. Whereas the recollection of an individual episode requires the differentiation of that from other experiences, more generic semantic recall does not require the separation of the many experiences that came together to build up that aspect of knowledge. If one thinks of experiences as being piled one on top of the other, then episodic memory requires the more or less accurate access to the residue of a single experience, whereas semantic memory is analogous to viewing the pile of experiences from above and abstracting what the various instances have in common.

Amnesia

Amnesic patients are assumed to have a deficit in the episodic learning mechanism, a problem that creates difficulties in adding to existing semantic memory.

Hence, they are typically unable to update their semantic memory, and are unaware of who is the current US President, and are not able to keep up with current developments in sport or to follow the plot of a play. They may, however, still be able to retrieve old information from semantic memory, since this has already been laid down. In short, I opt for a learning, rather than retrieval interpretation of the classic amnesic syndrome, while not, of course, denying that brain damage may also cause retrieval deficits in some cases.

I assume that the mechanism that is impaired in amnesia is not necessary for implicit or procedural learning, since this is typically preserved in most patients. This does not of course necessitate the assumption that implicit learning forms a unitary system; it is sufficient to assume that all implicit learning tasks have in common the fact that they do *not* need to rely on episodic learning. Indeed, it seems highly unlikely that classical conditioning, perceptual priming, pursuit tracking, and the acquisition of logical rules such as the Fibonacci series all depend on a single unitary system, despite the fact that all are preserved in amnesic patients (Richardson-Klavehn and Bjork, 1988; Squire and Zola-Morgan, 1988).

I have a similar problem in accepting the proposal made by Tulving and Schacter (1990) that perceptual priming represents the operation of a single system, apparently extending across modalities and across processing levels. The neuropsychological evidence alone seems to argue for separate perceptual processing modules for visual and auditory processing, which themselves appear to be fractionable into separable subsystems. Priming refers to a particular experimental paradigm that happens to be useful for detecting the persisting after-effects of earlier processing. The fact that it can be used in broadly analogous ways within different perceptual systems is, of course, important, but to refer to the assumed underlying process as a single system seems unnecessary and potentially rather misleading.

If the many implicit and procedural tasks that have been studied do indeed reflect different processes and subsystems, then one might expect to find differential disruption and preservation of aspects of this form of learning in neuropsychological patients, and such data are indeed beginning to appear (Butters, Heindel, and Salmon, 1990).

A Model of Working Memory

The overview of human memory just given assigns an important and central role to working memory. The next section gives a brief account of a preliminary model of a working memory system that might play such a role. More detailed descriptions are given elsewhere (Baddeley, 1986; 1992a–c).

The model evolved from the modal model of the 1960s that assumed a short-term store that acts as a working memory system. The most influential version of the modal model was that of Atkinson and Shiffrin (1968), which assumed a unitary short-term store of limited capacity that is responsible for a range of memory phenomena including memory span and the recency effect in free recall. This limited capacity store was also assumed to be essential for both learning and retrieval. The model received initial support from neuropsychological evidence that indicated a double dissociation between long- and short-term storage deficits (Baddeley and Warrington, 1970; Shallice and Warrington, 1970). However, the modal model also encountered problems in dealing with the neuropsychological evidence. Patients with grossly defective short-term storage appeared to show normal long-term learning, and indeed exhibited none of the gross cognitive impairment that one might have expected from an impairment in the functioning of an all-important working memory system (Shallice and Warrington, 1970).

Baddeley and Hitch (1974) investigated this issue through a series of experiments in which a short-term memory deficit was simulated by requiring subjects to rehearse a sequence of digits while performing simultaneous reasoning, comprehension, and learning tasks. Since the digit sequences were assumed to fill the working memory system to capacity, performance on the concurrent cognitive tasks was predicted to be markedly impaired. Across the range of tasks, a similar pattern of results occurred; concurrent digit span clearly impaired performance, but the degree of disruption was far from catastrophic.

To account for these and other results, Baddeley and Hitch proposed to abandon the idea of a single unitary working memory system, proposing instead a tripartite model. This assumed an attentional controller termed the *central executive*, aided by two active slave systems, the *articulatory* or *phonological loop*, which maintained speech-based information, and the *visuospatial scratch-pad* or *sketchpad*, which was capable of holding and manipulating visuospatial information. Patients with defective digit span were assumed to have an impairment in the functioning of the phonological loop; since the central executive and sketchpad were assumed to be unimpaired, they were still able to learn, and did not show any overwhelming problems in everyday cognition. The deficits they did show were broadly consistent with the proposed model of the phonological loop as described below (Vallar and Baddeley, 1984).

The phonological loop

This is assumed to have two components, a brief speech-based store that holds a memory trace that fades within approximately 2 seconds, coupled with an articulatory control process. This process, which resembles subvocal rehearsal, is capable of maintaining the material in the phonological store by a recycling process, and in addition is able to feed information into the store by a process of subvocalization. One final assumption is that auditory spoken information gains automatic and obligatory access to the store.

This simple model is able to account for a relatively rich array of laboratory findings. The *phonological similarity effect*, whereby memory span for similar sounding items such as the letters *B C G V T* is smaller than for dissimilar items (*F W Y K R*), is interpreted as reflecting the fact that the store is speech-based. Similar items have fewer distinctive features, and hence are more susceptible to trace decay (Baddeley, 1966a; Conrad and Hull, 1964). The phonological memory trace can also be disrupted by the *irrelevant speech effect*, whereby the presentation of unattended spoken material disrupts recall (Colle and Welsh, 1976; Salamé and Baddeley, 1982); such material is assumed to obtain obligatory access to the phonological store, corrupting the memory trace and leading to impaired performance.

Evidence for the articulatory control process comes from the *word length effect*, whereby memory span for long words is poorer than that for short (Baddeley, Thomson, and Buchanan, 1975). This is assumed to occur because subjects rehearse in real time; long words take longer to recycle, allowing a greater degree of trace decay to occur before the next rehearsal cycle. Subvocal rehearsal can be prevented by *articulatory suppression*, the requirement for the subject to utter some irrelevant sound. This prevents the material being rehearsed, and also interferes with any attempt to encode visual material by subvocalization. Articulatory suppression thus forces the subject to abandon the phonological storage of visually presented material, reducing the level of performance and also abolishing any effect of phonological similarity or irrelevant speech. Suppression also removes the effect of word length, in this case, whether presentation is auditory or visual, since the word-length effect relies on subvocalization (Baddeley, Lewis, and Vallar, 1984).

Vallar and Baddeley (1984) studied a patient, PV, with a very pure short-term phonological memory deficit, finding a pattern of results that was consistent with the assumption of a defective short-term phonological store. This pattern has subsequently been shown to be characteristic of such patients (see Vallar and Shallice, 1990, for a review).

Although the phonological loop model gives a reasonably good account of the performance of both normal subjects and neuropsychological patients on a range of memory-span tasks, the question remained as to the functional role of this subsystem.

There is some evidence to suggest that it plays a role in speech comprehension, although most STM (short-term memory) deficit patients are impaired on processing only relatively complex sentences (Vallar and Shallice, 1990).

This finding is open to at least two interpretations; one possibility is that the system is used only as an optional back-up mechanism for dealing with particularly demanding materials. The other possibility is that sufficient phonological storage is preserved in most patients to allow an experienced user of the language to cope with most sentences. Typically, although such subjects have a digit span of only one or two items, their span for structured sentential material tends to be six or seven words, which may provide a sufficiently wide mnemonic "window" to allow the comprehension of all but very complex material. A third possibility, that the phonological loop is not necessary for comprehension, is advocated by Butterworth, Campbell, and Howard (1986), who report the case of a subject with a developmental impairment in short-term memory who appears to have no comprehension problems. Interpretation of this case, however, remains controversial (see Howard and Butterworth, 1989; Vallar and Baddeley, 1989).

Baddeley, Papagno, and Vallar (1988) suggested that an important function of the phonological loop might be to facilitate long-term phonological learning. They demonstrated that patient PV, with a very pure short-term phonological memory deficit, showed normal paired associate learning for pairs of meaningful words, together with a severely impaired capacity to learn the novel words needed to acquire items of Russian vocabulary. Subsequent work using normal subjects showed that the acquisition of novel phonological material was substantially more disrupted than meaningful paired-associate learning by articulatory suppression (Papagno, Valentine, and Baddeley, 1991), and by the effects of length and phonological similarity (Papagno and Vallar, 1992), results that reinforce the conclusion that the phonological loop is particularly important for the acquisition of novel vocabulary.

If the phonological loop has evolved principally for the acquisition of language, then the failure to find major impairments in everyday functioning in STM patients becomes readily understandable, since they have already acquired a language, and typically would not be required to learn a new language following their brain damage. One might, however, expect deficits in the phonological store to be particularly problematic in children. This possibility was explored by Gathercole and Baddeley (1990a) in a sample of children who had been selected as having a specific language disability which involved a combination of normal or above-average nonverbal intelligence, coupled with a delay of at least 2 years in language development. The children did indeed prove to have a particularly marked impairment in the capacity to repeat back material, whether assessed by conventional memory-span measures, or in terms of their capacity for repeating back nonwords, varying in length.

Gathercole and Baddeley (1989) argued that nonword repetition provides a better estimate of phonological storage than digit span, since it does not rely on knowledge of digits or other lexical items, and is functionally more similar to the material involved in learning new vocabulary than the strings of unrelated lexical units that constitute the standard span procedure. Nonword repetition proved to be the best predictor of vocabulary acquisition in children tested over a range of ages between 4 and 8 years, and for the 4-year-olds at least, cross-lagged correlation suggests that good nonword repetition leads to good vocabulary, rather than the reverse.

Service (1989) showed in a study of Finnish children that their capacity for learning English was better predicted by their capacity for nonword repetition than by any of a range of other cognitive measures, while Gathercole and Baddeley (1990b) showed in a simulated vocabulary-learning task that children who were low in nonword repetition skills performed more poorly than high repetition children of equal nonverbal intelligence.

This pattern of results not only argues for an important role of the phonological loop in language acquisition, but also casts new light on the question of the role of short-term and working memory in long-term learning. The fact that patients with STS (short-term storage) deficits appeared to show normal long-term learning in studies such as that of Shallice and Warrington (1970) had previously seemed to rule out STS as a necessary stage in long-term learning. The observation that such patients have a specific deficit in working memory, which is clearly linked to a parallel deficit in long-term learning, reopens this question. There is, in addition, parallel evidence for the importance of both the visuospatial sketchpad and the central executive components of working memory in long-term learning, as we shall see below.

The visuospatial sketchpad

This again is assumed to involve a brief store, together with control processes responsible for registering visuospatial information, and for refreshing it by rehearsal. There is, however, rather less evidence as to the nature of this encode and refresh mechanism, and nothing equivalent to the word-length effect in phonological memory has so far been discovered. However, storage may be disrupted both by irrelevant visually presented items such as pictures or even patches of color (Logie, 1986), and by concurrent spatial processing. Such disruption may occur in the absence of visual input, as with the demonstration by Baddeley and Lieberman (1980) using blindfolded subjects, whose capacity to take advantage of a visual imagery mnemonic was disrupted by the requirement to track a moving sound source.

The two types of interference, pattern-based and spatial, may be associated with separate subcomponents of the sketchpad. The evidence for this is reviewed by Farah (1988), who presents evidence from studies of both normal subjects and neuropsychological patients, using both memory and psychophysiological measures, and argues for the anatomical and functional separation of the pattern-based and spatial components of visual short-term memory. The pattern-based system appears to be particularly dependent on the occipital lobes, while the spatial component appears to depend more on parietal processing. Subsequent work by Goldman-Rakic based on single cell recording in awake monkeys performing a visual STM task suggests that there may also be a frontal lobe involvement which may possibly be associated with the executive control of visual memory (Goldman-Rakic, 1988; Kojima and Goldman-Rakic, 1984).

As in the case of the phonological loop, there is evidence for an involvement of the sketchpad in long-term memory. Baddeley and Lieberman (1980) showed that a concurrent visuospatial tracking task disrupted the verbal learning performance of subjects using a spatial imagery mnemonic, while having no effect on their capacity for learning an equivalent list by rote rehearsal. Similarly, Logie (1986) found that presenting visual material such as color patches or pictures that the subject was instructed to ignore interfered with verbal paired-associate learning based on a visual imagery pegword mnemonic, while again having little or no effect on learning by verbal rote rehearsal.

The central executive

This is the most important but least well understood component of working memory. It was initially neglected on the grounds that the peripheral slave systems offered more tractable problems, but has subsequently begun to attract considerably more research. Baddeley (1986) proposed to use the Norman and Shallice (1980) model of attentional control as a working hypothesis for the central executive. This model assumes that action can be controlled at either of two levels, by the operation of a series of existing schemata, or via the Supervisory Attentional System (SAS), which takes control when novel tasks are involved, or when existing habits have to be overridden, for example, when danger threatens. A detailed account of the model is presented by Shallice (1992), and its application to working memory is discussed by Baddeley (1992b).

Shallice's principal concern was to provide a model of the very characteristic pattern of deficits shown by certain patients with bilateral damage to the frontal lobes. Such patients show marked problems in planning and in attentional control, sometimes perseverating on a single response, while in other situations they appear to be captured by whatever stimulus they encounter. Shallice argues that the frontal lobes are necessary for the operation of the SAS. In its absence, patients may become locked into an existing schema, or conversely, have their attention captured by any available triggering stimulus.

Within the working memory framework, Baddeley has used the Shallice model to explain existing data on the limited capacity for random generation. When subjects are asked to produce a random string of items such as letters of the alphabet, they are capable of performing the task well, provided the required rate is slow. As they speed up, however, they become progressively more biased in letter selection frequency and more stereotyped, producing sequences from the alphabet such as *PQR* and *RST*, and familiar acronyms such as *USA* and *BBC* (Baddeley, 1966b). The requirement to perform a concurrent task also decreases randomness. The capacity for random generation tends to be associated with overall intelligence, and to decline with age.

Although the data in this area are highly consistent and clear, they did not prove easy to interpret. However, the Norman and Shallice model offers a clear explanation as follows: The task of retrieving a sequence of letters in random order places the subject in a conflict situation; the names of letters of the alphabet are readily retrievable by reciting the alphabet, but this clearly infringes on the requirement to be random. Consequently, the subject must continually attempt to develop new retrieval strategies, at the same time as avoiding the existing alphabetic stereotypes, and avoiding the danger of any strategy becoming automated. The capacity of the supervisory system to function in this way is therefore directly challenged, with the randomness of the output providing an indication of its capacity. When used as a secondary task, random generation proves to be very disruptive of executive processes such as are, for example, involved in assessing a chess position and choosing an optimal next move (Baddeley, 1992b).

A good deal of recent work on the analysis of executive processes has been concerned with a study of patients with frontal lobe damage. In a typical study, patients with known frontal lesions might be required to perform a wide range of tasks that is expected to test different executive functions. The hope is to find one or two tasks that best characterize this deficit, and that might then throw light on the nature of the underlying executive processes. In practice, such studies tend not to have produced evidence pointing to certain crucial tasks; typically, the studies find very considerable variability among subjects in terms of both the nature and severity of their impairment, suggesting a constellation of subprocesses rather than a single controlling module (Duncan, 1992; Shallice, 1992). Given the size and complexity of the frontal lobes, and their richness of connection with other parts of the brain, such a result is perhaps not surprising. It suggests, however, that the central executive itself will need to be fractionated into a number of separable executive processes.

Given the probable complexity of the central executive, one approach is to attempt to isolate particular functions that are assumed, on a priori grounds, to be an important feature of the executive, and to design tasks that will measure these capacities. One example of this is given in the attempt to test the hypothesis that patients suffering from Alzheimer's disease (AD) show a particularly marked impairment in the functioning of the central executive (Spinnler, Della Sala, Bandera, and Baddeley, 1988).

The working memory model assumes that one very important function of the executive is to coordinate information from separate subsystems. This was studied by combining pursuit tracking, which is assumed to load on the sketchpad, with concurrent digit span, expected to make heavy demands on the phonological loop. Tracking speed and digit sequence length were adjusted so as to give an equivalent level of performance in three groups, patients suffering from AD, normal elderly subjects, and young controls. Subjects were then required to perform the two tasks simultaneously.

While the normal elderly were no more impaired than the young by the requirement to coordinate two tasks, the Alzheimer patients showed a marked deterioration in performance, supporting the view that their executive capacity was seriously impaired (Baddeley, Logie, Bressi, Della Salla, and Spinnler, 1986). In a subsequent longitudinal study, patients suffering from AD showed a steady deterioration in their capacity to combine tasks as the disease progressed, in contrast to their performance on the individual tasks, which remained relatively stable (Baddeley, Bressi, Della Sala, Logie, and Spinnler, 1992).

This latter approach has something in common with that adopted by Daneman and Carpenter (1980; 1983), who define working memory as the capacity to simultaneously store and process information. They have devised a number of tasks that combine storage and processing, and have shown that performance on these tasks correlates with important cognitive skills such as language comprehension and reading, with subjects who are low in working memory capacity having difficulty in coping with complex material such as that presented by garden path sentences, or by texts requiring inference for their comprehension (Daneman and Carpenter, 1980; 1983).

While Carpenter and her colleagues would not explicitly adopt the particular model of working memory just described, they do not deny the existence of more peripheral systems such as the phonological loop. Their work does, however, concentrate on the more executive aspects of working memory, typically using individual differences as a tool for analyzing the role of working memory in complex cognitive skills such as comprehension and reasoning. Such an emphasis on individual differences has the further advantage of linking up with more traditional psychometric approaches. This appears to be meeting with some success, since working memory measures appear to correlate very highly with performance on a range of reasoning tasks that have traditionally been used for measuring intelligence (Kyllonen and Chrystal, 1990).

In conclusion, although the concept of working memory has its roots in the more traditional and constrained concept of short-term memory, it appears to be successfully developing into a much broader model of the crucial interface between memory and cognition.

References

Atkinson, R. C., & Shiffrin, R. M. (1968). Human memory: A proposed system and its control processes. In K. W. Spence (ed.), *The psychology of learning and motivation: Advances in research and theory* (vol. 2, pp. 89–195), New York: Academic Press.

Baddeley, A. D. (1966a). Short-term memory for word sequences as a function of acoustic, semantic and formal similarity. *Quarterly Journal of Experimental Psychology*, **18**, 362–5.

Baddeley, A. D. (1966b). The capacity for generating information by randomization. *Quarterly Journal of Experimental Psychology*, **18**, 119–129.

Baddeley, A. D. (1986). *Working memory*. Oxford: Oxford University Press.

Baddeley, A. D. (1992a). Working memory. *Science*, **255**, 556–9.

Baddeley, A. D. (1992b). Working memory or working attention? In A. Baddeley & L. Weiskrantz (eds), *Attention: Selection, awareness and control. A tribute to Donald Broadbent*, Oxford: Oxford University Press, in press.

Baddeley, A. D. (1992c). Is working memory working? *Quarterly Journal of Experimental Psychology*, **44A**, 1–31.

Baddeley, A. D., Bressi, S., Della Sala, S., Logie, R., & Spinnler, H. (1991). The decline of working memory in Alzheimer's Disease: A longitudinal study. *Brain*, **114**, 2521–42.

Baddeley, A. D., & Hitch, G. (1974). Working memory. In G. A. Bower (ed.), *The psychology of learning and motivation* (vol. 8, pp. 47–89), New York: Academic Press.

Baddeley, A. D., Lewis, V. J., & Vallar, G. (1984), Exploring the articulatory loop. *Quarterly Journal of Experimental Psychology*, **36**, 233–52.

Baddeley, A. D., & Lieberman, K. (1980). Spatial working memory. In R. S. Nickerson (ed.), *Attention and performance* (pp. 521–39), Hillsdale, NJ: Lawrence Erlbaum.

Baddeley, A. D., Logie, R., Bressi, S., Della Sala, S., & Spinnler, H. (1986). Dementia and working memory. *Quarterly Journal of Experimental Psychology*, **38A**, 603–18.

Baddeley, A. D., Papagno, C., & Vallar, G. (1988). When long term learning depends on short-term storage. *Journal of Memory and Language*, **27**, 586–95.

Baddeley, A. D., Thomson, N., & Buchanan, M. (1975). Word length and the structure of short-term memory. *Journal of Verbal Learning and Verbal Behavior*, **14**, 575–89.

Baddeley, A. D., & Warrington, E. K. (1970). Amnesia and the distinction between long- and short-term memory. *Journal of Verbal Learning and Verbal Behavior*, **9**, 176–89.

Butters, N., Heindel, W. C., & Salmon, D. P. (1990). Dissociation of implicit memory in dementia: Neurological implications. *Bulletin of the Psychonomic Society*, **28**, 359–66.

Butterworth, B., Campbell, R., & Howard, D. (1986). The uses of short-term memory: A case study. *Quarterly Journal of Experimental Psychology*, **38A**, 705–38.

Colle, H. A., & Welsh, A. (1976). Acoustic masking in primary memory. *Journal of Verbal Learning and Verbal Behavior*, **15**, 17–32.

Conrad, R., & Hull, A. J. (1964). Information, acoustic confusion and memory span. *British Journal of Psychology*, **55**, 429–32.

Daneman, M., & Carpenter, P. A. (1980). Individual differences in working memory and reading. *Journal of Verbal Learning and Verbal Behavior*, **19**, 450–66.

Daneman, M., & Carpenter, P. A. (1983). Individual differences in integrating information between and within sentences. *Journal of Experimental Psychology: Learning, Memory and Cognition*, **9**, 561–84.

Duncan, J. (1992). Selection of input and goal in the control of behaviour. In A. D. Baddeley & L. Weiskrantz (eds), *Attention: Selection, awareness and control. A tribute to Donald Broadbent*, Oxford: Oxford University Press, in press.

Farah, M. J. (1988). Is visual memory really visual? Over-looked evidence from neuropsychology. *Psychological Review*, **95**, 307–17.

Gathercole, S., & Baddeley, A. D. (1989). Evaluation of the role of phonological STM in the development of vocabulary in children: A longitudinal study. *Journal of Memory and Language*, **28**, 200–13.

Gathercole, S., & Baddeley, A. (1990a). Phonological memory deficits in language-disordered children: Is there a causal connection? *Journal of Memory and Language*, **29**, 336–60.

Gathercole, S., & Baddeley, A. D. (1990b). The role of phonological memory in vocabulary acquisition: A study of young children learning new names. *British Journal of Psychology*, **81**, 439–54.

Goldman-Rakic, P. W. (1988). Topography of cognition: Parallel distributed networks in primate association cortex. *Annual Review of Neuroscience*, **11**, 137–56.

Howard, D., & Butterworth, B. (1989). Short-term memory and sentence comprehension: A reply to Vallar & Baddeley, 1987. *Cognitive Neuropsychology*, **6**, 455–63.

Jacoby, L. L., Baker, J. G., & Brooks, L. R. (1989). Episodic effects on picture identification: Implications for theories of concept learning and theories of memory. *Journal of Experimental Psychology: Learning, Memory and Cognition*, **15**, 275–81.

Johnson-Laird, P. N. (1983). *Mental models*. Cambridge: Cambridge University Press.

Kojima, S., & Goldman-Rakic, P. S. (1984). Functional analysis of spatially discriminative neurons in prefrontal cortex of rhesus monkey. *Brain Research*, **291**, 229–40.

Kyllonen, P. C., & Chrystal, R. E. (1990). Reasoning ability is (little more than) working-memory capacity?! *Intelligence*, **14**, 389–433.

Logie, R. H. (1986). Visuo-spatial processing in working memory. *Quarterly Journal of Experimental Psychology*, **38A**, 229–47.

Norman, D. A., & Shallice, T. (1980). Attention to action: Willed and automatic control of behavior. University of California San Diego, CHIP Report 99.

Papagno, C., Valentine, T., & Baddeley, A. (1991). Phonological short-term memory and foreign language vocabulary learning. *Journal of Memory and Language*, **30**, 331–47.

Papagno, C., & Vallar, G. (1992). Phonological short-term memory and the learning of novel words: The effect of phonological similarity and item length. *Quarterly Journal of Experimental Psychology*, **44A**, 47–67.

Richardson-Klavehn, A., & Bjork, R. A. (1988). Measures of memory. *Annual Review of Psychology*, **39**, 475–543.

Roediger, H. L. (1990). Implicit memory: Retention without remembering. *American Psychologist*, **45**, 1043–56.

Rumelhart, D. E. (1991). Connectionist concepts of learning, memory and generalisation. Paper given at the International Conference on Memory, Lancaster, England.

Salamé, P., & Baddeley, A. D. (1982). Disruption of short-term memory by unattended speech: Implications for the structure of working memory. *Journal of Verbal Learning and Verbal Behavior*, **21**, 150–64.

Service, E. (1989). Phonological coding in working memory and foreign-language learning. University of Helsinki, *General Psychology Monographs*, No. B9.

Shallice, T. (1992). Neuropsychological investigation of supervisory processes. In A. Baddeley & L. Weiskrantz (eds), *Attention: Selection, awareness and control. A tribute to Donald Broadbent*, Oxford: Oxford University Press, in press.

Shallice, T., & Warrington, E. K. (1970). Independent functioning of verbal memory stores: A neuropsychological study. *Quarterly Journal of Experimental Psychology*, **22**, 261–73.

Spinnler, H., Della Sala, S., Bandera, R., & Baddeley, A. D. (1988). Dementia, ageing and the structure of human memory. *Cognitive Neuropsychology*, **5**, 193–211.

Squire, L. R., & Zola-Morgan, S. (1988). Memory: Brain systems and behavior. *Trends in Neurosciences*, **11**, 170–5.

Tulving, E. (1972). Episodic and semantic memory. In E. Tulving & W. Donaldson. (eds), *Organization of memory* (pp. 381–403), New York: Academic Press.

Tulving, E. (1983). *Elements of episodic memory*. Oxford: Oxford University Press.

Tulving, E., & Schacter, D. L. (1990). Priming and human memory systems. *Science*, **247**, 301–6.

Vallar, G., & Baddeley, A. D. (1984). Fractionation of working memory: Neuropsychological evidence for a phonological short-term store. *Journal of Verbal Learning and Verbal Behavior*, **23**, 151–61.

Vallar, G., & Baddeley, A. D. (1989). Developmental disorders of verbal short-term memory and their relation to sentence comprehension: A reply to Howard and Butterworth. *Cognitive Neuropsychology*, **6**, 465–73.

Vallar, G., & Shallice, T. (eds) (1990). *Neuropsychological impairments of short-term memory*. Cambridge: Cambridge University Press.

Understanding Implicit Memory:
A Cognitive Neuroscience Approach

Daniel L. Schacter

In the introduction to an excellent review of memory and amnesia research, Rozin (1976) wistfully remarked, "I find myself wishing that I were writing this paper a little less than a hundred years ago, in 1890, at the close of a decade that I would consider the golden age of memory" (p. 3). Considering the lasting achievements of that decade – Ebbinghaus's pioneering experiments, Ribot's observations on disorders of memory, Korsakoff's description of the amnesic syndrome that now bears his name, and William James's (1890/1983) superb chapters on memory in the epic *The Principles of Psychology* – Rozin's characterization is highly appropriate.

It is too early to say whether future writers will someday look back on the decade of the 1980s as another golden age of memory. Nevertheless, it already seems clear that the 1980s will be viewed as a golden age, or at least the beginning of a golden age, for one issue in memory research: the investigation of *implicit memory* (Graf and Schacter, 1985; Schacter, 1987). Implicit memory is an unintentional, nonconscious form of retention that can be contrasted with *explicit memory*, which involves conscious recollection of previous experiences. Explicit memory is typically assessed with recall and recognition tasks that require intentional retrieval of information from a specific prior study episode, whereas implicit memory is assessed with tasks that do not require conscious recollection of specific episodes.

Although the explicit–implicit distinction was introduced during the 1980s, the sort of contrast that it captures is not new; related distinctions between conscious and unconscious memories, to take just one example, have been around for more than a century (for historical considerations, see Roediger, 1990b; Schacter, 1987). The critical development during the past decade has been the systematic demonstration, exploration, and attempted explanation of dissociations between explicit and implicit memory. Some of these dissociations have been provided by experiments demonstrating that brain-damaged amnesic patients with severe impairments of explicit memory can exhibit intact implicit memory; others come from studies showing that specific experimental variables produce different and even opposite effects on explicit and implicit memory tasks (for reviews, see Richardson-Klavehn and Bjork, 1988; Roediger, 1990b; Schacter, 1987; Shimamura, 1986). Fueled by these striking and frequently counter-intuitive dissociations, the study of implicit memory emerged from the decade of the 1980s at the forefront of memory research.

In this chapter I outline a general research strategy for attempting to understand implicit memory that I refer to as a *cognitive neuroscience approach*. This approach is motivated by the general idea that it is useful to combine cognitive research and theory, on the one hand, with neuropsychological and neurobiological observations about brain systems, on the other, making use of data from brain-damaged patients, neuroimaging techniques, and even lesion and single-cell recording studies of nonhuman animals. The cognitive neuroscience orientation has itself undergone rapid development during the past decade and is now a major force in the study of perception, attention, language, and emotion (cf. Gazzaniga, 1984; Kosslyn, Flynn, Amsterdam, and Wang, 1990; LeDoux and Hirst, 1986; Weingartner and Lister, 1991). A growing number of investigators have adopted a cognitive neuroscience approach to the study of human memory (for a representative sampling, see Olton, Gamzu, and Corkin, 1985; Squire and Butters, 1984; Squire, Weinberger, Lynch, and McGaugh, 1992; for a historical review, see Polster, Nadel, and Schacter, 1991).[1]

I will discuss the cognitive neuroscience orientation in relation to a major issue that has arisen in implicit memory research: the debate between memory systems and processing accounts of implicit–explicit dissociations. The former account holds that implicit memory effects depend on brain systems that are distinct from the memory system that supports explicit remembering (cf. Cohen, 1984; Hayman and Tulving, 1989; Keane, Gabrieli, Fennema, Growden, and Corkin, 1991; Schacter, 1990; Squire, 1987; Tulving and Schacter, 1990; Weiskrantz, 1989); the latter account holds that postulation of multiple memory systems is neither necessary nor justified and that relevant dissociations can be understood in terms of relations between processing operations carried out during study and test (cf. Blaxton, 1989; Jacoby, 1983; Masson, 1989; Roediger, Weldon, and Challis, 1989).

I suggest that a cognitive neuroscience orientation may help to resolve, or at least guide the investigation of, several key issues in the systems-versus-processes debate. More specifically, I will discuss four important features of a cognitive neuroscience approach in relation to this debate: (a) it provides an empirical basis for postulating memory systems that is independent of dissociations observed in implicit–explicit memory experiments; (b) it aids development of well-specified systems views that can suggest helpful constraints for processing approaches; (c) it encourages the use of *cross-domain hypothesis testing*; and (d) it also encourages the use of *cross-domain hypothesis generation*. I will illustrate each of these features with relevant examples from my own and others' laboratories.

Basis for Postulating Memory Systems

As noted earlier, interest in implicit memory has been fueled by the observation of dissociations between tasks that tap implicit and explicit memory, respectively. Consider, for example, the stem completion task, in which subjects are given three-letter word beginnings (e.g., TAB) and are asked to complete them with the first word that comes to mind; no reference is made to a prior study episode. Implicit memory is indicated when subjects complete a stem more frequently with a word that was recently presented on a study list (e.g., TABLE) than with a word that was not presented on the list (e.g., TABLET); this facilitation of task performance is known as direct or repetition priming (e.g., Tulving and Schacter, 1990). It is well-established that priming effects on the stem completion task can be dissociated from explicit memory. For instance, as indicated initially by the classic studies of Warrington and Weiskrantz (1974), patients with organic amnesia can show normal priming effects on stem completion performance, despite severely impaired explicit memory (cf. Graf, Squire, and Mandler, 1984; Warrington and Weiskrantz, 1974). Dissociations between stem completion priming and explicit memory have also been observed with normal, nonamnesic subjects. One of the more compelling phenomena involves the well-known depth-of-processing effect, which was initially established during the 1970s in studies of explicit memory (e.g., Craik and Tulving, 1975): Semantic study processing (i.e., thinking about the meaning of a word) generally produces much higher levels of subsequent recall and recognition performance than does nonsemantic study processing (i.e., thinking about the physical features of a word). By contrast, the magnitude of priming effects on the stem completion task are little affected – and sometimes entirely unaffected – by differences in depth of processing that are produced by different study tasks (cf. Bowers and Schacter, 1990; Graf and Mandler, 1984). Study–test modality shifts can also yield striking implicit–explicit dissociations: When a word is presented in one modality during the study task (e.g., auditory) and presented in another during test (e.g., visual), stem completion priming effects are reduced significantly, whereas explicit memory performance is little affected (Graf, Shimamura, and Squire, 1985; Schacter and Graf, 1989).

These kinds of dissociations are now familiar to memory researchers, and a comparable list could be readily constructed for various other implicit and explicit tasks. The critical question for the present purposes concerns their relation to the multiple memory systems debate: Do dissociations between implicit and explicit memory tasks constitute either a necessary or a sufficient condition for postulating that different memory systems support performance on the two types of task? Although dissociations clearly constitute a necessary condition for making such claims – it would be difficult to argue convincingly for multiple memory systems in the absence of any evidence that they operate differently – it seems equally clear that they do not constitute a sufficient condition. There are several reasons why one cannot make simple leaps from empirical dissociations to postulation of memory systems (e.g., Dunn and Kirsner, 1988; Jacoby, 1983), but perhaps the most compelling argument is related to the apparent ubiquity of dissociations in memory research. It has been known for many years that dissociations can be produced between explicit memory tasks – recall and recognition are prime examples – and it has been established more recently that dissociations can be produced between implicit memory tasks (cf. Blaxton, 1989; Witherspoon and Moscovitch, 1989). Thus, if we were to accept the idea that an empirical dissociation between, say, Explicit Task X and Implicit Task Y is alone sufficient to claim that different memory systems support performance on the two tasks, theoretical chaos would likely ensue: A long list of explicit memory systems, to say nothing of implicit memory systems, would be quickly composed (Roediger, 1990a). On the other hand, we have already acknowledged that empirical dissociations constitute a necessary condition for postulating multiple memory systems. How, then, can we extricate ourselves from the apparent impasse?

I suggest that it is crucial to have a basis for postulating different memory systems that is independent of dissociations observed in implicit–explicit memory experiments and that a cognitive neuroscience orientation can help to provide it. If claims about memory systems are supported by independent evidence – and are not made simply in response to the latest experimental dissociation between implicit and explicit memory tasks – then the aforementioned theoretical chaos can be greatly reduced by applying the logic of converging operations (Garner, Hake, and Eriksen, 1956).

To illustrate the point concretely, consider a criticism of the multiple memory systems approach offered by Roediger (1990a, 1990b) and Blaxton (1989). These investigators noted that one account of dissociations between word completion and word identification tasks, on the one hand, and recall and recognition tasks, on the other, is that priming effects are mediated by a semantic memory system, whereas explicit remembering depends on an episodic memory system (e.g., Tulving, 1983). In contrast, Roediger and Blaxton argued that both explicit and implicit memory are mediated by different types of processing in a single (episodic) memory system. Specifically, they invoked the principle of transfer-appropriate processing (Morris, Bransford, and Franks, 1977), which holds that memory performance depends on the extent to which processing operations performed during a study task match or overlap with processing operations performed during a memory test. They suggested further, in conformity with previous suggestions by Jacoby (1983), that implicit tasks such as stem completion and word identification depend largely on data-driven processing (i.e., bottom-up processing that is driven primarily by perceptual properties of study and test materials), whereas explicit tasks such as recall and recognition depend largely on conceptually driven processing (i.e., top-down processing that is driven primarily by subject-initiated activities such as elaborating and organizing). This general position allowed Roediger and Blaxton to account for the previously mentioned finding that semantic–elaborative study processing increases explicit but not implicit memory, whereas changes in modality and other physical features of target stimuli can affect implicit more than explicit memory.

In an attempt to compare directly the processing and systems accounts, Roediger (1990b) and Blaxton (1989) noted that claims for different memory systems had been based on comparisons between data-driven implicit tests (e.g., word completion) and conceptually driven explicit tests (e.g., recall and recognition). In line with their argument that type of processing is the crucial determinant of dissociations, they contended that it should be possible to produce dissociations between data-driven implicit tasks, such as word completion, and conceptually driven implicit tasks, such as answering general knowledge questions (see Blaxton for further discussion and details). Blaxton has indeed reported several experiments in which such dissociations were found, even though both types of tasks could be construed, according to her logic, as "semantic memory" tasks.

How does the multiple systems theorist respond to such results? As Blaxton (1989) and Roediger (1990b) noted, it is possible to postulate separate memory systems for data-driven and conceptually driven implicit tasks in response to the observed dissociation, but such an account is unparsimonious and lacks explanatory power. I concur entirely: An unprincipled, post hoc postulation of additional systems in response to a new experimental dissociation is the quickest route to the sort of theoretical chaos that we all wish to avoid. However, consider the issue in light of the aforementioned point that independent evidence is required to support claims for multiple memory systems. We are then led to ask whether data exist independently of Blaxton's results that support the hypothesis that priming on data-driven and conceptually driven tests is mediated by different systems.

Research from various sectors of cognitive neuroscience suggests a positive answer to this question. The critical evidence is provided by studies of patients who show relatively intact access to perceptual–structural knowledge of words or objects, despite severely impaired access to semantic knowledge of the same items (e.g., Riddoch and Humphreys, 1987; Schwartz, Saffran, and Marin, 1980; Warrington, 1982). These studies suggest that representation–retrieval of the visual form of words and objects depends on a system other than semantic memory. Similarly, studies of lexical processing using positron emission tomography (PET) indicate that visual word form information and semantic information are handled by separate brain regions (e.g., Petersen, Fox, Posner, Mintun, and Raichle, 1988). These kinds of observations suggest the existence of a perceptual representation system (PRS; cf. Schacter, 1990; Tulving and Schacter, 1990) that can function independently of (although it typically interacts extensively with) semantic memory.

We have argued that PRS plays a significant role in priming effects observed on data-driven implicit tests, an idea that fits well with previously mentioned findings that priming on such tasks is relatively unaffected by semantic versus nonsemantic study processing and greatly affected by study–test changes in modality and other kinds of perceptual information (see Schacter, 1990; Schacter, Cooper, and Delaney, 1990; Schacter, Cooper, Tharan, and Rubens, 1991; Schacter, Rapcsak, Rubens, Tharan, and Laguna, 1990; Tulving and Schacter, 1990). By contrast, semantic memory is held to be critically involved in priming on conceptually driven implicit tests (Schacter, 1990; Tulving and Schacter, 1990; see also Keane et al., 1991). The critical point here is that the idea that perceptual and conceptual priming depend on different systems was motivated by evidence from brain-damaged patients and PET imaging that is independent of the dissociation between data-driven and conceptually driven tasks reported by Blaxton (1989). Thus, a cognitive neuroscience orientation allows the formulation of a multiple systems framework that can accommodate – even though it was not formulated in response to – the Blaxton data. Indeed, recent studies have provided more direct evidence that different systems are involved in perceptual and conceptual priming (Keane et al., 1991; Tulving, Hayman, and Macdonald, 1991).

This example illustrates how a cognitive neuroscience orientation can help multiple systems approaches to avoid the pitfalls associated with unprincipled, post hoc postulation of memory systems. There are other ways to minimize these problems, such as by paying careful attention to the functional properties and computational capacities of putative memory systems (cf. Kosslyn et al., 1990; Sherry and Schacter, 1987; Tulving, 1983). Combining such considerations with a cognitive neuroscience orientation is clearly desirable.

Constraints for Processing Views

A difficulty with processing views is that they do not always allow one to specify, independently of experimental outcomes, the pattern of results that would indicate the presence of transfer-appropriate processing effects (cf. Graf and Ryan, 1990; Roediger et al., 1989). For example, imagine a word completion experiment in which a physical feature of a word (e.g., upper or lower case, type font) is either changed or held constant between study and test. If there is less priming when the feature is changed than when it is held constant, this can be taken as evidence for transfer-appropriate processing: The processing operations performed at study and test do not match as well in the former as in the latter condition. However, if priming is the same in the two conditions, it can always be argued that the manipulated feature was not relevant to study or test processing. In fact, both outcomes have been observed (e.g., Graf and Ryan, 1990).

A cognitive neuroscience orientation can help to clarify this interpretive ambiguity. Specifically, I suggest that it can facilitate the development of systems views that provide useful *constraints* for processing approaches, which in turn allow for firmer a priori predictions about experimental outcomes. Two examples help to illustrate the point. The first comes from a recent study by Marsolek, Kosslyn, and Squire (1992), in which subjects saw a list of familiar words and were then asked to complete three-letter stems with the first word that came to mind. On the completion test, the stems were presented either to the left hemisphere or to the right hemisphere through brief visual exposures in either the right or left hemifield. In the most directly relevant experiments, the case of target items (i.e., upper or lower case) was either the same or different at study and test. Marsolek et al. found that priming was reduced by case changes when stems were presented to the right hemisphere, but was unaffected by this manipulation when stems were presented to the left hemisphere.

It is not clear how a transfer-appropriate processing view would account for this pattern of results because the same materials and processing requirements were present in both the left and right hemifield conditions. However, Marsolek et al. (1992) drew on independent evidence from cognitive neuroscience concerning the characteristics of the hemispheres to argue that a left-hemisphere subsystem computes abstract word form representations that do not preserve specific features of particular inputs, whereas a right-hemisphere subsystem computes perceptually specific word form representations (in the present terminology, both could be viewed as PRS subsystems). From this perspective, it follows that priming in the right but not the left hemisphere is influenced by changes in the visual form of studied words. More important, the cognitive neuroscience analysis developed by Marsolek et al. provides just the sort of constraints that a processing view requires to make sense of the results: Given some knowledge of the characteristics of the two subsystems, processing theorists might well predict the occurrence of specific priming when the right hemisphere is queried and abstract priming when the left hemisphere is queried. But for processing theorists to make such predictions, they must incorporate the constraints provided by the cognitive neuroscience-based systems analysis.

A second example that illustrates a similar point is provided by a series of studies that Lynn Cooper and I have conducted on implicit memory for novel visual objects

(Cooper, Schacter, Ballesteros, and Moore, 1992; Schacter, Cooper, and Delaney, 1990; Schacter, Cooper, Delaney, Peterson, and Tharan, 1991; Schacter, Cooper, Tharan, and Rubens, 1991). In our paradigm, subjects study line drawings of novel objects (figure 23.1) and are then given either an explicit memory task (yes or no recognition) or an implicit memory task. To assess implicit memory, we developed an object decision task that exploits an important property of the target objects: One half of them are structurally possible (they could actually exist in three-dimensional form), whereas the other half are structurally impossible (they contain structural ambiguities and impossibilities that would prevent them from being realized in three dimensions). On this task, subjects are given brief (e.g., 50 ms) exposures to studied and nonstudied objects and decide whether each object is possible or impossible; no reference is made to the study episode. Priming or implicit memory on this task is indicated by more accurate object decisions about studied than nonstudied items.

A series of experiments has documented the existence of object decision priming and delineated several of its properties. For the present purposes, a few key findings are worth noting explicitly. First, robust priming on the object decision task is observed for structurally possible objects, but not for structurally impossible objects (Schacter, Cooper, and Delaney, 1990); indeed, we failed to observe priming of impossible objects even following multiple study–list exposures that produced high levels of explicit memory (Schacter, Cooper, Delaney, et al., 1991). Second, priming of possible objects is observed following study tasks that require encoding of information about

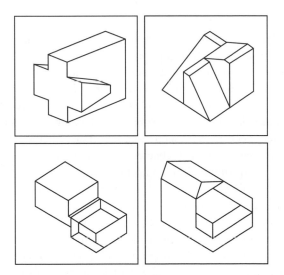

Figure 23.1 Examples of stimuli used in experiments on implicit and explicit memory for novel objects.
Note. The objects in the upper row are structurally possible, whereas the objects in the lower row are structurally impossible. Subjects study both types of objects in various encoding conditions. Implicit memory is tested with an object decision task, in which studied and nonstudied objects are flashed briefly and subjects decide whether each one is possible or impossible; explicit memory is assessed with a "yes or no" recognition task, in which subjects indicate whether they recollect having seen each object during the study task. From "Implicit memory for unfamiliar objects depends on access to structural descriptions," by D. L. Schacter, L. A. Cooper, and S. M. Delaney (1990), *Journal of Experimental Psychology: General, 119*, p. 7. Copyright 1990 by the American Psychological Association. Adapted by permission.

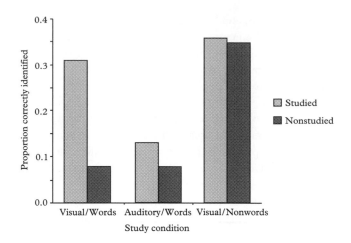

Figure 23.2 Summary of results from experiments by Schacter, Rapcsak, Rubens, Tharan, and Laguna (1990), in which patient P. T., a letter-by-letter reader, studied a list of five- to six-letter words or nonwords and was then given a visual identification task in which studied and nonstudied items were presented for 500 msec.

Note. Proportion correct on the identification task is displayed in three different conditions. The leftmost bars show that visual exposure to a list of familiar words produced substantial priming, as indicated by significantly more accurate identification of studied than of nonstudied words. The center bars show lack of priming following auditory study of familiar words, as indicated by a nonsignificant difference between identification of studied and nonstudied words. The rightmost bars show lack of priming following visual study of illegal nonwords, as indicated by no differences between the proportion of letters identified correctly in studied and nonstudied items.

the global three-dimensional structure of an object (e.g., judging whether an object faces primarily to the left or to the right) but is not observed following study tasks that require encoding of information about local two-dimensional features (e.g., judging whether an object has more horizontal or vertical lines; Schacter, Cooper, and Delaney, 1990). Third, the priming effect for possible objects is not increased, and is sometimes reduced, by encoding tasks that require subjects to link target objects with preexisting semantic knowledge, even though such encoding manipulations greatly enhance explicit memory for the same objects (Schacter, Cooper and Delaney, 1990; Schacter and Cooper, 1991). Fourth, priming on the object decision task appears to be preserved in patients with memory disorders (Schacter, Cooper, Tharan, and Rubens, 1991) and in elderly adults (Schacter, Cooper, and Valdiserri, in press).

These findings, taken together with the previously mentioned dissociations between structural and semantic knowledge in patients with object processing deficits (cf. Riddoch and Humphreys 1987; Warrington, 1982), have led us to argue that object decision priming is mediated to a large extent by a PRS subsystem that computes structural descriptions (Sutherland, 1968) of objects – that is, representations of the global relations among parts of an object. By this view, priming of impossible objects is not observed because it is difficult to represent internally their global structure (there is no globally consistent structural description of an impossible object), and semantic–functional encoding tasks do not enhance priming because the structural description system operates at a presemantic level. Note that several independent lines of evidence from studies of brain-lesioned monkeys and single-cell recordings indicate that regions of inferior temporal cortex (IT) play a major role in computing the global form and structure of visual objects (for a review, see Plaut and Farah, 1990). It is thus possible that IT or the analogous system in humans plays a significant role in object decision priming.

Many studies have shown that the response of IT cells is typically little affected or entirely unaffected by changes in the retinal size of an object (see Plaut and Farah, 1990). Thus, if object decision priming depends significantly on a system like IT, then the magnitude of the effect should not be influenced by a simple study–test change in an object's retinal size. Cooper et al. (1992) have recently performed such an experiment, and the data indicate clearly that object decision priming is unaffected by changing the size of an object between study and test, even though explicit recognition memory is lower in the different size than in the same size condition. We also found that changing the left–right reflection of target objects (i.e., mirror image reversal) between study and test had little effect on priming, again consistent with known properties of IT (see Plaut and Farah, 1990; for similar priming results with familiar objects, see Biederman and Cooper, 1991).

Now consider these results from the perspective of transfer-appropriate processing, using the data on size-invariant priming to illustrate the point (the same argument could be made with respect to the mirror-image results). Applying the logic that has been used to account for the effects of changing surface features of target items on other perceptually based implicit tests, it would be expected that in the different size condition, processing operations performed at study and test do not match as well as in the same size condition. Accordingly, size change should produce a decrement in priming. Because the data show otherwise, an advocate of transfer-appropriate processing might argue that priming was unaffected by size change because neither the study nor test tasks required specific processing of object size. The problem with this argument is that size change *did* affect recognition performance, even though subjects were not specifically required to process size information on this task; they simply indicated whether they had seen the object earlier, whether or not it was the same size as on the study list.

These interpretive ambiguities can be clarified by making use of the constraints provided by a cognitive neuroscience analysis: If a system similar to IT plays an important role in object decision priming and if retinal size is not a relevant property for this system, then the absence of size change effects is no embarrassment to a transfer-appropriate processing view. As in the earlier example, hypotheses about the properties of a system that is involved in a particular type of priming can help to guide and refine predictions about the kinds of transfer-appropriate processing effects that should be observed. Stated slightly differently, the nature of transfer-appropriate processing may be different in different systems, depending on the computational constraints that characterize a specific system.

Cross-Domain Hypothesis Testing

The typical research strategy in studies of implicit memory is to test theoretical hypotheses in the same domain in which they were generated – for cognitive psychologists, by examining the performance of college students, and for neuropsychologists, by examining the performance of patients with memory disorders. Although there has been considerable interaction in recent years between students of normal and abnormal memory, a cognitive neuroscience orientation can help to broaden our research horizons even further by encouraging the use of what I will refer to as *cross-domain hypothesis testing*: evaluating ideas and theories about the nature of implicit memory in domains other than the ones in which the hypotheses were originally formulated.

The easiest way to illustrate the strategy is with an example. To do so, I consider a recent study in which we (Schacter, Rapcsak et al., 1990) examined priming in a patient with a reading deficit known as *alexia without agraphia* or *letter-by-letter reading*. Such patients are unable to read words unless they resort to a laborious letter-by-letter strategy. The deficit affects all types of words, is indicated by the presence of a strong influence of word length on reading time, and is typically associated with lesions to the left occipital cortex (e.g., Reuter-Lorenz and Brunn, 1990).

Research and theorizing about letter-by-letter readers has typically proceeded separately from and independently of the implicit memory literature. There is, however, a potential link between the two domains, provided by the visual word form system. On the one hand, we have suggested that the visual word form system can be viewed as a PRS subsystem that is critically involved in word priming effects on data-driven implicit tasks (Schacter, 1990). On the other hand, issues concerning the status of the word form system have been central to debates about the nature of the deficit in letter-by-letter reading. Warrington and Shallice (1980) argued that the reading problems of these patients are produced by deficits in the word form system, which normally supports whole word reading. With the word form system dysfunctional, patients read letter-by-letter by somehow making use of their preserved spelling systems. In contrast, Patterson and Kay (1982) argued that the word form system is preserved in these patients and that their deficit is attributable to a problem with parallel, but not serial, transmission of information from letter representations to the word form system. Although the locus of the deficit may vary from patient to patient, recent evidence suggests that the word form system is largely preserved in at least some letter-by-letter readers (e.g., Reuter-Lorenz and Brunn, 1990).

We had the opportunity to study a patient, P.T., whose performance on various cognitive and neuropsychological tests yielded evidence of a preserved word form system (see Schacter, Rapcsak et al., 1990, for details). On the basis of our ideas about the role of this subsystem in implicit memory, we hypothesized that P.T. should show robust priming despite her reading impairment. To examine the issue, we performed an experiment in which P.T. studied a list of common words that appeared one at a time on a computer screen; she was given ample time to read each word in a letter-by-letter manner. To assess priming, we used a perceptual identification test, in which words are exposed for brief durations and the subject attempts to identify them; priming is indicated by more accurate identification of studied than of nonstudied words (e.g., Jacoby and Dallas, 1981). Although exposure rates of under 50 ms are typically used in studies with normal subjects, P.T. reported that she was unable to see even a single letter at such brief durations. Accordingly, we used a 500-ms test exposure (normal control subjects perform perfectly under such conditions, so we did not use control subjects in this study). As indicated by figure 23.2, P.T. showed large priming effects under these conditions, even though she had great difficulty identifying nonstudied words. Figure 23.2 also presents representative data from experiments showing that priming in P.T. was modality specific and that it was not observed for illegal nonwords (e.g., BTLEA). The latter finding indicates that priming cannot be attributed to activation of individual letter representations, and thus strengthens the case that the word form system was critically involved.

However investigators ultimately conceive the role of the word form system in priming, this case study illustrates how the strategy of cross-domain hypothesis testing can link two previously separate sets of ideas: Hypotheses about preservation of the word form system in letter-by-letter readers were formulated independently of implicit memory research, and hypotheses about the role of the word form system in implicit memory were formulated independently of research on letter-by-letter readers. Cross-domain hypothesis testing of this kind can serve at least two interrelated functions. First, it can help to ensure that implicit memory research does not develop in an overly narrow or insular manner, without regard to cognate fields of interest. Second, if hypotheses that are generated in one domain receive support when tested in a separate domain, they acquire a degree of external validity that is not readily conferred by repeated testing within a single domain. Although a cognitive neuroscience orientation is certainly not the only way to build bridges among separate research areas that are relevant to implicit memory (cf. Jacoby, 1991), it seems clear that it can provide a rich source of research opportunities that might otherwise be overlooked.

Cross-Domain Hypothesis Generation

The final feature of a cognitive neuroscience orientation that I will consider, *cross-domain hypothesis generation* can be thought of as a complement to the hypothesis testing strategy outlined in the previous section. The idea here is to draw on ideas and findings from various sectors of cognitive neuroscience to generate hypotheses about implicit memory that are then tested in implicit – explicit memory studies. This kind of strategy has already been illustrated in examples considered earlier, such as using observations of structural–semantic dissociations in patients with reading and object processing deficits to generate hypotheses about the role of PRS in priming (Schacter, 1990; Schacter, Cooper, and Delaney, 1990) and drawing on findings of size invariance in IT to generate hypotheses about the characteristics of object decision priming (Cooper et al., 1992). To conclude, I will consider some recent research in which we (Schacter and Church, in press) have used cross-domain hypothesis generation to guide a series of experiments on auditory implicit memory. We have used observations from cognitive neuroscience at two points in this research: first, to motivate the experiments theoretically, and second, to suggest and test a possible account of findings from our initial experiments.

Our approach to auditory implicit memory was guided by neuropsychological studies of patients who exhibit dissociations between access to form and semantic information in the auditory domain that are similar to those discussed earlier in the visual domain (e.g., Riddoch and Humphreys, 1987; Schwartz et al., 1980; Warrington, 1982). More specifically, patients with so-called word meaning deafness are unable to understand spoken words (e.g., Ellis and Young, 1988). However, they can repeat spoken words quite well and show some ability to write words to dictation, thus suggesting that they can gain access to stored auditory word form representations. It is interesting that such patients show normal access to semantic information in the visual modality, indicating that the impairment in these cases may be attributable to disconnection between a relatively intact system that handles acoustic–phonological properties of spoken words and a relatively intact semantic system (Ellis and Young, 1988). Unfortunately, these patients are extremely rare, so inferences based on their performance must be treated cautiously. Rather more frequently encountered are patients with transcortical sensory aphasia (e.g., Kertesz, Sheppard, and MacKenzie, 1982), who exhibit spared abilities to repeat spoken words and write them to dictation, together with impaired comprehension. In these patients, however, the comprehension deficit is also observed in other modalities, thus indicating damage to the semantic system itself.

These dissociations point toward the existence of a PRS subsystem that handles information about auditory word forms separately from semantic information (cf. Ellis and Young, 1988). If this reasoning is correct and if PRS subserves implicit memory in the auditory domain, then it should be possible to show that implicit memory on an appropriate auditory test is relatively unaffected by manipulations of semantic versus nonsemantic study processing. To examine the possibility, we (Schacter and Church, in press) used an implicit task that requires identification of auditorily presented words that are masked in white noise. Priming on this task is indicated by more accurate identification of previously studied words than of nonstudied words (e.g., Jackson and Morton, 1984). Explicit memory was assessed with an auditory yes or no recognition task. For the study task, all of the subjects heard a series of words spoken by various male and female voices. To manipulate semantic versus nonsemantic processing, one half of the subjects made a category judgement about each word (i.e., they indicated to which of four categories the word belongs), whereas the other half made a pitch judgement about each word (i.e., they judged the pitch of the voice on a four-point scale).

We also examined the specificity of auditory priming by testing one half of the words with the *same* voice that was used during the study task and the other half in a *different* voice; when a different voice was used at study and test, the voice change always entailed a change of gender (i.e., male–female or female–male). Jackson and Morton (1984) included a similar manipulation and found no effects of voice change on priming of auditory word identification. Note, however, that all of the subjects in their experiment performed a semantic study task (judging whether a word represents an animate or inanimate object). A recent experiment by Graf and Ryan (1990) suggested that specificity effects in visual word identification are observed only when subjects focus on visual characteristics of words during the study task. Analogously, it is possible that voice specificity effects in auditory word identification requrie specific encoding of voice characteristics during the study task. If so, then we should observe greater voice specificity effects in the pitch encoding condition than in the category encoding condition.

Two experiments using this basic design yielded a consistent pattern of results (see Schacter and Church, in press, for details of individual experiments). Explicit memory was much higher following the category than the pitch encoding task, whereas priming of auditory word identification was either less affected or entirely unaffected by the study task manipulation (figure 23.3). These data are largely consistent with the idea generated from studies of transcortical sensory aphasics and word meaning deafness patients that a presemantic PRS subsystem contributes significantly to auditory

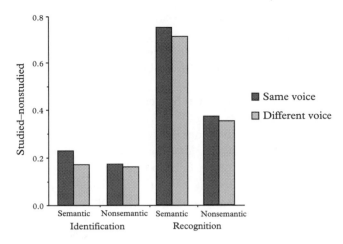

Figure 23.3 Summary data from two experiments by Schacter and Church (in press) on priming of auditory word identification.

Note. Subjects initially heard a list of familiar words spoken by a series of male and female voices, engaging in either a semantic or a nonsemantic encoding task. Priming was then assessed with an auditory word identification test in which studied and nonstudied words were masked in white noise, and explicit memory was assessed with a "yes or no" recognition test. The figure presents priming scores that were computed by subtracting the proportion of nonstudied words that were identified correctly from the proportion of studied words that were identified correctly and corrected recognition scores that were computed by subtracting the proportion of "yes" responses to nonstudied items (i.e., false alarms) from the proportion of "yes" responses to studied items (i.e., hits). Recognition memory, but not priming on the identification test, was higher following the semantic than the nonsemantic encoding task. Performance on both recognition and identification tasks was not significantly affected by whether the speaker's voice was the same or different at study and test.

priming. However, there were no significantly effects of voice change on priming (or explicit memory), even in the pitch encoding condition (figure 23.3).

Why did we (Schacter and Church, in press) fail to observe any effects of the voice change manipulation on priming? The result does not appear to be attributable to a simple inability of subjects to discriminate between male and female voices when they are masked in white noise; follow-up work indicated that subjects can do so quite readily on our task. Although any number of other explanations could be advanced (e.g., Jackson and Morton, 1984), we drew on the cognitive neuroscience literature to generate a hypothesis that draws on research concerning auditory processing in the left and right hemispheres. The hypothesis consists of three key components: (a) both left- and right-hemisphere subsystems play a role in auditory priming, (b) voice specificity effects may depend on a right-hemisphere subsystem, and (c) the auditory identification test that we used minimized the possible contribution of the right-hemisphere subsystem. Let me elaborate briefly on these ideas.

Various investigators have argued that auditory processing differs in the two hemispheres. The left hemisphere relies on categorical or abstract auditory information and operates primarily on phonemes, whereas the right hemisphere relies more on "acoustic gestalts" and operates primarily on prosodic features of speech, including voice information (cf. Liberman, 1982; Zaidel, 1985). Several lines of evidence link the right hemisphere with access to voice information. Right hemisphere lesions are associated with voice recognition deficits (e.g., Van Lancker, Cummings, Kreiman, and Dobkin, 1988) and are also associated with impairments in processing various features of prosody (e.g., Ross, 1981). In addition, studies of normal subjects using dichotic listening techniques have shown a left-ear (i.e., right-hemisphere) advantage for certain types of voice information, in contrast to the usual right-ear advantage for speech (e.g., Blumstein and Cooper, 1974; Shipley-Brown, Dingwall, Berlin, Yeni-Komshian, and Gordon-Salant, 1988).

Assuming that some sort of link exists between the right hemisphere and access to voice information, how does this relate to the absence of voice specificity effects in priming of auditory word identification? Zaidel (1978) reported evidence from the study of split-brain patients indicating that the right hemisphere has great difficulty processing spoken words that are embedded in background noise. Because the words on our (Schachter and Church, in press) auditory identification task were masked with white noise, it is conceivable that we inadvertently minimized or even excluded the effective participation of the right hemisphere in the task. In view of the link between the right hemisphere and voice information – as well as the previously discussed link between the right hemisphere and specificity effects in visual priming (Marsolek et al., 1992) – it is tempting to conjecture that the voice-independent priming that we observed may be partly attributable to the functional exclusion of the right hemisphere from implicit task performance.

Although speculative, this hypothesis does have a testable consequence: When an auditory implicit task is used that does *not* involve background noise, thus allowing the right hemisphere to contribute significantly to performance, priming should be reduced by voice change between study and test. Data bearing on this issue are provided by experiments that we have performed using an auditory stem completion task (cf. Bassili, Smith, and MacLeod, 1989), in which the subject hears either a male or a female voice pronounce the first syllable of a word (the speaker actually enunciates the entire word, and the utterance is edited on the Macintosh). The subject's task is to report the first word that comes to mind upon hearing the auditory stem, and priming is indicated by higher completion rates for stems that represent studied words than for stems that represent nonstudied words. To test explicit memory, subjects are given the identical stem together with cued recall instructions to think back to the study list and try to remember the correct word.

We (Schachter and Church, in press) have completed two experiments using these tests. In each experiment, subjects initially heard a list of words that were spoken by the same male and female voices used in previous studies. One group of subjects performed a nonsemantic study task that required attention to voice characteristics, and another group performed a semantic study task that did not require specific encoding of voice characteristics; one half of the studied words were tested with the same voice, and the other half were tested with a different voice. The critical outcome of both experiments was that priming effects (but not explicit memory) were reduced significantly by the voice change manipulation. Figure 23.4 summarizes the data from one of the experiments, in which the semantic study task required rating the number of alternative meanings for each word and the nonsemantic study task required rating how clearly each voice enunciated a target word. It is interesting that there was no evidence that voice change effects were greater following the nonsemantic study task than following the semantic study task. As in previous experiments, however, there was a strong interaction between type of study task and type of test: Explicit memory was

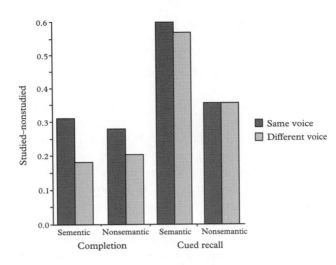

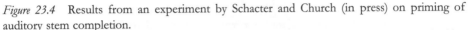

Figure 23.4 Results from an experiment by Schacter and Church (in press) on priming of auditory stem completion.

Note. Subjects initially heard a list of familiar words spoken by a series of male and female voices, engaging in either a semantic or a nonsemantic encoding task. Priming was then assessed with an auditory stem completion task, in which subjects heard the first syllable of studied and nonstudied words and responded with the first word that came to mind. Explicit memory was assessed with a cued recall test. The figure presents priming and corrected recall scores that were computed by subtracting the proportion of nonstudied stems that were completed correctly from the proportion of studied stems that were completed correctly. Cued recall performance, but not priming on the completion task, was significantly higher following semantic than nonsemantic encoding. By contrast, priming, but not cued recall, was significantly higher when speaker's voice was the same at study and test than when it was different.

much higher following semantic than nonsemantic encoding, whereas priming was essentially identical following the two study tasks.

These data are consistent with the hypothesis that voice specificity effects in auditory priming are attributable, at least in part, to the involvement of a right-hemisphere PRS subsystem. Clearly, however, the evidence supporting this idea is rather indirect; until and unless there is direct evidence for a link between voice specificity in priming and the right hemisphere, this hypothesis must be viewed as merely suggestive (see Schacter and Church, in press, for further discussion and alternative hypotheses). More important for the present purposes, these studies illustrate how a cognitive neuroscience perspective can facilitate the use of cross-domain hypothesis generation and thereby suggest novel experiments and ideas that might otherwise have been overlooked.

Concluding Comments

The systematic study of implicit memory is a relatively recent development. Although numerous reliable experimental procedures have been developed and robust experimental phenomena have been established, theoretical understanding of the nature of implicit memory is still rather rudimentary. It may well turn out, for example, that multiple systems and processing accounts are ultimately viewed as complementary, and not mutually exclusive, theoretical approaches (cf. Hayman and Tulving, 1989; Nelson, Schreiber, and McEvoy, 1992; Roediger, 1990b; Schacter, 1990; Tulving and Schacter, 1990). Whatever the outcome of this particular debate, it seems clear that at this early stage of research, the existence of a variety of theoretical viewpoints and investigative strategies is desirable.

Although I have emphasized the virtues of adopting a cognitive neuroscience orientation, the approach is not without its own limitations and pitfalls. Consider, for example, the point made earlier that neurophysiological data on size- and reflection-invariant object representation in inferior temporal cortex helped us to predict, and to some extent understand, findings of size- and reflection-invariant priming on the object decision task (Cooper et al., 1992). Note, however, that we were able to make use of these neural constraints only because the neurophysiological data on size- and reflection-invariance of IT representations are relatively clear-cut (Plaut and Farah, 1990). By contrast, when we initiated new experiments examining the effects of study-to-test changes in picture-plane orientation and color on object decision priming (Cooper, Schacter, and Moore, 1991), the cognitive neuroscience literature proved less helpful, primarily because data concerning the neural basis of these aspects of object representation are less clear-cut than are the data on size and reflection (e.g., Plaut and Farah, 1990). Thus, when neurophysiological and neuropsychological evidence is weak or unclear, a cognitive neuroscience orientation will not provide the sort of useful constraints discussed earlier.

A related limitation is that the cognitive neuroscience literature may often be mute concerning a particular finding or hypothesis. Returning again to the studies by Cooper et al. (1992), we found that study-to-test transformations of object size and reflection significantly impaired explicit memory. The neurophysiological studies on single-cell recordings and lesion effects that helped to illuminate the priming data simply do not speak directly to these findings on explicit memory, so our attempts to understand them relied entirely on cognitive concepts (Cooper et al., 1992). More generally, investigators studying implicit and explicit memory in human subjects who wish to make use of cognitive neuroscience evidence would do well to avoid an overly simplistic reductionist approach, in which explanatory efforts go no further than attempting to identify the brain locus of a particular phenomenon; theoretical accounts must also be couched at, and do justice to, the cognitive level of analysis (cf. Polster et al., 1991; Schacter, 1986).

As implied by the foregoing, the cognitive neuroscience orientation discussed here represents just one avenue of approach to implicit memory, and it should be pursued in addition to, rather than instead of, other strategies. Perhaps the main virtue of the cognitive neuroscience orientation is that it encourages us to draw on data and ideas from diverse areas of investigation. In so doing, it also encourages reliance on the logic of converging operations (cf. Roediger, 1990b) and can thus help to ensure that research on implicit memory remains broadly focused on fundamental issues concerning the nature of mind and brain.

Notes

The work described in this article has been supported by Air Force Office of Scientific Research Grant 90–0187, National Institute on Aging Grant 1RO1 AG08441–01, and a grant from the McDonnell-Pew Cognitive Neuroscience Program.

I am grateful to Barbara Church, Lynn Cooper, and Steve Rapcsak for their collaborative efforts on several of the experiments summarized in the article. I thank Douglas Nelson and Henry L. Roediger for comments on an earlier draft of the paper and Dana Osowiecki for help with preparation of the manuscript.

1   Much of what is discussed in this article could just as easily be described with the phrase *cognitive neuropsychology* as with the phrase *cognitive neuroscience*. However, the term *cognitive neuropsychology* often connotes a purely functional approach to patients with cognitive deficits that does not make use of, or encourage interest in, evidence and ideas about brain systems and processes. Because I believe that neural constraints can be important for cognitive theorizing, I use the term cognitive neuroscience instead of cognitive neuropsychology.

References

Bassili, J. N., Smith, M. C., & MacLeod, C. M. (1989). Auditory and visual word stem completion: Separating data-driven and conceptually driven processes. *Quarterly Journal of Experimental Psychology*, **41A**, 439–53.

Biederman, I., & Cooper, E. E. (1991). Priming contour deleted images: Evidence for intermediate representations in visual object recognition. *Cognitive Psychology*, **23**, 393–419.

Blaxton, T. A. (1989). Investigating dissociations among memory measures: Support for a transfer-appropriate processing framework. *Journal of Experimental Psychology: Learning, Memory, and Cognition*, **15**, 657–68.

Blumstein, S., & Cooper, W. E. (1974). Hemispheric processing of intonation contours. *Cortex*, **10**, 146–58.

Bowers, J. S., & Schacter, D. L. (1990). Implicit memory and test awareness. *Journal of Experimental Psychology: Learning, Memory, and Cognition*, **16**, 404–16.

Cohen, N. J. (1984). Preserved learning capacity in amnesia: Evidence for multiple memory systems. In L. R. Squire & N. Butters (eds), *Neuropsychology of memory* (pp. 83–103), New York: Guilford Press.

Cooper, L. A., Schacter, D. L., Ballesteros, S., & Moore, C. (1992). Priming and recognition of transformed three-dimensional objects: Effects of size and reflection. *Journal of Experimental Psychology: Learning, Memory, and Cognition*, **18**, 43–57.

Cooper, L. A., Schacter, D. L., & Moore, C. (1991, November). *Orientation affects priming of structural representations of three-dimensional objects*. Paper presented at the meeting of the Psychonomic Society, San Francisco.

Craik, F. I. M., & Tulving, E. (1975). Depth of processing and the retention of words in episodic memory. *Journal of Experimental Psychology: General*, **104**, 268–94.

Dunn, J. C., & Kirsner, K. (1988). Discovering functionally independent mental processes: The principle of reversed association. *Psychological Review*, **95**, 91–101.

Ellis, A. W., & Young, A. W. (1988). *Human cognitive neuropsychology*. Hove, England: Erlbaum.

Garner, W. R., Hake, H. W., & Eriksen, C. W. (1956). Operationalism and the concept of perception. *Psychological Review*, **63**, 149–59.

Gazzaniga, M. (1984). *Handbook of cognitive neuroscience*. New York: Plenum Press.

Graf, P., & Mandler, G. (1984). Activation makes words more accessible, but not necessarily more retrievable. *Journal of Verbal Learning and Verbal Behavior*, **23**, 553–68.

Graf, P., & Ryan, L. (1990). Transfer-appropriate processing for implicit and explicit memory. *Journal of Experimental Psychology: Learning, Memory, and Cognition*, **16**, 978–92.

Graf, P., & Schacter, D. L. (1985). Implicit and explicit memory for new associations in normal and amnesic patients. *Journal of Experimental Psychology: Learning, Memory, and Cognition*, **11**, 501–18.

Graf, P., Shimamura, A. P., & Squire, L. R. (1985). Priming across modalities and priming across category levels: Extending the domain of preserved function in amnesia. *Journal of Experimental Psychology: Learning, Memory and Cognition*, **11**, 385–95.

Graf, P., Squire, L. R., & Mandler, G. (1984). The information that amnesic patients do not forget. *Journal of Experimental Psychology: Learning, Memory and Cognition*, **10**, 164–78.

Hayman, C. A. G., & Tulving, E. (1989). Is priming in fragment completion based on a "traceless" memory system? *Journal of Experimental Psychology: Learning, Memory, and Cognition*, **15**, 941–56.

Jackson, A., & Morton, J. (1984). Facilitation of auditory word recognition. *Memory and Cognition*, **12**, 568–74.

Jacoby, L. L. (1983). Remembering the data: Analyzing interactive process in reading. *Journal of Verbal Learning and Verbal Behavior*, **22**, 485–508.

Jacoby, L. L. (1991). A process dissociation framework: Separating automatic from intentional use of memory. *Journal of Memory and Language*, **30**, 513–41.

Jacoby, L. L., & Dallas, M. (1981). On the relationship between autobiographical memory and perceptual learning. *Journal of Experimental Psychology: General*, **110**, 306–40.

James, W. (1983). *The principles of psychology*. Cambridge, MA: Harvard University Press (original work published 1890).

Keane, M. M., Gabrieli, J. D. E., Fennema, A. C., Growdon, J. H., & Corkin, S. (1991). Evidence for a dissociation between perceptual and conceptual priming in Alzheimer's disease. *Behavioral Neuroscience*, **105**, 326–42.

Kertesz, A., Sheppard, M., & MacKenzie, R. (1982). Localization in transcortical sensory aphasia. *Archives of Neurology*, **39**, 475–8.

Kosslyn, S. M., Flynn, R. A., Amsterdam, J. B., & Wang, G. (1990). Components of high-level vision: A cognitive neuroscience analysis and accounts of neurological syndromes. *Cognition*, **34**, 203–77.

LeDoux, J., & Hirst, P. (eds) (1986). *Mind and brain: Dialogues in cognitive neuroscience*. New York: Cambridge University Press.

Liberman, A. M. (1982). On finding that speech is special. *American Psychologist*, **37**, 148–67.

Marsolek, C. J., Kosslyn, S. M., & Squire, L. R. (1992). Form-specific visual priming in the right cerebral hemisphere. *Journal of Experimental Psychology: Learning, Memory, and Cognition*, **18**, 492–508.

Masson, M. E. J. (1989). Fluent reprocessing as an implicit expression of memory for experience. In S. Lewandowsky, J. C. Dunn, & K. Kirsner (eds), *Implicit memory: Theoretical issues* (pp. 123–38), Hillsdale, NJ: Erlbaum.

Morris, C. D., Bransford, J. D., & Franks, J. J. (1977). Levels of processing versus transfer appropriate processing. *Journal of Verbal Learning and Verbal Behavior*, **16**, 519–33.

Nelson, D. L., Schreiber, T. A., & McEvoy, C. L. (1992). Processing implicit and explicit representations. *Psychological Review*, **99**, 322–48.

Olton, D. S., Gamzu, E., & Corkin, S. (eds) (1985). Memory dysfunctions: An integration of animal and human research from clinical and preclinical perspectives. *Annals of New York Academy of Sciences*, **444**, 1–546.

Patterson, K., & Kay, J. (1982). Letter-by-letter reading: Psychological descriptions of a neurological syndrome. *Quarterly Journal of Experimental Psychology*, **34A**, 411–41.

Petersen, S. E., Fox, P. T., Posner, M. I., Mintun, M., & Raichle, M. E. (1988). Position emission tomographic studies of the cortical anatomy of single-word processing. *Nature*, **331**, 585–9.

Plaut, D. C., & Farah, M. J. (1990). Visual object representation: Interpreting neurophysiological data within a computational framework. *Journal of Cognitive Neuroscience*, **2**, 320–43.

Polster, M. R., Nadel, L., & Schacter, D. L. (1991). Cognitive neuroscience analyses of memory: A historical perspective. *Journal of Cognitive Neuroscience*, **3**, 95–116.

Reuter-Lorenz, P. A., & Brunn, J. L. (1990). A prelexical basis for letter-by-letter reading: A case study. *Cognitive Neuropsychology*, **7**, 1–20.

Richardson-Klavehn, A., & Bjork, R. A. (1988). Measures of memory. *Annual Review of Psychology*, **36**, 475–543.

Riddoch, M. J., & Humphreys, G. W. (1987). Visual object processing in optic aphasia; A case of semantic access agnosia. *Cognitive Neuropsychology*, **4**, 131–86.

Roediger, H. L., III (1990a). Implicit memory: A commentary. *Bulletin of the Psychonomic Society*, **28**, 373–80.

Roediger, H. L., III (1990b). Implicit memory: Retention without remembering. *American Psychologist*, **45**, 1043–56.

Roediger, H. L., III, Weldon, M. S., & Challis, B. H. (1989). Explaining dissociations between implicit and explicit measures of retention: A processing account. In H. L. Roediger III & F. I. M. Craik (eds), *Varieties of memory and consciousness: Essays in honor of Endel Tulving* (pp. 3–41), Hillsdale, NJ: Erlbaum.

Ross, E. D. (1981). The aprosodias: Functional–anatomic organization of the affective components of language in the right hemisphere. *Archives of Neurology*, **38**, 561–9.

Rozin, P. (1976). The psychobiological approach to human memory. In M. R. Rosenzweig & E. L. Bennett (eds), *Neural mechanisms of learning and memory* (pp. 3–48), Cambridge, MA: MIT Press.

Schacter, D. L. (1986). A psychological view of the neurobiology of memory. In J. E. LeDoux & W. Hirst (eds), *Mind and brain: Dialogues in cognitive neuroscience* (pp. 265–9), New York: Cambridge University Press.

Schacter, D. L. (1987). Implicit memory: History and current status. *Journal of Experimental Psychology: Learning, Memory, and Cognition*, **13**, 501–18.

Schacter, D. L. (1990). Perceptual representation systems and implicit memory: Toward a resolution of the multiple memory systems debate. *Annals of the New York Academy of Sciences*, **608**, 543–71.

Schacter, D. L., & Church, B. A. (in press). Auditory priming: Implicit and explicit memory for words and voices. *Journal of Experimental Psychology: Learning, Memory, and Cognition*.

Schacter, D. L., & Cooper, L. A. (1991). *Implicit memory for novel visual objects: Function and structure*. Paper presented at the meeting of the Psychonomic Society, San Francisco.

Schacter, D. L., Cooper, L. A., & Delaney, S. M. (1990). Implicit memory for unfamiliar objects depends on access to structural descriptions. *Journal of Experimental Psychology: General*, **119**, 5–24.

Schacter, D. L., Cooper, L. A., Delaney, S. M., Peterson, M. A., & Tharan, M. (1991). Implicit memory for possible and impossible objects: Constraints on the construction of structural descriptions. *Journal of Experimental Psychology: Learning, Memory, and Cognition*, **17**, 3–19.

Schacter, D. L., Cooper, L. A., Tharan, M., & Rubens, A. B. (1991). Preserved priming of novel objects in patients with memory disorders. *Journal of Cognitive Neuroscience*, **3**, 118–31.

Schacter, D. L., Cooper, L. A., & Valdiserri, M. (in press). Implicit and explicit memory for novel visual objects in older and younger adults. *Psychology and Aging*.

Schacter, D. L., & Graf, P. (1989). Modality specificity of implicit memory for new associations. *Journal of Experimental Psychology: Learning, Memory, and Cognition*, **15**, 3–12.

Schacter, D. L., Rapcsak, S. Z., Rubens, A. B., Tharan, M., & Laguna, J. M. (1990). Priming effects in a letter-by-letter reader depend upon access to the word form system. *Neuropsychologia*, **28**, 1079–94.

Schwartz, M. F., Saffran, E. M., & Marin, O. S. M. (1980). Fractionating the reading process in dementia: Evidence for word-specific print-to-sound associations. In M. Coltheart, K. Patterson, & J. C. Marshall (eds), *Deep dyslexia* (pp. 259–69), London: Routledge & Kegan Paul.

Sherry, D. F., & Schacter, D. L. (1987). The evolution of multiple memory systems. *Psychological Review*, **94**, 439–54.

Shimamura, A. P. (1986). Priming effects in amnesia: Evidence for a dissociable memory function. *Quarterly Journal of Experimental Psychology*, **38A**, 619–44.

Shipley-Brown, F., Dingwall, W. O., Berlin, C. I., Yeni-Komshian, G., & Gordon-Salant, S. (1988). Hemispheric processing of affective and linguistic intonation contours in normal subjects. *Brain and Language*, **33**, 16–26.

Squire, L. R. (1987). *Memory and brain*. New York: Oxford University Press.

Squire, L. R. & Butters, N. (eds). (1984). *Neuropsychology of memory*. New York: Guilford Press.

Squire, L. R., Weinberger, N. M., Lynch, G., & McGaugh, J. L. (eds) (1992). *Memory: Organization and locus of change*, New York: Oxford University Press.

Sutherland, N. S. (1968). Outline of a theory of pattern recognition in animal and man. *Proceedings of the Royal Society, London*, **B 171**, 297–317.

Tulving, E. (1983). *Elements of episodic memory*. Oxford, England: Clarendon Press.

Tulving, E., Hayman, C. A. G., & Macdonald, C. (1991). Long-lasting perceptual priming and semantic learning in amnesia: A case experiment. *Journal of Experimental Psychology: Learning, Memory, and Cognition*, **17**, 595–617.

Tulving, E., & Schacter, D. L. (1990). Priming and human memory systems. *Science*, **247**, 301–6.

Van Lancker, D. R., Cummings, J. L., Kreiman, J., & Dobkin, B. H. (1988). Phonagnosia: A dissociation between familiar and unfamiliar voices. *Cortex*, **24**, 195–209.

Warrington, E. K. (1982). Neuropsychological studies of object recognition. *Philosophical Transactions of the Royal Society*, **B298**, 15–33.

Warrington, E. K., & Shallice, T. (1980). Word-form dyslexia. *Brain*, **30**, 99–112.

Warrington, E. K., & Weiskrantz, L. (1974). The effect of prior learning on subsequent retention in amnesic patients. *Neuropsychologia*, **12**, 419–28.

Weingartner, H., & Lister, R. (1991). *Perspectives on cognitive neuroscience*. New York: Oxford University Press.

Weiskrantz, L. (1989). Remembering dissociations. In H. L. Roediger III & F. I. M. Craik (eds), *Varieties of memory and consciousness: Essays in honor of Endel Tulving* (pp. 101–20), Hillsdale, NJ: Erlbaum.

Witherspoon, D., & Moscovitch, M. (1989). Stochastic independence between two implicit memory tasks. *Journal of Experimental Psychology: Learning, Memory, and Cognition*, **15**, 22–30.

Zaidel, E. (1978). Concepts of cerebral dominance in the split brain. In P. A. Buser & A. Rougeul-Buser (eds), *Cerebral correlates of conscious experience* (pp. 263–84), Amsterdam: Elsevier.

Zaidel, E. (1985). Language in the right hemisphere. In D. F. Benson & E. Zaidel (eds), *The dual brain: Hemispheric specialization in humans* (pp. 205–31), New York: Guilford Press.

Action and Executive
Function

INTRODUCTION TO PART VII

The point of the brain is obviously to control behavior, a topic we've barely touched on so far. Mountcastle's description of visuomotor neurons in the parietal lobe and Goodale et al.'s ideas on the dorsal stream have given some hint of the blurry distinction between perception and action, and this section may blur the lines more. The cortex's most obvious output pathway is the primary motor cortex (M1), projecting directly onto spinal motor neurons and causing local muscular contraction when electrically stimulated. The article by Georgopoulos and colleagues describes a basic scheme by which this is thought to take place. In many ways, the primary motor cortex appears analogous to the primary visual cortex: each has a reasonably direct connection with the outside world, each is organized in an orderly map corresponding to the layout of the periphery.

The primary visual cortex, though, has its own output pathways. One of its main projections is to the superior colliculus, an ancient midbrain sensorimotor structure described by Robert Wurtz. This structure, though vastly overshadowed in humans by the cerebral cortex, nevertheless plays a vital role in orienting the organism towards objects and locations of interest. The V1's projection to it is very much analogous to the primary motor cortex's projection to the spinal cord. One might well ask whether the primary motor cortex has a corresponding role in sensation.

The subcortical theme continues with Thach et al.'s discussion of the basal ganglia and cerebellum, two major systems of the brain without which no discussion of motor function, and possibly cognition, would be complete. The obviously very different roles of these two systems are often mixed up in the general confusion as to the exact function of either one of them; Thach and colleagues attempt to dispel some of the chaos with a description of the cerebellum as a combiner of multiple muscle groups into context-appropriate movements and the basal ganglia as a "parking brake" on unwanted motor programs. Though not mentioned in this article, these structures' clearly crucial roles in movement may be rivaled by important contributions to cognition.

How behavior is organized on a higher level is even less clear, but a fascinating issue. Norman and Shallice conceive of multiple autonomous mutually competing "schemas" that are influenced by a "Supervisory Attentional System" (SAS) that can enhance a given schema over others and thereby allow it to attain dominance. The notion is very reminiscent of Posner's anterior attentional system, presented in the attention section, and in fact they explicitly identify the SAS with the capacities of the frontal cortex.

Some of these capacities are examined in detail by Patricia Goldman-Rakic, who records from the dorsolateral prefrontal cortex of behaving monkeys. She finds Baddeley's tripartite working memory model unconvincing, preferring a distribution of the "central executive" throughout the same areas responsible for storing information.

We have seen earlier, though, that working memory, or the maintenance of persistent thought or imagery following perception or recall, seems to require the same regions involved in perceiving those concepts or images in the first place. What then is the role of the prefrontal cortex? The question does not seem to be satisfactorily settled, but the fact remains that the prefrontal cortex is crucially involved in the effortful maintenance of the contents of the mind in a constantly changing stream of sensations.

Cognitive Neurophysiology of the Motor Cortex

Apostolos P. Georgopoulos, Masato Taira, and Alexander Lukashin

The recording of the activity of single cells in the brain of behaving animals provides a tool for directly studying the functional properties of single cells, interactions between cells, and the dynamics of neuronal populations involved in a variety of cognitive processes, including attention, memory, perception, and motor intention. This method was introduced 36 years ago by Ricci, Doane, and Jasper (*1*) and was perfected and popularized later by Evarts (*2*). Evarts saw it as the only way to study voluntary movement, a function that by definition cannot be studied in anesthetized preparations. His and subsequent studies showed that changes in cell activity in the motor cortex precede the development of the motor output and relate quantitatively to its intensity (*3*) and spatial characteristics (*4–7*).

The main challenge with data obtained with this technique in studies of cognitive function is their interpretation. For example, a common finding is that cell activity changes in a certain brain area during a particular cognitive process. The crucial question is: how can we deduce the time-varying cognitive process from the single-cell recordings? How can purely temporal series of action potentials (spike trains) yield information about a cognitive process unfolding in time?

To solve this problem, one must realize that a cognitive process usually operates on a variable; for example, mental arithmetic operates on numbers. The process, then, is the operation, and the puzzle of how the brain performs multiplication is transformed to the problem of how numbers are being multiplied. The crucial idea is that if we can decipher the neural coding of numbers, then we have a good chance of deciphering the cognitive process of mental multiplication by observing neural activity during this process, recovering the numbers by decoding, and inferring how they are being operated upon in this particular process. The essence of the idea is that solving the problem of neural coding of a particular variable provides the means for potentially solving the problem of cognitive processing of that variable. These logical steps are shown in table 24.1. The crucial step is step 2, namely that of neural coding. This is the step that connects cell activity with the variable of interest — that is, the step that

Table 24.1 Steps in deciphering brain mechanisms of cognitive processes.

1   Select a variable of interest.
2   Find the neural coding of the variable outside the cognitive process.
3   Select a cognitive process operating on the variable of interest.
4   Record brain activity during cognitive processing and infer how the variable is operated on.

provides the link between the neural dimension and the dimension of the variable. We illustrate, below, the successful application of this sequence of investigation to the study of cognitive processes involving motor operations in space. For that purpose, we chose the direction of reaching movement as the spatial variable of interest. We wanted to know how directional information is encoded in the motor cortex and how cognitive processes operating on direction (for example, memory or mental rotation) are reflected in motor cortical activity.

The Problem of Coding: Single Cells and Neuronal Populations

The problem with the coding of the direction of movement in space is that direction is a closed (circular or spherical) variable and as such does not lend itself to simple monotonic coding by the intensity of cell activity. A possible simple solution to the problem would be to allocate cells that would be specifically activated only with movements in a particular direction – that is, for cells to be sharply tuned to the direction of movement. However, this is not the case. Instead, cells in the motor cortex (*4–7*) as well as in other structures (*8, 9*) are broadly tuned to the direction of movement. This means that the cell activity is highest for a movement in a particular direction (the cell's preferred direction) and decreases progressively with movements farther away from this direction. The changes in cell activity relate to the direction and not the target of the reaching movement (*10*). Quantitatively, the crucial variable on which cell activity depends is the angle formed between the direction of the movement and the cell's preferred direction: the intensity of cell activity can be approximated as a linear function of the cosine of this angle (*4–9*). The directional tuning equation is

$$D_i(M_k) = b_i + a_i\cos\theta_{C_iM_k} \qquad (1)$$

where $D_i(M_k)$ is the discharge rate of the ith cell with movement in direction M_k, b_i and a_i are regression coefficients, and $\theta_{C_iM_k}$ is the angle between the direction of movement M_k and the cell's preferred direction C_i. An example is shown in fig. 24.1. Some points concerning preferred directions are noteworthy. First, cells in a cortical column tend to have very similar preferred directions (*11*). Second, particular preferred directions are multiply represented in the motor cortex (*11*). And third, the preferred directions of single cells are not clustered in particular directions but range throughout the directional continuum (*4–9*) (fig. 24.2). This indicates a distributed vectorial coding rather than coding of a coordinate frame (*12*); for example, if such a frame were Cartesian, the preferred directions would have clustered along the three cardinal directions.

The broad directional tuning indicates that a given cell participates in movements of various directions; from this result and from the fact that preferred directions range

Figure 24.1   Three-dimensional directional tuning. The axes meet at the origin of the movement. For a particular movement, the discharge rate of the cell predicted by Eq. 1 is proportional to the length of a line pointing in the direction of the movement and drawn from the origin to the surface of the tuning volume. The cell's preferred direction is indicated by the cone.

Figure 24.2   Three-dimensional preferred directions of 634 motor cortical cells studied in three monkeys.

widely, it follows that a movement in a particular direction will involve the engagement of a whole population of cells. How, then, is the direction of reaching encoded in an unambiguous fashion in a population of neurons, each of which is directionally broadly tuned? To answer this question, we hypothesized that the motor cortical command for the direction of reaching can be regarded as an ensemble of vectors (*13, 14*) in which each vector represents the contribution of a directionally tuned cell. A particular vector points in the cell's preferred direction and has a length proportional to the change in cell activity associated with a particular movement direction. For a given movement M_k, the vector sum of these weighted cell vectors (the neuronal population vector P) can be regarded as the outcome of the ensemble operation

Figure 24.3   The population vector obtained from the set of cells with preferred directions shown in fig. 24.2.

$$P(M_k) = \sum_i V_i(M_k)C_i \tag{2}$$

where C_i is the preferred direction (*4*) of the ith cell and $V_i(M_k)$ is the activity of the ith cell averaged over a period of time (for example, the reaction time). The population vector points at or near the direction of the movement (*12–16*) (fig. 24.3). Three aspects of the population vector are noteworthy: its simplicity, its robustness, and its spatial characteristics. First, the calculation of the population vector is a simple procedure for it (i) assumes directional selectivity of single cells, which is apparent; (ii) weights vectorial contributions by single cells on the basis of the change in cell activity, which is reasonable; and (iii) is the outcome of the vectorial summation of these contributions, which is practically the simplest procedure to obtain a unique outcome. Second, the population vector is a robust measure, for it can still convey a good directional signal even with relatively few (100 to 150) cells (*15*). And third, the population vector is a spatial measure. The population analysis transforms aggregates of purely temporal spike trains into a spatiotemporal population vector.

The neuronal population performing the vectorial operation consists only of directionally tuned cells. Given that the preferred direction seems to be represented in cortical columns (*11*) and that the population operation involves cells with different preferred directions, it follows that this operation has to be intercolumnar. Moreover, the population vector is a good predictor of the direction of movement when it is calculated separately from subsets of cells recorded in the upper or lower cortical layers (*17*).

The neuronal population vector has proved to be a robust and accurate measure of the directional tendency of a neuronal ensemble under a variety of conditions, including movements from different origins (*9, 18*), continuous drawing movements (*19*), and isometric force pulses (*6*). Moreover, the analysis holds in other structures concerned with sensorimotor control (*8, 9*) or visual processing (*20*). Single cell activity is broadly tuned in other areas (*21*) and for other movements (*22*), although a population vector analysis has not been performed. Finally, a cosine directional tuning was observed in the elements of the hidden layer of a three-layer artificial network trained to perform the population vector operation (*23*).

Especially interesting is a recent generalization of the application of the population vector analysis to the coding of faces in the discharge of cells in the inferotemporal cortex of monkeys (*24*). In the studies of the motor cortex, the population vector and the vectorial contributions of single cells were in directions in physical space. The face coding study generalized the vector approach to an arbitrary space of multidimensional scaling of the similarity of face features. Thus, space need not be physical but can be any *n*-dimensional feature space. Even for motor function, this can be a powerful approach. For example, an interesting question is how the motor cortex controls finger movements during hand manipulation of objects that involve a large number of combinations of finger movements. The hypothesis would be that (i) single cells code for combinations of manipulatory movements, (ii) a particular cell discharges most for a preferred combination, (iii) the intensity of cell activation follows a broad, possibly cosine, tuning with the various movement combinations when they are expressed in a continuum of similarity in a reduced "movement combination space," and (iv) when cell contributions are expressed as weighted vectors in the latter space, their vector sum (population vector) would provide an unequivocal signal for the coding of a particular manipulatory movement combination. Given a task that can provide the requisite variety of movement combinations, the hypothesis above can be tested rigorously.

The Population Vector as a Temporal Probe of Direction

The population vector can be used as a probe by which to monitor in time the changing directional tendency of the neuronal ensemble. One can obtain the time evolution of the population vector (Eq. 2) by calculating it at short successive intervals t (for example, every 10 or 20 ms) or continuously, during periods of interest:

$$P(M_k; t) = \sum_i V_i(M_k; t)C_i \qquad (3)$$

Thus, cortical mechanisms that underlie specific processes (for example, memorization) could be followed by observation of the time-varying population vector.

The feasibility of this approach was first documented when it was shown that the neuronal population vector predicts the direction of movement during the reaction time (*11, 14*). The visual reaction time is a period of approximately 300 ms that intervenes between the appearance of a visual target and the initiation of movement; during this period, the upcoming movement is being planned and its execution initiated. This is the simplest case of predicting the direction of the upcoming movement. In addition, the population vector predicts well the direction of movement during an instructed delay period (*25*). In these experiments, monkeys were trained to withhold the movement for a period of time after the onset of a visual cue signal and to move later in response to a "go" signal. During this instructed delay period, the population vector gave a reliable signal concerning the direction of the movement that was triggered later for execution. Finally, in an even more complex task, the population vector predicted well the direction of movement during a memorized delay period (*26*). In these experiments, the target of the movement was shown for only 300 ms. The monkeys were trained to withhold the movement for a subsequent period of time, during which the target was off, and then moved in the direction of the memorized target in response to a "go" signal. During this memorized delay period, the population vector pointed in the direction of the memorized movement.

Neural Mechanisms of a Cognitive Process: Mental Rotation

The cognitive process we chose for study involved a transformation of an intended movement direction. Our general approach in studying the brain mechanisms of a cognitive function involves (i) defining the cognitive task, (ii) performing psychological experiments in human subjects, the results of which lead to hypotheses concerning the nature of the cognitive process, (iii) training monkeys to perform the same task and recording the activity of single cells in the brains of these animals during performance of the task, and (iv) connecting the neural results with those of the human studies and interpreting the psychological results on the basis of the neurophysiological ones. This cycle is illustrated in fig. 24.4: the objective is to get as close as possible to relating neurophysiology and cognitive psychology. Below, we describe these steps as they were applied to a particular problem of a mental transformation of movement direction. Subjects were required to move a handle at an angle from a reference direction defined by a visual stimulus on a plane. Because the reference direction changed from trial to trial, the task required that in a given trial the direction of movement be specified according to this reference direction.

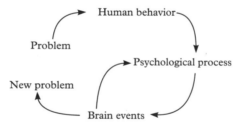

Figure 24.4   Cognitive neuroscience loop.

In human studies, subjects performed blocks of 20 trials in which the angle and its departure (counterclockwise or clockwise) were fixed, although the reference direction varied (*27*). Seven angles (5° to 140°) were used. The basic finding was that the reaction time increased in a linear fashion with the angle. The most parsimonious hypothesis to explain this result is that subjects arrive at the correct direction of movement by shifting their motor intention from the reference direction to the movement direction, traveling through the intermediate angular space. This idea is very similar to the mental rotation hypothesis advanced by Shepard and co-workers (*28*) to explain the monotonic increase of the reaction time with orientation angle about when a judgment has to be made about whether a visual image is normal or mirror-image. Interestingly, the mean rates of rotation (approximately 400° per second) and their range among subjects are very similar in both kinds of study. When the same human subjects performed both perceptual and motor rotation tasks, their processing rates were positively correlated (*29*), a result that indicates similar processing constraints for both tasks.

The results of neurophysiological studies (*30*, *31*) provided direct evidence for the mental rotation hypothesis. Rhesus monkeys were trained to move the handle 90° and counterclockwise from a reference direction. The population vector rotated during the reaction time from the stimulus (reference) direction to the direction of the movement through the counterclockwise angle. This is illustrated in fig. 24.5. The occurrence of a

Figure 24.5   Rotation of the neuronal population vector during the reaction time from the direction of the stimulus to the direction of the movement. Data from all eight stimulus directions used (*31*) are shown.

true rotation was further documented by showing that there was a transient increase during the middle of the reaction time in the recruitment of cells with preferred directions between the stimulus and movement directions (*31*). This neural rotation process, sweeping through the directionally tuned ensemble, provided for the first time a direct visualization of a dynamic cognitive process (*32*). The mean rotation rate and the range of rates observed for different reference directions (*31*) were very similar to those obtained in the human studies (*27*, *29*).

The Motor Cortex as a Network: Real and Artificial

The population vector and its transformations are the results of operations within an ensemble of cells. The cell activity is, in turn, the result of converging influences on the motor cortex of both external signals from other brain areas and of intrinsic interactions among the motor cortical cells. We investigated these local interactions by recording the impulse activity of several cells simultaneously by using seven independently movable microelectrodes (*33*). The data used here come from recordings of impulse activity during the reaction and movement time in the motor cortex of five monkeys during the performance of a reaching task (*4*). The seven electrodes were arranged in a linear array every 0.6 mm; cells were recorded at all interelectrode distances. A total of 1728 pairs were used in this analysis; in 1126 pairs, both cells in a pair were directionally turned, whereas in the remaining 602 pairs none of the two cells in a pair were tuned. We wanted to know whether the prevalence of significant interactions differed significantly between the tuned and nontuned pairs and whether the strength of interaction was correlated with the similarity of preferred directions of

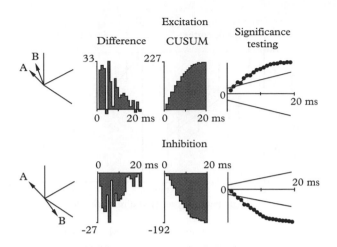

Figure 24.6 Dependence of cell interactions on their preferred directions. Two cases illustrate the methods described in (*34*). Upper row, a case of cells with similar preferred directions (arrows). The "difference distribution" and the CUSUM are positive, which indicates an excitatory effect. The statistical significance of the CUSUM (*P* < 0.04) is established when it crosses the upper chance line. Lower row, a case of cells with very different preferred directions. The "difference distribution" and the CUSUM are negative, which indicates an inhibitory effect.

cells in a pair. For that purpose, we estimated the strength of presumed interaction (synaptic weight) from the ith to the jth neuron in a pair using an analysis based on waiting time probability density function (*34*). An example is illustrated in fig. 24.6.

There were two major findings of our analysis. First, significant interactions were 2.25 times more frequent in the directionally tuned (203 of 1126 cells or 18%) than in the nontuned (48 of 602 or 8%) group (*P* < 10^{-5}; chi-square test); significant interactions in the tuned cell group were observed for cells recorded at all interelectrode distances. Second, the mean synaptic strength (*34*) was negatively correlated with the angle (0° to 180°) between the preferred directions of the two neurons [correlation coefficient $(r) = -0.815; P < 0.004$] (fig. 24.7A) throughout the range of connections from positive (excitation) to negative (inhibition).

The presence of interactions among cells in the motor cortex has been suggested on morphological grounds (*35*) and demonstrated by electrophysiological techniques (*36*). Our results demonstrate that the directional tuning of motor cortical cells is a significant factor governing the strength of interactions between cells. This finding is qualitatively similar to that observed in the visual cortex regarding the association of cells with similar orientation tuning (*37*).

The importance of directional tuning for the presence of cell interactions and the dependence of the strength of these interactions on the similarity of preferred directions provide a fertile ground on which to test hypotheses concerning the organization of artificial neural networks performing a population operation (*23, 38*). For that purpose we used a single-layer, extensively interconnected nonsymmetric network that consisted of directionally tuned cells and performed the calculation of the neuronal population vector. We wanted to know whether the strength of interactions between its elements depended on the similarity of their preferred directions, as observed in the motor cortex. The fact that the neuronal population vector remains stable after an

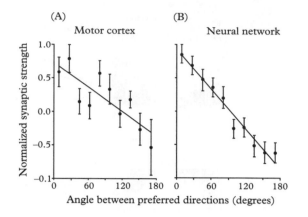

Figure 24.7   The dependence of the mean value (± SEM) of synaptic strength on the angle between preferred directions of neurons involved in the connection. We calculated the mean value of synaptic strength by averaging over synaptic strengths between neurons, the preferred directions of which did not differ from each other by more than 18°. (**A**) Results from 203 pairs of directionally tuned neurons with significant interactions recorded simultaneously in the monkey motor cortex. The total number of values averaged for each of ten points plotted (from left to right) are 25, 33, 22, 24, 16, 21, 15, 15, 18, and 14. (**B**) Results of simulations for $N = 32$, $K = 32$, and $d = 0.2$. The total number of values averaged for each of ten points plotted (from left to right) are 134, 104, 104, 94, 94, 90, 96, 108, 100, and 100.

initial growth (*11, 15*) implies that during this steady-state period the activities V_i (Eq. 3) cease to change, so that $dV_i/dt = 0$ for all *i*. Activities V_i can be represented as $V_i = g(u_i)$, where u_i is the internal state of the ith neuron (*u*, for example, might represent the membrane potential of the neuron averaged over a reasonable time interval) and *g* is an activation function having a saturation nonlinearity. Assuming that the internal state *u* is a linear function of inputs received by the neuron from the other neurons in the network, then at a stable state ($dV_i/dt = 0$) the equality

$$V_i(M_k) = g[\sum_j w_{ij} V_j(M_k)] \tag{4}$$

is valid for all neurons (*39*) and, generally, for all directions M. The weights w_{ij} in Eq. 4 can be regarded as synaptic connection strengths. If activities V_i at a stable state are known for a given number of neurons and for an appropriate number of directions M, Eq. 4 can be used for determining the parameters w_{ij}.

Equation 4 shows that the stability of the population vector could be ensured by an appropriate set of synaptic connection strengths w_{ij}. To determine the general features of the sets of these strengths that would ensure stability, we searched for parameters *w* within different ranges of possible values $|w| < d$ (where *d* is a restriction parameter) and for different numbers of neurons *N* in a network. In routine calculations, the activation function *g* in Eq. 4 was specified as $g(u) = \tanh u$. A cosine tuning function was chosen for activities $V_i(M_k)$ in accordance with experimental findings (*4*): $V_i(M_k) = a_i\cos\theta_{ik}$ (Eq. 1), where a_i is a positive number and θ_{ik} is the angle between the preferred direction of the ith cell (C_i) and the direction of upcoming movement (M_k). Directions C_i and M_k were randomly and uniformly distributed in space, and the values of a were randomly and uniformly distributed on the interval [0, 1]. For each set of N randomly selected, cell-preferred directions and of K randomly selected movement directions, we obtained values of the w parameters that ensured the conditions described in Eq. 4 above by minimizing a cost function without assuming a symmetry of the matrix w_y (*40*).

Figure 24.7B shows the result of the calculations for $d = 0.2$ and $N = 32$. The normalized mean value of synaptic connection strength w is plotted against the angle between the preferred directions of interconnected neurons: these parameters are negatively correlated ($r = -0.984$). Our calculations for different values of d and N confirmed that this correlation is always strong enough if possible values of synaptic connection strengths are restricted to $d \sim 1/N$ but practically disappears when the restriction becomes weak ($d \sim 1$) (*41*).

These simulation studies showed that weakly interconnected but correlated neurons can ensure the stability of the population vector. It is likely that converging external inputs initiate the changes in activity in the motor cortex and contribute to the ongoing activity of the population. However, such external contributions can be understood and evaluated properly only within the context of the dynamics of the cortical network itself. Our results show that the network can by itself support a stable process, which leads to the idea that external inputs may act as initiators or modifiers but need not be the exclusive determinants of this intrinsic process.

There are three points worth mentioning in comparing our data from the neural artificial networks. First, the interactions between directionally tuned cells predicted by the network model were confirmed by the results of the neurophysiological studies. Second, the emphasis in our modeling on intrinsic cell interactions as means for sustaining cell activities within the network is warranted by the recent emphasis on intrinsic cortical interactions as means for amplifying and sustaining cortical excitation (*42*). And third, the prediction by our model that extensive but weak interactions are sufficient for the stability of a network operation provides a reasonable explanation of, and a possible function for, the extensive (*35*) but weak interactions observed between cortical cells (*43*).

Conclusion

Major progress has been made during the past decade toward determining the functional properties of single motor cortical cells with respect to behavior and the understanding of operations by neuronal populations. This knowledge, combined with an elucidation of the interactions among cells and rigorous network modeling, should lead to an understanding of how the cortex works and how cognitive operations are processed in specific brain areas. A limitation of the single cell recording technique is that usually it can be applied only to one restricted brain area at a time. Other techniques, including positron emission tomography, can provide a greater picture of areas of activation in the brain during performance of a task. A new major tool is the oxygen-based functional imaging of the brain with the use of nuclear magnetic resonance (*44*). This technique is noninvasive, sensitive, does not require averaging of data from more than one subject, possesses adequate resolution, and has already been successfully applied to imaging of the human motor cortex

(*45*). This method provides information complementary to that obtained by single-cell recordings and, together with the latter, can lead to major insights into brain function.

References and Notes

1   G. Ricci, B. Doane, H. Jasper, in *Volume publié à l'occasion du IVe Congrès International d'Electro-encéphalographie et de Neurophysiologie clinique et de la VIIIe Réunion de la Ligue internationale contre l'Epilepsie* (Snoeck-Ducaju, Brussels, 1957), pp. 401–15. See also R. N. Lemon, *Methods for Neuronal Recordings in Conscious Animals* (Wiley, Chichester, United Kingdom, 1984).

2   E. V. Evarts, *J. Neurophysiol.*, **27**, 152 (1964).

3   ——, ibid., **32**, 375 (1969); A. M. Smith, M.-C. Hepp-Reymond, U. R. Wyss, *Exp. Brain Res.*, **23**, 315 (1975); W. T. Thach, *J. Neurophysiol.*, **41**, 654 (1978); B. Conrad, M. Wiesendanger, K. Matsunami, V. B. Brooks, *Exp. Brain Res.*, **29**, 85 (1977); M.-C. Hepp-Reymond, U. R. Wyss, R. Anner, *J. Physiol. (Paris).*, **74**, 287 (1978); P. D. Cheney and E. E. Fetz, *J. Neurophysiol.*, **44**, 773 (1980); E. V. Evarts, C. Fromm, J. Kröller, von A. Jennings, ibid., **49**, 1199 (1983); D. R. Humphrey and D. J. Reed, *Adv. Neurol.*, **39**, 347 (1983); J. H. Martin and C. Ghez, *Exp. Brain Res.*, **57**, 427 (1985); J. F. Kalaska, in *Motor Control: Concepts and Issues*, D. R. Humphrey and H.-J. Freund, eds (Wiley, New York, 1991), pp. 307–30. See also R. Lemon, *Trends Neurosci.*, **11**, 501 (1988); J. F. Kalaska and D. J. Crammond, *Science*, **255**, 1517 (1992).

4   A. P. Georgopoulos, J. F. Kalaska, R. Caminiti, J. T. Massey, *J. Neurosci.*, **2**, 1527 (1982); A. B. Schwartz, R. E. Kettner, A. P. Georgopoulos ibid., **8**, 2913 (1988).

5   A. B. Schwartz, *J. Neurophysiol.*, **68**, 528 (1992).

6   A. P. Georgopoulos, J. Ashe, N. Smyrnis, M. Taira, *Science*, **256**, 1692 (1992).

7   J. F. Kalaska, D. A. D. Cohen, M. L. Hyde, M. Prud'homme, *J. Neurosci.*, **9**, 2080 (1989); R. Caminiti, P. B. Johnson, A. Urbano, ibid., **10**, 2039 (1990); R. Caminiti and P. B. Johnson, *Cereb. Cortex*, **2**, 269 (1992).

8   J. F. Kalaska, R. Caminiti, A. P. Georgopoulos, *Exp. Brain Res.*, **51**, 247 (1983); P. A. Fortier, J. F. Kalaska, A. M. Smith, *J. Neurophysiol.*, **62**, 198 (1989).

9   R. Caminiti et al., *J. Neurosci.*, **11**, 1182 (1991).

10 A. P. Georgopoulos, J. F. Kalaska, R. Caminiti, *Exp. Brain Res. Suppl.*, **10**, 176 (1985).

11 A. P. Georgopoulos, J. F. Kalaska, M. D. Crutcher, R. Caminiti, J. T. Massey, in *Dynamic Aspects of Neocortical Function*, G. M. Edelman, W. E. Gall, W. M. Cowan, eds (Wiley, New York, 1984), pp. 501–24.

12 J. F. Soechting and M. Flanders, *Annu. Rev. Neurosci.*, **15**, 167 (1992).

13 A. P. Georgopoulos, R. Caminiti, J. F. Kalaska, J. T. Massey, *Exp. Brain Res. Suppl.*, **7**, 327 (1983).

14 A. P. Georgopoulos, A. B. Schwartz, R. E. Kettner, *Science*, **233**, 1416 (1986).

15 A. P. Georgopoulos, R. E. Kettner, A. B. Schwartz, *J. Neurosci.*, **8**, 2928 (1988).

16 A. P. Georgopoulos and J. T. Massey, *Exp. Brain Res.*, **69**, 315 (1988).

17 A. P. Georgopoulos, *Atten. Perform.*, **XIII**, 227 (1990).

18 R. E. Kettner, A. B. Schwartz, A. P. Georgopoulos, *J. Neurosci.*, **8**, 2938 (1988).

19 A. B. Schwartz and B. J. Anderson, *Soc. Neurosci. Abstr.*, **15**, 788 (1989).

20 M. A. Steinmetz, B. C. Motter, C. J. Duffy, V. B. Mountcastle, *J. Neurosci.*, **7**, 177 (1987).

21 R. H. Schor, A. D. Miller, D. L. Tomko, *J. Neurophysiol.*, **51**, 136 (1984); V. J. Wilson, K. Ezure, S. J. B. Timerick, ibid., p. 567; I. Suzuki, S. B. J. Timerick, V. J. Wilson, ibid., **54**, 123 (1985); J. B. Maunsell and D. C. Van Essen, ibid., **49**, 1127 (1983).

22 G. M. Murray and B. J. Sessle, ibid., **67**, 775 (1992).

23 A. V. Lukashin, *Biol. Cybern.*, **63**, 377 (1990).

24 M. P. Young and S. Yamane, *Science*, **256**, 1327 (1992).

25 A. P. Georgopoulos, M. D. Crutcher, A. B. Schwartz, *Exp. Brain Res.*, **75**, 183 (1989).

26 N. Smyrnis, M. Taira, J. Ashe, A. P. Georgopoulos, ibid., **92**, 139 (1992).

27 A. P. Georgopoulos and J. T. Massey, ibid., **65**, 361 (1987).

28 R. N. Shepard and J. Metzler, *Science*, **171**, 701 (1971); R. N. Shepard and L. A. Cooper, *Mental Images and their Transformations* (MIT Press, Cambridge, MA, 1982).

29 G. Pellizzer and A. P. Georgopoulos, *Exp. Brain Res.*, in press.

30 A. P. Georgopoulos, J. T. Lurito, M. Petrides, A. B. Schwartz, J. T. Massey, *Science*, **243**, 234 (1989).

31 J. T. Lurito, T. Georgakopoulos, A. P. Georgopoulos, *Exp. Brain Res.*, **87**, 562 (1991).

32 J. J. Freyd, *Psychol. Rev.*, **94**, 427 (1987).

33 V. B. Mountcastle, H. J. Reitboeck, G. F. Poggio, M. A. Steinmetz, *J. Neurosci. Methods.*, **36**, 77 (1991). The implantation of a recording chamber was performed aseptically under general pentobarbital (28 mg per kilogram of body weight) anesthesia.

34 C. E. Osborn and R. E. Poppele, ibid., **24**, 125 (1988). See also D. R. Cox, *Renewal Theory* (Butler & Tanner, Frome, United Kingdom, 1962) and D. R. Cox and P. A. W. Lewis, *The Statistical Analysis of Series of Events* (Chapman & Hall, London, 1966). We estimated the synaptic connection strength w'_{ij} from the ith to the jth neuron by calculating the "difference distribution" between the observed and randomly shuffled distributions of waiting times (mean of 100 shuffles) for a period of 2 to 20 ms. This is essentially the probability distribution, above chance, of the occurrence of a spike in the jth train following a spike in the ith train. The statistical significance of the cumulative sum. (CUSUM) of the differences was then tested [P. Armitage, *Sequential Medical Trials* (Wiley, New York, 1975)], and for significantly different distributions, the peak signed value of the CUSUM was taken as the estimate of the strength of the interaction.

35 S. R. y Cajal, *Histologie du Système Nerveux, Tome II* (Instituto Ramón y Cajal, Madrid, 1955); R. Porter, in *Handbook of Physiology*, Section 1: *The Nervous System*, volume II: *Motor Control*, Part 2, J. M. Brookhart, V. B. Mountcastle, V. B. Brooks, S. R. Geiger, eds (American Physiological Society, Bethesda, MD, 1981), pp. 1063–81; J. DeFelipe, M. Conley, E. G. Jones, *J. Neurosci.*, **6**, 3749 (1986).

36 C. Stefanis and H. Jasper, *J. Neurophysiol.*, **27**, 828 (1964); ibid., p. 855; V. B. Brooks and H. Asanuma, *Arch. Ital. Biol.*, **103**, 247 (1965); K. Takahasi, K. Kubota, M. Uno, *J. Neurophysiol.*, **30**, 22 (1967); H. Asanuma and I. Rosén, *Exp. Brain Res.*, **16**, 507 (1973); J. H. J. Allum, M.-C. Hepp-Reymond, G. Gysin, *Brain Res.*, **231**, 325 (1982); W. S. Smith and E. E. Fetz, *Soc. Neurosci. Abstr.*, **12**, 256 (1986); H. C. Kwan, J. T. Murphy, Y. C. Wong, *Brain Res.*, **400**, 259 (1987); J. T. Lurito, A. B. Schwartz, M. Petrides, R. E. Kettner, A. P. Georgopoulos, *Soc. Neurosci. Abstr.*, **14**, 342 (1988).

37 D. Y. Tso, C. D. Gilbert, T. N. Wiesel, *J. Neurosci.*, **6**, 1160 (1986).

38 L. N. Eisenman, J. Keifer, J. C. Houk, in *Analysis and Modelling of Neural Systems*, F. Eeckman, ed. (Kluwer Academic, Norwell, MA, 1991), pp. 371–6; Y. Burnod et al., *J. Neurosci.*, **12**, 1435 (1992).

39 Equation 4 is the usual condition for a desired state of the neuronal ensemble $V_i(M)$ to be an attractor of standard dynamical rules used in neural network theory [S. Amari, *IEEE Trans. Syst. Man Cybern.*, **SMC-2**, 643 (1972); T. J. Sejnowski, *Biol. Cybern.*, **22**, 203 (1976); S. Grossberg and M. Cohen, *IEEE Trans. Syst. Man Cybern.*, **SMC-13**, 815 (1983); J. J. Hopfield, *Proc. Natl. Acad. Sci. USA*, **81**, 3088 (1984); A. Atiya and P. Baldi, *Int. J. Neural Syst.*, **1**, 103 (1989)].

40 The cost function (F) was the following:

$$F(w) = (1/NK) \sum_{k}^{K} \sum_{i}^{N} |a_i \cos \theta_{ik}$$

$$-g(\sum_j w_{ij}a_j\cos\theta_{jk})| \tag{5}$$

In routine calculations, the number of neurons N and the number of directions K were varied from 8 to 64. Initially, all w values were assigned randomly ($F \sim 0.5$) on the interval $|w| < d$, where d is the restriction parameter, and then the parameters w were adjusted to reduce the F function down to 10^{-5}. The latter procedure was carried out for $|w| < d$ by means of the simulated annealing algorithm [S. Kirkpatrick, C. D. Gelatt, Jr, M. P. Vecchi, *Science*, **220**, 671 (1983)] with an annealing schedule fitted for the present problem. The cost function above was treated as "energy" of the system. Standard Monte Carlo procedures of changes in the w parameters were used to obtain the Boltzmann distribution over states (that is, sets of the w parameters) for a given "temperature." Generally, if the cooling of the system is slow enough (annealing procedure) the approach guarantees the achievement of the global minimum of the system at zero "temperature": this means that the resulting set of the w parameters provides the global minimum $F(w) = 0$ of the energy function (Eq. 5). We checked additionally that sets of the w parameters ensuring $F < 10^{-5}$ indeed yielded stable attractors when standard dynamical equations (*39*) were used to describe the temporal behavior of the neuronal ensemble. Moreover, we have checked the robustness of the results in respect to different series of random numbers used in the generation of a particular set of preferred directions and during the realization of the simulated annealing procedure (ten trials for each set of N and d values).

41 A. V. Lukashin, M. Taira, A. P. Georgopoulos, unpublished data.

42 K. A. C. Martin, *J. Physiol. (London)*, **440**, 735 (1991).

43 ——, *Q. J. Exp. Physiol.*, **73**, 637 (1988).

44 S. Ogawa, T.-M. Lee, A. S. Nayak, P. Glynn, *Magn. Reson. Med.*, **14**, 68 (1990); S. Ogawa and T.-M. Lee, ibid., **16**, 9 (1990); S. Ogawa, T.-M. Lee, A. R. Kay, D. W. Tank, *Proc. Natl. Acad. Sci. USA*, **87**, 9868 (1990).

45 P. A. Bandettini, E. C. Wong, R. S. Hinks, R. S. Tikofsky, J. S. Hyde, *Magn. Reson. Med.*, **25**, 390 (1992); S.-G. Kim et al., *J. Neurophysiol.*, **69**, 297 (1993).

46 Supported by US Public Health Service grants NS17413 and PSMH48185, Office of Naval Research contract N00014-88-K-0751, and a grant from the Human Frontier Science Program.

Vision for the Control of Movement

Robert H. Wurtz

Our vision is not uniform across the visual field but benefits from the striking foveal specialization that allows analysis of fine detail in the center of the visual field. This specialization is made more effective because we can move our eyes to direct this fine analysis to any part of the visual field. Thus, we have a remarkable coupling of a fine-grained visual detector and a movement controller that directs this detector with great precision. The movement, in turn, is controlled by the demands of visual processing. It is perhaps the most closely coupled sensory–motor system in the human brain and arguably the one that is best understood. It is this visual motor control system and its physiological basis within the brain that I would like to concentrate on in this article.

The eye movement that controls this continual redirection of the center of visual analysis is referred to as a rapid, or saccadic, eye movement, and it has been recognized as a separate type of eye movement at least since the work of Dodge[1] early in this century. Figure 25.1 illustrates these eye movements in the now classic work of the Russian psychologist Yarbus,[2] who had a subject view the picture of the girl from the Volga for 3 minutes and recorded the eye movements of the viewer. The lines in the lower part of figure 25.1 indicate when the eye moves rapidly from one point in the scene to another; the dots indicate when the eye stopped at those points. A large part of the girl's face is viewed, but clearly areas of interest, such as the eyes, occupy a disproportionate number of visual fixations, indicating that eye movements are directed toward aspects of importance. The main point to emphasize in this figure is that our vision can be regarded as falling into two phases: the rapid movement of the eyes from one part of the scene to another and the pauses or periods of fixation that hold the eyes steady at a particular part of the field. It is during these periods of fixation that virtually all our useful vision occurs. If we want to understand this system in the brain, we must explain how the eyes are moved rapidly and how they are held steady.

The systems within the brain controlling this visual oculomotor interaction have been studied during the last 25 years in a number of laboratories throughout the world. This work has been possible because of animal models of the human visual–oculomotor system, particularly the Old World monkey (*Macaca mulatta*). These marvelous primates also have a specialized foveal region in the retina and visual abilities

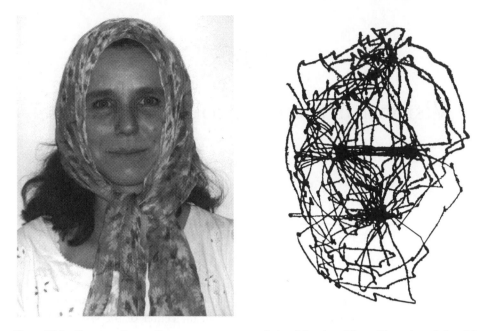

Figure 25.1   Pattern of saccadic eye movements and visual fixation. The subject viewed the girl from the Volga (*top*) for 3 minutes, and the recorded eye movements are indicated below the picture. Lines indicate the saccades that move the eye rapidly from one position to another, and dots indicate periods of visual fixation, when nearly all normal vision occurs. Reproduced with permission from Yarbus, A. L., *Eye Movements and Vision*, New York: Plenum Press (1967): 180.

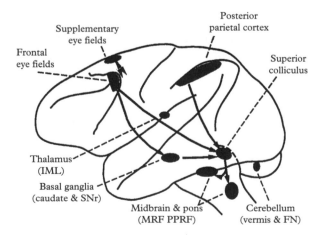

Figure 25.2   Areas of the primate brain related to saccadic eye movements. Areas indicated all have been shown to have single neuron discharge that changes before the onset of saccadic eye movements. Note the prominent location of the superior colliculus lying between the cerebral cortex and the brainstem.

that are very similar to those of humans.[3,4] In addition, their saccadic eye movements are so similar to ours[5] that it would be difficult in most cases to distinguish them. Monkeys' eye movements can be exactly recorded using the magnetic search coil technique,[6-8] and they are readily trained to make saccadic eye movements to examine targets in the visual field for a reward.[5] Single-cell activity can be recorded both while they fixate and when they make saccadic eye movements.[9] Given this ability to study a system in the primate brain while the system is actually in use, a number of laboratories have investigated the areas of the brain in which cells change their discharge in relationship to saccadic eye movements, and figure 25.2 illustrates the salient areas that have been identified. These include areas of parietal cortex, frontal cortex, thalamus, basal ganglia, and cerebellum (see ref. 10 for more detailed descriptions). Although it is clear that this system is distributed throughout much of the forebrain, it is equally clear that many (though not all) of the projections reach the brainstem oculomotor areas through the superior colliculus, a structure on the roof of the midbrain. From the superior colliculus, projections reach the midbrain reticular formation and the paramedian pontine reticular formation, and from there they project to the pontine and midbrain regions that contain the extraocular muscle motor nuclei. Because we know the visual input through the lateral geniculate nucleus to striate cortex (not shown in fig. 25.2) and the projections from striate cortex through extrastriate cortex to the parietal and frontal regions, we know in outline the complete retinal-to-extraocular muscle circuit within the brain.

I will concentrate on the superior colliculus in this extended system within the brain for two reasons. First, as figure 25.2 indicates, the colliculus acts as a funnel through which much of the input from cortex reaches the brainstem, so it is a key structure in the final pathway for the generation of saccades. Second, it is the last structure in this pathway that has a map of the visual field spread across its layers, and I will argue that these maps are critical for understanding the control of saccadic eye movements. I would like to use this chapter to illustrate how neuronal elements within the superior colliculus of the primate brain might be organized to produce this relatively simple visual-motor control system. Although the details and the interpretations will certainly change over time, I think the study of the superior colliculus illustrates general approaches used throughout this field to understand the functional organization of a system within the brain.

I will try to present this work at two levels. For those who are interested in an overall view of the rationale of the experiments and their conclusions, the introduction, the cartoon sections of the figures, and the conclusion should provide this general view. For those interested in the salient observations that support these conclusions, the text and data segments of the figures should fill out the nature of the arguments. For the sake of focus, several aspects of superior colliculus function are omitted altogether.

Neuronal Elements of the Superior Colliculus

The superior colliculus lies on the roof of the midbrain; in the monkey, each side of the brain represents the contralateral visual field and controls saccadic eye movements to that contralateral field. Figure 25.3 shows a schematic section of a frontal or coronal

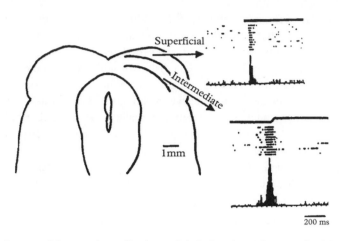

Figure 25.3   Layers of the superior colliculus and their function. The superficial layers have cells that discharge after the onset of visual stimuli in the appropriate region of the visual field. Cells in the intermediate layers increase their discharge before the onset of saccadic eye movements. In the rasters, each dot represents the cell discharge, and successive lines represent either a successive visual target presentation (*top*) or successive eye movements (*bottom*). Below each raster is a histogram showing the discharge summed over trials.

section through the brain showing the colliculus on the roof of the midbrain. The salient point of collicular organization is that it is a layered structure. In the superficial layers, neurons have visual responses to stimuli located in limited parts of the visual field, as indicated in the sample visual response in figure 25.3. A retinotopic map is spread over the collicular surface in the primate, as it is in all other mammals that have been studied. Below these visual cells are cells in the intermediate layers that also give responses to the onset of visual stimuli but that also demonstrate another characteristic: they increase their discharge before the onset of saccadic eye movements. This is illustrated in figure 25.3 by showing the rapid transition of eye position from one point to another, the saccadic eye movement, and the increased activity of the cells that occur in these intermediate layers before the eye movement actually occurs and that first revealed the relation of the colliculus to saccades.[11–16]

Burst neurons

Because of their activity before the onset of saccades, these neurons have been referred to as saccade-related burst neurons[17] or simply burst neurons.[18] Just as cells with visual responses have visual receptive fields, these cells discharging before the saccadic eye movements have what are referred to as movement fields.[13] Figure 25.4A illustrates this concept of a movement field by showing the screen that the monkey faces during experiments and the fixation point at which the monkey looks. In the usual experimental procedure, the fixation point is turned off, and the monkey makes a saccade to a visual target in another part of the field. The particular cell recorded discharges vigorously before saccades to one point in the field, less vigorously to other adjacent points, and not at all to more remote points. Thus, saccades to one part of the field (the movement field) will be preceded by an increase in discharge rates, with a peak

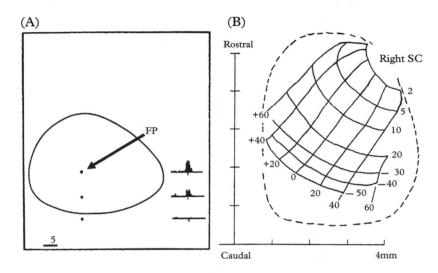

Figure 25.4 (**A**) Schematic drawing of the screen on which the monkey fixates and the fixation point (FP) that goes off as the target (*dot*) comes on. When the monkey makes a saccade to the target, the cell discharge increases if the saccade is to the center of the movement field (*top histogram*), and it increases less before saccades to other targets. (**B**) Schematic map of the intermediate layers of the monkey superior colliculus. The map of the amplitude and direction of saccades was made by electrically stimulating the colliculus. Modified from Robinson, D. A., "Eye movements evoked by collicular stimulation in the alert monkey," *Vision Res.* (1972) 12: 1795–1808.

discharge rate for saccades made close to the center of this movement field and a gradient of declining intensity of discharge at greater distances from the center. Electrical stimulation of these layers of the superior colliculus also evoke saccades, as was first demonstrated in the monkey by Robinson[19] and by Schiller and Stryker.[20] Looking at either the peak discharge of individual cells or the effect of stimulation of the colliculus reveals a map for the amplitude and direction of saccades in the intermediate layers roughly comparable to the map for visual responses in the superficial layers.[13,19] Figure 4B shows such a map derived from the electrical stimulation studies.[19] Stimulation in the rostral colliculus evoked small saccades, stimulation in the caudal colliculus evoked large saccades, stimulation closer to the midline produced upward saccades, and stimulation more lateral generated downward saccades.

Thus, burst neurons in the intermediate layers discharge before the onset of saccades, neurons in different parts of the colliculus discharge in relationship to saccades of different amplitudes and directions, and these neurons are organized into a consistent movement field map. This organization of the burst cells in the intermediate layers of the superior colliculus can be represented by a cartoon such as that in figure 25.5A; the visual field is represented on the surface extending from the fovea (0°) to the periphery (40°), going from rostral to caudal in the colliculus on one side of the brain. This summary also emphasizes that not just one or even a few cells are active before any saccadic eye movement but that a large fraction of the population within the superior colliculus is active.[21,22] The mounds indicate the peak of activity before a saccade – the activity of those cells that discharge for a given amplitude and direction

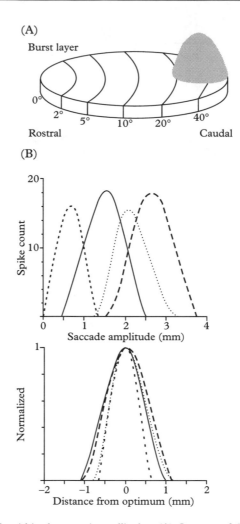

Figure 25.5   Burst cells within the superior colliculus. (**A**) Cartoon of the organization of burst cells within a layer of the superior colliculus. The visual field is represented as a two-dimensional surface extending from rostral to caudal, from the fovea (0°) to the periphery (40°). The mound in the caudal colliculus represents the population of cells that are active before a large saccade. (**B**) Size of the active zone in the burst cell layer estimated by analysis of movement fields of single burst cells. The upper graph shows spline curves through the activity of each cell for a series of saccadic amplitudes. The four representative cells all had closed movement fields. The optimal saccade amplitude for each cell was 2° (*short dashed line*), 5° (*solid line*), 9° (*dotted line*), and 16° (*long dashed line*). Saccade amplitudes have been converted from the degrees of arc measured during the experiment into millimeters along the collicular surface using an equation derived from the map shown in figure 25.4B. This allows a clearer demonstration that once allowance is made for the near logarithmic compression on the collicular map, the size and shape of the movement fields in different parts of the map are similar in shape and extent. In the lower graph, the same curves have been normalized on the peak of each curve, and the curves have been superimposed to show this similarity of shape even though each curve is related to saccades of differing amplitude. In this and subsequent figures, the illustrative samples of data are taken from the references cited in the text.

of saccade. Cells at increasing distances from the peak of the mound still discharge with this given amplitude saccade but with decreasing levels of activity. Recent experiments[23] have shown that the cells active before any given saccade include approximately one-quarter of the neurons in one colliculus. Furthermore, 25% of the cells are active regardless of the size of the saccade, whether the cell is in the caudal colliculus related to large saccades (as in fig. 25.5A) or in the more rostral colliculus related to smaller saccades.

The evidence for this large fraction of activity, and even distribution of the activity for different sizes of saccade, is indicated in figure 25.5B. Each curve shows the activity of a single cell for saccades of different amplitudes (2°, 5°, 9°, and 16°). If we consider the width of the curves in figure 25.5B to be from 25% of the peak value on both the ascending and the descending sides of the peak, we find that these curves span roughly 25% of the rostral-to-caudal extent of the colliculus. The curves are also symmetrical because saccade amplitude in degrees of arc is converted to millimeters across the superior colliculus using equations derived from the map shown in figure 25.4B. It becomes clear that the size of the population activated is the same no matter where that population lies on the collicular map – as originally proposed by McIlwain.[24, 25]

Thus, the superior colliculus represents an exceptionally clear instance of coding within a population of neurons: It is the output of a population of broadly coded neurons that carries the information, not just the output of a few highly specific neurons.

Buildup neurons

That there is a variety of neurons related to the generation of saccadic eye movements in the colliculus has been known since some of the earliest studies on the colliculus.[13–16, 26] Recent experiments have codified the characteristics of one of these neuron types and referred to them as buildup neurons.[18] These neurons are different from the burst neurons though they still have a movement field map, as do the burst neurons. The cartoon in figure 25.6A, therefore, represents them as lying on a separate layer from the layer of burst neurons.

The defining characteristic of the buildup neurons is a continuing discharge between the onset of the target to which the saccade should be directed and the onset of the saccade itself, and this is accompanied by a buildup of activity that precedes the onset of the saccadic eye movement.[18] Figure 6B illustrates these characteristics. Both the burst neuron (fig. 25.6B, top) and the buildup neuron (fig. 25.6B, bottom) have an increased discharge after the onset of the visual target. In this particular paradigm, the target comes on before the fixation point goes off, and the monkey is required to continue fixating until that point goes off. The burst neuron has little activity during this interval, whereas the buildup neuron continues to discharge during this period. When the fixation point is turned off and the saccade occurs, the burst neuron has a clear burst of activity, as do most buildup neurons. The distinguishing feature, however, is the continuing activity during the intervening period.

Another characteristic of the buildup neurons is that as the saccade becomes larger and larger, the cells continue to discharge; the cells have what is referred to as an open-ended movement field. This is in contrast to the burst neurons, which increase their activity as saccade amplitude increases. Beyond a certain amplitude, the discharge

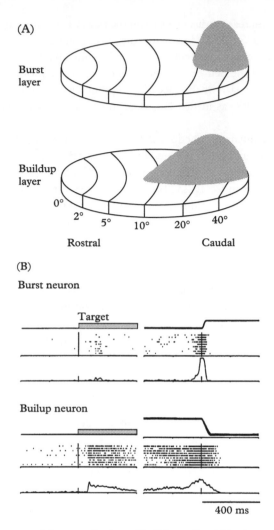

Figure 25.6 (**A**) Cartoon of the organization of buildup cells within the superior colliculus with a map of the field as is the case for burst cells (fig. 25.5A). (**B**) Comparison of the activity of burst and buildup cells. The task required of the monkey was to continue fixating after the target point came on (target) until the fixation point went out. In each panel are the individual rasters, the spike density profiles, and the horizontal eye position traces for 8 to 10 trials. The traces in the left column are aligned on target onset, and the same data are aligned on saccade onset in the right column. Saccade direction and amplitude were selected for the strongest movement-related response. (*Top*) Burst neuron. The discharge shown is for the optimal saccadic amplitude and direction. This cell was classified as a burst cell rather than a buildup cell because there was little activity between the initial visual response and the burst before the saccade. (*Bottom*) Buildup neuron. Discharge for saccades 10° to the right. The activity of the cell continues during the interval between the initial visual response and the increased activity just before the saccade, which is the defining characteristic of the buildup cell.

decreases; they have closed movement fields. In addition, the buildup neurons tend to be encountered more deeply within the intermediate layers of the superior colliculus, although there is some overlap with the burst cells. Because of this tendency for increased depth, the buildup layer is shown in figure 25.6A as lying beneath the burst cell layer.

Fixation neurons

The third and last neuron type to be considered is one referred to as a fixation neuron.[27] Its activity is opposite that of the burst and buildup neurons considered so far. The activity decreases during saccades and increases during active visual fixation. Figure 25.7B shows an example of the activity of such a neuron and compares it with the activity of a burst neuron. The fixation neuron has a high discharge rate during active visual fixation, pauses during the saccade, and resumes its higher discharge rate after the saccade, frequently with a briefly enhanced level of activity. In contrast, the burst neuron is relatively inactive during fixation, bursts before the saccade, and returns to a low level of activity after the saccade. Fixation cells were first identified in the cat

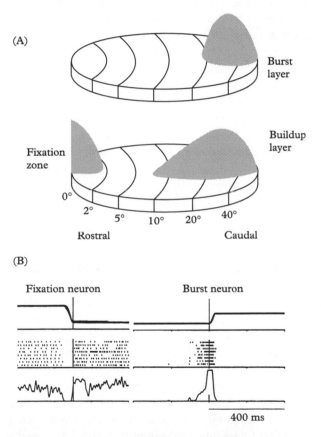

Figure 25.7 (**A**) Cartoon of the location of fixation neurons within the superior colliculus at the rostral end of the buildup layer. (**B**) Comparison of activity of fixation and burst neurons. On the left is an example of the discharge of a fixation cell during active fixation, and on the right is an example of a burst cell for comparison. Rasters and spike density histograms are aligned on the end of the saccade (*left*) or on the beginning of the saccade (*right*) indicated by the horizontal eye traces.

superior colliculus by Munoz and Guitton[28] and were found to lie in the rostral pole of the superior colliculus; in the monkey, fixation cells also have been found to lie at the rostral pole. In the monkey, it has been possible to exclude the possibility that the activity of these cells simply represents a visual response. As the monkey fixates, it directs its fovea toward the fixation spot. The cells that are active are those in the rostral colliculus, whose visual receptive fields fall on the fovea; hence, the higher activity during fixation could simply be a visual response. There are indeed cells in the rostral colliculus of the monkey that give visual responses for just this reason, but the fixation cells continue to discharge when the fixation point is blinked off for a period of several hundred milliseconds (some with a slightly reduced rate and others with a higher rate), indicating that these cells are responding to input other than simply the visual one.[27]

These cells also tend to be found at the same depth in the superior colliculus as the buildup cells and have characteristics that overlap those of the buildup cells.[27,18] There seems to be a transition zone between fixation cells and buildup cells. Cells in this zone pause during all saccades made to targets in the visual field ipsilateral to the collicular cells and to all large saccades to the contralateral visual field, but there is an increase in activity before small saccades made to the contralateral visual field. It is as if the cells in this transition zone have the characteristics of both fixation cells and buildup cells, whose preferred saccadic amplitude is only a few degrees.

These characteristics lead to the placement of the fixation cells in the rostral extent of the buildup cell layer shown as the fixation zone in figure 25.7A. Although this cartoon shows only one superior colliculus, it should be emphasized that fixation cells exist at the rostral poles of the superior colliculus on both sides of the brain and that they are active during all active visual fixations and pause with all saccades, both to the ipsilateral and the contralateral fields, with the exception of the small contralateral saccades mentioned above. Thus, fixation cells change their activity with all saccades, whereas burst and buildup cells change their activity primarily with saccades to one region of the contralateral visual field.

Sequence of Activity in the Colliculus

The sequence of activity of these elements within the superior colliculus is really the critical factor in understanding how the structure contributes to the generation of saccades. This sequence can be shown best by considering what happens over the population of collicular cells during the generation of saccades; figure 25.8 shows this activity across such a sample of neurons. Each graph on the successive lines shows the activity at successive times before, during, and after the generation of a large $50°$ saccade. On each line of the figure are two graphs. On the left is a graph for the burst cells (squares), and on the right is a graph for the fixation and buildup cells (Xs and squares); this distinction follows the separation of the burst cells and the fixation and buildup cells onto separate layers as in figure 25.7A. Each point on these graphs represents the activity of a single cell recorded during a $50°$ saccade. The abscissa shows the anterior–posterior position of the cell determined first by finding the optimal saccadic amplitude to which the cell is related – the center of its movement field – and then by using the collicular map shown in figure 25.4B to place the cell at

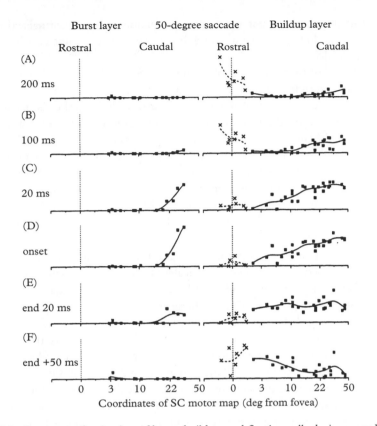

Figure 25.8 Sequence of activation of burst, buildup, and fixation cells during saccade generation. The spatial distribution of activity in burst and buildup cell layers is illustrated for just one amplitude saccade: 50°. Each buildup cell (*right*) and each burst cell (*left*) is represented by a filled square on each of the successive lines that show the magnitude of that cell's response at successive times from 200 msec before saccade onset to saccade onset. Fixation cells are represented by the crosses in the rostral pole of the buildup layer. The position of a cell on the abscissa corresponds to the cell's optimal saccade amplitude converted to mm from the rostral pole using the superior colliculus map shown in figure 25.4B. The zero point on the abscissa corresponds to the fixation zone. Cells lying to the right of the zero point were located in the superior colliculus contralateral to the direction of the saccade. Cells lying to the left of zero were located in the ipsilateral superior colliculus. The solid lines were produced by a spline fitting function through the data points for each group of burst, buildup, and fixation cells. The largest tick marks on the abscissa indicate mm from the rostral pole of the superior colliculus (–1 mm to 4 mm full scale), but, for ease of comparison with saccadic amplitude, the location of 10° and 50° amplitudes are indicated. See text on sequence of activity for description of event sequence.

one particular anterior–posterior position on the collicular map, be it the burst cell or fixation–buildup cell map. The ordinate represents the activity of each cell during the 50° saccade. This activity is normalized with respect to the cell's maximum activity before the optimal saccade amplitude. For example, in this graph of activity during a 50° saccade, a cell whose optimal amplitude is for a 10° saccade will not reach its peak discharge rate but will instead achieve only a fraction of that amplitude. Burst cells are normalized to the peak of their burst activity; buildup cells are normalized of their buildup activity, excluding any burst before the saccade because some cells have such a burst and others do not.

During a period of fixation (represented in fig. 25.8A by the period 200 msec before the onset of the saccade), fixation cells are the only ones active within the superior colliculus. The earliest indication of activity in the saccade-related cells occurs in the buildup cells (fig. 25.8B); there is no change of activity in the burst cells at this early time. Just before the onset of the saccade (fig. 25.8C), there is an increase of activity in these burst cells. At the same time, the activity of the buildup cells has increased, and the activity of the fixation cells has fallen substantially. At this time (20 msec before saccade onset), activity also begins to increase among the buildup cells lying rostral to the initially active buildup cells. At the onset of the saccade, fixation cell activity at the rostral pole has ceased, but both the burst and the buildup cells in the more caudal superior colliculus are maximally active.

Probably the most interesting point of the graph is that the spatial distribution of activity across the two layers differs dramatically as the saccade progresses (fig. 25.8D to 25.8F). Within the burst layer, there is little change in the spatial distribution of activity during the movement. The discharge of cells in the initially active zone diminishes from a peak before saccade onset to near zero at saccade termination; those cells that were not active at the saccade initiation remain inactive throughout the entire saccadic period. In contrast, among the buildup cells that lie rostral to the initially active cells in the caudal colliculus, all increase their discharge rate during the saccade. The peak discharge tended to occur progressively later during the saccade as the cell was located more and more rostrally (fig. 28.8E). By the end of the saccade (fig. 28.8F), the fixation cells in the rostral superior colliculus were once again activated, and the buildup cells showed an increase in activity close to the rostral superior colliculus but a decrease in activity near their initially active site in the caudal colliculus. Looking down the column related to the buildup cells, one sees an increase in activity beginning in the caudal superior colliculus at saccade onset and an increase of this activity rostral in the superior colliculus by the time the saccade ends. The increased activity in the more rostral buildup cell layer, with peak activity at successively later times, led Munoz and Wurtz[23] to interpret this as a spread of activity across the buildup cell layer. The spread of activity always moved rostrally, not caudally: When the activity during a small 2° or 5° saccade was investigated, which would have allowed a spread of activity across the inactive buildup cells more caudal in the colliculus, no such spread of activity was seen. Thus, there appears to be a spread of activity in the buildup cells, and this spread of activity moves rostrally in the colliculus. Such a shift in activity during the saccade was first seen in the cat by Munoz and Guitton,[29,30] but the shift was much more discrete, and they described it as a moving hill of activity rather than the more amorphous spread of activity just described in the monkey superior colliculus.

Hypotheses of Saccade Generation

Once the elements within the colliculus and their sequence of activity are known (at least in outline), the next task is to attempt to understand how the activity of these cells could contribute to the generation of saccadic eye movements. Clearly, only part of

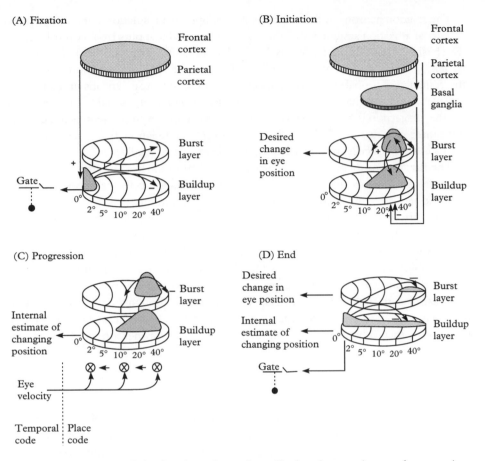

(A) Fixation

Frontal cortex

Parietal cortex

Burst layer

Gate

Buildup layer

0°

2° 5° 10° 20° 40°

(B) Initiation

Frontal cortex

Parietal cortex

Basal ganglia

Desired change in eye position

Burst layer

Buildup layer

0°

2° 5° 10° 20° 40°

(C) Progression

Burst layer

Buildup layer

Internal estimate of changing position

0°

2° 5° 10° 20° 40°

Eye velocity

Temporal code : Place code

(D) End

Desired change in eye position

Burst layer

Buildup layer

Internal estimate of changing position

0°

2° 5° 10° 20° 40°

Gate

Figure 25.9   Cartoons of the function of superior colliculus elements in saccade generation. During fixation (**A**), saccade initiation (**B**), saccade progression (**C**), and saccade end (**D**). See text on hypotheses of saccade generation for details.

the activity related to this generation lies within the superior colliculus, so the task is to relate the collicular events to those of other parts of the visual–oculomotor system to understand saccade generation. Figure 25.9 summarizes the activity during saccade generation in four steps and shows what inputs to the colliculus are assumed to be present, what the key outputs of the colliculus are thought to be, and what is the proposed function for each step.

Fixation

During fixation (fig. 25.9A), the cells most active in the colliculus are the fixation cells in the rostral pole of the buildup layer. Activation of these cells has been shown to suppress the generation of saccades.[31] These cells have been shown to inhibit burst and buildup cells in the caudal colliculus because stimulation of the fixation cells suppresses activity of burst and buildup cells,[32] and, by this suppression, controls when the burst and buildup cells can increase their activity, thereby controlling when saccades occur.

The fixation neurons in the colliculus do not operate in isolation but are thought to be part of a fixation system within the brain, with probable inputs from cortical areas in which similar fixation activity has been observed, including the posterior parietal cortex[33-35] and the frontal cortex.[36-38] The output of these fixation cells from the colliculus is probably a direct projection to the omnipause neurons in the pontine reticular formation that, like the fixation cells, pause with each saccade.[39] The evidence for this projection is first a selective anatomic projection from the rostral colliculus to the omnipause neurons.[40] In addition, antidromic stimulation from the omnipause neurons activates cells in the colliculus, particularly fixation cells.[41, 42]

The function of these fixation neurons, then, is most likely to be that of a gate that determines when saccades can be made. When the fixation cells are maximally active, saccadic activity in the caudal colliculus is suppressed, and saccades do not occur. This gate is different from the gate hypothesized to be a function of the omnipause neurons in the pontine reticular formation that pause at the beginning and end of the saccade.[39] Although the differences in these cells have not been explored throughly at this point, the likely distinction is that the omnipause neurons turn on and off to shape the burst of activity transmitted to the extraocular muscle neurons. In contrast, the fixation cells in the superior colliculus, though possibly contributing critical input to the omnipause neurons, directly control when a saccade can be initiated because of their inhibitory effect on the burst and buildup neurons in the colliculus itself.

Saccade initiation

The earliest change in saccade-related activity in the superior colliculus before a saccade is an increase of buildup cell activity at the site related to the amplitude and direction of the impending saccade (fig. 25.9B), which is coupled with a reduction in fixation activity. It seems clear from this that the selection of one part of the visual field – one part of the girl's face in figure 25.1 – as the target of the next saccade is evident first in the buildup cells. The fall of activity in the fixation cells also can be regarded as underlying the disengagement of the current site of attention, which has been proposed to be necessary for the shift of attention and the shift of gaze.[43] Inputs to the colliculus from cerebral cortex, including frontal eye fields,[44-46] supplementary eye fields,[47] and posterior parietal cortex,[48] as well as from the basal ganglia, particularly the substantia nigra pars reticulata,[49] are likely to contribute to this buildup of activity. Those from the basal ganglia are definitely inhibitory, and the initiation of the saccade would be expressed as a reduction of inhibitory input; input from cortex is presumably excitatory and would be an increase in that activity. These areas are also likely to be involved in the selection of the saccadic target, and the colliculus may be the output pathway for executing this selection. That these inputs are only to the buildup cells as shown in figure 25.9B is not known but is inferred because these cells are the ones showing the earliest change of activity.

There is no direct evidence on the connection between buildup and burst cells, but figure 25.9B shows that burst cells just above the most active buildup cells became active because of the increase in buildup cell activity in the underlying cells. In the model developed by Optican,[50, 51] once a set of burst neurons becomes active, these neurons inhibit other burst neurons so that only one peak of activity is present in the burst cell layer. In addition, this inhibition acts to reduce the activity of the fixation cells, a case of competing reciprocal inhibition. Recent evidence[32] has indicated that stimulation of burst cells does inhibit other burst cells and fixation cells. Thus, at the start of the saccade, the burst cells are maximally active, the buildup cells in the same part of the saccade movement map remain active, and the fixation cell activity has been all but obliterated.

An important output from the colliculus at this stage of activity is that from the burst cells. As indicated in figure 25.9B, this is interpreted as indicating the desired change in eye position – that is, the burst cells convey the desired amplitude and direction of the impending saccadic eye movement.

Saccade progression

In the next stage of saccade generation, the progression of the saccade (fig. 25.9C) activity in the burst layer begins to decline as the saccade progresses and activity in the buildup cell layer spreads more rostrally. This spread of activity varies in duration, depending on the site in the colliculus at which it starts. The spread, therefore, could play a function in providing an internal representation within the brain of how far the saccade has progressed. The larger the saccadic eye movement, the more caudal within the superior colliculus the buildup cells would initially be active, the farther the spread of activity would have to extend, and the longer the duration of that spread of activity. A shorter saccade would have initial activity more rostral in the colliculus, and the activity would have a relatively shorter distance over which to spread, thus producing a short duration appropriate for a short saccade. This interpretation of the spread has been made for the cat[29, 30, 52] and for the monkey.[50, 51]

Figure 25.9C shows a schematic representation of the idea for the monkey developed by Optican,[50, 51] which assumes that the velocity signal conveyed by burst cells in the brainstem is fed back onto all parts of the superior colliculus. The feedback is only effective, however, on those collicular cells that are initially active themselves, that is, the buildup cells that are active for the appropriate amplitude and direction of the current saccade. By a multiplicative interaction, this velocity feedback enables the spread of activity rostrally within the superior colliculus. Optican's interpretation of the output of these buildup cells during the saccade is that these cells then provide an internal estimate of changing eye position or how far the saccade has progressed toward its target. This interpretation of the spread as an indicator of how far the eye has moved has the remarkable feature of converting a velocity signal in temporal coordinates (the higher the discharge rate and the greater the number of spikes, the faster and longer the saccade) into the spatial coordinates of the superior colliculus. This conversion is made by feeding the temporal signal back to all parts of the map within the colliculus; it is the map that maintains the spatial coordinates and allows the conversion from temporal back to spatial. Thus, the output of the buildup cells during saccade generation is taken as a representation of the current eye position. The identification of this internal representation of changing eye position fills a missing niche in the model of saccadic eye movement control and, therefore, is a particularly satisfying aspect of this interpretation. It is, however, certainly the most controversial among the interpretations of the collicular activity shown in figure 25.9.[53]

Note that the same buildup cells provide critical activity in two phases of saccade generation: The buildup cells are active before onset of the saccade as the first indicator of target selection, the buildup cells continue to be active during the saccade, and the spread of activity on the collicular buildup map is potentially useful in determining where the eye is during the saccade.

Saccade end

Figure 25.9D shows the activity at the end of the saccade, which really represents a return to the initial conditions. There is no activity left in the burst cell layer, and the fixation cells have been relieved of the inhibition on them from the burst cells and are again active. The activity of the fixation cells in turn inhibits cells in the burst and buildup cell layers, which returns those cells more closely to the quiescent condition seen before the saccade was initiated.

Incorporating the Superior Colliculus into Saccadic Models

Models of the saccadic system have essentially been designed to solve the problem outlined in figure 25.1: to move the eye to a new target and to hold it there. The most widely accepted model for accomplishing this is the feedback control theory model based on the initial proposal of Robinson[54] outlined in figure 25.10A. When the eye position shifts from one position (E) to a new one (T), the goal of the movement is to reduce the retinal error (e_r) between the current object of interest and the new target. This can be viewed in the model as a summing junction between E and T, and, as long as there is a difference between them, there remains a retinal error. It is this retinal error that drives the saccade. In the brain, this retinal error (after a visual delay) leads to the production of an eye velocity signal that is then integrated to produce a new eye position signal. This cycle continues until the eye position and the target position are the same, the retinal error is zero, and the eye is on target. For a number of reasons, including the strong likelihood that this loop would be too long to produce a stable control system, Robinson[54] hypothesized that there was an internal loop that controlled the generation of the pulse – that is, there was an internal representation of the current eye position during a saccade and that internal representation was compared to the desired eye position in an internal feedback loop. This approach was modified subsequently by Jürgens, Becker, and Kornhuber[55] to monitor not eye position but the change of eye position that would occur with each saccade. All this takes place within the pulse generator, which is expanded in figure 25.10B. Here the desired change in eye position (ΔE) is compared to the output of a displacement integrator that keeps track of the change in eye position during each saccade ($\Delta E'$), and the resultant eye movement error (e_m) produces the pulse. The eye velocity signal is then integrated to produce the new eye position as in figure 25.10A.

The types of colliculus neurons already described might provide the elements demanded by this model of saccade generation. The burst cells generally have been assumed to provide the desired change in eye position because the subset of these cells active before each saccade is related to the direction and amplitude of the impending saccade. The ΔE signal in figure 25.10B is most likely to be conveyed by the burst

(A) Model of saccadic system

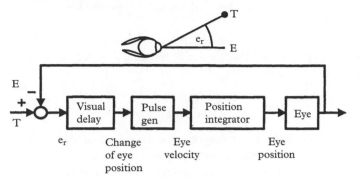

(B) Pulse generator

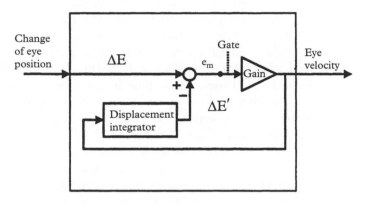

Figure 25.10   Outline of neuronal models of saccade generation that incorporate the superior colliculus. (**A**) The outline of steps for saccade generation in the control theory model of saccade generation. The saccade is controlled by the size of the eye velocity signal from the pulse generator. (**B**) The hypothesized structure of the pulse generator, which compares the desired change in eye position (ΔE) with an internal representation of where the eye currently is located ($\Delta E'$).

neurons. The spread of activity among the buildup cells might convey information about how far the eye has moved during a saccade; therefore, it could act as a displacement integrator – the $\Delta E'$ signal in figure 25.10B. The fixation cells contribute to the occurrence of a saccade by inhibiting within the superior colliculus (not shown in fig. 25.10) and by contributing to the omnipause neurons that gate the occurrence of the saccade indicated in figure 25.10B.

Thus, we can understand the contribution of the elements within the superior colliculus and their sequence of activity in general terms, as in figure 25.9, and more specifically in terms of a model of the saccadic system, as in figure 25.10. Optican and colleagues[50,51] have developed a model that simulates the elements outlined in figure 25.10, using the sequence outlined qualitatively in figure 25.9, that not only produces saccadic output but produces the sequence of activity observed experimentally within the superior colliculus.

Tests of the Collicular Hypotheses

The hypotheses on collicular organization for saccade generation (figs. 25.9, 25.10) make a number of predictions that are readily testable. Two such tests are described for the purposes of illustration.

Spread and saccade trajectory

One hypothesis considered above suggests that the spread of activity during a saccade provides information about the current eye position during a saccade (fig. 25.9C). If this is true, altering the spread of activity should alter the saccade. Because the buildup layer is a two-dimensional map incorporating vertical and horizontal eye position, altering the map should alter both the horizontal and vertical components of the saccade. This should change the trajectory of a saccade. This type of alteration was attempted by injecting the γ-aminobutyric acid (GABA) agonist muscimol to inhibit cells in the superior colliculus,[56] using the logic illustrated in figure 25.11A. It would be ideal to have an injection localized just to buildup cells. Technically, though, this is not feasible because even in the ideal scenario, the cells are too close together, and in actuality there is some variation in depth at which the cells are encountered. To circumvent this problem, the experiment was designed to make an injection of muscimol into the colliculus at a point that would affect the spread of activity in the buildup cell layer but would minimally alter the activity in the burst layer. To do this, an injection was made at a rostral-caudal point in the colliculus, at a point in the buildup layer that would certainly be included in the spread of activity occurring during a saccade, but that would spare burst cells related to larger saccades.

A sample of such an experiment is shown in figure 25.11B in which the injection was made so as to maximally affect saccades at 5° to 10° amplitude, as indicated on the superior colliculus map on the left. Previous work[57] had shown that the injection of muscimol into the superior colliculus disrupts the saccades made to the area of the visual field related to the injection site, and similar disruptions were found for saccades to targets around the 5° to 10° eccentric target location (as in saccades to the 10° targets in fig. 25.11B). For saccades made to more eccentric targets, the saccades reach the target, but the trajectory of the saccade is curved (fig. 25.11B, −20 deg targets). This is evident by comparing the sample saccade taken before the injection (thin line) with the saccade made to the target after the injection (thick line). An interpretation of this observation is that the burst cells for 20° to 30° saccades were largely unaffected, and the information from them about the desired target was left intact. However, the spread of activity across more rostral buildup cells crossed the area of muscimol deactivation, and the spread of activity was disrupted, producing the curved saccade. This aspect of the experiment is predicted by the hypotheses developed and described in relation to figures 25.9 and 25.10 and supports the idea that the superior colliculus is in the feedback loop controlling the amplitude of the saccades. However, these experiments also changed saccades in ways not clearly predicted by the hypotheses. For example, note that the saccades begin their curved trajectory immediately at saccade initiation. One would think, from the spread of activity analysis, that the saccade would start in the right direction and only be deflected as the spread of activity

(A)

GABA Agonist
muscimol

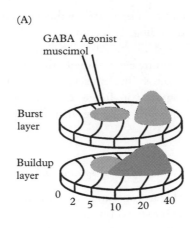

Burst
layer

Buildup
layer

0
2   5   10   20   40

(B)

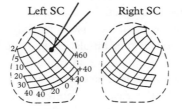

Left SC   Right SC

2
/5
/ 10
/ 20
/ 30
40 40   20   0
+60
+40
+20

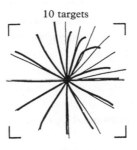

10 targets

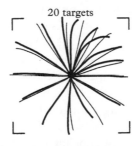

20 targets

Figure 25.11 Alteration of saccades by muscimol injection into the superior colliculus. (**A**) Logic of the experiment. The injection is made at a rostral location that should spare the activity of the burst cells related to larger saccades but should alter the spread of activity accompanying these saccades. (**B**) Effect on eye movements after an injection in the superior colliculus related to 5° to 10° saccades (*left*, SC map). Amplitude of short saccades are altered (5° targets, *middle*), the amplitude of larger saccades (20° targets, *bottom*) is not, but their trajectory is curved.

progressed across the rostral colliculus altered by the muscimol, but this is clearly not the experimentally observed finding. In addition, very large (40° to 50°) saccades after an injection at the 2° area in the rostral colliculus frequently do not always show the disruption of curvature even though the rostral spread of activity of these saccades should pass across the muscimol-deactivated zone. These results indicate that the approach outlined in figure 25.9 cannot be correct in a number of important aspects, but they do illustrate that the approach is experimentally testable.

Fixation control of saccade initiation

A second issue that is amenable to experimental test is the interaction of the fixation neurons on one hand and the burst and buildup neurons on the other hand. Because these cell types are spatially separated within the colliculus, it ought to be possible to alter the fixation cells and see the effect on the generation of saccades. This has been done by increasing and decreasing activity among the fixation cells.[31]

Figure 25.12A shows the logic of increasing the activity of the fixation cells, in this case by electrical stimulation. If the stimulation increased the activity of the fixation cells, the inhibition acting on the burst and buildup cells should increase, making it more difficult to generate a saccade. The experimental results shown in figure 25.12B indicate that this is true. In this case, the monkey normally made saccades (dashed lines) after approximately 180 msec after the target point came on and the fixation point went off. When electrical stimulation was applied to the rostral pole of both colliculi for 500 msec, the onset of the saccade was delayed until the stimulation ceased (solid traces). Once the saccade was generated, however, the velocity seemed to be similar to that of saccades made in the absence of stimulation so that the dynamics of the saccade were minimally affected. The same effect could be produced by the injection of the GABA antagonist, bicuculline, which, by reducing the normally present GABAergic action on the superior colliculus fixation neurons, increased their activity in the same way electrical stimulation did and had the same effect regarding increasing the latency of the saccades.

By injecting the GABA agonist muscimol into the region of the fixation cells, the opposite effect can be produced. The muscimol should increase the inhibition on fixation cells, decrease their activity, decrease the inhibition acting on the burst and buildup cells, and increase the activity of the burst and buildup cells. This should have increased the tendency to make saccadic eye movements, and it did. In these experiments, the monkey was trained to make a saccade to a remembered target; the target was flashed while the monkey fixated, but it was required to withhold the saccade to the remembered location of the target until the fixation point went off. It was rewarded only for those saccades made after the offset of the fixation point. In the normal case, the monkey had no difficulty in with holding the saccade until the fixation point went off, but after injection of muscimol into the fixation zone of one superior colliculus, the monkey made many saccades right after the target was flashed rather than waiting until the fixation point went off.

Thus, in these logically reciprocal experiments, increasing the activity of the fixation cells decreases the likelihood of saccade onset, whereas decreasing the activity of the fixation cells increases the likelihood of saccade onset. This is fully consistent with the

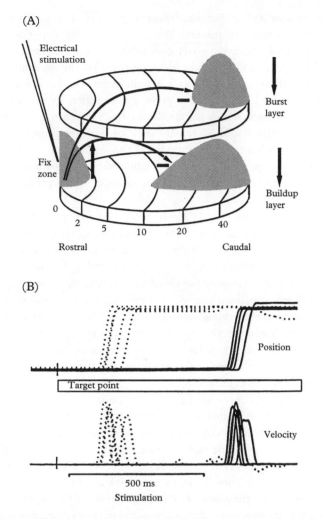

Figure 25.12 Suppression of saccades by activation of the superior colliculus fixation cells. (**A**) Logic of the experiment. Suppression was produced by bilateral stimulation of both fixation zones simultaneously. This should increase their activity and their inhibition on the burst and buildup cells, making it more difficult to activate these cells and, therefore, harder to make saccades. (**B**) Five control trials (*dotted traces*) and five stimulation trials (*solid traces*) are superimposed in each panel as the monkey made visually guided saccades initiated when the fixation point went off and the target point simultaneously came on. The horizontal bar under the eye position traces indicates the time of stimulation. Low-frequency, long-duration stimulation (150 Hz, 500 msec, 30 μA) of both fixation zones prevented the initiation of centrifugal saccades.

role of the fixation cells in controlling when saccades are made, suggested in the collicular organization hypotheses outlined above.

Conclusion

In considering what aspects of eye movements have to be controlled in our normal viewing of the visual scene, it became clear not only that the eyes must move rapidly from one point to another but that there must be periods of steady fixation that allow us to see clearly the objects of interest. We now find in the superior colliculus two systems that accomplish these two goals: cells related to the generation of the saccade (burst and buildup cells) and cells related to suppressing the generation of saccades (fixation cells). For these two behaviorally salient events in our vision, we know the types of neurons involved in the superior colliculus and their sequence of activity, and we have strong hypotheses of how these cells are organized into computational maps to produce these movements. There remain areas of substantial uncertainty about the role of buildup cells within the colliculus, about the inputs to a number of these cell types, and about the outputs from these elements, but the organization of activity in the superior colliculus is certainly the best understood in the primate brain for any sensorimotor system.

This level of understanding also suggests organizational principles that might be relevant beyond the superior colliculus. Preeminent among them is the importance of maps, particularly of the visual field in the case of the superior colliculus. But what the colliculus reveals most clearly is that these maps are critical for the control of movement as well as the representation of the visual field. Each map may serve very different functions: Activity may remain at one locus to provide the same information throughout the movement, or it may spread across a map and provide changing information about the movement. Within these maps, the burst cells illustrate the coarse coding in a population of neurons in which at least one quarter are active before every saccade, with only the location of the peak of activity on the map changing for saccades of different amplitudes and directions.

The goal of this research has been to discover not only *where* in the brain saccades are organized, but *how*. Had we limited our experiments to imaging techniques, we would have learned that the superior colliculus is active in association with saccades. By recording the activity of single neurons in awake monkeys, we were able to begin to decipher the timing of the chain of neural events that break fixation, move the eye, and resume fixation – the very events that allow us to look at a picture of a Russian peasant girl or explore our visual environment. The importance of timing was evident in the first experiments on the superior colliculus, that the neurons discharge *before* a saccade. We now know that activity in the buildup cells is a harbinger of a saccade, that the saccade is almost inevitable when the fixation cells pause and burst cells discharge, and that the saccade ends with the reactivation of the fixation cells. This understanding of the timing of neural events at a resolution of milliseconds has proven essential for proposing a model of how the system actually may work. One cannot help but expect that a similar understanding of timing will illuminate the events by which the cerebral cortex directs the infinitely more complex functions that we call human visual-motor behavior.

References

1   Dodge, R. Five types of eye movement in the horizontal meridian plane of the field of regard. *Am. J. Physiol.* (1903) **8**: 307–29.
2   Yarbus, A. L. *Eye Movements and Vision* (New York: Plenum Press, 1967).

3   De Valois, R. L., Morgan, H. C., Polson, M. C., Mead, W. R., Hull, E. M. Psychophysical studies of monkey vision, I: Macaque luminosity and color vision tests. *Vision Res.* (1974) **14**: 53–67.

4   De Valois, R. L., Morgan, H. Psychophysical studies of monkey vision, III: Spatial luminance contrast sensitivity tests of macaque and human observers. *Vision Res.* (1974) **14**: 75–81.

5   Fuchs, A. F. Saccadic and smooth pursuit eye movements in the monkey. *J. Physiol. (Lond)* (1967) **191**: 609–31.

6   Robinson, D. A. A method of measuring eye movement using a scleral search coil in a magnetic field. *IEEE Trans. Bio. Med. Eng.* (1963) **BME-10**: 137–45.

7   Fuchs, A. F., Robinson, D. A. A method for measuring horizontal and vertical eye movement chronically in the monkey. *J. Appl. Physiol.* (1966) **21**: 1068–70.

8   Judge, S. J., Richmond, B. J., Chu, F. C. Implantation of magnetic search coils for measurement of eye position: An improved method. *Vision Res.* (1980) **20**: 535–8.

9   Wurtz, R. H. Visual receptive fields of striate cortex neurons in awake monkeys. *J. Neurophysiol.* (1969) **32**: 727–42.

10 Wurtz, R. H., Goldberg, M. E. *The Neurobiology of Saccadic Eye Movements*: Reviews of Oculomotor Research, vol. III (Amsterdam: Elsevier, 1989).

11 Wurtz, R. H., Goldberg, M. E. Superior colliculus responses related to eye movement in awake monkeys. *Science* (1971) **171**: 82–4.

12 Schiller, P. H., Koerner, F. Discharge characteristics of single units in superior colliculus of the alert rhesus monkey. *J. Neurophysiol.* (1971) **34**: 920–36.

13 Wurtz, R. H., Goldberg, M. E. Activity of superior colliculus in behaving monkey, III: Cells discharging before eye movements. *J. Neurophysiol.* (1972) **35**: 575–86.

14 Sparks, D. L. Response properties of eye movement-related neurons in the monkey superior colliculus. *Brain Res.* (1975) **90**: 147–52.

15 Mohler, C. W., Wurtz, R. H. Organization of monkey superior colliculus: Intermediate layer cells discharging before eye movements. *J. Neurophysiol.* (1976) **39**: 722–44.

16 Sparks, D. L., Holland, R., Guthrie, B. L. Size and distribution of movement fields in the monkey superior colliculus, *Brain Res.* (1976) **113**: 21–34.

17 Sparks, D. L. Functional properties of neurons in the monkey superior colliculus: Coupling of neuronal activity and saccade onset. *Brain Res.* (1978) **156**: 1–16.

18 Munoz, D. P., Wurtz, R. H. Saccade-related activity in monkey superior colliculus, I: Characteristics of burst and buildup cells. *J. Neurophysiol.* (1995) **73**: 2313–33.

19 Robinson, D. A. Eye movements evoked by collicular stimulation in the alert monkey. *Vision Res.* (1972) **12**: 1795–1808.

20 Schiller, P. H., Stryker, M. Single-unit recording and stimulation in superior colliculus of the alert rhesus monkey. *J. Neurophysiol.* (1972) **35**: 915–24.

21 Lee, C., Rohrer, W. H., Sparks, D. L. Population coding of saccadic eye movements by neurons in the superior colliculus. *Nature*, (1988) **332**: 357–60.

22 Sparks, D. L., Lee, C., Rohrer, W. H. Population coding of the direction, amplitude, and velocity of saccadic eye movements by neurons in the superior colliculus. *Cold Spring Harbor Symp. Quant. Biol.* (1990) **55**: 805–11.

23 Munoz, D. P., Wurtz, R. H. Saccade-related activity in monkey superior colliculus, II: Spread of activity during saccades. *J. Neurophysiol.* (1995) **73**: 2334–48.

24 McIlwain, J. T. Large receptive fields and spatial transformations in visual system. *Int. Rev. Physiol.* (1976) **2**: 223–48.

25 McIlwain, J. T. Distributed spatial coding in the superior colliculus: A review. *Vis. Neurosci.* (1991) **6**: 3–13.

26 Sparks, D. L., Mays, L. E. Movement fields of saccade-related burst neurons in the monkey superior colliculus. *Brain Res.* (1980) **190**: 39–50.

27   Munoz, D. P., Wurtz, R. H. Fixation cells in monkey superior colliculus, I: Characteristics of cell discharge. *J. Neurophysiol.* (1993) **70**: 559–75.

28   Munoz, D. P., Guitton, D. Control of orienting gaze shifts by the tectoreticulospinal system in the head-free cat, II: Sustained discharges during motor preparation and fixation. *J. Neurophysiol.* (1991) **66**: 1624–41.

29   Munoz, D. P., Pélisson, D., Guitton, D. Movement of neural activity on the superior colliculus motor map during gaze shifts. *Science,* (1991) **251**: 1358–60.

30   Munoz, D. P., Guitton, D., Pélisson, D. Control of orienting gaze shifts by the tecto-reticulospinal system in the head-free cat, III: Spatiotemporal characteristics of phasic motor discharges. *J. Neurophysiol.* (1991) **66**: 1642–66.

31   Munoz, D. P., Wurtz, R. H. Fixation cells in monkey superior colliculus, II: Reversible activation and deactivation. *J. Neurophysiol.* (1993) **70**: 576–89.

32   Munoz, D. P., Wurtz, R. H. Interactions between fixation and saccade neurons in primate superior colliculus. *Soc. Neurosci. Abstr.* (1993) **19**: 787.

33   Lynch, J. C., Mountcastle, V. B., Talbot, W. H., Yin, T. C. T. Parietal lobe mechanisms for directed visual attention. *J. Neurophysiol.* (1977) **40**: 362–89.

34   Mountcastle, V. B., Lynch, J. C., Georgopoulos, A., Sakata, H., Acuña, C. Posterior parietal association cortex of the monkey: Command functions for operations within extrapersonal space. *J. Neurophysiol.* (1975) **38**: 871–908.

35   Sakata, H., Shibutani, H., Kawano, K. Spatial properties of visual fixation neurons in posterior parietal association cortex of the monkey. *J. Neurophysiol.* (1980) **43**: 1654–72.

36   Bon, L., Lucchetti, C. The dorsomedial frontal cortex of the macaca monkey: Fixation and saccade-related activity. *Exp. Brain Res.* (1992) **89**: 571–80.

37   Schlag, J., Schlag-Rey, M., Pigarev, I. Supplementary eye field: Influence of eye position on neural signals of fixation. *Exp. Brain Res.* (1992) **90**: 302–6.

38   Suzuki, H., Azuma, M. Prefrontal neuronal activity during gazing at a light spot in the monkey. *Brain Res.* (1977) **126**: 497–508.

39   Keller, E. L. Participation of medial pontine reticular formation in eye movement generation in monkey. *J. Neurophysiol.* (1974) **37**: 316–32.

40   Büttner-Ennever, J. A., Horn, A. K. E. Neuroanatomy of saccadic omnipause neurons in nucleus raphe interpositus. In: Fuchs, A. F., Brandt, T., Büttner, U., Zee, D. S., eds, *Contemporary Ocular Motor and Vestibular Research: A Tribute to David A. Robinson* (Stuttgart: Thieme, 1994): 488–95.

41   Raybourn, M. S., Keller, E. L. Colliculo-reticular organization in primate oculomotor system. *J. Neurophysiol.* (1977) **40**: 861–78.

42   Istvan, P. J., Dorris, M. C., Munoz, D. P. Functional identification of neurons in the monkey superior colliculus projecting to the paramedian pontine reticular formation. *Soc. Neurosci. Abstr.* (1994) **20**: 141.

43   Fischer, B., Weber, H. Express saccades and visual attention. *Behav. Brain Sci.* (1993) **16**: 553–67.

44   Leichnetz, G. R., Spencer, R. F., Hardy, S. G. P., Astruc, J. The prefrontal corticotectal projection in the monkey: An anterograde and retrograde horseradish peroxidase study. *Neuroscience,* (1981) **6**: 1023–41.

45   Segraves, M. A., Goldberg, M. E. Functional properties of corticotectal neurons in the monkey's frontal eye field. *J. Neurophysiol.* (1987) **58**: 1387–1419.

46   Stanton, G. B., Bruce, C. J., Goldberg, M. E. Frontal eye field efferents in the macaque monkey; II: Topography of terminal fields in midbrain and pons. *J. Comp. Neurol.* (1988) **271**: 493–506.

47   Shook, B. L., Schlag-Rey, M., Schlag, J. Primate supplementary eye field, I: Comparative aspects of mesencephalic and pontine connections. *J. Comp. Neurol.* (1990) **301**: 618–42.

48   Lynch, J. C., Graybiel, A. M., Lobeck, L. J. The differential projection of two cytoarchi-
     tectonic subregions of the inferior parietal lobule of macaque upon the deep layers of the
     superior colliculus. *J. Comp. Neurol.* (1985) **235**: 241–54.

49   Hikosaka, O., Wurtz, R. H. Visual and oculomotor functions of monkey substantia nigra
     pars reticulata, IV: Relation of substantia nigra to superior colliculus. *J. Neurophysiol.* (1983)
     49: 1285–1301.

50   Optican, L. M. Control of saccade trajectory by the superior colliculus. In: Fuchs, A. F.,
     Brandt, T., Büttner, U., Zee, D. S., eds, *Contemporary Ocular Motor and Vestibular Research: A
     Tribute to David A. Robinson* (Stuttgart: Thieme, 1994): 98–105.

51   Optican, L. M. A field theory of saccade generation: Temporal-to-spatial transform in the
     superior colliculus. *Vision Res.* (1995) **35**: 3313–20.

52   Lefevre, P., Galiana, H. L. Dynamic feedback to the superior colliculus in a neural network
     model of the gaze control system. *Neural Networks* (1992) **5**: 871–90.

53   Gandhi, N. J., Keller, E. L., Hartz, K. E. Interpreting the role of the collicular buildup
     neurons in saccadic eye movement control. *Soc. Neurosci. Abstr.* (1994) **20**: 141.

54   Robinson, D. A. Oculomotor control signals. In: Lennerstrand, G., Bach-y-Rita, P., eds,
     Basic Mechanisms of Ocular Motility and their Clinical Implications, (Oxford: Pergamon Press,
     1975): 337–74.

55   Jürgens, R., Becker, W., Kornhuber, H. H. Natural and drug-induced variations of velocity
     and duration of human saccadic eye movements: Evidence for a control of the neural pulse
     generator by local feedback. *Biol. Cybern.* (1981) **39**: 87–96.

56   Aizawa, H., Wurtz, R. H. Control of trajectory of saccadic eye movements by monkey
     superior colliculus. *Soc. Neurosci. Abstr.* (1994) **20**: 141.

57   Hikosaka, O., Wurtz, R. H. Modification of saccadic eye movements by GABA-related
     substances, I: Effect of muscimol and bicuculline in monkey superior colliculus. *J. Neuro-
     physiol.* (1985) **53**: 266–91.

Combining versus Gating Motor Programs: Differential Roles for Cerebellum and Basal Ganglia?

W. T. Thach, J. W. Mink, H. P. Goodkin, and J. G. Keating

Introduction

Surely the actions of the cerebellum and of the basal ganglia must be fundamentally different. For over a century it has been known that their lesion in man and in animals impairs behavior in very different ways. In clinical neurology it is axiomatic that lesion of the cerebellum produces deficits usually seen only during movement. This is best appreciated as clumsiness or awkwardness, a lack of fine control or of coordination of movement. Movement always occurs; there is no paralysis or akinesia. Various attempts to parse the disorder into putative components have documented delays in initiation and termination of movement, and irregularity in its direction, velocity and force. There are abnormalities peculiar to body part and/or of task, such as difficulty in leg and trunk during standing and walking, of arm in reaching and pointing, of hand in fine finger movements and object manipulation, and of eye in saccade termination, smooth pursuit, and the vestibulo-ocular reflex. Whether abnormalities in compound (multijoint = synergic), rapid alternating, and sequential movements are simply additives of the above or are uniquely and qualitatively different is a debate that continues to this day. Classically, cerebellar movement disorders are unaccompanied by any abnormality of sensation (except weight discrimination, which requires movement), perception, memory, mood, or intellect.

By contrast, lesion of the basal ganglia produces deficits usually seen during attempts to relax and "rest." One of the deficits is a rigidity of posture due to the maintained co-contraction of agonist and antagonist muscles that may hold the body in distorted bizarre attitudes of excessive flexion or extension (dystonia). The co-contraction may persist through attempts to move, and be associated with slowing of movement (bradykinesia) or even prevention of movement (akinesia). Paradoxically, unwilled and unwanted movement may interrupt attempts to rest, and be of sufficient fluency and coordination as to resemble purposeful movement (chorea = dance; "pill-rolling" tremor). Additional features may include decreased range or size of movements (micrographia = small writing), and the inabilities to suppress repeatedly elicited reflex movements (eye-blink), to follow smoothly with the eyes slowly moving visual targets, or to sustain repetitive or sequential movements. Debate continues as to whether these additional abnormalities are additive expressions of those first mentioned. Also, whether the first one (rigidity, bradykinesia and akinesia) is primary and the others secondary.

However, research over the past decade has tended to blur the distinctions between the basal ganglia and the cerebellum. Roles have been proposed for each as if the two structures were interchangeable. How can this be?

The cerebellum had long been known to project to many elements of the motor system (fig. 26.1). But since its removal was thought to result only in loss of fine control or coordination, it was felt by the majority to be only modulatory, adjusting the gain of (or tuning up) downstream executive centers[1]. Nevertheless, work on the cerebellum has promoted its role beyond that of modulation. First, transients in neural activity recorded in the cerebellar denate nucleus were found to precede activity in motor cortex, which in turn preceded the first EMG activity associated with movement onset. Inactivation of the dentate nucleus delayed onset of activity in motor cortex and of movement. These observations suggested a role for the cerebellum in movement initiation. Second, electroanatomical and anatomical tracing studies in macaques have shown projections from cerebellum to thalamus that in turn project further anterior in the cerebrum than primary motor cortex (area 4). These extend into premotor (area 6),

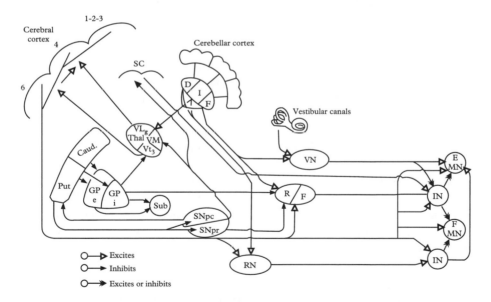

Figure 26.1 Descending pathways to the spinal cord, and their origins in brainstem, cerebellum and cerebrum. Caud., caudate; Put., putamen; GPe, globus pallidus, external segment; GPi, globus pallidus, internal segment; Thal., thalamus; VLc, caudal ventrolateral nucleus; VLo, oral ventrolateral nucleus; VM, ventromedial nucleus; Sub, subthalamic nucleus; D, dentate nucleus; I, interposed nucleus; F, fastigial nucleus; SNpc, substantia nigra pars compacta; SNpr, substantia nigra pars reticulata; RN, red nucleus; RF, reticular formation (e.g., reticular nucleus of the pontine tegmentum); VN, vestibular nuclei; IN, interneuron; E MN, extensor motoneuron; F MN, flexor motoneuron (from [7]).

frontal eye fields (area 8) and possibly even parts of prefrontal cortex (areas 9 and 10). These more rostral projections have suggested control functions in motor programming and even "cognition." PET studies of the human brain have shown increased blood flow in the cerebellum during purely mental tasks such as thinking (without saying) verbs and rhymes[5]. These cerebellar activation studies have been supplemented by deficits in these and other cognitive task performances in patients with cerebellar lesions[6].

By contrast, the output of the basal ganglia was initially thought to project only to the postural control nuclei in the brainstem, parallel to the corticospinal tract (fig. 26.1). Hence, it was easy to endorse the view that the basal ganglia output (extrapyramidal) primarily supported automatic posture and the motor cortex output (pyramidal) controlled voluntary movement. With the discovery that the major part of basal ganglia output is directed via thalamus to motor parts of the cerebral cortex (fig. 26.1), it was appreciated to be *pre*pyramidal as well as extrapyramidal. Thus, it was proposed that the basal ganglia play pivotal roles in "cognitive" activities, motor programming, and movement initiation. A second argument for a role of the basal ganglia in movement initiation hinged on the facts that lesions of GPi resulted in akinesia – the inability to produce voluntary movement. This was abetted by the fact that lesions of striatum and subthalamic nucleus resulted in chorea, athetosis, and hemiballismus – which resembled normal voluntary movement. It was thus easy to imagine that the GPi was a movement generator normally held under control by the striatum. Lesion of the GPi would abolish movements, lesion of the caudate putamen would release movements.

Thus, both the cerebellum and the basal ganglia are proposed to play cardinal roles in the planning, initiation and execution of movement. These contributions would seem to argue for their equivalency. What then *are* the important functional differences between the basal ganglia and cerebellum, and how do they operate together so as to have created the false impression that they "do the same thing"?

Experimental Results

Is the cerebellum a "tuner-upper" of its targets (optimizing their function) or is it a synthesizer of compound movements (from simpler components in downstream generators), or is it both? It is known that cerebellar nuclear cell activity leads most movements: transient changes correlate with movement parameters; maintained levels correlate with different postures [cf. 1]. In contrast, wrist movements so loaded as to require activity only of flexors or extensors engaged no cerebellar unit activity that was correlated with movement parameters – force, position, velocity or direction[8]. In the following experiments, monkeys were trained to produce a variety of movements at the wrist, and were observed as they sat, stood, walked, reached and pinched[1]. Fastigius inactivation by muscimol had no effect on any trained wrist movement; interpositus, only a slight tremor across all movements; and dentate, only a tremor during visuo-manual slow tracking and a slight delay (20–40 ms) on visual-triggered ballistic moves. In contrast to the minor deficits during learned single-joint movements, nuclear inactivation produced dramatic deficits on "natural" multijoint movements. Fastigial inactivation led to inability of the animal to sit, stand or walk without falling to the side of the injection; interposed, a gross action tremor (as much as 30°, 3–5 Hz) in all reaching movements; and dentate, overshoot on reach of as much as 6 cm and an inability to pinch. Independent movement of wrist, thumb and index finger were preserved. We conclude that cerebellar activity co-varies with and controls compound movements and not (directly) simple movements.

Are the basal ganglia responsible for the planning and initiation of movements and postures? A different idea was suggested by the following experiments[2–4]. Monkeys were trained to produce a variety of movements at the wrist. Unit recordings in the globus pallidus pars interna (GPi) (basal ganglia output) showed a late onset that for the most part followed the onset of the EMG. During movement, 70% of cells showed an increase and 30% a decrease in firing. There was no exclusive relation to any class of movement nor to any parameter of movement. Inactivation of the GPi cells by muscimol injection produced co-contraction of agonist and antagonist muscles (rigidity), slowed movement (bradykinesia) without a delay in movement initiation, and produced a preferential disability in *turning off* preloaded muscle vs. *turning on* preloaded muscle. These results suggest that a role of the basal ganglia is not to initiate movement, but rather to turn off mechanisms that hold the wrist in position, allowing initiatory mechanisms to operate unimpeded. The holding mechanisms would include long-loop reflexes through motor cortex, tonic neck and labyrinthine reflexes.

Discussion

Normal functions of the cerebellum and the basal ganglia

Based on cerebellar anatomy, timing of neural discharge and its relation to behavior, and focal ablation syndromes, we have proposed a model of cerebellar function which we believe is both comprehensive as to the available information (at these levels) and unique in several respects[1]. The unique features are the inclusion of new information on: (1) cerebellar output – its replicative representation of body maps in each of the deep nuclei, each coding a different type and context of movement, and each appearing to control movement of multiple body parts more than of single body parts (fig. 26.2); and (2) the newly assessed long length of the parallel fiber. The parallel fiber, by virtue of its connection through Purkinje cells to the deep nuclei, appears optimally designed to combine the actions at several joints (e.g. combining motor cortex representations of individual thumb and forefinger movements into a pinch) and to link the modes of adjacent nuclei (possibly linking a dentate-controlled pinch to an interpositus-brainstem controlled reach) into more complex coordinated acts (fig. 26.3). We have reviewed the old question of whether the cerebellum is responsible for the coordination of body parts as opposed to the tuning of downstream executive centers, and conclude that it is both, through mechanisms that have been described in cerebellar cortex. We have argued that such a mechanism would require an adaptive capacity, and support the evidence and interpretation that it has one. We have pointed out that many parts of the motor system may be involved in different types of motor learning for different purposes, and that the presence of the many does not exclude an existence of the one in cerebellar cortex. The adaptive role of cerebellar cortex would appear to be

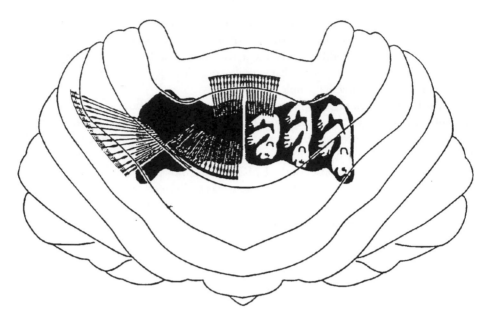

Figure 26.2   Diagram showing linkage into beams of Purkinje cells by parallel fibers. Beams project down onto the somatotopically organized nuclei. Purkinje cell beams thus link body parts together within each nucleus, and link adjacent nuclei together. Such linkage could be the mechanism of the cerebellar role in movement coordination (from [1]).

specialized for combining simpler elements of movement into more complex synergies, and also in enabling simple stereotyped reflex apparatus to respond differently, specifically and appropriately under different task conditions and specific contexts. "Context" would include all aspects of the performance: location, size, shape, orientation, weight and texture of an object to be grasped in space, visual medium and position of head and eyes in foveating the object; weight of the limb, clothing and any impediments or hindrances on it such as gravity, wind, roughness of terrain, etc. The essence of our proposal is that a movement that is unique for the context is synthesized by combining lower motor program elements. The combining is done by a unique subset of parallel fibers that contact many Purkinje cells through synapses which are adjusted through climbing fiber activity (fig. 26.3). This context specificity would take account of the fact that we may learn to hit a baseball with a new bat, but that the adaptation will not affect our performance at tennis with a familiar racket. Similarly, that we may adapt a vestibulo-ocular reflex to each of the different media of air, trifocal spectacles, and underwater, without one of the gains affecting the others. Speed of learning and magnitude of memory for both novel synergies and task-specific performance modifications are other attributes of cerebellar cortex (number of granule cells and their Purkinje cell contacts).

By contrast, the late pallidal discharge and the ablative deficits of co-contraction rigidity, bradykinesia, relative "turn-offs" of postural holds being more impaired than "turn-ons" – all with normal initiation (reaction time) – have all suggested quite a different model for the basal ganglia (fig. 26.4)[2–4]. At rest, the tonic inhibitory output of GPi restrains *all* movement generators of many different types – those for voluntary grasping, reaching, long loop postural holding, tonic neck, contact, righting reflexes,

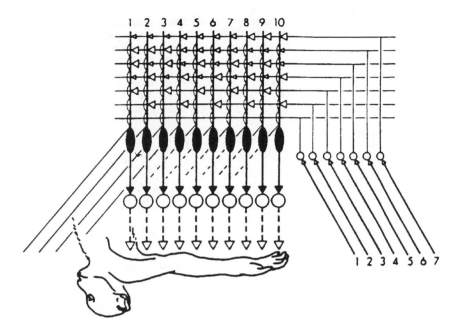

Figure 26.3   Model of granule cell parallel fiber control of muscular coordination.

a. Within each nucleus, there is a use-specific (modal) representation of somatic musculature.

b. The orientation of the myotome is in the coronal plane.

c. The orientation of the parallel fibers is also in the coronal plane.

d. The output of the parallel fiber beam of Purkinje cells falls on the nuclear representation of the myotome.

e. Different uses of the muscles in a limb may be coded by different subsets of parallel fibers and their differential effects on the Purkinje cells (coordination of synergist muscles).

f. Parallel fiber beams that span the nuclei in their Purkinje cell projection may influence two or more nuclei simultaneously (coordination of modes of movement).

g. The effect of a parallel fiber on each and any Purkinje cell in the beam may be individually adjusted by the action of the climbing fiber which is private to each Purkinje cell (from [1]).

and locomotor activity. When one or a combination of these generators is selected to operate the body, several things must happen: 1. The desired generator circuit must be turned *on* – with the help of the cerebellum if the movement is compound. 2. The basal ganglia inhibition of that generator must be turned *off*. 3. The basal ganglion inhibition of competitive generators must be turned *on*. In theory, one might accomplish steps 1–3 all at once, and in many types of motor performance this might be the quickest and most efficient way to achieve movement initiation and execution. In some tasks, however, where a position is held against a load that would tend to displace the member from its position[2,3], the movement must be initiated before the held posture is turned off. We have previously suggested an analogy for holding and moving to braking and accelerating a car parked on a hill. If the brake is removed before the accelerator is applied, the car may roll down the hill. In normal practice, the accelerator is applied and forward motion begun before the brake is removed. In starting up a car on the level and in movements made from a stable postural base, the brake or restraint may be withdrawn before the movement is started with no ill effect.

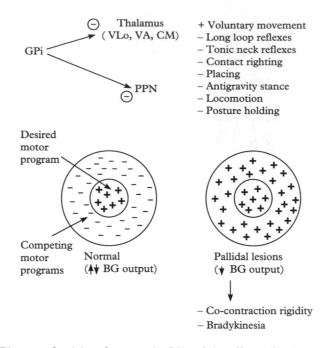

Figure 26.4   Diagram of activity of neurons in GPi and the effects of its increase and decrease on downstream movement generators (see text).

Pathophysiology of cerebellar and basal ganglia disease

These models appear to explain not only some of the necessities of behavior but also some of the deficits of cerebellar and pallidal disease. After fastigial lesion, the inability to sit upright, stand and walk without falling would be due to lack of the proper tuned interfacing of spinal locomotor and brainstem antigravity mechanisms to gravity, terrain, loads, or other pertinent contexts. The tremor after interposed lesions would signify the improper tuning of agonist and antagonist stretch reflexes and possibly instability of uncontrolled brainstem reach mechanisms. The excessive co-contraction would result from the inability to properly combine agonist and antagonist activity (seen only during movement, in contrast to the co-contraction of pallidal ablation). The overreach after dentate lesion would reflect a mismatch of reach (interpositus-brainstem) and grasp (dentate-motor cortex) mechanisms; the lack of pinch, defective combination of motor cortex "simple movements."

As for pallidal lesions, co-contraction rigidity is the final common path mixture of the many active movement and hold generators that cannot be "turned off." The same is true of bradykinesia. Consistent also is the normality of reaction time (motor initiatory mechanisms), and the rarity of "akinesia," where there is no voluntary movement at all. One might object that co-contraction rigidity cannot explain bradykinesia, since they do not co-vary and the one may occur in the relative absence of the other. In response to this argument, the number of competitive motor generators may be large, the competition may exist at a number of model points in the neuraxis, and the mixture may vary considerably depending on the location and extent of the pallidal lesion. Finally, we should point out that the evidence and models which would appear to be directly contradictory to the one proposed here are not necessarily so. The suggestion that the co-contraction rigidity of Parkinson's Disease and MPTP poisoning is caused by a pathologically increased pallidal output would seem to be at variance with the co-contraction rigidity caused by GPi lesions (where it clearly is decreased). Ablation of the STN (assumed to reduce GPi discharge [9]), and even of GPi itself [10], is reported to alleviate MPTP rigidity and bradykinesia, rather than make it worse. These results are not necessarily contradictory with the model we have proposed above. If, in MPTP co-contraction rigidity, the problem is in the dual inabilities to *increase* the surround inhibition and to *decrease* the center inhibition, then focal ablation of GPi (at the center) or of STN (affecting the GPi center) might well remove inhibition from the desired motor program, thereby actually improving movement. But we would predict that if the ablation of GPi (or STN) is large or complete, the co-contraction rigidity and bradykinesia should increase rather than diminish.

Cerebellar–basal ganglia interaction

What then are the differences between the cerebellum and the basal ganglia? Both are proposed to use inhibition to disinhibit/initiate/"turn on" downstream activity as well as to turn it off. Both are proposed to operate within a motor generator/motor program (e.g., acting on arm while sparing leg), and both may operate across motor generators/motor programs (e.g., controlling antigravity, long loop holding reflexes, reach and grasp).

We propose relationships that are diagrammed in fig. 26.5 with regard to movement initiation and control. The cerebellum recognizes a context and links it through learning to a unique combination of motor components residing in downstream motor nuclei. The cerebellum alone has the variety of input information to so fully represent the many possible contexts of movement, the long associational fibers needed to combine the motor elements, the number of cells required to store the context–movement linkages, and the demonstrated learning capacity. It also fires before the basal ganglia.

Once the particular movement generators are engaged by the cerebellum, then their activity triggers the basal ganglia to release them from inhibition and to inhibit competitive motor generators. This function does not require the large cell numbers for the storage of all the many learned combinations of task context – body part synergy.

The movement pattern that the cerebellum selects and initiates is a combination of elements from within the motor generators A and B. These elements are combined in a mix that, through trial and error learning, is optimally tuned to one specific context and goal (e.g., picking a grape from a vine). One can alternatively, and especially in cerebellar disease, trigger elements in motor programs A and B without the cerebellum. The movement elements will occur as primitives, not properly combined (thumb and forefinger occurring singly but not in combination, finger movements uncoupled from reach) and poorly directed to the goal of locating and closing on the desired object with force sufficient to grip, pluck, retrieve and not to squash it. The primitives will be performed without the cerebellum. They will look as though they had lost their fine control and coordination.

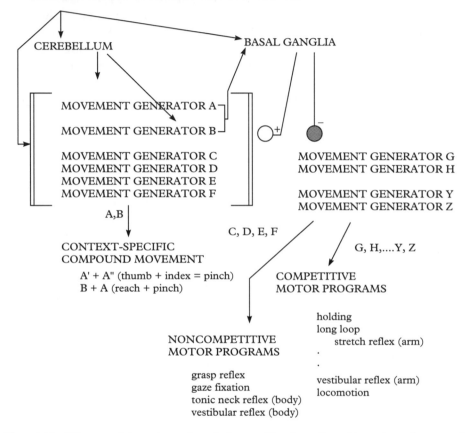

CONTEXT

Intention to move hand to object
Position of head and eyes in foveating the object
Location, size, shape, orientation, weight, and texture of an object to be grasped in space
Visual medium
Weight of the limb, clothing and any impediments or hindrances on it such as gravity, wind, footwear, roughness of terrain, etc.
Feedback from movement generators and from movement

CEREBELLUM   BASAL GANGLIA

MOVEMENT GENERATOR A
MOVEMENT GENERATOR B

MOVEMENT GENERATOR C   MOVEMENT GENERATOR G
MOVEMENT GENERATOR D   MOVEMENT GENERATOR H
MOVEMENT GENERATOR E
MOVEMENT GENERATOR F   MOVEMENT GENERATOR Y
                              MOVEMENT GENERATOR Z
          A,B
                    C, D, E, F
CONTEXT-SPECIFIC   G, H,....Y, Z
COMPOUND MOVEMENT   COMPETITIVE
    A' + A" (thumb + index = pinch)   MOTOR PROGRAMS
    B + A (reach + pinch)

                                      holding
                                      long loop
                                          stretch reflex (arm)
          NONCOMPETITIVE   .
          MOTOR PROGRAMS   .
            grasp reflex   vestibular reflex (arm)
            gaze fixation   locomotion
            tonic neck reflex (body)
            vestibular reflex (body)

Figure 26.5   Diagram of the actions of cerebellum and basal ganglia and how they relate to each other (see text).

We have pointed out elsewhere the fact that the elements or primitives, in motor programs A and B, despite cerebellar disease, may themselves be performed almost or entirely normally. We also point out that this can be and has been used in rehabilitating such patients. The patients can and do use simple single-jointed movements effectively. They may even learn to make them *seriatim* at shoulder and elbow to reach to objects in space (decomposition of movement).

These movements cannot be initiated by GPi simply by removing the tonic inhibition from movement generator A and B. Even though GPi activity is, like cerebellar activity, context initiated, it has neither the breadth and grain of context information nor the selectivity and combining capability, nor especially does it have the linkage of the two together that occurs in the cerebellum. But its inhibitory brake must be removed if the cerebellar-created synergies are to operate unimpeded.

More important, once the GPi is informed that the cerebellum has created a compound movement (from context and from movement generator information), its activity can then inhibit motor generators whose activity is competitive with that selected by the cerebellum (motor generators G–Z). This is necessary to prevent the simultaneous activities of MOVE and HOLD programs (long loop holding, tonic neck, and labyrinthine reflexes' action on the arms) which would otherwise result in bradykinesia or akinesia.

The motor generators (C–F) that are involved in tasks that are not competitive with activities selected and combined by the cerebellum are allowed to operate under their own excitatory drives free from inhibition. Examples would be the grasp reflex, gaze fixation, tonic neck, labyrinthine, spinal activities acting on the trunk, and legs in stance. (This is probably oversimplified: the cerebellum probably compensates for interaction torques upon trunk and legs generated by reaching.)

In summary, we outline here a model in which the functions of the cerebellum and the basal ganglia, though integrated and cooperative, are very different. We point out how these functions are consistent with what is known about the external connections, the intrinsic circuitry, the neural activity and particularly the timing data, and the results of ablation both in animals and in humans. The cerebellum creates a movement through trial and error learning that matches optimally both the situational context and the intended goal. The basal ganglia release this movement from widespread tonic restraint, permit non-competitive posture and movement to proceed, and restrain competitive activity.

References

1   Thach, W. T., Goodkin, H. P., and Keating, J. G. *Ann. Rev. Neurosci.* (1992) **15**: 403–42.
2   Mink, J. W. and Thach, W. T. *J. Neurophysiol.* (1991a) **65**: 273–300.
3   Mink, J. W. and Thach, W. T. *J. Neurophysiol.* (1991b) **65**: 301–29.
4   Mink, J. W. and Thach, W. T. *J. Neurophysiol.* (1991c) **65**: 330–51.
5   Petersen, S. E., Fox, P. T., Posner, M. I., Mitten, M. and Raichle, M. E. *J. Cognitive Neurosci.* (1989) **1**: 153–70.
6   Fiez, J. A., Petersen, S. E., Cheney, M. K., and Raichle, M. E. A single case study. *Brain* (1990) **115**: 758–78.
7   Thach, W. T. and Montgomery, E. B. Motor System. In: Pearlman, A. L. and Collins, R. C. (eds), *Neurobiology of Disease*, New York: Oxford University Press, 1990, p. 170.
8   Schieber, M. H. and Thach, W. T. *J. Neurophysiol.* (1985) **55**: 1228–70.
9   Bergman, H., Wichmann, T. and Delong, M. R. *Science* (1990) **249**: 436–8.
10 Baron, M. S., Wichmann, T. and Delong, M. R. (1992) Inactivation of the sensorimotor territory in the internal pallidum reverses Parkinsonian signs in MPTP-treated monkeys. *Soc. Neurosci. Abstr.* (1992) **18**: 693.

Attention to Action: Willed and Automatic Control of Behavior

Donald A. Norman and Tim Shallice

Much effort has been made to understand the role of attention in perception; much less effort has been placed on the role attention plays in the control of action. Our goal in this chapter is to account for the role of attention in action, both when performance is automatic and when it is under deliberate conscious control. We propose a theoretical framework structured around the notion of a set of active schemas, organized according to the particular action sequences of which they are a part, awaiting the appropriate set of conditions so that they can become selected to control action. The analysis is therefore centered around actions, primarily external actions, but the same principles apply to internal actions – actions that involve only the cognitive processing mechanisms. One major emphasis in the study of attentional processes is the distinction between *controlled* and *automatic* processing of perceptual inputs (e.g., Shiffrin and Schneider, 1977). Our work here can be seen as complementary to the distinction between controlled and automatic processes: we examine action rather than perception; we emphasize the situations in which deliberate, conscious control of activity is desired rather than those that are automatic.

In this chapter we will be particularly concerned with the different ways in which an action is experienced. To start, examine the term *automatic*: it has at least four different meanings. First, it refers to the way that certain tasks can be executed without awareness of their performance (as in walking along a short stretch of flat, safe ground). Second, it refers to the way an action may be initiated without deliberate attention or awareness (as in beginning to drink from a glass when in conversation). Third, it is used in cases such as the orienting response, in which attention is drawn *automatically* to something, with no deliberate control over the direction of attention. And finally, within contemporary cognitive psychology, the term *automatic* is often defined operationally to refer to situations in which a task is performed without interfering with other tasks. In this situation, *automatic* is principally defined to mean that the task is performed without the need for limited processing resources (Shiffrin and Schneider, 1977), although variations on this theme are prevalent (e.g., Kahneman and Treisman, 1983; Posner, 1978).

It is possible to be aware of performing an action without paying active, directed attention to it. The most general situation of this type is in the initiation of routine actions. Phenomenally, this corresponds to the state that Ach (1905) describes as occurring after practice in reaction time tasks. Over the first few trials, he said, the response is preceded by awareness that the action should be made, but later there is no such awareness unless preparation has been inadequate. In such well-learned tasks the subject does experience the response as proceeding with "an awareness of determination," even if it is not immediately preceded by any experience of intention to act. Awareness of determination can, however, be absent. One example comes from the study of slips of action (Norman, 1981; Reason, 1979; Reason and Mycielska, 1982): one may find oneself doing a totally unexpected set of actions, much to one's own dismay.

In contrast to acts undertaken without active, directed attention being paid to them are those carried out under deliberate conscious control. This distinction corresponds closely to Williams James's (1890) distinction between "ideo-motor" and "willed" acts. To James, "wherever movement follows unhesitatingly and immediately the notion of it in the mind, we have ideo-motor action. We are then aware of nothing between the conception and the execution." He contrasted these with acts which require will, where "an additional conscious element in the shape of a fiat, mandate, or expressed consent" is involved.

Experientially, a number of different sorts of tasks appear to require deliberate attentional resources. These tasks fit within the following categories:

1   They involve planning or decision making.
2   They involve components of troubleshooting.
3   They are ill-learned or contain novel sequences of actions.
4   They are judged to be dangerous or technically difficult.
5   They require the overcoming of a strong habitual response or resisting temptation.

The general principle involved is that these are special situations in which the uncontrolled application of an action schema is not desired for fear that it might lead to error.

1   Theory

Our goal is to account for several phenomena in the control of action, including the several varieties of action performance that can be classified as automatic, the fact that action sequences that normally are performed automatically can be carried out under deliberate conscious control when desired, and the way that such deliberate control can be used both to suppress unwanted actions and to enhance wanted ones. In addition, we take note both of the fact that accurate, precise timing is often required for skilled performance and of the fact that it is commonly believed that conscious attention to this aspect of performance can disrupt the action. Finally, in normal life numerous activities often overlap one another, so that preventing conflicts between incompatible actions is required.

These phenomena pose strong constraints upon a theory of action. The theory must account for the ability of some action sequences to run themselves off automatically, without conscious control or attentional resources, yet to be modulated by deliberate conscious control when necessary. Accordingly, we suggest that two complementary processes operate in the selection and control of action. One is sufficient for relatively simple or well learned acts. The other allows for conscious, attentional control to modulate the performance. The basic mechanism, *contention scheduling*, which acts through activation and inhibition of supporting and conflicting schemas, is proposed as the mechanism for avoiding conflicts in performance. Precise timing is handled by means of "triggers" that allow suitably activated schemas to be initiated at the precise time required. The mechanisms for contention scheduling and triggers follow those developed by McClelland and Rumelhart (1981) and Rumelhart and Norman (1982).

Start by considering a simple, self-contained, well-learned action sequence, perhaps the act of typing a word upon the receipt of a signal. This action sequence can be represented by a set of schemas, which when triggered by the arrival of the appropriate perceptual event result in the selection of the proper body, arm, hand, and finger movements. Whenever the action sequence is effected, its representation by means of action schemas constitutes a "horizontal thread." The important point is that the processing structures which underlie a horizontal thread can in principle be well specified. The general nature of the processing structure for a simple action sequence is shown in figure 27.1.

When numerous schemas are activated at the same time, some means must be provided for selection of a particular schema when it is required. At times, however, there will be conflicts among potentially relevant schemas, and so some sort of conflict resolution procedure must be provided. This is a common problem in any information-processing system in which at any one moment several potential candidates for operation might require access to the same resources or might result in incompatible actions. (McDermott and Forgy, 1978, discuss this issue for production systems and Bellman, 1979, discusses the problem with respect to animal behavior.)

The procedure we propose is constrained by the desire to transmit properties by means of the single variable of amount of activation, a concept consistent with current

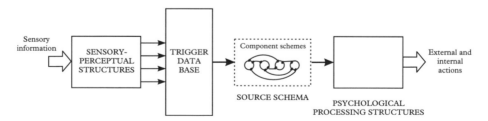

Figure 27.1   A horizontal thread. For well-learned, habitual tasks an autonomous, self-sufficient strand of processing structures and procedures can usually carry out the required activities without the need for conscious or attentional control. Selection of component schemas is determined, in part, by how well the "trigger conditions" of the schema match the contents of the "trigger data base." Such a sequence can often be characterized by a (relatively) linear flow of information among the various psychological processing structures and knowledge schemas involved: a horizontal thread.

psychological theory. We propose that the individual schemas of the horizontal threads each have an activation value that is determined by a combination of factors, some that operate among schemas, some that result from special processes that operate upon the schemas.

A schema is selected once its activation level exceeds a threshold. Once selected, it continues to operate, unless actively switched off, until it has satisfied its goal or completed its operations, or until it is blocked when some resource or information is either lacking or is being utilized by some more highly activated schema. The activation value is important primarily in the selection process and when the selected schema must compete either for shared resources or in providing components schemas with initial activation values.

The scheduling is, therefore, quite simple and direct. No direct attentional control of selection is required (or allowed). Deliberate attention exerts itself indirectly through its effect on activation values. All the action, therefore, takes place in the determination of the activation values of the schemas.

1.1   Contention scheduling

To permit simultaneous action of cooperative acts and prevent simultaneous action of conflicting ones is a difficult job, for often the details of how the particular actions are performed determine whether they conflict with one another. We propose that the scheduling of actions takes place through what we call *contention scheduling*, which resolves competition for selection, preventing competitive use of common or related structures, and negotiating cooperative, shared use of common structures or operations when that is possible. There are two basic principles of the contention scheduling mechanism: first, the sets of potential source schemas compete with one another in the determination of their activation value; second, the selection takes place on the basis of activation value alone – a schema is selected whenever its activation exceeds the threshold that can be specific to the schema and could become lower with use of the schema.

The competition is effected through lateral activation and inhibition among activated schemas. What degree of lateral inhibition exists between schemas on the model remains an open issue. Schemas which require the use of any common processing structures will clearly need to inhibit each other. Yet the degree of inhibition cannot be determined simply *a priori*. Thus, some aspects of the standard refractory period phenomena can be plausibly attributed to such inhibition between schemas; explanations based upon conflicts in response selection fit the data well (Kahneman, 1973). Unfortunately, it is not always clear how to determine when two tasks use common processing structures. The experimental literature on refractory periods reveals interference between tasks involving the two hands. This suggests that responses involving the two hands may use common processing structures. However, one cannot assume that the two hands inevitably involve a common processing structure, as refractory period effects can disappear if highly compatible tasks are used (Greenwald and Shulman, 1973). On the model, as tasks become better learned, the schemas controlling them could become more specialized in their use of processing structures, reducing potential structural interference and minimizing the need for mutual inhibition among schemas.

1.2   Determination of activation values

We divide activational influences upon a schema into four types: influences from contention scheduling, from the satisfaction of trigger conditions, from the selection of other schemas, and from "vertical thread" influences. Trigger conditions specify under what conditions a schema should be initiated, thus allowing for precise environmental control of performance. How well existing conditions match the trigger specifications determines the amount of activation contributed by this factor.

Selection of one schema can lead to the activation of others. Any given action sequence that has been well learned is represented by an organized set of schemas, with one – the source schema – serving as the highest-order control. The term *source* is chosen to indicate that the other component schemas of an action sequence can be activated through the source. We assume that the initial activation values of component schemas are determined by means of their source schema. For example, when the source schema for a task such as driving an automobile has been selected, all its component schemas become activated, including schemas for such acts as steering, stopping, accelerating, slowing, overtaking, and turning. Each of these component schemas in turn acts as a source schema, activating its own component schemas (braking, changing gear, signalling, and so on).

1.3   The supervisory attentional system

The horizontal thread specifies the organization structure for the desired action sequence. However, a schema may not be available that can achieve control of the desired behavior, especially when the task is novel or complex. In these cases, some additional control structure is required. We propose that an additional system, the Supervisory Attentional System (SAS), provides one source of control upon the selection of schemas, but it operates entirely through the application of extra activation and inhibition to schemas in order to bias their selection by the contention-scheduling mechanisms. (A planning mechanism which performs an analogous function in problem-solving programs has been simulated by various researchers; see, for example, Boden, 1977). The overall system is shown in figure 27.2. Note that the operation of the SAS provides only an indirect means of control of action. *Attention*, which we will associate with outputs from SAS, controls only activation and inhibition values, not selection itself. Moreover, it is control overlaid on the horizontal thread organization. When attentional activation of a schema ceases, the activational value will decay back to the value that other types of activating input would produce.

In addition, we assume that motivational factors supplement the activational influences of the SAS. We take motivation to be a relatively slow-acting system, working primarily to bias the operation of the horizontal thread structures toward the long-term goals of the organism by activating source schemas (and through their selection component schemas).

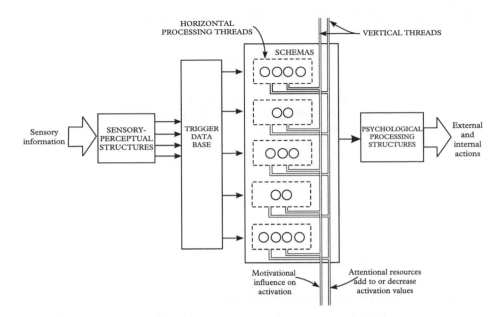

Figure 27.2 The overall system: vertical and horizontal threads. When attention to particular tasks is required, vertical thread activation comes into play. Attention operates upon schemas only through manipulation of activation values, increasing the values for desired schemas, decreasing (inhibiting) the values for undesired ones. Motivational variables are assumed to play a similar role in the control of activation, but working over longer time periods. To emphasize that several tasks are usually active, with the individual components of each task either being simultaneous or overlapping in time, this figure shows five different horizontal threads. Some means of selecting the individual schemas at appropriate times while providing some form of conflict resolution becomes necessary. The interactions among the various horizontal threads needed for this purpose are indicated by the lines that interconnect schemas from different threads.

2 Evidence

That horizontal thread control of action may be viewed within a schema framework is too well known to need reviewing here (see, e.g., Pew, 1974; Schmidt, 1975). There are four major aspects of the model that require assessment:

1 Actions under deliberate conscious control involve a specific mechanism in addition to those used in automatic actions.
2 Attentional processes can modulate the selection process only by adding activation or inhibition. Attention to action is neither sufficient nor necessary to cause the selection of an action sequence.
3 Attentional processes are primarily relevant to the initiation of actions, not for their execution.
4 Selection between competing action sequences takes place through the mechanism of contention scheduling.

Now let us examine the evidence for these aspects of the model.

2.1   *Evidence for a distinct supervisory attentional system: neuropsychological findings*

A major feature of our model is that for well-learned action sequences two levels of control are possible: deliberate conscious control and automatic contention scheduling of the horizontal threads. Possibly the strongest evidence for the existence of both levels comes from neuropsychology. The functions we assume for the supervisory attentional control – those that require "deliberate attention" – correspond closely with those ascribed by Luria (1966) to prefrontal regions of the brain, thought by Luria to be required for the programming, regulation, and verification of activity. In this view, if the Supervisory Attentional System were damaged, the resulting behavior should be similar to that exhibited by patients with prefrontal lesions.

On the model, well-learned cognitive skills and cognitive procedures do not require the higher-level control system. Higher-level control becomes necessary only if error correction and planning have to be performed, if the situation is novel, or temptation must be overcome. It is well known in clinical neuropsychology that lesions confined to prefrontal structures leave the execution of basic skills such as the use of objects, speaking, and writing unaffected (see Walsh, 1978, for review). "Well able to work along old routine lines" is a classical characterization of such patients (Goldstein, quoted by Rylander, 1939). Quantitatively it has, for instance, been shown by McFie (1960) that performance of WAIS subtests is relatively unaffected by lesions to the frontal lobes. The model does predict impairments in the performance of tasks that require error correction or planning, or are in some basic way novel – just the constellation of deficits that are observed clinically in the so-called frontal syndrome (see Walsh, 1978).

Evidence for the contrast in performance in the two types of situations can be obtained from case studies of patients with frontal lobe lesions. A classic study was that carried out by Lhermitte, Derouesne, and Signoret (1972). Their two principal patients could perform certain Verbal and Performance WAIS subtests at normal level (Derouesne, personal communication). These were tasks which required the use of well-learned skills in routine fashion. Thus digit span, which uses maintenance rehearsal schemas, was well performed. When much novel programming of the external and internal action sequence was required, performance was extremely poor. Examples were WAIS Block Design or the reproduction of a complex figure – the Figure of Rey. However, performance could be greatly improved by providing a program for the patient; in the case of the Figure of Rey, this involved breaking down the total design into a series of hierarchically organized subcomponents.

Group studies of neurological patients also provide support. It is well established that patients with frontal lobe lesions have difficulties with error correction. The Wisconsin card-sorting test involves multidimensional stimuli and requires the patient to switch from sorting on one dimension to sorting according to another. In this task, frontal patients show a strong tendency to perseverate in sorting on the previously correct dimension, even when they are told they are wrong (Milner, 1964; Nelson, 1976). Planning, too, has been shown to present difficulties for these patients. The simplest example of such a defect is Gadzhiev's finding (see Luria, 1966) that frontal patients presented with a problem tend to miss out the initial assessment of the situation. Shallice and McCarthy (see Shallice, 1982) showed that patients with left frontal lesions are significantly more impaired than those with lesions in other sites in look-ahead puzzles related to the Tower-of-Hanoi; comparison of performance on this task with that on other tasks suggested that it was the planning component of the task that was affected. Novel learning tasks have also been shown to produce specific difficulties for frontal lobe patients. Petrides and Milner (see Milner, 1982) found that both patients with left frontal and those with right frontal lesions were significantly impaired in learning new arbitrary pairings presented one at a time in a random sequence.

Prediction about the effect of an impairment to the Supervisory Attentional System can be approached in another way. On the model, the failure of this single mechanism can give rise to the apparent contradiction between increased perseveration and increased distractability, depending on the pattern of trigger–schema relations. What would be expected if behavior is left under the control of horizontal thread structures plus contention scheduling? If one schema is more strongly activated than the others, it will be difficult to prevent it from controlling behavior. By contrast, when several schemas have similar activation values, one should obtain another clinical characteristic of frontal patients: an instability of attention and heightened distractability (see Rylander, 1939; Walsh, 1978). Both types of results are also observed in animals with prefrontal lesions (see Fuster, 1980, for review).

If the properties of the Supervisory Attentional System seem to correspond fairly well with neuropsychological evidence, does the same apply to the properties of contention scheduling? One possible relation is with mechanisms in the corpus striatum of the basal ganglia, often thought to be involved in the selection of actions (see Denny-Brown and Yangisawa, 1976; Marsden, 1982). The basal ganglia are innervated by one of the major dopamine projections, and dopamine release is in turn facilitated by amphetamine. Robbins and Sahakian (1983) have provided an explanation of the effects of increased doses of amphetamine based on the work of Lyon and Robbins (1975), in terms closely related to ours. The account goes like this: Increased amphetamine results in an increase in the speed with which response sequences are carried out and a decrease in the interval between them. At higher levels "competition for expression via the motor or executive system begins to occur between different sequences with the result that some sequences are aborted and their terminal elements are lost. Eventually, the performance of a complete sequence is drastically attenuated and the stereotype occurs." Robbins and Sahakian argue that increased dopamine release potentiates the activation level of schemas and leads to an increasing number of schemas being activated above threshold. In our terms, if the potentiation becomes too great, the lateral inhibitory control of contention scheduling is broken. Many schemas are selected at the same time, producing a jamming of almost all objects of behavior. Parkinsonism appears to provide a complementary condition.

2.2   *Attentional processes only modulate schema selection*

The motivation for this aspect of the model is that attentional control is probably too slow and unwieldly to provide the high precision of accuracy and timing needed to perform skilled acts. Deliberate conscious control is generally agreed to involve serial processing steps, each step taking on the order of 100 msec or more. Such control would simply be too slow to account for skilled human behavior that requires action sequences to be initiated just when environmental or internal conditions call for them; in some situations they must be accurate to the nearest 20 msec. This is consistent with the general view that deliberate control of skilled performance leads to deterioration of performance. Accordingly, in the model we allow attentional processes only to bias or modulate the operation and selection of schemas. Precise timing is controlled by the fit of stimulus input to that required by the set of trigger conditions for a schema.

Other factors are also involved. Thus, despite one's desire to attend to one set of signals, if the trigger conditions of another are sufficiently well met, the other may be selected in contention scheduling despite the attention directed toward the one: triggering activation can be more powerful than activation from the Supervisory Attentional Mechanisms. A classic example of this difficulty is the Stroop phenomenon. Another set of relevant findings comes from the classical literature on selective attention in which an attempt is made to keep the subject concentrating upon a primary task while other signals are presented. Certain classes of words presented upon a secondary channel can intrude upon or bias primary task performance, such as a word that fits within the context of the primary channel, or that has been conditioned to electric shock, or that has high emotional value. Performance of the other task is impaired when the interrupt occurs (e.g., Treisman, 1960, or in the refractory period paradigm, Helson and Steger, 1962). In terms of our model, these "intrusions" result from data-driven entry of action schemas into the contention-scheduling mechanism, and their selection there is due to the strongly activating properties of such triggers.

Further evidence that attention serves a biasing or modulating role comes from a study by McLean and Shulman (1978) that examined the role of attention on the speed of performance in a letter-matching task. Once a subject's attention had been directed toward a particular expectation, performance remained biased toward that expectation even after the subjects had been told that the expectation was no longer valid. The bias decayed slowly, lasting for around one second, thereby acting more like the decay of activation from a memory structure than of an attentional selection that could be quickly added or taken away. Although the emphasis in this experiment was on perception rather than action, their conclusion that attention acts by means of an activation level on memory units (schemas, in our vocabulary) is support for this aspect of the model.

Possibly the strongest evidence that conscious attentional control is not necessary for the initiation or execution of action sequences comes from the study of slips of action (Norman, 1981; Reason and Mycielska, 1982). In the class of errors known as "capture errors," the person appears to perform the action without either conscious control or knowledge. Capture errors are easily illustrated by an example: one of Reason's subjects described how, when passing through his back porch on the way to get his car out, he stopped to put on his Wellington boots and gardening jacket as if to work in the garden.

Consider what would happen on the model if a routine task is being carried out that does not require continuous monitoring and activation from the Supervisory Attentional System. Its component schemas can be selected using contention scheduling alone, so the Supervisory Attentional System could be directed toward activating some other noncompeting schema (i.e., "thinking about something else"), and the component schemas in the routine action would still be satisfactorily selected by contention scheduling alone. Occasionally, though, a schema that controls an incorrect action could become more strongly activated in contention scheduling than the correct schema, and capture the effector systems. The supervisory system, being directed elsewhere, would not immediately monitor this, and a capture error would result.

Findings from the diary study of Reason (1983) provide support for an interpretation of this type of error in terms of the model. The data show that people typically rate themselves as being "preoccupied" and "distracted" in the situations wherein lapses occur. This would correspond in our model to the case in which no activation is being received for the "appropriate" schema from the supervisory system: instead, the supervisory system is activating a different, noncompeting schema. In Reason's data, both captured and capturing actions are rated as occurring "very often" and being "automatic." Moreover, the captured and capturing actions were rated as having very similar stimulus characteristics. These characteristics are all consistent with the model: frequently performed action sequences are apt to have developed sufficient horizontal thread structure that they could be carried out by contention scheduling alone – "automatically." The similarity of the captured and capturing actions is consistent with the suggestion that some data-driven activation of the capturing schema might take place and that trigger conditions appropriate for one sequence are likely to be appropriate for the other as well. All these factors maximize the chance of an incorrect schema's being more activated in contention scheduling than the correct one, thus leading to a capture error.

2.3   *Attentional resources are primarily relevant for action selection*

One theme of the model is that attentional resources are relevant only at the specific points in an action where schema selection is required. Thus, control of a hand movement in response to a signal will usually require attentional resources twice: once to initiate the schemas that start the motion, once to initiate the schemas that control termination of the motion (see Keele, 1973). This fits with the results of probe studies during movement where responses to probes at the start or end of the movement can be more delayed than those during execution (Posner and Keele, 1969). (The interpretation of probe studies is not straightforward – see McLeod, 1980 – but U-shaped functions of the type obtained by Posner and Keele seem unlikely to arise artifactually.) When a simple movement is made to an external stop, the response time to a probe during the movement appears to be no greater than if no movement is being made (Posner and Keele, 1969; Ells, 1973). This suggests that when hand motion can be stopped by an external device the movement can be stopped without initiating an action sequence and without attentional control.

2.4   *Competition between tasks*

On the model, the degree to which two tasks will interfere with each other depends upon a number of factors. These include structural factors critical for the contention scheduling mechanism, the balance of activation and inhibition in that mechanism, and the degree of learning which is relevant mainly for the degree of involvement required of the Supervisory Attentional System.

For most task combinations, precise prediction of the degree of interference depends on too many unknown parameters (see Shallice, McLeod, and Lewis, 1985). One obvious prediction is that "parallel" dual task performance should be most easily possible when one or both of the tasks can be performed without attentional control. This fits the experimental literature on monitoring (see Duncan, 1980, for review). When two response streams have to be initiated, the model makes the standard prediction that parallel performance is more likely if subjects are skilled and well practiced (see Allport, Antonis, and Reynolds, 1972; McLeod, 1977; Spelke, Hirst, and Neisser, 1976). Note that even in these situations performance normally deteriorates somewhat when two tasks are combined, even though there appear to be no obvious grounds for structural or attentional interference. We feel this indicates that even when the individual tasks are well learned, at times there will be a need for schemas that require vertical thread activation for rapid selection. Thus, as Allport (1980) pointed out, in experiments involving piano playing conducted by Allport, Antonis, and Reynolds (1972), the one subject who showed no interference "was also the most competent of our pianists." The other subjects all found some technical challenge in the music such that "moments of emergency occurred" when recovery required some relatively unpracticed applications of keyboard technique and therefore, on our model, attentional resources.

2.5   *Will and deliberate conscious control*

A major goal of our approach has been to produce an explanation for the different types of experience one can have of an action. Consider the types of information the Supervisory Attentional System would require in order to carry out its complex functions. Representations of the past and present states of the environment, of goals and intentions, and of the repertoire of higher-level schemas it could activate would all have to be available. Yet more would be necessary. The system would need to know aspects of the operation of a selected schema or, to be more precise, of those selected schemas which it could potentially activate (source schemas). It would need to know not only which source schemas had been selected but also the action sequences they produced and probably the eliciting triggers as well. Without such information, error correction would be a hopeless task, but it is a key function of the supervisory system.

How an action is experienced is dependent upon what information about it is accessed by the Supervisory Attentional System and upon whether the supervisory system activates source schemas itself and, if so, how strongly. This, therefore, allows a variety of states of awareness of actions to exist.

Consider the different meanings of *automatic* discussed earlier. The first two meanings, which refer to automaticity in the initiation and carrying out of an action, correspond to the selection and operation, respectively, of a schema without the supervisory system's assessing information relevant to it. In contrast are those occasions when a trigger not only activates a schema strongly and directly but also produces an interrupt in the supervisory system itself. This corresponds to the third, very different, meaning of *automatic*, wherein what is automatic is the attention-demanding characteristics of the stimulus. When the supervisory system does access some aspect of the triggering or selection of schema, or where it monitors the action sequence itself while at the same time providing no attentional activation to assist in schema selection, we have a correspondence for James's ideomotor acts. Schema selection is elicited solely by triggers, but information about the process is accessed at the higher level.

What happens when the supervisory system does produce attentional activation to modulate schema selection? We propose that *will* directs action by deliberate conscious control. This definition is consistent both with the popular meaning of the term and with the discussions of will in the earlier psychological literature (e.g., James, 1890; Pillsbury, 1908). Thus, strongly resisting a habitual or tempting action or strongly forcing performance of an action that one is loathe to perform seem to be prototypical examples of the application of will. The former would appear to result from deliberate attentional inhibition of an action schema; the latter, from deliberate activation.

In our view, will varies along a quantitative dimension corresponding to the amount of activation or inhibition required from the supervisory attentional mechanisms. The assumption that this activation values lies on a continuum explains why the distinction between willed and ideomotor actions seems quite clear in considering extreme actions but becomes blurred in considering those that require very little attentional effort. Thus, introspection fails in determining whether will is involved in the voluntary lifting of the arm. But there is no need to make a distinction if this act is simply identified as being near the zero point of the quantitative scale of attentional activation.

The idea that will corresponds to the output of the Supervisory Attentional System has certain other useful consequences. Consider the errors that occur with brief lapses of attention, when there is a failure to sustain will adequately. One type of error results following a decision not to do a step within a habitual sequence of actions. To eliminate the step requires deliberate (willful) inhibition of the relevant schema. If there is a momentary lapse of attention to the deliberate inhibition, the step may get done anyway. Closely related is the error that occurred to one of us, who decided not to take another bite of a delicious but extremely rich dessert; with only a brief lapse of attention, the cake got eaten.

Certain aspects of will require elaboration. In some circumstances an action may seem to require no will at all, yet at other times it will require extreme demands. Thus, getting out of bed in the morning is at times an automatic act and at other times requires great exertion of will. One explanation for this phenomenon is that activation of an action schema by the attentional mechanisms necessarily involves knowledge of consequences. When these are negative, they lead to inhibition of the source schemas, which then must be overcome. In some cases, the self-inhibition can be so intense as to prevent or at least make very difficult the intended act. Thus, inflicting deliberate injury to oneself (as in pricking one's own finger in order to draw blood) is a difficult act for many people.

The elicitation of strong activation from the supervisory attentional mechanism is not necessarily unpleasant. Indeed, many sports and games seem to be attractive because they do necessitate such strong activation. In this case *concentration* is perhaps the more appropriate experiential equivalent rather than *will*. In addition, will is not just a matter of attention to actions. As Roy D'Andrade (personal communication) has pointed out, a willed act demands not only strong attentional activation; it also depends on the existence of a "mandated decision," independent of one's attending – a conscious knowledge that the particular end is to be attained. This mandate, in our view, would be required before the supervisory attentional mechanisms will produce their desired activation output. However, the critical point for the present argument is that the phenomenal distinction between willed and ideomotor acts flows from the separation of the supervisory attentional mechanisms from the systems they oversee. The phenomenology of attention can be understood through a theory of mechanism.

Acknowledgments

We thank members of the Skills group of the Cognitive Science Laboratory at UCSD, especially David Rumelhart, Geoffrey Hinton, Wynne Lee, Jonathan Grudin, and Bernie Baars. We appreciate thoughtful reviews and comments by Roy D'Andrade, Steve Keele, John Long, George Mandler, and Peter McLeod.

Research support to D. A. Norman was provided by the Personnel and Training Research Programs, Office of Naval Research, under contract N00014–79-C-0323. The collaboration was made possible by a grant from the Sloan Foundation to the Program in Cognitive Science at UCSD. Support was also provided by grant MH-15828 from the National Institute of Mental Health to the Center for Human Information Processing.

References

Ach, N. (1905). *Uber die Willenstätigkeit und das Denken*. Gottingen: Vardenhoek.

Allport, D. A. (1980). Attention and performance. In G. L. Claxton (ed.), *New directions in cognitive psychology*. London: Routledge.

Allport, D. A., Antonis, B., & Reynolds, P. (1972). On the division of attention: A disproof of the single channel hypothesis. *Quarterly Journal of Experimental Psychology*, **24**, 225–35.

Bellman, K. (1979). *The conflict behavior of the lizard*, Sceloporus Occidentalis, *and its implication for the organization of motor behavior*. Unpublished doctoral dissertation, University of California, San Diego.

Boden, M. (1977). *Artifical intelligence and natural man*. New York: Basic Books.

Denny-Brown, D., & Yanagisawa, N. (1976). The role of the basal ganglia in the initiation of movement. In M. D. YAHR (ed.), *The basal ganglia*, New York: Raven Press.

Duncan, J. (1980). The locus of interference in perception of simultaneous stimuli. *Psychological Review*, **87**, 272–300.

Ells, J. G. (1973). Analysis of temporal and attentional aspects of movement control. *Journal of Experimental Psychology*, **99**, 10–21.

Fuster, J. M. (1980). *The prefrontal cortex*. New York: Raven Press.

Greenwald, A. G., & Shulman, A. G. (1973). On doing two things at once, II: Elimination of the psychological refractory period. *Journal of Experimental Psychology*, **101**, 70–6.

Helson, H., & Steger, J. A. (1962). On the inhibitory effect of a second stimulus following the primary stimulus to react. *Journal of Experimental Psychology*, **64**, 201–5.

James, W. (1890). *The principles of psychology*. New York: Holt.

Kahneman, D. (1973). *Attention and effort*. Englewood Cliffs, NJ: Prentice-Hall.

Kahneman, D., & Treisman, A. M. (1983). Changing views of attention and automaticity. In R. Parasuraman, R. Davies, & J. Beatty (eds), *Varieties of attention*, New York: Academic Press.

Keele, S. W. (1973). *Attention and human performance*. Pacific Palisades, CA: Goodyear.

Lhermitte, F., Derouesne, J., & Signoret, J.-L. (1972). Analyse neuropsychologique du syndrome frontale. *Revue Neuropsychologique*, **127**, 415–40.

Luria, A. R. (1966). *Higher cortical functions in man.* London: Tavistock.

Lyon, M., & Robbins, T. (1975). The action of central nervous system drugs: A general theory concerning amphetamine effects. In W. B. Essmann & L. Valzelli (eds), *Current developments in psychopharmacology*, vol. 2, New York: Spectrum.

Marsden, C. D. (1982). The mysterious motor function of the basal ganglia. *Neurology*, **32**, 514–39.

McClelland, J. L., & Rumelhart, D. E. (1981). An interactive activation model of context effects in letter perception; Part 1: An account of basic findings. *Psychological Review*, **88**, 375–407.

McDermott, J., & Forgy, C. (1978). Production system conflict resolution strategies. In D. A. Waterman & F. Hayes-Roth (eds), *Pattern-directed inference systems*, New York: Academic Press.

McFie, J. (1960). Psychological testing in clinical neurology. *Journal of Nervous and Mental Diseases*, **131**, 383–93.

McLean, J. P., & Shulman, G. L. (1978). On the construction and maintenance of expectancies. *Quarterly Journal of Experimental Psychology*, **30**, 441–54.

McLeod, P. D. (1977). A dual task response modality effect: Support for multiprocessor models of attention. *Quarterly Journal of Experimental Psychology*, **29**, 651–8.

McLeod, P. D. (1980). What can probe RT tell us about the attentional demands of movement? In G. E. Stelmach & J. Requin (eds), *Tutorials in motor behavior*, Amsterdam: North-Holland.

Milner, B. (1964). Some effects of frontal lobectomy in man. In J. M. Warren & K. Akeri (eds), *The frontal granular cortex and behavior*, New York: McGraw-Hill.

Milner, B. (1982). Some cognitive effects of frontal-lobe lesions in man. *Philosophical Transactions of the Royal Society of London, Series B.*, **298**, 211–26.

Nelson, H. (1976). A modified card sorting test sensitive to frontal lobe defects. *Cortex*, **12**, 313–24.

Norman, D. A. (1981). Categorization of action slips. *Psychological Review*, **88**, 1–15.

Pew, R. W. (1974). Human perceptual motor performance. In B. H. Kantowitz (ed.), *Human information processing: Tutorials in performance and cognition*. Hillsdale, NJ: Erlbaum.

Pillsbury, W. B. (1908). *Attention.* London: Swan Sonnenschein.

Posner, M. I., & Keele, S. W. (1969). Attention demands of movement. In *Proceedings of the 16th International Congress of Applied Psychology*, Amsterdam: Swets and Zeitlinger.

Posner, M. I. (1978). *Chronometric explorations of mind.* Hillsdale, NJ: Erlbaum.

Reason, J. T. (1979). Actions not as planned. In G. Underwood & R. Stevens (eds), *Aspects of consciousness*, London: Academic Press.

Reason, J. T. (1983). Lapses of attention. In R. Parasuraman, R. Davies, & J. Beatty (eds), *Varieties of Attention*, New York: Academic Press.

Reason, J. T., & Mycielska, K. (1982). *Absentminded? The psychology of mental lapses and everyday errors.* Englewood Cliffs, NJ: Prentice-Hall.

Robbins, T. W., & Sahakian, B. (1983). Behavioral effects of psychomotor drugs: Clinical and neuropsychological implications. In I. Creese (ed.), *Stimulants: Neurochemical, behavioral and clinical perspectives*, New York: Raven Press.

Rumelhart, D. E., & Norman, D. A. (1982). Simulating a skilled typist: A study of skilled cognitive-motor performance. *Cognitive Science*, **6**, 1–36.

Rylander, G. (1939). Personality changes after operations on the frontal lobes. *Acta Psychiatrica Neurologica Scandinavica, Supplement no. 30.*

Schmidt, R. A. (1975). A schema theory of discrete motor skill learning. *Psychological Review*, **82**, 225–60.

Shallice, T. (1982). Specific impairments of planning. *Philosophical Transactions of the Royal Society of London, Series B*, **298**, 199–209.

Shallice, T., McLeod, P. D., & Lewis, K. (1985). Isolating cognitive modules with the dual task paradigm: Are speech perception and production separate processes? *Quarterly Journal of Experimental Psychology* (in press).

Shiffrin, R. M., & Schneider, W. (1977). Controlled and automatic human information processing, II: Perceptual learning, automatic attending, and a general theory. *Psychological Review*, **84**, 127–90.

Spelke, E., Hirst, W., & Neisser, U. (1976). Skills of divided attention. *Cognition*, **4**, 205–30.

Treisman, A. M. (1960). Contextual cues in selective listening. *Quarterly Journal of Experimental Psychology*, **12**, 242–8.

Walsh, K. W. (1978). *Neuropsychology: A clinical approach*. Edinburgh: Churchill Livingstone.

Architecture of the Prefrontal Cortex and the Central Executive

Patricia S. Goldman-Rakic

Introduction

The mind/brain discussion is now the subject of cross-disciplinary research, with the result that mental phenomena are becoming recognized by brain researchers and the structure of the nervous system is being increasingly acknowledged by behaviorists and theorists. Nevertheless, scholars and scientists on both sides of the issue remain skeptical of one another's approach, and doubts prevail concerning whether neurobiology, based largely on the study of nonhuman experimental models and tissues, can add insight to cognition and mental processing, and, conversely, whether cognitive sciences can enrich an understanding of brain function. In this chapter I hope to illustrate from recent research on nonhuman primates that (1) a genuine neurobiology of mental representation is possible, and (2) significant contributions concerning the organization of the human thought process can be derived from neurobiology. The work I will describe relies on behavioral analysis as much as on neurobiology.

The Supervisory Attentional System, Central Executive, and Domain-Specific Slave Systems

One of the most powerful and influential ideas in cognitive psychology is Baddeley's working memory model.[1] This tripartite model of cognitive architecture invokes a supervisory controlling system called the Central Executive and two slave systems, the Articulatory Loop and the Visuospatial Scratch Pad or Sketch Pad, specialized for language and spatial material, respectively. The model, reproduced in figure 28.1, recognizes the separation of informational domains for lower-level tasks handled by the "slave" systems, but retains the traditional notion of a general purpose, panmodal processor, the central executive, that manages control and selection processes, similar

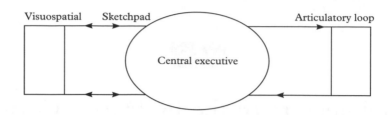

Figure 28.1　Diagrammatic representation of central executive according to Baddeley. Reproduced, with permission, from Baddeley.[1]

to the supervisory attentional system of Shallice.[2] It is interesting that Baddeley acknowledged that a single central controller was not essential to his model. "If the control functions could be carried out by the interaction of the various cognitive subsystems, as suggested by Barnard,[3] we would be happy to accept this" (ref. 1, p. 71). In what follows, I present evidence from experimental studies in nonhuman primates that decomposes the central executive into segregated information processing modules each with its own sensory, mnemonic, and motor control features. This multiple domain model reduces but does not necessarily eliminate "the residual area of ignorance" called the central executive. Our evidence is based mainly on the study of visuospatial working memory in nonhuman primates, and our premise is that understanding this information processing system will serve to explicate general principles applicable to other informational processing domains.

Localization of the Central Executive and the Visuospatial Sketchpad

The localization of the components of the working memory model has puzzled and challenged cognitive psychologists. Baddeley was himself very skeptical that neuroanatomical localization could be helpful to functional analysis and went so far as to comment with reference to the localization of long-term memory systems that "I would...argue that those aspects of the long-term memory deficit that have proved most amenable to interpretation through localization have shown the least theoretical development" (ref. 1, p. 237). Almost 10 years have passed since that statement and perhaps it is now possible to look more favorably on the contributions of cognitive neuroscience. The proposition we will support in this article is that the central executive is associated with a compartmentalized prefrontal architecture and a compartmental organization can explain a number of aspects of cognitive function. I review the findings from studies in monkeys that support the following tenets: (1) that working memory – the basic ability to keep track of and update information at the moment – is the cardinal specialization of the granular prefrontal cortex; (2) that the central executive is composed of multiple segregated special purpose processing domains rather than one central processor served by convergent slave systems; and (3) that each specialized domain consists of local and extrinsic networks with sensory, mnemonic, motor, and motivational control elements.[4] This process-oriented view explains the disorientation, perseveration, and distractability of patients with frontal lobe lesions or dysexecutive syndromes as a default in the working memory system and accounts for dissociations in memory problems. According to this view, the prefrontal cortex has a specialized function that is replicated in many, if not all, of its various cortical subdivisions, and the interactions of these working memory centers with other areas in domain-specified cortical networks constitute the brain's machinery for higher-level cognition. This view is supported by a large experimental, clinical, and neurobiological data base (summarized in Goldman-Rakic[4]).

The Visuospatial Sketchpad

We previously described a cortical area in the rhesus monkey with many if not all characteristics that could qualify as a visuospatial sketchpad. The region in question is area 46, which surrounds and lines the principal sulcus in the prefrontal cortex of the nonhuman primate brain (fig. 28.2). Lesions restricted to this region have been shown repeatedly to impair performance on spatial delayed-response tasks that tax an animal's ability to hold information "in mind" for a short period of time and to update information from moment to moment. It is important to note that the same lesions do not impair performance which relies on associative memory or sensory-guided responses.[4,5] In general, the consistent rules of a task or its sensorimotor requirements do not cause a problem for the prefrontally lesioned animal. The monkey's difficulty

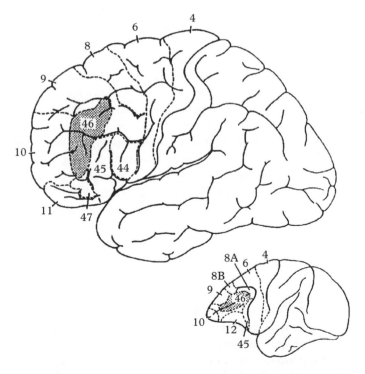

Figure 28.2   Views of the human and monkey brain illustrating the approximate location of area 46. Arabic numerals indicate the location of other cortical areas in the frontal lobe. The diagonal line that runs through area 46 on the monkey brain is the principal sulcus. This is the area associated with spatial working memory.

lies in recalling information and using it to guide a correct response. Thus, on the basis of neuropsychological evidence, I have suggested that the brain obeys the distinction between working and associative memory, and that prefrontal cortex is preeminently involved in the former, whereas other areas – for example, the hippocampal formation and posterior sensory association regions – are critical for associative memory.[4]

Animal models are valuable because the phenomenon of working memory can be pursued at a number of different levels in order to fully comprehend the relevant neural circuit and cellular mechanisms and equally the cell biology of this unique process. Single-neuron recording in nonhuman primates has especially been used extensively to dissect the neuronal elements involved in working memory processes. In the oculomotor delayed-response (ODR) paradigm developed for this purpose, briefly presented visuospatial stimuli are remembered in order to provide guidance *from memory* for subsequent saccadic eye movements. The essential feature of this task is that the item to be recalled (in this case, the location of an object) has to be updated on every trial as in the moment-to-moment process of human mentation. The prefrontal cortex contains classes of neurons engaged respectively in registering the sensory cue, in holding it "on line," and in releasing the motor responses in the course of task performance.[6] These cells with diverse subspecializations are organized in modular or columnar units[7,8] and are thought to have common spatial selectivities.[9] In aggregate, dorsolateral prefrontal cortex contains a local circuit that encompasses the entire range of subfunctions necessary to carry out an integrated response: sensory input, retention in short-term memory, and motor signaling.

A particular focus in our laboratory are the prefrontal neurons that express "memory fields"; that is, the removal of a particular target from view is the trigger for an individual prefrontal neuron to increase its firing maximally and to remain activated until the end of the delay when the response is made (usually a period of 3–5,000 ms). The concept "memory field" is based on the finding that the same neuron appears to always code the same location and different neurons code different locations. In instances where the memory field of a neuron is not maintained throughout the delay and the activity falters, the animal is highly likely to make an error.[10] Thus, a default in the neuronal firing mechanism provides a neural basis for the oft-quoted phrase: "out of sight" is "out of mind." The finding that content-specific neuronal firing is directly associated with accurate recall provides an important example of how a compartmentalized and constrained architecture for memory processing can mirror the anatomical organization of the underlying neural circuitry. These and other results provide strong evidence at a cellular level for the theorized role of prefrontal neurons in working memory, that is, maintenance of representational information in the *absence* of the stimulus that was initially present. Accordingly, it is no wonder that monkeys and humans with prefrontal lesions have little difficulty in moving their eyes to a visible target or reaching for a desired object; their problem is directing these same motor responses to *remembered* targets and objects. At the same time, damage to the prefrontal cortex can and does spare knowledge about the outside world but destroys the ability to bring this knowledge to mind in order to guide behavior.

Working Memory: Storage and Process

It has been emphasized by cognitive theorists that working memory has at least two components – a storage component and a processing component.[1, 11] The question can be raised as to whether working memory is sufficiently developed in nonhuman species and whether it can be studied in them. This question seems easily answered in the affirmative because monkeys are capable of remembering briefly presented information over short temporal delays and repeatedly updating that information as demonstrated by performance on the classical spatial delayed-response tasks (for review see refs. 4 and 12) as well as in the more demanding eight-item oculomotor version of that task,[10] in various match-to-sample paradigms,[13, 14] and in "self-ordering" tasks.[15] It is less easily shown that monkeys can *process* information, that is, transform it mentally. A recent study in my laboratory addressed this issue in part by training monkeys on an anti-saccade task similar to that used by Guitton et al.[16] to study the effects of unilateral frontal cortical damage in humans. The anti-saccade paradigm required the monkeys to suppress the automatic or prepotent tendency to respond in the direction of a remembered cue and instead respond in the opposite direction, a transformation that is not particularly easy for human subjects. The anti-saccade task could be viewed as a member of a class of tasks such as the extremely valuable Stroop test that pits strong response tendencies against opponent responses. As is well known, the Stroop test requires the subject to overcome the prepotent tendency to read a printed word and instead name the discordant color of the ink in which it is printed.

We have recorded from the prefrontal cortex in our trained monkeys to isolate and characterize neuronal activity in the principal sulcus and surrounding cortex in a compound delayed-response paradigm in which, on standard trials, the monkey learned to make deferred eye movements to the same direction signaled by a brief visual cue (standard ODR task); on other trials, it learned to suppress that response and direct its gaze to the opposite direction. The type of trial was cued by a change in the color or size of the fixation point. The monkeys succeeded in learning this difficult task at high (85% and above) levels of accuracy. In itself, their acceptable learning performance indicates that monkeys are capable of holding "in mind" two sequentially presented items of information – the color of the fixation point and the location of a spatial cue – and of transforming the direction of response from left to right (or the reverse) based on a mental synthesis of that information. If "if-then" mental manipulations can be equated with propositional thought, the anti-saccade task may be a way of assaying the thought process in nonhuman species. Further, the task provides an elegant way of dissociating the direction of the cue from the direction of the response to allow us to determine the coding strategy of prefrontal neurons.

A major finding from these studies is that the great majority (approximately 60%) of prefrontal neurons was selectively activated during a silent 3-s period intervening between a particular antecedent stimulus and the prospective response, *regardless* of whether the intended movement was toward or away from the designated target. Figure 28.3 illustrates a neuron that exhibited enhanced activity in the delay-period of the ODR task whenever the visual cue to be remembered was presented on the right

(A) Standard

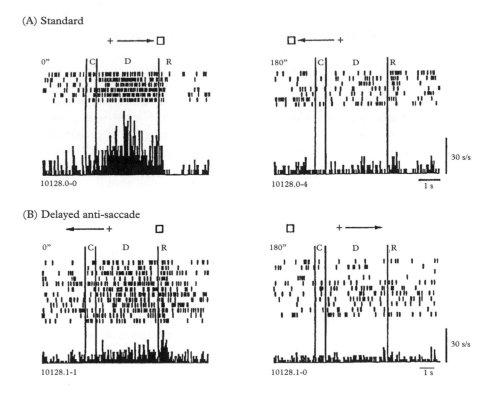

(B) Delayed anti-saccade

Figure 28.3   The neuron shown in the figure was tested during concurrent administration of standard ocular delayed-response (ODR) and anti-saccade ODR trials. (**A**) On ODR trials, the cell's activity was significantly higher during the delay when the target to be recalled was to the right compared to the left. (**B**) This neuron was also activated in the delay period on the anti-saccade trials, even though the target on the right now signaled the animal to respond to the left. Thus, the neuron's activity was not dictated by the direction of responding, but by the direction of the remembered cue. This pattern of activity also indicates that the same neuron is engaged whether the monkey activates or inhibits a motor intention. (Modified from Funahashi et al.).[37]

(Fig. 28.3A, left). For targets presented on the left, by contrast, delay-period activity was not above baseline (Fig. 28.3A, right). On the anti-saccade ODR trials, the neuron was again activated preferentially in the delay period when the visual cue was presented on the right, in spite of the fact that the monkey's response was now directed to the left at the end of the delay. The absence of motor planning activity in this neuron is further demonstrated by the absence of enhanced activity before saccades to the right in the anti-saccade task condition (Fig. 28.3B, right), demonstrating that it was not the rightward saccade in the ODR condition that was driving the unit. This result thus establishes that the same neuron involved in commanding an oculomotor response is also engaged when this response is suppressed and/or redirected. Such findings argue for at least a rudimentary form of propositional thinking on the part of nonhuman primates as well as pointing toward a cellular basis for mental processing in the nonhuman primate prefrontal cortex.

Multiple Working Memory Domains

According to the working memory analysis of prefrontal function, a working memory function should be demonstrable in more than one area of the prefrontal cortex and in more than one knowledge domain. Thus, different areas within prefrontal cortex will share in a common process – working memory; however, each will process different types of information. Thus, informational domain, not process, will be mapped across prefrontal cortex. Evidence on this point has recently been obtained in our laboratory from studies of nonspatial memory systems in prefrontal cortex.[17, 18] In particular, we explored the hypothesis that the inferior convexity of the prefrontal cortex may contain specialized circuits for recalling the attributes of stimuli and holding them in short-term memory – thus processing nonspatial information in a manner analogous to the mechanism by which the principal sulcus mediates memory of visuospatial information. The inferior convexity cortex lying below and adjacent to the principal sulcus is a likely candidate for processing nonspatial – color and form – information. Lesions of this area produce deficits on tasks requiring memory for the color or patterns of stimuli (e.g., refs. 13 and 14), and the receptive fields of the neurons in the posterior portion of this area, unlike those in the dorsolateral cortex above, represent the fovea, the region of the retina specialized for the analysis of fine detail and color – stimulus attributes important for the recognition of objects.[19, 20]

We recorded from the inferior convexity region in monkeys trained to perform delayed-response tasks in which spatial or feature *memoranda* had to be recalled on independent, randomly interwoven trials. For the spatial delayed-response (SDR) trials, stimuli were presented 13° to the left or right of fixation while the monkeys gazed at a fixation point on a video monitor. After a delay of 2500 ms, the fixation point disappeared, instructing the animal to direct its gaze to the location where the stimulus appeared before the delay. For the pattern delayed-response (PDR) trials, various patterns were presented in the center of the screen; one stimulus indicated that a left-directed and the other a right-directed response would be rewarded at the end of the delay. Thus, both spatial and feature trials required exactly the same eye movements at the end of the delay, but differed in the nature of the mnemonic representation that guided those responses.

We found that neurons were responsive to events in both delayed-response tasks. However, a given neuron was generally responsive to the spatial aspects or the feature aspects, but not both. Thus, a large majority of the neurons examined in both tasks were active in the delay period when the monkey was recalling a stimulus pattern that required a 13° response to the right *or* left. The same neurons did not respond above baseline during the delay preceding an identical rightward or leftward response on the PDR trials. Neurons exhibiting selective neuronal activity for patterned memoranda were found almost exclusively in or around area 12 on the inferior convexity of the prefrontal cortex, beneath the principal sulcus, whereas neurons that responded selectively in the SDR were rarely observed in this region. Spatially responsive neurons appear instead in the dorsolateral cortical regions where spatial processing has been localized in our previous studies. In addition, we discovered that the neurons in the inferior convexity were highly responsive to complex stimuli, such as pictures of faces or specific objects. We subsequently used face stimuli as memoranda in a working memory task and demonstrated that such stimuli could indeed serve as memoranda in

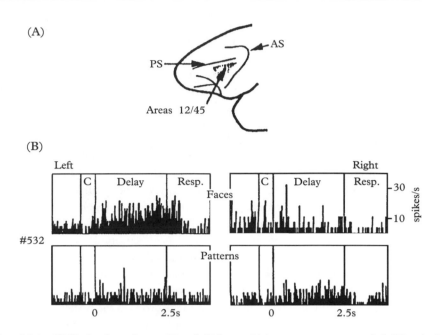

Figure 28.4   (**A**) Brain view of areas 12 and 45 from which neurons were recorded. PS, principal sulcus; AS, arcuate sulcus. (**B**) The neuron illustrated was activated in the delay when the stimulus to be recalled was a particular face (*left panel*), but not for another face (*right panel*). The same neuron was not differentially activated by the recall of patterned cues (*lower panels*). This result illustrates that prefrontal neurons can code selective features of or complex images in working memory. (Modified from Wilson et al.)[18]

memory tasks. Figure 28.4 shows a neuron that encoded a face stimulus in the delay period of our working memory paradigm (Fig. 28.4A). The same cell was unresponsive on trials when the monkey had to remember a different face (Fig. 28.4B) as well as when patterns were used as memoranda (Fig. 28.4C and D). It should be noted that even though the same response is required on trials shown in Figure 28.4A and C, the neuron responds in the delay only in Figure 28.4A. These results provide strong evidence that the neuron in question is encoding information about the identifying features of a stimulus and not about the direction of an impending response. Further-more, different neurons encode different features. Altogether, our results establish that nonspatial aspects of an object or stimulus may be processed separately from those dedicated to the analysis of its spatial location and vice versa. Thus, feature and spatial memory – what and where an object is – are dissociable at both area and single-neuron levels. These findings support the prediction that different prefrontal subdivisions represent different informational domains rather than different processes and that more than one working memory domain exists in prefrontal cortex.

Implication for Human Cognition: Activation Studies Using Positron Emission Tomography

Numerous PET and several fMRI studies of the human brain support the role of the dorsolateral prefrontal cortex as a key site of activation during performance of working memory tasks.[21–28] The application of PET and other promising methods like fast scan magnetic resonance spectroscopy for the study of cognitive activation in human subjects offers an unprecedented opportunity to test hypotheses about cortical organization derived from studies of experimental animals and from human neuropsychology. The prefrontal cortex, in particular, is activated by working memory tasks, and several recent studies have pinpointed areas 9 and 46 as functional sites in the normal performance of spatial working memory processes. McCarthy et al.,[26, 27] Smith et al.,[29] and Sweeney et al.[28] have all examined spatial working memory paradigms that were similar to those that have been employed in studies of spatial working memory in nonhuman primates. Petrides et al.[22] found similar areal activation in a spatial self-ordering task. In these studies of spatial cognition in humans, the functional organization of the cortex bears a remarkable correspondence to that in nonhuman primates.

With respect to nonspatial working memory, the results are less clear. Petrides et al. have recently provided evidence that area 46 was activated in a verbal[23] working memory task. Likewise, Frith et al.[30] have reported that area 46 was activated during tasks calling for the open-ended generation of words or finger movements. As with spatial working memory tasks, these nonspatial tasks had a working memory component in that the information needed to guide correct responses was not present in the immediate environment and had to be recalled and/or generated *de novo* at the time of response. The differentiation between spatial and object memory thus remains an issue.

The clearest dissociations that can so far be discerned in imaging studies appear to be between tasks that involve explicit verbal processing, on the one hand, and explicit spatial or location processing, on the other. Less clear differences have been observed between location versus object memory, as would be expected from the monkey-lesion and neurophysiological literature. At present, the variety of findings with respect to regional localization of spatial and nonspatial working memory tasks raises several possibilities that need to be considered in future research. It is possible that in the human prefrontal cortex, functions that are distributed within a hemisphere of the nonhuman primate have been allocated to different hemispheres in line with the increased hemispheric specialization that appears to be a hallmark of human cortical organization. Many studies report a predominant right hemisphere activation for spatial tasks, and a left hemisphere predominance for verbal paradigms. A second consideration is the strong potential for interactions with verbal mediation in human studies. In spite of efforts to prevent verbal mediation in many studies, spatial as well as nonspatial tasks could have engaged verbal encoding, and, conversely, nonspatial tasks could have engaged spatial processes, depending on how the stimuli are presented. "Functional cross-overs" might explain to some degree the overlap in regional localization that is commonly observed when comparing spatial versus nonspatial processing in prefrontal cortex. Perhaps the most nagging problem in the PET and to a considerable extent the fMRI studies is that of spatial resolution. If an object or feature processing and visuospatial modules were close to one another as they are in the rhesus monkey, and further if they were coactivated during task performance because of problems inherent in task design, it would be difficult to tease them apart.

Where Then is the Central Executive?

Studies in nonhuman primates are beginning to model the basic processes that are central to cognitive operations. The modular parallel organization of memory circuits in the macaque cerebral cortex suggests a neural basis for similarly modular and segregated cognitive processing systems demonstrable in humans behaviorally, and by neuropsychological deficits following relatively circumscribed injuries, and by non-invasive imaging of the brain during cognitive processing.

It is important to underscore that although the domains of information processing are modular and parallel, the process carried out within these systems is complex, integrative, and temporally regulated. An outstanding feature of the memory cells of the prefrontal cortex is that different groups of cells respond at different time points as the process unfolds within a trial. Assuming conservatism in evolution of cortical structure and function, experimental studies in animals may help to decide controversial issues in cognitive psychology and may also shed light on the phylogenetic origins and neural basis of intelligence. Currently, the comparative analysis of working memory functions across monkeys and humans favors the idea of multiple working memory domains – that is, multiple special purpose systems organized in parallel rather than the concept of a central panmodal executive processor to account for the diversity and complexity of the human thought process. As suggested in Figure 28.5, these working memory domains have the complexity of neural machinery necessary to accommodate both passive storage functions for specified information and the processing of that very same information. Presumably, the more demand placed on the system, the more neurons within a domain would be recruited to meet that demand within the limits of the particular system. The activation of prefrontal loci would require a sufficient load to be resolved by PET or fMRI. If a task is insufficiently demanding, too few neurons might be activated to be resolved by present imaging modalities. Negative findings in PET and fMRI studies or in neuropsychological investigation should therefore be interpreted cautiously when drawing inferences about localization of function. On the other hand, positive findings must also be regarded with caution if behavioral analysis is insufficient to confirm the strategy employed by versatile human subjects. The same

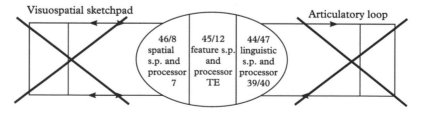

Central executive

Figure 28.5 Provisional neurologically based model of the central executive proposed in this chapter: domain-specific working memory modules can register information, hold it "on line," *and* process it by interacting with the relevant sensory and motor areas with which each is connected. The number of neurons engaged by any given task will depend upon the level or depth of processing.

cautions apply to nonhuman primate research where monkeys can and do at times outwit investigators with respect to behavioral strategies.

It may be argued that the organization of the human brain differs in architecture from the nonhuman primate brain by virtue of its greater cognitive and linguistic capacity, and, accordingly, the human brain may have a cortical center or network that is truly a central processor oblivious to informational domain. If so, imaging studies could in the future reveal the location of this area but thus far they have not. What area would we expect it to be? The architecture of cognitive processing in human and nonhuman primates is a topic of great challenge and one which can only be enriched by collaborative efforts among researchers from neurobiology and psychology and allied fields.

References

1   Baddeley, A. (1986). *Working Memory*, pp. 1–289. Oxford University Press, London.

2   Shallice, T. (1982). Specific impairments in planning. *Phil. Trans. R. Soc. Lond. B.*, **298**: 199–209.

3   Barnard, P. (1985). Interacting cognitive subsystems: A psycholinguistic approach to short-term memory. In *Progress in the Psychology of Language*, vol. 2, A. Ellis, ed.: 197–258, Lawrence Erlbaum, London.

4   Goldman-Rakic, P. S. (1987). Circuitry of primate prefrontal cortex and regulation of behavior by representational memory. In *Handbook of Physiology: The Nervous System, Higher Functions of the Brain*, F. Plum, ed.: 373–417, American Physiological Society, Bethesda, MD.

5   Goldman, P. S. & H. E. Rosvold (1970). Localization of function within the dorsolateral prefrontal cortex of the rhesus monkey. *Exp. Neurol.*, **27**: 291–304.

6   Goldman-Rakic, P. S., S. Funahashi & C. J. Bruce (1990). Neocortical memory circuits. *Q. J. Quant. Biol.*, **55**: 1025–38.

7   Goldman-Rakic, P. S. (1984). Modular organization of prefrontal cortex. *Trends Neurosci.*, **7**: 419–24.

8   Kritzer, M. & P. S. Goldman-Rakic (1995). Intrinsic circuit organization of the major layers and sublayers of the dorsolateral prefrontal cortex in the rhesus monkey. *J. Comp. Neurol.*, **359**: 131–43.

9   Goldman-Rakic, P. S. (1995). Cellular basis of working memory. *Neuron*, **14**: 477–85.

10   Funahashi, S., C. J. Bruce & P. S. Goldman-Rakic (1989). Mnemonic coding of visual space in the monkey's dorsolateral prefrontal cortex. *J. Neurophysiol.*, **61**: 331–49.

11   Just, M. A. & P. A. Carpenter (1985). Cognitive coordinate systems: Accounts of mental rotation and individual differences in spatial ability. *Psychol. Rev.*, **92**: 137–72.

12   Fuster, J. M. (1989). *The Prefrontal Cortex*, 2nd edn, pp. 1–255. Raven Press, New York.

13   Passingham, R. E. (1975). Delayed matching after selective prefrontal lesions in monkeys (*Macaca mulatta*). *Brain Res.*, **92**: 89–102.

14   Mishkin, M. & F. J. Manning. (1978). Non-spatial memory after selective prefrontal lesions in monkeys. *Brain Res.*, **143**: 313–23.

15   Petrides, M. (1991). Functional specialization within the dorsolateral frontal cortex for serial order memory. *Proc. R. Soc. Lond. B*, **246**: 293–8.

16   Guitton, D., H. A. Buchtel & R. M. Douglas (1985). Frontal lobe lesions in man cause difficulties in suppressing reflexive glances and in generating goal-directed saccades. *Exp. Brain Res.*, **58**: 455–72.

17   O Scalaidhe, S. P., F. A. W. Wilson & P. S. Goldman-Rakic (1992). Neurons in the prefrontal cortex of the macaque selective for faces. *Soc. Neurosci. Abstr.*, **18**: 705.

18 Wilson, F. A. W., S. P. O. Scalaidhe & P. S. Goldman-Rakic (1993). Dissociation of object and spatial processing domains in primate prefrontal cortex. *Science*, **260**: 1955–8.

19 Mikami, A., S. Ito & K. Kubota (1982). Visual response properties of dorsolateral prefrontal neurons during a visual fixation task. *J. Neurophysiol.*, **47**: 593–605.

20 Suzuki, H. & M. Azuma (1983). Topographic studies on visual neurons in the dorsolateral prefrontal cortex of the monkey. *Exp. Brain Res.*, **53**: 47–58.

21 Jonides, J., E. E. Smith, R. A. Koeppe, E. Awh, S. Minoshima & M. A. Mintun (1993). Spatial working memory in humans as revealed by PET. *Nature*, **363**: 623–5.

22 Petrides, M., B. Alivisatos, A. C. Evans & E. Meyer (1993a). Dissociation of human mid-dorsolateral from posterior dorsolateral frontal cortex in memory processing. *Proc. Natl. Acad. Sci. USA*, **90**: 873–7.

23 Petrides, M., B. Alivisatos, E. Meyer & A. C. Evans (1993b). Functional activation of the human frontal cortex during the performance of verbal working memory tasks. *Proc. Natl. Acad. Sci. USA*, **90**: 878–82.

24 Cohen, J. D., S. D. Forman, T. S. Braver, B. J. Casey, D. Servan-Schreiber & D. C. Noll (1994). Activation of prefrontal cortex in a non-spatial working memory task with functional MRI. *Hum. Brain Map*, **1**: 293–304.

25 Swartz, B. E., E. Halgren, J. Fuster, F. Simpkins, M. Gee & M. Mandelkern (1995). Cortical metabolic activation in humans during a visual memory task. *Cereb. Cortex*, **3**: 205–14.

26 McCarthy, G., A. M. Blamire, A. Puce, A. C. Nobre, G. Bloch, F. Hyder, P. S. Goldman-Rakic & R. Shulman (1994). Functional magnetic resonance imagining of human prefrontal cortex activation during a spatial working memory task. *Proc. Natl. Acad. Sci. USA*, **91**: 8690–4.

27 McCarthy, G., A. Puce, R. T. Constable, J. H. Krystal, J. Gore & P. S. Goldman-Rakic (1996). Activation of human prefrontal cortex during spatial and object working memory tasks measured by functional MRI. *Cereb. Cortex*, in press.

28 Sweeney, J. A., M. A. Mintun, B. S. Kwee, M. B. Wiseman, D. L. Brown, D. R. Rosenberg & J. R. Carl. A positron emission tomography study of voluntary saccadic eye movements and spatial working memory. *J. Neurophysiol.*, in press.

29 Smith, E. E., J. Jonides & R. A. Koeppe (1996). Dissociating verbal and spatial working memory using PET. *Cereb. Cortex*, in press.

30 Frith, C. D., K. Friston, P. F. Liddle & R. S. J. Frackowiak (1991). Willed action and the prefrontal cortex in man. *Proc. R. Soc. Lond. B*, **244**: 241–6.

31 Rajkowska, G. & P. S. Goldman-Rakic (1995). Cytoarchitectonic definition of prefrontal areas in the normal human cortex, II: Variability in locations of areas 9 and 46 and relationship to the Talairach Coordinate System. *Cereb. Cortex*, **5**: 323–37.

32 Stuss, D. T. & D. F. Benson (1986). *The Frontal Lobes*, pp. 1–303. Raven Press, New York.

33 Paulescu, E., C. D. Frith & F. S. J. Frackowiak (1993). Localization of a human system for sustained attention by positron emission tomography. *Nature*, **362**: 342–5.

34 Zatorre, R. J., A. C. Evans, E. Meyer & A. Gjedde (1992). Lateralization of phonetic and pitch discrimination in speech processing. *Science*, **256**: 846–9.

35 Petersen, S. E., P. T. Fox, M. I. Posner, M. Mintun & M. E. Raichle (1988). Positron emission tomographic studies of the cortical anatomy of single-word processing. *Nature*, **331**: 585–9.

36 McCarthy, G., A. M. Blamire, D. L. Rothman, R. Gruetter & R. G. Shulman (1993). Echo-planar magnetic resonance imaging studies of frontal cortex activation during word generation in humans. *Proc. Natl. Acad. Sci. USA*, **90**: 4952–6.

37 Funahashi, S., M. V. Chafee & P. S. Goldman-Rakic (1993). *Nature*, **365**: 753–6.

Language

INTRODUCTION TO PART VIII

The efficient communication of complicated ideas is one of the secrets of human success. How this highly specialized ability is organized is a source of great interest. It has long been known that the left hemisphere is preferentially endowed with linguistic capabilities; indeed, as we have seen, this has cost the left hemisphere some capacity for spatial processing. Greater detail, however, is hard-won. Unlike most other cognitive capacities, language can obviously not be studied in nonhuman animals. Neuroscientists are thus restricted to more indirect techniques than might otherwise be used.

Observing the results of incidental brain damage is the oldest technique in existence, pre-dating neuroscience and actually language itself. In a modern scientific context, this approach can be very illuminating. Hart, Berndt, and Caramazza report on a patient with the extremely exclusive difficulty of being unable to name fruits or vegetables. This conceptual-category-selective impairment presumably argues for a content-based map of object names over the surface of the cortex.

Surgical intervention for clinical treatment offers further opportunities for serendipitous research. Patients whose interhemispheric connections have been severed for treatment of epilepsy offer a unique glimpse at the relative abilities of their disconnected hemispheres. In "Right Hemisphere Language Following Brain Bisection," I review results from a number of such patients that strongly suggest both that the left hemisphere is almost always overwhelmingly dominant in linguistic ability and that, when right hemisphere language exists at all, it varies greatly between individuals in nature and degree and does not appear to follow any particular pattern of specialization.

A very popular technique in neurolinguistics is the use of scalp recordings, enabling precise measurement of the time courses of the neural events involved in language comprehension. Marta Kutas presents some insightful observations of the processes involved, emphasizing that many fundamental components are by no means exclusive to language, but must be more general mechanisms of working memory and, presumably, attention and imagery.

Category-Specific Naming Deficit Following Cerebral Infarction

John Hart Jr, Rita Sloan Berndt, and
Alfonso Caramazza

Studies aimed at characterizing the operation of cognitive functions in normal individuals have examined data from patients with focal cerebral insult. These studies assume that brain damage impairs functions of the cognitive processes along lines that honour the 'normal' pre-morbid organization of the cognitive system.[1] For example, detailed study of individual brain-damaged patients has revealed apparently selective disruption of cognitive functions such as auditory/verbal working memory,[2] phonological processing ability,[3] grapheme-to-phoneme translation procedures[4] and semantic processing.[5] Warrington et al. have studied patients with even more fine-grained selective disturbances of the semantic system.[6, 7] The most selective deficits have been reported for four patients who were significantly better at identifying inanimate objects than they were at identifying living things and foods.[8] These patterns of selective deficit after localized brain damage provide important information about the normal organization of the lexicon, and ultimately about how components of the lexical system are related to particular neural substrates. Here, we report a case study of a patient demonstrating a very selective disturbance of the ability to name items from two related semantic categories. Despite normal performance on a large battery of lexical/semantic tasks, the patient shows a consistent and striking disability in naming members of the semantic categories of 'fruits' and 'vegetables'. The selectivity of this deficit supports a category-specific organization of the mental lexicon, and suggests independence of the processing routes involving naming and name recognition.

The patient studied here (M.D.) is a 34-year-old, right-handed male college graduate who works as a systems analyst for a large United States government agency. In August of 1981 he suffered a left-hemisphere cerebrovascular accident, which resulted acutely in a global aphasia and right hemiparesis. Within 1 month, he recovered to a mild expressive aphasia and mild hemiparesis. M.D. subsequently experienced several transient ischaemic attacks, and a left internal carotid artery occlusion was diagnosed.

In December 1981, he was treated with extra-cranial/intra-cranial bypass surgery, which has been successful in averting further ischaemic episodes. A computerized tomography scan obtained at 1 month post-onset revealed an infarction involving the left frontal lobe and basal ganglia.

Early in 1983 M.D. was referred as a potential candidate for a research project on naming deficits in aphasia. His initial performance on all subtests of a standard language battery[9] indicated that he was not clinically aphasic, although he had some difficulty naming objects. He maintained that he was experiencing considerable difficulty with certain words. Further experimental testing suggested that these difficulties were focused on the semantic categories of 'fruits' and 'vegetables'. M.D. showed a striking inability to name such common items as Peach and Orange while able to name easily less frequent items such as Abacus and Sphinx.

To chart the boundaries and stability of this unusual deficit, M.D. was tested over 1 year with a variety of materials that were designed to evaluate the structure of his lexical/semantic system. Performance on a large battery of tests was excellent. This battery included: visual and auditory lexical decision; oral reading; word-picture matching (nouns and verbs); semantic categorization (words and pictures); and picture naming (oral and written). Unless some member of the semantic categories of fruits and vegetables were a stimulus item, M.D.'s scores were almost perfect.

Special tests were designed to focus on the problematic categories. M.D. was asked to name a large number of items (line drawings, coloured drawings, colour photographs and actual objects) from several semantic classes; table 29.1 summarizes his performance for all stimulus types.

M.D. showed considerable difficulty in naming individual fruits and vegetables, but was able to name easily a large range of other pictures and objects. His seven naming errors outside the fruits/vegetables category involved two household items, four geometric shapes (for example, diamond) and one tree. He named correctly a total of 13 food products outside the categories of fruits and vegetables. The 'other' items given to M.D. for naming were chosen to cover a wide range of semantic categories. Some of these categories (for example, 'body parts') have members with a very high frequency of usage in the language, hence the mean frequency of occurrence[10] for the fruit/vegetable items (11.8 per million) was considerably lower than the mean for the other items (32.8 per million). This disparity does not explain M.D.'s selective impairment, however, as 73% of items in the 'other' group were in the same frequency range as the fruit/vegetable items and were named without difficulty.

Table 29.1 Number of correct naming responses

	Semantic category		
	Fruit	Vegetables	Other
Line drawings	5/11	7/11	11/11
Coloured drawings	4/6	5/7	18/18
Photographs	11/18	12/18	222/229
Real objects	10/13	13/23	11/11
Total	30/48 (0.63)	37/59 (0.63)	262/269 (0.97)

The 'other' category includes vehicles, toys, tools, animals, body parts, food products, school, bathroom, kitchen and personal items, clothing, colours, shapes and trees.

To investigate M.D.'s knowledge of the semantic category of these items, he was shown pictures of 75 items from the categories fruits, vegetables, animals, vehicles and food products and he was asked to sort them into piles on the basis of their semantic classification. He was then asked to label the categories thus produced; his errors consisted entirely of confusions involving the categories of fruits and vegetables. He categorized 3 out of 24 fruits as vegetables and 6 out of 23 vegetables as fruit. He also incorrectly classified two food products (butter, cheese) as vegetables, although he named them correctly. Although the absolute number of errors committed on this task was not very large, M.D. had considerable difficulty with it, performing slowly and complaining of uncertainty.

In another attempt to determine M.D.'s knowledge of the members of semantic categories, he was asked to generate as many names as possible from 17 categories. The mean number of fruits and vegetables generated in 1 minute was 6.5, with an additional four vegetable names generated incorrectly as fruits. The mean number of items generated for the other 15 categories was 12.4, including 12 instances in the category 'food products'.

M.D.'s ability to name and to categorize pictures of fruits and vegetables is compromised relative to his ability to name and to categorize members of other categories. A further set of tasks was designed to assess the possibility that this impairment is limited to stimuli processed through the visual modality. A set of 20 verbal definitions, containing perceptual, functional and category information, was developed for 10 fruit/vegetable items and 10 other items (animals, furniture and clothing). M.D. named two out of 10 fruits and vegetables and all of 10 other items from their definitions. Next, M.D. was asked to name a set of objects that he could feel with either the left or right hand, but could not see. Fruit/vegetable items were selected on the basis of their tactile discriminability from other similar items. M.D. named 6 of 13 fruits, 11 of 21 vegetables, and 11 of 12 other items (he failed on tea bag). There was no difference in performance based on the hand used.

M.D.'s selective naming deficit for fruit/vegetable items is not modality-specific, and therefore may be the result of a selective disturbance within the semantic system itself, rather than a problem with access to the semantic system. To assess this possibility, a series of tasks was designed to probe M.D.'s comprehension of the names that he has difficulty producing. A 45-item word/picture matching task was developed in which M.D. was required to point to one of two pictures in response to an aurally presented word. Fruit and vegetable items were represented, as well as vehicles, food products and animals. For half the items, the incorrect pictures were closely semantically related to the target. M.D.'s one error (confusion between rhinoceros and hippopotamus) was not within the fruits/vegetables category; he pointed immediately and with certainty to pictured fruits and vegetables on hearing their names.

M.D.'s comprehension of the properties of objects was assessed by asking him for judgements about the category, size, colour, texture and shape of eight fruit/vegetable items that he had previously misnamed, and four animals. Item names were presented aloud. Although some responses on this task were hesitant for the fruits/vegetables categories, they were correct for all properties.

Note that M.D. could categorize items correctly as fruits or vegetables when their names were presented aurally, suggesting that his difficulty in categorizing pictures of fruits and vegetables was related to his inability to name them. This possibility was supported by his ability to categorize correctly all the written names of the fruits and vegetables whose pictures he had found difficult to classify. On two separate occasions approximately 6 months apart, M.D. easily sorted 14 printed fruit/vegetable names into their proper categories, together with the names of 21 items from other categories.

The impairment to the semantic system revealed in this patient appears to be limited to two specific and related semantic categories and to situations that require him to name the objects or to categorize them without having first been given their names. M.D. is aware of this problem, and expresses some frustration with it. Although he confesses to knowing little about cooking or food in general, it is clear that his difficulty with these items is not consonant with his ability to name many other types of foods and food-related items; in this respect he differs from the patients studied by Warrington and Shallice,[8] who had difficulty identifying all types of food products. Further, his failure to learn the names of these items after many test sessions that focused on this deficit suggests that this phenomenon does not reflect a simple pre-morbid lack of interest in these categories.

Although a unified lexical/semantic theory cannot be formulated on the basis of this one case, there are three important implications of these findings for the ultimate development of such a theory. First, the selective impairment of information in specific superordinate categories suggests that the organization of the semantic system in some sense honours those categorical distinctions. These results support and considerably extend previous neuropsychological investigations which have indicated a category-specific organization of the semantic system.[6, 8] Second, the dissociation in categorization ability between performance with lexical instances (which is normal) and with pictorial instances (which is impaired) suggests that lexical categorization could be accomplished on the basis of strictly lexical, as opposed to semantic, information. Third, although a general dissociation between 'name recognition' and 'name retrieval' has been supported previously by results from aphasic patients,[9] the category-specific dissociation found in M.D. indicates that the output lexicon is addressed by semantically categorized information that can be disrupted highly selectively.

The results reported here suggest that the lexical/semantic system is organized categorically and specifically at the level of the input and output processes to and from the system.

Acknowledgments

This study was supported by NINCDS grants NS-21054 to the University of Maryland School of Medicine and NS-14099 to the Johns Hopkins University. We thank Charlotte Mitchum for assistance with many aspects of this research.

References

1   Saffran, E. M., *Br. J. Psychol.*, **73**, 317 (1982).
2   Warrington, E. K. & Shallice, T., *Brain*, **92**, 885 (1969).
3   Caramazza, A., Berndt, R. S. & Basili, A., *Brain Language*, **18**, 128 (1983).

4   Beauvois, M. F. & Derousne, J., *J. Neurol. Neurosurg. Psychiat.*, **42**, 1115 (1979).
5   Schwartz, M. F., Marin, O. S. M. & Saffran, E. M., *Brain Language*, **7**, 277 (1979).
6   Warrington, E., *Br. J. Psychol.*, **72**, 175–96 (1981).
7   Warrington, E. & McCarthy, R., *Brain*, **106**, 859 (1983).
8   Warrington, E. & Shallice, T., *Brain*, **107**, 829 (1984).
9   Goodglass, H. & Kaplan, E., *The Assessment of Aphasia and Related Disorders* (Philadelphia: Lea & Febiger, 1972).
10 Francis, N. & Kucera, H., *Frequency Analysis of English Usage* (Boston: Houghton Mifflin, 1982).

Right Hemisphere Language Following Brain Bisection: A 20-Year Perspective

Michael S. Gazzaniga

In the early 1960s at the California Institute of Technology, Sperry and I initiated a long series of studies on the psychological and neurological consequences of brain bisection in humans (see Gazzaniga, 1970; Sperry, 1968). The patients were a small, select group of epileptics who suffered intractable seizures. Cerebral commissurotomy including both the corpus callosum and the anterior commissure was carried out in one operation to limit the interhemispheric spread of seizure activity (Bogen, Fisher, and Vogel, 1965). The early results contributed to a number of advances concerning the functional organization of the human brain, including findings concerning somatosensory representation (Gazzaniga, Bogen, and Sperry, 1963), visual function (Gazzaniga, Bogen, and Sperry, 1965), praxis (Gazzaniga, Bogen, and Sperry, 1967), language processes (Gazzaniga and Sperry, 1967), and nonverbal processes (Bogen and Gazzaniga, 1965). These findings also had philosophical implications with respect to generally accepted views on the unity of conscious experience (Gazzaniga, 1972; Sperry, 1968).

Research with the California Institute of Technology patients has been continued by a number of subsequent investigators under Sperry's direction, with much of the theoretical emphasis of this work arguing for the importance of differences in cognitive style between the hemispheres (Levy, Trevarthen, and Sperry, 1972) and the special properties of right hemisphere language (Levy and Trevarthen, 1977; Zaidel, 1978a). More traditional neuropsychological tests of auditory function (Zaidel, 1976), memory skills (Zaidel and Sperry, 1974), and other general observations concerning behavior as assessed on a battery of psychological tests have also been conducted (Zaidel and Sperry, 1973).

In the early 1970s I was invited to test another group of patients undergoing similar surgery by Donald Wilson (Wilson, Reeves, Gazzaniga, and Culver, 1977) at Dartmouth Medical School. The surgical approach, as well as the structures sectioned and the staging of the operation itself, provided an opportunity to confirm, modify, and extend the earlier findings. The new series also provided a small group of patients with a range of right hemisphere language skills.

In addition, we have been testing another split-brain patient operated on by Mark Rayport of the Medical College of Ohio. This patient has also proved to be linguistically sophisticated in each hemisphere. What follows is a review of studies of these three series of patients focusing on issues concerning right hemisphere language. In general, the data collected so far show that (a) most split-brain patients do not possess right hemisphere language of any kind and (b) when right hemisphere language does occur, it varies widely in its organization and extent of sophistication.

General Background and Critical Review

Traditionally, the clinical neurological literature has shown that language processes in the adult brain are largely a property of the left cerebral hemisphere (Geschwind, 1965). In recent years this view has been enhanced by new neuroanatomical correlations (Geschwind, 1965; Galaburda, LeMay, Kemper, and Geschwind, 1978) as well as by behavioral measures of language lateralization, including event-related potentials (Hillyard and Woods, 1979; Kutas and Hillyard, 1980), blood-flow measures (Lassen, Ingvar, and Skinhojie, 1978), dichotic listening procedures (Milner, Taylor, and Sperry, 1968), and unilateral sodium amytal tests (Milner, Branch, and Rasmussen, 1966).

As a consequence of the early testing of the California split-brain patients, however, there was the suggestion that the extent of right hemisphere involvement in language processing had been underestimated. With separate testing of each hemisphere, we found that two of the three commissurotomy patients tested (N.G. and L.B.) possessed some right hemisphere language capacity (Gazzaniga and Sperry, 1967). In general, what was meant by "language capacity" in these patients was the ability to understand written or spoken words. Other than the observation that bimorphemic "er" nouns derived from verbs could not be processed by the right hemisphere, we did not further delineate the semantic capacity of the right hemisphere.

It is important to note a major methodological constraint of split-brain testing: One can only be assured that the right hemisphere is performing a task if either the question or the mode of response is strictly lateralized to the right hemisphere. The only modality that allows for this is vision (figure 30.1). Any conclusions concerning right hemisphere language capacity based on auditory or tactile stimulation are therefore somewhat suspect. For example, if the experimenter asks a blindfolded patient to retrieve a particular object with the left hand, a correct response cannot be interpreted as evidence for right hemisphere language. Although stereognostic information from the left hand is primarily projected to the right hemisphere, it has been shown that if the left hemisphere also knows what is being sought, it can use ipsilateral somatosensory cues to make the correct match. This fact brings into question several early conclusions concerning auditory comprehension in the right hemisphere (Gazzaniga and Sperry, 1967).

A somewhat anecdotal argument for the existence of right hemisphere language capacity commonly advanced is that the right hemisphere is capable of following verbal instructions and, therefore, must possess some language skills. It seems fallacious, however, to argue that right hemisphere competence to carry out a nonverbal task implies a language capacity because successful completion of the task signifies an

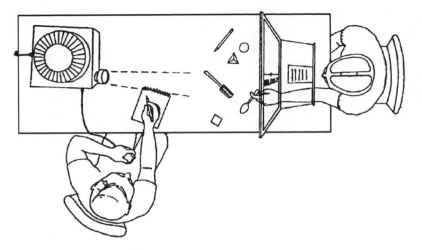

Figure 30.1 General purpose testing system.

Visual information is presented tachistoscopically in either visual half field, thereby assuring lateralized testing of each separate cerebral hemisphere. Unimanual presentation of objects for somesthetic exploration favors contralateral identification. The ipsilateral hemisphere, however, can also be accurate at identifying the object if the total response set is known to the subject.

Box 30.1 Guide and glossary to split-brain research

The so-called *split-brain operation* was initially carried out by Joseph E. Bogen and P. J. Vogel in an effort to control otherwise intractable epilepsy. The operation was further developed by the late Donald H. Wilson of the Dartmouth Medical School and has now been put to use at a number of medical centers.

In brief, the brain is bilaterally organized, with the left and the right half connected by the corpus callosum. This is the brain fiber system that is responsible for the exchange of information between the two hemispheres. During the surgery, this structure is sectioned by the neurosurgeons. The medical consequence of this procedure is that generalized convulsions are markedly reduced, or eliminated completely.

The neuropsychological analyses of the separate functions of each half-brain are made possible by simple lateralized testing techniques that capitalize on the normal organization of the human visual and tactile sensory systems. In brief when a point is fixated in space, all visual information to the right of the point is exclusively projected to the left half-brain. Information presented to the left of fixation is projected to the right half-brain. This makes easily possible the separate testing of each hemisphere.

Touch information is also lateralized to a large extent. Information related to object recognition coming from the right hand is projected to the left hemisphere; the opposite is true for the left hand. More details on basic testing techniques and the simple brain anatomy that is associated with these studies can be found in Gazzaniga (1970).

understanding of the experimenter's verbal instructions. Tasks given to a split-brain patient are not only described verbally, they are also demonstrated. Just as no one would claim that a chimp understands a human's instructions when it learns how to perform a complicated association (see Premack, 1976), such a claim should not be made for the right hemisphere of humans (Gazzaniga, 1970).

With these points clearly in mind, we obtained further evidence that the right hemisphere language capacity of N.G. and L.B. was limited (Gazzaniga and Hillyard, 1971). A series of tests measuring syntactic competence as well as linguistic function suggested that these two patients had only a limited language capacity. Still, at the time, these studies implied that a reassessment of the frequency with which right hemisphere language occurs in normal adults was necessary. We stated:

> The language capacity of the minor hemisphere in Case 1 proved to be almost negligible and was decidedly inferior to that of the other two subjects. Also, Case 1, unlike the others, had sustained considerable brain damage, especially in the minor hemisphere prior to surgery. For these reasons it was assumed that findings in Cases 2 and 3 could be relied upon to reflect more accurately the typical effects of cerebral disconnection per se, whereas Case 1 is more representative of the kinds of disconnection syndrome seen in cases of brain tumor, vascular accidents, or other cerebral pathology.   (Gazzaniga and Sperry, 1967)

We concluded:

> Though based on only two cases and clearly at variance with many reports in a literature filled with contradictions, there nevertheless are reasons at this time for thinking that the general picture seen in these two individuals may represent, by and large, a common and perhaps the typical picture.   (Gazzaniga and Sperry, 1967)

In this light, we initiated studies on another clinical population with the aim of demonstrating more language competence in the right hemisphere (Glass, Gazzaniga, and Premack, 1973). In a study of a group of patients who were globally aphasic due to left hemisphere strokes, no natural language facility was observed other than the ability to recognize an occasional noun and a curious ability to carry out word versus nonword judgments. These observations discouraged the view that right hemisphere language was common to the general population.

As more cases were added to the split-brain series, it became clear that our early reports and conclusions were based on an unrepresentative set of split-brain patients and that the generality of our findings to normal brain organization was suspect. Work with these additional cases also suggested that perhaps we had overestimated the amount of auditory comprehension present in the two cases, N.G. and L.B. As noted above, several of the tests reported were flawed because auditory comprehension of words was assessed by the ability to retrieve the correct object with the left hand.

In the new East Coast series (see below), we have now seen evidence for right hemisphere language of varying degrees in only 3 of 28 patients. Taken together, our findings imply that right hemisphere language is not common. When present, it can be attributable in almost every case to the presence of early left hemisphere brain damage.

At the same time, the relative incidence of right hemisphere language in these patients is consistent with other clinical data on the frequency of right hemisphere language as assessed by unilateral injection of amytal (Milner et al., 1966).

Nonetheless, the claim persists that not only is right hemisphere language common, it is of a different quality and kind than the normal system coexisting in the left half-brain. For example:

> It is argued that right hemisphere language represents the experience-reinforced linguistic capacity of a special purpose cognitive apparatus as opposed to the innate language mechanisms in the left hemisphere which specializes in syntactic and phonetic analysis. (Zaidel, 1978a)

and

> Results of the Rhyming Objects Test strongly suggest that the right hemisphere lacks a phonetic analyzer that can also generate phonetic images and that its verbal capacities depend on special right hemisphere processes which although adequate for understanding simple written and spoken language are probably quite deficient for complex linguistic tasks and are certainly incapable of integrating all but the simplest articulation. The articulations of which the right hemisphere may be capable are probably formed as motor Gestalts and are not constructed analytically from phoneme-elicited articulemes as many linguists would claim to be necessary for speaking.   (Levy and Trevarthen, 1977)

Zaidel's hypotheses are based on observations of two split-brain patients, N.G. and L.B., the same patients studied earlier, plus one patient who had undergone a left hemispherectomy. There are 6 frequently studied patients in the California series and approximately 15 patients altogether (Bogen and Vogel, 1975). Levy and Trevarthen (1977) also base their conclusions on observations of these 6 patients. Yet, 4 of the 6 have not been independently assessed for language using lateralized visual techniques. In initial testing of these 6 patients by the present author, only N.G. and L.B. evidenced clear right hemisphere language function. Unless there has been a dramatic change in the language skills of the other 4 patients in the interim, all of the evidence for right hemisphere language in the West Coast group is derived solely from cases L.B. and N.G., and there are no published data to date to suggest that such a change has occurred.

Although these two patients are not characteristic of split-brain patients as a whole, they alone have led to several general hypotheses concerning the role of the right hemisphere in recovery from stroke (Zaidel, 1976) and its possible involvement in deep dyslexia (Coltheart, 1980). They have even been used as a rationale for why aphasics might be able to regain language skills (Hécaen, 1978). These claims are made despite the fact that most patients who have suffered left hemisphere strokes show little or no recovery of language beyond that which immediately follows the acute phase of illness (e.g., Luria, 1970; Sarno and Levita, 1971; Woods and Carey, 1979).

In this context, it is of interest to identify the specific claims that have been made for the special nature of right hemisphere language and to examine in some detail the underlying data base.

Phonetic processing and the right hemisphere

Levy and Trevarthen (1977) were the first to observe that N.G. and L.B. were unable to carry out rhyming tasks in the right hemisphere. Zaidel (1978b) extended these observations by including a word-to-sound matching test and also found that N.G. and L.B. were unable to demonstrate evidence for phonetic processing. Comparable results were obtained in our laboratory for Case J.W. (Sidtis, Volpe, Rayport, Wilson, and Gazzaniga, 1981).

At the same time, we have also shown that the right hemispheres of two other patients are capable of rhyming, even when tested before the right hemisphere developed access to speech (Gazzaniga, LeDoux, and Wilson, 1977; Sidtis et al., 1981). Thus, the inability to perform rhyming tasks is not an absolute property of right hemisphere language. This inability also raises the question of whether performance on a rhyming task is a true index of phonetic processing in general. In follow-up studies on Case J.W., who showed no phonetic processing using the tests just described, phonological capacity was demonstrated in a semantic priming paradigm (Sidtis and Gazzaniga, in press).

In this light, it would seem premature to interpret rhyming deficits as a general phonological deficit and to conclude that, therefore, the auditory processing strategy of the right hemisphere differs from that of the left.

Language comprehension in the right hemisphere with prolonged lateralized assessment procedures

Several other studies have reinforced the notion that the right hemisphere processes linguistic information in a unique fashion (Zaidel, 1976; 1978c). In one instance the use of a special system of stimulus presentation was combined with the administration of standardized tests of auditory and visual language comprehension. Based on these studies, Zaidel concluded that (a) auditory comprehension is superior to visual comprehension in N.G. and L.B.; (b) syntactic competence is generally poor; and (c) if word frequency is taken into account, there is no difference between the comprehension of nouns and verbs. Each of these conclusions is considered in detail below.

Auditory versus visual comprehension

The claim for the superior auditory comprehension of the right hemisphere of N.G. and L.B. is based largely on the results of the Peabody Picture Vocabulary Test. N.G. has a raw score of 82; L.B. scores 103. Mental age equivalents are then determined using the established norms for the test. The mental ages for auditory stimuli were 11 and 16, respectively. The visual version of the test produced mental ages of 6.5 and 10.5, respectively. Since the highest chronological age category is 18, the values of N.G. must be considered an approximation. L.B., on the other hand, was at approximately the correct age for the mental age determination.

We administered the same test to J.W. – the patient in the Wilson series who possesses right hemisphere language that is comparable in sophistication to that found in N.G. and L.B. Lateralized presentation of the picture choices for the test

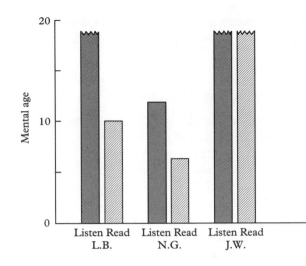

Figure 30.2 Combined raw scores of three split-brain cases.

Shows differences in overall capabilities of the left and right hemisphere as well as differences in auditory versus visual processes for Cases N.G. and L.B. but not J.W. (Adapted from Zaidel [1978a] and Gazzaniga et al. [note 2].)

were easily managed tachistoscopically (Gazzaniga, Smylie, Baynes, Hirst, and McCleary, note 1). The testing procedures differed only in whether the test word was spoken or written. We found no difference between the visual and auditory verbal processing skills of J.W. (figure 30.2). Additionally, the overall scores for the left hemisphere were higher (133) than those for the right hemisphere (109). An error analysis suggested that both hemispheres tended to miss the same words.

The difference between these results and those for N.G. and L.B. may merely reflect yet another different profile of right hemisphere language. Yet Zaidel (1978a, 1978c) argues that the difference between visual and auditory verbal processing is a real property of all right hemispheres and that the auditory processing capacity of the left hemisphere of a split-brain patient can appear to be subnormal. This conclusion is based on the left hemisphere score of a new patient, R.Y., who is a "representative commissurotomy patient" and who was actually tested under free-field conditions. The patient's subnormal performance, he concluded, was due to the fact that the right hemisphere did not contribute its normal input for auditory language functions.

This analysis raises serious questions, R.Y., a bilingual Mexican-American, is a patient who has never demonstrated right hemisphere language under any condition. This makes it questionable to argue that poor left hemisphere performance is a result of commissural section. For the claims made about the right hemisphere's normal contribution to auditory comprehension, the left hemisphere auditory comprehension of L.B. and N.G. also should be considered. In fact, these data exist (Zaidel, 1978c), and the language performance appears to be normal.

Syntactic capacity of the right hemisphere

Both patients in the California series (N.G. and L.B.) exhibited little if any syntactic capacity in the right hemisphere (Gazzaniga and Hillyard, 1971; Zaidel, 1978c). These results are also consistent with results on J.W. from the Wilson series. This is not the case, however, for patients with both language and speech in the right hemisphere (see below).

Noun versus verb understanding in the right hemisphere

Early reports on N.G. and L.B. suggested that whereas the right hemisphere could comprehend nouns, it was unable to carry out lateralized written commands (Gazzaniga and Sperry, 1967). This has been reconfirmed for N.G. and L.B. by myself (Gazzaniga, 1970) and has been noted for patient J.W. (Sidtis et al., 1981). Zaidel (1978a) reported that in N.G. and L.B. these findings were not due to a failure of the right hemisphere to comprehend action verbs: When word frequency was taken into account, the right hemisphere could define action verbs and nouns equally well. Sidtis et al. (1981) obtained comparable results for patient J.W. It should be stressed, however, that verb comprehension should not be confused with the capacity to generate a behavior. One would not necessarily predict that a patient who could correctly select a picture of a runner when the word *running* is lateralized to the right hemisphere would also be capable of carrying out the lateralized command *run*. It is this difference in generative capacity that distinguishes the left and right hemispheres of these patients, not a differential capacity to comprehend nouns and verbs. It should be pointed out, however, that both P.S. and V.P. were able to carry out commands lateralized to their right hemispheres even prior to the emergence of right hemisphere access to speech (figure 30.3).

In sum, the foregoing results support the notion that the right hemisphere language skills of the few cases studied to date exhibit a wide range of sophistication. The variability of right hemisphere language comprehension is even more apparent for the recent split-brain cases. Two of these patients (P.S. and V.P.) demonstrate extensive and more complex right hemisphere language capacities than previously noted, which ultimately has included the ability to generate speech. Additional data collected from these patients are discussed below.

Language competence of the Wilson and Rayport series

Commissural surgery of the three patients described below differed in two respects from that performed on the California patients (see figure 30.4). First, in all of these cases, the anterior commissure was left intact; in the California series, commissural section included the anterior commissure. Second, in two instances (J.W. and V.P.), commissurotomy was performed in two stages, with a several-month interoperative period. The posterior portion of the callosum was initially transected in J.W.; the anterior portion was initially transected in V.P.

One might argue that because of these differences, behavioral measures of the California patients are not comparable to those of the East Coast patients. For example, it could be asserted that differences in performance between the two patient groups are accountable in terms of the functional role of the anterior commissure. This interpretation is implausible for several reasons. For one, in general, the performance of the East Coast and West Coast patients in right hemisphere language tasks is very similar. Of the 28 East Coast patients, only 3 have demonstrated evidence of right

Figure 30.3   Lateralized commands given to the mute right hemisphere.

These tests were possible only in Cases P.S. and V.P. These same tests were not possible for J.W. and L.B. and N.G.

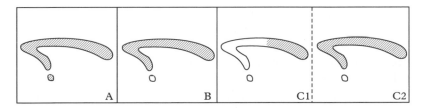

Figure 30.4   The variable method and extent of cerebral commissurotomy.

As shown in **A**, Bogen et al. (1965) sectioned the corpus callosum and anterior commissure in one operation without the aid of an operating microscope; in **B**, Wilson et al. (1977) cut only the callosum; and in **C**, Wilson and Rayport cut the callosum in two stages.

hemisphere language, a ratio consistent with the California series. Second, the right hemisphere language profile of patient J.W. is very similar to that obtained for the two West Coast patients with right hemisphere language, despite an intact anterior commissure in this patient. J.W. was also one of the patients who underwent the staged surgical procedure. It therefore seems unlikely that the manner in which the callosum is sectioned has an impact on the quality of right hemisphere language.

It should be pointed out that two of the patients discussed below (V.P. and P.S.) have developed right hemisphere speech, whereas none of the West Coast patients have done so. It remains an as yet unsubstantiated possibility that the anterior commissure provides a means of access to the speech system from the right hemisphere. It should be emphasized that if this is the case, it cannot be argued that this invariably takes place; J.W. has shown no sign of right hemisphere access to speech in the four years following surgery.

In sum, it would appear that the quality of right hemisphere language does not depend on the presence of the anterior commissure nor does it depend on the manner in which commissural section is performed.

Language comprehension

A summary of the language comprehension skills of the 3 patients who possess some right hemisphere language in the Wilson and Rayport series, along with those of the Bogen and Vogel series, is presented in table 30.1. Of the 44 split-brain patients living in the United States, only these 5 have shown clear evidence of language processes in the right hemisphere, the quality and extent of which ranges from rudimentary naming skills to language skills essentially identical to left hemisphere processes.

When several aspects of language processes are considered, two levels of language competence emerge. For example, J.W., N.G., and L.B. demonstrate clear evidence of right hemisphere semantics. Further analysis of J.W. revealed that within his right hemisphere semantic network, superordination, synonyms, antonyms, and other semantic relationships were all present. It might be expected that similar results would be found in L.B. and N.G., but despite the ability of each to comprehend verbs, neither could carry out simple verbal commands.

For P.S. and V.P., on the other hand, language comprehension in the right hemisphere appears essentially normal (Gazzaniga and LeDoux, 1978; Sidtis, 1981). In addition, the ability to carry out verbal commands for both axial and distal movement was unimpaired. Both were able to detect semantic incongruity in sentences lateralized to the right hemisphere as assessed by the N400 event-related potential (Kutas and Hillyard, in press), in a series of studies carried out by Kutas, Hillyard, and ourselves. Cases N.G., L.B., and J.W. showed much smaller N400 responses. In other behavioral tests, P.S. was able to perform well in each hemisphere on the token test, which examined a variety of syntactic skills.

The results for P.S. and V.P. indicate that, by a number of criteria, right hemisphere language is essentially normal; it is not frozen into an intermediate stage of competence as in L.B., N.G., and J.W.

Speech and writing

Case P.S. was the first split-brain patient to develop expressive speech controlled by the right hemisphere (Gazzaniga, Volpe, Smylie, Wilson, and LeDoux, 1979). Approximately 26 months after callosal section, P.S. began to provide verbal descriptions of stimuli appearing in either visual field. This was the case for both pictorial and verbal stimuli. Our first assumption was that remaining interhemispheric connections had "opened up" and that the sensory information presented to the right hemisphere was being transferred to the left. This did not prove to be the case. For example, P.S. was able to compare two stimuli only if they both appeared in the same visual half-field. If half of the information was presented to the left hemisphere and half to the right, P.S.'s performance did not exceed chance. Additional paradigms involved brief presentation of complex scenes to the left visual field. A picture of a man holding a gun, for

Table 30.1 Right hemisphere language comprehension: summary of skills in five patients

Skill	Patient				
	P.S.	V.P.	J.W.	N.G.	L.B.
Phonetic					
Rhyming (visual)	+	+	−	−	−
Rhyming (priming task)	*n.a.*	*n.a.*	+	*n.a.*	*n.a.*
CV discrimination (auditory)	*n.a.*	+	−	−	−
Semantic					
Picture/word – word/picture	+	+	+	+	+
Synonym	+	+	+	+	+
Antonym	+	+	+	*n.a.*	*n.a.*
Function	+	+	+	*n.a.*	*n.a*
Class membership:					
Superordinate	+	+	+	+	+
Subordinate	+	+	+	+	+
Verbal commands	+	+	−	−	−
Action verbs	+	+	+	+	+
Electrophysiological response to semantic violation (N400)	+	+	−	−	−
Syntax					
Active/passive sentences	*n.a.*	+	−	−	−
Token test	+	*n.a.*	+/−	+/−	+/−

Note. + = capable, − = incapable, +/− = intermediate, *n.a.* = not available.

example, prompted the exclamation "holdup." Yet, when the patient was questioned as to the details of the stimulus, an erroneous account of its actual nature was provided. Most likely, this account was generated by the left hemisphere, which remained in charge of extended dialogue (figure 30.5).

The surprising development of right hemisphere speech in P.S., which is described in more detail below, was also noted in Case V.P. In early postoperative testing, it was clear that her right hemisphere language system was evolving in a manner much like that of P.S. (Sidtis et al., 1981). Shortly after surgery, her right hemisphere was able to generate responses to verbal commands and showed signs of syntactic competence. Approximately nine months postoperatively, V.P.'s right hemisphere began to generate speech. As with P.S., at first she could only name single-field stimuli presented to either the left or right half-brains. Subsequently, her naming of double-field stimuli improved.

For both P.S. and V.P., shortly after surgery the right hemisphere was able to generate written responses to questions put to it. J.W., on the other hand, was unable to do so. At the same time, however, J.W., a skilled artist, was able to draw the picture corresponding to words presented to the right hemisphere. The writing and drawing skills of N.G. and L.B. are not extensive (Gazzaniga and Sperry, 1967).

Paracallosal integration of phonetic information

Just as P.S. was the first to demonstrate right hemisphere speech, he also was the first to demonstrate interhemispheric communication between the two language-competent

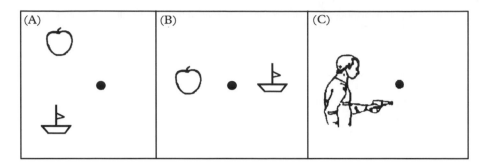

Figure 30.5   A variety of tests demonstrated that the right hemisphere had gained access to speech.

In a within-field condition (**A**), same/different judgments were easily carried out, whereas across-field judgments (**B**) were not. In **C**, complex scenes were apprehended by the right in a short verbal description such as "holdup" only to then be explained away in erroneous detail by the more talkative left half-brain (from Gazzaniga et al., 1979).

hemispheres without overt voicing movements (Gazzaniga et al., 1982). In a series of tests, a target word was flashed to one hemisphere, and P.S. was instructed not to report the word but to call it something else. For example, if the word *apple* was flashed to the right hemisphere, the right hemisphere would be taught to respond *petunia*. Once the *apple/petunia* association was established in the right hemisphere, a series of other words was presented to either the left or right hemisphere. They were all named normally. During the series, if the word *apple* was presented to the trained hemisphere, P.S. promptly responded *petunia*. To our surprise, however, when the word *apple* was presented to the left hemisphere, P.S. also responded *petunia*. In other words, a hemisphere that had never been perceptually exposed to the word *apple* was able to associate it with the word taught only to the opposite hemisphere. This would be expected only if a transfer of information between the hemispheres had occurred. In follow-up studies, the results of a control test revealed that interhemispheric transfer in P.S. did not include the figural properties of the stimulus. These findings suggested that phonetic encoding of a stimulus is required before interhemispheric communication can occur. It is not yet clear whether such transfer relies on midbrain and brain stem systems or on afferent information provided by the speech musculature.

This skill appeared in P.S. approximately one year after the right hemisphere began to initiate speech. In V.P., although she has developed right hemisphere speech, she has not, at this writing, demonstrated evidence of interhemispheric transfer. We predict that she will.

Right Hemisphere Language and Speech: An Overview

It is clear from the foregoing that language and speech in the right hemisphere can exist at either a sophisticated or a rudimentary level. It is present in a small subset of the split-brain patients and in almost every case can be attributed to brain pathology occurring prior to commissural section.

It would also appear that in language systems that possess generative skills such as writing and the ability to carry out verbal commands, the probability that speech will develop is high – even in a maturational state beyond the period commonly believed to allow for such brain plasticity.

With two separate but coexisting language systems in one cranium competing for a single vocal apparatus, it might be predicted that with continual practice, interactions between the two systems would develop. This in fact has occurred in P.S. Through some as yet poorly understood language-processing mechanism, the phonetic activities of one hemisphere are known to the other.

Interhemispheric interactions

Still more recently, we have demonstrated other, more subtle indications of interhemispheric interactions. In a series of experiments on split-brain patients (Holtzman, Sidtis, Volpe, Wilson, and Gazzaniga, 1981; Sidtis and Gazzaniga, in press), it has been demonstrated that both attentional and semantic interactions occur not only within the two cerebral hemispheres but also between the separated hemispheres (figure 30.6A). These are the first studies to demonstrate that cognitively based information activated in one half-brain can influence specific processes in the other. Prior to this work, interhemispheric interactions were linked to emotional aspects of stimuli, and the spreading of emotional tone helped the speaking hemisphere narrow down possible responses (Gazzaniga, 1970; LeDoux, Wilson, and Gazzaniga, 1977; Sperry, Zaidel, and Zaidel, 1979).

In brief, attentional interactions were demonstrated in a spatial priming task. Here, a 3 × 3 cell grid appeared in each visual field on either side of a central fixation dot. On each trial an X appeared in one of the cells followed by a digit, either in the same cell or a different cell of the same or different grid. The subject then made an odd/even judgment, and response latencies were recorded. Performance in the within- and between-field conditions was compared. Split-brain subjects showed normal facilitation of response under both conditions. Despite this outcome, patients performed at

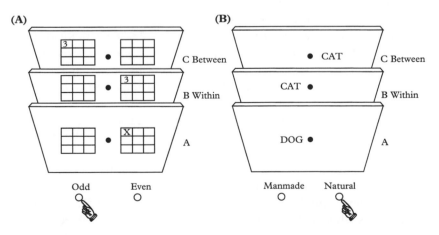

Figure 30.6   Attentional interactions.

Demonstrated by showing a facilitation on an RT measure to the judgment of whether a flashed number was odd or even. If the prime appeared in the same cell as the number, facilitation was seen both within and between visual fields. Semantic priming was observed for related items on a natural versus fabricated discrimination.

chance when asked to provide a same/different judgment of the relative location of two Xs, each appearing in a different visual field.

In an analogous fashion, semantic interactions were discovered on a priming task that required one hemisphere to judge whether or not a word designated something "natural" or fabricated. Prior to this judgment, a related or unrelated word was presented to either the same or the opposite hemisphere. Priming was observed under both the within- and between-field conditions (see figure 30.6B).

These results suggest that subcortical structures may play a significant role in relaying information to both hemispheres. Yet, it must be stressed that these kinds of results only obtain in patients with bilateral language. Does this mean that such observations are only of limited interest since they describe what is clearly a set of idiosyncratic patients?

On the contrary, their results provide provocative dissociates that require consideration for models of normal cognition. In the case of the semantic priming results, it has always been of interest where in the informational processing system priming effects occur. Our results suggest that priming effects do not occur at the perceptual level or the phonological level since these loci for interaction are not available to patients such as Case J.W. The data appear to support the view that priming effects occur at the level of the semantic representation.

Language and personal awareness

One intriguing aspect of patients who have developed right hemisphere speech is that the right hemisphere becomes an assertive agent. It must be remembered that most split-brain patients have little or no right hemisphere language, resulting in extremely passive mental systems capable of performing, at best, simple match-to-sample non-verbal perceptual tasks. With a mental system that can perform transformations on stimuli, can carry out commands with ease, and can write, draw, and even talk, new questions emerge. Principally, how does the dominant left hemisphere cope with actions and even statements generated by a mental system that exists separately and initiates actions for its own discrete reasons?

One question that has concerned psychologists and philosophers for years can be tested directly in new split-brain paradigms. The effect of what traditionally has been called unconscious processes can be approached directly by observing how the verbal left hemisphere copes with overt behaviors produced by the newly verbal right hemisphere.

It should be noted that these studies were conducted at two points along the postoperative course of patients with right hemisphere speech: In Phase 1, the observations were made prior to the emergence of right hemisphere speech; Phase 2 took place subsequent to the emergence of right hemisphere speech.

Even during Phase 1, the left hemisphere's language system interpreted actions taken by the right hemisphere as meaningful (Gazzaniga and LeDoux, 1978). For example, in one study a single stimulus was lateralized to each hemisphere on each trial, and the subject was required to select related items from pairs of flashed stimuli. Thus, if a cherry was one of the stimuli flashed, the correct answer might have been an apple as opposed to a toaster, chicken, or glass, with the superordinate concept being, of course, fruit.

Each hemisphere could perform this task under conditions of both unilateral and bilateral stimulation. Only rarely did the response of one hemisphere inhibit a response by the other hemisphere. Of particular interest was the manner in which the subject verbally interpreted double-field responses. When a snow scene was presented to the right hemisphere and a chicken claw was presented to the left, P.S. responded correctly by selecting pictures of a shovel and a chicken from among a series of pictures before him. He was then asked, "What did you see?" He responded, "I saw a claw and I picked the chicken, and you have to clean out the chicken shed with a shovel" (figure 30.7).

A similar example of creative fabrication was observed in patient V.P. In this case, a simple line drawing of a Christmas tree was lateralized to her right hemisphere. When asked to describe the picture, her left verbal hemisphere, knowing that something had been presented, responded, "A house ... with smoke ... coming out of a chimney." She was then asked to close her eyes and with her left hand write the name of the person usually associated with the picture. The right hemisphere, knowing very well that it saw a Christmas tree, wrote, "Sata Mein." When asked what she had written, her verbal system said, "fireman," which is consistent with her earlier left-hemisphere-generated description. Next, using her left hand and with her eyes closed, she was asked to write

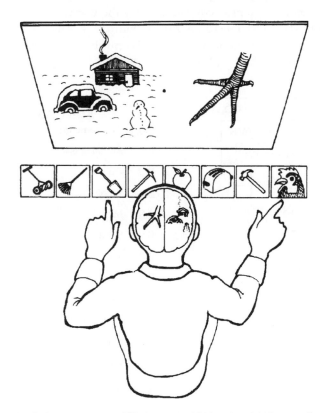

Figure 30.7 Method for presenting different cognitive tasks simultaneously to each hemisphere.

The left hemisphere was required to process the answer to the chicken claw, and the right dealt with the implications of being presented with a snow scene. After each hemisphere responded, the left hemisphere was asked to explain its choices (from Gazzaniga & LeDoux, 1978).

the date usually associated with the picture. The right hemisphere wrote, "Dec 25." After the left hemisphere saw this response, she exclaimed, "Oh...Christmas! The picture must have something to do with Christmas." Asked once more to describe the picture, she replied, "Oh, you guys are going to think I'm crazy, but it was a house with smoke coming out of the chimney and a Christmas tree."

These results imply that the right hemisphere knows exactly what the picture is and can abstract information about it but cannot directly express this information to the left verbal hemisphere. The left hemisphere, on the other hand, when confronted with the fact that it wrote something totally unrelated to its initial verbal response, chooses to integrate the written message into its description.

In the case of P.S., a different experimental approach could be taken. Having developed right hemisphere speech, problems proposed to it could be remarked upon, which leads us to Phase 2. We now see in P.S. an interesting interweaving of spoken reports, one from each hemisphere (figure 30.8).

In this study, P.S. was shown a series of slides with two words on each slide. Read normally from left to right, the series of slides told a logical story (Story 1: Mary + Ann, May + Come, Visit + Into, The + Town, Ship + Today). P.S., of course, cannot read the story from left to right, but rather, each hemisphere on a given trial receives a single word. The left hemisphere proceeds to read only the words on the right side of the screen, which by design also make up a story (Story 1: + Ann, + Come, + Into, + Town, + Today), and the right hemisphere reads only the words on the left side of the screen (Story 3: Mary +, May +, Visit +, The +, Ship +).

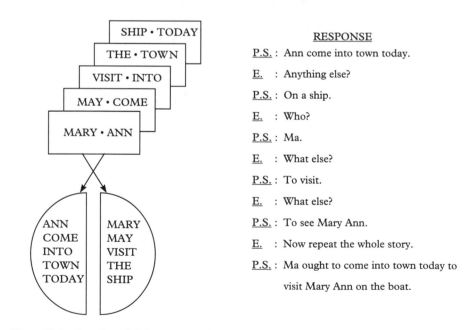

Figure 30.8   A series of slides presented to the subject

Normals read them from left to right, resulting in Story 1. Split-brain subjects read the words on the right in series, making Story 2, and the words on the left in series, making Story 3.

Following presentation of the entire story, P.S. was asked to recall it. He immediately responded, "Ann come into town today." This was the more robust left hemisphere expressing what it had perceived. Then, P.S. was asked if that was the full story. He paused briefly and blurted out, "on a ship... to visit... to visit Ma." When asked to repeat the whole story, he replied, "Ann came into town today to visit Ma on the ship."

Once again we see the integration of disparate behaviors into a coherent framework. With the development of bilateral access to speech, behaviors generated by the right hemisphere, which now initiates the spoken word, are incorporated into the conscious stream of the left hemisphere.

Conclusions

My intention has been to review the relevant split-brain studies to date that concern aspects of right hemisphere language and speech. I would now like to consider how these observations contribute to our understanding of the role of language in our conscious awareness.

The emerging picture is that our cognitive system is not a unified network with a single purpose and train of thought. A more accurate metaphor is that our sense of subjective awareness arises out of our dominant left hemisphere's unrelenting need to explain actions taken from any one of a multitude of mental systems that dwell within us (Gazzaniga and LeDoux, 1978). These systems, which coexist with the language system, are not necessarily in touch with language processes prior to a behavior. Once actions are taken, the left, observing these behaviors, constructs a story as to the meaning, and this in turn becomes part of the person's understanding of the language system.

Many problems, of course, remain. It is too simple to say language is identical with "consciousness" or "subjective awareness." Language can exist in virtually perfect repair in an otherwise demented or cognitively deficient neurologic patient who is incapable of solving the simplest kind of perceptual or conceptual task. As a result, it would seem more prudent to think that the left language system is intimately linked to a cognitive system that strives for consistency and order in the buzzing chaos of behaviors that are constantly being produced by the total organism.

Second, a half-brain system does not seem to be cognitively sophisticated without language despite certain visual-spatial skills. In testing right hemispheres without language skills, simple perceptual matching tests are frequently not possible (Gazzaniga, Bogen and Sperry, 1962). Indeed, it could well be argued that the cognitive skills of a normal disconnected right hemisphere without language are vastly inferior to the cognitive skills of a chimpanzee. This raises intriguing ontogenetic questions. Since the right hemisphere during normal development most likely goes through a phase of being able to become language competent, the subsequent consolidation of language processes in the usually dominant left hemisphere seems to lead to a freezing of the overall cognitive competence of the right. Of course, this fact only emerges in these special split-brain cases and in left-hemisphere-damaged patients. It would appear, nonetheless, that the price of lateral specialization for language on the left is a state of rudimentary cognition for the right hemisphere, which is revealed only if the latter has to serve alone following brain bisection or left-brain damage.

Finally, the fresh awareness that the two separate cognitive systems do interact at important levels in the realms of both attentional process and semantics suggests that any of a variety of subcallosal brain mechanisms may be involved in these functions. It has been suggested, for example, that specific pathways involving pulvinar/parietal systems may integrate the visual half-fields for the control of attention (Holtzman et al., 1981). Possible linking systems for semantic processes are less definite.

Notes

This research was aided by US Public Health Service Grant no. NS15053-02, National Science Foundation Grant no. BNS578-16531, the McKnight Foundation, and the Alfred P. Sloan Foundation.

The author would like to thank Jeffrey D. Holtzman, George A. Miller, Steven A. Hillyard, and John J. Sidtis for their many helpful criticisms of the manuscript.
1   Gazzaniga, M. S., Smylie, C. S., Baynes, K., Hirst, W. and McCleary, C. *Profiles of right hemisphere language and speech following brain bisection.* Manuscript submitted for publication, 1983.

References

Bogen, J. E., Fisher, E. D., & Vogel, P. J. Cerebral commissurotomy: A second case report. *Journal of the American Medical Association* (1965), **194**, 1328–9.

Bogen, J. E., & Gazzaniga, M. S. Cerebral commissurotomy in man: Minor hemisphere dominance for certain visual-spatial functions. *Journal of Neurosurgery* (1965), **23**, 394–9.

Bogen, J. E., & Vogel, P. J. Neurologic status in the long term following complete cerebral commissurotomy. In F. Michel & B. Schott (eds), *Les syndromes de disconnexion calleuse chez l'homme* (Lyon: Hôpital Neurologie, 1975).

Coltheart, M. Deep dyslexia: A right hemisphere hypothesis. In M. Coltheart, K. Patterson, & J. C. Marshall (eds), *Deep dyslexia* (London: Routledge & Kegan Paul, 1980).

Galaburda, A. M., LeMay, M., Kemper, T. L., & Geschwind, N. Right–left asymmetries in the brain. *Science* (1978), **199**, 852–6.

Gazzaniga, M. S. *The Bisected Brain* (New York: Appleton-Century-Crofts, 1970).

Gazzaniga, M. S. One brain – two minds? *American Scientist* (1972), **60**, 311–17.

Gazzaniga, M. S., Bogen, J. E., & Sperry, R. W. Some functional effects of sectioning the cerebral commissures in man. *Proceedings of the National Academy of Sciences* (1962), **48**, 1765–69.

Gazzaniga, M. S., Bogen, J. E., & Sperry, R. W. Laterality effects in somesthesis following cerebral commissurotomy in man. *Neuropsychologia* (1963), **1**, 209–15.

Gazzaniga, M. S., Bogen, J. E., & Sperry, R. W. Observations of visual perception after disconnexion of the cerebral hemispheres in man. *Brain* (1965), **88**, 221–30.

Gazzaniga, M. S., Bogen, J. E., & Sperry, R. W. Dyspraxia following division of the cerebral commissures. *Archives of Neurology* (1967), **16**, 606–12.

Gazzaniga, M. W., & Hillyard, S. A. Language and speech capacity of the right hemisphere. *Neuropsychologia* (1971), **9**, 273–80.

Gazzaniga, M. S., & LeDoux, J. E. *The Integrated Mind* (New York: Plenum Press, 1978).

Gazzaniga, M. S., LeDoux, J. E., & Wilson, D. H. Language, praxis and the right hemisphere: Clues to some mechanisms of consciousness. *Neurology* (1977), **27**, 1144 –7.

Gazzaniga, M. S., Sidtis, J. J., Volpe, B. T., Smylie, C. S., Holtzman, J. D., & Wilson, D. H. Evidence for para-callosal transfer after callosal section: A possible consequence of bilateral language organization. *Brain* (1982), **105**, 53–63.

Gazzaniga, M. S., & Sperry, R. W. Language after section of the cerebral commissures. *Brain* (1967), **90**, 131–8.

Gazzaniga, M. S., Volpe, B. T., Smylie, C. S., Wilson, D. H., & LeDoux, J. E. Plasticity in speech organization following commissurotomy. *Brain* (1979), **102**, 808–15.

Geschwind, N. Disconnexion syndromes in animal and man. *Brain* (1965), **88**, 237–67.

Glass, A. S., Gazzaniga, M. S., & Premack, D. Artificial language training in global aphasics. *Neuropsychologia* (1973), **11**, 95–103.

Hécaen, H. Right hemisphere contributions to language functions. In P. A. Buser & A. Rougeul-Buser (eds), *Cerebral Correlates of Conscious Experience* (Amsterdam: Elsevier/North-Holland, 1978).

Hillyard, S. A., & Woods, D. L. Electrophysiological analysis of human brain function. In M. S. Gazzaniga (ed.), *Handbook of Behavioral Neurobiology*, vol. 2: *Neuropsychology* (New York: Plenum Press, 1979).

Holtzman, J. D., Sidtis, J. J., Volpe, B. T., Wilson, D. H., & Gazzaniga, M. S. Dissociation of spatial information for stimulus localization and the control of attention. *Brain* (1981), **104**, 861–62.

Kutas, M., & Hillyard, S. A. Reading senseless sentences: Brain potentials reflect semantic incongruities. *Science* (1980), **207**, 203–5.

Kutas, M., & Hillyard, S. Event related potentials in cognitive science, In M. S. Gazzaniga (ed.), *Handbook of Cognitive Neuroscience* (New York: Plenum Press, in press).

Lassen, N. A., Ingvar, D. H., & Skinhojie, E. Brain function and blood flow. *Scientific American* (1978), **239** (4), 62–71.

LeDoux, J. E., Wilson, D. H., & Gazzaniga, M. S. A divided mind: Observations of the conscious properties of the separated hemisphere. *Annals of Neurology* (1977), **2**, 417–21.

Levy, J., & Trevarthen, C. Perceptual, semantic, and phonetic aspects of elementary language processes in split-brain patients. *Brain* (1977), **100**, 105–18.

Levy, J., Trevarthen, C., & Sperry, R. W. Perception bilateral chimeric figures following hemispheric disconnection. *Brain* (1972), **95**, 61–78.

Luria, A. R. *Traumatic aphasia* (The Hague: Mouton, 1970).

Milner, B., Branch, C., & Rasmussen, T. Evidence for bilateral speech representation in some non-right handers. *Transactions of the American Neurological Association* (1966), **91**, 306–8.

Milner, B., Taylor, L., & Sperry, R. W. Lateralized suppression of dichotically presented digits after commissural section in man. *Science* (1968), **161**, 184–5.

Premack, D. *Intelligence in Apes and Man* (New York: Wiley, 1976).

Sarno, M. T., & Levita, E. Natural course of recovery in severe aphasia. *Archives of Physical Medicine and Rehabilitation* (1971), **52**, 175–9.

Sidtis, J. J. On the nature of central cortical function underlying right hemisphere auditory perception. *Neuropsychologia* (1980), **18**, 321–30.

Sidtis, J. J., & Gazzaniga, M. S. Competence versus performance after callosal section: Looks can be deceiving. In J. B. Hellige (ed.), *Cerebral Hemisphere Asymmetry: Method, Theory, and Application* (New York: Praeger, in press).

Sidtis, J. J., Volpe, B. T., Rayport, M., Wilson, D. H., & Gazzaniga, M. S. Variability in right hemisphere language function after callosal section: Evidence for a continuum of generative capacity. *Journal of Neuroscience* (1981), **1**, 323–31.

Sperry, R. W. Mental unity following surgical disconnection of the cerebral hemispheres. *The Harvey Lecture Series* (1968), **62**, 293–323.

Sperry, R. W., Zaidel, E., & Zaidel, D. Self-recognition and social awareness in the deconnected minor hemisphere. *Neuropsychologia* (1979), **17**, 153–66.

Wilson, D. H., Reeves, A. G., Gazzaniga, M. S., & Culver, C. Cerebral commissurotomy for the control of intractable seizures. *Neurology* (1977), **27**, 708–15.

Woods, B. T., & Carey, S. Language deficits after apparent clinical recovery from childhood aphasia. *Annals of Neurology* (1979), **6**, 405–09.

Zaidel, D., & Sperry, R. W. Performance on Raven's colored progressive matrices tests by commissurotomy patients. *Cortex* (1973), **9**, 34.

Zaidel, D., & Sperry, R. W. Memory impairment following commissurotomy in man. *Brain* (1974), **97**, 263–72.

Zaidel, E. Auditory vocabulary of the right hemisphere following brain bisection or hemi-decortication. *Cortex* (1976), **12**, 191–211.

Zaidel, E. Auditory language comprehension in the right hemisphere following cerebral commissurotomy and hemispherectomy: A comparison with child language and aphasia. In A. Caramazza & E. Zurif (eds), *Language Acquisition and Language Breakdown: Parallels and Divergencies* (Baltimore, MD: Johns Hopkins University Press, 1978a).

Zaidel, E. Concepts of cerebral dominance in the split brain. In P. A. Buser & A. Rougeul-Buser (eds), *Cerebral Correlates of Conscious Experience* (Amsterdam: Elsevier/North-Holland, 1978b).

Zaidel, E. Lexical organization in the right hemisphere. In P. A. Buser & A. Rougeul-Buser (eds), *Cerebral Correlates of Conscious Experience* (Amsterdam: Elsevier/North-Holland, 1978c).

Current Thinking on Language Structures

Marta Kutas

Language is not just sandwiched
between Broca's and Wernicke's.
Heard, spoken or seen
meaning emerges from activities
in multiple sites
each scheming by all rights
at much the same time
to yield both the literal
and the metaphorical,
the banal
and the sublime.

Introduction

What is current thinking on language structures? The answer to this question is not as obvious as it may seem, as certainly in isolation, and sometimes even within context, language input is ambiguous at many levels. In fact, I will assert that it is pointless to view language simply as a code which combines context-invariant meanings of words via a set of rules (grammar); rather it makes more sense to view language as providing clues to the language user for flexibly addressing his/her knowledge base so as to make sense of a particular utterance within the current context (for elaboration see Coulson, 1997). Without some background knowledge, in other words, more context than is literally a part of this chapter's title, no one can know exactly what meaning its author intended. The title "current thinking on language structures" is ambiguous in meaning. Moreover, several of its individual words are lexically ambiguous. For example, is "current" serving as an adjective or a noun in this case? Which meaning was intended – the swiftest part of a stream, or a flow of electric charge? And what about "structures," does it refer to something constructed or to the organization of the parts as dominated by the general character of the whole? This is not to mention "on," which many people may not consider ambiguous until they look it up in the dictionary only to find over twenty different definitions.

How does the reader's brain choose and the writer's mind come to know which of these dictionary entries is the right one? In other words – which "current," which "structures," and which "on" are to be accessed and recombined to yield the title's intended meaning? Perhaps it is those structures in the brain that turn changes in air pressure on the eardrums into a meaningful sound as well as those that allow us to know that "I am pleased as punch to be here" does not mean that I am thirsty (for punch) or that I want to be punched (i.e., hit).

Language is an exquisite medium for passing along propositions, for talking about the past and the future, and for getting people to do or to think what you want them to do or think, respectively. But decoding linguistic input, especially in real time, is a difficult analytic problem. Human brains are massively parallel in their processing but linguistic input (speech) enters as an essentially serial stream of acoustic inputs: words come in one at a time, perhaps with a little forewarning (e.g., co-articulation) but more often than not it is necessary to hold onto parts of the input, i.e., to wait for more than a word or two in order to figure out the structure and the meaning of an utterance or a line of text. Perhaps this is the language structure to which my title refers.

So, What Are some Current Thoughts on Language Structures?

Some current thinking on language (brain) structures is that the traditional view of Wernicke's area in the temporal lobe near its junction with the parietal lobe as taking in linguistic information and Broca's area in the frontal cortex of the left hemisphere as controlling its output needs to be modified (Damasio, 1997). However one defines language, the cognitive neuroscience literature attests to the involvement of many more than two areas of the brain in understanding a single sentence much less an entire discourse. Areas in the left and right hemispheres in both anterior and posterior regions of the brain have been implicated in some aspect of language processing (e.g., Binder, Frost, Hammeke, Cox, Rao, & Prieto, 1997). Damage somewhere in the peri-sylvian region of the left hemisphere can be devastating to certain aspects of language, especially speech. But damage to the right hemisphere seriously compromises an individual's ability to appreciate the meaning of an indirect request, a metaphor, an idiom or a joke (Joanette and Brownell, 1990; Joanette, Goulet, and Hannequin, 1990). The traditional model of language representation in the brain is undergoing fine-tuning and expansion based on what is now known about the size of brain areas, about various language functions and brain activity and/or damage to the brain, and about the functions of language as well as about various linguistic phenomena.

For instance, it is quite unlikely that what has traditionally been called Broca's area refers to a single brain area. Based on the numbers and sizes of visual, auditory, somatosensory and motor areas in macaques, the average brain area in the human probably covers about 1000 mm^2 of cortex. If what is typically labeled Broca's area does in fact subsume 4 to 5 distinct brain areas, it is easier to explain the substantial variability in the behavioral symptoms reportedly observed after damage to this region. Note that a similar argument could be made for Wernicke's area. The newer brain imaging techniques such as computerized axial tomography (CAT) and magnetic resonance imaging (MRI) scans have made it possible to define the exact areas damaged by a stroke, and thus have forced neuropsychologists to reconsider the view that damage to Broca's (and no other) area always leads to Broca's aphasia. In fact, brain images such as by positron emission tomography (PET) have revealed that functional damage often extends beyond the boundaries of the observed structural damage. Some researchers argue that this is simply an inferential limit inherent in neuropsychological data, which therefore can be overcome by measuring brain activity instead of brain damage or by localizing the damaged areas with greater anatomical precision. But, in fact, we can never make the inferential part of the mapping problem vanish fully. fMRI and PET data map brain activity, not linguistic or psychological functions, and it is function that we hope to specify so as to account for the understanding and/or production of utterances or reading of texts.

In fact, many researchers do seem to have abandoned the simple one-to-one mapping between Broca's area and production and Wernicke's area and comprehension. But this view has been replaced with the equally simplistic view that Broca's area is responsible for syntax and Wernicke's area is responsible for semantics, or Broca's area is mainly involved in rule-based processing (e.g., regular verbs) whereas Wernicke is a memory store for exceptions (e.g., irregular verbs). Naturally, there are some data consistent with each of these alternatives. Thus we come back to our original question – what functions does Broca's area perform? This is a difficult question to answer given our current state of knowledge, but I suggest that knowing that Broca's area probably comprises four or five different areas rather than one will help to constrain hypotheses about the functions of its different sub-areas (Deacon, 1996).

Another language-sensitive area identified recently is the Basal Temporal Language Area at the bottom of the temporal lobe (e.g., Luders, Lesser, Hahn, Dinner, Morris, Resor, and Harrison, 1986). It is in this general area (anterior fusiform gyrus) within the brains of individuals with epilepsy that Nobre, Allison, and McCarthy (1994) observed a large electrical response whose amplitude was sensitive to semantically anomalous words in sentence context. Nobre et al.'s data also revealed that cells in both hemispheres respond not just to faces but also to words both in and out of context, lending support to the hypothesis that the basal temporal regions are involved in language processing.

In summary, there appear to be multiple "language areas" distributed throughout the brain. We might ask what the functions of these areas are and whether these functions are specific to language processing. Clearly, in order to link these areas with language processing functions in real time it is necessary to determine not only where they are located (in space) but also their temporal characteristics (duration and order of involvement). Most psycholinguists agree that different types of linguistic and non-linguistic information can influence how sentences are understood, but they disagree on when and how different sorts of information are used. In other words, they disagree on the temporal structure of processing, and on which processes work on input from only one level of analysis and which are typically influenced by input from more than one level. To choose among the existing hypotheses, psycholinguists need to know more about the temporal coordination of all the (distributed) brain areas involved in comprehension and production. This is where event-related brain potential (ERP) methodology can be useful. If the average ERPs from two experimental conditions differ reliably at any given point in time, it can then be inferred that the associated brain and mental activity also differ at least by that point. In fact, the onset latency of the ERP difference can serve as an upper limit for the minimum time it takes the brain to differentiate two or more classes of stimuli.

ERPs provide an exquisite measure of the brain's activity at any moment across scales from milliseconds to tens of seconds. Its temporal resolution ranges from the crucial milliseconds that differentiate one phoneme from another to the more extended time course needed to determine that "pencilist" is not a word, or that "pencils" does not fit with the sense of the phrase "The pigs were herded into their pencils" as well as the seconds that may be required to determine who did what to whom after reading... "The American that the Frenchman that the Russian telephoned perplexed contacted the Spanish electrophysiologist about running a study." ERP records can tell cognitive neuroscientists *when* certain events in the brain take place. And, as this last example implies, ERPs can provide such timing information beyond the level of the single word. With the exception of the magnetoencephalogram (MEG), no other currently-used neuroimaging technique has the temporal precision of the ERP technique. Neither PET nor fMRI methods will ever attain the resolution of electromagnetic recordings because they are based on hemodynamic changes, which occur on the order of a second or more. By contrast, both PET and fMRI have a higher spatial resolution than ERP/MEG although electromagnetic methods have gained considerable ground in this arena with the advent of high EEG resolution methods (see Kutas and Federmeier, 1998, for a review). Moreover it is important to note that measures dependent on hemodynamic or metabolic changes are indirect reflections of neural activity whereas the EEG/MEG are direct indices. Recently it has been suggested that optical imaging may someday rival both ERPs/MEG and PET/fMRI if it can be determined that the optical changes reflect changes in neural activity per se (Gratton, Fabiani, and Corballis, 1997).

It is unlikely that you would tell someone who couldn't make it to a talk what it was all about via a string of isolated words. Language has structure – the very structure that Chomsky (1966) said could never be accounted for strictly in terms of chains of stimulus–response pairings in his devastating review of Skinner's *Verbal Behavior*. The exact same words occurring in different orders mean something different. Thus, it is the structure of language that makes "Kutas understood Jean" different from "Jean understood Kutas" but similar to "Kutas was understood by Jean," and "understood Jean was Kutas" not a meaningful sentence at all, and "Kutas who you understand understands that you understand her understanding" not so easy to understand. Structures have processing consequences which make some sentences easier to deal with than others.

The brain is sensitive to the structure(s) of language, as it encodes light and sound to yield meaning, a primary aim of many language exchanges. The details of the psychological or physiological processes that extract intended meaning from sensory input are unknown and highly controversial. But it is generally agreed that one outcome is some type of (re)depiction of activities of various people, places, and things in the comprehender's mind. The so-called discourse entities must be selected. Further, their interactions need to be encoded in a dynamic mental model that supports the kinds of inferences that are required to generate new information or new construals of old information by the comprehender. To understand "Jacques who Marta commented on presupposed the existence of a special purpose innate processor for language" requires keeping some temporary representation of Jacques and Marta until it becomes clear who did what to whom. Sentential structure notwithstanding, there are still many moments of syntactic ambiguity during a sentence's processing when it isn't clear who is doing and who is being done unto, as in "Jacques who Marta . . .". Moreover, as has become all too clear from the many failed attempts at machine translation from one language to another, to understand the meaning of such a sentence, information needs to be retrieved from long-term memory; language comprehension and knowledge in long-term memory go hand in hand. For example, knowing that Jacques's title included the phrase "language acquisition device" frames the sentence under discussion differently than simply knowing that Jacques and Marta both gave a presentation. The point, for present purposes, is that understanding the bulk of language requires processing at levels beyond words. Processing of units larger than single words, in turn, implies temporary representations in some form of working memory.

While the nature of the units of working memory (e.g., discrete chunks, activations within a production system, across units of a neural network, an articulatory loop) is highly contentious, it is commonly agreed that working memory is capacity limited and that its "contents" are temporary (for reviews, see Richardson, Engle, Hasher, Logie, Stoltzfus, and Zachs, 1996). Furthermore, there is a growing appreciation for the importance of temporal sequencing of working memory operations in separating processes and thereby in our ability to comprehend and produce language. The capacity limitations and the temporal characteristics of working memory impact language comprehension in important ways, which as yet are not fully understood. Thus, I believe we need to track both working and long-term memory use during online language comprehension so as to get a better picture of how different regions in neural space are coordinated in time to yield sense from a serial linguistic stream.

In our laboratory, we have been using ERPs recorded from the scalp as people read clauses or sentences as a way to look at word processing, language structure, and the relation between the two. Most recently, we have used ERPs to examine the hierarchical relations between words independent of their actual meanings, with the eventual aim of investigating how meaning influences the processing of sentences with certain structures. We started by recording ERPs across the human scalp to simple transitive sentences like "The doctor examined the child" – where there is a subject (S), a verb (V), and an object (O). The data revealed electrophysiological properties that emerge across sentences that are more than the responses to individual words lined up end to end: namely, very slow potentials that cumulate and fluctuate across the course of the sentence.

An informative way of looking at such slow potential effects is to apply a low pass digital filter to the cross-sentence ERPs such that only the slow activity remains. The filtering simplifies the representation of the data but still leaves a temporally and spatially rich and complex pattern of activity over the head. The slow potentials vary in time across the clause as sentence constituents are processed, and in space from the front to the back of the head as well as between the hemispheres. An important characteristic of these types of simple transitive sentences is that they do not draw any special attention to themselves but do nonetheless engage orthographic, lexical, semantic, and syntactic information and processes as well as working and long-term memory systems.

Let us briefly examine the pattern of slow potentials (see figure 31.1). Electrodes over the lateral occipitotemporal cortex are over brain areas that are critical for the early processing of visual stimuli including words. We cannot assume that electrical activity at the scalp is generated directly beneath the electrode. But as a first working hypothesis, we suggest that the sustained occipital potential reflects neural activity involved in processing of visual features. This negativity may reflect the continuous processing of the visual input in the ventro-lateral occipital areas proposed by Petersen and Fiez (1993) to be involved in processing word forms on the basis of their PET data. If our hypothesis is correct, then we would expect to record similar slow potentials during spoken sentences; however, these potentials would have a more central distribution characteristic of early auditory processing generated in or near the superior temporal gyrus. This prediction was borne out in subsequent work, as seen in figure 31.3 (Mueller, King and Kutas, 1997).

Over temporal sites, both the fast and slow potential activity are sensitive to lexical class and even higher-level features of the input. The low-pass filtered data show a phasic positivity beginning at the verb of the clause (see figure 31.1). Our current working hypothesis is that this phasic positivity is an index, at least in part, of the processing of thematic role information contained in the lexical representation of the verb; loosely this means the positivity is being linked to processes responsible for

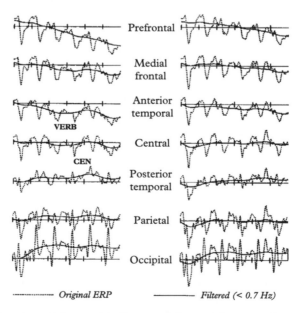

Figure 31.1   Superimposed are originally recorded cross-clause grand average ERPs and the slow potentials only (low pass filtered at 0.7 Hz) to simple transitive clauses for 7 pairs of sites from anterior to posterior sites across the head over left and right hemispheres separately. Negative is up on this and all subsequent figures. Words were presented one at a time every 500 ms for a duration of 200 ms. The positivity associated with verbs and the clause ending negativity (CEN) are labeled.

correctly associating a verb with its noun arguments. If our hypothesis is correct then we would expect the amplitude of the response to the verb to vary systematically with the number of thematic roles assigned by that verb. Specifically, we would expect amplitude differences for intransitive verbs ("sleep") that assign one thematic role, transitive verbs ("kill") that assign two thematic roles, and ditransitive verbs ("give") that assign three thematic roles.

Also over temporal sites, following the object of the verb ("child") comes the slow CEN, or clause ending negativity (see figure 31.1). Clause boundaries have been shown to make very heavy demands on working memory capacity; this is evidenced in generally slowed reading times whether measured by manual responses or eye movements (e.g., Aaronson and Ferres, 1986). If we are correct about our proposed link between the phasic verb positivity and thematic role assignments and the clause ending and the CEN, we would expect to see them both during speech processing as well.

At the same time, over the front of the head there is an extremely slow (< 0.2 Hz), cumulative positivity. The combination of its frontal maximum and the role of the frontal lobes in executive functions of working memory (Pennington, Bennetto, McAleer, & Roberts, 1996) have led us to suggest that this ultra-slow positivity may reflect integration of recently encoded information in working memory with information from long-term memory. As with the verb-related positivity and CEN, we would expect this activity to be relatively independent of input modality, insofar as it is related to some aspect of language processing as opposed to reading or listening per se. On the other hand, even if such effects turn out to be modality-independent, this does not necessarily mean that they are language-specific.

In brief, we have described four slow potential effects, all of which are laterally asymmetric: a sustained negative shift over occipital sites presumably related to early visual processing, a temporal positivity time-locked to verb processing (possibly thematic role assignment), a negativity that indexes clause ending, and an ultra-slow cumulative positivity over frontal sites that might reflect the processing involved in building a mental model of the sentence. These slow potential effects show that the different temporally overlapping processes that are called into play in multiple brain areas can be monitored via ERP recordings.

The pattern of these slow potential effects during the processing of simple transitive sentences is markedly different for "good" and "poorer" comprehenders. Poor and good comprehenders were grouped according to a median split on their scores to comprehension questions following a subset of the sentences. Over occipital sites, poorer comprehenders show larger and more asymmetric early visual components (P1-N1-P2) and larger and more asymmetric slow potentials. By contrast at the prefrontal sites, it is the good rather than poor comprehenders who show a larger and more asymmetric slow positivity that builds over the sentences – which we linked to integration. Perhaps there is a tradeoff in resource allocation: more resources devoted to early visual processing (feature extraction, accessing wordforms) by poor comprehenders and more resources devoted to higher order integrative processes by good comprehenders.

We would expect integrative processes, in particular, to be more readily completed for simple transitives than for sentences with more complex syntactic structures that describe more complex discourse relations, such as those with relative clauses. There are, however, different types of relative clauses; two that we have investigated are subject and object relative sentences. In subject relative sentences, the subject of the main clause is also the subject of the relative clause (e.g., "The professor who advised the dean made a public statement."). In object relative sentences, the subject of the main clause is also the object of the relative clause verb (e.g., "The professor who the dean advised made a public statement."). These sentences are similar in that they both include a relative clause but they differ in the structure of the relative clause and in the role the main clause subject plays in the relative clause. Neither sentence type is ambiguous. However, object relatives are typically considered to be more difficult than the subject relatives (King and Just, 1991).

It has been suggested that object relatives are more difficult primarily because they put a greater load on working memory resources than do subject relatives, although both make greater demands on working memory than do simple transitive sentences. Object relatives require the reader or listener to hold an unattached constituent in working memory for a longer time than in subject relatives. This greater memory load is assumed to lead to processing difficulty (i.e., slower processing or lower accuracy). This has been inferred from reading time measures, taken as subjects press a key to present each word of a sentence one after another, one at a time, at their own pace. In reading time data, the first reliable sign of such a greater memory load occurs at the end of the relative clause ("advised"), which is just about when the load goes away. Moreover, the largest reading time effects are observed right after that at the main clause verb ("made"). Another potentially difficult aspect of object relatives is that they require multiple shifts in focus between the discourse participants. In this example, first the professor is at the center of focus, then the dean, then the professor again. In contrast, the professor remains the focus in subject relative sentences.

Electrophysiological data, at the sentence location where the largest RT effects are generally observed, namely, at the main clause verbs, reveal a much greater left anterior negativity (LAN) for the object relatives (King and Kutas, 1995). This type of effect was first described by Kluender (1991) for wh-Questions versus simple yes–no questions. In wh-Questions, it takes a while before the reader or listener knows who the who is in "Who do you think that...?" Kluender proposed that this greater LAN for wh-Questions reflects the maintenance of items in working memory (Kluender and Kutas, 1993). An alternative view links the LAN to a disruption of the first stages of syntactic processing (e.g., Friederici and Mecklinger, 1996). Our data do not fit readily with this latter view. We have observed a LAN for both types of relative clauses compared with verbs in sentences that do not have any embedded clauses, so this relative negativity does appear to vary with working memory load. This finding meshes well with the reading-time data. As an aside, note that it may well be that there is more than one negativity subsumed by the LAN, one of which may reflect working memory processes. Moreover, it follows that if the LAN reflects working memory load it should be present with non-language materials as well. Although it is difficult to compare ERPs elicited in different experimental paradigms directly, the work of Roesler and his colleagues (Roesler, Heil, and Roder, 1997) shows that increased memory load is associated with greater long-lasting negativities. The negativities are sensitive to the same sorts of manipulations but vary in their scalp maxima as a function of the stimulus materials. We consider this pattern to be non-language-specific in its elicitation but language-specific in its scalp distribution.

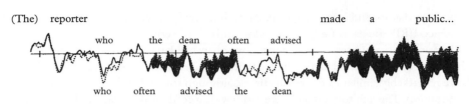

Figure 31.2 Comparison of the grand average cross-sentence ERPs elicited by subject-relative (*solid line*) and object-relative (*dotted line*) sentences recorded over a left frontal location. The two sentence types are equivalent both before and after the relative clause. The relative clause above the baseline is a sample object-relative sentence and that below the baseline is a sample subject-relative sentence. Words were presented one at a time every 500 ms for a duration of 200 ms. The shaded area represents the difference between the two conditions on the average; object relatives are reliably more negative than subject relatives here.

Back to the issue at hand, one could ask whether the LAN effects at the main clause verb add any new information. Some researchers say that the presence of this LAN effect could be informative, but only if its neural generator were known. However, even without knowledge of neural generators, ERPs can provide information that reading time could not provide. By contrasting sentence length ERPs for the two relative clause sentence types, we can see that processing differences between the two object relative types occur much earlier in the sentence than reading time data suggested (figure 31.2). The first sign of a reliable ERP difference occurs as soon as the working memory load is different – at the relative clause, when the reader has to deal with the word "dean" without yet knowing what to do with "professor." The difference is a sustained negativity over central and frontal sites for the object compared with the subject relatives. There is a further ERP differentiation as the reader returns to the main clause, encounters the main clause verb "made," and can in fact finally decide who did what to whom.

A median split of Good (87%) versus Poorer (60%) comprehenders reveals strikingly different patterns, with the good comprehenders showing a large difference between the subject and object relatives and poorer comprehenders showing almost none. In fact, the ERP data suggest that poorer comprehenders find even the subject relative sentences pretty difficult; they generate mostly negativities as if their WM were loaded down even by the embeddings in subject relatives. Moreover, the over-sentence ERPs of poorer comprehenders show a much attenuated version of the slow frontal positivity characteristic of the subject relatives in good comprehenders, suggesting that the poorer comprehenders are not integrating as regularly or as well as the good ones.

One criticism that has been leveled against this work, however, is that reading two words per second is abnormally slow, when normal reading is closer to three to four words per second. Thus, it has been suggested that the ERP differences we have observed between the relative clause sentence types were merely an artifact of our one-word-at-a-time, presentation rate. Moreover, even at normal reading rates it has been argued that "real" language is speech, not reading. But segmenting speech raises both theoretical and practical problems; it is difficult to record clear ERP components even from semi-connected speech. However, because the slow potentials we have observed are not triggered by individual word onsets, but rather by the continuous mental processes that extend across larger units such as clauses, we decided to examine the sentence ERP effects as people listened to embedded sentences.

Just as in visually-presented sentences, we observed large ERP differences between the subject and object relative sentence types (Mueller, King, and Kutas, 1996). These were remarkably similar to the visual effects, although somewhat different in their scalp distribution. The auditory effects were more widespread on the scalp, and much larger over the right hemisphere than the visual effects. However, at some electrode sites, such as left frontal regions, the effects during the relative clause are remarkably similar in the two modalities. We view the difference in negativity for subject and object relative sentences for both written and spoken language as a modality-general effect. In other words, we view the presence of a negative difference with a similar timecourse and sensitivity as an index of language processing in general, rather than a process specific to either reading or listening.

As expected, however, there are other aspects of the ERP that are modality specific. The slow potentials reveal that visual and auditory sentences generate dynamically similar but topographically distinct effects. We believe that the negativities across the course of sentences in the visual and auditory modalities are similar; however, since the stimulus input features are different, the particular brain areas involved in their processing are also different to some extent. As a consequence, the relative distributions of potentials across the scalp also differ. For example, in the visual modality, the resting negativity is large at a (left) occipitotemporal site, but absent at a site on top of the head. In the auditory modality, the opposite pattern is seen (figure 31.3). We have previously argued that the visual negativity is related to sustained word processing; we make a comparable argument for the auditory data. We also found that the processing

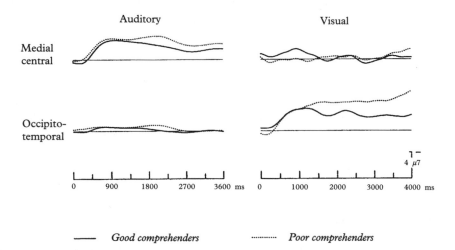

Figure 31.3   Grand average slow potential ERPs (low pass filtered at 0.7 Hz) to sentences of various structures for good (*solid line*) and poor (*dotted line*) comprehenders in the visual and auditory modalities at one medial central and one occipito-temporal recording site. In the auditory modality, the prolonged negative potential over the clause is pronounced over central and occipital sites whereas in the visual modality it is maximal over occipito-temporal sites. Note that the reading (King & Kutas, 1995) and listening data (Muller et al., 1997) are from two different groups of subjects.

differences connected with comprehension skill as reflected in the ERP patterns are similar for reading and listening.

With such data in hand, we have begun to examine what types of information (e.g., lexical, semantic, discourse, pragmatic) the brain is sensitive to while processing object relatives. In this way we can begin to understand why some embedded sentences like "The student that the committee that the results surprised summoned listened closely" seem to be much harder to understand than others like "The painting that the artist that everyone loves painted hung in the living room" although they have exactly the same syntactic structure with the same number of embeddings. It is our belief that the difference must rest in the content of the words – in other words, in their meaning. Theories of parsing differ considerably on when meaning is allowed to play any role and exactly what role it is allowed to play. Jill Weckerly, Jeff Elman, and I have pursued this by doing connectionist modeling, reading time studies and ERP studies (see Weckerly and Elman, 1992). All three approaches indicate that a noun's animacy does influence sentence parsing, perhaps by supporting tentative estimates on likelihood of the roles that a noun might play even before any verbs are encountered (Weckerly, 1995).

Thus far I have described how ERP data are used to study language processing in real time. I would like to conclude by relating my comments and data to Professor Mehler's position. Mehler wrote that "language has to be studied as an endowment that is genetically determined and culturally clinched." In other words, that language is innate but influenced by cultural input. If from this we are to understand that language is an inborn capacity that is not learned, then it is not particularly useful since almost all behavior is subject to some kind of learning. If on the other hand we are to understand by this that language is innately specified in the genome, then it is a bit misleading in that every phenotypic feature and hence also every behavioral trait is codetermined by an individual's genome and by environmental variables past and present. PET evidence was offered as "additional data that may make it easier to understand our language processing device (LAD)." I cannot see how PET data, per se, regardless of the task, can ever be evidence for a language acquisition device given that the participants in these experiments were molded both by their genetic endowment and by their experiences. The existence of a language acquisition device is a hypothesis but in this type of presentation, it seems to be a given. Presumably, this language processing device is a cortical structure that is specific to processing language and no other cognitive function, and thus studying the brain seems a reasonable approach. However, the LAD is not presented as a hypothesis but rather mentioned as if there were already evidence for its existence, although in fact there is no agreement as to what data would constitute evidence for it. Moreover, the brain data are presented as relevant to issues in language acquisition. But this link hinges on the assumption that language is innately specified, from which it would then follow that this innate specification in the genome would be manifest in cortical organization. But again there is no consensus that language is innately specified. Finally, Professor Mehler presented neural imaging data from bilinguals as a means of determining how their first and second languages compete for this cortical structure (i.e., the LAD); again, this approach is based on the presupposition that such a cortical structure exists. The neuroimaging data do show, not surprisingly, that somewhat different regions of the brain are involved in first and second languages. What they do not show, however, is that there is an LAD in monolinguals or bilinguals; nor could they ever.

By contrast, our research does not start with the assertion that language is innate or that there is a language acquisition device. Rather we take the view that there may be a relatively direct relationship between processes of language comprehension and general cognitive processes, and that linguistic data can suggest constraints on memory access and organization of background knowledge. Work in my laboratory as well as my reading of the literature lead me to conclude that there are multiple areas of the brain involved in language processing. I have shown that the ERP methodology is one technique for temporally tracking sentence comprehension and that so doing reveals that working memory operations and background knowledge are critical to normal comprehension. Our data show that many of the processes of language include large parts of the brain, are neither modality nor language-specific, are quite sensitive to individual differences, and overlap in space and time, such that both dimensions are needed to tease them apart.

Acknowledgments

Thanks to M. Besson and C. van Petten for comments on a previous draft of this manuscript and J. Requin for many discussions throughout the years. Some of the work reported herein was supported by grants from HD22614, MH52893, and AG08313 to M. Kutas.

References

Aaronson, D., & Ferres, S. (1986). Reading strategies for children and adults: A quantitative model. *Psychological Review*, **93**, 89–112.

Binder, J. R., Frost, J. A., Hammeke, T. A., Cox, R. W., Rao, S. M., & Prieto, T. (1997). Human brain language areas identified by functional magnetic resonance imaging. *Journal of Neuroscience*, **17**, (1), 353–62.

Chomsky, N. (1966). Review of Skinner's "Verbal behavior". *Language*, **35**, 26–58.

Coulson, S. (1997). Semantic leaps: The role of frame-shifting and conceptual blending in meaning construction. Ph.D. dissertation, University of California, San Diego, La Jolla, CA.

Damasio, A. R. (1997). Brain and language: What a difference a decade makes. *Current Opinion in Neurology*, **10**, 177–8.

Deacon, T. W. (1996). Prefrontal cortex and symbol learning: Why a brain capable of language evolved only once. In B. Mitrofanovich Velichkovsky & D. M. Rumbaugh (eds), *Communicating meaning: The evolution and development of language* (pp. 103–38), Mahwah, NJ: Lawrence Erlbaum Associates.

Friederici, A. D., & Mecklinger, A. (1996). Syntactic parsing as revealed by brain responses: First-pass and second-pass parsing processes. *Journal of Psycholinguistic Research*, **25** (1), 157–76.

Gratton, G., Fabiani, M., & Corballis, P. M. (1997). Can we measure correlates of neuronal activity with non-invasive optical methods? *Advances in Experimental Medicine and Biology*, **413**, 53–62.

Joanette, Y., & Brownell, H. H. (eds) (1990). *Discourse ability and brain damage: Theoretical and empirical perspectives*. New York: Springer-Verlag.

Joanette, Y., Goulet, P., & Hannequin, D. (1990). *Right hemisphere and verbal communication*. New York: Springer-Verlag.

King J., & Just, M. (1991). Individual differences in syntactic processing: The role of working memory. *Journal of Memory and Language*, **30**, 580–602.

King, J., & Kutas, M. (1995). Who did what and when? Using word- and clause-related ERPs to monitor working memory usage in reading. *Journal of Cognitive Neuroscience*, **7**, 378–97.

Kluender, R. (1991). Cognitive constraints on variables in syntax. Ph.D. dissertation, University of California, San Diego, La Jolla, CA.

Kluender, R., & Kutas, M. (1993). Bridging the gap: Evidence from ERPs on the processing of unbounded dependencies. *Journal of Cognitive Neuroscience*, **5**, 196–214.

Kutas, M., & Federmeier, K. (1998). Minding the body. *Psychophysiology*, **35**, 1–16.

Luders, H., Lesser, R. P., Hahn, J., Dinner, D. S., Morris, H., Resor, S., & Harrison, M. (1986). Basal temporal language area demonstrated by electrical stimulation. *Neurology*, **36**, 505–10.

Mueller, H. M., King, J. W., & Kutas, M. (1997). Event-related potentials to relative clause processing in spoken sentences. *Cognitive Brain Research*, **5** (3), 193–203.

Nobre, A. C., Allison, T., & McCarthy, G. (1994). Word recognition in the human inferior temporal lobe. *Nature*, **372**, 260–3.

Pennington, B. F., Bennetto, L., McAleer, O., & Roberts, R. J. Jr (1996). Executive functions and working memory: Theoretical and measurement issues. In G. R. Lyon & N. A. Krasnegor (eds), *Attention, memory, and executive function* (pp. 327–48), Baltimore, MD: Paul H. Brookes Publishing.

Petersen, S. E., & Fiez, J. A. (1993). The processing of single words studied with positron emission tomography, *Annual Review of Neuroscience*, **16**, 509–30.

Richardson, J. T. E., Engle, R. W., Hasher, L., Logie, R. H., Stoltzfus, E. R., & Zachs, R. T. (1996), *Working memory and human cognition*. New York: Oxford University Press.

Roesler, F., Heil, M., & Roder, B. (1997). Slow negative brain potentials as reflections of specific modular resources of cognition. *Biological Psychology*, **45**, (1–3), 109–41.

Weckerly, J. (1995). Object relatives viewed through behavioral, electrophysiological, and modeling techniques. Ph.D. dissertation, University of California, San Diego, La Jolla, CA.

Weckerly, J., & Elman, J. (1992). A PDP approach to processing center-embedded sentences. In *Proceedings of the 14th annual conference of the Cognitive Science Society*, Hillsdale, NJ: Erlbaum.

Evolution

INTRODUCTION TO PART IX

Understanding any biological system can only be helped by knowledge of its evolutionary history. The brain's horrendous complexity is the result of billions of years of incremental modification. On the level of psychology, awareness of the selective pressures on our ancestors can make the bottom lines of social interaction very clear, and hint at less obvious tendencies that might be obscured by social graces. On a physiological level, observation of organizational features common to many species may indicate what matters most.

Jon Kaas addresses the complexity of primates' visual systems, asking "why?" Why, if each area is specialized to detect a different set of visual attributes, can some species get by with far fewer areas while apparently still being able to detect many of the same features? Why have visual areas multiplied in primates rather than increasing in intrinsic complexity? His answers are inconclusive, but the questions he raises are an important counterbalance to comfortingly simple ideas.

In "Antibodies and Learning: Selection versus Instruction," Niels Kaj Jerne reviews the history of several lines of thought in biology and observes that processes that are initially thought to be based on learning consistently turn out to be based on a selective mechanism. He asks the provocative question of whether the learning processes of the mind might in fact result from some competitive, selective process. One might reconsider Norman and Shallice's model in this light.

The differences between humans and animals, Todd Preuss argues in the final article, are played down by neuroscientists invested in the notion of the ready applicability to humans of insight gleaned from studying animals. Preuss points out that other life forms, rather than representing throwbacks stuck at an earlier point of human evolution, have in fact been energetically evolving much as we have in the millennia since the lines diverged. He illustrates the point with evidence of dramatic differences in structure and wiring between mammalian species. One would hope that an implication is that we can ignore the differences as nonessential species-specific adaptations, concentrating on the common organizational principles that presumably underlie the fundamentals.

Why Does the Brain Have So Many Visual Areas?

Jon H. Kaas

Introduction

The visual system of an advanced mammal, such as a macaque monkey, includes a number of subcortical and cortical centers (see Kaas and Huerta, 1988, for review). The retina projects to the suprachiasmatic nucleus, the pregeniculate nucleus, the lateral geniculate nucleus, nuclei of the accessory optic system, the pretectal nuclei, and the superior colliculus. Most of the very large pulvinar complex, which includes at least 7 or 8 nuclei, is also involved in vision. Parts of the reticular nucleus, the basal ganglia, pons, and cerebellum are predominantly visual in function, and the parabigeminal nucleus and oculomotor nuclei of the brain stem are visual centers. But much of visual processing, especially processing related to conscious aspects of vision, occurs in visual cortex, where some 15–30 visual areas participate. An obvious question, given this multiplicity, is why so many areas?

Of course an obvious question is not often new. Cowey (1981), for example, titled a paper "Why are there so many visual areas?" Kaas (1982) subtitled a paper "Why do sensory systems have so many subdivisions?", and Barlow (1986) recently asked "Why have multiple cortical areas?" Cowey (1981) noted that "the answer to the question ...is not clear" and "that is why it is worth discussing." The general consensus is that the different visual areas are specialized to mediate different aspects of vision, but there are varying opinions about the nature of these different aspects, and about what is gained by increasing the numbers of visual areas. The present chapter considers what is a visual area, how species vary in numbers of visual areas, and the possible advantages of having larger numbers of visual areas.

1   What is a Visual Area?

Brodmann (1909) regarded cortical areas as the "organs" of the brain, with specific functions or sets of functions. Because of their functional distinctiveness, the "organs" of the brain were expected to differ in histological structure, and Brodmann used architectural differences in the brains of humans and a wide range of other mammals to parcel cortex into areas of presumed functional significance. Eight decades of subsequent research support Brodmann's assumption that cortex is sharply divided into a mosaic of functionally distinct areas or fields. However, the architectonic method, when used by itself, is often unreliable.

Because the architectonic method and other approaches all have the potential for error, cortical areas are most reliably defined by multiple criteria. If cortical areas are functionally distinct subdivisions of the brain, areas are likely to differ along a number of parameters including histological structure, connections, and neuron properties (see Kaas, 1982). In addition, areas in sensory systems often systematically represent a sensory surface. If a region of the brain contains a complete and orderly representation of the hemiretina (or contralateral visual hemifield), is histologically distinct (a wide range of procedures are now available, including traditional stains for cell bodies or myelinated fibers as well as more recently developed reactions for metabolic enzymes and neurotransmitters), has unique patterns of inputs, outputs and intrinsic connections, has a population of neurons with distinctively different response properties, and deactivation produces specific impairments, then the region is likely to be a valid visual area.

Early investigators, largely limited to relating histological appearance to rather sparse evidence from experimental animal studies and clinical reports, produced brain maps that differ greatly from current maps. In any study, the significance of architectonic distinctions can be misinterpreted so that parts of areas can be considered to be complete areas, a single area can be incorporated into several different fields, several fields can be incorrectly combined (e.g., borders misidentified), and identified subdivisions can be incorrectly homologized across species (see Kaas, 1982). Brodmann, because of the extent of his studies, and the number of species considered, has had great and lasting impact, even though his brain maps correctly identified only a few sensory areas of the cortex. For visual cortex, Brodmann usually, but not always, identified the primary field, V-I (his area 17), sometimes located the second field, V-II (his area 18), but failed to identify any of the other of the currently recognized visual fields (with the possible exception of "area 19" as V-III in cats). In proposing subdivisions of cortex in squirrels (fig. 32.1B), Brodmann (1909) correctly identified part of the primary field, V-I or area 17, but incorrectly identified the less developed medial portion of area 17 that is devoted to monocular vision as the second field, area 18 (V-II). No primary somatosensory field (area 3b) or primary auditory field (area 41) was found, and only part of the primary motor field (area 4) was identified. Most other proposed subdivisions have little relationship to present understandings of cortical organization. The point is not to devalue the contributions of Brodmann and other earlier investigators, but to stress the potential for error when only one method is used to subdivide the brain. The older, highly inaccurate maps are part of our scientific legacy, but further progress depends on evaluation, revision, and replacement. Given

(A) Proposed subdivisions of cortex in squirrels

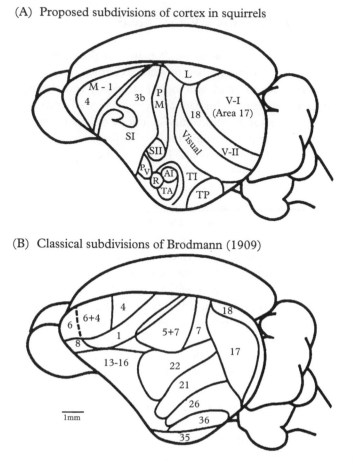

(B) Classical subdivisions of Brodmann (1909)

Figure 32.1   Current (**A**) and classical (**B**) views of how neocortex of squirrels is subdivided into areas. **A**. Some of the proposed areas are supported by a convergence of evidence from microelectrode recordings or stimulation, architectonic studies, and studies of connections. Other proposed subdivisions are based on more limited evidence. See text and Kaas et al., 1989, for details. **B**. Subdivisions of cortex according to the cytoarchitectonic studies of Brodmann (1909). Note that there is little correspondence with the modern view other than the partial overlap of primary visual cortex (area 17) and primary motor cortex (area 4 or M-I), and that Brodmann recognized no primary somatosensory (area 3b or S-I) or auditory (area 41 or A-I) fields. Brains are dorsolateral views with rostral (olfactory bulbs) to the left.

the power of current methods, especially when used in combination, there is no need to rely on the proposals and guesses of the past.

Current maps of the neocortex of a common rodent, the grey squirrel, illustrate some of the basic progress that has been made in defining cortical areas, and some of the questions that remain (figure 32.1A; see Krubitzer et al., 1986; Luethke et al., 1988; Kaas et al., 1989b). The primary visual area, V-I or area 17, has been defined by many criteria, including cyto- and myeloarchitecture, histological procedures such as reactions for cytochrome oxidase activity, microelectrode recordings that reveal a topographic representation of the contralateral visual hemifield, and systematic patterns of

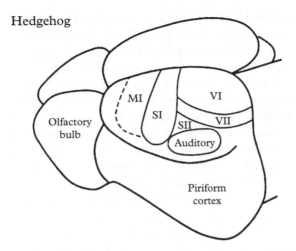

Hedgehog

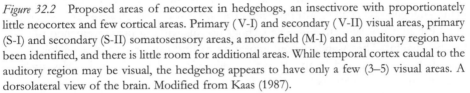

Figure 32.2 Proposed areas of neocortex in hedgehogs, an insectivore with proportionately little neocortex and few cortical areas. Primary (V-I) and secondary (V-II) visual areas, primary (S-I) and secondary (S-II) somatosensory areas, a motor field (M-I) and an auditory region have been identified, and there is little room for additional areas. While temporal cortex caudal to the auditory region may be visual, the hedgehog appears to have only a few (3–5) visual areas. A dorsolateral view of the brain. Modified from Kaas (1987).

connections with other cortical and subcortical structures. The second visual area, V-II or area 18, has also been delimited by the same set of multiple criteria. More laterally, cortex defined as visual has interconnections with V-I and V-II, but it is presently uncertain if the region is one or several visual fields. In the caudal temporal lobe, presumptive areas TI and TP are architectonically distinct, and have connections with the visual pulvinar, but more evidence is needed to determine if they correspond to functionally distinct visual areas. Elsewhere, primary motor cortex M-I, somatosensory fields S-I, S-II, and PV, and auditory areas A-I and R have been defined by multiple criteria, while other proposed subdivisions are supported by more limited evidence. However, methods for obtaining more evidence are available, and further investigation can and should modify and improve the map. Similarly, in other mammals such as cats and various monkeys, the evidence for proposed subdivisions varies area by area.

2 Are There Many Visual Areas?

The question of number of visual areas is part of a larger issue of how many areas of cortex exist. Until recently, one could be a "lumper" or a "divider" and propose that there are many or few brain areas, since there was no unequivocal way to evaluate the various proposals based on architectonic appearance. The two major contributors to theories of cortical organization, Brodmann (1909) and von Economo (1929), agreed that the number is species variable, that an increase represents an advance in evolution, and that the human brain has on the order of 50 or more areas. Other estimates for the human brain were of over 200 areas. Lashley, in contrast, argued that there was little reason to believe that rats and humans differ in number of fields, and that the brains of both contain about ten areas (e.g., Lashley and Clark, 1946). We now have strong evidence that primitive mammals with small brains and limited behavioral range have few cortical areas, perhaps as few as 10–15, while advanced mammals with large brains and considerable behavioral range have many cortical areas (50–100 or more).

The common European hedgehog, an insectivore, is an example of a mammal with very few cortical areas (figure 32.2). The brain is small, and it has very little neocortex, no more than a cap on the rest of the forebrain and about the same amount as the first mammals, as suggested from endocasts of the brain cavity. In hedgehogs, microelectrode recordings and stimulations have demonstrated first and second visual areas, motor cortex, first and second somatosensory areas, and an auditory region (see Kaas, 1987a). The auditory region may contain two or more fields, there is room in temporal cortex for one or two additional visual fields, a taste area remains to be identified, a supplementary motor field may exist medially, there appear to be several orbitofrontal and midline limbic fields, and transitional cortex is found along the rhinal fissure. Altogether, hedgehogs get along just fine with probably 10–15 cortical areas, as Lashley supposed for all mammals. Of course hedgehogs do this without being tremendously flexible in behavior. They wander about appearing to find carrion and other helpless food largely by accident, and escape danger by rolling into a ball of spines. Thus, the Greek poem from about 680–640 BC, "The fox knows many tricks, the hedgehog only one. One good one!"

The upper limit on the number of cortical areas in hedgehogs can be deduced from the strong evidence for the location and existence of some areas and the fact that there isn't much cortex in addition to these fields. Another example is the cortex of the common mouse, where we have some concept of cortical organization based on experimental data from mice and rats. The small amount of neocortex can be easily removed, flattened between glass plates, sectioned parallel to the surface, and stained to reveal myeloarchitectonic fields that have been previously related to sensory representations (figure 32.3; see Kaas et al., 1989b; Krubitzer et al., 1986, for review). Again, the conclusion is clear. Mice have few cortical areas, on the order of 10–15, and at best 3–5 visual areas (Wagor et al., 1980; however, see Montero et al., 1973).

Behaviorally advanced mammals with larger brains certainly have more fields. The best examples come from the domestic cat, several species of New World monkeys, and Old World macaque monkeys where considerable experimental evidence has been gathered (see Kaas, 1989a, for review). Cats appear to have as many as 10–15 visual areas, five somatosensory areas, and at least eight auditory areas. Monkeys also have large numbers of cortical areas, especially visual areas, and it is probable that higher primates including humans have even more.

Much of our research on the organization of cortex has been on the relatively small-brained New World monkey, the night or owl monkey (*Aotus*). In this monkey, the cortex can be removed and flattened, much as in the mouse, by placing a cut in primary visual cortex (area 17) so it can spread out (figure 32.4). In this form, all of the neocortex can be viewed as a single, flat sheet with only slight distortions produced by flattening. Fiber stains and other histological procedures provide landmarks so that experimentally determined fields can be superimposed on the flattened cortex with considerable accuracy.

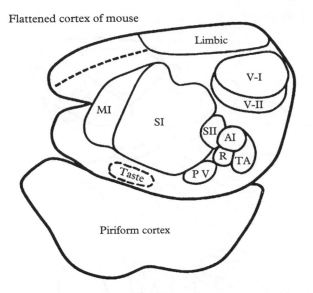

Figure 32.3 Some of the subdivisions of neocortex in a mouse. The drawing is based on architectonic distributions apparent in cortex that has been separated from the brain, unfolded, flattened between glass plates, and cut parallel to the surface. Somatosensory fields (S-I or primary somatosensory cortex, S-II or secondary somatosensory cortex, and PV or parietal-ventral), the visual fields (V-I or primary visual, V-II or secondary visual), motor field (M-I), and auditory fields (primary or AI, rostral or R, temporal anterior or TA) have been identified in micro-electrode mapping studies where results were related to architecture in rodents (see Krubitzer et al., 1986; Luethke et al., 1988; Kaas et al., 1989, for reviews). Because of the flattening, cortex of the medial wall including limbic cortex is to the top and parts of piriform cortex are at the bottom. The olfactory bulbs are missing. Rostral is left.

The caudal half of the cortex in owl monkeys contains a large number of visual areas (see Kaas, 1986 and 1989a, for review). The experimental support is extensive for the existence, location and extent of the primary field (V-I or area 17), the secondary field (V-II or area 18), and the middle temporal visual area (MT): Other proposed subdivisions have less compelling and varying amounts of experimental support. Thus it is likely that the present scheme will be modified, and given the history of progress in this type of research, several of the larger fields will prove to be composed of more than one visual area. However, there is now evidence for about 15 visual areas in caudal neocortex and at least 3 visuomotor areas in the frontal lobe. Similar numbers of visual areas have been proposed for macaque monkeys, where different groups of investigators have produced somewhat different summaries and use partially different terminologies (figure 32.5; see Van Essen, 1985; Desimone and Ungerleider, 1986). The clear conclusion, however, is that these advanced mammals, cats and monkeys, have on the order of 15–30 visual areas.

3 What Do Neurons in Visual Areas Do?

There is general agreement that neurons in different visual areas respond to visual stimuli with different response profiles (see Baker et al., 1981; Zeki, 1978). The point of

Owl monkey

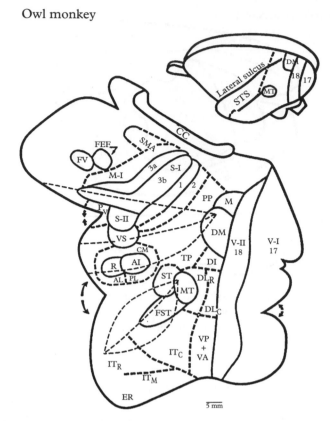

Figure 32.4   Cortical areas superimposed on an outline of a section from cortex that has been removed, flattened and cut parallel to the surface for a New World owl monkey. A dorsolateral view of the brain with reference areas is on the upper right. The opened lateral (Sylvian) sulcus and superior temporal sulcus (STS) are marked with dashed lines. The corpus callosum (CC) and limbic cortex have been unfolded from the medial wall of the cerebral hemisphere. The visual, somatic, auditory, and motor areas are from published reports on owl monkeys (see Kaas, 1982; 1988, for review and references). A dashed line on the outline of the intact brain (upper right) and the shaded region on the flattened cortex (below) indicate the approximate extent of visual cortex. This includes primary (V-I) and secondary (V-II) fields, the middle temporal visual area (MT), rostral (DL_R) and caudal (DL_C) division of the dorsolateral complex, the dorsointermediate area (DI), the dorsomedial area (DM), the medial area (M), the ventroposterior (VP) and ventroanterior (VA) areas, the superior temporal area (ST), the area of the fundus of the superior temporal sulcus (FST), the temporal parietal area (TP), and caudal (IT_C), rostral (IT_R) and medial (IT_M) areas of inferotemporal cortex (IT). Neurons in posterior parietal cortex (PP) are activated by visual stimuli. In addition, the frontal eye field (FEF), the frontal ventral area (FV) and the eye region of the supplementary motor area (SMA) are visual or visuomotor in function. Thus, owl monkeys have on the order of 20 or more visual or visuomotor areas. Somatosensory (3a, S-I or 3b, 1, 2, S-II PV, VS) and auditory (A-I, R, CM, AL, PL) areas have been identified as well. ER, entorhinal cortex.

disagreement is what these differences in responsiveness suggest for theories of processing in the visual system. One view is that neurons that are apparently responding best to a particular stimulus feature are in fact signaling that the feature is present.

(A) Van Essen (1985)

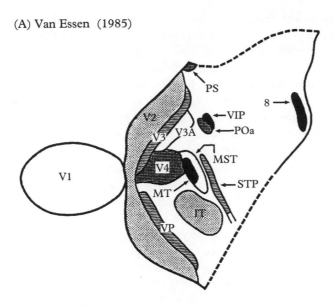

(B) Ungerleider and Desimone (1986)

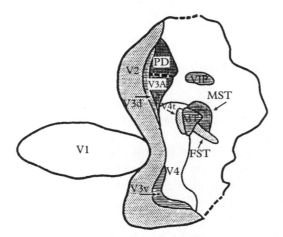

Figure 32.5 Proposed subdivisions of visual cortex on artificially flattened views of cortex in Old World macaque monkeys. The two proposals differ slightly in the amount of cortex included and in how visual cortex is subdivided. Both reconstructions separate most of primary visual cortex (V-I) from secondary visual cortex (V-II) rather than splitting V-I as in figure 32.4. Thus, in the intact brain, V-II would fold around V-I. Both proposals underestimate the number of visual areas. See Van Essen (1985) and Ungerleider & Desimone (1986) for details and terminology.

Neurons detect stimulus features and by doing so participate in the function of object identification. An extension of this view is that greater specificity occurs over stages of processing so that at higher stations only a small subset of neurons are activated, and their activity signals the presence of a specific object, such as a face (see Barlow, 1972).

The obvious problem with this line of reasoning is that the proposal ultimately seems unworkable because too many classes of very specific neurons would be needed at the highest levels. Others hold that neurons, though responding best to certain stimulus features, are encoding multidimensional properties of visual stimuli (e.g., Optican and Richmond, 1987). According to some holding this view (e.g., Desimone et al., 1985), the response characteristics of neurons become less specific and more abstract in reflecting stimulus features in the higher stages of processing. According to this concept, large numbers of neurons participate in all perceptual tasks and individual neurons are active during many perceptual tasks. In support of this view, network models have demonstrated that problems can be solved when activity is distributed across an array of elements and when the nature of the task is not obvious from the activity profiles of the individual elements (e.g., Andersen and Zipser, 1988; Hopfield and Tank, 1986).

Remarkably, the same sorts of response profiles for neurons in different areas of visual cortex have been used as evidence for both types of theories. In one view, the "best response" is the key, and other responsiveness is "noise." In the other view, all responses of neurons, even at low rates, are significant. While the basic issue is not easily resolved, Marrocco (1986) has critically reviewed the evidence for what he terms "attribute-specific areas" with attribute-specific neurons, and provides guidelines for evaluating visual areas for specificity. Marrocco (1986) concludes that the weight of the evidence is against the theory that neurons in each field are devoted to a single stimulus attribute (as suggested in figure 32.7).

4   Why Not Have Just One Big Visual Area?

Reptiles appear to get along with only one visual "area" in dorsal or general cortex (neocortex; see Kaas, 1987b; Ulinski and Mulligan, 1987), with much of the visual processing being done in the optic tectum (superior colliculus) of the midbrain. The optic tectum is extremely well differentiated into layers in some species, but the structure is not subdivided horizontally into a number of areas. Mammals appear to have addressed the problem of increasing visual abilities largely by increasing the number of visual areas, rather than the size of a single field such as V-I. An increase in number rather than just size isn't a result of some unknown factor that limits size. Area 17 varies greatly in size across species, with larger brains having a larger area 17. For example, area 17 can be as much as 1000 times larger in the human than the mouse brain (figure 32.6), so areas can be increased greatly in size.

To some extent, some mammals probably do enhance or specialize their visual abilities by enlarging and differentiating an existing visual area or areas. An extreme in specialization where a single visual area is emphasized may be the tarsier, where area 17 is very large, extending over the caudal third of the cerebral hemisphere and more differentiated into layers (and sublayers) than in any other mammal (e.g., Hassler, 1966; Woolard, 1925). The large size and sharp laminar distinctions of area 17 in tarsiers are reminiscent of the optic tectum of highly visual birds, and indeed there may be further similarities in function. Tarsiers are specialized as visual predators (Polyak, 1957), and need to be extremely proficient in detecting and tracking prey, but there is little evidence for varied or complex visual behavior.

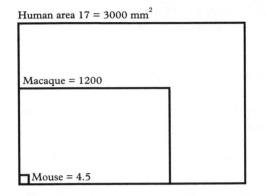

Figure 32.6   The sizes of primary visual cortex (V-I or area 17) in mice (unpublished measurements), macaque monkeys (typical values from Van Essen et al., 1984), and humans (typical values from Stensaas et al., 1979).

In a sense, laminar specializations such as that seen in area 17 of tarsiers and the optic tectum of some birds are equivalent to producing more visual areas by stacking representations one on top of the other. The potential of this method of increasing visual abilities is limited, however, by restrictions on the thickness of cortex, which varies only slightly across species.

Another way of creating multiple representations within a single visual area is to have a mosaic of vertical arrays of neurons (local processing modules), with each location in visual space repeated in several types of arrays. Thus, rather than containing a single representation with continuous change across the surface, an area can have repetitions and local discontinuities to produce several fractionated, interdigitated representations, each with its own functions (see Kaas, 1989b). To some extent, all visual areas may multiply functions in this way, but clear evidence for distinct classes of modules is available only for area 17 and 18 of monkeys. In area 17, there is evidence for separate laminar systems relating to processing information from the parvocellular and magnocellular geniculate layers, and for separate vertical systems for the cytochrome oxidase (CO) blob and interblob regions, devoted to different aspects of the parvocellular inputs (perhaps stimulus orientation and color, respectively, see Livingstone and Hubel, 1988). In area 18, three types of vertical bands of cells, the M stripe, the P stripe, and the interstripe regions form three fractionated maps of the visual hemifield, each processing a different type of information from area 17 (figure 32.9; see Livingstone and Hubel, 1988, for review). In principle, the number of fractionated representations within a single visual area could increase to any number, thus providing an alternative to increasing the number of separately located and internally coherent visual areas. That the number appears to be small suggests that there are major disadvantages to increasing the number of dispersals of functionally distinct processing modules within a field. The most obvious disadvantage is that as the number increases, interactions between modules of the same set and between modules of different sets become dependent on longer connections. Thus, the problem of interconnections within a field may be the major limit on multiplying function within a field (Cowey, 1981; Kaas, 1977; see below). Thus, limits on cortical thickness and therefore numbers of functionally distinct layers, and limits on numbers of functionally distinct vertical modules, mean that major advances in visual processing cannot result by simply increasing the size of one visual area.

5   Concepts of How Multiple Areas are Interconnected

In the classical view of the visual system, there was a simple hierarchy of only two or three functionally distinct subdivisions of cortex (see Merzenich and Kaas, 1980, for review). Thus, a primary "visuosensory" area (area 17 or striate cortex) activated a secondary "visuopsychic" area (Bolton, 1900; Campbell, 1905) divided into two sequential bands, areas 18 and 19 of Brodmann (1909) or the parastriate and peristriate areas of Elliot-Smith (1906). Visuopsychic cortex then fed into bimodal or multimodal association cortex ("interpretive cortex"). Even relatively recent proposals for the organization of visual cortex in humans added to these early views only by allowing several functional subdivisions of interpretive cortex (e.g., Konorski, 1967). For mammals with large numbers of visual areas, these early to more recent views are obviously too simple (see figures 32.4 and 32.5). Yet, the concept of serial processing along a chain of visual areas remains important in theories of cortical organization (e.g., Hubel and Wiesel, 1965). Another concept, that of parallel processing, has become increasingly discussed in terms of cortical function. More recently, the complexities of cortical processing have been described in terms of a network of interconnected areas. These concepts are discussed and related to current information on the interconnections of visual areas below.

5.1   Serial processing across visual areas

Serial processing is certainly an important feature of the visual system. In an overly simple view of visual cortex as a single chain of visual areas, the significance of multiple visual areas is that each area represents a successive step in a serial chain of processing. Such a restricted view of visual processing is no longer common, but it is suggested by some of the terminology in current use. The early and long-standing use of terms such as V-I and V-II, S-I and S-II, and A-I and A-II, implies serial processing (although Woolsey introduced the terms to indicate order of discovery). The subsequent use of the term "V-III" by Hubel and Wiesel (1965) further implies a serial model, although it wasn't clear from the reported data on single neurons that serial processing across fields accomplished much more than the serial processing within V-I (simple to complex to hypercomplex). A chain of processing areas also is implied, intended or not, by the more recent use of the terms V1, V2, V3, V4, V5 and V6 for proposed visual areas (e.g., Zeki, 1978; figure 32.7). While Ungerleider and Mishkin (1982) argue for the alignment of visual areas in two parallel streams (see below), only one stream is considered important in the recognition of visual stimuli. According to this view, the areas in the object recognition system are "primarily organized in a serial hierarchy," although parallel processing may occur within a field (Desimone et al., 1985).

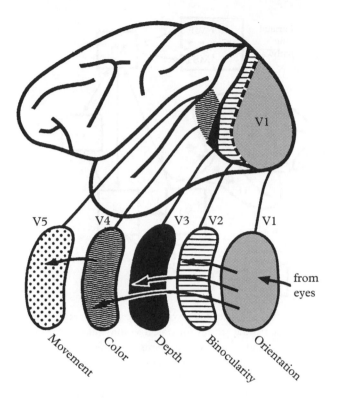

Figure 32.7 One concept of serial processing in visual cortex in macaque monkeys. A sequence of visual areas (V-1–V-5) successively compute and add different features (attributes) of the visual array to result in object vision. The proposal stresses serial processing and the specializations of visual areas for the detection of stimulus attributes, but does not recognize the known complexity of the system. Modified from Young (1978).

5.2 Parallel processing across visual areas

Parallel processing streams within visual systems appear to address the problem of the basic slowness of strictly serial systems. Modern views of parallel processing in the mammalian visual system stem from the discoveries that three broad categories of ganglion cells of the retina of cats, the X, Y, and W cells, project in parallel to the lateral geniculate nucleus where the inputs remain largely segregated and project separately to cortex. One hypothesis for cats is that V-I, V-II and V-III, rather than being successive stages in a hierarchy, are three end targets for the parallel pathways, with V-I being devoted to X cells, V-II devoted to Y cells, and V-III devoted to W cells (Stone et al., 1979). In primates, where the W (koniocellular) cell system is typically reduced, and the geniculate projection is almost exclusively restricted to V-I (see Kaas and Huerta, 1988), there is evidence instead for parallel processing of X (parvocellular) and Y (magnocellular) cell information within V-I and V-II (figure 32.9; see Kaas, 1986; Livingstone and Hubel, 1988). In addition, Ungerleider and Mishkin (1982) present evidence for a divergence of outflow from V-I into two parallel hierarchies of areas,

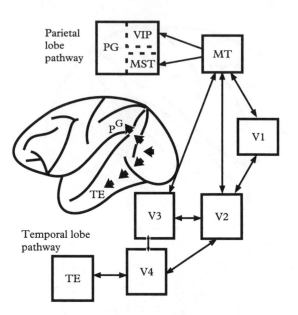

Figure 32.8   A simplified scheme of processing in visual cortex of macaque monkeys stressing two parallel pathways, with the ventral stream for object vision and the dorsal stream to PG (parietal area "G") for visual attention and spatial relations. Modified from Ungerleider (1985). See text and Ungerleider (1985) for details and abbreviations.

with one sequence of fields ending in the temporal lobe and mediating object vision and the other sequence of fields ending in posterior parietal cortex and mediating visual attention and spatial vision (figure 32.8). While more elaborate hierarchies have been subsequently proposed (e.g., figure 32.9; Ungerleider and Desimone, 1986; Maunsell and Van Essen, 1983; Weller & Kaas, 1987), patterns of connections support the view that many of the visual areas largely belong to one or the other of the two major streams in both New and Old World monkeys. More recent evidence (see Livingstone and Hubel, 1988) suggests that the X (parvocellular) stream subdivides into two parallel streams in V-I, which remain segregated in V-II, and project in parallel to DL (V4) (figure 32.9). Thus, at least the early stages of processing in visual cortex of primates are characterized by three parallel streams of sequences of modules connected across several visual areas.

Within the parallel streams in primates, and within the overall hierarchy of visual areas, there are "feedforward" projections from lower to higher levels, and "feedback" projections from higher to lower levels (Maunsell and Van Essen, 1983). The feedforward projections presumably activate the neurons in the higher stations and provide inputs for further computations. The significance of the feedback connections is less certain, but presumably feedback connections modulate the activity of the neurons at the lower level. For areas 17 and 18 of monkeys, the feedback from MT, which is in the Y cell or M stream, distributes across all three processing streams (Krubitzer and Kaas, 1988). Therefore one function of feedback may be to integrate processing across the semi-independent parallel pathways.

5.3 Networks

A number of models of how neuronal systems function have employed large numbers of simulated neurons that are widely interconnected. Such models may have stages of processing, but they are basically concerned with the outcomes (emergent properties) of multiple interactions at the neuronal level (e.g., Andersen and Zipser, 1988; Hopfield and Tank, 1986; Linsker, 1986). In addition, the term "network" has been used, especially recently, in another way to refer to a collection of cortical areas, presumably functioning together, that are interconnected in a manner that is not obviously hierarchical, or at least in a manner where hierarchical processing across areas is not the dominant feature. For example, Mesulam (1981) and Goldman-Rakic (1988) describe a collection of interconnected fields in the frontal, parietal, and temporal lobes of macaque monkeys as a "network." While feedforward and feedback types of connections clearly exist, many of the connections of visual cortex are of intermediate types that do not clearly identify areas as "higher" or "lower" (see Maunsell and Van Essen, 1983; Weller and Kaas, 1981), supporting the viewpoint that, in some sense, there is validity in describing the organization of visual cortex as a "network" of areas. However, a notion embedded in the concept of a network, whether at the level of neurons or cortical areas, is that widespread interconnections provide widespread accessibility of components to each other (e.g., Hopfield and Tank, 1986). The cortical areas are not so broadly interconnected. If extremely sparse and variable connections are not considered, then cortical areas typically have interconnections with 3–6 fields of the same hemisphere, 2 or 3 fields of the opposite hemisphere, and with 2–3 thalamic nuclei (see Cusick and Kaas, 1986; Merzenich and Kaas, 1980). Only some of these connections have a major activating role, and most of the major connections can be classified as feedforward or feedbackward across series of fields. Thus, the term "network" can be misleading.

5.4 A manifold system

Clearly the visual systems of advanced mammals are capable of performing many different functions at once, and include a large number of parts with complex patterns of interconnections. Figure 32.9 is a greatly oversimplified diagram of how visual cortex is interconnected in owl monkeys. Cortical visual areas are not arranged in a single hierarchy for processing from sensation to perception. Rather, each visual area is interconnected with 3–6 other visual areas with the inclusion of serial, parallel, recurrent, and network-like components. In addition, each visual area directly accesses a number of subcortical regions and receives inputs from parts of the pulvinar complex (see Kaas and Huerta, 1988). In general, current theories of visual system organization and function do not adequately address the complexities of the connectional framework, which suggests that visual processing is manifold in nature (Kaas, 1977), with wide regions of cortex including many cortical fields interacting during even simple visual tasks. Furthermore, the outputs from many visual areas, via subcortical connections, have the potential to directly influence behavior. Perhaps it is the multitude of possible influences on neurons in the motor system that allows the flexibility in behavior that occurs in advanced mammals.

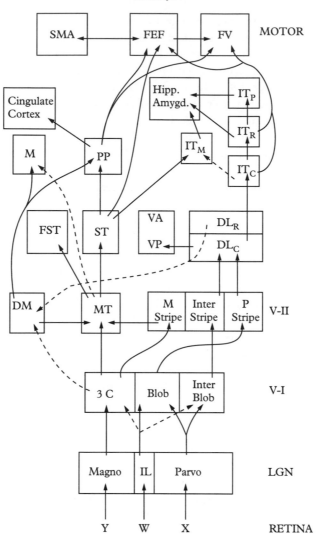

Processing hierarchy of visual cortex in owl
monkeys

Figure 32.9   A processing hierarchy for visual areas in owl monkeys. The simplified outline includes major feedforward (see Maunsell and Van Essen, 1983) connections, does not consider all feedback or "intermediate" connections, and does not include all visual areas. Also, the many subcortical and callosal connections are not shown. Serial and parallel processing components are evident. In addition, a given visual area such as MT typically receives inputs from several levels in the system. Thus, higher levels of the sequence may be described by "network" concepts (see text). Functionally distinct classes of cells in the retina (X, Y, and W) project to parvocellular, magnocellular, and interlaminar (IL) regions of the lateral geniculate nucleus (LGN), which in turn project to neurons in V-I that relay to output neurons in layer 3C (Hassler's 1966 terminology), blobs, or interblob regions. Subsequent relays are of the magnocellular pathway to the M stripes, and one parvocellular (blob) pathway to the P stripes and the other (interblob) parvocellular pathway to the interstripe regions of V-II (area 18). Layer 3C neurons also project directly to the middle temporal visual area (MT), which also receives an

6 How Do Connection Patterns Develop and How are they Maintained?

Obviously what any visual area does, that is the computations that occur in an area, depends on inputs and local connections. An understanding of the details of connections, how they form and how they are maintained, can contribute to understanding what visual areas do by placing constraints, by making theories more or less likely.

The idea that connections can be guided to very specific and predetermined targets, even over considerable distances, has been with us for some time (e.g., Sperry's chemospecificity theory – see Sperry, 1945). However, the bulk of the evidence now suggests that only the crude outlines of patterns of connections are formed by such guidance. Selection among many possibilities for synaptic targets and synaptic strength provides the details of the connection pattern during development, and maintains and modifies local connections in adults (see Kaas, 1988; Merzenich et al., 1988, for reviews). The critical point of this theory, which has the concept of the "Hebbian" synapse (Hebb, 1949) as its cornerstone, is that synaptic inputs are selected (reinforced) on their ability to be correlated in their activity patterns to the extent that they are active together when the activity is powerful enough to result in the discharging of the target neuron (see Changeux and Danchin, 1976; Willshaw and Von der Malsburg, 1976). If this is the way that the nervous system constructs and maintains itself, then certain connection patterns and therefore modes of functioning seem more likely than others.

Since much of the processing in a sensory system has a hierarchical component, within and across areas, it is instructive to imagine what the selection of inputs with correlated activity would do at successive stages in the visual system. Some of the functional implications of current concepts of the development of connections within and across sensory areas have been reviewed and outlined elsewhere (Kaas, 1988).

One implication is that selection for correlated activity would tend to create and preserve retinotopic and visuotopic organization (see, for example, Constantine-Paton, 1982). Obviously, a powerful factor in correlating neural activity is retinal location. Neurons in the same retinal location are likely to fire together, both initially because they are likely to be interrelated by local, perhaps initially random, interconnections, and later in development because they have a high probability of being activated together by the same stimuli. Selection for activity correlated by retinal position would counter the divergences and convergences of potential connections across stations, and retinotopic organization would tend to be preserved across stations.

---

input from the M stripes of V-II. MT projects to cortex in the fundus of the superior temporal sulcus (FST) and the superior temporal area (ST), which relay to posterior parietal cortex as part of a subsystem specialized for visual attention and spatial relations (see Ungerleider and Mishkin, 1982, for details). Most of the output of V-II is directed to the dorsolateral visual area (DL or V-4 of macaque monkeys), where information is relayed over sequence of fields in inferior temporal (IT) cortex (note caudal, C, rostral, R, polar, P, and medial, M, divisions). Higher levels access cingulate cortex, presumably for motivational components, the hippocampus and amygdala for mechanisms related to the storage of memories, and visuomotor centers (frontal ventral, frontal eye field, supplementary motor area) in the frontal lobe (see Kaas, 1986; 1988, for references and details).

After vision starts, the alignment of the eyes would allow stimuli to activate matched locations in the two eyes, so that in late maturing connections, inputs from the two eyes merge and create visuotopic organization, the systematic representation of visual space.

Another implication is that neurons will become less selective at higher processing levels. Because it is difficult to precisely preserve the timing of neural discharges across multiple relays, each station in the relay will accept, in order to maintain synaptic density, inputs with a greater range in correlations. One consequence is that the receptive fields get bigger. Thus, whatever functions neurons in higher stations perform, they must do it with larger receptive fields. Neurons in early stations are more likely to be activated by spatially local events; neurons in higher stations are more likely to be activated by more global events. Of course, the amount of selectivity for correlation within a given field may be modifiable in evolution, so that receptive fields for neurons in area 17, for example, may vary in size from species to species, and area 17 may have a role in more global or more local functions accordingly. An advantage of more cortical areas is that this could provide a greater range of levels of local to global processing.

A third implication is that parallel paths will occur and increase in number across higher stations. Location on the receptor sheet is only one way to influence correlations. Another is through neural transductions and computations. The different sensitivities of adjacent receptors discorrelates the activity of some of the neurons with inputs from the same retinal location and decreases the probability that they will synapse on the same neuron at the next station. This tends to create local populations of neurons that are interconnected and computing on the basis of stimulus properties related to the transduction process, as well as to stimulus location. Post-receptor processing mechanisms, such as those that create the X, Y and W cell classes in the retina, would tend to create parallel pathways across visual areas and semi-isolated processing modules (columns) within areas. Moreover, the construction of any new cell classes (in terms of response properties) at higher stations would tend to increase the number of parallel paths at higher levels in a hierarchy. However, the tendency for an increase in parallel paths would be countered somewhat if higher neurons are more broadly tuned for correlation. Thus, a merging of parallel paths would occur to some extent. Because of a probable relaxation of the correlation requirements, higher areas, by merging streams, would be expected to more closely resemble a broadly interconnected network, and the processing would less closely resemble the predominantly hierarchical processing at early levels. Thus, connection patterns between higher areas would be less clearly feedforward or feedback.

If the requirements for correlation become more relaxed across stations, a fourth implication is that feedback connections would be more promiscuous but less effective than feedforward connections. Neurons within a system clearly have synaptic contacts that range in effectiveness. The highly correlated feedforward inputs would acquire the most synaptic strength, and be the most powerful. Because the neurons providing feedback, callosal, and widespread intrinsic connections are less correlated in activity than those providing the feedforward inputs, the feedback, callosal, and widespread intrinsic connections would be less effective and have modulatory roles on neural activity. However, neurons throughout the visual system seem to be making center–surround or local–global comparisons (see Allman et al., 1985), and the modulatory inputs may be very important in providing the surround or global effects. Providing more global effects is a consequence of broader connections across cell classes and across more visual space as a result of degraded correlations.

7   Where in Processing Hierarchies do Visual Areas get Added?

All mammals appear to have the primary (area 17 or V-I) and secondary (area 18 or V-II) visual fields (Kaas, 1980) and the end stations of visual processing, such as entorhinal cortex; the amygdala and hippocampus, related to object identification and visual memories (Mishkin, 1982); the medial limbic cortex, related to visual attention and motivation (Mesulam, 1981); and the motor and visuomotor fields and subcortical structures mediating motor behavior. The simple hierarchies of visual areas, with little more than beginning and end stations, that characterize the brains of mice and hedgehogs become complex hierarchies, like those of monkeys and cats, by the addition of new visual areas in the middle stages of processing. As a result, a change occurs from the situation where the first cortical station, area 17, directly accesses some of the end or near-end cortical stations in frontal and limbic cortex, as in rats and mice (e.g., Miller & Vogt, 1984), to where area 17 relates to only early stages of a lengthy hierarchy, as in monkeys (figure 32.6).

8   Theories of Why Multiple Visual Areas Exist

Several proposals have been made for the advantages provided by having larger rather than smaller numbers of areas in visual cortex. The proposals, to some extent, address different issues, and are, to a large extent, mutually compatible. The first proposals are different versions of the basic theme that visual area are specialized for analyzing different aspects of the visual world, and that having more visual area allows the analysis of more aspects.

8.1   Increasing the number of visual areas increases the number of visual abilities

This widespread assumption seems valid, though poorly supported. Clearly there is an overall relationship between the magnitude of brain development and abilities. To consider extremes, the visual capabilities of some fish seem to be so limited that they select prey on the basis of retinal image size (see Wetterer and Bishop, 1985) rather than real size (which can be determined only with information in addition to image size), while human vision includes complex and varied inferences about the visual world that allow, for example, mental rotations of objects, accurate predictions about where obscured moving objects will appear, and the rapid identification (categorization) of a wide range of objects. By being less extreme and considering only mammals, we see that no doubt mammals with few visual areas, such as hedgehogs and mice, have visual capacities vastly inferior to those of mammals with many visual areas, such as cats, monkeys, and presumably humans. Of course there are several nagging concerns. Mammals with more visual areas also have larger brains (relative to body size), and it is not certain that number of areas rather than brain size is important. There probably is an interaction, but it would be difficult to evaluate the relative contributions of brain size and number of fields. Another problem is that studies of animal behavior have concentrated on species with simple nervous systems, and we do not have a comprehensive understanding of how visual abilities vary in mammals. Finally, we have an understanding of the broad outlines of cortical organization and these outlines are available for only a few species. Presently, we can't be precise about the number of visual areas for any species. For these reasons, it is unlikely that we will have strong evidence in the near future for the assumption that increases in numbers of areas lead to increased abilities.

Opinions differ on how having more visual areas increases visual abilities. A common view is that visual information is distributed to a number of visual areas where each visual area processes different "attributes" (contrast, spatial frequency, orientation, movement, retinal disparity, size, color) of a complex visual stimulus (Cowey, 1979; Young, 1978; Zeki, 1978). According to Zeki (1974; 1978), for example, multiple visual areas are for the "division of labor" and "simultaneous analysis" of different components of vision. Different functions are emphasized in different cortical areas. More specifically, according to this view, V1 emphasizes the analysis of stimulus contours, V2 relates to depth, V4 (DL) is devoted to color, and V5 (MT) is critical for detecting movement. However, most mammals, including some with the fewest visual areas, are sensitive to these basic attributes of visual stimuli. Thus, species differences in numbers of areas are not explained, unless one holds that other (unspecified) stimulus features are analyzed by advanced but not by primitive mammals.

Another approach is to be less specific about what identified visual areas do, but simply propose that having more visual areas allows more stimulus parameters to be considered. Thus, Ballard (1986) concludes that neurons within any field have "multi-modal" responses, but the number of parameters that can be handled by any topographic representation is limited (on the order of 5–15). Given that it is beneficial to compute a large number of parameters, multiple areas are needed. A related concept is that multiple visual areas allow the system to detect "suspicious coincidences" along more stimulus parameters. According to Barlow (1986), the primary and other areas distribute information to a number of visual areas, each organized to detect different "suspicious coincidences" or "linking factors" (e.g., attributes such as orientation, direction of motion, or color) of the stimulus (also see Phillips et al., 1984). Topographic representations preserve neighborhood relations, and therefore are useful in detecting coincidences in restricted regions of visual space. However, associations that do not depend on proximity in space are psychologically important, and non-topographic maps or transformations, according to Barlow, would seem better suited for most detections. Somewhat differently, Desimone et al. (1985) argue that object vision depends on the flow of information along a pathway from striate cortex to the temporal lobe, where processing is serial, yet multi-dimensional and increasingly abstract at each stage. According to this view, having more, rather than fewer, visual areas would allow more complex processing that would enrich perception and reduce perceptual errors.

Multiple areas also provide more links to motor outputs. Each visual area projects to approximately 5–15 subcortical structures and nuclei (e.g., Graham et al., 1979), and many of these structures are closely related to motor performance. Most of these structures have inputs from a number of visual areas, although the pattern of subcortical targets is different for each visual area. Creutzfeldt (1985) has emphasized that there may be behavioral advantages to having such multiple links between the sensory organ and the motor output. One possible advantage may be that more possible influences on motor outputs increases behavioral flexibility.

8.2   Multiple areas simplify the problem of interconnecting functionally related groups of neurons

Cowey (1979; 1981) and others (i.e., Barlow, 1986; Kaas, 1977) have argued that having multiple visual areas is an effective way of allowing neurons to have the connections needed for their roles in perception. Cowey (1979) starts with the premise that the different visual areas are concerned with "different aspects of the visual world" (attributes). Most areas have retinotopic maps because the interactions between neurons with similarly located receptive fields that create selectivity for specific attributes of a complex stimulus depend on connections that are best if short and local and would be "cumbersome or impossible" if long. Cowey (1979) also supposes that it is genetically easier to program local rather than far-reaching connections. Thus, within visual areas "the retina is topographically mapped in order to keep intracortical connections short and to simplify developmental specificity." Multiple visual areas exist "for the same reasons." More specifically, the local connections that would be needed to sharpen the tuning of individual neurons for one of the many attributes (see above) of a complex stimulus would be long if neurons for all the different attributes were in the same visual area. Having many retinotopic maps allows most of the computing to be done with short local connections, although the receiving and sending information would require long connections between areas and subcortical structures. Most visual areas are semiretinotopic; that is, at the global level there is a retinotopic map, but locally other features of organization dominate. In the development of the brain, crude guidance could set up the long connections that interrelate these separate maps, and the order of these connections, including aspects important for retinotopic and local features, could be refined by rules for reinforcing correlated activity (see above). Neurons in these visual areas seem to be connected in ways that allow comparisons between more local and more global features of the stimulus (see Allman et al., 1985). Connections that allow such computations would be long and widespread if visual functions were expanded by enlarging a single visual area. In the largest visual area, V-I, some of the intrinsic connections are very long, up to 5–6 mm in some mammals, and widespread, yet they interrelate neurons that are typically concerned with only 10° or so of visual space, and in monkeys, at least, involve only a limited subset of neurons. To widely interconnect neurons, and to have many different types of neurons with different connection patterns within a single field, would seem to require an unreasonable amount of genetic programming.

8.3   Adding visual areas overcomes constraints on modifying existing visual systems that are imposed by the ongoing needs of the individuals, and allows new capacities to evolve

Allman and Kaas (1971; 1974) have discussed the possible significance of multiple visual areas in the general context of evolution. Existing body plans clearly have constraints on change that may be difficult or impossible to overcome. For example, we can presume that most vertebrates have not evolved human-like hands or bird-like wings because the forelimbs are part of the basic walking and support system, and it is difficult to gradually, over many generations, switch from an effective four-legged system to an effective two-legged system. Perhaps hands and wings would have become much more common if it were possible to add pairs of limbs to the basic four in vertebrates. However, the replication of existing parts has been common in evolution (see Gregory, 1935), and the number of visual areas has increased in several lines of evolution, possibly by the replication of existing areas or (and) by the subdivision of existing areas (see Kaas, 1986). Existing visual areas in any species presumably are performing functions critical to the existence of that species, and therefore only limited changes in organization may be compatible with current requirements for ongoing functions basic for survival and reproduction. Large-scale changes that may seem logical in terms of body design may just not be possible due to impaired function during the period of change. The creation of new visual areas allows this constraint to be avoided. If a genetic mutation occurs that results in the replication of an existing cortical area, either area would be capable of performing the functions of the old area, and the new area or the old area could be modified gradually for new functions, or the two areas could divide old functions between them and each modify for new functions.

Acknowledgments

This manuscript is based on an invited presentation given at the 3rd Annual Meeting of the American Academy of Clinical Neurology. I thank R. Blake, J. Bullier, P. Garraghty, S. Florence, L. Krubitzer, and M. Powers for comments on the manuscript.

References

Allman, J. M., Meizin, F., & McGuinnes, E. (1985). Stimulus specific responses from beyond the classical receptive field: Neurophysiological mechanisms for local–global comparisons in visual neurons. *Annual Review of Neuroscience*, **8**, 407–30.

Allman, J. M., & Kaas, J. H. (1971). A representation of the visual field in the posterior third of the middle temporal gyrus of the owl monkey (*Aotus trivirgatus*), *Brain Research*, **31**, 85–105.

Allman, J. M., & Kaas, J. H. (1974). A crescent-shaped cortical visual area surrounding the middle temporal area (MT) in the owl monkey (*Aotus trivirgatus*). *Brain Research*, **81**, 199–213.

Allman, J. M., Baker, J. F., Newsome, W. T., & Peterson, S. E. (1981). Visual topography and function: Cortical areas in the owl monkey. In C. N. Woolsey (ed.), *Cortical Sensory Organization, vol. 2: Multiple Visual Areas* (pp. 17–185), Clifton, NJ: Humana Press.

Andersen, D. A., & Zipser, D. (1988). The role of the posterior parietal cortex in coordinate transformations for visual-motor integration. *Canadian Journal of Physiology and Pharmacology*, **66**, 488–501.

Baker, J. F., Peterson, S. E., Newsome, W. T., and Allman, J. M. (1981). Response properties in four extrastriate visual areas of the owl monkey (*Aotus trivirgatus*): A quantitative comparison of medial, dorsomedial, dorsolateral, and middle temporal areas. *Journal of Neurophysiology*, **45**, 397–416.

Ballard, D. H. (1986). Cortical connections and parallel processing: Structure and function. *The Behavioral and Brain Sciences*, **9**, 67–120.

Ballard, D. H. (1987). Cortical connections and parallel processing: Structure and function. In M. A. Arbib and A. R. Hanson (eds), *Vision, Brain, and Cooperative Computation* (pp. 563–621), Cambridge, MA: MIT Press.

Barlow, H. B. (1972). Single units and sensation: A neuron doctrine for perceptual psychology. *Perception*, **1**, 371–94.

Barlow, H. B. (1985). Cerebral cortex as model builder. In D. Rose and V. G. Robson (eds), *Models of the Visual Cortex* (pp. 37–46), New York: John Wiley and Sons.

Barlow, H. B. (1986). Why have multiple cortical areas? *Vision Research*, **26**, 81–90.

Bolton, J. S. (1900). On the exact histological localization of the visual area of the human cerebral cortex. *Philosophical Transactions*, **193**, 165–222.

Brodmann, K. (1909). *Vergleichende Lokalisationslehre der Grosshirnrinde*. Leipzig: Barth.

Campbell, A. W. (1905). *Histological Studies on the Localization of Cerebral Function*. Cambridge: Cambridge University Press.

Changeux, J. P., & Danchin, A. (1976). Selective stabilization of developing synapses as a mechanism for the specification of neuronal networks. *Nature*, **264**, 705–12.

Constantine-Paton, M. (1982). The retinotectal hookup: The process of neural mapping. In S. Subtelny (ed.), *Developmental Order: Its Origin and regulation* (pp. 317–49), New York: Liss.

Cowey, A. (1979). Cortical maps and visual perception. The Grindley Memorial Lecture. *Quarterly Journal of Experimental Psychology*, **31**, 1–17.

Cowey, A. (1981). Why are there so many visual areas? In F. O. Schmitt, F. G. Warden, G. Adelman, & S. G. Dennis (eds), *The Organization of the Cerebral Cortex* (pp. 395–413), Cambridge, MA: MIT Press.

Creutzfeldt, O. (1985). Multiple visual areas: Multiple sensori-motor links. In D. Rose & V. G. Dobson (eds), *Models of the Visual Cortex* (pp. 54–61), New York: John Wiley and Sons.

Creutzfeldt, O. (1986). Comparative aspects of representation in the visual system. In C. Chagas & R. Gattas (eds), *Experimental Brain Research Supplement*, **11**, 53–82.

Cusick, C. G. & Kaas, J. H. (1986). Interhemispheric connections of cortical, sensory and motor maps in primates. In F. Lepore, M. Ptito, & H. H. Jasper (eds), *Two Hemispheres – One Brain* (pp. 83–102), New York: Alan R. Liss.

Cusick, C. G., & Kaas, J. H. (1988). Cortical connections of area 18 and dorsolateral visual cortex in squirrel monkeys. *Visual Neuroscience*, **1**, 211–37.

Desimone, R., & Ungerleider, L. G. (1986). Multiple visual areas in the caudal superior temporal sulcus of the macaque. *Journal of Comparative Neurology*, **248**, 164–89.

Desimone, R., Schein, S. J., Moran, J., & Ungerleider, L. G. (1985). Contour, color and shape analysis beyond the striate cortex. *Vision Research*, **25**, 441–52.

DeYoe, E. A., & Van Essen, D. C. (1985). Segregation of efferent connections and receptive field properties in visual area V2 of the macaque. *Nature*, **317**, 58–61.

DeYoe, E. A., & Van Essen, D. C. (1988). Concurrent processing streams in monkey visual cortex. *Trends in Neuroscience*, **11**, 219–26.

Economo, von C. (1929). *The Cytoarchitectonics of the Human Cortex*. Oxford: Oxford University Press.

Elliot-Smith, G. E. (1906). A new topographic survey of human cerebral cortex, being an account of the distribution of the anatomically distinct cortical areas and their relationship to the cerebral sulci. *Journal of Anatomy and Physiology*, **41**, 27–254.

Goldman-Rakic, P. S. (1988). Topography of cognition: Parallel distributed networks in primate association cortex. *Annual Review of Neuroscience*, **11**, 137–56.

Graham, J., Lin, C. S., & Kaas, J. H. (1979). Subcortical projections of six visual cortical areas in the owl monkey, *Aotus trivirgatus*. *Journal of Comparative Neurology*, **187**, 557–80.

Gregory, W. K. (1935). Reduplication in evolution. *Quarterly Review of Biology*, **10**, 272–90.

Gross, C. G., Rocha-Miranda, C. E., & Bender, D. B. (1972). Visual properties of neurons in inferotemporal cortex. *Journal of Neurophysiology*, **35**, 96–111.

Hassler, R. (1966). Comparative anatomy of the central visual systems in day- and night-active primates. In R. Hassler & H. Stephan (eds), *Evolution of the Forebrain* (pp. 419–34). Stuttgart: Thieml Verlag.

Hebb, P. O. (1949). *Organization of Behavior*. New York: John Wiley and Sons.

Hopfield, J. J., & Tank, D. W. (1986). Computing with neural circuits: A model. *Science*, **233**, 625–33.

Hubel, D. H., & Wiesel, T. N. (1965). Receptive fields and functional architecture in two non-striate visual areas (18 and 19) of the cat. *Journal of Neurophysiology*, **28**, 229–89.

Kaas, J. H. (1977). Sensory systems in mammals. In G. S. Stent (ed.), *Function and Formation of Neural Systems* (pp. 65–80), Berlin: Drahlem Konferehzen.

Kaas, J. H. (1980). A comparative survey of visual cortex organization in mammals. In S. O. E. Ebbesson (ed.), *Comparative Neurology of the Telencephalon* (pp. 483–502), New York: Plenum Press.

Kaas, J. H. (1982). The segregation of function in the nervous system: Why do sensory systems have so many subdivisions? In W. P. Neff (ed.), *Contributions to Sensory Physiology*, vol. 7 (pp. 201–40), New York: Academic Press.

Kaas, J. H. (1986). The structural basis for information processing in the primate visual system. In J. D. Pettigrew, W. R. Levick, & K. J. Sanderson (eds), *Visual Neuroscience* (pp. 315–40), Cambridge: Cambridge University Press.

Kaas, J. H. (1987a). The organization of neocortex in mammals: Implications for theories of brain function. *Annual Review of Psychology*, **38**, 124–51.

Kaas, J. H. (1987b). The organization and evolution of neocortex. In S. P. Wise (ed.), *Higher Brain Functions* (pp. 347–78), New York: John Wiley and Sons.

Kaas, J. H. (1988). Development of cortical sensory maps. In P. Rakic & W. Singer (eds), *Neurobiology of Neocortex* (pp. 41–67), New York: Springer Verlag.

Kaas, J. H. (1989a). Changing concepts of visual cortex organization of primates. In J. W. Brown (ed.), *Neurobiology of Visual Perception*, Hillsdale, NJ: Lawrence Erlbaum Associates.

Kaas, J. H. (1989b). Processing modules in sensory-perceptual cortex. In *Signal and Sense: Local and Global Order in Perceptual Maps*, in press.

Kaas, J. H., & Huerta, M. F. (1988). Subcortical visual system of primates. In H. P. Steklis (ed.), *Comparative Primate Biology, vol. 4: Neurosciences* (pp. 327–91), New York: Alan R. Liss.

Kaas, J. H., Krubitzer, L. A., & Johanson, K. L. (1989). Cortical connections of areas 17 (V-I) and 18 (V-II) of squirrels. *Journal of Comparative Neurology*, in press.

Konorski, J. (1967). *Integrative Activity of the Brain*. Chicago: University of Chicago Press.

Krubitzer, L. A., & Kaas, J. H. (1988). Cortical integration of parallel pathways in the visual system of primates. *Brain Research*, in press.

Krubitzer, L. A., Sesma, M. A., & Kaas, J. H. (1986). Microelectrode maps, myeloarchitecture, and cortical connections of three somatotopically organized representations of the body surface in parietal cortex of squirrels. *Journal of Comparative Neurology*, **253**, 415–34.

Lashley, K. S., & Clark, G. (1946). The cytoarchitecture of the cerebral cortex of Ateles: A critical examination of architectonic studies. *Journal of Comparative Neurology*, **85**, 223–305.

Linsker, R. (1986). From basic network principles to neural architecture: Emergence of spatial-opponent cells. *Proceedings of the National Academy of Sciences, USA*, **83**, 7508–12.

Livingstone, M. S., & Hubel, D. H. (1988). Segregation of form, color, movement, and depth: Anatomy, physiology, and perception. *Science*, **240**, 740–9.

Luethke, L. E., Krubitzer, L. A., & Kaas, J. H. (1988). Cortical connections of electrophysiologically and architectonically defined subdivisions of auditory cortex in squirrels. *Journal of Comparative Neurology*, **268**, 181–203.

Marrocco, R. T. (1986). The neurobiology of perception. In J. E. LeDoux & W. Hirst (eds), *Mind and Brain, Dialogues in Cognitive Neuroscience* (pp. 33–79), Cambridge: Cambridge University Press.

Maunsell, J. H. R., & Newsome, W. T. (1987). Visual processing in monkey extrastriate cortex. *Annual Review of Neuroscience*, **10**, 363–401.

Maunsell, J. H. R., & Van Essen, D. C. (1983). The connections of the middle temporal visual area (MT) and their relationship to a cortical hierarchy in the macaque monkey. *Journal of Neuroscience*, **12**, 2563–86.

Merzenich, M. M., & Kaas, J. H. (1980). Principles of organization of sensory-perceptual systems in mammals. In J. M. Sprague and A. N. Epstein (eds), *Progress in Psychobiology and Physiological Psychology* (pp. 1–42), New York: Academic Press.

Merzenich, M. M., Recanzone, G., Jenkins, W. M., Allard, P. T., Nudo, R. J. (1988). Cortical representational plasticity. In P. Rakic & W. Singer (eds), *Neurobiology of Neocortex* (pp. 41–67), New York: Springer Verlag.

Mesulam, M. M. (1981). A cortical network for directed attention and unilateral neglect. *Annals of Neurology*, **10**, 309–25.

Miller, M. W., & Vogt, B. A. (1984). Direct connections of rat visual cortex with sensory, motor, and association cortices. *Journal of Comparative Neurology*, **226**, 184–202.

Mishkin, M. (1982). A memory system in the monkey. *Philosophical Transactions of the Royal Society of London [Biology]*, **248**, 85–95.

Montero, V. M., Rojas, A., & Torrealba, F. (1973). Retinotopic organization of striate and peristriate visual cortex in the albino rat. *Brain Research*, **53**, 197–201.

Optican, L. M., & Richmond, B. J. (1987). Temporal encoding of two-dimensional patterns by single units in primate inferior temporal cortex, III: Information theoretic analysis. *Journal of Neurophysiology*, **57**, 162–78.

Phillips, C. G., Zeki, S., & Barlow, H. B. (1984). Localization of function in the cerebral cortex: Past, present and future. *Brain*, **107**, 327–61.

Polyak, S. (1957). *The Vertebrate Visual System*. Chicago: University of Chicago Press.

Shipp, S., & Zeki, S. (1985). Segregation of pathways leading from area V2 to areas V4 and V5 of macaque monkey visual cortex. *Nature*, **315**, 322–5.

Sperry, R. (1945). Chemoaffinity in the orderly growth of nerve fiber patterns and connections. *Proceedings of the National Academy of Science, USA*, **50**, 703–10.

Stensaas, S. S., Eddington, D. K., & Dobelle, W. H. (1979). The topography and variability of the primary visual cortex in man. *Journal of Neurosurgery*, **40**, 747–55.

Stone, J., Dreher, B., & Leventhal, A. (1979). Hierarchical and parallel mechanisms in the organization of visual cortex. *Brain Research Reviews*, **1**, 345–94.

Treisman, A., & Gormican, S. (1988). Feature analysis in early vision: Evidence from search asymmetries. *Psychological Review*, **95**, 15–48.

Ulinski, P. S., & Mulligan, K. A. (1987). Representation of visual space in the visual cortex of turtles. *Society of Neuroscience Abstracts*, **13**, 1048.

Ungerleider, L. A. (1985). The corticocortical pathways for object recognition and spatial perception. In C. Chagas, R. Gattass, and C. Gross (eds), *Pattern Recognition Mechanisms. The Pontifical Academy of Sciences*, 21–37.

Ungerleider, L. A., & Desimone, R. (1986). Cortical connections of visual area MT in the Macaque. *Journal of Comparative Neurology*, **248**, 190–222.

Ungerleider, L. G., & Mishkin, M. (1982). Two cortical visual systems. In D. J. Ingle, M. A. Goodale, and R. J. W. Mansfield (eds), *Analysis of Visual Behavior* (pp. 549–86), Cambridge, MA: MIT Press.

Van Essen, D. C. (1985). Functional organization of primate visual cortex. In A. Peters & E. G. Jones (eds), *Cerebral Cortex, vol. 3* (pp. 259–329), New York: Plenum Press.

Van Essen, D. C., Newsome, W. T., & Maunsell, J. H. R. (1984). The visual field representation in striate cortex of the macaque monkey: Asymmetries, anisotropies, and individual variability. *Vision Research*, **24**, 429–48.

Wagor, E., Mangini, N. J., Pearlman, A. L. (1980). Retinotopic organization of striate and extrastriate visual cortex in the mouse. *Journal of Comparative Neurology*, **193**, 187–202.

Weller, R. E., & Kaas, J. H. (1981). Cortical and subcortical connections of visual cortex in primates. In C. N. Woolsey (ed.), *Cortical Sensory Organization, vol. 2: Multiple Visual Areas* (pp. 121–55), Clifton, NJ: Humana Press.

Weller, R. E., & Kaas, J. H. (1987). Subdivisions of connections of inferior temporal cortex in owl monkey. *Journal of Comparative Neurology*, **256**, 137–72.

Wetterer, J. K., & Bishop, C. J. (1985). Planktivore prey selection: The reactive field volume model vs. the apparent size model. *Ecology*, **66**, 457–64.

Willshaw, D. J., & Von der Malsburg, C. (1976). How patterned neural connections can be set up by self-organization. *Proceedings of the Royal Society of London, Series B*, **194**, 431–45.

Woolard, H. H. (1925). The cortical lamination of Tarsius. *Journal of Anatomy*, **60**, 86–105.

Young, J. Z. (1978). *Programs of the brain.* Oxford: Oxford University Press.

Zeki, S. M. (1974). The mosaic organization of the visual cortex in the monkey. In R. Bellairs & E. G. Gray (eds), *Essays on the Nervous System – A Festschrift for Professor J. Z. Young* (pp. 327–43), Oxford: Clarendon Press.

Zeki, S. M. (1978). Functional specialization in the visual cortex of the rhesus monkey. *Nature*, **274**, 423–38.

Antibodies and Learning: Selection versus Instruction

Niels Kaj Jerne

Until less than ten years ago, there was an almost unanimous consensus among immunologists that antibody formation was equivalent to a learning process in which the antigen played an instructive role. The main basis for this belief was that the number of different antibody specificities, or the number of different antibody molecules that one animal can produce, is so large that it would be impossible for a cell nucleus to accommodate genes for this entire range of potentialities for protein synthesis. The number of different antigens is immense. Every species of animal, for example, must have several species-specific antigens. Against any one of these millions of antigens the immune system of one individual animal can produce a specific antibody. Therefore, the argument went, the number of different antibodies that an animal can produce must be virtually unlimited. Furthermore, the work of Landsteiner and his school[1] had shown that an animal produces antibodies even against artificially synthesized substances (haptens) that were made in a chemical laboratory and had never before existed in the world. The immune system of an animal could not possibly have anticipated the arrival of such antigens and must therefore have been "instructed" by the antigen itself in the formation of the antibody. The instructive mechanism proposed was that the antigen, after having entered a competent cell, guides the tertiary folding of polypeptide chains into globulin molecules, thereby imposing upon those molecules a conformation complementary to a surface region on the antigen.[2-5]

Instruction versus Selection in Antibody Formation

In contrast to this view, a selection mechanism was proposed, based on a logical argument concerning "recognition." The precision of recognition by the immune system can be illustrated by examining the antigenic properties of the "constant" part of the kappa light chain of human immunoglobulin. This constant portion comprises 107 amino acids (numbered 108 to 214) at the carboxyl end of the light chain, which have been found to be identical in sequence in all individual cases so far examined, except for amino acid number 191. In some individuals, this is valine; in others it is leucine. This difference is known as an allotypic difference. Those individuals that have valine at the 191 position belong to allotype Inv b[+], whereas those that have leucine at this position belong to allotype Inv a[+]. This allotypic difference was detected by immunological methods involving the formation of allotype-specific antibodies.[6] The immune system is thus capable of recognizing the replacement of one amino acid within a long sequence of amino acids of a protein molecule. It is a characteristic feature of the immune system that an animal does not normally appear to produce antibodies against its own circulating antigents, which *do* elicit antibody formation when injected into a different animal. How does the animal recognize that an antigen arriving in its tissues is, in fact, an antigen against which an antibody should be produced and not one of its own antigens to which no response is desired?

The immune system, then, must not let itself be stimulated to produce antibodies before having recognized that the antigen with which it is confronted differs from its own antigens. In order to recognize its own antigens, which differ among themselves in innumerable ways, the animal would have to possess a large set of self-recognizing molecules, and it would not be able to decide that a given antigen was its own before this entire set had been applied – a scrutiny, moreover, that would have to be interminably repeated. It would therefore seem impossible for the animal to recognize its own antigens. The recognizing agent must recognize foreign antigens, and the obvious molecules to accomplish this task are antibody molecules.

It follows that an animal cannot be stimulated to make specific antibodies, unless it has already made antibodies of this specificity before the antigen arrives. It can thus be concluded that antibody formation is a selective process and that instructive theories of antibody formation are wrong.[7–10]

Many immunologists were not convinced by the logical argument presented above, and only because of direct experimental evidence, accumulated during the last three or four years, have instructive theories of antibody formation finally been abandoned. Antibody molecules have been shown to consist of two identical heavy polypeptide chains and two identical light polypeptide chains.[11] It has also been shown that these polypeptide chains are assembled on ribosomes[12] and that the specificity of an antibody molecule is determined by the primary structure of its polypeptide chains.[13,14] This leaves no room for instructive action by the antigen. Furthermore, it has been demonstrated that certain antibody-producing cells, which turn out more than 1000 antibody molecules per second, contain no antigen.[15] The experimental methods would have detected the antigen if more than ten molecules of antigen had been present per cell. At one ribosomic site, a light or heavy polypeptide chain cannot be synthesized in less than 15 seconds. Therefore more than 100,000 ribosomes in an antibody-producing cell must simultaneously be able to turn out specific chains in the absence of antigens.

Although it is thus clear that the antigen plays a selective and amplifying role, we do not yet know by what mechanism the selective stimulus is transmitted. All we know with certainty is that, one day and later after having injected an antigen into an animal, we can find, in its spleen or lymph nodes, cells that are both multiplying and producing specific antibody. The simplest assumption would seem to be that an animal contains, among its population of 10^9 to 10^{12} lymphocytes (depending on species and age), a very large number of subpopulations, each of which is capable of being stimulated by certain antigens to grow, divide, and produce antibody-secreting cells among their offspring (perhaps because on their surface the cells display the antibodies they can synthesize).

Cellular Dynamics in Immunology

This picture can be illustrated by experiments that make use of an agar plaque method for counting, in a cell suspension obtained from a mouse spleen, the number of cells secreting a certain antibody. A certain amount of such a suspension – say 10^6 mouse spleen cells, as well as 4×10^8 sheep red blood cells (SRC) – is added to 2 milliliters of fluid 0.7 per cent agar at 45° C. The mixture is immediately poured into a petri dish, where it solidifies into a layer less than 1 mm thick. Each spleen cell is now surrounded by many SRC in a fixed position in the agar layer. If a spleen cell, during incubation of the petri dish at 37° C, secretes antibody molecules directed against an antigen of the SRC surface, the molecules diffuse into the agar and become fixed to the SRC in the immediate surroundings. Red blood cells, to the surface of which an antibody has attached, are said to be sensitized. Such sensitized cells will lyse in the presence of a serum factor called complement. By flooding the petri dish with complement after one-hour incubation, the sensitized SRC will lyse and lose their hemoglobin. Thus, around each mouse spleen cell that secretes hemolytic antibodies against sheep red blood cells, a pale plaque, visible to the naked eye, appears. Microscopic observation reveals the antibody-producing lymphocyte, or plasma cell, in the precise center of each plaque.[16,17]

The spleen of an untreated eight-weeks-old inbred mouse contains about 80 plaque-forming cells (PFC) among a total of about 1.5×10^8 spleen cells. These 80 PFC produce antibody against sheep red blood cells, although the mice have never experienced sheep antigen. As always in immunological observations, there is a great variation among individual animals. The normal level of 80 PFC is an average. Among a group of 50 apparently identical mice, the normal level could range from, say, 10 to 500 PFC.

We now give each of a few hundred mice one injection of 4×10^7 SRC into a tail vein. Every day we sacrifice 20 mice and determine the total number of plaque-forming cells in each spleen. Twenty-four hours after the antigen injection, the number of PFC starts to rise above the normal level, proceeding exponentially to reach an average of 10^5 PFC per spleen at four days, after which there is a rapid decline.

The following two observations appear to support the assumption that the exponential rise in PFC between day one and day four reflects cell multiplication.

If, on day two, an animal is given one microgram of colcimid per gram body weight and is killed three hours later, about 20 percent of the PFC in its spleen is found to have been arrested in metaphase of mitosis. If, on day three, the spleen cells are suspended for 30 minutes in vitro in a medium containing tritiated thymidine, about 55 percent of the PFC can be shown by autoradiography to have synthesized DNA, whereas the remainder have not.

The rate of appearance of PFC after an intravenous dose of 4×10^7 SRC corresponds to a cell-doubling time of seven hours. Although smaller doses of SRC evoke smaller responses, it is not possible to obtain a larger response than that elicited by 4×10^7 SRC, even if the dose is increased to 4×10^8 or 4×10^9 SRC. Each dose within this hundredfold range produces the same maximum response, indicating that all cells capable of being stimulated by sheep red blood cell antigen are maximally engaged.

The experiments described above can be repeated with similar results if rabbit red blood cells are used as antigen. The antibodies produced by mice against SRC and rabbit red blood cells do not cross-react. Also, the PFC that arise after a mouse has been injected with SRC do not form plaques in agar with rabbit red blood cells, and vice versa. Furthermore, the following experiment shows that the class of cells in the mouse spleen initially stimulated by an SRC injection is different from the class of cells initially stimulated by a rabbit red blood cell injection. The number of PFC against rabbit red blood cells appearing after a single injection of 10^6 rabbit red blood cells is the same, whether or not 10^8 SRC are injected simultaneously. The two types of antigen clearly do not compete for the same target.[18]

In summing up, we can conclude that the mouse spleen possesses, among its more than 10^8 cells, small classes of cells that can be stimulated to grow and divide by particular antigens, and that antibody-secreting cells arise from these subclasses by cellular proliferation.

We can now try to estimate the number of cells in a mouse spleen that belong to the class that can respond to SRC antigen. We have reasons to believe that these cells are not the PFC that form the normal level in nonstimulated animals. First, the normal level PFC are mostly plasma cells, whereas the cells that respond to a primary antigen stimulus are probably small lymphocytes. Second, the magnitude of the response of individual mice appears unrelated to their normal level of PFC. We therefore do not believe that the normal PFC belong to the class of cells that can respond to a primary stimulus of SRC antigen, nor that they become the ancestors of the PFC arising after a stimulus.

The exponential curve describing the appearance of PFC extrapolates below the normal level of PFC at less than 24 hours after the sheep red blood cell stimulus, suggesting that the average size of the class of responding cells might be less than 80. Other experiments appear to leave little doubt, however, that the size of the class of initially responding cells is of the order of several thousand. These experiments involve (1) the exponential decay of this class of cells after increasing exposure of nonstimulated mice to X-radiation, and (2) the transfer of a small fraction of the cells from a normal mouse spleen to the spleen of a mouse that has been rendered immunologically incompetent by X-irradiation.[19–21] Thus, only a small fraction of the immediate descendants of the initially responding cells are PFC, i.e., secrete an antibody that can cause lysis of sheep red blood cells.

The initially responding cells and most of their immediate descendants might then display or secrete antibodies of a degree of specificity that enables the antigen to stimulate these cells to divide, but which is not serologically recognizable. This might also explain the finding that certain serologically unrelated antigens, such as different *Salmonella flagellar* antigens[22] and different protein subunits of lactodehydrogenase,[23] can induce immunological tolerance with respect to each other. In both of these cases, tolerance may be due to the removal of a class of initially responsive cells that display cross-specific antibodies not detected by serological methods.

The picture that emerges for the initial stages of antibody formation is that the antigen first selects a class of initially responding cells. These are stimulated to differentiate and to divide. For each division they may require a new antigenic stimulus. All daughter cells do not necessarily produce the same antibody, and the antigen preferentially stimulates those descendant cells that produce the antibody best fitting the antigen.

This brings me to another relevant immunological phenomenon, the increase in "avidity" of the antibodies produced during the time following an antigenic stimulus. In the early days of immunology, the term avidity was introduced to express the degree of firmness of the bond formed between serum antibody and antigen in vitro. If the antigen dissociated easily from the antigen–antibody complex on dilution, the antibody was said to be of low avidity. Avidity is thus a measure of the goodness of fit of antibody toward the antigen. It was shown that the antibody present in animal serum is a heterogeneous population of molecules varying widely in avidity, and that the average avidity of the antibody present in an animal increases after repeated antigenic stimulation, or even with time after a single primary stimulus.[24,25]

Recent studies have confirmed that antibody molecules produced by one animal shortly after a single primary antigenic stimulus have a lower average association constant with respect to the antigen than later, and that this applies to a single class of antibody (IgG) with respect to a single antigenic determinant.[26]

This indicates that a further selection of cells producing better-fitting antibody takes place among the descendants of the cells first stimulated after the initial antigenic stimulus. Avidity does not increase as quickly after a large dose of antigen as after a small dose. As might be expected, a large dose of antigen is less selective, and in extrapolation we might relate tolerance following excessive doses of antigen to the absence of progressive selection. The immunological tolerance observed after repeated minimal doses of antigen might be caused by stimulation of the entire class of available responding cells, followed by a decay of their descendants because of the absence of antigen needed for further stimulation.

The assumption underlying the above discussion, that the descendants of the initially stimulated cells require further antigenic stimulation in order to continue to multiply, is supported by the finding that the exponential rate at which PFC appear in the spleens of mice after one intravenous injection of SRC decreases with decreasing antigen doses. Thus the doubling times of PFC per spleen after one dose of 4×10^7, 4×10^6, 4×10^5, and 4×10^4 SRC are 7, 9, 21, and 36 hours, respectively. The simplest explanation of this remarkable fact is that the cells require, and must therefore wait for, a new antigenic stimulus for each division.

In the picture developed above, a continuing selective-role has thus been assigned to the antigen. Among the general population of antigen-responsive cells, a particular antigen first selects the small class of cells that can respond to the primary presence of that antigen. These cells are stimulated to grow and divide. A secondary selection by the antigen then takes place among the differentiating descendants of these cells, resulting in the production of increasingly better-fitting antibodies.

Instruction versus Selection in Learning

In accordance with this general picture of the selective role of antigen in antibody formation, the view that antigen acts instructively at the intracellular level has been abandoned. It may be useful, therefore, to examine in a broader biological context whether there exist situations in which instructive mechanisms operate or to which the term "instruction" is applicable. It would seem that an answer to this question requires a specification of the organizational level at which a process is described. Thus, although the mechanism by which an antigen brings about antibody formation in the tissues of a mouse must be purely selective, the antigen does not select a mouse. When viewing the situation at the level of the entire mouse, we may still say that the antigen "instructs" the animal to produce an adequate antibody.

Similar reasoning can be applied to examples from other areas of biology. For instance, in the case of the selection by streptomycin of streptomycin-resistant mutants among a population of bacteria, it is clear that the streptomycin molecules did not cause these mutants to arise. They were already present before the streptomycin arrived; no instructive role can therefore be assigned to streptomycin. On the level of the entire bacterial culture, however, we may still say that streptomycin instructs the transition to streptomycin resistance.

Let us consider a more complicated example of Darwinian selection. A large population of brown moths spend a major part of their time sitting on a factory wall of the same color. These moths are the prey of certain birds. Now the wall is repainted white. One or two years later we observe that the moths sitting on the wall are likewise white. In this case, the signal that entered into the system, i.e., the color change, was not even received by the moths, but by the birds. The mechanism by which the color change in the moths came about was obviously selective, in that moths of lighter color were already present among the original population before the signal arrived. Again we might say, however, on the level of the entire system, that the signal "instructed" the population of moths to mimic the color change.

A clear example of an instructive process would be the role of messenger RNA in protein synthesis. The messenger RNA molecules arriving in their ribosomal habitat do not select already existing protein molecules and may therefore be said, at the organizational level of protein, to play an instructive role. The messenger RNA does recognize and select, however, already available subunits, namely, species of amino acid-charged transfer RNA. At this lower level, therefore, the process is a selective one.

I will finally turn to the question of the analogies between the immune system and the central nervous system.

Both systems have a history that develops during the lifetime of the individual. Each antigen that makes its appearance irreversibly changes the immune system. In the same way, the state of the central nervous system reflects the experience of the individual.

The immune system appears to be learning by responding to antigens entering from the outside world. The central nervous system also appears to learn in response to sensory signals.

Like the central nervous system, the immune system appears to have a memory that enables it to benefit from previous experience. It produces more and better antibodies if the antigen enters a second time, or repeatedly.

The experience gathered by the immune system of an individual cannot be transferred to its progeny. As with the central nervous system, each newborn must start, so to speak, from scratch.

In the remaining, speculative part of this chapter, I shall try to make the most of these analogies. Let us consider the kappa light chains of the antibodies of mice and man. Each of these light chains consists of a "constant" sequence of 107 amino acids and a "variable" sequence of 107 amino acids.

The constant part of human light chains is identical in all individuals and in all antibodies they produce. It differs, however, from the constant part of mouse light chains by some 40 amino acid substitutions that have obviously arisen by mutation during phylogeny. The variable part of human light chains, on the contrary, differs between different antibody molecules of one individual, and the differences are similar in nature to the differences between mouse and man in the constant part. This is reminiscent of the old saying that ontogeny mimics phylogeny: phylogenic differences between species in the constant part of the light chain are mimicked by the ontogenic plasticity of the variable part.[27–30]

Similarly, in the central nervous system, instincts are fixed in one species, but each individual (particularly man) has also a plasticity in learning capacity, which mimics the total of all phylogenically developed instincts of different species. In the immune system, the constant part of the light chain is obviously laid down in the DNA of the zygote, and it is equally clear that there is DNA in the zygote that represents the variable part of the light chain, although, ontogenically, this DNA may exhibit an immense plasticity.

In the central nervous system, instincts are also obviously encoded in the zygote, most probably in the DNA. But if DNA acts only through transcription into RNA and translation into protein, and if the phenotypic expression of instincts is based on particular arrangements of neuronal synapses, then DNA through RNA and protein must govern the synaptic network in the central nervous system.

Analogous to the utilization of the diversity of the variable part of the antibody light chain in the immune system, it would seem probable to me that, in the central nervous system, learning from experience is based on a diversity in certain parts of the DNA, or is due to plasticity of its translation into protein, which then controls the effective synaptic network underlying the learning process. I would, therefore, find it surprising if DNA were not involved in learning, and envisage that the production by a neuronal cell of certain proteins, which I might call "synaptobodies," would permit that cell to enhance or depress certain of its synapses, or to develop others.

Pursuing these analogies even further, we might now ask whether one can distinguish between instructive and selective theories of learning in the central nervous system. Looking back into the history of biology, it appears that wherever a phenomenon resembles learning, an instructive theory was first proposed to account for the underlying mechanisms. In every case, this was later replaced by a selective theory. Thus the species were thought to have developed by learning or by adaptation of individuals to the environment, until Darwin showed this to have been a selective process. Resistance of bacteria to antibacterial agents was thought to be acquired by adaptation, until Luria and Delbrück showed the mechanism to be a selective one.[31] Adaptive enzymes were shown by Monod and his school to be inducible enzymes arising through the selection of pre-existing genes.[32] Finally, antibody formation that was thought to be based on instruction by the antigen is now found to result from the selection of already existing patterns.

It thus remains to be asked if learning by the central nervous system might not also be a selective process; i.e., perhaps learning is not learning either.

Several philosophers, of course, have already addressed themselves to this point. John Locke held that the brain was to be likened to white paper, void of all characters, on which experience paints with almost endless variety.[33] This represents an instructive theory of learning, equivalent to considering the cells of the immune system void of all characters, upon which antigens paint with almost endless variety.

Contrary to this, the Greek Sophists, including Socrates, held a selective theory of learning. Learning, they said, is clearly impossible. For either a certain idea is already present in the brain, and then we have no need of learning it, or the idea is not already present in the brain, and then we cannot learn it either, for even if it should happen to enter from outside, we could not recognize it. This argument is clearly analogous to the argument for a selective mechanism for antibody formation, in that the immune system could not recognize the antigen if the antibody were not already present. Socrates concluded that all learning consists of being reminded of what is pre-existing in the brain.[34]

Summary

In concluding this analysis, it would seem that selection refers to a mechanism in which the product under consideration is already present in the system prior to the arrival of the signal, and is thus recognized and amplified.

Each system that is capable of receiving a signal, however, is subject to instruction by this signal. Thus, at the level of an entire system, all such processes are instructive, whereas all instructive processes at a lower level imply selective mechanisms. In learning, and in all processes resembling learning, a discussion of instruction versus selection serves only to determine the organizational level of the elements upon which selective mechanisms operate.

During recent years the belief that antigen plays an instructive role in antibody formation by intracellular guidance of the formation of the tertiary structure of globulin molecules has been replaced by the idea that antibody formation is based on a selective process in which antigen selects pre-existing patterns and causes molecules representing these patterns to be produced at increased rates. The logical arguments for selection have been enforced by experimental evidence showing that the general mechanism of protein biosynthesis also applies to antibody production, that primary polypeptide structure determines antibody specificity, and that plasma cells can produce antibody in the absence of intracellular antigen. The antibody response appears to depend on multiplication of cells of the immune system. Attempts are being made to describe the cellular dynamics involved and to understand the nature of the antigenic stimulus.

The replacement of instructive by selective theories appears to be a general trend in the development of biology. A number of analogies are drawn between the central nervous system and the immune system, and the question is posed whether a selective mechanism may also underlie the learning process. An analysis of this question leads to the conclusion that the terms "instruction" and "selection" can apply to descriptions of the same process at different levels. Each system that is capable of receiving a signal is subject to instruction by this signal. Thus, at the level of an entire system, all such signals are instructive, whereas all instructive processes at some lower level imply selective mechanisms, through which products that were already present in the system prior to the arrival of the signal are selected and amplified. In learning, as in all processes resembling learning, a discussion of instruction versus selection serves only to determine the organizational level of the elements upon which selective mechanisms operate.

Notes

1   K. Landsteiner (1945), *The Specificity of Serological Reactions*. Cambridge: Harvard University Press, revised edition.

2   F. Breinl and F. Haurowitz (1930), Chemische Untersuchung des Präzipitates aus Hämoglobin und Anti-Hämoglobin-Serum und Bemerkungen über die Natur der Antikörper. *Z. Physiol. Chem.*, **192**, 45–57.

3   S. Mudd (1932), A hypothetical mechanism of antibody formation. *J. Immunol.*, **23**, 423–7.

4   J. Alexander (1931), Some intracellular aspects of life and disease. *Protoplasma*, **14**, 296–306.

5   L. Pauling (1940), A theory of the structure and process of formation of antibodies. *J. Am. Chem. Soc.*, **62**, 2643–57.

6   C. Baglioni, L. Alescio Zonta, D. Ciolo and A. Carbonara (1966), Allelic antigenic factor Inv(a) of the light chains of human immunoglobulins: chemical basis. *Science*, **152**, 1517–19.

7   N. K. Jerne (1955), The natural-selection theory of antibody formation. *Proc. Natl. Acad. Sci. U.S.*, **41**, 849–57.

8   F. M. Burnet (1957), A modification of Jerne's theory of antibody production using the concept of clonal selection. *Australian J. Sci.*, **20**, 67–9.

9   F. M. Burnet (1959), *The Clonal Selection Theory of Acquired Immunity*. Cambridge: Cambridge University Press.

10   J. Lederberg (1959), Genes and antibodies. *Science*, **129**, 1649–53.

11   G. M. Edelman and J. A. Gally (1964), A model for the 7S antibody molecule. *Proc. Natl. Acad. Sci. U.S.*, **51**, 846–53.

12   B. A. Askonas and A. R. Williamson (1966), Biosynthesis of immunoglobulins on polyribosomes and assembly of the IgG molecule. *Proc. Roy. Soc. (London), Ser. B*, **166**, 232–43.

13   E. Haber (1964), Recovery of antigenic specificity after denaturation and complete reduction of disulfides in a papain fragment of antibody, *Proc. Natl. Acad. Sci. U.S.*, **52**, 1099–106.

14   P. L. Whitney and C. Tanford (1965), Recovery of specific activity after complete unfolding and reduction of an antibody fragment. *Proc. Natl. Acad. Sci. U.S.*, **53**, 524–32.

15   G. J. V. Nossal, G. L. Ada, and C. M. Austin (1965), Antigens in immunity: IX. The antigen content of single antibody-forming cells. *J. Exptl. Med.*, **121**, pp. 945–54.

16   N. K. Jerne and A. A. Nordin (1963), Plaque formation in agar by single antibody-producing cells. *Science*, **140**, p. 405.

17   N. K. Jerne, A. A. Nordin, and C. Henry (1963), The agar plaque technique for recognizing antibody-producing cells. In *Cell-Bound Antibodies* (B. Amos and H. Koprowski eds). Philadelphia: The Wistar Institute Press, pp. 109–25.

18   N. K. Jerne, A. A. Nordin, C. Henry, A. Koros, and H. Fuji (1965), unpublished observations.

19 J. C. Kennedy, J. E. Till, L. Siminovitch, and E. A. McCulloch (1965), Radiosensitivity of the immune response to sheep red cells in the mouse, as measured by the hemolytic plaque method. *J. Immunol.*, **94**, 715–22.

20 J. C. Kennedy, J. E. Till, L. Siminovitch, and E. A. McCulloch (1966), The proliferative capacity of antigen-sensitive precursors of hemolytic plaque-forming cells. *J. Immunol.*, **96**, 973–80.

21 J. H. L. Playfair, B. W. Papermaster, and L. J. Cole (1965), Focal antibody production by transferred spleen cells in irradiated mice. *Science*, **149**, 998–1000.

22 C. M. Austin and G. J. V. Nossal (1966), Mechanism of induction of immunological tolerance: III. Cross-tolerance amongst flagellar antigens. *Australian J. Exptl. Biol. Med. Sci.*, **44**, pp. 341–54.

23 K. Rajewski, personal communication.

24 N. K. Jerne (1951), A study of avidity based on rabbit skin responses to diphtheria toxin-antitoxin mixtures. *Acta Pathol. Microbiol. Scand., Supl. 87.*

25 N. K. Jerne and P. Avegno (1956), The development of the phage-inactivating properties of serum during the course of specific immunization of an animal: reversible and irreversible inactivation. *J. Immunol.*, **76**, pp. 200–8.

26 H. N. Eisen (1964), The immune response to a simple antigenic determinant. *Harvey Lectures, Ser. 60*, pp. 1–34.

27 N. Hilschmann and L. C. Craig (1965), Amino acid sequence studies with Bence-Jones proteins. *Proc. Natl. Acad. Sci. U.S*, **53**, 1403–9.

28 F. W. Putnam, K. Titani, and E. Whitley, Jr (1966), Chemical structure of light chains: amino acid sequence of type K Bence-Jones proteins. *Proc. Roy. Soc. (London), Ser. B*, **166**, 124–37.

29 C. Milstein (1966), Chemical structure of light chains. *Proc. Roy. Soc. (London), Ser. B*, **166**, 138–49.

30 L. E. Hood, W. R. Gray, and W. J. Dreyer (1966), On the mechanism of antibody synthesis: a species comparison of L-chains. *Proc. Natl. Acad. Sci. U.S.*, **55**, 826–32.

31 S. E. Luria and M. Delbrück (1943), Mutations of bacteria from virus sensitivity to virus resistance. *Genetics*, **28**, 491–511.

32 J. Monod (1956), Remarks on the mechanism of enzyme induction. In *Enzymes: Units of Biological Structure and Function* (O. H. Gaebler, ed.), New York: Academic Press, pp. 7–28.

33 J. Locke (1689), *An Essay Concerning Human Understanding.*

34 Socrates, in *Menon.*

The Argument from Animals to Humans in Cognitive Neuroscience

Todd M. Preuss

During the past two decades, neuroscientists have developed a host of new techniques for studying the organization of the nervous system at a level of detail and precision scarcely imaginable by earlier generations of researchers. However, many of the most useful and informative techniques, including those used to trace neural connections, require invasive or terminal procedures. For this reason, they are used to study nonhuman species almost exclusively, and provide no direct information about the human nervous system. As a result, much of what neuroscientists believe to be true about the human brain, particularly about its connectional and areal organization, is based on inference or extrapolation from studies of other species.

From an evolutionary standpoint, it is reasonable to expect that we can learn much about humans by studying other species, especially closely related species. After all, humans share a long history of common ancestry with other primates and with mammals generally. Evolution necessarily entails change, however, and change poses a problem for those who would extrapolate findings from one species to another. Neuroscientists rarely confront this challenge directly. It is entirely commonplace to read reports of studies of a single primate species, usually the rhesus macaque, that purport to be studies of "the monkey" or "the primate." This practice discourages critical evaluation of evolutionary differences. Furthermore, since humans are primates, it tempts one to conclude that what is true of "the primate" will also be true of humans. The problem is that, strictly speaking, there is no such thing as "the primate" or "the monkey." Rather, there are approximately 200 living species of primates (Fleagle, 1988; Nowak, 1991), representing several distinct phyletic groups: prosimians, New World monkeys, Old World monkeys, and hominoids (apes and humans). Unless evolution has produced very few changes in neural organization, we have no prior grounds to conclude that what is true of any single primate species – rhesus macaque, squirrel monkey, owl monkey, or whatever – is true of primates generally, or of humans in particular.

Furthermore, if it is the case that evolution has produced so few differences between the brains of humans and other primates that we can comfortably ignore them, why should we suppose there is anything unusual about primates? Perhaps the features of cerebral organization found in humans evolved early in mammalian history. If so, the choice of species to be studied becomes largely a matter of cost and convenience, and it would be difficult to defend the study of anything other than rats. Indeed, Kolb and colleagues have vigorously defended the status of rats as "representative" mammals, and regard rat cortex as a good model system for understanding the structure and function of the human cortex, even the higher-order association regions (Kolb and Tees, 1990; Kolb and Whishaw, 1990). People who study primates may scoff at this, but if one accepts that evolution produced important differences between rodents and primates, one must acknowledge that it could have produced important differences between rhesus macaques and humans as well.

The purpose of this chapter is to consider how ideas about evolution affect the practice of neuroscience. First, I will contrast the modern conception of evolution, which embraces both similarities and differences, with the traditional view adopted by many neuroscientists, which emphasizes similarity and continuity. Next, I will review some of the evidence for phyletic differences in mammalian cerebral organization. I will then propose procedures for making inferences about human neural organization from the study of animals that are grounded in modern evolutionary principles, and thus do not rely on the traditional (and unwarranted) assumption that all primates or all mammals possess, in a fundamental sense, the same brain. Finally, I will consider how the evolutionary model advocated here can provide new perspectives on human cognition and its relationship to other varieties of animal cognition.

The Evolutionary Tradition in Neuroscience

To illustrate the potential pitfalls involved in making inferences about the human brain from studies of macaques or other putative model species, imagine trying to make inferences about the *non*-neural characteristics of humans by studying macaques (Fleagle, 1988; Richard, 1985). To be sure, we would get some things right. Humans, like macaques, have eyes set together in the front of the face rather than on the sides of the head, have dexterous hands with opposable thumbs and digits tipped with nails instead of claws, and live in complex societies. Unfortunately, we would also make many mistakes. For example, we would conclude that humans walk on all fours, have a tail, and possess a thick coat of fur. We would infer that humans possess a pouch of tissue in the cheek, where food can be hidden from higher-ranking individuals (figure 34.1). Furthermore, we would conclude that human social groups are centered on a stable core of closely related adult females, with males leaving their natal groups when they reach puberty. Besides leading us to ascribe erroneous characteristics to humans, the study of macaques would provide us no information about the unique evolutionary specializations of humans: bipedalism, functional hairlessness, unique hand muscles, a new layer of fatty tissue, and language, among others (Aiello and Dean, 1990; Napier, 1993).

In extrapolating from macaques to humans, why would we get some features right and others wrong? The answer lies in the geometry of evolution. Evolution is like a

Figure 34.1 A rhesus monkey (*Macaca mulatta*), marked for identification as part of a field study, showing cheek pouches distended with food. Cheek pouches are evolutionary specializations of the Old World monkey subfamily Cercopithecinae, to which macaques belong. (Courtesy of A. Richard)

branching tree (figure 34.2). Every species is a composite of characteristics that evolved at different points in its ancestry; closely related species share more features, distant relatives fewer features. Macaques and humans share a long history of common ancestry. This is reflected in the characteristics they have in common, which are the characteristics we correctly attribute to humans based on the study of macaques. However, the macaque and human lineages separated about 25 million years ago, and since that time each has evolved its own unique features: the cheek pouch and "sisterhood" social organization in the case of macaques, bipedalism and language in the case of humans. It is features such as these, the evolutionary specializations of particular taxonomic groups, that confound attempts to make extrapolations from one group to another. When we consider a particular feature of macaque neural organization, how are we to know whether this is a feature present in humans rather than some unique product of macaque evolution? How can we tell whether we are studying the neural analogues of the opposable thumb and frontated orbits, rather than something akin to a cheek pouch? And how can we ever hope to understand what is distinctive about the human brain by studying macaques?

Given the diversifying nature of phyletic change, it is difficult to imagine a modern evolutionary biologist endorsing the use of macaques (much less rats or cats) as model humans. Why are neuroscientists not troubled by this procedure? The answer seems to be that neuroscientists, for the most part, do not view brain evolution as treelike. There is a tradition in neuroscience and psychology that holds that the important events in brain evolution involved mainly progressive increases in the size and "differentiation" of the brain and its components, without fundamental changes in basic structures and functions (in mammals, at least). That is to say, the pattern of brain evolution has been likened to a unitary scale or ladder rather than to a branching tree.

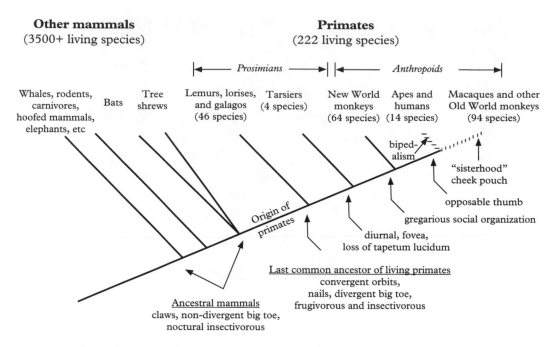

Figure 34.2   An evolutionary tree, showing the relationship of primates to other mammals, and the relationships among primates. The origins of evolutionary specializations distinctive of different groups, inferred from comparative and paleontological studies, are mapped onto the tree diagram. So, for example, the origin of primates was marked by the evolution of convergent orbits and the modification of claws into nails, among other changes. The features are shared by later primates. Humans and macaques differ due to evolutionary events that occurred subsequent to the divergence of their respective lineages (marked with horizontal and vertical bars, respectively). The number of species of primates and other mammals is derived from Nowak (1991).

The view that evolution is like a scale is certainly not unique to neuroscientists: this was the predominant view of evolution among biologists from Darwin's era until well into the twentieth century, and it remains the predominant view in our culture at large. Nevertheless, modern evolutionary biologists are inclined to view the phylogenetic scale as a relic of the nineteenth century, with its emphasis on the march of Progress and the inevitable ascent of Man (Richards, 1987; 1992). Faced with the fact that lineages tend to evolve distinctive specializations, and unable to document a unitary, progressive trend in the history of life, evolutionary biologists consider the branching tree a more suitable metaphor for evolution than the scale (Gould, 1989; Williams, 1966; 1992).

In continuing to embrace the phylogenetic scale, therefore, the neurobehavioral sciences are out of step with modern evolutionary biology (Hodos and Campbell, 1969; Kaas, 1987; Povinelli, 1993; Preuss, 1993). How are we to understand this adherence to an otherwise discredited idea? Without question, the scale holds particular appeal for students of the brain and cognition. The scale ranks animals from lower to higher, and few of us would question the placement of humans at the top, at least with regard to cognition. Yet even as it affirms the special status of humans, the scale metaphor suggests a unity among animal brains, and so provides a rationale for extrapolating from animals to humans. For the scale permits change only within very narrow limits: Along the scale, change is strictly cumulative, so that brains may become improved, added to, and enlarged, but they do not *diverge*. Thus, lower forms can serve as simplified models of higher forms. The appeal of the phylogenetic scale may also reflect the fact that neurobiology has deep roots in a particular anatomical doctrine closely linked to the phylogenetic scale. According to this doctrine, known as typological or idealistic morphology, the member species of each major taxonomic group are regarded as manifestations or elaborations of an ideal, inherent form or archetype (Richards, 1992). Under this theory, the goal of comparative anatomy was to glimpse the common archetype through the haze of variations, the different expressions of the archetype presented by actual organisms.

Typological morphology was the dominant anatomical doctrine of the eighteenth and nineteenth centuries, pre-dating the theory of evolution. The idea that differences between related species are not fundamental – that variations represent different expressions of a shared type – was held by many early evolutionists, including Darwin. This is evident in Darwin's insistence that humans possess no structures that are not also present in other animals, and by his emphasis on continuity between living forms in both physical and mental characteristics (Darwin, 1871, chap. 1). For example, in *The Descent of Man*, Darwin asserted that "the difference in mind between man and the higher animals, great as it is, is certainly one of degree and not of kind" (Darwin, 1871, p. 105). The only uniquely human characteristic he acknowledged (grudgingly, it seems) is language. For Darwin, human evolution was largely a process of improving upon faculties present in other animals, rather than adding new ones (Povinelli, 1993; Preuss, 1993; Richards, 1987).

Evolutionary biologists today take a different view of the evolutionary process: The changes organisms undergo in evolution represent departures or deviations from an ancestral condition, rather than different expressions of a common type (e.g., Williams, 1992). Yet, neurobiologists embraced Darwin's narrow doctrine of evolution, along with its typological foundations, early in the development of their discipline; and the influence of typological morphology continues to this day. For example, Cajal (1904) maintained that structures corresponding to the higher-order cortical areas of humans are present in other mammals, although smaller than in humans. Later, Elliot Smith (1924) and his student Le Gros Clark (1959), both central figures in the development of primate neuroanatomy, acknowledged that the number of cortical areas increased in evolution. However, they rationalized these changes as improvements or refinements of common brain structures rather than as the evolution of new structures. Ebbesson's (1980) idea that brain evolution is largely a matter of "parcellation" – the progressive segregation of elements originally mixed in one structure into multiple daughter structures – also belongs within this tradition: The brain is enlarged, and the parts rearranged, but nothing new appears.

Recently, Kolb and his colleagues have developed a framework for thinking about brain evolution and its relevance to animal models of human neuropsychology (Kolb and Whishaw, 1983; 1990; Kolb and Tees, 1990). Their approach is very much in the traditional vein, in that they acknowledge that mammalian species differ in brain size and in the number of cortical areas while denying that such differences are fundamental or qualitative. They specifically deny that evolution has produced new connectional or functional systems: the major features of cortical organization are present throughout the class Mammalia and are therefore said to be "class common." They conclude, "There is no strong evidence for unique brain–behavior relations in any species within the class Mammalia, including *Homo sapiens*" (Kolb and Whishaw, 1990, p. 110). From this perspective, it follows that the rat can serve as a "representative mammal" for the purposes of generalizing from animals to humans, even regarding such functionally higher-order regions as prefrontal and parietal cortex (Kolb and Tees, 1990).

The Diversity of Cortical Structure

I now turn to the evidence for variation in neural organization among mammals, focusing on the cortex and related structures. The fact of variation is not at issue: No one suggests that all mammalian brains are exactly the same. What is at issue is the nature of variation. Is it the case, as many neuroscientists have supposed, that brains vary only by degrees from a common mammalian type, such that the study of a few species would lead to an accurate picture of all other species, including humans? Or is there evidence of more substantial differences? A review of the literature suggests that mammalian brains display a number of remarkable variations, at several levels of organization. (For further discussion of neural diversity, see Kaas, 1987; Kaas and Preuss, 1993; and Preuss, 1993.)

Histology

Ever since techniques were first developed to stain nerve cell bodies, biologists have been struck by the distinctive, laminated appearance of neocortex. Figure 34.3A presents a Nissl-stained section through the primary visual area (V1, area 17) of an owl monkey. The laminated appearance of the cortex reflects in part the segregation of cell types into different strata, for example, the concentration of small, granular cells in layer IV and of larger, pyramidal cells in layers III and V. (Six main layers are usually distinguished in neocortex.) Lamination is developed to an extreme degree in the visual cortex of anthropoid primates, but similar (if less vivid) patterns can be discerned in cortical areas in almost all mammals that have been examined (Brodmann, 1909). But there is at least one outstanding departure from this pattern among mammals – the cortex of cetaceans (whales and dolphins). Figure 34.3B shows a Nissl-stained section through the visual cortex of a bottlenose dolphin. Clearly, this is cortex with a difference. Layer I is enormously thick in these animals, compared with the other layers. No granular layer IV can be distinguished in adult dolphins, although granule cells are present in other cortical layers. Moreover, Golgi studies indicate that the pyramidal cells of dolphin visual cortex include a variety of unusual morphologies (Garey, Winkelmann, and Brauer, 1985; Glezer, Jacobs, and Morgane, 1988). These characteristics are found throughout the cortical mantle of cetaceans that have been studied to date. Some workers believe that the distinctive characteristics of cetaceans represent the retention of a primitive stage in the evolution of mammalian cortex (Glezer, Jacobs, and Morgane, 1988), while others believe they constitute evolutionary specializations (Johnson, 1988; Preuss, 1993). In either case, the unusual character of cetacean cortex is very interesting, in view of the reputedly high intelligence of these

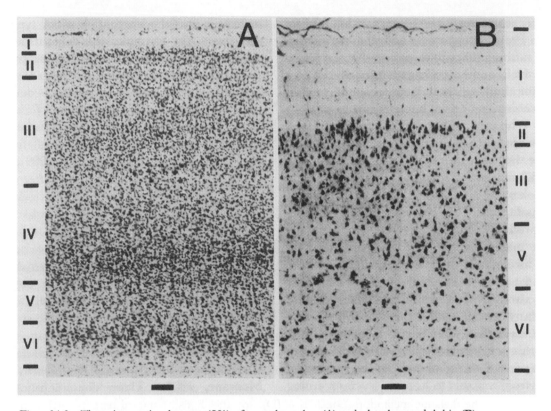

Figure 34.3   The primary visual cortex (V1) of an owl monkey (**A**) and a bottlenose dolphin (**B**), stained with cresyl violet. Owl monkey V1 is highly stratified: Note for instance the concentration of small (granular) cells in layer IV and the concentration of large, pyramidal cells in the deepest part of layer III. Dolphin visual cortex displays a very different pattern of lamination: Layer I is extremely thick, layer IV is absent, and stratification is generally less marked. The apparent difference in overall cell density between these two sections may be due in part to differences in histological processing. (**A**) A 40 μm thick frozen section. (**B**) A 20 μm thick section from a paraffin-embedded brain. The larger average cell size in (**B**) presumably reflects the fact that dolphins are much larger-bodied animals than owl monkeys. Scale bars represent 100 μm. (**B** modified from Garey, Winkelmann, and Brauer, 1985, and reproduced courtesy of Lawrence Garey)

animals: if cetaceans are indeed intelligent in a manner recognizable to humans, their intelligence rests on a very different neural foundation than does ours.

Cetaceans pose a challenge for the view that there is a "basic uniformity in structure of the neocortex" across mammals (Rockel, Hiorns, and Powell, 1980). Although cetaceans are probably an extreme case, there is evidence of more subtle variations in the laminar and cellular organization of cortex between mammalian species and between cortical areas in the same species (Beaulieu and Collonier, 1989; Beaulieu, 1993).

Connectivity

Although it is now widely accepted that the number of cortical areas differs among mammalian groups, it is not as commonly recognized that the connectional and functional relationships between areas also vary. Even the relationship between primary sensory areas and secondary areas may change. For example, inactivation of V1 by cooling or lesion in anthropoid primates produces functional deactivation of the immediately adjoining visual area, V2, and other extrastriate visual areas (Rocha-Miranda et al., 1975; Schiller and Malpeli, 1977; Kaas and Krubitzer, 1992). Inactivation of V1 in cats has a less profound effect on the visually driven activity of neurons in extrastriate visual areas (e.g., Sherk, 1978; Guido, Tong, and Spear, 1991), presumably because in cats (unlike in primates), there are significant projections from the lateral geniculate nucleus to visual areas beyond V1 (Rosenquist, 1985). A similar evolutionary "rewiring" of thalamocortical and corticocortical connections in the somatosensory system of primates has also been documented (Garraghty et al., 1991).

The cortical connections of rats and primates appear to differ in several respects. For example, the primary motor area (M1) of rats is connected with orbital cortex (Reep, Goodwin, and Corwin, 1990; Paperna and Malach, 1991); despite intensive study of M1 in non-human primates, no orbital connections have been reported (e.g., Stepniewska, Preuss, and Kaas, 1993). The rat primary visual area (V1) also differs from that of primates and carnivores, having direct projections to medial limbic and possibly frontal cortex (Vogt and Miller, 1983; Reep, Goodwin, and Corwin, 1990; Paperna and Malach, 1991); visual–limbic connections have also been described in tree shrews (Sesma, Casagrande, and Kaas, 1984).

The carnivore literature provides two interesting examples of species differences. In rats and macaques, it is well established that the amygdala sends strong projections to the thalamic mediodorsal nucleus (MD), specifically to its medial part (Krettek and Price, 1977; Russchen, Amaral, and Price, 1987), which projects in turn to medial frontal and orbitofrontal cortex. However, studies with comparable techniques indicate that the amygdala does not project significantly to MD in cats (Krettek and Price, 1977; Velayos and Reinoso-Suárez, 1985). In cats, as in primates, there is a region of cortex anterior to the somatic motor region from which eye movements can be elicited by electrical stimulation; this is usually called the frontal eye field, although this region is actually composed of multiple areas in both primates and cats (Schlag and Schlag-Rey, 1987; Stepniewska, Preuss, and Kaas, 1993). While it is tempting to view this as a case of class-common organization, the connectional evidence suggests otherwise. In nonhuman primates, the frontal oculomotor areas receive their main cortical inputs from parietal and temporal areas located at the fringe of the extrastriate visual region (Huerta, Krubitzer, and Kaas, 1987). In cats, by contrast, the main input to frontal oculomotor cortex arises from cortex near the insula, at a distance from the main extrastriate zone, a region that includes the anterior ectosylvian visual area (EVA) (Nakai, Tamai, and Miyashita, 1987; Olson and Graybiel, 1987). EVA is unlike any visual area known in primates, being separated from the rest of extrastriate visual cortex by intervening territories of auditory and somatosensory cortex, and having unusual receptive field properties (Olson and Graybiel, 1987; Mucke et al., 1982). It seems likely that EVA is a cat area that has no homologue in primates. So, although both primates and carnivores possess frontal oculomotor cortex, they differ with respect to the major cortical connections of the region. This suggests that one or more of the frontal oculomotor fields of primates and carnivores are the products of convergent evolution and are therefore not homologous. There is evidence of other differences in frontal lobe organization between primates and nonprimates (Preuss and Goldman-Rakic, 1991a; 1991b; Preuss, 1993).

Modular and Laminar Organization

In cortical areas, the terminal fields of input fibers and the cells of origin of outputs are typically segregated in different laminae, and are sometimes also segregated into repeating "columns" or "modules" oriented orthogonally to the laminae. These patterns of segregation vary across mammalian groups. The best-known examples of modular segregation are the ocular dominance columns of primary visual cortex. In most mammals, dense projections from the lateral geniculate nucleus of the thalamus terminate in layers III and IV of cortical area V1; these projections relay visual information from the left and right eyes to V1 on each side of the brain. In some primate species, inputs from the left and right eye are segregated into alternating bands within layers III and IV, known as ocular dominance columns. The degree of segregation varies considerably among primates, however, and some New World monkeys exhibit virtually no segregation at all (reviewed by Florence, Conley, and Casagrande, 1986). Ocular dominance columns are absent in other mammals that have been examined, with the exception of carnivores (reviewed by Casagrande and Kaas, in press). Ocular dominance columns probably evolved independently (convergently) in primates and carnivores. One reason for concluding this is that carnivores, which possess columns, are distantly related to primates, whereas tree shrews, which are thought to be closely related to primates (Novacek, 1992), lack columns (Hubel, 1975). However, tree shrews offer an interesting twist to the ocular dominance story. Although they lack ocular dominance columns, inputs from each eye are differentially distributed within layers III and IV of the primary visual area. Specifically, inputs from both eyes converge in the upper and lower tiers of layer IV, but inputs from the contralateral eye have additional terminations in the middle tier of layer IV and in layer III (Hubel, 1975). This laminar arrangement of ocular inputs is unique among mammals studied to date.

Area V1 of primates exhibits another form of modular organization. As shown in figure 34.4, sections cut parallel to the cortical surface and stained for the metabolic enzyme cytochrome oxidase (CO), exhibit a regular pattern of darkly stained spots, termed "puffs" or "blobs." CO blobs have been described in at least seven genera of anthropoid primates (including *Homo*) as well as in a number of prosimians, but have not been clearly demonstrated in any nonprimate mammal (Horton, 1984; Kaas and Preuss, 1993; Preuss, Beck, and Kaas, 1993; Casagrande and Kaas, in press). These results are consistent with the suggestion of Horton (1984) that CO blobs are an evolutionary specialization of primate V1. CO blobs are thought to constitute a specialized processing channel within the visual cortex, a point I will consider in a later section.

Neurochemical Distribution

It is axiomatic among cell biologists that macromolecular pathways and systems have been highly conserved during the evolution of eukaryotic organisms. This conservatism is reflected in the presence of a common set of neurotransmitter, neuromodulator,

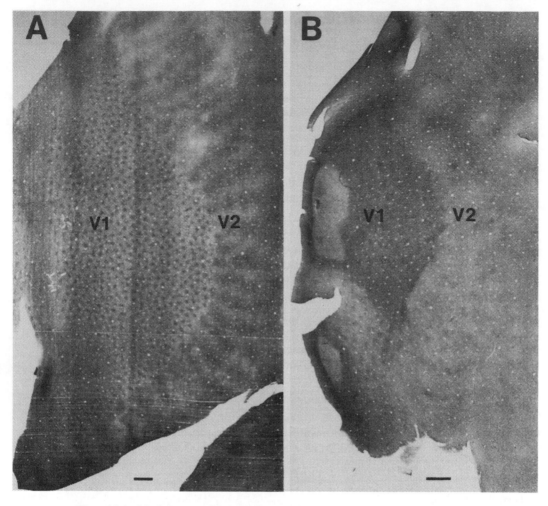

Figure 34.4   Modular organization of areas V1 and V2 in (**A**) a squirrel monkey (*Saimiri sciureus*), a diurnal, anthropoid primate, and (**B**) a galago (*Galago garnetti*), a nocturnal, prosimian primate. In both cases, the cortex was separated from the underlying white matter, flattened, and sectioned parallel to the cortical surface. Sections were then stained for cytochrome oxidase, a metabolic enzyme. Many small, dark, cytochrome oxidase–rich "blobs" are visible in area V1 of both animals. Squirrel monkeys and other anthropoid primates also possess well-marked cytochrome oxidase–dense stripes in area V2, whereas stripes are very poorly developed in V2 of galagos and other prosimian primates. Scales bars: 1 mm.

and receptor molecules across a spectrum of invertebrate and vertebrate groups. Nevertheless, there are phyletic differences even at this level of organization, particularly with regard to the biochemical phenotypes of specific classes of neurons and the distribution of specific transmitter- and modulator-containing axons within the cortex.

One of the best-studied examples is the differential distribution of dopamine (DA)-containing axons in the frontal cortex of rats and macaques (Berger, Gaspar, and Verney, 1991; Berger, 1992). Dopaminergic neurons, with cell bodies located in the substantia nigra and ventral tegmental area of the midbrain, send strong projections to the frontal cortex, where they appear to modulate the responses of target neurons to other afferents. In rats, DA-containing fibers are concentrated in the medial frontal and orbitofrontal regions, with relatively weak projections to the primary motor cortex (M1) and supplementary motor area. Macaques and humans also have DA projections to medial and orbital cortex, but in addition exhibit very dense DA innervation of M1 and the supplementary motor area, with fibers distributed across all layers of cortex (see also Williams and Goldman-Rakic, 1993). In rat motor cortex, by contrast, DA-containing fibers are essentially restricted to layers V and VI. In rats, furthermore, the DA-containing fibers of frontal cortex also contain neurotensin, whereas in macaques, DA and neurotensin are localized in different fibers, which project to different laminae (Berger, Gaspar, and Verney, 1991).

To take another example, there is now good evidence that rats possess a population of intrinsic neurons in cerebral cortex that contain acetylcholine (ACh); these have been identified using several different antibodies raised against choline acetyltransferase, the synthetic enzyme that is a definitive marker for ACh (Houser et al., 1985). Studies employing similar techniques provide no evidence of ACh-containing cortical neurons in macaques (Lewis, 1991), humans (Mesulam and Geula, 1991), or cats (Kimura et al., 1981).

From Nonhumans to Humans

The diversity of mammalian neurological organization cannot be denied or dismissed as trivial. We need to consider how the fact of diversity affects the practice of neuroscience. If we cannot simply extrapolate results from nonhumans to humans, how are we to advance our understanding of the human brain?

We can, of course, carry out more intensive studies of human beings, as suggested by Crick and Jones (1993). The problem, as Crick and Jones recognize, is that the techniques currently available for studying the connectional organization of the human brain are markedly inferior to those available for studying nonhumans. Certainly, innovations that improve our ability to study the human brain directly are only to be welcomed. For the immediate future, however, our methods for studying animals will remain superior to our methods for studying people. A second approach, to be advocated here, seeks to improve the inferences we make about humans from animal studies. One major goal of this approach is to determine those features of nonhuman neurological organization that are likely to be present in humans, as determined through a program of comparative research, guided by our understanding of evolutionary relationships. This approach promises fruitful interactions with more direct studies of human organization. Another goal of this approach is to understand in what respects the brains of species differ from each other, and how and why those differences evolved. Of particular interest and importance are those characteristics that distinguish humans from other animals.

The manner in which comparative studies can yield inferences about humans, and the potential for interaction between human and animal studies, are illustrated by recent investigations of extrastriate visual cortex (see also Kaas, 1993). This region has been extensively studied in Old World monkeys, mainly macaques, which have been taken as models for human organization. Crick and Jones (1993) have criticized this approach, arguing that macaque studies can provide only a working hypothesis about human organization, about which we have little direct knowledge. Humans and macaques presumably differ in ways we cannot determine at present. This is a reasonable expectation on evolutionary grounds, but it must be recognized that our knowledge of visual organization in nonhuman primates is not restricted to Old World monkeys: New World monkeys and prosimians have been studied in detail as well. One can identify a number of visual areas, based on similarities in architectonics, location, connections, and physiological properties, that are present in species belonging to each of these major primate groups (reviewed by Kaas, 1993; Krubitzer and Kaas, 1993; Preuss, Beck, and Kaas, 1993). As shown in figure 34.5A, the shared areas include the primary visual area (V1), second visual area (V2), dorsolateral area (DL; also known as V4), middle temporal area (MT; also known as V5), and the dorsomedial area (DM). There is also evidence that all major primate groups possess posterior parietal and inferotemporal cortex, although much remains to be learned about the organization of these regions, especially in New World monkeys and prosimians. While there are doubtless additional visual areas, these are the areas which, based on current evidence, appear to be shared by the major primate groups and thus are likely to have been present in ancestral primates.

The fact that we can identify a common pattern of extrastriate organization, shared across a wide variety of nonhuman primates, suggests that human extrastriate cortex is organized in similar fashion. This organization may have been modified during human evolution, but the common pattern of primate organization – inferred from studies using multiple techniques and diverse species – provides a solid foundation from which to pursue human investigations. Efforts are currently being made to identify homologues of extrastriate areas in humans, using evidence from architectonics, location, and function (Kaas, 1992). For example, there is good evidence that humans possess a homologue of MT, located anteriorly to V1 and V2 in the lateral occipitotemporal region (figure 34.5B), as one would expect based on comparative studies (Clarke and Miklossy, 1990; Zeki et al., 1991). By contrast, the location of area V4 is controversial. Zeki and colleagues (1991) argue that this area is located in the inferior and medial part of the occipital lobe, because they regard V4 as the cortical color center, and the inferomedial region is activated metabolically when subjects view colored stimuli. In response, Kaas (1992) has noted that if Zeki and colleagues are correct, human V4 differs in its location from that of all other primates studied. In nonhuman primates, V4 or DL is located on the lateral surface, between area MT and the foveal representation of V2. While it is possible that evolution has "relocated" V4 in humans, the spatial arrangement of anatomical structures tends to be highly conserved in evolution (Darwin, 1859), a principle illustrated nicely by the stability of extrastriate organization across nonhuman primates. The comparative evidence thus suggests that the cortical region activated by colored stimuli in the study by Zeki and colleagues (1991) corresponds to some visual area other than V4, or perhaps to a limited portion of V4.

It is common to hear neuroscientists assert that they are not really interested in comparative issues; what they care about is *function*. Yet a comparative perspective can provide unique insights on function. Consider the cytochrome oxidase–rich "blobs" in the primary visual area of primates (figure 34.4). Physiological investigations in Old World and New World monkeys have shown that blobs contain a higher proportion of color-opponent cells than surrounding cortex (Livingstone and Hubel, 1984). Blobs

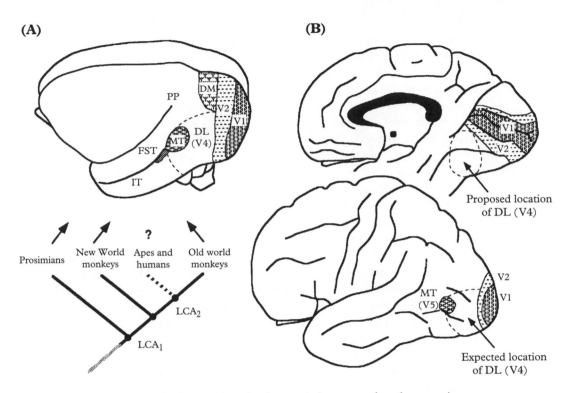

Figure 34.5   The organization of extrastriate visual cortex in humans and nonhuman primates. (**A**) Visual areas shared by nonhuman primates. Studies of prosimians, New World monkeys, and Old World monkeys have made it possible to identify a set of visual areas common to these groups, depicted in the figurine at the top. In addition to the primary visual cortex (V1; striate cortex), the common areas include the second visual area (V2), dorsomedial area (DM), dorsolateral area (DL; and known as V4), middle temporal area (MT; also known as V5), and the area of the fundus of the superior temporal sulcus (FST). There is also evidence for multiple divisions of posterior parietal (PP) and inferotemporal (IT) cortex in these groups. Given the similarities among prosimians, New World monkeys, and Old World monkeys, it is likely that these visual areas were present in the last common ancestor of the living primates (LCA$_1$), as indicated in the tree diagram at the bottom. The phylogenetic distribution of visual areas also implies that these areas were present in the last common ancestor of apes, humans, and Old World monkeys (LCA$_2$). (**B**) The organization of visual cortex in humans, based on recent architectonic and in vivo imaging studies (modified from Kaas, 1992). The area denoted as MT in humans is very densely myelinated and is reponsive to moving stimuli, as is MT in other primates. The location of human DL (V4) is controversial. Zeki et al. (1991) have identified a region of cortex on the ventromedial surface of the occipital lobe that is metabolically active while subjects view colored stimuli; they regard this as the homologue of DL (V4) of nonhuman primates, an area they consider to be the color-processing area. By contrast, Kaas (1992) suggests that in humans DL (V4) should be located at the lateral surface of the occipital lobe, between V2 and MT, as it is in all other primates examined.

have thus come to be regarded as components of a specialized color-processing "channel" within the visual system – as indeed they may be, in diurnal primates such as macaques and squirrel monkeys (figure 34.4A). However, the comparative evidence puts the relationship between blobs and color vision in a different light (as it were). In addition to diurnal primates, which have well-developed color vision, CO blobs are present in such nocturnal primates as galagos (figure 34.4B), lorises, and owl monkeys (Horton, 1984; Livingstone and Hubel, 1984; Preuss, Beck, and Kaas, 1993), in which color vision is not well developed. What is more, because nocturnality is probably the ancestral condition for primates (Fleagle, 1988), it is likely that blobs originally evolved in animals with poor color vision. For this reason, researchers have considered other possible functions of blobs. Along with color-opponent cells, blobs contain broad-band, brightness-selective cells (Livingstone and Hubel, 1984), prompting the sugges-tion that in primates generally, blobs constitute part of a perceptual brightness constancy system (Allman and Zucker, 1990). Furthermore, Allman and Zucker propose that when diurnal primates evolved, the brightness constancy system was modified to accommodate color-specific brightness differences. That is, they propose that evolution constructed primate color vision using structures that originally sub-served other aspects of vision.

The foregoing example illustrates an important evolutionary principle. Evolution is a tinkerer, building new structures and systems by modifying existing structures, rather than by designing them from scratch (Simpson, 1967; Jacob, 1982). If we ask, Why is this system constructed in this way? we must consider not only what the system does but also where it came from. And that is a question about evolution to be addressed through comparative studies.

It is because evolution adapts old structures to new ends that we may find studies of nonhuman species helpful in understanding the structural basis of even uniquely human functions. Consider the case of language. It has long been argued that the ventral premotor area (PMV) of nonhuman primates resembles Broca's area in cytoarchitecture and location (e.g., Bonin, 1944; figure 34.6). Recent studies provide additional evidence that Broca's area and PMV are homologous. Connectional and microstimulation studies in nonhuman primates indicate that PMV represents forelimb and orofacial movements (Preuss, 1993; Stepniewska, Preuss, and Kaas, 1993). Meta-bolic and surface stimulation studies in humans suggest that Broca's area also repre-sents nonlinguistic forelimb and orofacial movements (Fox et al., 1988; see also Roland et al., 1980; Uematsu et al., 1992). Results such as these have led Fox and colleagues (1988) to suggest that Broca's area is a general premotor area without specific linguistic functions. Alternatively, it might be the case that Broca's area has both linguistic and somatic motor functions, and that evolution constructed the neural systems of language in part by "recruiting" existing motor areas, as Bonin (1944) suggested. The latter hypothesis suggests why language can be conveyed as naturally and fully with manual signs as with speech (Klima and Bellugi, 1979).

The foregoing examples demonstrate how we can make reasonable inferences about the structure of the human brain by comparing the neural organization of animals closely related to humans. This procedure does not require that the animals we compare be alike in *all* features of organization, merely that they possess *some* features in common by virtue of shared ancestry. Studies of nonhuman primates are of particular relevance for identifying likely features of human organization, for these are the animals with which humans share the longest period of common descent.

The matter of inferring human brain structure represents only one aspect of comparative neuroscience, a specific aspect that is best addressed by studying animals closely related to humans. There are other neurobiological issues of a more general

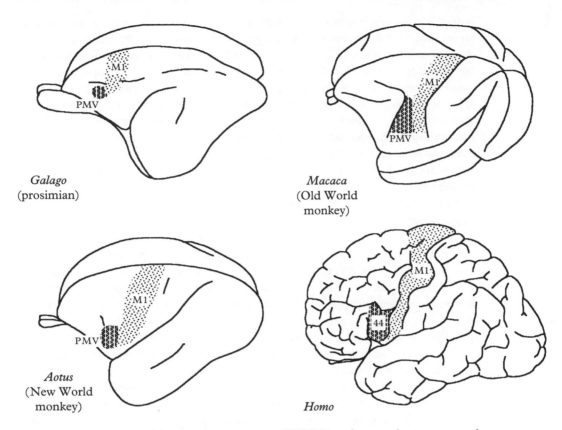

Galago
(prosimian)

Macaca
(Old World
monkey)

Aotus
(New World
monkey)

Homo

Figure 34.6 The location of the ventral premotor area (PMV) in nonhuman primates compared to that of Brodmann's area 44 (the posterior part of Broca's area) in humans. PMV has been identified in prosimians, New World monkeys, and Old World monkeys, as a discrete region that represents forelimb and orofacial movements and is located immediately anterior to the inferior part of primary motor cortex (M1) (Preuss, 1993). Brodmann's area 44 occupies the same location with respect to M1 in humans. Recent metabolic and stimulation studies in humans suggest that Broca's area is involved in the control of forelimb and orofacial movements.

nature, though still pertinent to understanding humans, for which different comparative strategies are appropriate. For example, if we want to know why information processing in the human visual system is compartmentalized into blobs and columns, it is useful to consider the range of circumstances under which compartments develop and the structural and functional consequences of compartmentalized processing. Such an inquiry properly extends to whatever species and systems exhibit compartmentalization, from the barrel fields of rat somatosensory cortex (Kaas, Merzenich, and Killackey, 1983) to the optic tectum of three-eyed frogs, with its artificially induced visual columns (Constantine-Paton, 1982).

A Diversity of Minds

Providing the basis for making inferences about humans from the study of other species is just one way that evolutionary ideas can inform cognitive neuroscience.

Indeed, if we accept the modern metaphor of evolution as a branching tree, and if we accept that neural organization varies among mammals, we are led to a new and challenging conception of the relationship between human minds and animal minds, one that is fundamentally different from that suggested by the scale metaphor. Under the older view of life represented by the phylogenetic scale, humans stand at the zenith of a continuum of mental development, and other beings are ranked according to a human standard. The modern conception of evolution as a branching tree removes this standard, so that nonhuman species are seen not as steps on the ladder to humanity but as alternative outcomes of the evolutionary process. Under this view, the human mind represents not the highest expression of a common animal mind, but rather one mind among many.

What are the consequences of acknowledging a diversity of minds? For one thing, it suggests new questions about the human brain and cognition. If the human mind is one evolutionary outcome among many, we must ask: Why this outcome and not some other? What specific cognitive capacities were selected for in human evolution? How were the components of neural and cognitive systems present in our primate ancestors modified to produce new systems in humans? Questions like these make little sense under the phylogenetic scale, in which the emergence of the human mind is the almost inevitable outcome of a general process of improvement. And these are fundamental questions about human nature rarely asked by neuroscientists.

To view evolution as treelike is to raise new questions about other animals as well. We should expect that nonhuman species are in some respects truly different from humans, with neural systems and functional capacities that humans lack. Understanding what other animals are like, when they are not like humans, is perhaps the most profound and intriguing challenge faced by cognitive neuroscientists.

Acknowledgments

The author would like to thank Michael Gazzaniga, Leda Cosmides, John Tooby, Jon Kaas, Mary Anne Case, and Sherre Florence for their support and assistance in preparing this chapter. Conversations with Patricia Gaspar, Jon Kaas, and Frederick Szalay were instrumental in developing the ideas presented here. The author's research is supported in part by the McDonnell-Pew Program in Cognitive Neuroscience.

References

Aiello, L., and C. Dean, (1990). *Human Evolutionary Anatomy*. London: Academic Press.

Allman, J., and S. Zucker (1990). Cytochrome oxidase and functional coding in primate striate cortex: A hypothesis. *Cold Spring Harb. Symp. Quant. Biol.*, **55**: 979–82.

Beaulieu, C., (1993). Numerical data on neocortical neurons in adult rat, with special reference to the GABA population. *Brain Res.*, **609**: 284–92.

Beaulieu, C., and M. Collonier, (1989). Number of neurons in individual laminae of areas 3B, 4γ, and 6aα of the cat cerebral cortex: A comparison with major visual areas. *J. Comp. Neurol.*, **279**: 228–34.

Berger, B. (1992). Dopaminergic innervation of the frontal cerebral cortex: Evolutionary trends and functional implications. In *Frontal Lobe Seizures and Epilepsies*, P. Chauvel, A. V. Delgado-Escuerta, E. Halgren, and J. Bancaud (eds), New York: Raven, pp. 525–44.

Berger, B., P. Gaspar, and C. Verney (1991). Dopaminergic innervation of the cerebral cortex: Unexpected differences between rodent and primate. *Trends. Neurosci.*, **14**: 21–7.

Bonin, G. von (1944). The architecture. In *The Precentral Motor Cortex*, P. C. Bucy (ed.), Urbana: University of Illinois Press, pp. 7–82.

Brodmann, K. (1909). *Vergleichende Lokalisationslehre der Grosshirnrhinde*. Leipzig: Barth.

Cajal, S. Ramon Y (1904). *Textura del Sistema Nervioso del Hombre y de los Vertebrados*, vol. 2. Madrid: N. Moya. English translation in *Cajal on the Cerebral Cortex*, J. DeFelipe and E. G. Jones (eds), 1988, New York: Oxford University Press, pp. 465–90.

Casagrande, V. A., and J. H. Kaas, in press. The afferent, intrinsic, and efferent connections of primary visual cortex in primates. In *Cerebral Cortex*, vol. 10: *Primary Visual Cortex in Primates*, A. Peters and K. Rockland (eds), New York: Plenum.

Clarke, S., and J. Miklossy (1990). Occipital cortex in man: Organization of callosal connections, related myelo- and cytoarchitecture, and putative boundaries of functional visual areas. *J. Comp. Neurol.*, **298**: 188–214.

Constantine-Paton, M. (1982). The retinotectal hookup: The process of neural mapping. In *Developmental Order: Its Origin and Regulation*, S. Subtelny (ed.), New York: Liss, pp. 317–49.

Crick, F., and E. G. Jones (1993). Backwardness of human neuroanatomy. *Nature*, **361**: 109–10.

Darwin, C. (1859). *On the Origin of Species*. London: Murray; reprinted, 1984, Cambridge, MA: Harvard University Press.

Darwin, C. (1871). *The Descent of Man, and Selection in Relation to Sex*. London: Murray; reprinted, 1981, Princeton: Princeton University Press.

Ebbesson, S. O. E. (1980). The parcellation theory and its relation to interspecific variability in brain organization, evolutionary and ontogenetic development, and neuronal plasticity. *Cell. Tissue Res.*, **213**: 179–212.

Elliot Smith, G. (1924). *The Evolution of Man: Essays*. London: Oxford University Press.

Fleagle, J. G. (1988). *Primate Adaptation and Evolution*. San Diego: Academic Press.

Florence, S. L., M. Conley, and V. A. Casagrande (1986). Ocular dominance columns and retinal projections in New World spider monkeys (*Ateles ater*). *J. Comp. Neurol.*, **243**: 234–48.

Fox, P., S. Petersen, M. Posner, and M. Raichle (1988). Is Broca's area language specific? *Neurology*, **38** (suppl. 1): 172.

Garey, L. J., E. Winkelmann, and K. Brauer (1985). Golgi and Nissl studies of the visual cortex of the bottlenose dolphin. *J. Comp. Neurol.*, **240**: 305–21.

Garraghty, P. E., S. L. Florence, W. N. Tenhula, and J. H. Kaas (1991). Parallel thalamic activation of the first and second somatosensory areas in prosimian primates and tree shrews. *J. Comp. Neurol.*, **311**: 289–99.

Glezer, I. I., M. S. Jacobs, and P. J. Morgane (1988). The "initial brain" concept and its implications for brain evolution in Cetacea. *Behav. Brain Sci.*, **11**: 75–116.

Gould, S. J. (1989). *Wonderful Life*. New York: Norton.

Guido, W., L. Tong, and P. D. Spear (1991). Afferent bases of spatial- and temporal-frequency processing by neurons in the cat's posteromedial lateral suprasylvian cortex: Effects of removing areas 17, 18, 19. *J. Neurophysiol.*, **64**: 1636–51.

Hodos, W., and C. B. G. Campbell (1969). Scala naturae: Why there is no theory in comparative psychology. *Psychol. Rev.*, **76**: 337–50.

Horton, J. C. (1984). Cytochrome oxidase patches: A new cytoarchitectonic feature of monkey visual cortex. *Philos. Trans. R. Soc. Lond. [Biol.]*, **304**: 199–253.

Houser, C. R., G. D. Crawford, P. M. Salvaterra, and J. E. Vaughn (1985). Immunocytochemical localization of choline acetyltransferase in rat cerebral cortex: A study of cholinergic neurons and synapses. *J. Comp. Neurol.*, **234**: 17–34.

Hubel, D. H. (1975). An autoradiographic study of the retino-cortical projections in the tree shrew (*Tupaia glis*). *Brain Res.*, **96**: 41–50.

Huerta, M. F., L. A. Krubitzer, and J. H. Kaas (1987). Frontal eye field as defined by intracortical microstimulation in squirrel monkeys, owl monkeys, and macaque monkeys, II: Cortical connections. *J. Comp. Neurol.*, **265**: 332–61.

Jacob, F. (1982). *The Possible and the Actual.* New York: Pantheon Books.

Johnson, J. I. (1988). Whose brain is initial-like? *Behav. Brain Sci.*, **11**: 96.

Kaas, J. H. (1987). The organization and evolution of neocortex. In *Higher Brain Function: Recent Explorations of the Brain's Emergent Properties*, S. P. Wise (ed.), New York: Wiley, pp. 347–78.

Kaas, J. H. (1992). Do humans see what monkeys see? *Trends. Neurosci.*, **15**: 1–3.

Kaas, J. H. (1993). The organization of visual cortex in primates: Problems, conclusions, and the use of comparative studies in understanding the human brain. In *Functional Organization of the Human Visual System*, B. Gulyas, D. Ottoson, and P. E. Roland (eds), Oxford: Pergamon, pp. 1–11.

Kaas, J. H., and L. A. Krubitzer (1992). Area 17 lesions deactivate area MT in owl monkeys. *Vis. Neurosci.*, **9**: 399–407.

Kaas, J. H., M. M. Merzenich, and H. P. Killackey (1983). The reorganization of somatosensory cortex following peripheral nerve damage in adult and developing mammals. *Annu. Rev. Neurosci.*, **6**: 325–56.

Kaas, J. H., and T. M. Preuss (1993). Archontan affinities as reflected in the visual system. In *Mammal Phylogeny: Placentals*, F. S. Szalay, M. J. Novacek, and M. C. McKenna (eds), New York: Springer, pp. 115–28.

Kimura, H., P. L. McGeer, J. H. Peng, and E. G. McGeer (1981). The central cholinergic system studied by choline acetyltransferase immunohistochemistry. *J. Comp. Neurol.*, **200**: 151–201.

Klima, E. S., and U. Bellugi (1979). *Signs of Language.* Cambridge, MA: Harvard University Press.

Kolb, B., and R. C. Tees (1990). The rat as a model of cortical function. In *The Cerebral Cortex of the Rat*, B. Kolb and R. C. Tees (eds), Cambridge, MA: MIT Press, pp. 3–17.

Kolb, B., and I. Q. Whishaw (1983). Problems and principles underlying interspecies comparisons. In *Behavioral Approaches to Brain Research*, T. E. Robinson (ed.), New York: Oxford University Press, pp. 237–63.

Kolb, B., and I. Q. Whishaw (1990). *Fundamentals of Human Neuropsychology*, edn 3. New York: Freeman.

Krettek, J. E., and J. L. Price (1977). Projections from the amygdaloid complex to the cerebral cortex and thalamus in the rat and cat. *J. Comp. Neurol.*, **172**: 687–722.

Krubitzer, L. A., and J. H. Kaas (1993). The dorsomedial visual area (DM) of owl monkeys: Connections, myeloarchitecture, and homologies in other primates. *J. Comp. Neurol.*, **334**: 497–528.

Le Gros Clark, W. E. (1959). *The Antecedents of Man.* Edinburgh: Edinburgh University Press.

Lewis, D. A. (1991). Distribution of choline acetyltransferase-immunoreactive axons in monkey frontal cortex. *Neurosci.*, **40**: 363–74.

Livingstone, M. S., and D. H. Hubel (1984). Anatomy and physiology of a color system in the primate visual cortex. *J. Neurosci.*, **4**: 309–56.

Mesulam, M.-M., and C. Geula (1991). Acetylcholinesterase-rich neurons of the human cerebral cortex: Cytoarchitectonic and ontogenetic patterns of distribution. *J. Comp. Neurol.*, **306**: 193–220.

Mucke, L., M. Norita, G. Benedek, and O. Creutzfeldt (1982). Physiologic and anatomic investigation of a visual cortical area situated in the ventral bank of the anterior ectosylvian sulcus of the cat. *Exp. Brain Res.*, **46**: 1–11.

Nakai, M., Y. Tamai, and E. Miyashita (1987). Corticocortical connections of frontal oculomotor areas in the cat. *Brain Res.*, **414**: 91–8.

Napier, J. (1993). *Hands*, R. H. Tuttle (ed.), Princeton: Princeton University Press.

Novacek, M. J. (1992). Mammalian phylogeny: Shaking the tree. *Nature*, **356**: 121–5.

Nowak, R. M. (1991). *Walker's Mammals of the World*, vol. 1, edn 5. Baltimore, MD: Johns Hopkins University.

Olson, C. R., and A. M. Graybiel (1987). Ectosylvian visual area of the cat: Location, retinotopic organization, and connections. *J. Comp. Neurol.*, **261**: 277–94.

Paperna, T., and R. Malach (1991). Patterns of sensory intermodality relationships in the cerebral cortex of the rat. *J. Comp. Neurol.*, **308**: 432–56.

Povinelli, D. (1993). Reconstructing the evolution of mind. *Am. Psychol.*, **48**: 493–509.

Preuss, T. M. (1993). The role of the neurosciences in primate evolutionary biology: Historical commentary and prospectus. In *Primates and their Relatives in Phylogenetic Perspective*, R. D. E. MacPhee (ed.), New York: Plenum Press, pp. 333–62.

Preuss, T. M., P. D. Beck, and J. H. Kaas (1993). Areal, modular, and connectional organization of visual cortex in a prosimian primate, the slow loris (*Nycticebus coucang*). *Brain Behav. Evol.*, **42**: 321–35.

Preuss, T. M., and P. S. Goldman-Rakic (1991a). Myelo- and cytoarchitecture of the granular frontal cortex and surrounding regions in the strepsirhine primate *Galago* and the anthropoid primate *Macaca*. *J. Comp. Neurol.*, **310**: 429–74.

Preuss, T. M., and P. S. Goldman-Rakic (1991b). Ipsilateral cortical connections of granular frontal cortex in the strepsirhine primate *Galago*, with comparative comments on anthropoid primates. *J. Comp. Neurol.*, **310**: 507–49.

Reep, R. L., G. S. Goodwin, and J. V. Corwin (1990). Topographic organization in the corticocortical connections of medial agranular cortex in rats. *J. Comp. Neurol.*, **294**: 262–80.

Richard, A. F. (1985). *Primates in Nature*. New York: Freeman.

Richards, R. J. (1987). *Darwin and the Emergence of Evolutionary Theories of Mind and Behavior*. Chicago: University of Chicago Press.

Richards, R. J. (1992). *The Meaning of Evolution: The Morphological Construction and Ideological Reconstruction of Darwin's Theory*. Chicago: University of Chicago Press.

Rocha-Miranda, C., D. Bender, C. G. Gross, and M. Mishkin (1975). Visual activation of neurons in inferotemporal cortex depends on striate cortex and the forebrain commissure. *J. Neurophysiol.*, **38**: 475–91.

Rockel, A. J., R. W. Hiorns, and T. P. S. Powell (1980). The basic uniformity of structure of the neocortex. *Brain*, **103**: 221–4.

Roland, P., E. Skinhøj, N. A. Lassen, and B. Larsen (1980). Different cortical areas in man in organization of voluntary movements in extrapersonal space. *J. Neurophysiol.*, **43**: 137–50.

Rosenquist, A. C. (1985). Connections of visual cortical areas in the cat. In *Cerebral Cortex*, vol. 3: *Visual Cortex*, A. Peters and E. G. Jones (eds), New York: Plenum, pp. 81–117.

Russchen, F. T., D. G. Amaral, and J. L. Price (1987). The afferent input to the magnocellular division of the mediodorsal thalamic nucleus in the monkey, *Macaca fascicularis*. *J. Comp. Neurol.*, **256**: 175–210.

Schiller, P. H., and J. G. Malpeli (1977). The effect of striate cortex cooling on area 18 in the monkey. *Brain Res.*, **126**: 366–9.

Schlag, J., and M. Schlag-Rey (1987). Evidence for a supplementary eye field. *J. Neurophysiol.*, **57**: 179–200.

Sesma, M. A., V. A. Casagrande, and J. H. Kaas (1984). Cortical connections of area 17 in tree shrews. *J. Comp. Neurol.*, **230**: 337–51.

Sherk, H. (1978). Area 18 responses in cat during reversible inactivation of area 17. *J. Neurophysiol.*, **41**: 204–15.

Simpson, G. G. (1967). *The Meaning of Evolution*, revised edn. New Haven: Yale University Press.

Stepniewska, I., T. M. Preuss, and J. H. Kaas (1993). Architectonics, somatotopic organization, and ipsilateral cortical connections of the primary motor area (M1) of owl monkeys. *J. Comp. Neurol.*, **330**: 238–71.

Uematsu, S., R. Lesser, B. Gordon, K. Hara, G. L. Krauss, E. I. Vining, and R. W. Webber (1992). Motor and sensory cortex in humans: Topography studied with chronic subdural stimulation. *Neurosurgery*, **31**: 59–72.

Velayos, J. L., and F. Reinoso-Suárez (1985). Prosencephalic afferents to the mediodorsal thalamic nucleus. *J. Comp. Neurol.*, **242**: 161–81.

Vogt, B. A., and M. W. Miller (1983). Cortical connections between rat cingulate cortex and visual, motor, and post-subicular cortices. *J. Comp. Neurol.*, **216**: 192–210.

Williams, G. C. (1966). *Adaptation and Natural Selection: A Critique of Some Current Evolutionary Thought*. Princeton: Princeton University Press.

Williams, G. C. (1992). *Natural Selection: Domains, Levels, and Challenges*. New York: Oxford University Press.

Williams, S. M., and P. S. Goldman-Rakic (1993). Characteristics of the dopaminergic innervation of the primate frontal cortex using a dopamine-specific antibody. *Cerebral Cortex*, **3**: 199–222.

Zeki, S., J. D. G. Watson, C. J. Lueck, K. J. Friston, C. Kennard, and R. Frackowiak (1991). A direct demonstration of functional specialization in human visual cortex. *J. Neurosci.*, **11**: 641–9.

Index